Encyclopedia
of Women
in Religious Art

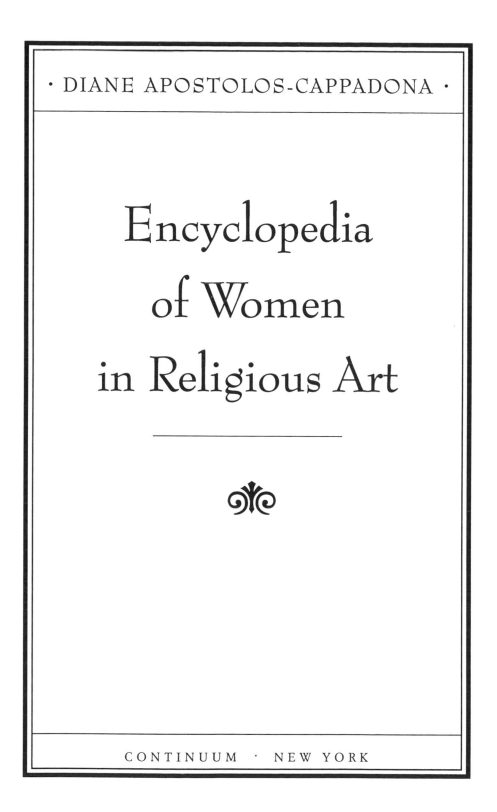

· DIANE APOSTOLOS-CAPPADONA ·

Encyclopedia
of Women
in Religious Art

CONTINUUM · NEW YORK

1996
The Continuum Publishing Company
370 Lexington Avenue New York, NY 10017

Library of Congress Cataloging-in-Publication Data

Apostolos-Cappadona, Diane.
    Encyclopedia of women in religious art / Diane Apostolos
—Cappadona.
      p. cm.
    Includes bibliographical references and index.
    ISBN 0-8264-0915-6
    1. Women in art—Encyclopedias. 2. Art and religion—
Encyclopedias. I. Title.
    N7793.W65A66 1996
    704.9'424'03—dc20   96-41647
                                      CIP

Printed in the United States of America

For Anna Brownell Murphy Jameson

Contents

ᘒᕀᘓ

Introduction

❧

The study of the iconography of women in religious art should extend the knowledge of women's positions in the religious and social orders. The three images on the cover of this book—*The Goddess Isis with the Child Horus* (fig. 1), *Yashodā with Krishna* (fig. 2), and the *Virgin and Child* (fig. 3)—represent more than just three distinctive historical cultures. This group of three sculptures also provides a visual argument for the multivalent nature of religious art *and* for the elasticity of women's images. Some viewers will immediately, and perhaps only, *see* three representations of a mother and a child and, worse yet, may simply interpret these as one more example of the patriarchal dominance of a society in which a "woman's place is in the home." These three sculptures span several centuries, several continents, and several religious and cultural traditions. The common denominator is that of portrayals of motherhood, thereby raising the question whether motherhood—especially when *only* the mother is depicted with her child—is a situation of dependence and powerlessness. As each of these three women merit individual en-

tries in the *Encyclopedia of Women in Religious Art,* readers are referred to those entries either to refresh their memories about the identities of Isis, Yashodā, or Mary or to learn their identities for the first time.

As exemplars of motherhood, the Egyptian Isis, the Hindu Yashodā, and the Christian Mary all signify "unnatural" modes of maternity from the ithyphallic conception of Horus to the surrogate maternity of Krishna and to the miraculous conception of Jesus of Nazareth. Thus, these extraordinary women stand as mothers *alone,* that is, without the requisite male partner who was extraneous to these conceptions and births and who remains unnecessary in the nurturing of these three male children. As such, I would suggest that these otherwise "powerless" women are in fact female images of empowerment, signifying at once the creative female energies of fertility, fecundity, and independence. Their individual postures and gestures testify to their independence and singular authority from the enthroned regality of Isis to the sensuous physicality of Yashodā to the elegant strength of Mary. Ironically, when these three sculptures are placed side by side as on the cover of this book, we note the powerful upward movement in the posturing of the child from the frontal-postured thighs of Isis to the elevated pelvis of Yashodā to the swerved hip of Mary. As with objects from the natural order, bodily postures and gestures signify meaning in religious art; and the careful viewer of the images of women such as these will take time to consider the several possible interpretations of motherhood, of woman, and of woman's roles in society that are being visualized. With a mind and an eye open to the symbolism and the multiple meanings of the details found in the many entries in the *Encyclopedia of Women in Religious Art,* the reader will come not simply to learn about the cultural history of women but commensurately to re-evaluate and thereby learn about the cultural history of men. The fullness of the human experience to which the art of world religions stands as an elegant and profound witness argues persuasively for the necessary duality and parity of the sexes, and thereby for a new definition of society.

This one-volume *Encyclopedia of Women in Religious Art* is composed of upwards of 2,000 entries. During my research for this book, I was surprised to note how few images of women in religious art have survived and yet how my initially proposed list of entries expanded geometrically. Given the fact that a majority of the entries for a specific female figure or symbol are represented by a small number of visual references or even just one, the number and nature of the entries in this present book are extraordinary in their scope and categories. Certainly many more images of women perished than sur-

vived through the ravages of religious persecution, iconoclasm, inquisition, religious patriarchalism and misogyny, war, and lack of care. In those instances where few representations of a particular female figure or symbol were originally created, the motif most probably has perished thereby making those surviving depictions that much more precious. It is, of course, probable that more and more "lost" works will be found and that previously cryptic motifs will be deciphered.

I am convinced that the introduction of visual images as documentary evidence in the ever-evolving study of women's cultural history will not only create a revolution in the boundaries of source materials for historical interpretation but also provide a firm and informative foundation for the "missing" elements in understanding the historical roles of women in social and cultural history. Given the fact that so many of the persons in the western world were verbally illiterate but visually literature, the role of art historical and cultural analyses must be acknowledged and recognized as legitimate as any written text or archaeological artifact. Art can be used as a fundamental and appropriate resource in establishing new methodologies for studying women's cultural history.

While reading through this *Encyclopedia of Women in Religious Art,* consider not merely the necessary position of art in the study of women's cultural history but more importantly the contexts for that art. For example, why was religious art with women's imagery produced? Where was it produced, and by whom? How were women depicted— that is, beyond the adequate rendering of the bodily distinctions between men

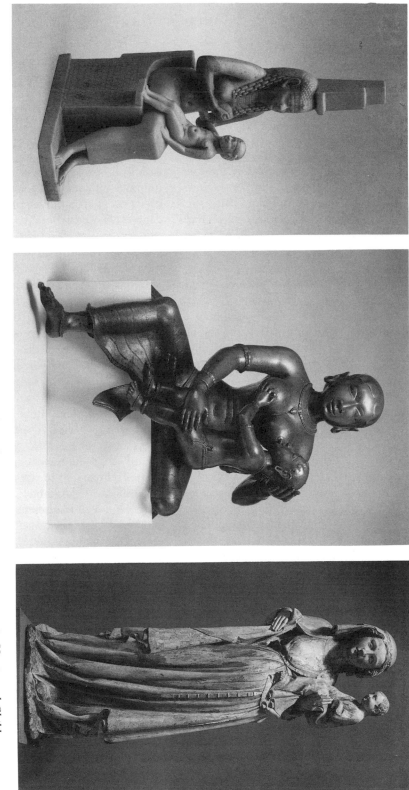

1. The Goddess Isis with the Child Horus

2. Yashoda with Krishna

3. Virgin and Child

and women, the postures, activities, and situations in which women were represented? What if any were the roles of women in the production of religious art with women's imagery? Were they nothing more than subject matter, or also possibly artists, patrons, collectors, or sources of inspiration? Did these images of women merely mirror the social order or more significantly did they announce transformations in women's roles; and thereby the cultural definitions of gender, sexuality, and social order?

Throughout the entries on female figures in the *Encyclopedia of Women in Religious Art*, I have attempted to provide identifying information about each female figure as well as a description of her iconographic pattern in religious art. At this particular moment in cultural history, however, it is not always possible to discern the necessary data on each and every figure who has merited her own entry. Therefore, the reader will find a disparity in the length and context of these entries. Rather than eliminate those entries on female figures for whom a discernible iconographic pattern has not been identified or about whom very little is known, I have chosen to include as many female figures as possible and to provide whatever information is available at this time. I do this both to announce that these otherwise silent and anonymous women have "names" and to indicate that there is much work to be done by current and future generations of scholars not simply on the iconography of women but on the larger question of religious art outside of the comfortable context of western culture. The majority of the shorter entries identifying female figures are from outside the west—from Asia, Africa, Oceania, and Meso-America.

Any comprehensive examination of the relationships among religion, art, and women's history would necessarily need to be a multi-volume project and would still be found wanting by readers with specialized interests or scholarly training. This present volume has been designed as a basic reference for students interested in both religious art and women's images from the varied disciplines of art history, gender studies, history of religions, and women's studies as well as a useful guide for nonspecialists and those museum visitors who have found the wall labels or catalogue entries of a work of art insufficient as to the identity of a particular legendary or long-forgotten female figure or to why certain objects are included within the context of a particular painting. My goal in the development of the *Encyclopedia of Women in Religious Art* has been to be as comprehensive as possible with regard to art historical and religious studies scholarship of women's imagery while still providing a book useful to the broadest possible audience of readers with the most generic of queries on this topic. It is my hope that the *Encyclopedia of Women in Religious Art* will serve as an introduction to a fascinating field of study and as an acknowledgment of the need for future exploration of women's imagery in the art of the world's religions.

It is unfortunate that few images of women in religious art created by women artists have survived. Feminist art historians have argued persuasively that many of those works of art labeled "anonymous" were most probably made by women artists as women were discriminated against in terms of educational opportunities as well as vocational options and denied the appropriate credit for their work, especially in the western world. Since the body of extant works of art by women artists is so small, and the number of texts on women artists (aside from recent scholarship on women artists in the west) equally minimal, I have erred on the side of inclusivism and included *all* those women artists credited with even one work which can be categorized as "religious."

The entries on legendary, mythological, and saintly women have been narrowed down from a much larger listing of *all* the goddesses, heroines, and female figures of world mythologies, *all* the women of the Old and New Testaments, and *all* the female saints of Christian history. Every attempt has been made to include those women, real or legendary, who either have been the subject of a large array of works of art throughout the history of religious art, or who were popular topics during a specific period of religious art and thereby merit mention.

Symbols and subjects in religious art are susceptible to multiple readings or interpretations, and often for the most accurate presentation a particular motif, figure, sign, symbol, or topic must be placed within the context of the time period in which the work of art was created and the artist lived. Popular recitations of the stories of heroines or goddesses, legendary and devotional texts, lay spirituality, pious devotionalism, iconographic innovations, and personalized artistic style played a more significant role in the history of religious art than did the theological tenets, institutional documents, and canonized scriptures of world religions. The selected bibliography lists common reference books and basic texts on the iconography of women in religious art which should be readily available in libraries and bookstores.

As with my earlier *Dictionary of Christian Art,* I have made one concession to contemporary scholarship in using the *New Revised Standard Version of the Bible* for the Jewish and Christian entries in this book. However, the reader is again advised that should she find a particular symbol or topic of interest, she may find the NRSV (as it is commonly referred to by biblical scholars) insufficient. Such readers should turn to a translation of either Jerome's *Vulgate* for their curiosities or the *Douay-Rheims Bible.* For example, few readers will readily connect the parable of the "ten bridesmaids" (NRSV) with that of the "wise and foolish virgins." For this reason, readers are advised to look for specific topics, titles, and biblical figures in the index should an initial alphabetical search for an entry prove fruitless. Similarly, the various spellings and transliterations of foreign names, especially those from the Arabic, Egyptian, Mesopotamian, Sanskrit, and Sumerian languages, are listed in the subject index where the reader is referred to the actual entry that appears in this volume. Readers should be advised that every effort has been made to indicate the many variations in spelling or variant names used for the major goddesses and heroines. Throughout this text, I have made an effort to conform to those spellings or transliterations which predominate in major American museum collections.

I realize that my concern with iconographic patterns may appear to be the preoccupation of a western-trained scholar and that, in fact, other cultures do not identify or create such patterns. A similar caveat could be made with regard to the imposition of order and clarity as again a western preoccupation which may be inappropriate or inapplicable to other cultures or its religious art. So, for example, extensive study in the iconographies of women in the religious art of Africa may in fact result in the conclusion that gender distinctions and their visualization are more subtly rendered and defy the type of iconographic patterning for which I am searching. Perhaps future studies in these "understudied" traditions of religious art will provide us with innovative methods for evaluating both the visual image and its place in cultural history. If nothing more, these future studies will affirm the revelatory and multivalent nature of religious art.

Acknowledgments

❧

Like all authors, I am indebted to those colleagues and friends who have supported me throughout the drafts and re-writes of this present study and to those research librarians who assisted my searches in a myriad of untold ways. Although these individuals and libraries are too numerous to mention, several must be acknowledged for their tireless efforts. I am pleased to acknowledge the research services provided me at the Bibliothèque Nationale, the British Library, the National Gallery of Art Library, the University of Maryland Library, and, most especially, the Lauringer Library at Georgetown University. As the reader should be aware, any reference work such as the present one is dependent upon all those which have preceded it. Given the innovative nature of the *Encyclopedia of Women in Religious Art,* I am especially indebted to the authors of all those reference sources upon which I have built the arrangement, list of entries, and descriptive texts of this present volume.

The development of any illustrated book, especially one on such an all-encompassing subject as the *Encyclopedia of Women in Religious Art,* requires the patient assistance and professional skills of those individuals engaged in the administration of photographic archives. I have been fortunate in the informative assistance I have always received from a critical group of photographic resources. Thereby, I am pleased to thank Joanne Greenbaum, Permissions Director, and her staff at Art Resource; Mary Doherty, Beatrice Epstein, and their staffs at the Photograph Library of the Metropolitan Museum of Art; and as always, Ira Bartfield, Coordinator of Visual Services, and his staff at the National Gallery of Art, Washington, D.C., for their time and efforts on my behalf.

Of the many individuals who generously supported me throughout the preparation of this book, I would like especially to thank those who reviewed the initial entries lists or who listened intently as iconographic conundrums arose within their areas of specializations. Several scholars read carefully and caringly through the various drafts of this text and offered critical admonitions, historical and linguistic precision, and intelligent advice. Among these several colleagues, I am most deeply indebted to Annmari Ronnberg, of the Archive for Research in Archetypal Symbolism, whose mutual interest in the iconography of women in religious art and whose knowledge of Scandinavian mythology added immeasurably to the scope of this book; Lucinda Ebersole, feminist author and specialist in popular culture, whose concern for the symbolic transformations of women's images and the "missing" history of women critically appraised this project from its inception; and Robley E. Whitson, anthropologist, linguist, and theologian extraordinaire, whose encyclopedic breadth of knowledge remains a continual amazement. All these readers have prevented countless anthropological, art historical, linguistic, mythological, and theological errors and throughout the process of their readings and my revisions have reminded me of the precious gift of intellectual exchange which makes the life of the mind such a rewarding experience. It goes without saying that I am responsible for my interpretations of all resource materials as well as the judgments made with regard to iconographic patterns, inclusion or exclusion of entries, styles of cross-references, and bibliographic listings. Without doubt, there are unintended omissions and a disparity in entry lengths, some of which will become more apparent as research continues in the study of women's images. Therefore, I would be grateful to those readers who can provide additional materials that may be incorporated in revised future editions of the *Encyclopedia of Women in Religious Art.*

John L. Esposito, Director, Center for Muslim-Christian Understanding:

History and International Affairs at Georgetown University, offered me a scholarly haven and unremitting collegial support throughout the research and writing of this volume. A series of conversations with my colleague, Amira El-Azhary Sonbol, Assistant Professor of Society, History, and Law, helped to clarify my purposes in the final development of the *Encyclopedia of Women in Religious Art.* Pat Gordon and Ethel Stewart, also at the Center for Muslim-Christian Understanding, cheerfully provided those often unmentioned forms of support—computer skills, duplication services, a careful eye to needed supplies, and a supportive smile—which are necessary for the successful completion of any research project. I am grateful to these four individuals for their contribution to this book.

For better or worse, Werner Mark Linz of the Continuum Publishing Company employed all of his persuasive skills to convince me to enlarge my original proposal for a book on *Women in Christian Art and Legend* into the realm of world religions. Also at Continuum, Frank Oveis continued to provide his editorial precision with his ever present concern for the clarity of my prose; while Ulla Schnell once again handled all production and design problems with such professional alacrity that I often never even knew there was a problem.

A note on the dedication of the *Encyclopedia of Women in Religious Art:* Anna Brownell Murphy Jameson (1794–1860) was one of the first women writers on art. Self-educated in aesthetics and art and church history, she authored two catalogues of London galleries, a widely influential account of

Italian painting from the thirteenth to the sixteenth century, six volumes that comprise the first systematic study of Christian iconography, and numerous articles. An advocate for women's education, Mrs. Jameson wrote and lectured widely on behalf of improved employment and educational opportunities for women. She has served as both an inspiration and a role model ever since I first encountered her books as an erstwhile undergraduate newly infatuated with the study of Christian iconography. Therefore, it seems only fitting that I dedicate this book—one whose subject matter and breadth of scale she would have understood—to "Mrs. J" as a hoped-for extension of her own legacy in the cultural history of women.

A

Ab. Heart organ of man or woman in Egyptian art and mythology. The ab was the center of the spiritual and intellectual life, and of the "conscience." The ab of the dead was weighed on the scales of justice against the *feather of *Maat in accordance with the *Book of the Dead.

Abacus. *Attribute of Arithmetic as one of the *Seven Liberal Arts in classical Greco-Roman, *medieval, and *renaissance western art.

Abbess. From the Aramaic for the familiar term for "father." The female equivalent of the abbot in Christian monasticism. The abbess was the elected head or superior of an abbey or community of nuns, or the superior of the Second Franciscan Order, the *Poor Clares. Upon her election, she must be at least forty years old and have been a professed *nun for ten years. During the medieval period, they had temporal powers that were restricted by the *Council of Trent. In western Christian art, an abbess was signified by a ring of authority and a pastoral staff or crosier. She may be depicted with a crown at her feet or on her head. Famed abbesses in western Christian art include *Bridget of Sweden, *Clare of Assisi, *Teresa of Avila, *Walburga, *Werburg, and *Winifred.

Abigail (I Sm 25:2–42). Old Testament figure who saved her rich but foolish husband, Nabal of Maon, from the wrath of the young David for refusing to pay tribute for the protection of his flocks. She appeased the angry king with food that she brought on a convoy of asses. Following Nabal's death, David married the beautiful Abigail. In western Christian art, Abigail was depicted as a beautiful young woman who signified female prudence. If depicted kneeling before David on her husband's behalf, she prefigured *Mary's intercession on behalf of humanity.

Abishag the Shulammite (I Kg 1:1–4; 2:13–25). Old Testament maiden renowned for her youthful beauty selected by the faithful servants of David who suffered from severe cold in his bed and was unable to be warmed by blankets. Although Abishag placed herself upon him, the aged King remained physically and sexually cold. Given the tradition that an impotent king could only rule a barren land, David's inability to be "warmed" by Abishag's "heat" indicated a symbolic end to his reign. Relegated to the royal harem, Abishag was sought in marriage by Adonijah, the brother of Solomon. Fearing the loss of the throne, Solomon had his brother killed. According to some interpreters, Abishag was the Shulammite maid described in the *Song of Songs* (Sg 6:13). Throughout the ancient Mediterranean cultures and in parts of Asia, monarchical recognition came with the mating of the king with the goddess's surrogate, her chief priestess. In such practices, the king symbolized his people and the goddess's surrogate the land; her pregnancy insured the harvests. In western Christian art, Abishag was represented as a very young and beautiful woman within the context of the narrative cycle of King David. Their unconsummated relationship was a foretype of the chaste marriage of *Mary and Joseph.

Ablution. Symbolic use of water for purificatory purposes according to the scriptural or ritual teachings of a religious tradition. In particular, for women, a ritual cleansing that may follow menstruation, sexual intercourse, or childbirth. According to Jewish ritual law and practice, "ritually tabooed" women were cleansed by partaking of a *mikveh*, or "pool of living water." According to tradition, *Bathsheba's bath was a mikveh after the end of her menstrual cycle signifying that she has not pregnant by her husband Uriah and that she was cleansed for David.

Abra. Name given to *Judith's maidservant. As both confidante and companion to the beautiful Jewish heroine, Abra played a significant role in the successful execution of Judith's plan to destroy Holofernes and his army at the cost of just one life. She was initially depicted as an older woman with graying hair and appropriate matronly dress, thereby signifying Judith's propriety. However as Judith became a more and more popular topic in *renaissance and *baroque art, Abra became more and more visually prominent in the artistic representations and eventually was depicted as a youthful coconspirator with her mistress, for example, Artemisia Gentileschi's *Judith and Holofernes*.

Abtu. From the Egyptian language for "abyss." Symbolic of the genitals, or "fish," of the goddess *Isis that engulfed the penis of the god Osiris.

Abuk. First woman in the cosmogony of the Dinka tribe of the Sudan. According to legend, Abuk and her male partner, Garang, were created from clay. In this creation myth, Abuk was deemed guilty of grinding more than the allotted amount of one grain of corn per day. The patron of women, gardens, and the grains brewed for beer, Abuk was symbolized by a little snake.

Abundance. Allegorical female figure signifying sufficient food supplies as a result of peace, justice, and good governance. Popular in Italian renaissance art, Abundance was represented as a beautiful and robust young woman often accompanied by domesticated animals, sheaves of corns, or several children like *Charity. Her *attributes included the *cornucopia filled with either fruits or jewels, the rudder symbolic of good government, and a sheaf of corn signifying *Ceres as her classical Roman foretype.

Acacia. A botanical symbol of friendship, the moral life, and the immortality of the soul in western Christian art. The red and white *flowers of the acacia represented life, death and rebirth. The tonguelike shape of the leaves of the acacia permitted a visual connection to the "burning bush" (Ex 3:2). Since the Church Fathers interpreted the *Burning Bush as a foretype of *Mary's perpetual virginity, the acacia was a botanical symbol of Mary. As the sacred wood of the Hebrew Tabernacle, acacia wood was reputed to have been used for the crown of thorns.

Acanthus. A botanical symbol whose thorns signified pain and the punishment for sin in western Christian art. As an emblem of the heavens, it also formed the basis of the design for the iconography of the *Tree of Jesse.

Acca Larentia. From the Greek for "she who fashions" or "mother of the ancestral spirits." The foster mother of Romulus and Remus, the legendary founders of Rome. Variously identified as the first of the *Vestal Virgins, a Roman courtesan, or a temple prostitute, Acca Larentia was midwife to *Rhea Silvia when she gave birth to her famed twin sons. As with *Akka of Akkad and the Pharoah's daughter, Acca Larentia drew the floating basket with Romulus and Remus out of the river, and raised the infants as her own children. She was both lover of Hercules and wife of Faustulus. According to tradition, she bequeathed her wealth to the citizens of Rome thereby indebting them to her memory. Acca Larentia was honored at the annual festival of the Larentalia.

Achamoth. Christian Gnostic mother goddess, daughter of *Sophia, sister of Christ, and mother of the material universe; of the Son of Darkness, Ildabaoth; and the five planetary spirits that produced archangels, angels, and humanity. Analogous to the northern European mythic triumvirate of Great-Grandmother, Grandmother, and Mother was the primordial female triad of the Gnostics: Sige, *Sophia, and Achamoth. According to legend, her spirit took the form of a *serpent named either Ophis or Christ who taught humanity disobedience and who led Adam to eat the fruit of the Tree of Knowledge.

Acheiropaeic image. A singular category of works in eastern and western Christian art that were deemed "not made by hands." The *Veil of Veronica and Mandylion of Edessa were two of the more famous acheiropaeic images in Christian art.

Acheiropoitos. From the Greek for "not made by hand(s)." Works of Christian art such as the *Veil of Veronica, the Mandylion of Edessa, or portraits of *Mary with the Christ Child by Luke the Evangelist were deemed to be miraculously made by divine intervention.

Adah and Zillah. From the Hebrew for "Brilliance" and "Shadow." Dialectical manifestations of the goddess such as light-and-dark or heaven-and-hell, they were identified as the biblical wives of Lamech (Gen 4:19, 23), the Two Ladies of Anatolia, and the Two Mistresses of Egypt. In religious art and metaphor, Adah and Zillah were signified by groupings that included *Isis, *Nephthys, *Ishtar, *Ereshkigal, *Kore, and *Persephone.

Aditi. From the Sanskrit for "infinity." This mother and wife of Vishnu, and mother of Krishna, was identified as a form of the Great Mother embracing all living beings. Personifying the generative powers of the earth, Aditi held dominion over the divine ordering of the world. As a redeemer figure, she saved devotees from illness, need, and the stain of sin. Aditi was the mother of the Adityas, or "Children of Aditi," who were the twelve zodiac spirits of the months. According to tradition, Aditi becomes a sun goddess.

Adraste. From the Celtic for "victory" or "she who is invincible." War goddess of Celtic mythology. Queen *Boadicea worshiped and sacrificed captured Roman women to this war goddess of ancient Britain.

Adrasteia. From the Greek for "the inescapable." Phrygian mountain goddess who was associated with the Greek *Nemesis as a guardian of justice and an avenger of evil.

Adultery. From the Latin for "to another." Illicit sexual intercourse outside of marriage, or social or kinship group. Throughout the history of world cultures, there have been a variety of attitudes towards adultery ranging from disgrace and the death penalty to honor and thanksgiving if the conception of a child, preferably male, resulted. Prohibitions against the adultery of married women were the clearest in definition and the severest in punishment. For example, while it was a *matrilineal privilege of women property owners to leave a former husband without financial resources, *patriarchal societies traditionally established strict legal and religious laws to insure the sexual fidelity of women. Originally defined as the sexual infidelity between a married woman with a man other than her husband, the theme of adultery abounded throughout world mythologies, legends, sacred scriptures, and art. For example, according to Hebraic custom, single women were not adulterous. Adultery was one of the sins—the others being homosexuality, idolatry, murder, and witchcraft—for which a *Hebrew was punished by death (Deut 22:21). Beyond the economic considerations, female adultery was condemned for fear of the paternity of male heirs. The Hebraic law of Levirate Marriage, in which widows were required to marry their brothers-in-law, retained property within the paternal tribe and ensured the family lineage. Following the practice of the Hebrew prophets, western Christian art depicted adulterous liaisons such as that between Solomon and the *Queen of Sheba as a visual metaphor for the worship of false gods. In classical Greco-Roman art and mythology, the "adulteries" of the goddess *Aphrodite (*Venus) were renowned and she was categorized as the most "male," that is sexually independent, of the goddesses.

Aedon. From the Greek for "nightingale." Wife of Zethus of Thebes in Greek mythology. Aedon mistakenly killed her own son, Stylus, whom she took for one of *Niobe's sons. In her grief, she attempted suicide but Zeus transformed her into a nightingale. In classical Greek art, Aedon was depicted as a beautiful matron grieving over her son's corpse or being transformed into the nightingale.

Aegis. Breastplate of a goat-skinned cloak embossed with the head of *Medusa and trimmed with *serpents. As a symbol of divine power and sovereignty, the aegis was an identifying garment of *Athena (*Minerva) and *Bast.

African art. Traditionally the art created by the peoples resident south of the Sahara Desert. African art—especially masks, figurines, and totems—was predominantly created for use in religious ceremonies and rituals. Given the spiritual and ritual nature of these works, they were not preserved for their aesthetic characteristics or accomplishments, but rather allowed to fade out of use and to be replaced. Most frequently created from the varied types and colored woods, African art incorporated the decorative embellishments of beads, shells, feathers, ivory, clay, and metals. Although regional and tribal differences in stylization abound, the generic identification of the elements of traditional African art include its emphasis on abstraction, the implementation of distortion as symbolic of spirituality, the simplification of facial features, and the reliance upon geometric formations. Beyond the ritual and ceremonial masks, figurines, and totems, indigenous African artists created stylized but striking headdresses, carved doorways, votive figures, and portrait heads. Singular among these were the realistic portraiture of Yoruban sculptures. African art has been distinguished by the energy and vitality of its execution and presentation of spiritual and human figures. With the opening of the Musée de l'homme in Paris in 1905, European artists, most notably the Fauves and Cubists (including Pablo Picasso and Henri Matisse), recognized the extraordinary nature and spiritual aesthetic of African art, and initiated its influence upon the development of modern art.

African religions. Multiplicity of indigenous ritual and ceremonial practices and belief systems of traditional African peoples. Although difficult to characterize or identify without careful consideration of tribal and regional study, there are a series of common elements which can be identified as "features of African religions." These include affirmation of a cosmology with a high god, most often a creator god, who existed in a ruptured relationship with humanity; the acknowledged existence of superhuman spirits (or gods) manifested through natural phenomena; a series of annual and life-cycle rituals; and the hereditary hierarchy of ritual leaders and spiritual healers. Predominant among these varied indigenous religious systems are those of the Yoruba of Nigeria, the Dogon of Mali, and the Ashanti of Ghana.

Agape, Saint (legendary). From the Greek for "love feast." Legendary woman transformed accidently into a virgin martyr when images of the *Horae were erroneously identified as Christian saints. In the cult of *Aphrodite, Agape was the female personification of the ritual practice of sexual intercourse. This rite was assimilated into several early Christian sects as a form of "spiritual marriage," but was declared heretical by the seventh century.

Agape, Saint (d. 304). Virgin martyr. One of three Thessalonian sisters and converts to Christianity who were martyred by Diocletian for their refusal to obey his decree of 303 forbidding the possession of scriptural texts. During their trial by Dulcitius, the Roman Governor of Macedonia, the three sisters—Agape, *Chionia, and *Irene—refused to offer sacrifice or incense to the Roman deities. Agape and Chionia were burned alive, while Irene was condemned to a brothel and eventually martyred. A rare topic in Christian art, Agape was usually depicted with her sisters either in an episode of their trial, their martyrdom, or as spiritual guide holding both a copy of the Christian scripture and a palm branch in *Byzantine art.

Agatha, Saint (third century). From the Greek for "kindly one." Early virgin martyr. This young Christian from Catania (Palermo) rejected the advances of the lecherous Roman governor, Quintianus. He attempted to corrupt her by forcing her to live in a house of prostitution for thirty days. When this failed, Quintianus had Agatha racked and further tortured by cutting off her *breasts. According to legend, Peter appeared to heal her wounds. Agatha was rolled in hot coals until she died. A year after her martyrdom, Mount Etna erupted and the citizens of Catania halted the lava flow with Agatha's *veil carried on a spear. Agatha was the patron of nurses, wet nurses, bell founders, and jewelers, and her name was invoked as protection against *fire, earthquakes, volcanic eruptions, and natural disasters. In western Christian art, Agatha was depicted as a beautiful young woman holding her *attributes of a *palm branch and a *dish with breasts. The visual resemblance of the shape of female breasts to loaves of *bread led to the practice of blessing bread on Agatha's feast day.

Aglaia. Youngest of the *Graces or *Charites. According to legend, she was married to Hephaestus.

Agnes, Saint (d. 304). Early virgin martyr. According to tradition, this youthful Christian refused to marry the son of the Roman prefect, having dedicated herself to God. Her suitor's father had the naked Agnes pulled by her *hair through the streets to a brothel. As she prayed, her hair grew to cover her naked body. Her virginity was protected in the brothel by an *angel. When the spurned suitor sought to ravish Agnes, he was struck dead, but her prayers restored his life. After a failed attempt to burn her to death, Agnes was decapitated with a *sword. According to pious legend and devotion, the martyred virgin—radiant with heavenly glory and accompanied by a *lamb—appeared at her grave, initiating it as a sacred site. Agnes was the patron of young maidens and was invoked for chastity. In western Christian art, she was depicted as a beautiful young woman who held her main *attribute, a lamb (which was both a pun on her name in Latin and a sign of her legendary claim to have been a bride of Christ). Her other attributes included long flowing hair, a palm branch, an olive branch, a crown of olives, a sword or dagger, and a flaming pyre.

Agnes of Assisi, Saint (c. 1197–1253). Sister of *Clare of Assisi, founding member of the Order of *Poor Clares, and later an *abbess. Initially a novice in the Benedictine convent of Sant'-

Angelo di Panzo, Agnes joined her elder sister, and after receiving a habit from *Francis, the two sisters established the Poor Clares. Committed to a life of penance and poverty, Agnes founded convents in Mantua, Venice, and Padua, and was named abbess of the Convent of the Poor Clares at Monticelli by Francis. She nursed Clare during her final illness, and then Agnes herself died three months later. In western Christian art, Agnes was portrayed as a young woman dressed in the habit of her order including all the *attributes of an abbess and often holding a model of one of the convents she established. She was included in depictions of the Death of Saint Clare.

Agrat Bat Mahalat. Hebraic Queen of the Demons. A granddaughter of Ishmael, the son of *Hagar and Abraham, Agrat Bat Mahalat was the concubine of Samael, the King of the Demons. According to the Talmud, the demonic couple seek destruction on Tuesday and Friday nights. Hebraic tradition advises that it was dangerous to sleep by the light of the full moon when Agrat Bat Mahalat searches for her human prey.

Agrippina (first century). Wife of the Roman general Germanicus and a classical Roman symbol for conjugal fidelity. Often identified by the epithet "the Elder" in distinction from the mother of Nero, Agrippina was remembered for her loyalty in returning from Syria with the ashes of her husband, the courageous Roman who had been poisoned on Imperial orders. According to Tacitus (*Annals*, 3:1), she and her two children were greeted by large crowds of mourners when the ship arrived at Brindisi. Agrippina was depicted in classical Greco-Roman and *renaissance art in the mode of a pious widow wearing a widow's veil and holding an urn with her husband's ashes as she either stands on or disembarks from the ship.

Agrona. Ancient British goddess of battle, slaughter, and death. Agrona was the British cognate of *Morrigan.

Aibell. From the Irish for "beautiful." Feminine guardian spirit and ruler also identified as a fairy in popular legend. Aibell possessed a magical harp whose music was heard as an announcement of death.

Aine. Irish goddess of love and fertility.

Akka. Akkad mother goddess identified as "the Old Woman," "the Grandmother," "the Midwife" and the "Water Drawer." Akka assisted in the birth of the gods from the primal deep. She was a prototype of a primordial goddess figure known as Acat or Akna in Mesoamerica, Acco or Acca in Greece, Mader Akka in Lapland and Finland, and Acca Larentia in Rome.

Ala. Earth goddess of the Ibo people of Nigeria. Ala personifies the duality of fecundity and death in the mystery of woman. She was symbolized by the abundance of the harvest and as the ruler of the underworld. In Nigerian art, Ala was represented as a naked female figure distinguished by her pendulant breasts and distended womb.

Alacoque, Saint Margaret Mary (1647–90). Christian visionary and advocate of the Devotion of the Sacred Heart. Sickly as a child, Margaret Mary Alacoque experienced a early devotion to the Blessed Sacrament. Although she entered the Visitation Convent at Paray-le-Monial at the age of twenty four, she had been having visions of Christ since she was twenty. Following the profession of her vows, Margaret Mary had a series of visions beginning on December 27, 1673, in which Christ reportedly selected her to begin the devotion to the *Sacred Heart of Jesus. Over the next eighteen months, these visions continued as she was instructed in the appropriate prayers, meditations, and rites that would become the Nine Fridays and the Holy Hour dedicated to the Sacred Heart. She was also directed to establish a Feast Day of the Sacred Heart. Initially rebuffed by her superior and later by a theological council, Margaret Mary continued in her obedience to her visions, and in 1683 was named assistant to the new Mother Superior of her order. The Sisters of the Visitation began private convent observances of the feast of the Sacred Heart in 1686 and built a chapel dedicated to the Sacred Heart in 1688, while other Visitadine convents began observance of this feast. Margaret Mary died on October 17, 1690, and the devotion to the Sacred Heart of Jesus was officially recognized by Clement XIII in 1765. Margaret Mary Alacoque was portrayed in the habit of her order and shown either receiving a vision of the Sacred Heart or in devoted prayer.

Alcestis. Greek mythic daughter of Pelias and wife of Admetus. Alcestis believed that *Medea could save Pelias from the ravagements of old age, thereby she followed the famed sorcerer's directions with great care. However, Medea tricked her into bringing about Pelias's death. *Artemis promised Admetus that he would be spared death if he found someone to die in his stead. As the model of wifely devotion, Alcestis offered herself to Death upon Admetus' appointed hour. She was later reunited with her husband when Hercules, moved by her sacrifice, descended to the underworld and successfully wrestled with death.

Alchemy. Esoteric quest to turn base metals or stones into gold by means of the legendary philosopher's stone. Alchemy flourished in ancient Babylonia, Egypt, and Greece; medieval Arabia and Europe; and sixteenth-century western Europe. The philosopher's stone was reputed to be the "Elixir of Life," or the secret of immortality. According to medieval legend, Solomon received the philosopher's stone from the *Queen of Sheba.

Alcmene. From the Greek for "power of the moon." Greek mythic virginal mother of Hercules, granddaughter of Perseus, and wife of Amphitryon. Alcmene was visited by Zeus in the guise of her husband who was avenging the deaths of his eight brothers-in-law. Alcmene's twin sons, Hercules the child of Zeus and Iphicles the child of Amphitryon, were born in due course. After learning the true identity of Hercules' father from the seer Tiresias, Alcmene abandoned the infant in fear of *Hera. *Athena found him and persuaded Hera to nurse him. As he suckled with great force, Hera pulled the young Hercules from her now painful breast and her milk spurted across the sky forming the Milky Way. Made immortal by Hera's nurture, the infant Hercules was returned to his mortal mother who eventually outlived him and protected his children. Variants of the mythology of Alcmene indicate significant parallels to the *Miraculous Conception and virgin birth of Jesus. She was a foretype of *Mary in classical Greek art and mythology. In classical Greco-Roman art, Alcmene was depicted as a beautiful young woman either in the act of encounter with Zeus or suckling Hercules. In *renaissance and *baroque art, she was represented suckling Hercules as a mythic foretype of Mary nursing the Christ child.

al-Lāt. One of the triad of goddesses—al-Lāt, *al-'Uzza, and *Manat—venerated by the Arabs at the Ka'ba in Mecca during pre-Islamic times. According to scholars, there are two distinct explanations for the derivation of her name. Arabic lexicographers identify the etymology of al-Lāt from the root *l-t-t* suggesting "to knead or mix barley meal" and arising from her association with "the idol of jealousy" *Astarte. For Semiticists, however, her name was the feminine form of Allah or his prototype al-lah, the unnamed god of the pre-Islamic pantheon. In her role as the goddess of fertility, al-Lāt was considered to be the mother of the gods. She was revered by the Arabs of Najd, the upland plateau of the Arabian peninsula, but was later eclipsed by her younger sister al-'Uzza, the favorite of the Quraysh, the tribe that inhabited Mecca and to which the prophet Muhammad belonged.

Alma Mater. From the Latin for "Soul Mother." Roman priestess renowned for her pedagogical skills, especially in the sexual mysteries. Etymologically associated with the Arabic *Al-Mah*, the moon goddess and her temple women, Alma Mater was a classical Mediterranean counterpart to the *Shaktī of Tantric Buddhism. Her *attributes included the *cowrie shell.

Almathea. From the Greek for "youthful aunt." Mythic Greek she goat or goat nymph who suckled the infant Zeus in a nymph's cave on Crete. Later, Zeus borrowed one of the goat's horns and transformed it into the *cornucopia, or "horn of plenty," which remained filled with desired, and constant, food and drink. As Lord of the Universe, Zeus placed Almathea's image in the form of Capricorn among the stars. Almathea was represented in classical Greek art as either a goat or a beautiful nymph suckling the infant Zeus, or as a she goat with a broken horn that was filled with the riches of the harvest and rests either under her arm or at her feet. In *renaissance and *baroque art, Almathea was depicted as a youthful nymph with the cornucopia at her feet and the infant Zeus at her breast.

Almond. The early blossoming of the almond tree symbolized spring. In Chinese art, a dual symbol for feminine beauty and sorrowful fortitude. The almond was a symbol of virginity, purity, and divine approval in western Christian art. A sweet *fruit with a hard shell, the almond implied the essential spiritual and hidden internal reality of the Incarnation of Christ. The almond symbolized divine approval, recalling to the flowering almond *staffs of Aaron (Nm 17:1–8) and Joseph (of Nazareth) (*Protoevangelium of James* 8:1). An *attribute of *Mary, the sweetness and delicacy of both the almond blossoms and the nuts themselves resulted in their ritual use at joyous feasts such as weddings and *baptisms. The almond-shaped frame that encased the head and body of a holy person was a *mandorla (from the Italian for "almond").

Alom. A Mayan mother goddess identified as "she who bore sons."

Alpan. Etruscan goddess of love and the underworld. She was associated with the female demons known as the Lasas. In classical Etruscan art, Alpan was depicted as a beautiful naked woman except for a cloak that magically conceals her body, heavily jeweled, and wearing sandals. She was a foretype of the Roman goddess of love, Venus.

Alphabetical symbolism. Decorative and compositional component in eastern and western Christian art. Specific *letters and/or combinations of letters, such as *initials or *monograms, had symbolic meanings. *See also A(ve) M(aria),* M with a Crown, and MA.

Altar. From the Latin for "high." A table of stone or wood, usually carved, which was the central focus of the sanctuary. In pre-Christian religious practice, the altar was a raised platform for sacrificial offerings. In early Christianity, the altar symbolized the Last Supper. By the fourth century, the altar implied a place of sanctuary and refuge. It was the site of liturgical offerings and symbolized the presence of Christ in the Eucharist. The altar faced *east towards Jerusalem and the rising *sun (Ex 43:4), in preparation for the Second Coming of Christ.

Althaea. Legendary Greek wife of Oeneus and mother of Meleager. Destined by the Fates to his death once the brand of wood then burning on the fire was consumed, Meleager's mother stopped the fire and hide the wood. Many years later as he claimed his prize in the Calydonian Boar Hunt, Meleager was criticized by his uncles whom he proceeded to slay in a sudden fury. Distraught at the news of her brothers' deaths, Althaea hurled the brand of wood into the fire and her son died. Cognizant of the violation of her maternal nature, Althaea hanged herself. In classical Greco-Roman art, Althaea was represented as a matron either in the act of burning the brand of wood or mourning the death of Meleager (including her suicide).

al-ʿUzza. From the Arabic for "Powerful One." One of the triad of goddesses—*al-Lāt, al-ʿUzza, and *Manat—venerated by the Arabs at the Kaʿba in Mecca during pre-Islamic times. Although al-ʿUzza was the youngest of the three, she overshadowed her two older sisters. She was particularly esteemed by the Quraysh, the tribe that inhabited Mecca at the time of the prophet Muhammad and to which he belonged. In her role as tutelary goddess of the sanctuary at Mecca, al-ʿUzza became the most important of the three goddesses. Her main sanctuary was in the valley of the Nakhla on the road leading towards Iraq and Syria.

Amata. From the Latin for "beloved." This was the ritual title of a *Vestal Virgin as a Bride of God as personified in the spirit of Rome manifested in the *Palladium, a symbolic lingam allegedly brought from Troy by Aeneas and a signifier of Rome. Amata was represented in *Roman art by the simultaneous presence of a Vestal Virgin and the Palladium, oftentimes inscribed with *Amor*, the secret name of Roma.

Amaterasu Omikami. From the Japanese for "shining from heaven." Shinto sun goddess and ancestor of the Emperors of Japan. Amaterasu was venerated at the great shrine of Isē as the divine progenitor of the Imperial Family, thus her epithet, Omikami, "great and exalted divinity." Daughter of the primal divinities, Izanagi-No-Mikoto and *Izanami-No-Mikoto, she was both sister and wife to Susano, the god of the ocean. His activities angered Amaterasu who withdrew to a cave and devastating darkness lay on the land until she was enticed to come out by the Three Sacred Relics, that is, the sacred mirror, sword, and necklace of *commas held by the dance of *Uzume. In Japanese art, Amaterasu was represented as a beautiful, kimono-clad woman with a solar *halo and a pagoda-shaped reliquary or *sharito*. Her attributes include the Yatagarasu, or eight-hand crow; the solar disk; arrows; cock; or, the Three Sacred Relics of the sacred mirror, sword, and necklace of commas.

Amazons. From the Greek for "without a breast." Legendary Greek race of female Scythian warriors who excluded men from their nation, which was governed by a queen. Sacrificing their right breasts for military prowess, these young women were hunters and fighters. Queen Hippolyta's girdle became the object of Hercules' famed ninth labor which ended in the deaths of many Amazons. In classical Greco-Roman art, the Amazons were depicted as martial female figures, dressed in short tunics with a bared right arm and armed with spears or shields. They were usually represented riding horses, an action that signified the strength and prowess of the rider as the one in control. They were the classical Greco-Roman images of the female warrior deities and female warrior saints such as *Joan of Arc.

Ambika. Vedic mythic name for *Ūma, the wife of Shiva or of Rudra.

Ambrosia. From the Greek for "supernatural red wine." Greek mythic fluid associated with *Hera as the mother of the gods. It was believed that partaking of ambrosia granted immortality. It was identified in Egyptian mythology as *sa*, Vedic mythology as *soma*, and Persian mythology as *haoma*. Ambrosia in all its mythic and linguistic variants retains a direct connection to the moon and the feminine, and may be a primordial expression of the potency of menstrual blood.

Amentit. From the Egyptian language for "hidden." Egyptian mother goddess of the necropolis and of the West, including Libyan provinces west of Lower Egypt. As a consort of Amen, she was known in Thebes as *Mut. Amentit assisted in the transformation of the bodies of the blessed into those who will live in the Kingdom of Osiris.

Ammavaru. Telugu mother goddess. She existed before the birth of the Four Ages that were before the creation of the world in *Hinduism. From the egg Ammavaru laid on the Sea of Milk came forth Brahmā, Vishnu, and Shiva. In Indian art, Ammavaru was depicted as riding on a jackal.

Ammit. From the Egyptian language for "devourer of the death." Egyptian female demon who remained by the scales of justice on the Day of Judgment and awaited the verdict to devour the sinner. In Egyptian art, Ammit was identified by the head of a *crocodile, torso of a predatory *cat, and the buttocks of a *hippopotamus.

Amphitrite. From the Greek for "all-encircling triad." Mythic Greek nereid or sea nymph, female personification of the sea, and wife of Poseidon and mother of Triton. In classical Greek art, Amphitrite was depicted as a beautiful young woman with either a net above her hair or crab-claws on her head. Her chariot of shells was drawn by Tritons.

Ana. From the Celtic for "the lasting one." Ancient Irish mother goddess of the earth and fertility. According to Irish tradition, Ana was the mother of all heroes. *See also* Buana, Danaan.

Anahit. From the Persian for "the immaculate;" from the Armenian for "mother of all knowledge." Parsee goddess of fertility and victory. In art, Anahit was depicted as a maiden clothed in a gleaming gold mantle and wearing a diadem and many jewels. In her left hand she held a water pot signifying her role as the goddess of water. As temple prostitution was characteristic of her cult, Anahit wore a *pomegranate blossom on her breast. Anahit was also identified as the chief goddess of fertility and wisdom in indigenous Armenian mythology.

Ananke. From the Greek for "she who guides the worlds." Greek goddess of fate and the female personification of the inevitable. She was associated with the Roman *Fortuna. In classical Greek art, Ananke was represented as a beautiful young woman holding a *spindle in her right hand.

Ananta. From the Sanskrit for "The Infinite." Eternal *serpent in which the deities rest during sleep or death in Hindu mythology. In the earliest tradition, Ananta was identified as female; while later Vedic texts viewed the serpent as male.

Anastacia, Saint. *See* Anastasia, Saint

Anastasia, Saint (d. 304). From the Greek for "resurrection." A fourth-century Christian convert and martyr. According to Christian legend, Anastasia was a noble Roman matron who was condemned for her acts on behalf of imprisoned Christians. She was rescued from an unseaworthy boat overcrowded with slaves by Saint Theodora who guided the ship to a safe landing. During this ordeal, Anastasia's exemplary faith brought about the conversion of the slaves who were later martyred for their newfound religion. Taken to Palmaria (Sirmium in Yugoslavia), she was tortured by being tied to a saltire cross and having her breasts cut off; then she was burned to death. Her relics were believed to have been enshrined in Constantinople or on the Palatine Hill where the Church of Sant' Anastasia was built and decorated with a narrative cycle of murals commissioned by Pope Saint Damascus I. In the Eastern Orthodox Church, she was identified as the *Pharmacolytria* as she rendered poisons harmless. In eastern Christian art, Anastasia was represented a veiled matron who held a covered jar of antidotes in her left hand.

Anat. From the Egyptian language for "lady of heavens and mistress of the gods." Egyptian goddess originally identified as *Anath, an Ugarit war goddess and sister/lover of Baal. She was famed for her fearlessness in slaying Mot, the killer of Baal. In Egyptian art, Anat was depicted as either an enthroned woman who holds a shield and spear in her right hand and a club in her left; or as an erect figure dressed in a panther skin and a white-feathered crown with a pair of horns at the base. In this mode, she holds a papyrus scepter in her right hand and an *ankh in her left.

Anath. From the Phoenician for "providence" or "precaution." Maiden sister of Baal. Anath was a Syrian war goddess. In religious art, she was more commonly identified as the Egyptian goddess *Anat.

Anchoress. From the Greek for "to withdraw." A Christian woman who withdraws from the world to devote herself to a religious life of prayer and solitude. The anchoress was confined to a cell or dwelling that was normally attached to a parish church, and was supported by the charitable gifts of food and life necessities donated by parishioners.

Androgyne. From the Greek for "man" and "woman." Legendary and historic human beings distinguished as being half male and half female, and often misidentified as a *hermaphrodite. Worldwide symbol for the mythic division of the bisexual creator figure such as the Mesopotamian *Tiamat or the Judeo-Christian scriptural Adam of Genesis 1:27. Such "splitting apart" of a bisexual creature was common to all world religions and/or philosophies from the famed passages in Plato's *Symposium* (189–191) and the Book of Genesis (1:27, 2:24) as well as the mythologies of the Navaho, Northwest Coast, and Zuni Indians of North America, the Sudanese Dogon tribes of Africa, and the Hindu tradition of India. In the Rabbinic literature of Judaism, the androgyne was identified as having both male and female characteristics as had Adam (Gn 1:27). In Hebrew law, an androgyne must be treated as a man, that is, circumcision and marriage to a woman. The commonality to representations of the androgyne in religious art was the representation of a human figure who was half man and half woman, the variation was in terms of the dividing line—either vertically or horizontally.

Andromache. Legendary Greek wife of Hector and mother of Astyanax who poetically mourned their deaths during the Trojan War. Following the defeat of Troy and the deaths respectively of her husband at the hands of Achilles and her son by the cruelty of the Greeks, Andromache was awarded as a captive concubine to Achilles' son, Neoptolemus. In classical Greek art, and later during in *renaissance art, Andromache was depicted as an elegant matron who either watched worriedly from the parapet of Troy as her husband struggled against Achilles, or at the moment of her son's death as he was thrown from the parapet, or as the "great mourner."

Andromeda. From the Greek for "ruler of men." Legendary Greek princess of Ethiopia, daughter of Cepheus and Cassiopeia. Her mother defiled the honor of Poseidon by publicly stating that her daughter was more beautiful than his nereids. A wrathful sea god sent an eternally famished sea monster that could only be sated with the sacrifice of Andromeda. Perseus discovered the princess chained to a seaside cliff awaiting her gruesome fate. The young hero proceeded to slay the sea monster and married the princess. During the wedding banquet, a former suitor usually identified as Phineas entered uninvited and publicly claimed his bride. Perseus responded to the physical attack by exposing the severed head of the *Medusa, which immediately transformed Phineas and his supporters into stone. Later after her death, Andromeda was placed among the stars by *Athena. In *classical and *renaissance art, Andromeda was represented as a beautiful young maiden either awaiting the sea monster or being rescued by Perseus. She was the classical foretype of the "maiden in distress."

Anemone. A botanical symbol of death and mourning that also implied illness and decline. A classical Greco-Roman symbol for sorrow and death, the anemone was reputed to have sprung from the *blood of Adonis. In western Christian art, this floral *attribute of *Mary signified her sorrow over the Passion and Death of Jesus Christ. The red-spotted petals of this flower symbolized the blood of Christ. According to legends, the anemone sprung up on Calvary on the eve of the Crucifixion and was therefore found in depictions of this scriptural event. The triple-leafed anemone signified the Trinity in early Christian art.

Angelica. Literary heroine of the romantic epic poem *Orlando Furioso* by Ariosto (1474–1533). As the beloved of several knights in this story of the conflict between the Christians and the Saracens at the time of Charlemagne, Angelica's choice of the Moor Medoro for her husband drove the Christian hero, Orlando, to madness (*furioso*) in his grief and jealousy. A popular topic among baroque and romantic painters, Angelica was depicted as a beautiful young woman elegantly clad and bejeweled in the medieval style. The most popular episodes of her story depicted in art were Angelica and the Hermit, Ruggiero frees Angelica, and Angelica and Medoro. In each of these episodes, she employs the use of magical symbols and was interpreted as a secularized image of the medieval Christian heroines such as Isolde.

Angelico, Fra (c. 1387 or 1400–55). A Dominican Friar whose simple and direct style of painting was used for didactic, not mystical, purposes. Also known as Beato Angelico, his first attributed painting, *Linaccioli Madonna* dated from 1433. When the Dominican Order took over the Convent of Saint Mark in Florence, Fra Angelico created over fifty *frescoes in the monastic cells as aids to contemplation. The altarpieces he painted for this and two other convents led to the development of the format known as the *sacra conversazione* ("sacred conversation"), especially in regard to the *Madonna and Child as the central figures in an altarpiece. His renderings of *Mary revealed a new attitude towards delicate and gentle display of maternal love and female humility.

Angels. From the Greek for "messenger." Spiritual attendants and messengers of the deities in religious art. In Egyptian art, winged human and animal figures guarded the entrances to temples, altars, and *mammisi. The winged mythic messenger deities of classical Greek and Roman art provided routes of communication between humanity and the divinities, and also protected sacred spaces. The *angirases*, youthful demigods, as carriers of divine gifts to humanity, and the *apsarāses*, celestial nymphs, as attendants in the heavenly paradise of Indra, served as the Hindu mythic angels. In Hindu art, these wingless creatures were characterized as sensuous figures engaged as dancers and musicians. The Chinese *t'ien-jen* and the Japanese *tennin* were represented as winged and with lotus flowers. The initial Christian *iconography of angels was derived from the winged *beasts guarding the royal palaces of Assyria and Babylonia. In fifth-century Christianity, the classification of angels was defined by Pseudo-Dionysus the Areopagite according to the political structure of the Byzantine Empire. The first hierarchy of angels consisted of the seraphim, cherubim, and thrones. The seraphim as representatives of divine love were red-colored, bodiless creatures with six wings and flaming *candles. As the signifiers of divine wisdom, the golden-yellow or blue cherubim carried *books. Thrones, garbed in judicial green robes, symbolized divine justice. The second hierarchy of angels were the dominations (dominions), virtues, and powers. As the representatives of the power of God, dominations were depicted as crowned angels who carried the scepter and orb as symbols of authority. The *virtues had as their *attribute either the white *lilies of purity, the red *roses of Jesus' Passion, or the *censer as the symbol of pleas and prayers. Signifying God's eventual triumph over the Devil and evil, the powers were fully armored, victorious warriors. The third, and lowest, hierarchy of angels was composed of the princedoms (principalities), archangels, and angels. Princedoms (principalities) were the dispensers of the Fates of nations; archangels were the warriors of heaven; and angels were the guardians of the innocent and the just, and messengers of God's presence. In the *Old Testament, the angels composed God's heavenly court and were his servants guarding the entrance to the *Garden of Eden, protecting the faithful while punishing the guilty, and conveying divine messages to humanity. The cherubim and the seraphim guarded God's throne, decorated Solomon's temple, and protected the Ark of the Covenant. In the *New Testament, the angels were present at all the major events in the life of Jesus, either to assist him or to announce God's will. In Christian art, the figuration of the angels related to both contemporary artistic style and the angelology. For example, in the fourth century, angels appeared as male figures (usually without feet) dressed in long white robes with *wings. By the High Middle Ages, these personages were more elegantly garbed (depending on their station in the hierarchies) and appeared to be androgynous. In the Renaissance, angels were depicted as being either female figures dressed in the latest fashions (making them more approachable) or plump little children with wings (as influenced by classical Greco-Roman art). The archangels—Michael, Gabriel, and Raphael—were the most frequently depicted angels in western Christian art.

Angerona. Roman goddess of silence. According to tradition, the goddess was the female personification of the secret name of Rome, which was forbidden to be pronounced. She was associated with the gnostic Sige, the female personification of the dark and silent womb in which the first deities were gestated. In Roman art, Angerona was portrayed with a finger in front of her closed lips.

Anglicanism. From the Latin for "English." Medieval identification for the ecclesiastical province of Britain. From the sixteenth century forward, Anglicanism denoted the reformed independent Church of England affiliated with Canterbury not Rome, thereby the Anglican communion. This Christian tradition was established under Henry VIII with his declaration of independence and clarified by Elizabeth I in the Thirty-Nine Articles. It affirmed the historic episcopacy but not the primacy of Rome. Anglicanism has supported a wide body of theological positions including the High Church or Anglo-Catholicism which favored sacramental worship and a high doctrine of the church; the Low Church or Evangelicalism which affirmed the centrality of scripture and doctrine over sacramental worship; the Broad Church which maintained a theological posture between the High and Low Churches; and the Episcopalian Church or the Anglican Church of America.

Aniconism. From the Greek for "without an image, or a likeness." Religious art distinguished by the absence of the human figure. The concept of aniconic religious art implies the presence of a divine or human presence by the implementation of symbols, and/or symbolic referents, such as a *lotus or empty throne. Many religious art traditions, such as Buddhist art, begin aniconically and then develop iconically, that is, by the inclusion of the human figure, particularly in terms of the anthropomorphic presentation of the divine.

Animals, symbolism of. A decorative compositional component while specific animals and/or combinations of animals, such as the *lion and the *lamb, conveyed symbolic meanings. As such, they were media of revelation, and bearers of supernatural powers and archetypal qualities. In those religions with animal cults, the animal signified the earthly image of transcendent or primeval forces. These sacred animals represented an aspect of the sacred entity and had eternal souls. Thereby, their images were interpreted as an anthropomorphized form of the divine image. In religious art, the use of animal imagery had several forms: the actual animal image as a sign or symbol; the anthropomorphized form with an animal head; or an animal as attribute. Sources for animal symbolism were the classical writings such as the *Physiologus and the *Historia Animalium, and the medieval bestiaries. See also Ant, Antelope, Apes, Asp, Ass, Basilisk, Bat, Bears, Beaver, Bee, Bestiary, Boar, Buffalo, Bull, Camel, Cat, Chameleon, Chimera, Cow, Crab, Crocodile, Deer, Dog, Donkey, Dragon, Elephant, Ermine, Fabulous Beasts, Fish, Fly, Fox, Frog, Gazelle, Giraffe, Goat, Grasshopper, Griffin, Gryphon, Hare, Hart, Hedgehog, Hind, Hippocampus, Hippopotamus, *Historia Animalium*, Hog, Horse,

Hyena, Ladybug, Lamb, Leopard, Lion, Lizard, Lynx, Minotaur, Mole, Monkeys, Mythical Beasts, Ox, Ox and Ass, Panther, *Physiologus*, Pig, Rabbit, Ram, Rat, Rhinoceros, Salamander, Scorpion, Serpent, Sheep, Shrew, Snail, Snake, Sphinx, Spider, Squirrel, Stag, Starfish, Swine, Toad, Tortoise, Unicorn, Vulture, Weasel, Whale, Wild Beast, Wolf, and Worms.

Ankamma. *Kālī as the female personification of the disease cholera.

Ankh. Egyptian language for "life." This Egyptian symbol for eternal life and the imperishable vital force was found regularly on the walls of temples and tombs as a sign of divine protection for the dead. Also identified as the "key of the Nile," the ankh purportedly imaged the sexual engagement of the female oval and the male cross. In Egyptian art, the ankh was an *attribute of several goddesses including *Hathor, *Isis, and *Sekhmet. In Coptic Christian art and spirituality, the ankh was transformed into the *crux ansata*, that was a Greek cross with a looped handle over the horizontal bar.

Ankhat. An epithet of the Egyptian goddess Isis as "giver of life."

Anna. An ancient Hebrew prophetess who recognized the infant Jesus of Nazareth during the *Presentation in the Temple. Widowed for eighty-four years after only seven years of marriage, Anna lived her life in prayer, fasting, and supplication in anticipation of the coming of the Messiah. In Christian art, Anna was characterized as an aged woman by her stooped posture and her heavy cloak that covers her head and body. She was positioned near Simeon whose prophecy about the infant Jesus she joyously repeats. Her attribute was the scroll inscribed with Simeon's prophecy (Lk 2:22–28).

Anna-Purna. From the Sanskrit for "full of food." Vedic mythic aspect of *Pārvāti, the wife of Shiva, in her role as provider. In Hindu art, Anna-Purna was portrayed seated on a waterlily while she holds a bowl overflowing with rice in one hand and a spoon in the other.

Anne, Saint (first century). The mother of *Mary and the wife of Joachim. Anne's story and her place in Christian art and spirituality were derived from the apocryphal *Gospel of Mary* and the *Protoevangelium of James*. Although of the House of David, Anne and Joachim were childless, thereby causing his sacrifice to be rejected by the High Priests. Joachim ventured into the desert to offer his sacrifice directly to God. After his offering was completed, Joachim had a vision that his wife would bear a child as an *angel simultaneously announced this special birth to Anne. On his return to Jerusalem, Joachim met Anne at the Golden Gate and they rejoiced in this news. Anne was the patron of pregnant women and was invoked during childbirth. In western Christian art, Anne was depicted in the extrascriptural narrative scenes of the Marian narrative of the *Annunciation of the Birth of Mary (*Protoevangelium of James* 4:1), the *Meeting at the Golden Gate (*Protoevangelium of James* 4:4), the *Nativity of the Virgin Mary (*Protoevangelium of James* 5:2), and the *Presentation of the Virgin Mary in the Temple (*Protoevangelium of James* 7:2). In single paintings, Anne taught Mary to read or embroider, and was represented seated with Mary on her lap. Prior to condemnation by the *Council of Trent, images of Anne with Mary on her lap, and Jesus on his mother's lap were popular. This scene was replaced by the motif of the Holy Family. In western Christian art, Anne was represented as a middle-aged matron who signified perfect motherhood. She was depicted in a *red dress with a *green mantle signifying divine love and immortality.

Annunciation of the Death of the Virgin Mary (*The Golden Legend* 119). Rarely depicted in Christian art, the Annunciation of the Death of Mary was the first scene in the narrative of her *Dormition. Having completed a full life, Mary prayed for the release offered by death. The Archangel Michael, the carrier of *souls, appeared and presented her with a *palm branch. He told Mary that in three days she would join her son. The symbol of the oasis, and therefore of heaven, the palm branch was later carried by John in Mary's burial procession. Presented in a similar manner to the *Annunciation to Mary, the Annunciation of the Death of Mary was comprised of the kneeling or praying figure of Mary who was offered the palm branch by the Archangel Michael.

Annunciation to the Virgin Mary (Lk 1:26–38). Scriptural event signifying the announcement of the miraculous conception of the Son of God. The Archangel Gabriel appeared to *Mary to tell her that she would bear God's special child. One of the most popular themes in the history of Christian art, rivaled only by images of the Crucifixion and the *Madonna and Child, the Annunciation was described in both canonical and apocryphal texts. In the earliest Christian renderings of this theme, Mary was placed to the viewer's left and Gabriel to the right. She was initially depicted as a simple maiden who held a spindle or a piece of embroidered cloth signifying her weaving the veil of the Temple, according to the *Protoevangelium of James* (10:1). A visual metaphor for gestation, weaving was a reminder of the parallels between Marian imagery and that of *Athena. Gabriel was originally represented as a youthful erect male figure who raised his right hand in a gesture of greeting. By the medieval period, the *iconography of the Annunciation became more complex, from the elaborate garments of Mary and Gabriel (including his rainbow-colored *wings) to the inclusion of such botanical symbols as the *lily and the *rose without thorns (influenced by the Song of Songs), and several signs of cleanliness such as the water jar, white *towels, and the *washbasin. Mary was characterized as the enthroned queen of *heaven who received the kneeling messenger of God. Her garments, throne, and bodily gestures, along with the posture of the archangel, indicated the esteem with which Mary was revered. In the twelfth century, the Virgin Annunciate held a *book either in her hands or open before her on her lap or prie-dieu. This new iconographic motif related directly to the concept of Mary as *Sophia (*Wisdom) and to the economic position of women book owners. Theologically, this image of the Virgin Annunciate reading a book denoted Mary's foreknowledge that her child was born to die in her own lifetime, thereby making her acceptance of God's request that much greater and her sacrifice more meaningful. The *dove, the

4. Gerard David, *The Saint Anne Altarpiece*

5. *The Birth of Aphrodite* from the Ludovisi Throne

symbol of the Holy Spirit, became more prominent as it either hovered over Mary's womb or descended towards her from a clear glass window. This new motif developed in northern *medieval art as a visual defense of Mary's perpetual virginity: for just as light descended through the window without destroying the clean glass, so Mary conceived and bore this special child while her physical virginity remained intact. The setting for this scene was defined in the medieval period; southern artists painted this scene in gardens or palazzo porches, while northern artists favored interior domestic or ecclesiastical settings. One unique variation of Annunciation iconography in late medieval art was Simone Martini's *Annunciation*. In his version, Gabriel wore a *wreath of *olive leaves and carried an *olive branch to present to Mary, while the more typical vase of lilies rested in the background. As a Sienese artist, Martini could not have allowed Gabriel to present Mary with the symbol of the rival city of Florence! Beginning with the Renaissance, Mary was represented as a simple young maiden whose reading of her *Book of Hours was interrupted by the unexpected visitor. With the revival of Mariology in *baroque art, the topic of the Annunciation to Mary was revived as the initial moment of Mary's glorification.

Anointing at Bethany (Jn 12:1–8; Lk 7:36–50). Differing scriptural accounts exist of the anointing of Jesus by a woman who recognized his uniqueness. According to John, Jesus went to the home of Lazarus and his two sisters, *Martha and *Mary of Bethany, for the evening meal on the sixth day before Passover. After Martha served the meal,

Mary anointed Jesus' *head and *feet with precious ointments. Then she dried his feet with her hair. Judas rebuked her for this extravagance that could have benefited the poor, while Jesus defended her as he knew his time was short. Luke, however, related that Jesus was dining in the house of Simon the Pharisee when an anonymous, sinful woman entered and anointed his feet. Both the anonymous anointer of Luke and Mary the sister of Martha became conflated with *Mary Magdalene.

Ant. Symbol of diligence, organized communal life, and foresight in western Christian art.

Antelope. Fleet creature with beautiful eyes and antlers. Misidentified in the *Physiologus* with the reindeer, the antelope was reputed to encounter death at the Euphrates River where it seeks water. As it played with the herbecine shrub, the antelope's antlers became ensnared. As the trapped animal bellowed in fear, it was killed by a hunter. In Egyptian art and mythology, the antelope was an attribute of the Egyptian goddess, *Satis, as the antelope's horns signified the annual Nile flood. In Christian art, the antelope symbolized the wise man who heeds the warnings of feminine entanglements and the dangers of drink, lest he be trapped for the waiting Devil.

Antigone. Legendary Greek daughter of Oedipus and Jocasta, and a classical symbol of filial piety and devotion. She followed her unfortunate blinded father condemned by the Furies into exile. After his death, she buried him in the appropriate manner at Colonnus, and then returned to Thebes. She supervised the burial rites of both her brothers, Eteocles and Polynices, who killed each other in the war of the Seven against Thebes. However she suffered burial while alive as punishment for providing the rebel Polynices with a proper burial. In classical Greek art, Antigone was depicted as a pious maiden either in the act of accompanying her blinded father or burying her brothers.

Antiope. *Amazon and sister of Queen Hippolyta in Greek mythology. According to legend, she was raped by Theseus and bore his son Hippolytus. She fought with Theseus on behalf of Athens in the war with Amazons. Antiope reputedly met her fate at the hands of her sister Amazons in battle. Another version recounts that when she tried to prevent Theseus's marriage to Phaedra, he killed Antiope. According to the Roman mythographers Hyginus and Ovid, Antiope was a Greek nymph who was ravished in her sleep by Jupiter in the form of a satyr. Artistic representations of the beautiful Antiope asleep in the woods and being uncovered by the horned and goat-footed satyr were a popular medium for the portrayal of the female nude in *classical and *renaissance art.

Anuket. From the Greek for "to embrace." Greek form of the Egyptian goddess, Anukis. *See* Anukis.

Anukis. Egyptian goddess of lust and/or fertility. Anukis was the wife of Khnum and the mother of Satis. As the goddess of the First Cataract of Aswan and the Triad of Elephantine, her cult was known in Nubia, hence her attributes of the red parrot and the gazelle.

In Egyptian art, Anukis was portrayed as a woman holding a tall papyrus scepter and wearing a crown of feathers. She may be accompanied by either of her animal attributes.

Anunītu. Babylonian goddess of childbirth as an aspect of *Inanna.

Aparājīta. From the Sanskrit for "the unconquered (female) one." Indian Tantric Buddhist female deity. In Buddhist art, Aparājīta was denoted by her yellow color, and her one head and two arms. Bedecked with *jewels, she aroused terror with her countenance and was more often depicted trampling the elephant god, Ganesha.

Apes. In religious art, apes were identified as solar animals whose screeches at sunrise were homages to the sun and a form of worship to the indigenous solar deity, e.g., the Japanese goddess *Amaterasu Omikami. In Egyptian art and mythology, the ape was the attribute of the god Thoth, patron of scribes, inventor of hieroglyphs, and lord of divine writings. Signifying the baser forces of human and *animal existence such as lust, envy, cunning, and malice, apes represented the Devil in western Christian art. An ape eating an *apple denoted the *Fall of Adam and Eve. Depictions of enchained apes in scenes of the *Adoration of the Magi were personifications of sin conquered by Christ. Mirroring human failure such as lust and sloth, apes were associated with orgiastic sexuality. In particular, female apes were believed to have lascivious natures, and thereby exposed their buttocks to male apes. As such, apes symbolized prostitutes or lustful women.

Aphrodite. From the Greek for "she who is born of foam" or "she who arises from the sea." Greek goddess of love, beauty, and the generative powers of nature who was born of sea foam and carried to land on a seashell. With her earthly lover, Anchises, she conceived Aeneas, the Trojan ancestor of Rome, and was identified as "the Mother of Rome and the Romans." As a fertility goddess, she was connected visually and literally with the oriental goddesses *Astarte and *Ishtar. The goddess to whom Paris awarded the Golden Apple, Aphrodite was integral to the Trojan War and the downfall of Troy. *Incense and *flowers were sacrificed to her; the apple, *rose, *poppy, and *myrtle were her botanical *attributes. She was also seen with the *ram, *goat, *hare, *dove, *sparrow, *swan, and *swallow. In classical Greco-Roman and *renaissance art, Aphrodite was depicted as a beautiful young woman who was either nude or lightly clad, and was identified by any of her *attributes. Pearls, the tears of the oyster (a sea creature), were sacred to her. As the "Mother of Rome," a fertility goddess, the temptress who won the Golden Apple, and from her associations with the *sea, love, and certain *flower and *animal symbols, Aphrodite prefigured *Mary.

Apocalypse. From the Greek for "uncovering" or "revelation." A form of visionary literature found in the *Old and *New Testaments. Exemplified by the prophecies of Ezekiel and Daniel, apocalyptic literature predicted the end of the world. In the New Testament, the Book of Revelation attributed to John (not to be identified with John the Apostle) was influential on western Christian art, especially the medieval depictions of the last days. The revelatory image of the *Woman Clothed with the Sun (Rv 12:1–6) was a popular theme in *medieval and *baroque art. Other iconographic motifs developed from the Book of Revelation, such as the Four Horsemen of the Apocalypse, were popular in medieval manuscript *illuminations, tapestries, and woodcuts, especially during the times of the Black Plague.

Apocrypha. From the Greek for "obscure" or "hidden." These fifteen books were written after the fifth to fourth century B.C.E. and not included in the later rabbinic Hebrew canon of Scripture, but were part of the earlier Septuagint Greek canon. Though often regarded as extracanonical, these texts were removed from the Hebrew canon but as included in the Greek canon were influential upon Christian art and in the consciousness of Christian believers. The *Old Testament apocryphal texts included twelve significant books such as those of *Judith and *Susanna. All the texts of the Old Testament Apocrypha, except for I and II Esdras and the Prayer of Manasseh, formed an accepted part of the Roman Catholic Canon. The Protestant traditions follow the rabbinic canon and identified all fifteen books as apocryphal and usually have excerpted them into an appendix to the Bible. The *Council of Trent declared these books to be "deuterocanonical"; that is, inspired texts equal in rank but later in date to the other books of the bible.

Apocryphal Gospels. A series of legendary and devotional narrative texts written after the second century C.E. which relate extraordinary and strange tales about scriptural figures. An important source for writers and artists, these texts were identified as untrue or false stories. Among the Apocryphal Gospels crucial for the imagery of women in Christian art were the *Protoevangelium of James, Gospel of Pseudo-Matthew, Gospel of Thomas*, and *Infancy Gospel of Mary*.

Apollonia, Saint (d. 249). Alexandrian Christian noted for her *charity, piety, and purity. A *deaconess of the *church, she refused to worship pagan idols, which broke into a thousand pieces as she made the sign of the *cross. According to early Christian accounts, Apollonia was tortured by having her jaws broken. Medieval legend, however, described the painful removal of her *teeth with flaming *pincers. In any event, following these tortures, Apollonia dedicated her *body to Christ and fell upon a burning pyre. The patron of dentists, she was invoked against toothaches. In western Christian art, Apollonia was depicted as a beautiful young woman who held either a pincer with teeth or a *dish with pincers and teeth and a *palm branch.

Appearance to His Mother. Without any scriptural or apocryphal foundation, and first advocated by Ambrose in his *Liber de Virginitate*, this postresurrection event was described in detail in the *Meditations on the Life of Christ*. This motif was popular in northern *medieval art and legend, was a special devotion of the Jesuits, and was declared official teaching of the church by the *Council of Trent. *Mary prayed for solace following the death and burial of her son, while the Risen Christ, who was holding the victorious *banner and displaying his wounds, interrupted her prayers. This motif was alternatively identified as Christ Appearing before His Mother or Christ Taking Leave of His Mother.

Appearance to Mary Magdalene (*Noli me tangere*) (Jn 20:1–18). Scriptural event signifying both the Resurrection of Christ and denoting *Mary Magdalene as the first witness to the Resurrection. Having found the tomb of Jesus empty, the other Marys went to tell *Peter and the other apostles, while Mary Magdalene remained at the tomb crying over the loss of the body of Jesus. The two *angels in the sepulcher inquired why she wept, and when she turned to respond she encountered a man she thought was a gardener. However, when he called her name she recognized him as the Resurrected Christ. Reaching out to touch him, he warned her he had not yet ascended to his Father. He then sent her to affirm his resurrection to the apostles. This dramatic scene was originally included within the context of the Passion and Resurrection narratives, but by the medieval period became an independent topic influenced in part by the development of the passion plays. *See also* Noli me tangere.

Appiades. Collective Roman name for the five goddesses: *Concordia, *Minerva, *Pax, *Venus, and *Vesta.

Apple. A classical Greco-Roman *attribute for *Aphrodite, who was awarded the Golden Apple by Paris, an action that led to the Trojan War. The goddess gave Hippomenes three golden apples to drop before *Atalanta thereby permitting him to win the race and her hand in marriage. The apple bough signified both the minor Greek goddess *Nemesis and the price of entry into the Elysian Fields. A botanical attribute of the *Graces. In Christian art, the apple was an ambivalent symbol for sin and salvation. The primary botanical symbol for sin, especially *Original Sin, the apple was depicted in the *hands of either Adam, *Eve, or the *serpent, or in the mouth of an *ape to signify the *Fall. The apple nonetheless became the *fruit of the *Tree of Good and Evil because the Latin word for apple, *malum*, had derived from the same root as the word for evil, *malus*. When held by either the infant or young Jesus, or by his mother, *Mary, the apple became a fruit of salvation, as they bore the burden of human sinfulness and restored humanity to God (Song 2:3). Three apples, usually in a *basket, were an *attribute of *Dorothea. Wild apple blossoms symbolize female beauty in Chinese art.

Apples of Hesperides. Mythic Greek wedding gift of a tree bearing golden apples to *Hera from *Gaia. Planted in the far west, the daughters of Atlas known as the Hesperides guarded the tree.

Apsarās, Apsarāses. Celestial beings characterized in the Vedas as the water nymphs who serve as attendants to the Hindu sky god, Indra, in his Paradise. The apsarāses were transformed into celestial musicians and dancers, and became the attendants of the god of love, Kama, and thereby the mistresses of deities and heroes. In their Buddhist forms, they joined the service and ceremonial processions of the Buddha and became a popular motif on temples and sanctuaries. In Hindu art, the apsarāses were portrayed as beautiful young women, often winged and/or bare to the waist, who were otherwise richly adorned with much *jewelry and elegant headdresses. Their *attributes included the *swan and the *drum. In Buddhist art, the apsarāses were winged and bejeweled young nymphs found either in processional groups surrounding the Buddha, or hovering over a stupa or a pagoda.

Arachne. Legendary Greek maiden of extraordinary skill in spinning and weaving. Challenging *Athena to a contest, Arachne reputedly wove such a delicate and flawless cloth that the jealous goddess destroyed it in a rage. An alternate version of the myth reports that Athena wove the more delicate and flawless cloth. In despair at the outcome of the contest, the maiden hanged herself as the goddess completed her revenge by transforming the beautiful mortal into a spider that was condemned eternally to hang and to spin. In the Roman version as recounted by Ovid in his *Metamorphoses* (6:129–45), Arachne wove a pattern of the loves of Olympus on her flawless cloth. The depiction enraged *Minerva who tore the cloth into pieces. In despair at the goddess's wrath, the maiden hanged herself but was saved from death by Minerva who transformed Arachne into a spider dangling eternally on her thread. In *classical and *renaissance art, Arachne was represented as a beautiful young maiden weaving at her loom as the armored goddess either sat watching intently or stood with her raised hand pointing to the loom; or at the moment of her transformation into a spider dangling from a web.

Aradia. Daughter of *Diana. Aradia was identified as the "queen of the witches" in medieval Europe. Her *attribute was the *moon.

Aranrhod. Powerful mother goddess in Celtic mythology. She was the keeper of the Silver Wheel of the Stars, a symbol for Time. Her name was derived from the Latin *corona borealis* and was the Welsh form of *Ariadne.

Arethusa. *Nereid companion of *Artemis and *inspiration for pastoral poetry. Artemis transformed Arethusa into a spring in order to aide her escape from the unwanted advances of the river god, Alpheius. She was also identified as one of the *Hesperides for whom the springs at Chalcis and Euboea were named. A rare topic in classical Greco-Roman art, Arethusa was represented as either a beautiful young nereid with Artemis or being transformed into a water.

Ariadne. From the Greek for "high fruitful mother." Mythic Greek daughter of King Minos and Pasiphae, lover of Theseus, and wife of the god Dionysius. According to tradition, Greece sent a tribute of fourteen youths and maidens to the Minotaur of Knossos every nine years. Ariadne became enamored of the youth, Theseus, whom she aided in killing the Minotaur and escaping from the famed maze of Knossos. She gave the youth a ball of string to form an exit path from the labyrinth. She escaped with the Greeks but was deserted by Theseus on Naxos. The god Dionysius found her and fell in love with her. As a marriage gift, Zeus made Ariadne immortal and placed her bridal crown among the stars (Corona Borealis). She

became identified as a vegetation goddess. In classical Rome, she was identified with the wine goddess, Liberia, just as Bacchus was with the wine god Liber. In *classical Greco-Roman and *renaissance art, Ariadne was portrayed as a beautiful young woman within the context of the Minotaur narrative or in scenes of her abandonment by Theseus, or in her marriage to Dionysius.

Armaiti. Female personification of compliant speech in *Hinduism. Intimately related to the earth, Armaiti was simultaneously a goddess of the earth, of fertility, and of the dead who have "entered" the earth.

Armor. A sign of chivalry and defense against evil. Female warriors and belligerent goddesses wore armor to denote their aggressive, "male," natures. Armor was a metaphor for Christian faith as a protection against the Devil or evil (Eph 6:11–18). Most of the Christian military saints, like George of Cappadocia, William of Aquitaine, and *Joan of Arc, were depicted in their armor and carried a *sword. The Archangel Michael was distinguished by his armor, which was covered with the sign of the *cross.

Arrow. A weapon that signified spiritual or physical disease, especially the plague, or love. In Buddhist art, the arrow with a bow connoted the destruction of the passions, the gift of concentration and wisdom, or love. In *classical Greco-Roman art, a bow and arrow signified either the advent or departure of love, or the hunt. It was an *attribute of Amor, *Aphrodite, Apollo, *Artemis, Cupid, *Diana, Eros, Putti, and *Venus. In western Christian art, a spiritual weapon signifying the dedication of one's life to God. As an instrument of torture, the arrow was an attribute of Sebastian and *Ursula. A symbol of war and death, the arrow was an attribute of most military saints, including George of Cappadocia and *Joan of Arc. The flaming arrow was an attribute of *Teresa of Avila, and three arrows identified Bartholomew and Edmund. Arrows piercing the heart signified *Augustine, and an arrow piercing both the *stag and his *hand represented Giles.

Artemidos, Saint. Legendary Christian virgin saint erroneously interpreted from a votive image of *Artemis.

Artemis. Greek virgin goddess of the *moon, the night, and the hunt. Artemis was the guardian and huntress of wild *animals and the protector of youth, particularly maidens. Twin sister of *Apollo, she was associated with other virgin goddesses including *Diana of Ephesus and *Astarte. As a vegetation and fertility goddess, Artemis was invoked by women in childbirth. She was attended by virgins who were severely punished if they strayed from their vows of chastity. In classical Greco-Roman and *renaissance art, she was depicted as a beautiful young woman, often winged, dressed in a short chiton, wearing *sandals, carrying a bow and quiver, and with the crescent moon in her *hair. Her companions were does, *lions, and *dogs. She was a classical Greco-Roman foretype of *Mary, especially through her connection to Diana of Ephesus and most of her *attributes were assimilated into Marian *iconography.

Artemisia (fourth century B.C.E.). Roman symbol of widow's devotion to the memory of her husband. Following the death of her husband, Mausolus, in 353 B.C.E., Artemisia succeeded him as satrap of Caria. She built a major memorial, i.e., mausoleum, to him that became one of the "seven wonders of the world." According to the Roman historian, Valerius Maximus, the bereaved widow became a living tomb by drinking her husband's ashes. In *renaissance and *baroque art, Artemisia was depicted as a well-dressed matron holding either a goblet or urn.

Artio. Gallic-Helvetian goddess of forests and hunting. Her primary center of worship was near Berne, meaning "bears." Her attribute was the *bear. Artio was related to the Roman *Diana and the Greek *Artemis. Artio was also identified as a Celtic priestess of the bear clan and was characterized as seated before or offering fruit to a great bear.

Āryajangulī. *Tārā "who removes poison" in Tantric Buddhist art. Found only in paintings and mandalas, Āryajangulī was a multiarmed and many headed female figure seated on a *lotus. She held *peacock feathers in her right hands and *serpents in her left hands.

Asceticism. From the Greek for "to train the body." Religious practice of self-denial characterized by starvation, self-inflicted physical injury, austerity, and sexual renunciation. This form of religious activity was found in religious traditions, sometimes with an emphasis on a particular form of denial, most often sexuality as for example among the Essenes.

Asera. From the Semitic for "Mother of the Gods" or "Queen of the Sea."

Semitic-Amorite goddess of love and fertility. She was related to the Babylonian *Astarte. Asera was represented as a beautiful naked woman.

Asertu. Semitic goddess famed for her acts of infidelity with the weather god.

Asherah. From the Semitic for "in wisdom the mistress of the gods." The Canaanite form of the *Great Goddess also known as *Astarte, *Demeter, *Hathor, *Isis, and *Venus. Asherah was a fertility goddess and the consort of the god, Baal. In Canaanite art, she was characterized as a naked female figure who wore a horned headdress. Her *attributes included flocks of sheep, sacred tress, or a carved wooden pole that was usually placed near her altar.

Ashes. Sign of the transitory nature of human existence and penance. In early Christian and medieval times, repentant sinners rubbed ashes over their bodies and wore sackcloth as signs of denial of material goods. Ashes from the *palms of the previous Palm Sunday were blessed and then placed on the forehead of Christian believers as a sign of the penance of Lent.

Ashokakāntā. Popular variation of the Buddhist female deity, *Mārīcī. In Buddhist art, Ashokakāntā was depicted as bedecked with jewels, clothed in white, and as golden yellow in color. She rode on a *pig or stood on a *moon above a *lotus. Her right hand gesture of *varadamudrā* revealed that wishes had been granted.

Ashthābhuja-Kurakulla. From the Sanskrit for "eight-armed one." Special iconographic form of the Tantric Red *Tārā, Kurakulla, featuring one *head and eight arms, red in color, and seated in meditation on the *sun above a red *lotus with eight leaves.

Asnan. Mesopotamian wheat goddess.

Asp. A reptilian symbol for evil and venom, and thereby death, in western Christian art.

Aspen. A symbol of the Crucifixion in Christian. According to legend, the wood of the aspen was chosen for the cross of Jesus, and the leaves of the *tree trembled with shame. According to another legend, when Jesus died on the cross, all the other trees bowed their heads in sorrow and respect, except for the aspen. As a punishment for its hubris, the aspen's leaves were condemned to eternal trembling.

Ass. An ambivalent but common animal symbol in religious art simultaneously signifying humility and torment. In Egyptian art, the ass was an attribute of the evil god Seth and signified torment and burden. It was also an attribute of the sun god as a beneficent creature and protector against evil. The ass was a symbol of the simplest and most humble of all created beings in western Christian art. Known for its docility, humility, patience, and stubbornness, the ass was a common presence in Christian art, and was included in narrative presentations of the Sacrifice of Isaac, *Nativity, *Flight into Egypt, *Rest on the Flight into Egypt, *Return from Egypt, and Entry into Jerusalem. Both *Mary and Jesus rode an ass to signify their humility. The presence of the ass in Nativity scenes fulfilled the prophecy of Isaiah 1:3 and signified that even the lowest of the *animals recognized the Messiah. As a domestic animal, the ass was depicted with *Old Testament figures, such as Abigail, or Christian *saints, including *Jerome and Anthony of Padua.

Assumption of the Virgin Mary (*The Assumption of the Virgin* and *The Golden Legend* 119). Event signifying *Mary's entry into *heaven following her *dormition and burial. Without scriptural foundation, this event was described in legendary and devotional materials, and was accepted as common belief. The word assumption implied assistance or help, so that Mary was depicted surrounded by *clouds and *angels who carried her upwards to her heavenly reward. Originally, the representation of the assumption of Mary's soul was a motif in the byzantine *iconography of the *Koimesis. Once a part of the narrative and iconography of the *Dormition, the Assumption of Mary became an independent topic in western Christian art during the late medieval period. This theme flourished in the art of southern baroque artists who visually defended Mary's uniqueness against the outcries of the Reformers. The Assumption of Mary was interpreted as central to her position as intercessor or mediator for human beings who hoped for salvation and protection within the Christian faith. This common belief was declared an article of faith for all Roman Catholics by Pope Pius XII in 1950. In depictions of this theme, Mary was surrounded by music making or singing *angels, wispy clouds, and many *attributes from the Song of Songs and the Book of Revelation, including a *crown of twelve *stars and roses of sharon. The apostles stood below in total amazement, while God the Father and the Risen Christ awaited her arrival. In byzantine and late medieval renderings of this theme, Mary dropped her girdle, the last symbol of her earthly chastity and her perpetual virginity according to legend and apocryphal texts, upon the *head of Thomas, who doubted both her dormition and assumption.

Astarte. From the Canaanite for "mother of mankind." Near Eastern mother goddess identified with the Babylonian goddess of sky and fertility, *Ishtar. The principal goddess of Phoenicia and Canaan, Astarte personified love and fertility. Among the Philistines, she was known as a goddess of war "clad in terror." Mentioned in the *Old Testament, Astarte received occasional homage from Solomon (I Kgs 11:5; II Kgs 23:13). In Egypt, she was revered as the daughter of the sun god, Ra, and as a goddess of war. She was also identified with the Queen of Byblos who served as wet nurse to Horus when *Isis went in search of Osiris. In Near Eastern art, Astarte was depicted as a beautiful naked woman with visual emphasis placed on her breasts and womb. In Egyptian art, she was represented as a naked woman riding bareback and carrying weapons; or standing of a lioness as she held a mirror and lotus in her hands; or with a lioness head surmounted by a disk of the sun and standing on a horse-drawn chariot. As the "queen of the stars" and the mother of the solar god, Astarte was a classical foretype of *Mary.

Asteria. Mythic Greek sister of *Leto. To save herself from Zeus's unwelcome pursuit, Asteria transformed herself first into a *quail and then into the island of

6. Antonio Vivarini, *Saint Apollonia Destroying a Pagan Idol*
7. *Asherah, or Goddess of Fertility, from a cover of a box
which contained unguents and medicine*

8. *Astarte*

9. *Athena Flying Her Owl*

Ortygia (Delos). Fleeing *Hera's wrath, a pregnant Leto sought refuge on Ortygia in order to give safe birth to *Artemis.

Astlik. From the Armenian for "star." Indigenous Armenian goddess of nature and love was identified with *Ishtar and *Aphrodite.

Astraea. From the Greek for "starry one." Greek virgin goddess of justice and one of the *Horae. This daughter of Zeus and Themis was translated into the heavens as the constellation identified as Virgo. In classical Greco-Roman art, Astraea was represented as a young maiden who held the scales of justice in her right hand and a *cornucopia in her left.

Ataecina. Indigenous Hispanic goddess of the underworld associated with *Proserpina.

Ataentsic. Legendary Iroquois and Huron female ancestor of the human race. According to tradition, Ataentsic was a woman of the sky people who came to earth and conceived twins by the lord of the winds.

Atalanta (*Metamorphosis* 10:560–707). Mythological huntress famed for her beauty, physical agility, virginity, and distrust of men. According to legend, she was abandoned at birth by her father who wanted a son. Raised by hunters and nursed by she bears, Atalanta grew up to be a proverbial hater of men and perpetually avowed virgin. She challenged each of her suitors to a race: if he won, she was the prize; if he lost, he lost his life. In her race with Hippomenes (Melanion), he won not by physi-

cal skill but by dropping three golden *apples given him by *Venus in order to entrap Atalanta who lost the contest when she stopped to gather the apples. In a moment of intense passion, Atalanta and Hippomenes made love in a temple dedicated to *Cybele. Outraged, the goddess transformed the offending couple into *lions that drew her chariot. In *classical, *renaissance, and *baroque art, Atalanta was depicted as a beautiful and physically powerful woman, either nude or wearing a chiton like the huntress *Diana, who bends over to pick up the discarded apples as Hippomenes runs past.

Atargatis. Syrian mother goddess. Atargatis was portrayed seated on a lion-flanked throne and holding her attributes of an ear of corn and a stone.

Atchet. From the Egyptian language for "to nurse." Egyptian female counterpart to the sun god, Ra. Atchet was the goddess of nurturing and nursing children. In Egyptian art, she was represented in the act of nursing a child or children.

Até. Greek goddess of disaster. Até was the feminine embodiment of that blind folly that stupefies man and results in disaster.

Athaliah (2 Chr 22:10–12; 23:1–17). *Daughter of *Jezebel and Old Testament feminine embodiment of idolatry. Advocate of the worship of Baal, Athaliah as ruler of Judah antagonized the people. She commanded a massacre of all male children of the House of David following the death of her own son. However, her young stepson, Joash, was rescued by the priests and upon his maturity, was proclaimed king. Despite her cries of "treason," Athaliah was dragged from the Temple and executed. Simultaneously, the images of and the altar dedicated to Baal were destroyed. In early Christian art, Athaliah was depicted garbed as a queen either in the act of idol worship or at the moment of her death. She was a popular topic of the moralizing prints created by northern artists.

Athena. Greek virgin goddess of *wisdom, war, and weaving. The protector of eternal virginity who ruled over the moral and intellectual life of the Greeks, Athena was responsible for inventions and innovations in the arts and sciences. As the goddess of wisdom and peace, she was venerated by poets and philosophers. The protector and defender of Athens, her greatest temple was the Parthenon on the Acropolis. In classical Greco-Roman and *renaissance art, she was depicted as a physically strong woman dressed in a long chiton and a breastplate, her *head covered with a *helmet, and carrying *shield emblazoned with the head of the *Medusa. She was accompanied by an *owl, the symbol of wisdom, who sat on her arm. She held either a spear as the goddess of war or a distaff as the goddess of weaving and the domestic arts. The *olive tree, sea eagle, *serpent, and *rooster were sacred to Athena. An imposing physical figure, she was the descendent of the Egyptian goddesses *Isis and *Neith, and the classical Greco-Roman foretype of the heroines and female warrior *saints of the Hebraic and Christian traditions. As the embodiment of chastity and the female personification of wisdom, she prefigured *Mary.

Athena Nike. Small temple on the Acropolis of Athens that was dedicated to *Athena as the goddess of victory, both in military encounters and political intrigues.

Athena Parthenos. Famed gold and silver statue of *Athena as the goddess of wisdom, war, and weaving made by Phidias for the Parthenon.

Athletes of God. An early Christian visual and verbal metaphor derived from the writings of Paul and the early church fathers who saw an analogy between the disciplined physical and spiritual training of the Olympian and Pythian athletes and the sufferings of the early Christian martyrs. In their fatal competition against the gladiators or the *lions in the Roman arenas, these Christian "athletes of God" were depicted receiving the *laurel wreath of victory, which represented the victory over death, from *angels. This image was revived and reinterpreted by renaissance artists, including *Michelangelo.

Atirat. From the Arabic for "brilliance, brightness." Semitic solar goddess.

Atropos. From the Greek for "cutter." One of the *Moirai. This daughter of Zeus and Themis cut the thread spun by her sister *Clotho and measured by her sister *Lachesis. In classical Greco-Roman and renaissance art, Atropos was represented as a matron or old woman who held a scissors or knife and was about to cut the thread of life.

Attribute. An emblem or an object that identified a biblical, historic, legendary, or mythological figure in religious art. In Christian art, the attribute was connected to either the style of martyrdom, e.g., a spiked wheel for *Catherine of Alexandria; the central legend or moral the person represented, e.g., the *dragon for *Martha of Bethany; or the prophecy foretold by the person, e.g., a *scroll with the inscription of verse 7:14 for Isaiah or a shut gate for Ezekiel.

Auge. Minor Greek goddess of birth or an epithet of *Artemis.

Augustine of Hippo, Saint (354–430). A *Doctor of the Church and one of the four great fathers of the Western Church. Born to a pagan father and a Christian mother, *Monica, the story of his lengthy journey to the Christian faith was reported in the first autobiography in western literature, *Confessions*, which was also a classic work of Christian mysticism. One of the most influential theologians of the early *church, Augustine wrote the first Christian philosophy of history, *The City of God*, which had a great influence on the Holy Roman Emperor Charlemagne and the establishment of the western medieval feudal system. He was famed for his treatises against the Manichaean and the Pelagian controversies, and he established or codified the church's official position on many aspects of the Christian life, including the teachings on *Original Sin. Augustine and his later western interpreters identified Eve's hubris as the cause of the Fall and of the resulting uncontrollable lust of women as the downfall of men. Augustine was the patron of theologians and scholars. In western Christian art, he was depicted as a middle-aged man, either beardless or with a short beard, dressed as a bishop and holding a *book or a *pen signifying his many influential texts. *See also* Lucretia.

Aureole. From the Latin for "golden." A circle or orbit of light signifying the radiance of divinity. Transported to western art from Oriental art by the armies of Alexander the Great, the origin of the aureole was similar to that of the *mandorla, which signified the radiance of the holy person. In western Christian art, the mandorla came to be reserved for representations of Jesus Christ and *Mary as a signifier of their unique bodily glory, and the aureole or halo came to encase only the head of a holy person. *See also* Cakra, Glory.

Aurora. Roman goddess of the dawn characterized as "rosy-fingered and saffron-robed." Aurora left her aged husband, Tithonius, asleep, to lead her brother, the sun god Helios, into the sky every morning. She was simultaneously mother and wife of Tithonius whom she imbued with immortality at his birth but not eternal youth. According to some legends, he becomes gray and shrunken, ultimately transforming into a cicada that chirps with great intensity at the rising of the sun. Destined to become infatuated with youthful mortals, Aurora engaged in daring sexual encounters including a famous liaison with Cephalus who resisted the goddess until she was alleged to have raped him. In *classical Greco-Roman art, Aurora was depicted as a winged and beautiful young maiden who drove a four-horse chariot. She was often depicted in postures mourning of her beloved son, Memnon, killed by Achilles in the Trojan War. In this motif, the dew was reputed to be her tears. A popular theme in *baroque art, especially the great ceiling paintings, Aurora was represented in her chariot or riding the winged white horse, Pegasus, and often surrounded by the *Horae.

Australian Aboriginal art. Rich and complex indigenous symbolism characterized by Dreaming, or Dream Time, understood as the "seeing of eternal things." Ritual experience or spiritual encounter with this primordial moment led to a recognition of eternity and of universe, and thereby led to a world order in which humanity existed and forever found renewal. This primeval unity of humanity and nature undergird the symbol-laden universe of the Australian Aborigines and was expressed through a variety of the arts from cave paintings, totem carvings, and graphic signs, coordinated with the performance arts of chanting, dancing, and acting. Visually, Australian aboriginal art was characterized by abstracted simplifications of nature from human and animal figures to geological objects, and empowered by a spiritual vitality.

Australian Aboriginal religion. Belief and ritual systems of the indigenous people of Australia. Premised upon the concept of Dreaming, or Dream Time, as the "seeing of eternal things," Australian aboriginal religion emphasized a cosmology based upon the periodic renewal of primordial time by the Dream Time ancestors at the sacred sites. Ceremonies and rituals followed a life-cycle pattern of initiations and were characterized by a symbolic fusion of gestures, songs, myths, chants, dance, narration, and the visual arts such as body-painting and totems.

Auxo. Greek goddess of growth. A daughter of Zeus and Themis, Auxo was one of the *Horae.

Avalokiteshvara. From the Sanskrit for "Lord who looks down with compas-

sion." Most popular of all *bodhisattvas of *Buddhism. This human embodiment of compassion had an extraordinary path of cultural and iconographic transformation beginning with the pre-twelfth century figuration of a male *bodhisattva who then became feminized as the identification of compassion became a descriptive category of motherhood. Thereby, this bodhisattva image was converted from that of *Padmapăni into the initially masculine and later androgynous depictions of the Indian Avalokiteshvara to the feminine *Kuan-yin of China and the *Kwannon of Japan. As the tutelary spirit of Tibet, Avalokiteshvara was depicted uniquely with four arms in Tibetan Buddhist art. In Indian Buddhist art, Avalokiteshvara had many modes of depictions that were initially male with variations of eleven heads or one thousand arms. He wore a long flowing garment and a crown inscribed with an image of Amitābha; and either held or stood upon a blue *lotus. *Attributes included a *vase, sprig of *willow, Wheel of the Law, *Rosary, *book, *scroll, conch shell, or a small *child.

A(ve) M(aria) (Lk 1:28). Latin for "Hail Mary." Opening words of the salutation of the Archangel Gabriel as he greeted *Mary at the *Annunciation (to the Virgin Mary). This initial form for *Mary as the Virgin Mother was incorporated either into representations of her in Christian art, especially depictions of the Annunciation, or within the symbolic and decorative designs of liturgical vesture.

Aya. Mesopotamian goddess of the dawn associated with the Greek *Eos and the Roman *Aurora.

B

Ba. Chinese goddess and female personification of drought. As the daughter of Huang Di, she supported her father's war against Chi Yu almost destroying the earth with a great drought.

Baalath. Middle Eastern generic name for a goddess; hence, the Baalath of Byblos was *Astarte.

Baba. From the Sumerian for "female doctor of the black-headed." Sumerian tutelary mother goddess identified in Babylonia as the goddess of healing. In Mesopotamian art, Baba was identified by her *attribute the winnowing fan.

Baba-yaga. Legendary *witch of Eastern European folk tales. A forest spirit, Baba-yaga was the leader of demonic spirits. In indigenous Russian art, she was portrayed as an old hag holding a kettle and riding a broomstick. According to the Slavonic tradition, Baba-yaga was a monstrous witch and she was depicted as a man-eating hag who lived within a fenced area littered with human bones. Her giant size and huge mouth extended from one side of the earth to the other, thereby accounting for earthquakes and earth cracks.

Bacchantes. Female followers of the Greek Dionysius or the Roman Bacchus. Also known as the Bacchae or the *Maenads, these women, frenzied with drink, participated in orgiastic activities that were described by Ovid (*Metamorphosis* 4). In *classical and *renaissance art, Bacchantes were portrayed as beautiful young women in varied stages of dress and engaged in lascivious and riotous activities from drinking to dancing to sexual intercourse.

Bachue. Mother Goddess who originated humanity according to the mythology of the Indians of Colombia.

Badb. From the Irish for "crow" or "raven." Irish goddess of battles and death. Badb was part of the feminine triad known as the *Morrigan. She was characterized as a blackbird that shrieked over the heads of warriors who were about to die in battle. Her *attribute was the raven.

Balls. In classical Greco-Roman art, the jugglers of fortune, *Tyché and *Fortuna, were signified by the ball, while *Ariadne was identified by the ball of thread that she gave Theseus as an aid in his return from the labyrinth. In Christian art, three balls denoted the dowries that Nicholas (of Myra or Bari) donated to the three marriageable daughters of an impoverished count. In *renaissance art, *Avarice as one of the *Seven Deadly Sins was accompanied by the *Harpies carrying the golden balls of greed.

Banba. Member of the feminine triad of Banba, Futla, and Éire that signified the sovereignty and spirit of Ireland, and characterized as "Mother of Ireland."

Banner. Sign of victory, the nature of which was characterized by the *colors or design of the banner. A white-ground banner with a red cross symbolizing victory represented *Constantine's conversion to Christianity, or the victory of George of Cappadocia and *Ursula over evil. When carried by the Lamb of God, a banner indicated victory over death. The Resurrected *Christ carried the Banner of Victory in postresurrection narrative depictions. *John the Baptist held a banner inscribed with either a cross or the words *Ecce Agnus Dei* ("Behold the Lamb of God"). All military saints including George of Cappadocia, Ansanus, James Major, *Ursula, *Reparata, and *Joan of Arc, carried banners. The use of the banner as a symbol of military victory was adapted by the fourth-century *church, and became a common symbol in western Christian art.

Banshee. From the Gaelic for "woman of the fairy mounds." Legendary white female ghost whose eerie shriek brought death to her hearers. Associated with the *Crone form of the *Great Goddess; the central European death-priestesses, the Vila, and the Oriental death priestesses, the Dākīnī, the banshee proved to be either gentle or tormented in her death song. In religious art, the banshee was represented as a ghostly white lady whose gestures indicate her death wail. She was best known in the representations of the *Crone in western art.

Baptism. From the Greek for "to dip" or "to dip under." Act of ritual purification and regeneration by which the cleansed one was initiated into a religious tradition, such as Christianity. Baptism was the first of the Seven Sacraments and was symbolized by three *fish in early Christian art. Along with the Eucharist, it was one of the two central sacraments shared by most Christian traditions.

Barbara, Saint (late third century). Popular medieval *saint and one of the *Fourteen Holy Helpers. Converted to Christianity by an emissary of the Christian theologian Origen, this beautiful young woman was imprisoned in a *tower by her father to separate her from possible suitors. She spent her time reading philosophical texts and became interested in Christianity. Feigning an illness, she was visited by a Christian missionary in the guise of a physician. He proceeded to baptize her into the Christian faith. Barbara's father learned about her conversion when she asked that a third *window be put into her tower. In response to her father's query as to why she needed another window, Barbara proclaimed for the Holy

Trinity. Angered at her conversion, her father tried to kill her, but she was miraculously delivered from him. Civil authorities subjected her to torture until her father decapitated her. He was immediately struck dead by lightning. Barbara was the patron of artillery soldiers, gunsmiths, architects, builders, and miners, and was invoked against lightning, thunderstorms, and sudden death. A popular topic in northern *medieval art, she was depicted as a richly dressed and beautiful young woman seated before a tower and reading a *book. She was the only female saint who was accorded the *attribute of a *wafer and a sacramental *cup in honor of her dying request that those who honored her martyrdom would receive the sacrament. In some depictions, she held a *peacock *feather as a reference to Heliopolis, her native city, where the *phoenix rejuvenated itself. Since the phoenix was an unknown entity to northern artists, the phoenix feather of Heliopolis became a peacock feather in Barbara's *hand.

Baroque art. From the Portuguese for "irregularly shaped pearl." Style of architecture, painting, and sculpture that succeeded *Mannerism and lasted into the eighteenth century. The purest presentation was identified as the High Baroque (1630–80), which corresponded with the artistic maturity of *Gian Lorenzo Bernini in Rome. The premise of the baroque tradition was the union of architecture, painting, and sculpture, which worked together to allow the spectator's participation in the spiritual dramas being depicted before them. Emphasizing an asymmetrical composition, simple subject matter, unidealized naturalism, complex *iconography, and

chiaroscuro (theatrical dark light identified as tenebrism in northern European art), baroque art sought to overwhelm the viewers's emotional sensibilities. Northern baroque art, contemporary to the establishment of *Lutheranism and the Protestant traditions, no longer favored religious themes; instead, northern baroque artists turned their attention to the topics of history painting, portraiture, *landscape, *still life, and genre scenes. Leading northern baroque artists included *Rembrandt van Rijn, Pieter de Hooch, and Jacob van Ruisdael. Southern baroque art and artists defended the teachings and traditions of the Roman Catholic Church affirmed by the *Council of Trent; as a result, a new series of iconographic motifs were developed that defended the teachings and the *saints of the Roman Catholic Church against the Reformers' critiques. Leading southern baroque artists included *Michelangelo Merisi da Caravaggio, the Carracci Brothers, *Bartolomé Murillo, Vélasquez, Guido Reni, and *El Greco. Although northern by birth, *Peter Paul Rubens was a devout Roman Catholic; in theme and symbolism his art was southern baroque, but it was northern baroque in terms of his use of color.

Basilisk. A fabulous *animal composed of the three-crested *head of a *cock, the *body of a lizardlike *serpent, and a three-pointed tail. Medieval *bestiaries described the basilisk as born of a yokeless *egg laid by a *cock and hatched by a *toad on a bed of dung. According to legend, the basilisk killed merely by glancing at an animal or a person. A popular symbol in early Christian, *byzantine, and *medieval art, the basilisk was a symbol of the Devil and of the Antichrist (Ps 90:13).

Basket. An open container with a handle used to carry items, especially foods and flowers. In religious art and rituals, a basket signified sacrifice, fertility, or salvation. In Egyptian art, *Nephthys wore the plan of a house surmounted by a basket on her head. *Hecate was identified with a basket on her head in classical Greek art. In western Christian art, a basket with *roses and *apples was an *attribute of *Dorothea. A basket containing an infant denoted Moses. An empty basket or one filled with *bread and *fish signified the Multiplication of Loaves and Fishes. A basket filled with *scrolls signified both the classical philosopher and Jesus Christ as the Philosopher-Teacher in early Christian art. In *renaissance art, a basket of flowers identified *Hope and a basket of fruit Taste.

Bast. From the Egyptian language for "eye of the moon." Egyptian goddess who protected pregnant women, and reveled in dance and music. As the counterpart to *Sekhmet, Bast personified the beneficence and fertilizing energies of the sun. As the female personification of ointment, she protected against disease and evil spirits. Originally associated with the *lion, Bast became the cat-headed goddess who was the guardian of grain and the defender against *snakes. Ezekiel prophesied that the city of Bast would fall by the sword (Ez 30:17). In Egyptian art, Bast was represented by a cat-headed woman who held an aegis with the head of a cat or lioness in her left hand and a sistrum for music in her right.

Bat. A widespread symbol in religious art for the night. In western Christian art, the bat signified an impure animal signifying duplicity, hypocrisy, sexuality, melancholia, evil, and the Devil. This night creature haunted *ruins and lonely places. The bat was understood to be an incarnation of the Prince of Darkness.

Bat Mitzvah. From the Hebrew for "daughter of the commandments." Recent Jewish ritual of female initiation into the adult community. Upon the age of twelve years and one day, a girl became a woman under Jewish law and was required to keep the commandments. In modern practice among Reform and Conservative Jews, the young woman is called to read the *Torah as a public sign of her physical and spiritual maturity. The major ceremonial distinction between a bat mitzvah and a bar mitzvah is that the young man reads Torah by himself whereas the young women read as a group of initiates.

Bath(ing). Ritual of purification and cleansing. This immersion into water, especially as understood as "prima materia," signified an act of regeneration or rebirth. Among a variety of ancient Mediterranean cultures, the ritual bath(ing) of an image of the goddess—particularly *Aphrodite, *Cybele, *Hera, or *Venus—represented the restoration of her *virginity and her preparation for sexual intercourse. In Greco-Roman mythology and art, there was a severe penalty for any human who witnessed the actual bath(ing) of a goddess, as in *Athena's blinding of Tiresias. In other cultural contexts, such as those of the *Old Testament heroines *Bathsheba or *Susanna, the ritual bath depicted in western Christian art was a *mikveh, the ritual cleansing required by Judaic law of women after childbirth, sexual intercourse, or the menstrual cycle. In other contexts, the bath(ing) signified *baptism.

Bathsheba (2 Sm 11–12). The wife of Uriah the Hittite and later of David, and mother of Solomon. Overcome by her beauty as he watched her bathe, the king sent for Bathsheba and they became lovers. Wishing to marry his now pregnant mistress, David arranged for Uriah to be killed in battle. Reproached by the prophet Nathan, the king repented of his sin of adultery, but the *child born of Bathsheba sickened and died. Later she bore David a second son, Solomon. According to the *Talmud, Bathsheba was a virgin as her marriage to Uriah had not been consummated. Further, in keeping with Jewish tradition, Uriah had given his wife a conditional *get*, or bill of divorcement, before he went into battle. Therefore, Bathsheba was an unmarried (divorced) virgin who did not commit adultery with David according to the rules of Jewish law. David, however, was guilty of adultery. In *medieval art, Bathsheba was represented either in the act of adultery with David or bathing as he espied her. Since David was interpreted as a foretype of Jesus, Bathsheba as his beloved bride was understood to represent the *church undergoing purification by cleansing, while Uriah signified the Devil. Late northern medieval, renaissance, and baroque artists turned their attention to depictions of Bathsheba at the bath, so that by the seventeenth century this motif became a scriptural excuse for painting the female nude.

Batō Kwannon. Japanese Buddhist form of *Avalokiteshvara. Batō Kwan-

non was a destroyer of evil and a protector of horse and cattle. She was depicted with the head of a horse or with a crown inscribed with a horse's head.

Battle for the Trousers. Legendary topos of this item of male clothing as a sign of physical superiority and domestic power. A popular theme in moralizing prints and the arts of popular culture, the Battle for the Trousers was represented by the struggle between a man and a woman or several women over a pair of trousers.

Baubo. Female personification of fecundity in Asia Minor. According to the Orphic tradition, Baubo was an old woman who made the grieving *Demeter laugh by the display of her aging pudenda. Her obscene gesture became an amulet against death. In classical Mediterranean and Middle Eastern art, Baubo was represented by a headless woman who indicates her pudenda with an obscene gesture or by a crouched woman with her head between her legs.

Baucis. Mythic Greek wife of Philemon. As models of hospitality and humility, the impoverished elder couple offer hospitality to a disguised Zeus and Hermes. The couple was rewarded for their exemplary behavior with a never-emptied wine jug, and were spared the sorrow of each other's death by being transformed into intertwined *elm and *oak *trees. A popular topic in *medieval, *renaissance, and *baroque art, Baucis and Philemon were interpreted as foretypes of the Philoxeny of Abraham, Last Supper, and the Supper at Emmaus. As a pious and devoted wife, Baucis was a classical foretype of *Anne. The Latin version of her story was

10. Rembrandt van Rijn, *Bathsheba*

11. Gian Lorenzo Bernini, *Death of the Blessed Ludovica Albertoni*

recorded in Ovid's *Metamorphosis* (8:621–96).

Beans. Vegetable symbol for both the female genitals and fertility in varied ancient religious traditions. A popular yonic symbol in classical Rome, beans were believed capable of enabling conception, possessing spirits, and naming the sacred king. While the linguistic and symbolic properties of beans were magnified in Sanskrit as the word *mudrā* could be translated as "kidney beans" or "woman" or "magical gesture (as in that made by a *shaktī)." Thereby, beans connoted female fecundity and female sexuality in religious art. Native American tradition, specifically that of the Zuni, required that a pregnant woman just prior to labor and childbirth swallow beans as a form of sympathetic magic for an easy birth.

Bean Sídhe. From the Irish for "woman of the hills" or "woman of the fairies." Following the gods' descent into the underworld, Bean Sídhe was transformed into the *banshee.

Bears. Animal symbol of multiple meanings including ideal mother, physical strength, and lust and greed. Among primal peoples, the bear was characterized as an ideal mother who protectively and independently nurtured her cubs. The power of the bear was reenforced by its representation of death and rebirth following each winter's hibernation. The bear was the sacred animal of *Artemis and also her Roman counterpart, *Diana, especially in their role as protectors of young animals and children, and an emblem of *Callisto in Greco-Roman art and mythology. It was an *Old Testament sign for cruelty and evil associated with Persia according to the prophecies of Daniel (7:5). According to the *Physiologus, bears were born shapeless and were formed by their mothers licking them, symbolizing the conversion of the infidels and barbarians to Christianity. The bear was an *attribute of *Euphemia; and of the *Seven Deadly Sins, especially Gluttony, Lust, and Anger. Among varied Native American tribes, the bear signified the female spirit of regeneration, healing, and nurture; and was an *attribute of the Earth as Mother.

Beasts (real and imaginary). *See* Animals, and Mythical Beasts.

Beata. From the Latin for "blessed." Spanish identification of a white *witch or hermit singled out for her ecstatic visions, trances, cures, and perhaps even the *stigmata. In Catholic Spain, these women were both feared and respected; they might alternately be canonized as a saint or condemned as a heretic.

Beatrice. Poetic idealization of feminine beauty and spirituality. Beatrice Portinari (1266–90) was a beautiful Florentine noblewoman who was the secret beloved of the poet Dante. He immortalized her as the epitome of feminine spiritual values as his guide in Purgatory and Heaven in his literary masterpiece, *The Divine Comedy*. Beatrice was represented in *medieval and *renaissance art as a beautiful young noblewoman; and was an inspiration for the spiritual conception of ideal love in nineteenth-century art, as in portraits by *Dante Gabriel Rossetti and Washington Allston.

Beatrice of Nazareth (1200–68). Belgian Beguine and mystic. From the age of ten, Beatrice lived in a Cistercian monastery for women religious. Gifted in the graphic arts and in writings, she was the author of a *Life*, her autobiography; and an account of her mystical experiences, *Seven mannieren van Minne* (*Seven Experiences of Love*). During the last thirty years of her life, Beatrice served as prioress for religious women at the monastery she named Nazareth. A rare topic in western Christian art, she was occasionally represented in a Cistercian habit or dressed as a Beguine, and posed at her desk writing.

Beaver. *Animal symbol for chastity, gentility, industriousness, and medicine. The beaver's testicles were reputed to have curative powers. The animal escaped certain death by castrating itself and speeding off as the hunter stops for the discarded testicles. Moralizers advocated that intelligent persons separated themselves from sexual lust and perversity, and thereby escaped the Devil. In western Christian art, the beaver signified chastity, asceticism, and vigilance.

Bee. Insect symbol of fertility, diligence, and eloquence common to religious art. In traditional Chinese art, the image of the bee combined with the peony signified a young man in love. In classical Mediterranean art, the bee was an attribute of *Artemis (*Diana), *Demeter (*Ceres), and the city of Ephesus. As the orgiastic nymph, Artemis (Diana), was signified by the busy bee; as the productive earth mother, Demeter (Ceres), by the honeycomb; and as a goddess of love and fertility, *Cybele, by the queen bee. In classical Greece and Crete, the Queen Bee signified the *Great Mother who was attended by

her priestesses identified as the Melissae (from the Greek for "bee"). Appropriately, the term "Melissae" also identified the priestesses of Artemis and Demeter. The three old women who reportedly taught Apollo the art of prophecy were known as Melissae. In western Christian art, it was a symbol for creativity, diligence, resourcefulness, and the industrious Christian. Reputed never to sleep, the bee was a sign of Christian vigilance in practicing the *Virtues. The bee's production of honey denoted sweetness and religious eloquence, and was a sign of Jesus Christ and of the virtue of *Mary. According to ancient legends, the female bee reproduced without the assistance of the male bee, thereby symbolizing the Virgin Birth and the Incarnation. The bee was an *attribute of Ambrose, Bernard of Clairvaux, and John Chrysostom.

Beehive. A symbol for the Christian *church as a unified community where all worked with diligence and harmony to spread the "honeyed" words of the *gospel. The beehive was an *attribute of Ambrose, Bernard of Clairvaux, John Chrysostom, and a symbol for *Mary as *Mater Ecclesia* (Mother Church).

Befana. From the Latin for "Epiphany." Legendary Italian beneficent female spirit. According to popular tradition, Befana was the old fairy woman who filled children's stockings with treats and sweets on Twelfth Night or the Eve of Epiphany. She was assimilated into Christian legend and art as the woman who was too busy with her domestic duties to accept the Magi's invitation to accompany them to see the newborn Christ child. However, she asked them to visit her on their return journey. Unfortunately for Befana, the Magi returned home on a different route but she reportedly seeks them out every Twelfth Night. A popular topic in folklore and folk art, Befana was characterized as an old female figure with graying hair, a pronounced perhaps even crooked nose, glasses, and a kerchief covering her head. She was dressed as a peasant woman with an apron whose deep pockets were filled with sweets and treats for young children. "Befana dolls" were a popular gift during the Christmas season.

Beguines. Medieval informal association of pious lay women who supported both reform and lay devotional movements, and sought a spiritual revival in western Christianity. The Beguines were characterized as a community of religious women who lived a simple, chaste, and charitable Christian existence apart from the world, took no vows, and had minimal hierarchical structure. They divided the day between work, prayer, and preaching. They were the northern European counterparts of the female tertiaries of the Dominicans and Franciscans caring for the poor, the sick, and the aged. They were significant as translators of the late medieval theological shift from the divinity of Christ to the humanity of Jesus, from the queenship of *Mary to her intercession. Through their work with the laity, the Beguines expanded the boundaries of medieval spirituality and mysticism. Rare topics in Christian art, the Beguines were represented by their most famous members, such as *Mechthild of Madgeburg and *Beatrice of Nazareth.

Bēletsēri. From the Babylonian for "book-keeper or clerk." Babylonian goddess of the underworld who recorded all human events.

Belili. Mesopotamian goddess of the moon, trees, love, and the underworld. She was associated with *Ishtar.

Bell. Common instrument of chiming sound used in religious rituals to announce the levels of worship or to scatter evil spirits. In Tantric Buddhist art and spirituality, the bell signified the universal womb. In Hindu art, it was an *attribute of *Sarasvatī and *Duūrgā (*Devi). In Christian art, a symbol for the Word of God. An attribute of lepers, the bell warned of their approach. Bells were also carried by *saints like Anthony the Abbot who were reputed to be exorcisers of demons. The ringing of *church tower bells to summon the faithful to prayer was an announcement of the Word of God. The ringing of the sanctus bell during the preparation of the Eucharist announced the presence of Christ. Bells were an *attribute of Aaron, David and *Agatha. A bell tied to a crutch was an attribute of Anthony the Abbot. In renaissance art, the bell was an attribute of *Music as one of the *Seven Liberal Arts.

Bellini, Jacopo (c. 1400–70), **Gentile** (c. 1429/30–1507), **Giovanni** (c. 1430–1516). A family of Venetian artists who had great influence on the development of Venetian art during the Renaissance. The father, Jacopo Bellini (who was also the father-in-law of *Andrea Mantegna), was an important teacher to aspiring young Venetian artists, including his sons. The most famous of the Bellinis was Giovanni, who was influenced by

Mantegna and was the teacher of Giorgione and Titian. An acute observer of nature, Giovanni filled his canvases with poetic but naturalistic details that never overwhelmed the human figures in his compositions. He was at his best in fulfilling official commissions, such as the votive offerings of the Doges, the large altarpieces offered by the varied Venetian guilds, and small devotional works. Iconographically, he was the most innovative painter of northern Italy, and was especially concerned with the *iconography of *Mary.

Bellona. Roman goddess of war and the female personification of war. Bellona was the wife of the Roman god of war, Mars. The famed *columna bellica* from whence war was declared with a symbolic spear thrust was in front of her temple on the Campus Marticus. In classical Greco-Roman and *renaissance art, Bellona was portrayed as a physically strong matron dressed in full armor and often holding a torch in her right hand.

Belt. A sign of virginity and chastity when worn by a woman. At puberty, a young girl would be given her "girdle" by her family as a sign of womanhood. The legend of the Virgin's girdle being dropped from heaven on Thomas's head after her *Assumption related to this cultural custom, and was interpreted as a sign of her perpetual *virginity. On a male figure, the belt signified preparation for service, as this was the last item one put on when dressing. *Old Testament *prophets wore belts as a sign of humility.

Bendis. Armor-bearing Thracian virgin goddess associated with *Artemis and *Hecate.

Benedictines. The "black monks" were an order of monastics established by Benedict at Monte Cassino. As the model for western monasticism, this close community of men religious was led by a spiritual father, the abbot, and adhered to the rule of a common life predicated upon a division of each man's time to contemplation, prayer, and manual labor. Benedictines emphasized the importance of education, liturgy, and the arts, and had a long and fruitful missionary history. In western Christian art, these monks were identified by their original *black *habit. Reforms led to the establishment of new orders, including the Carthusians, Cistercians, and Trappists, from the original Benedictine tradition.

Benten. Japanese Buddhist goddess of eloquence and music. As the divine patron of geishas, Benten was represented in Japanese art wearing a bejeweled diadem and holding a stringed *musical instrument.

Benu (*Book of the Dead*). Fantastic bird of Egyptian art and mythology. This huge golden bird had a heronlike head and was renowned for creating itself from the fire that burned the top of the sacred Persea tree of Heliopolis. As a sunbird, the benu was a symbol of the rising sun and of the dead sun god, Osiris, from whose heart it was allegedly to have sprung initially. Herodotus related that the benu was reborn every five hundred years and that it symbolized resurrection (*History*, Book II). It was associated with the *phoenix. According to tradition, the benu came to Egypt from Arabia with the body of its original father, Osiris, enclosed in an *egg of *myrrh for burial in the Temple of the Sun. In Egyptian and Hellenistic art, the benu was depicted as a long-legged gold and red heronlike wading bird.

Bercht. Indigenous Germanic midwinter spirit, sometimes depicted as a hag. As a good spirit, Bercht was the reputed "bringer of gifts" to children. Although characterized as a slovenly person, she insisted on regular domestic cleanliness with at least one annual cleaning by the eve of Epiphany or else disease permeated the household. With the advent of Christianity into Germany, she was transformed into the female personification of the eve of Epiphany.

Berenice II (c. 273–221 B.C.E.). Beautiful queen/wife of Ptolemy III who offered her *hair to the gods if her husband returned as the vanquisher of Asia. Her regal tresses were stolen on the first night of their display at the Temple of Arsinoë. According to tradition, Berenice's hair was blown by the wind gods to heaven where it was transformed into the tail of Leo, that is, the *Coma Berenices*. Berenice was represented in *classical and *renaissance art either cutting off her hair or hanging it from the temple.

Bernadette of Lourdes, Saint (1844–79). Christian visionary. A sickly and impoverished child, Bernadette reported having daily visions between February 11 and March 25, 1858, in which she saw a beautiful young woman standing before the cave of the River Gave in Lourdes. The woman initially identified herself as the Virgin Mary to the young Bernadette, and later before a crowd of believers on March 25th the apparition told Bernadette that she was the *Immaculate Conception, requested that a chapel be built on this spot, and directed her to a long-forgotten healing spring. Despite skepticism on the part of secular authorities, the site of Bernadette's visions became a center for devotions and the healing springs were responsible for miraculous cures, including seven that were accepted officially as the work of God by the *Roman Catholic Church. Since Bernadette's visions, Lourdes has become one of the most significant Christian pilgrimage centers. Distancing herself from the developments at Lourdes, Bernadette entered the Sisters of Charity in Nevers in 1866 and nursed the injured soldiers of the Franco-Prussian War. She died at the young age of thirty-five after suffering from tuberculosis. In western Christian art, Bernadette was depicted as a slender young woman either in the act of dropping her firewood or in the posture of prayer when she first saw the vision of *Mary at the grotto of Lourdes.

Bernice. From the Greek for "victorious." Jewish-born Roman noblewoman who knew Paul. A daughter of Herod Agrippa I and granddaughter of Herod the Great, Bernice and her brother, Herod Agrippa II, were members of the audience at Paul's defense in Caesarea. Her appropriate demeanor at the apostle's presentation of his case so impressed Luke that he noted her interest and her informed attention (Acts 25:13, 23; 26:30). Later, she and her brother examined Paul. Beyond her alleged scandalous relationship with her brother, Bernice was famed as a skilled and courageous diplomat who risked her own life to save Jews during the massacre by Gessius Florus. A rare topic in western Christian art, Bernice was depicted as a well-dressed Roman matron in the company of her brother in the narrative cycles of Paul.

Bernini, Gian Lorenzo (1598–1680). The greatest exponent of High Baroque architecture and sculpture. Influenced by classical Greco-Roman sculpture, *Michelangelo, and the *baroque art of *Caravaggio, the Carracci, and Guido Reni, Bernini developed the sculptural concept of a single frontal viewpoint that incorporated a clear expression of energy and psychological insight. A devout Roman Catholic, Bernini sought to express and defend the teachings, including *Mariology, of the *Council of Trent through his innovative *iconography. He was particularly noted for his attempts to visually express mystical experience by means of the female figure as witnessed in his *Ecstasy of Saint Teresa* and the *Death of the Blessed Ludovica Albertoni*.

Bes. Originally adapted from Semitic cult sources, a mythic Egyptian dwarf protector of the family, married women, and women in childbirth. As an ugly and deformed figure, Bes frightened away evil spirits. His image was found in Egyptian art, especially on the walls of the *mammisi, in conjunction with the protection of women from evil spirits and on the walls decorating birthing rooms. In Egyptian and Near Eastern art, Bes was portrayed as a bearded and terrifying dwarf who wore lion skins and a crown of feathers. His *attributes included a *sword, *harp, and tambourine.

Beset. Mythic Egyptian female counterpart of *Bes. As a patron of art, music,

and childbirth, Beset was identified in Egyptian art by a crown of feathers.

Bestiary. A moralizing natural history of ancient origins based on the Greek *Physiologus*, and rivaling the Bible, in popularity in the Middle Ages. There were three categories of *animals described in the medieval bestiaries: *beasts, *birds, and reptiles and *fish. On average, each bestiary described the history, legend, natural characteristics, and symbolism of one hundred animals as opposed to the original forty-nine animals studied in the *Physiologus*. The bestiaries became standard books used by medieval artists in the development of their complex iconographies, as moralizing parallels were regularly drawn between the animals and their human counterparts.

Betrothal and Marriage of the Virgin Mary (*Protoevangelium of James* 8:2–9:2 and *The Golden Legend* 131). Legendary events signifying the initiation of *Mary into womanhood and her role as the mother of Jesus Christ. As she approached the age of puberty, the High Priests began to make the arrangements for her marriage. Mary refused initially to marry, declaring that she had dedicated herself to God, but she eventually acceded to God's will. An *angel (an oracle) ordered the High Priests to call for the assembly of all eligible bachelors (aged widowers) from the House of David. Each man brought his staff and left it overnight in the Temple so that God could select the future husband of his special handmaiden. When the High Priests arrived the following morning, they found that the staff of Joseph (of Nazareth), a widowed carpenter, had flowered (fulfilling the prophecy of Aaron's Staff). The Marriage Ceremony, presided over by the High Priest, was depicted outside of the Temple as Mary and Joseph exchanged *rings and formed the ceremonial handclasp. In the background, the rejected suitors broke their staffs in a gesture. A narrative element in the Marian cycle, the individualized scenes of the Betrothal and Marriage became conflated into one theme by the mid-fourteenth century as the suitors's staffs were either placed on the high *altar or broken by the rejected suitors while the sacrament of marriage took place with Joseph distinguished by his flowering staff and the *dove hovering over his *head. In *baroque art, the wedding guests (and rejected suitors) were either greatly reduced in number or omitted completely as was Joseph's flowering staff; the visual emphasis became the solemn sacrament of marriage as Joseph placed a ring on Mary's finger and the High Priest gestured a blessing.

Bhrkuti. Buddhist deity. In Buddhist art, Bhrkuti was portrayed as a youthful four-armed woman with one head and yellow in color. In her left hand, she held a triple staff signifying that Brahman had renounced the world, and in her right hand a garland of roses. Bhrkuti's right hand formed the gesture that "wishes have been granted." More often than not, she stood on the moon with a likeness of Amitābha on her head.

Bible. Originally derived from the name of the Phoenician city of Byblos, then from the Latin for the Greek for "books." The composite collection of the sacred writings of the *Old and *New Testaments. Described as one

*book in this unitary view, the Bible presented God's plan of salvation history, beginning with the creation of the world and ending with the Day of Judgment. Originally written in Hebrew, the Old Testament was translated into Greek (the *Septuagint*), for the Greek-speaking Jews of Alexandria (the version cited throughout the New Testament). The New Testament was originally written in Greek, and was translated into Latin by *Jerome; a revision of his Vulgate was declared the authoritative version of the Roman Catholic Church at the *Council of Trent. *Martin Luther translated the Bible into German, and several English translations followed during the Reformation until the King James Bible was accepted as the authorized version.

Biblia Pauperum. From the Latin for "Bible of the poor." An illustrated *blockbook of forty images designed in a typological, or "moralizing," fashion, consisting of three columns in which the center illustration was the *New Testament type and to either side was the *Old Testament or classical foretype. For example, a depiction of the Baptism of Jesus was paralleled with images of Noah's Ark and of Moses Striking Water from the Rock in the Desert. Probably invented by Anschar of Bremen (801–865), this popular medieval book originally published in 1466 was inspired by Gregory the Great's defense of Christian art as the "biblia pauperum" or the bible of the poor (meaning "the illiterate"). Gregory advocated the idea that simultaneously seeing the image and reading the appropriate scriptural lessons sealed these Christian teachings in the heart of the believer.

Birds, symbolism of. Avian symbol for both the *soul and the mediator between *heaven and *earth. Following ancient Egyptian practice, the bird represented the soul. As such, birds symbolized the spiritual life, and in early Christian art, signified saved souls. When held by either *Mary or the Christ Child or tied to him by a string, individual birds had specific meanings. One of the most popular images in *late medieval art was that of *Francis of Assisi preaching to the birds, which denoted both his concern for all the creatures of the creator God and for the Christian faithful. *See also* Benu, Blackbird, Cock, Crane, Crow, Cuckoo, Dove, Duck, Eagle, Falcon, Goldfinch, Goose, Hawk, Hen, Heron, Ibis, Kingfisher, Lark, Magpie, Nightingale, Ostrich, Parrot, Partridge, Peacock, Pelican, Pheasant, Phoenix, Pigeon, Quail, Raven, Sparrow, Stork, Swallow, Swan, Turtledove, Vulture, and Woodpecker.

Birgitta of Sweden, Saint. *See* Bridget of Sweden, Saint.

Birth. First physical rite of passage in human existence. Surrounded by the sacred mysteries and dangers of blood, pain, new life, and death, birth was a liminal experience for both the mother and the child. It was a time fraught with risk and delight. Birth signified the triumph of female energy and power. Traditionally in many cultures, charms, chants, and customs have protected the mother and her newborn child both during and after the process of the birthing experience from both the physical dangers but especially a jealous goddess or spirit such as *Lilith. Rituals of purification were adhered among those cultures that respected a menstrual

blood taboo as the blood of the mother and the newborn signified simultaneously the mysterious and sacred force of life and the "stain" of *menstruation. According to Jewish tradition, a death in childbirth was caused by a previous negligence in the laws concerning menstruation, the baking of challah bread, or the lighting of the Sabbath lamp. It was also believed that during the nine-month period of gestation a candle in the womb allowed the unborn child to see from one end of the world to the other. Also during this time, an angel taught the unborn child *Torah but just before the actual birth, this same angel touched the baby's top lip causing simultaneously the infant to forget everything and the cleavage of the upper lip. Among other cultures, it was believed that the newborn child was in immediate danger of possession by evil spirits and must be ritually cleansed and protected by a combination of any of the following elements: water, oil, egg, or indigenous sacred fluids. *See also* Candlemas, Purification of the Virgin Mary.

Birth Goddess. Female deities who provided fertility to barren women, protected pregnant women throughout the period of gestation, and administered to women during labor and delivery.

Black. A dual symbol simultaneously denoting sacrifice, deprivation, sickness, mourning, and death; or the fertility of the earth and the nourishment of the night (sleep). As it was the practice of pagan religions to sacrifice black animals to the gods and goddesses of the underworld, the color became associated with death and the underworld. In Egyptian art and mythology, black was the color of the netherworld of Osiris and of *Isis, thereby it signified both death and resurrection. As the color of Isis, black symbolized divine generation and fertility. In Christian art, the color black was identified with the Devil— the color of the "Prince of Darkness." In medieval times, black was associated with witchcraft and magic. As a symbol of abstinence, penance, and humility, the color black was used for the *habits of several monastic orders including the Augustinians, Benedictines, Carmelites, and Dominicans. Women dressed in black in western Christian art were understood to be either widows or *nuns.

Black Madonna. Images of *Mary and the child Jesus that either turned *black from some natural cause (such as candle smoke or tarnish), or a chemical imbalance of the paints, or were naturally black. These images were predominantly found in medieval France, and had a series of interconnections with worship sites previously dedicated to fertility goddesses such as *Isis and *Diana of Ephesus, and with pilgrimage sites related to the *Holy Grail, and also with Albigensianism, the Knights Templar, and the Merovingian dynasty. Devotional images of the highest order, Black Madonnas were found all over Europe with the most famous ones being at Chartres, Czestoschowa, Einsiedeln, Montserrat, and Oropa. A fourth group of Black Madonnas were of a more recent (postrenaissance) vintage and their coloration was more directly related to the racial and ethnic types appropriate to their geographic location, such as Our Lady of Guadalupe.

Blackbird. The beautiful *black *feathers and melodious song denoted the

temptations of the flesh and human sinfulness. According to legend, Benedict of Nursia was tempted by a blackbird during his prayers. This blackbird was interpreted as a sign of the Devil it could be vanquished when the *saint made the sign of the cross.

Blancheflor. From the French for "white flower." Manifestation of the virginal aspect of the Goddess characterized as the "Lily Maid" and present at initiation ceremonies. Blancheflor was only one of the three aspects of the Goddess, the other two being the red flower of the mother and the black bird of the *crone, following the ancient Hindu tradition expounded in the Gunas, or threads of fate in ancient Indian traditions. A rare topic in religious art, Blancheflor was represented as a beautiful young woman, oftentimes holding a small child or infant, and dressed all in white.

Blindfold. Cloth that covered the eyes and signified spiritual as well as physical blindness and impartiality in justice. In *classical, Christian, and *renaissance art, blindfolded figures symbolized moral and spiritual ignorance. *Avarice, *Fortune, *Justice, *Nemesis, and *Synagoga were represented wearing blindfolds.

Blodeuwedd. From the Welsh for "flower aspect." Female personification and deity of the spring in Welsh mythology. Blodeuwedd was defined as virginal, composed of flower buds, and described as ideal beauty. She connoted the aspect of the earth that awaited the sacrifice of the sacred king's blood as a ritual to insure fertility and a good harvest. Conversely, she was also de-

12. *Birth of Krishna*

13. *Goddess Tlazolteotl in the Act of Childbirth*
15. *Birth of Buddha Cakyamuni*

14. Duccio di Buoninsegna, *The Nativity with the Prophets Isaiah and Ezekiel*

scribed as the legendary faithless lover who betrayed her betrothed and sought to bring about his death to marry her illicit lover. Her betrothed killed the illicit lover and Blodeuwedd was transformed into a screech owl—an outcast among birds. A rare topic in religious art, Blodeuwedd was identified by her animal emblem, the owl as a symbol of wisdom and lunar goddesses such as *Athena, and outcast seductresses such as *Lilith.

Blood. Common dual symbol of life and death in the art of world religions. Simultaneously, the power or "taboo" of menstrual blood has played a significant role in religious art. In Egyptian art and mythology, blood was the binary symbol of the life force from the creative power of women to the effluxes of the deities. The sun god Ra was circumcised and his sacrificial blood had great power, just as the "knot of Isis," or menstrual blood was interpreted as "life giver." In *Judaism, the potency of blood was central to its symbolism in cultic rites and practices. Menstrual blood and the menstruating woman were feared for their power; so well water must not be polluted with *Lilith's menstrual blood, that is, the unusual astronomical occurrences identified as solstices and equinoxes; and menstruating women were to be kept separate, that is, unable to participate in sexual intercourse and ritual activities, or to look into a mirror whose glass would become polluted instantly. In western Christian art, this dual symbol denoted both life and death, as well as the sacrament of the Eucharist. The *red *color of blood permitted association both with life-giving symbols such as the red *rose (for

true love), and with sacrificial symbols such as the red martyrdom (the sacrifice of life as opposed to the white martyrdom of the sacrifice of sexuality). The blood that spurted from the wounded side of the crucified Jesus was interpreted as a sign of both his sacrifice of life and of the new life available in the *church through the Eucharist. In byzantine *iconography, two streams of fluid flowed from Jesus' wounded side—one white and the other red. These denoted water and blood as color symbols for the two central *sacraments of the Christian traditions—*baptism and Eucharist. In medieval art, these red and white streams signified the life of the spirit and the life of the body.

Blue. A common binary symbol for water and sky, thereby for life and the heavens, in religious art. In Egyptian art, blue signified the life-giving and life-sustaining power of water, especially of the Nile; and the Pharoah worn a blue war crown to signify that he was empowered to victory by the Nile. In Christian art, this color denoted the heavens, spiritual love, constancy, truth and fidelity. Blue garments were worn by Jesus Christ and *Mary to signify their personification of these characteristics. The deep blue color favored for depictions of Mary was a very expensive color made from ground lapis lazuli; its use was interpreted as a form of adoration for both its monetary value and its symbolic properties (the deeper the color the truer the characteristics exemplified by the individual).

Bluebell. A floral symbol for luck and good fortune in western Christian art. Given its physical resemblance to a bell, a bluebell suspended over a doorway warded off or exorcised evil and the Devil.

Boadicea. From the Irish and the Welsh for "victorious." Most famous female warrior/champion of Celtic history. Boadicea led a rebellion against the Romans and almost emerged victorious. A rare topic in Celtic art, Boadicea was included in the iconographic tradition of women warriors and heroines.

Boar. An animal associated with feminine fertility deities such as *Demeter and *Freya. The boar signified brutality, evil, lust, and the sins of the flesh in western Christian art. It was depicted being trampled under the feet of *Chastity, one of the three monastic vows.

Boat. *See* Ship.

Bodhisattva. From the Sanskrit for "he whose essence is enlightenment." In *Buddhism, the reality and the symbol of a person reaching the final stage towards achieving enlightenment. Initially in Buddhism, this term was used to denote the historical Buddha prior to his enlightenment under the bodhi tree. In the development of Mahāyāna Buddhism, it connoted a "Buddha-to-be" in whom compassion was so great that he or she renounces the achievement of Buddhahood in order to teach others the path to salvation. It was most commonly employed to identify a transcendent, not a living, being who has been enlightened and residing in one of the celestial spheres, who was worshiped in ceremonial rites or invoked in situations of need or distress, such as *Avalokiteshvara, *Kuan-yin, or *Kwannon. In Buddhist art, a Bodhisattva was robed

and bejeweled as a prince or princess, and often wore a five-leaved crown. *Attributes included *sword, *vase, *scroll, and *lotus.

Boiuna. Goddess of the Amazon River in the religious tradition of the Brazilian Indians. Boiuna was visualized as a giant *serpent with shining eyes who was feared for her magical powers.

Bona Dea. From the Latin for "good goddess." Roman female personification of female fertility who was associated with the Greek Damia. Her annual festival held in the beginning of December represented a form of mystery cult reserved for women. The night ceremony was attended by the *Vestal Virgins. Wine and myrtle were excluded from these rites as a woman would be tortured with these by her father and/or her husband. In classical Greco-Roman art, Bona Dea was represented as a physically strong woman dressed in the appropriate style of a matron and holding or accompanied by *serpents as the sign of healing.

Book. A symbol for learning, teaching, and writing. The book was an *attribute of authorship or of erudition. An open book signified the dissemination of *wisdom and truth, and a closed book a hidden secret or mystery. A book with *pen and ink symbolized an author. In Hindu art, *Sarasvatī held a book as the goddess of learning. In classical Greco-Roman and *renaissance art, it was an attribute of *Athena (*Minerva), *Calliope, *Clio, *Grammar, *Melancholia, *Philosophy, *Prudence, *Rhetoric, and *Sophia. In Christian art, the usual convention was that a book signified the *New Testament and a *scroll, either classical Greco-Roman philosophy or the *Old Testament. The Hebrew *prophets were identified by a scroll that might have been inscribed with an appropriate verse. Classical Greco-Roman philosophers, like Aristotle or Plato, were represented by a *basket of scrolls, a symbol that also identified Jesus as the Philosopher-Teacher. In *medieval art, the size and shape of the book became significant as the small, thick, hardbacked book held by or on the lap of a lady was a *Book of Hours, the oversized book with encrusted covers in the *hands of the *Evangelists were the *gospels, sacramentaries, or psalters. A simply covered book held by any one of the Evangelists signifies their individual gospel. *Doctors of the Church each held a book to signify their theological erudition. In the hands of missionary *saints such as Francis Xavier, the book signified evangelization. A monastic with an open book was identified as the founder of an order, while a monastic with a book and pen or inkhorn was an individual author. The *Archangel Uriel held a book as the interpreter of judgments. Stephen the First Martyr held a book signifying the Old Testament. The symbolism of *Mary with a book at the *Annunciation related both to her role as the *sedes sapientiae* ("seat of wisdom") and her foreknowledge of future events. *Anne held a book when she taught Mary or Jesus to read, thereby symbolically imparting *wisdom. A book with the *Alpha and Omega symbolized Jesus as the Christ; with a *fish, Simon; pierced by a sword, Anthony of Padua. A book was an *attribute of *Barbara, *Catherine of Alexandria, *Jerome, and *Mary Magdalene.

Book of Hours. Popular prayer book of medieval Christians. Based on the "Little Hours of the Virgin" (a tenth-century addition to the Divine Office), these small, thick, hardbacked books contained the hours of the Divine Office, prayers, scriptural and devotional texts, and *illustrations or *illuminations. Commissioned individually, Books of Hours entered into the *iconography of the Virgin Annunciate and female saints in the twelfth century.

Book of the Dead. Renowned complex collection of hymns, ritual formulae, funerary incantations, and the notable ethical formulation referred to as the "negative confession," which was the foundation of the funerary literature of ancient Egypt. Selections from the *Book of the Dead* (more appropriately, the *Chapters on Coming Forth by Day*) were inscribed on the coffins and on the papyrus scrolls buried with the dead. Texts were accompanied with illustrations, thereby making these among the first examples of illuminated manuscripts and/or illustrated books. The title, *Book of the Dead*, was devised by Richard Lepsius, the German Egyptologist, who published the initial 1842 English translation.

(Tibetan) Book of the Dead. Alternatively, from the Tibetan for "liberation through hearing." Tibetan Buddhist texts and teachings on *bardo*, the stage between death and rebirth. The *(Tibetan) Book of the Dead* describes both the forty-nine day journey between death and rebirth, and also the proper pattern of action for this time. Chanted at the time of death, this text prepares one for death.

Botticelli, Sandro (c. 1445–1510). This leading painter of late fifteenth-century Florence, influenced by the development of renaissance ideas, sought to represent emotional (and later spiritual) expression in his art. Botticelli's early works reflected mythological themes as in his *Primavera,* but he progressed to inspired religious themes. Deeply affected, if not converted, by the preaching of Savonarola, the artist destroyed several important early works after hearing sermons on the "vanities" of the arts. Botticelli had a workshop dedicated to the production of devotional images of the Madonna from 1480 until the early 1500s. His greatest legacy to Christian art were his innovations in the gentility and devotionalism of his depictions of the *Madonna, such as his *Madonna of the Magnificat.*

Bow. An attribute of superior physical ability. The bow was the attribute of *Ishtar in Assyrian art, of *Astarte in Phoenician art, and of *Sarasvatī in Hindu art. In classical Greco-Roman art, the bow was an attribute of *Artemis (*Diana) as goddess of the hunt, as the weapon of the *Amazons; and as an agent of love of Eros (Cupid), especially when he was in the company of his mother, *Aphrodite (*Venus). In western Christian art, the bow was a symbol for war, hostility, and worldly power (Jer 49:35). The bow and arrows signified the hunt in classical art, torture and martyrdom in Christian art, and either destruction of the passions, attainment of wisdom, or love in Buddhist art.

Bowl. A worldwide symbol for sacrificial offerings or an *attribute of religious mendicants. In Hindu art, the bowl was an attribute of *Dūrgā (*Devi). In classical Greco-Roman and *renaissance art, it signified the *Sibyl of Cumea. Within the context of a *vanitas,* it represented emptiness.

Box. A simple square or rectangular container for the storage of varied items. In Christian art, the box represented the containment or concealment of an important item, such as a relic(s) or the severed *head of one's enemy. It also signified worldly possessions, as in a jewelry box or box for the storage of money.

Box of Ointment. The major *attribute of *Mary Magdalene, who reputedly anointed Jesus at the *Feast in the House of Simon (Jn 12:3), and who sought to anoint the crucified body of Jesus at the by-then-empty *tomb. A box of ointments was an attribute of Cosmas and Damian who were physicians.

Bramble. A sign of the Burning Bush (Ex 3:2). The bramble symbolized the purity of *Mary, who never experienced physical lust, since she was immaculately conceived, but did know divine love. The *Burning Bush was also a sign of the perpetual *virginity of Mary for just as the bush burned but was not consumed, so Mary conceived and bore a child but was still virginal.

Bread. Symbol of the sustenance of life in religious art. In the *Old Testament, bread in the form of *manna was a sign of God's nurture (Ex 16:15). In the *New Testament, it denoted the *body of Jesus (Lk 22:19) and the staff of life (Jn 6:35). Loaves of bread were an *attribute of several *saints, including

*Dominic, who was signified by one loaf of bread; *Mary of Egypt, by three loaves; Philip, by a loaf of bread incised with a *cross or *fish; and *Paul the Hermit, by a loaf of bread in the mouth of a *raven.

Breast. A symbol of love, nurture, nourishment, and protection, and thereby of maternity and motherhood. As a representative *Mother Goddess, *Lakshmi was portrayed holding one of her breasts in Hindu art. In Buddhist art, *Hariti was depicted in the act of suckling one or more children. In Egyptian art, representations of *Isis suckling Horus and *Renenutet suckling an infant were found in sanctuaries dedicated either to these goddesses, or to the protection of women in childbirth. In classical Mediterranean art, *Diana of Ephesus as the great goddess of fertility was represented with many breasts. *Hera nursed the eager Herakles who suckled so violently that the goddess's immortal milk spurt out into the heavens forming the Milky Way. In western Christian art, several women were depicted expressing breast milk, including *Charity, who was distinguished by the presence of more than one *child, and *Mary, who allowed Bernard of Clairvaux the singular gift of three drops of her milk directly expressed into his mouth. The *iconography of the *Maria Lactans* (Mary as the Nursing Mother) was derived from the byzantine icon of the *Galakotrophusa* ("Mother of God as Milk Giver"). As it would have been indecorous to display Mary's actual breast, a third unusually placed and distortedly large breast signified the nourishment of the Christian faithful by Mother Church. This Marian motif appeared and disappeared throughout the

history of medieval and renaissance art. The Maria Lactans was popular during periods of famine and plague. Breasts on a platter were an *attribute of *Agatha as a sign of her martyrdom.

Bridget of Sweden, Saint (1303–73). Founder of the Order of the Holy Savior ("Bridgettines") and famed medieval female mystic. The widowed mother of eight children, Bridget dedicated herself to Christianity following the untimely death of her husband after a pilgrimage to Spain. She recounted her mystical visions and communications from *Mary in the *Revelations of Saint Bridget of Sweden*. The vivid descriptions of her spiritual visions of the major events in the life of Jesus Christ, especially of the *Annunciation and the *Nativity, profoundly affected northern *medieval art and later Christian art. Bridget was the patron of Sweden and had the Bible translated into Swedish. A friend of *Catherine of Siena, Bridget was involved in the efforts to return the Avignon Papacy to Rome. In western Christian art, she was depicted dressed in a nun's black habit with a white wimple and veil banded in red. Her *attributes included the *candle, *crosier (as founder of her order), *pilgrim's *staff with *wallet, *book, *pen, and *crown at her feet.

Bridgettines. Order of the Most Holy Savior established by *Bridget of Sweden in 1346. This dual community of women and men followed the Rule of St. Augustine, shared a common chapel, were devoted to learning, and were cloistered in contemplation and prayer for the souls in Purgatory. In western Christian art, the Bridgettines were identified by their black or gray habits.

16. *Black Madonna of Dorres*

17. Sandro Botticelli, *Primavera*

Bridle. Bit and reins used by a rider to control the movement and direction of a horse; thereby a widespread symbol for control or power. In *classical and *renaissance art, the bridle was an *attribute of *Temperance, *Nemesis, and *Fortune.

Brigantia. From the Celtic for "hill, height." Goddess of victory for the Celtic peoples of Brigantes (Wales). She was associated with *Minerva (*Athena). In religious art, Brigantia was depicted as a large and physically powerful woman who wears a loose and flowing garment with an image of the *Medusa on her breast, and holds a spear in her right hand, and a skull or jug in her left while her shield rests in the upright position at her left foot.

Brigid, Saint (c. 450– c. 523/25). Most revered Irish saint after Patrick, founder of convents, and *abbess. According to legend, the youthful Brigid was baptized by Patrick who was a family friend, later was given the veil by Macaille at Croghan, and professed by Mel of Armagh who gave her abbatial authority. She was reputed to have established a house for herself and seven female companions near Croghan Hill before 468, and in Kildare founded the first Irish convent with herself as abbess in 470. The double monastery at Kildare became a thriving center for art, learning, and spirituality. Brigid established an art school that produced extraordinary illuminated manuscripts until the seventeenth century. She was characterized as a woman of unlimited energy, charm, and Christian compassion. She was reported to have died in Kildare on February 1. An alternate version of her life suggested that she was sold as a young girl to a *Druid who by her efforts became a Christian. As a young woman she defied her father and refused to marry the King of Ulster. In recognition of her Christian piety and devotion, the King freed Brigid from her slavery and her allegiance to her father, thereby allowing her to pursue the religious life. According to popular legend, she was identified as one of the unnamed midwives who attended *Mary at the *Nativity of Jesus Christ. Also known as the "Mary of the Gaels," Brigid became conflated with *Brigit in Irish legend and popular culture. She was the patron saint of Ireland, poets, blacksmiths, healers, cattle, dairymaids, midwives, newborn babies, and fugitives. Brigid was depicted as an *abbess holding a lamp or a candle and accompanied by a cow in western Christian art. Her *attribute was the cross of Saint Brigid.

Brigit. From the Gaelic for "power, authority." Irish goddess of fire, the hearth, medicine, metalwork, fertility, and poetry. According to tradition, Brigit was the daughter of Dagda and the patron of smiths, poets, and doctors. She was associated with the ritual fires of purification and honored at the feast of Imbolc on February 1, a fertility festival associated with the "coming into milk" of the ewes. She was identified as *Brigantia and later as *Minerva of the Gauls by Julius Caesar. The story and the image of Brigit were assimilated into Christianity, and she was venerated at Kildare as "Holy Brigit who tends the holy fire with nineteen nuns." *See also* Brigid, Saint.

Brimstone. From the Greek for "raging one." Epithet for *Athena, *Demeter, and *Hecate of classical Greek mythology and ritual. "Brimo" signified the fearsome and violent aspect of the goddess. As the female personification of sulphur, she was empowered to cleanse and purify either herself or a petitioner; while her stone, that is the brimstone, served as an amulet against disease, especially of plagues.

Brisingamen. From the old Germanic for "fire necklace." Solar *necklace of extraordinary beauty and magical power word by *Freya in Scandinavian mythology. According to popular legend and tradition, the goddess desired jewels and wealth. She willingly expressed herself as a goddess of love and fertility by spending four different nights of love with four different dwarfs who then forged the fabulous necklace for her. The brisingamen was made of amber, a fossil stone, which signified the power of the sun and fertility. Her feathered cloak, the Valhamar, and the brisingamen formed part of the treasure of the Aesir of Norse mythology.

Britomartia. From the Greek for "sweet virgin." This epithet of Rhea was transformed into a Cretan virgin goddess of nature, especially associated with wild animals, the earth, and trees. Originally a moon goddess, Britomartia was the protector of hunters, fishermen, and sailors. She was eventually merged with her companion, *Artemis (*Diana).

Broomsticks. Traditional and prevalent symbol associated with the significant rituals of the mysteries of womanhood, including the birth of a child or marriage. As an *attribute of *Hecate in classical Greco-Roman art and mythology, the broomstick had an ambiguous identity as a symbol of sexual union and as the most important instrument in the ritual emptying a home of evil spirits following the birth of a child. These associations eventually led to the development of the marriage ritual known as "broom jumping." In Tantric art and symbolism, the broomstick indicated the sexual union between male and female deemed a necessary element of religious ritual and spirituality. Eventually, the association with female sexuality and the goddess were negatively transformed in western religion art into one with witches, thereby signifying simultaneously a mode of transportation and of sexual encounter.

Brown. Color symbol for mortification, mourning, humility, and abstinence. As the sign of spiritual death (*ashes were brown) and physical degradation, this color became symbolic of renunciation of the world. This "lifeless" color, then, was used for the habits of the Franciscans and Capuchins.

Brynhild. Leading member of the *Valkyries. In Scandinavian and German mythology, Brynhild attracted the love of Sigurd (Siegmund) but married a mortal king instead. Later she disobeyed Odin by supporting the wrong victor in a battle. Brynhild was punished by imprisonment within a wall of fire. She was rescued by Sigurd whose own death she followed by fire. She was also the queen of Iceland in the *Nibelungenlied*. In art, Brynhild was portrayed as a monumental female figure often dressed in a flowing gown and covered in military armor. Her helmet has wings and she rides a winged white horse.

Buana. Manifestation of the mother goddess as a cow in Irish mythology.

Associated with *Hathor and *Hera, Buana was a mother goddess whose milk denoted riches and abundance.

Buddhism. From the Sanskrit *buddha* for "the Awakened One." Complex religious tradition established by Siddartha Gautama (c. 566–486 B.C.E.) in northern India, and which spread throughout Asia in varied forms including Mahāyāna, Theravāda (Hīnayāna), and Vajrāyāna. As a "middle path" between the extremes of self-indulgence and self-denial, Buddhism advocates the Middle Path that provided vision, knowledge, and nirvana. Buddhist teaching was centered on a practical path for living that simultaneously ended suffering and achieved enlightenment. To attain wisdom, *prajñā*, a Buddhist must be aware of the Four Noble Truths and the doctrine of no-self. As Buddhism spread throughout Asia, it assimilated indigenous cultic practices, mythologies, and religious iconographies. Theravāda, from the Pali for "Way of the Elders," was an early form of Buddhism which affirmed the monastic tradition. This school of Buddhism was also referred to as Hīnayāna, from the Sanskrit for "lesser vehicle;" however it is more appropriately identified as Theravāda Buddhism and is practiced in Sri Lanka and Southeast Asia. Mahāyāna, from the Sanskrit for "greater vehicle," began as an internal reform movement within Buddhism against the elaborate hierarchical structure that had evolved in Indian Buddhism. Mahāyāna Buddhism advocated the ideal of the *bodhisattva as the goal of Buddhist teaching and thereby urged all believers to become boddhisattvas. As Mahāyāna Buddhism spread through Tibet into China and eventually into Japan, it assimilated indigenous deities and cultic practices eventually leading to the development of the meditation traditions known as Ch'an in China and Zen in Japan. Vajrāyāna, from the Sanskrit for "the Diamond (Thunderbolt) Vehicle," designated the Tantric form of Buddhism practiced in Tibet. *See also* Tantra, Tantrism.

Buddhist art. Aesthetic representations of the Buddha, his teachings, and/or the varied Buddhist celestial beings and heroes, which either serve pedagogical, devotional, or meditation functions. Although initially an aniconic tradition, *Buddhism espoused religious iconography, especially anthropomorphic images of the Buddha, within its first five centuries. Although regional and cultic differences in stylization abound, the generic identification of the elements of traditional Buddhist art include its emphasis on simple elegant figures identified by the *mudrās; the implementation of the central symbols of Buddhist iconography such as the Buddha image, the *lotus, the dharmachakra ("wheel of the law"), footprint of the Buddha, the bodhi-tree, and the stupa; the simplification of facial features; and the reliance upon the dialectic of symmetrical and asymmetrical formations to delineate movement and eternality.

Buffalo. Symbol of the Hindu goddess *Durgā (*Devi).

Bulaing. Australian Karadjeri divinity of creation. As an immortal being, Bulaing lived in heaven and created all things and creatures. Her name was associated with mythical *serpents.

Bull. A worldwide symbol for the masculine principle in images of the sun and sky gods as sources of male fertility and creation. Bull worship formed a major cult within world religions and was linked to worship of the *Mother Goddess, especially in Crete and the Indus Valley. In classical Greco-Roman art and mythology, the bull signified Zeus (Jupiter) especially in the story of the abduction of *Europa. In Christian art, the bull was a symbol for brute force, strength, and fertility. The bull was an *attribute of *Thecla, Sylvester, and Eustace. A winged bull (ox) was the sign of Luke the Evangelist.

Bulrush. A common plant or weed, grew low to the ground, was thickly clustered, and flourished near *water. The bulrush became a sign of the Christian faithful, especially those from the "low walks of life," who followed the path of Christian humility and ecclesiastical laws. The story of the infant Moses found in the bulrushes was interpreted as a symbol of salvation and as a foretype of Jesus Christ (Ex 2:5–6).

Burning Bush (Ex 3:2). Sign of God's presence when he spoke to Moses in the wilderness. Miraculously, the bush that burned was not consumed. The Burning Bush was a foretype for the perpetual virginity of *Mary.

Buto. Greek name for the Egyptian cobra goddess, *Wadjet. As protector of Lower Egypt, Buto was a form of *Hathor and identified with the appearance of the sky in the Nile River waters during sunrise. She was the twin sister of Nekhebet, goddess of Upper Egypt. Buto aided *Isis when the grieving goddess hid from Seth and gave birth to Horus on the island of Khemmis. During Horus's childhood, he was pro-

tected by the camouflage of Buto's hair. In the Kingdom of the Dead, she destroyed the toes of the deceased. In Egyptian art, Buto was represented as a woman wearing the crown of Lower Egypt and holding a papyrus scepter entwined with a *snake. Alternately, she may hold the crown of Lower Egypt in her right hand as she is about to crown Pharoah. Buto is also signified by a winged serpent wearing the crown of Lower Egypt. Her symbol was the *uraeus—the forward falling cobra with spread hood.

Butterfly. A worldwide symbol for the soul. In classical Greek art, the butterfly signifies simultaneously the soul and its female personification as *Psyche. Thereby, the image of the butterfly leaving its chrysalis denoted the soul departing the body. In Chinese art and mythology, the butterfly with plum blossoms connoted beauty and longevity. In Japanese art and mythology, the butterfly represented the soul and woman. In Christian art, the butterfly was a dual symbol whose short life and transcendent beauty signified vanity and futility, but whose three-stage cycle as caterpillar, chrysalis, and butterfly denoted resurrection or new life. The chrysalis was interpreted as a symbol of sleep or death, and the butterfly as the new life that arises out of sleep or death. When either the Christ Child or his mother held the butterfly, it connoted the *Resurrection.

BVM. Alphabetical symbol for *Mary in western Christian art. These are the initials signifying the Latin phrase, "*Beata Virgo Maria*," which was translated as "Blessed Virgin Mary."

Byblos. From the Greek for "book." Most ancient and continuously occupied temple center for the worship of the *Great Goddess on the coast of Phoenicia who was identified at that time as *Asherah, Ashoreth, *Astarte, *Baalath, *Hathor, *Ishtar, *Isis, and Mari. As a result, any of the great goddesses were known by the honorific "Lady of Byblos." She provided the mandate and the ruling power for the kings of Byblos. Under the domain of these goddesses was learning and the libraries. As a form of reverence and adoration, the priestesses of the "Lady of Byblos" collected books.

Byzantine art. A style of painting associated with the *icons of the Eastern Orthodox Church. Whether created by artists in the eastern or western Mediterranean, byzantine art was generally characterized by a golden background signifying no particular geographic or historic site, a flatness of form, static figures, elongated proportions in the human forms, an emphasis upon frontality, and a code of *color symbolism, and was without a normal sense of perspective or spatial relationship. In Eastern Christianity, the rubrics and style of byzantine art begun in the fourth century continues into the present day. In western Christian art, the byzantine influence lasted into the twelfth and thirteenth centuries with the development known as Italo-Byzantine art, which merged many characteristics of byzantine art with the growing Italian interest in the expression of emotion and human relationships.

C

❧

Cabiria. Honorific of *Demeter as goddess of the Cabirian Mysteries and other similar rituals which effected fertility of the fields. Accompanied by her youthful consort, either Cabirius, Dionysus, or Ganymede, Demeter entered into a sexual union in order to insure a good harvest. The water ritually poured from a male into a female vessel connoted the encounter between Demeter and her consort. During the Middle Ages, Cabiria became a prevalent name for a witch.

Caduceus. Ancient magician's wand transformed into emblem announcing and granting safe passage to divine messengers, and as a symbol of the healer. The caduceus was formed from a combination of an *olive branch with minimal, if no, leaves that later became entwined with two *snakes and topped by circle, crescent, or *wings. It was an *attribute of *Iris as a divine messenger, and of *Eirene (*Pax).

Caillech. From the Irish for "old woman." Destroyer and fearsome aspect of the *Great Goddess in Irish art and mythology. Associated with *Kālī, Caillech was also represented as black in color signifying her fecundity and creative powers. Ironically as a bringer of disease, such as smallpox, small images of Caillech served as amulets against these physical plagues, especially during the medieval period. She was portrayed as an haggard old woman stooped with age, wearing flowing gray garments and a veil, and black in color.

Caipora. Female spirit of the forest for the Indians of Brazil. Caipora was the protector of animals and feared by hunters.

Cakra. *Halo or *aura signifying divinity or saintliness in Buddhist art. Cakras were of two basic types: encircling the body or encircling the head. Depending upon both the prevalent art style and the status of the figure, cakras were rendered as either simple or complex radiances.

Calf, Golden (Ex 32). Formed by Aaron at the repeated requests of the *Hebrews, who had despaired of God's promise during Moses's absence on Mount Sinai. When Moses returned with the Tablets of the Law, he was outraged to find the Hebrews dancing and acting lasciviously around the Golden Calf. Smashing the tablets, Moses condemned the Hebrews who had abandoned God and ordered the Levites to punish three thousand guilty Hebrews with death. In western Christian art, the theme of the Adoration of the Golden Calf or Dance around the Golden Calf was a sign of the lascivious and immoral nature of *dance and of women, and was a popular image during those periods in which liturgical dance was questioned and/or condemned by ecclesiastical officials.

Calliope. From the Greek for "she of the beautiful voice." Mythic Greek muse of epic poetry and learning, leader of the nine *Muses, and mother of Orpheus by Apollo. She negotiated with the goddesses, *Aphrodite and *Persephone, to spend a third of each year with her lover Adonis. In classical Greco-Roman and *renaissance art, Calliope was identified by her attributes the stylus and wax tablets or *scroll.

Callisto. From the Greek for "she who is most beautiful." Beautiful nymph companion of *Artemis in Greek mythology. Zeus became infatuated with her. There are two variants to the story. In the Greek myth, following the birth of their son, Arcas, the jealous goddess *Hera transformed Callisto into a bear. In this form, a fearful nymph lived in the forest until she was hunted by her son. Before he could kill his mother, Zeus transformed them into the constellations known as the Great Bear and the Little Bear. As her final revenge, Hera persuaded Poseidon to deny Cal-

listo the right to bathe in the sea, so these constellations never descended below the horizon. In the Roman myth as recounted by Ovid (*Metamorphoses* 2:442–453), *Diana became outraged that Callisto had sacrificed her *chastity to Jupiter. In anger, the virgin goddess transformed the nymph into a bear and set her dogs upon her. At just that moment, Jupiter sent the bear/nymph into the heavens and made her a constellation. In classical Greco-Roman and *renaissance art, Callisto was represented either as a beautiful nymph espied by Zeus, being transformed into a bear by Hera, being judged by Diana, or as a bear confronting her hunter son.

Calvary. Latin for the Hebrew "golgotha" for "skull." The location of the Crucifixion of Jesus. According to the fourth-century tradition, during her quest for the True Cross, *Helena identified the site of the Crucifixion and ordered the building of the Basilica Church of the Holy Sepulcher. Following the legendary and devotional texts, the linguistic connection between the names Calvary and *Golgotha and the word *skull led to a common belief that the cross was erected upon the site of Adam's grave. Medieval artists depicted either a skull and crossbones, a *skeleton (oftentimes in a casket), or male and female corpses (Adam and *Eve) seated upright in one casket beneath the foot of the cross.

Calvinism. The tradition of Reformed Protestantism established under the guidance of John Calvin (1509–64). Calvin's theology was based upon four central concepts: the Absolute Sovereign Will of God, Christocentricism, Scripture as the sole Supreme Rule of Faith and Life, and the Church. Calvin advocated a pessimistic view of humanity as totally corrupted by sin, a doctrine of election and predestination, and a vigorous morality. More thoroughgoing in his reform of ecclesiastical organization and liturgical worship than *Martin Luther, Calvin stripped away the nonessentials (that is, everything not expressly mandated in the biblical texts) from the worship environment to focus the congregation's attention upon the pulpit with the open Bible. In his proclamation against violent iconoclasm, Calvin formulated a median position on Christian art in his *Institutes of the Christian Religion* I.11. He allowed for the possibility of historical images for the sake of religious pedagogy, which gave rise to a select group of biblical themes such as the *Blessing of the Children* and the *Holy Kindred*, which were rendered by sixteenth-to eighteenth-century artists in Calvinist countries. Calvinism spread from Switzerland into southern Germany, the Netherlands, Scotland, England, France, and eventually the American colonies.

Calypso. From the Greek for "to cover or veil." Mythic Greek queen of Ogygia and a seducer of Odysseus. The sea-wrecked warrior-king was promised eternal youth and immortality if he remained with Calypso. After eight years of promises, *Athena persuaded Zeus to send Hermes with word that Odysseus be given a raft to continue his journey to Ithaca and to *Penelope. As the etymology of her name suggested her origin as a goddess of death, then Odysseus's departure can be interpreted as a triumph over death.

Camel. An *animal symbol for temperance and humility. Since the camel sustained itself for several days without water, it was interpreted as a sign of physical control and abstinence. When it knelt down to receive its burden of either a human passenger or material objects, the camel was described as a humble creature and was a sign of Jesus Christ. Since the camel traveled through the *desert (to or from the Orient), it was both a beast of burden and a royal sign. In western Christian art, the camel was placed in depictions of the Adoration of the Magi. John the Baptist wore camel skins as a sign of his life in the desert. According to several legends, the camel symbolized nymphomania and female lust, because the female camel was uncontrollable during her time of heat and copulated all day long with her mate.

Camênae. Indigenous Italic goddess of springs and wells. Camênae became associated with the *Vestal Virgins who drew water daily from the well. She became fused with the *Muses.

Campaspe. *See* Phyllis.

Câmundā. Manifestation of the Hindu goddess *Durgā. Câmundā slew the two demons, Cānda and Mundā, from whom her name was derived. In Hindu art, she was portrayed as being either red or black in color, and seated on a demon. A frequenter of graveyards, Câmundā's companion was the *owl.

Canaanite religion. Belief and ritual systems of the inhabitants of the southwestern Levant, and the precursor of Israelite religion. Canaanite religion was divided between the practices of a local cult and a royal cult. The former emphasized the fertility and sacrificial rituals necessary for an agrarian society, and was centered upon deities such as *Astarte, *Anat, and *Asherah, while the latter was a hierarchical sacrificial cult patronized by and supportive of the monarchy.

Canaanite Woman's Daughter (Mt 15:21–28; Mk 7:24–30). A mother whose daughter was possessed by the devil asked Christ for a cure. After some conversation, he rewarded this mother's faith by cleansing her daughter. When the woman went home, she found her daughter healed and resting upon her bed. This miraculous healing was rarely depicted in Christian art, and was fused with other healings.

Candace. From the Meroitic for "queen" or "queen mother." General term for the Queens of Nubia. One particular Candace, however, had as her treasurer an Ethiopian who had been a pilgrim to Jerusalem and was converted by Paul (Acts 8:27). A rare topic in Christian art, this particular queen was represented as a beautiful black woman dressed in regal garb including a crown, and included in the narrative cycles of Paul.

Candle. A widespread symbol of light in religious art. In Christian art, candles symbolized Jesus Christ as "the light of the world." The number or type of candles used in liturgical services had a symbolic value: six candles represented the church's constant prayers during liturgy or mass, twelve candles the exposition of the Blessed Sacrament, three candles the Trinity, seven candles the *sacraments, eucharistic candles the coming of Christ in the Eucharist, and the paschal candle the Resurrection. In Christian art, a lit, unlit, or extinguished candle signified Christ. In the *hands of Joseph (of Nazareth) at the *Nativity, the lighted candle denoted the light given to the world by the birth of this special *child. The candle was an *attribute of *Bridget of Sweden, *Geneviève, and the *Sibyl of Libya.

Candlemas. Liturgical feast celebrating the *Purification of the Virgin Mary and the *Presentation of the Jesus Christ in the Temple. As the conclusion to the Christmas cycle, the name "candlemas" was derived from the liturgical procession of *candles that symbolized the coming of "the light of the world" into the Temple.

Candlestick. A symbol of spiritual light and salvation in Christian art. The seven-armed candlestick, or menorah, signified *Judaism.

Cane. In Hindu art, sugar cane was an *attribute of *Sarasvatī.

Canoness. Female form of canon from the Greek for "rod of straightness" as in "that which was measured" or "against which another could be measured," thereby a rule or order of arrangement, hence the order of the clergy. All members of a corresponding community of women living under a rule—usually the Rule of Saint Augustine—although not necessarily under a perpetual vow. Although the term "canoness" has only been employed since the seventeenth century, there is little practical distinction from a *nun.

Caquixaha. One of the first women and wife of Iqui-Balam in the Mayan cosmology.

Caravaggio, Michelangelo Merisi da (1571–1610). First major painter of the Italian *Baroque and a major innovator in the *iconography of the *Counter-Reformation. Working directly on the canvas from a model, Caravaggio shunned the traditional practice of preparatory sketches for his works. Known best for his vivid realism and the intensity of the dramatic emotions his paintings conveyed, Caravaggio employed contemporary costumes and settings, an immediate simplicity of forms, and chiaroscuro (theatrical dark light identified as tenebrism in northern European art) to highlight specific details. More than a technical innovator, Caravaggio sought to redefine traditional symbols and images, thereby invigorating his presentations of biblical and devotional figures. Among his best-known works were *The Repentant Magdalene* and *The Death of the Virgin*.

Caritas. *See* Charity.

Carnation. A floral symbol for commitment, betrothal, and love. As with other flowers in Christian art, the color of the carnation characterized the nature of love; thus, *red carnations signified true love, marriage and passion; pink carnations young love, fidelity, and maternal love (especially that of *Mary); white carnations pure (platonic) or spiritual love; and yellow carnations rejection. According to legend, the carnation originated from the Virgin's tears on the Road to Calvary, and was therefore a sign of maternal love and eventually, of Mother's Day. The carnation's clove-scented aroma enhanced its association with the Crucifixion because the clove was shaped like a nail. As a sign of fidelity, it was a Flemish custom for a bride to hide a "pink" on her gown and to allow her bridegroom to search for it. The pink carnation became a symbol of fidelity in marriage, and newlyweds were depicted in portraits holding a pink.

Caryatid. From the Greek for "a woman of Caryae." Ornamental support in form of a sculpted female figure that supplanted column or pilaster. According to Greek myth, Dionysius was infatuated with a Laconian maiden who died suddenly at Caryae. The maiden was transformed into a walnut tree, thereby acquiring the epithet, *caryatis*, "of the walnut tree." *Artemis reported the maiden's death to the Laconians. The temple to Artemis at Caryae has female statues for columns. According to tradition, the postures of the caryatids mimicked those taken in the folk dances of the annual festival of Artemis Caryatis.

Cassandra. Legendary princess of Troy and blind prophetess. The most beautiful of Priam and Hecuba's twelve daughters, Cassandra learned prophecy from Apollo whom she later spurned as her lover. In a rage, he transformed her gift of prophecy into a perpetual curse of madness; thereby her prophecies went unheeded. For example, Cassandra foresaw the fall of Troy, the Trojan Horse, and the murder of Agamemnon. Immediately following the fall of Troy, she was raped by Ajax near a statue of *Athena. Later as a spoil of the Trojan War, she became a captive concubine to Agamemnon and was murdered by

*Clytemnestra and Aegisthus. Representations of Cassandra appeared within the context of either the Trojan War or the death of Agamemnon.

Cassiopeia. Mythic Greek mother of *Andromeda and Queen of Ethiopia. In an act of hubris, Cassiopeia declared her daughter, Andromeda, to be as beautiful as the *Nereids. An irate Poseidon wrecked havoc upon her people and her daughter. At Andromeda's wedding banquet, Cassiopeia was struck dead by the sight of the head of *Medusa. Poseidon placed her in the sky as a constellation in the form of a seated woman whose hands are extended in supplication, and whose overall image hangs upside down.

Cassone. Bridal chest reserved for her dowry. Decorated with scenes from mythology, history, or the *bible that illustrated motifs of happiness in marriage and/or of warnings on the power of women over men or of the consequences of female disobedience, the cassone was popular in medieval and renaissance Europe. Among the more popular themes inscribed on a cassone was that of the *Toilet of *Venus.

Castitas. *See* Chastity.

Cat. A sign of passivity, occult powers, and lust. Among the Egyptians, the cat was sacred to the sun god Ra as the destroyer of *snakes, and was the sacred animal of *Bast. As a sign of longevity in China and Japan, the cat must be propitiated throughout its life as demonic powers could be unleashed at the animal's death. In classical Mediterranean culture, *Isis, a goddess of the underworld and fertility, was accompanied by a cat. As Isis was black in coloration, the cat became associated with the Devil and with *witches in western Christian art. In particular, the black cat denoted death and evil. According to medieval legend, the cat of the Madonna (*gatta della Madonna*) was the exception to this symbolic rule. She had her litter in the stable as *Mary gave birth to Jesus. As a sign of her unique nature, the *gatta della Madonna* had a cross-shaped marking on her back.

Catacombs. From the Latin for "to the hollows." The underground burial chambers of *Jews and early Christians in Rome. These underground passageways and burial chambers were decorated with *frescoes and carvings representing scriptural stories and Jewish and Christian symbols. The catacombs were reputedly the original sites for communal worship until Christianity was declared a legal religion by the *Constantine in the fourth century.

Catherine of Alexandria, Saint (d. 310). Virgin martyr and model for the bride of Christ. According to historical and legendary texts, Catherine devoted herself as a young girl to a life of study and prayer after the death of her mother. A convert to the Christian faith, she pleaded with her legendary suitor, Emperor Maximus (Maxentius), to cease the persecution of Christians and the worship of idols. He challenged her to an intellectual confrontation with his greatest philosophers. According to tradition, her erudition was so great that she not only demolished their arguments, but all fifty philosophers converted to Christianity. Enraged at both her victory and her refusal to marry him, Maximus had Catherine tortured and

18. *Caryatids* from The Erechtheion, Acropolis, Athens

19. Pol, Jean, and Herman de Limbourg, *Saint Catherine of Alexandria Bound to a Column* from *The Belles Heures of Jean, Duke of Berry*

imprisoned without food or water. She was visited daily by *angels and *doves who fed her and nursed her *wounds. She also was visited by Christ in her cell. Maximus ordered that she be tortured with a spiked *wheel, but she prayed to God and an angel shattered the wheel allegedly killing over 4,000 heathens. She remained faithful to Christ, and her strength brought two hundred Roman soldiers to conversion. When she was beheaded, Catherine's veins flowed with *milk instead of *blood. Following her funeral rites, her body was translated to Mount Sinai and is today revered as a sacred relic in the Greek Orthodox Monastery at Mount Saint Catherine. There are many legends associated with Saint Catherine, including the vision that her *head glowed with an *aureole at her birth. The most famous legend associated with Catherine was that of her Mystical Marriage to the Christ Child. In one version of the story, *Mary appeared to a desert hermit and ordered him to show the young Catherine an image of the Virgin and Child, and to tell her that this would be her husband. Catherine became so enraptured with the Christ Child that she dedicated herself to him as his bride. In another legend, while awaiting *baptism the young Catherine had a dream in which Mary asked her son to take Catherine as his servant; he declined by turning his head away and saying she was not beautiful. After studying the dream, Catherine proceeded to be baptized and was found beautiful by the Christ Child, who placed a celestial *ring on her finger. One of the *Fourteen Holy Helpers, Catherine of Alexandria was the patron of young girls, spinsters, scholars, schools, universities, preachers, millers, and wheelwrights. Hers was one of the voices heard by Joan of Arc. A popular topic in western Christian art, Catherine was depicted as a beautiful young woman dressed as a princess in an elegant costume and wearing a *crown. She was identified by her *attributes: the Catherine Wheel, crown, *palm, *sword, wedding ring, and *book.

Catherine of Bologna, Saint (1413–63). Christian artist and visionary. Fragile as a child, Catherine of Bologna entered the *Poor Clares in Ferrara following the death of her beloved father. The only artist to be canonized, she was the creator of small religious works and the decoration of missals with miniatures and illuminations. The majority of her art was reportedly based upon her visions, including her small painting of the Infant Jesus renowned for its miraculous cures. The finest example of her artistry is her version of *Saint Ursula and Her Maidens*. Catherine of Bologna founded the Convent of Corpus Domini in Bologna, and served there as *Abbess. She was the author of a posthumously published autobiographical book of her visions and prophecies, *Le armi spirituali* (*The Seven Weapons*) (1511). The patron of Bologna and the Bolognese Academy of the Fine Arts, Catherine of Bologna was also the special patron of artists. In western Christian art, she was portrayed dressed as an *abbess of the Poor Clares, and in the act of painting a picture of one of her visions, the most famed being her visions of the Crucifixion, and of the *Maria Lactans*.

Catherine of Genoa, Saint (1447–1510). Christian mystic and visionary. Obedient to her family's wishes, sixteen-year-old Catherine entered into a marriage of convenience with Julian Adorno. Finding no favor with her husband, the youthful wife prayed for his spiritual salvation. Her marital torment ended when her husband lost his fortune. Their renewed and chaste marriage permitted Catherine to dedicate herself to the care of the sick in a hospital in Genoa. Granted profound spiritual visions at the end of her life, she was the author of *On Purgatory* and *A Dialogue between the Body and Soul*.

Catherine of Siena, Saint (1347–80). Christian mystic and *Doctor of the Church. Catherine dedicated herself at the age of seven to Christ, with whom she believed she had entered into a mystical marriage. A visionary since childhood, she became a significant correspondent to kings, popes, and emperors throughout her lifetime. A member of the Third Order of *Dominicans, she was reputedly protected during her prayers by a *white *dove on her *head. Catherine became an influential figure in fourteenth-century ecclesiastical and secular politics, including her role in persuading Gregory IX to end the Avignon Papacy and to return to Rome. Her intense periods of prayer and mystical unions ultimately led to her receipt of the *stigmata. She was the patron of all Italy, and especially of Siena. In western Christian art, Catherine was depicted as a young woman dressed in the *habit of a Dominican Tertiary *nun; she was identified by her *attributes of a white dove, *lily, *cross surmounted by a lily or a *heart, *rosary beads, *book, *crown of thorns, pierced heart, and an amanuensis writing her letters.

Cauldron. Symbol for an *enchantress, *sorcerer, or *witch, and of cyclical time. Among the ancient Egyptians, the cauldron denoted simultaneously female creative powers and the creation of the world. While for the Hindu tradition, it signified the cosmic womb of the Mother Goddess and the goddess *Kālī. In classical Greco-Roman art, *Medea was signified as a woman with a brewing cauldron. Later in western art and culture, the cauldron became transformed from the emblem of the three goddesses of fate known as the *Weird Sisters to that of the evil magical powers of *witches.

Cauldron of Oil. A symbol for both a means of torture and death, and a receptacle for evil. The cauldron of oil was an *attribute of John the Evangelist and Vitus.

Cave. Prevalent symbol for the womb of Mother Earth, the Mother Goddess, or fertility goddesses in religious art. From the caves associated with *Cybele, *Rhea, and *Kālī, evolved the symbolism of the cave as the site of the *Nativity of Jesus Christ in Christian art, and thereby as a symbol of the virginal womb of *Mary.

Cecilia, Saint (third century). Virgin martyr and saint. Converted as a child to Christianity, Cecilia married at her father's request but was unable to consummate her marriage, having vowed perpetual virginity. Her bridegroom, Valerian, respected her vow on the condition that he be allowed to see the *angel Cecilia claimed protected her. She sent him to her mentor, Urban, who was instructing catechumens in the *catacombs. Urban told the young husband to respect his bride's vow and he would see an angel upon his return home. When he entered his home, Valerian found the house filled with sweet smells and beautiful music. An angel presented him with a *wreath of *lilies for Cecilia, and a wreath of *roses for himself. He and his brother were converted to Christianity by Urban. They began to preach, were imprisoned, and executed. Seeking to obtain Valerian's property, the Roman governor ordered Cecilia to perform an act of idolatry, but she refused. Locked in a bathroom filled with hot steam, Cecilia survived her ordeal, only to have herself subjected to three attempts at decapitation. On the third day following the last execution attempt, Cecilia died after counseling Urban as to the distribution of her wealth to the poor in the Christian community. According to tradition, Cecilia was buried in the catacomb of Callistus, and her tomb was opened in 817 after Pope Paschal I had a vision of it. He ordered her body to be reburied alongside the remains of Urban, her husband, and her brother-in-law, in the crypt of Saint Cecilia-in-Trastevere. During renovations to the crypt in 1599, her sarcophagus was discovered and her body was miraculously found to be in perfect condition. This event—the incorruptible body of the saint—was documented by the sculptor Stefano Maderno. The patron of music and musicians, Cecilia became the patron of the Academy of Music in 1584. In western Christian art, she was depicted as a beautiful young woman with three wounds in her neck, and was represented playing a musical instrument and singing. Among her *attributes were the *harp, *organ, and a *crown of lilies and roses.

Cedar. Evergreen trees species and worldwide symbol for the afterlife and/

or resurrection. Cedar cones signified fertility and protection against disease in Mesopotamian art. A stately and majestic *tree signifying Christian incorruptibility. The Cedars of Lebanon, treasured as sources of wealth and the timber used to build the Temple of Solomon, were symbols of both *Mary, especially of the *Immaculate Conception, (Song 5:15) and Jesus Christ (Ez 17:22).

Celtic religion. Indigenous belief and ritual systems of Britain and Gaul prior to the invasion of the Roman Imperial Army, and later of Christian missionaries. Premised upon a reverence for nature especially as manifested in the deities and spirits, Celtic religion affirmed the fertility of the earth, the esoteric lore of the ancestors, the immortality of the soul, and the sacral nature of the arts. The *Druids were identified as the priests and intellectuals who oversaw the ceremonials and rituals of Celtic religion. Elements of the legacy of the sacred lore and ceremonials of Celtic religion were assimilated into Medieval Christian culture, especially of France and the Lowlands.

Ceres. An Italic goddess of grain, the harvest, fertility, marriage, and death. The Romans fused Ceres with the Greek goddess *Demeter. A daughter of Saturn and *Ops, Ceres was closely associated with the indigenous earth goddess *Tellus. The earth was interpreted as her bosom from which all living things emerged at birth and to which they returned at death. In classical Greco-Roman art, the iconography of *Ceres paralleled that of Demeter.

Ceres Africanus. North African goddess of the harvest. This indigenous fertility goddess was also identified as Ceres Placida. Her cult was attested to by the church father, Tertullian.

Cerialia. Annual Roman festival honoring *Ceres. Celebrated on April 19, the Cerialia was later transformed into a festival for the divine triad of Ceres, Liber, and Libera.

Cerridwen. Mythic Celtic-British witch goddess. As the prototypical witch, Cerridwen was identified by the witch's cauldron in which she created a potion for universal knowledge. Cerridwen became the model for the *iconography of witches in western art.

Cestus. Feminine symbol of fertility and sensuality in classical Mediterranean art and mythology. The Cestus was the magic girdle Hephaestus made for his wife, *Aphrodite, and that caused all those who beheld her to fall in love with her. The only time Aphrodite was reported to have been without her cestus was when it fell off during her passionate lovemaking with Ares. With Freya's *brisingamen and *Isis's knot, Aphrodite's cestus was a common symbol for the power and energy of feminine fecundity.

Chakra. From the Sanskrit for "rings." Levels of the spinal column associated with Kundālini, a serpent goddess, who resided in the spinal column, characterized as the source of *shaktī, and when unleashed provided enlightenment. Chakra was also the name given to the ritual circle dance involving men and women.

Chalchihuitlicue. From the Aztec for "the lady who has the green cloak of jewels." Aztec goddess of flowing waters and vegetation. Protector of newborn children and of marriages, Chalchihuitlicue was the wife of the rain god Tlaloc. She ruled the third hour of the day and the sixth hour of the night in the Aztec cosmology. In Aztec art, Chalchihuitlicue was depicted wearing a watery-green colored skirt and cloak adorned with water lilies. She was bare-breasted in order to suckle the young child she held in her arms. Her attribute was a rattle on a stick.

Chalice. An ambiguous symbol for nourishment, containment, tribulation, and protection. The chalice was the liturgical vessel used for the consecration and distribution of the wine of the Eucharist. In Christian art, the chalice signified the Last Supper, the Sacrifice of Jesus, and Christian faith. A chalice with a *serpent was an *attribute of John the Evangelist, a chalice with a *wafer of Barbara, and a broken chalice of Donatus. A chalice with a *cross was an attribute of *Thomas Aquinas and also signified the Agony in the Garden. A simple chalice was an attribute of Bonaventure. The quest for the *Holy Grail, the chalice used at the Last Supper, became a central theme in medieval art and legends.

Chameleon. A *animal symbol for the many guises of Satan, which he used to beguile humanity.

Chandashi. Supreme Mother Goddess of Central African peoples. Chandashi was the cause of earthquakes.

Ch'ang-O. *See* Heng-O.

Chantico. Aztec goddess of fire and the hearth.

Chaos. From the Greek for "eternal flux." Condition in the cosmic womb of the *Mother Goddess prior to creation and destruction of the world, and simultaneously of human life. As the category of unorganized creation, chaos was signified by the Babylonian goddess *Tiamat and the *Old Testament *Rahab.

Charites. From the Greek for "to rejoice." The title for the *Graces or the Roman *gratiae* in Greek mythology. As the female personifications of all that created beauty and charm, Aglaia from the Greek for "brilliance," Euprosyne from the Greek for "joy," and Thalia from the Greek for "bloom of life," inspired the arts and were associated with the *Muses and the *Horae. In classical Greco-Roman and *renaissance art, the Charites were depicted as three beautiful young women who held hands and either accompanied or encircled *Aphrodite, Apollo, Hermes, or Dionysus.

Charity. From the Latin for "selfless love." One of the *Virtues and of the Corporal Works of Mercy, and foremost among the theological virtues. In classical Greco-Roman and western Christian art, charity was typified by a mother who nursed and protected her children. A characteristic of *Mary whose charity was evident in those depictions in which she held her son in one arm while the little John the Baptist played at her *feet. In *renaissance and *baroque art, Charity was symbolized by a beautiful young woman suckling an infant, holding the hand of another small child, and encircled by other children.

Charity, Saint (second century). The female personification of the cult of Divine *Wisdom (*Sophia) in the eastern Mediterranean. According to this tradition, the Roman widow, Sophia, had three daughters—*Faith, *Hope, and Charity. The mother and her daughters were tortured and beheaded under the Emperor Hadrian.

Chasca. Incan goddess of the dawn and the twilight. According to the mythology of the Incas, Chasca controlled the weather and was the protector of young maidens. From her associations with the rising and the setting of the sun, Chasca was interpreted as an Incan form of *Venus. Fluffy clouds filled with dew were both her messengers and her *attribute.

Chastity. From the Latin for "pure, untouched." A sacred and religious virtue common to all world religions, and signifying the power of the spirit over the flesh. In classical Greco-Roman art, chastity was symbolized by the *Vestal Virgins, *Artemis (*Diana), *Danaë, *Daphne, or the figure of a beautiful young woman binding the eyes of Eros (Cupid) or any personification of Love. In Christian art, chastity was represented by a veiled young woman holding a palm branch in one hand and a shield with the sign of the *phoenix in the other, and who trampled a boar or pig under her feet; or by *Lady Poverty, any of the virgin martyrs and saints, any of the emblems of *Mary, and a *girdle, *tower, or *unicorn.

Chensit. Goddess of Lower Egypt. In Egyptian art, Chensit was represented bearing the crown of *Hathor or the *feather of *Maat.

Cherry. Cherry blossoms signified spring and feminine beauty in Chinese

20. *Ceres*

21. Guido Reni, *Charity*

22. Miniature from Christine de Pizan's *City of the Ladies (Cité des Dames)*
23. *Cihuateotl, kneeling death goddess*

and Japanese art. A sweet red fruit symbolizing the pleasant character resulting from good deeds in western Christian art. One of the "Fruits of Paradise," the cherry represented eternal life. When held by the Christ Child, the cherry signified the delights of the blessed or, on occasion, the "forbidden fruit" of the *Garden of Eden.

Cherubim. The second order of the first hierarchy of *angels. Led by the *archangel Jophiel, they guarded the Tree of Knowledge and the *Garden of Eden, and protected the Ark of the Covenant in the Temple of Solomon. In western Christian art, cherubim were depicted as either *blue or *yellow in *color, and as bodiless creatures who rode on winged *wheels. As symbols of God's *wisdom, cherubim held or read *books. In *baroque art, the cherubim became chubby, smiling, winged little babes, and were depicted most often as winged *heads or torsos.

Chestnut. A symbol of chastity and triumph over the temptations of the flesh, as the meat of this *nut laid in its husk, unharmed by its surrounding *thorns.

Chia. Moon goddess and female progenitor of the Musica Indians of Colombia. As wife of the great god Bochia, Chia tried to stop his imposition of order on the world. Invoking the displeasure of her husband, Chia as the female personification of the moon was punished with the monthly lunar cycle.

Chicomecoatl. From the Toltec for "seven snakes." Aztec goddess of corn and other foods. As the giver of maize, Chicomecoatl was identified by her attributes of an ear of corn and a ceremonial rattle.

Child/children. A human symbol for innocence and trust, spontaneity, new beginnings, and abundant possibilities. In Egyptian art and mythology, children signified the power of future beginnings and the special gift of divinization as signified in depictions of *Isis seeking Osiris or Isis with the young Horus. In the Jewish tradition, there was strict adherence to God's first command to Adam and *Eve, that is, "to be fruitful and multiply" (Gn 1:28). Thereby, faithful Jewish couples sought to have one son and one daughter in order to reproduce themselves as a couple. In western Christian art, child or children were *attributes of Anthony of Padua, Charity, Christopher, and Vincent de Paul.

Childbirth. *See* Birth; Nativity of Jesus Christ; Nativity of Mary.

Chimalman. From the Aztec for "hand shield" or "shield carrier." Triple goddess of Aztec art and mythology. Chimalman was the virgin mother of Quetzalcoatl, a war goddess, and revered as a virgin, a mother, and a *crone. Identified as an apparition of *Coatlicue, Chimalman was assimilated into her representations.

Chimera. From the Greek for "goat." A mythological beast believed to be female in nature and composed of the *head of a *lion, the *body of a *goat, and tail and *feet of a *dragon or *snake. The chimera was interpreted as a sign of the dark and sinister in several Mediterranean cultures. Following Middle Eastern legends, this monster ravaged Syria until it was slain by Bellerophon. Alleged to breathe *fire, the chimera was an invisible monster that regularly threatened Christian martyrs and, later, medieval princesses. It was a popular element in *medieval art, especially in the decorative carvings of *cathedrals and designs for tapestries.

Chinna-mastā. From the Sanskrit for "whose head is cut off." Terrifying Tantric goddess of Bengal. In Buddhist art, Chinna-mastā was identified as holding her own severed head in one hand and held so that she can drink the blood from her neck wound with her own mouth.

Chionia, Saint (d. 304). From the Greek for "snow queen." Virgin martyr. Originally one of the *Horae, Chionia was a foretype of the legendary medieval "ice queens." She was assimilated into the early Christian female martyr. One of three Thessalonian sisters and converts to Christianity who were martyred by Diocletian for their refusal to obey his decree of 303 by their possession of scriptural texts. During their trial by Dulcitius, the Roman Governor of Macedonia, the three sisters—*Agape, Chionia, and *Irene—refused to offer sacrifice or incense to the Roman deities. Chionia and Agape were burned alive, while Irene was condemned to a brothel and eventually martyred. A rare topic in Christian art, Chionia was usually depicted with her sisters either in an episode of their trial, their martyrdom, or as spiritual guide holding both a copy of the Christian scripture and a palm branch in *Byzantine art.

Chloe. Youthful beloved of Daphnis in Greek mythology. The pastoral ro-

mance of these two young lovers, Daphnis and Chloe, recounted their initial meeting, romantic escapades, separation, reunion, and marriage. In classical Greco-Roman art, she was depicted as a beautiful and lightly clad woman who was usually placed within a beautiful woodland setting as appropriate to the episode of her love affair with Daphnis. A popular theme in *baroque art, Daphnis and Chloe were represented as a shepherd and shepherdess in a landscape setting.

Chloris. Greek goddess of youth and youthful pleasures, and patron of flowers and spring. Chloris was identified with the Roman *Flora. She was portrayed as a beautiful young maiden wearing a *wreath and/or garlands of spring *flowers.

Chomiba. One of the first women in the Mayan Indian cosmology.

Christ Appearing before His Mother . *See* Appearance to His Mother.

Christian art. Traditionally, works of art created by Christian artists for any of the following uses within the Christian church: didactic, liturgical, devotional or contemplative, decorative, and/or any combination of these uses. The term Christian art has been employed as an identification for works of art created by Christian artists whether or not the theme or function was religious in nature; works of art created by Christian artists for religious purposes; or works of art with a Christian theme, religious or secular, created by non-Christian artists. *See also* Byzantine Art, Christian Iconography, Icons, Iconoclasm.

Christian iconography. The study and system of the signs, symbols, and images used in Christian art. Premised on the allegorical and metaphorical teachings of the early church fathers, Christian artists developed a typological reading of both classical Greco-Roman heroes and heroines and the *Bible. The "type" then was *Mary or Jesus Christ, or some *New Testament element as the fulfillment of the "foretype" from either classical Greco-Roman legend, literature, and mythology or the Bible.

Christian Scriptures. *See* New Testament.

Christina, Saint (third century). Virgin martyr. According to legend, this daughter of wealthy Romans smashed the family idols, distributed *gold and *silver pieces to the poor, and was imprisoned for filial infidelity and impiety. After burning, attempted drowning, and torture with a *knife and tongs failed to kill her or force her to recant, Christina died after being shot with three arrows. She was popular in *medieval art and legend, and northern Italian *renaissance art and spirituality. In western Christian art, Christina was depicted as a beautiful young woman with three arrows in her neck. Her other *attribute was the millstone as a sign of her attempted martyrdom by drowning. Christina was a companion to *Ursula.

Christine de Pizan (1363–c. 1431). First professional woman of letters in medieval France. Following the premature death of her beloved husband, Étienne de Castel, in 1390, Christine de Pizan was required to become the sole financial support of her family. Exceptionally well educated for her time, she earned her living by writing, and produced over twenty distinguished works on the subject of French politics and/or the defense of women, especially in terms of their obligations and the dignity of women. A distinguished advisor to leading court officials, she was best known for her book, *The City of the Ladies* in which she refuted the image(s) of woman described in the popular *The *Romance of the Rose*. She offered her female readers the vision of a utopian ideal city as the dwelling place of worthy women. Her companion text, *A Medieval Woman's Mirror of Honor*, was a practical guide for women who wished to live an honorable noble life—composed of hard work, honor of purpose, and strength of commitment—in order to enter into the City of the Ladies. An early feminist and advocate for women's education, Christine de Pizan was also a supporter of women artists, in fact in *The City of Ladies*, she entered into a lengthy conversation with Reason about the famous women artists from antiquity. She regularly commissioned illustrations for her books from the otherwise unknown woman artist identified as "Anastaise," who was also the apparent source of the many images of Christine de Pizan writing at her desk or instructing young women in medieval art.

Chrysanthemum. Floral symbol of autumn and longevity, especially in Chinese and Japanese art.

Church. From the Greek for "the Lord's Place." A term of dual meaning signifying either the social reality of the Christian community or an architectural edifice. As a social designation, church referred to the community of the people who had been called and gathered to follow Christ. As the place of gathering, the church was the building used for the assembly of the Christian faithful. This "House of God" was referred to as the Body of Christ or the Ark of Salvation. In Christian art, the image of a church building in the *hands of a *saint, bishop, or male figure signified that this person had been either the patron, *donor, bishop, or architect of the building. In the hands of either *Jerome or Gregory the Great, the image of the ecclesial building signified the larger sense of the church. The image of *Ecclesia, a crowned and wide-eyed female figure holding a *banner, *chalice, and/or a *book, represents the church, specifically the Church Triumphant, in opposition to *Synagoga.

Church of England. *See* Anglicanism.

Cihuacoatl. From the Toltec for "serpent woman." Aztec goddess of childbirth who aided Quetzalcoatl at the creation of the first man. In Aztec art, Cihuacoatl was depicted holding a child in her arms.

Cihuateotl. Aztec goddess of disease and misfortune. Cihuateotl was a woman who had died during childbirth and was transformed into a deity. She was reported to descend to earth only on preassigned days of the Aztec calendar. Cihuateotl was depicted as a skeletal figure who squatted in the birthing position with a protruding or oversized skull.

Cincture. *See* Girdle.

Cintāmani. Famed "wish-granting jewel" of Buddhist art and tradition. The cintāmani bestowed the fulfillment of wishes and desires, including the greatest of "all treasures"—the understanding of Buddhist Law that freed one from desire and satisfaction and freed the heart for compassion. In Buddhist art, the cintāmani was characterized as a circular or round jewel with a pointed top thereby similar in shape to a female *breast.

Circe. Legendary Greek sorcerer, mistress of herbs and amulets. Although renowned for her cruelty and for her magical transformation of men into animals, she cleansed her niece *Medea and Jason of their guilt in the murder of Apsyrtus. However when Glaucus rejected her for Scylla, Circe turned him into a terrifying monster. She seduced Odysseus and transformed his companions into pigs until she was overcome by Hermes's herbal magic (*Odyssey*, Book 10). This witchlike goddess restored Odysseus's companions to their human forms, and then sponsored a one-year banquet celebrating their departure for Ithaca with Odysseus. In classical Greco-Roman and *renaissance art, Circe was depicted as a beautiful woman with the attributes of a sorcerer, such as a magician's wand and potion vials, and in the act of transforming human beings into animals or monsters.

Circle. Worldwide religious symbol of the cosmos, the heavens, and the supreme deity. In Taoism, the circle represented the creative principle of the universe as the unification of the *Yin (female) and the Yan (male) parts. In Christian art, the circle's round shape with no apparent beginning or end signified eternity and God. The perfect shape within a *triangle, the circle signified the Trinity, as did the motif of three intertwined circles.

Clare of Assisi, Saint (c. 1194–1253). Founder of the Order of the *Poor Clares, dedicated to the cloistered contemplative life. A devoted follower of *Francis of Assisi, Clare was the greatest female Franciscan. Miraculously, the *bread supply at her convent was replenished daily as a sign of her extraordinary holiness. The patron of television, Clare was invoked against possession by the Devil or evil. *Francis receives Clare*: After leaving her family and receiving sanctuary from Francis, Clare knelt to make her confession at her feet. *Repulsion of the Saracens (The Golden Legend)*: Her deep devotion legendarily allowed her to repel Moslem invaders by holding up a monstrance before them. *Death of Clare*: Surrounded by her sister nuns, and varied female martyrs and saints, Clare has a final vision of *Mary and the Child, or alternately Mary holds Clare's head as the saint breathes her final breath. In western Christian art, she was depicted as an elderly woman wearing the gray tunic with knotted *girdle and the white coif and black veil of her order. Her *attributes included a monstrance, *lily, *cross, and crosier (as the founder of her order).

Claudia (*Festivals* 4:291–348). Legendary *Vestal Virgin. Claudia defended her honor from an unjust accusation of unchastity. Invoking *Cybele as the *Great Mother as witness to her innocence, the Vestal attached her *girdle to the prow of a ship that was imbedded in the mud of the mouth of the Tiber. Cognizant that a sacred stone image of the goddess was part of the ship's cargo, Claudia was able to tow the ship up the river. In classical Roman and *renaissance art, she was portrayed as a beautiful matron dressed in flowing white garments with the ship tied to her girdle as she pulls it to the amazement of the elders, including her accusers. Representations of Claudia holding a boat in her hands signified confidence or trust.

Clement, Clara Erskine. *See* Waters, Clara Erskine Clement.

Cleopatra VI (69–30 B.C.E.). Beautiful romantic heroine and final Ptolemaic queen of Egypt. She was restored to the throne of Egypt by an infatuated Julius Caesar following his defeat of her husband/brother Ptolemy XII in 48 B.C.E. The mother of Caesar's son, Caesarion, Cleopatra lived with him for two years in Rome. Following Caesar's assassination, she returned to Egypt where she ruled as queen until falling in love with Mark Antony who abandoned his wife, Octavia. Antony died at the Battle of Actium fighting against his former brother-in-law, Octavius. Shortly thereafter, Cleopatra committed suicide by the bite of a poisonous asp. *Banquet (Feast) of Cleopatra*: The Egyptian queen stunned Mark Antony with the lavish elegance of a banquet on her Nile barge. She emphasized her disinterest in material wealth by dissolving a pearl in her wine and then drinking the wine. This scene was popular in *baroque and *romantic painting. Cleopatra and Mark Antony were seated at a banquet table as servants carried trays laden with foods and drink passed by. Visual focus was directed towards the beautiful queen who held the pearl in one hand and the wineglass in the other. *Cleopatra and Octavius*: As a sign of her defeat, Cleopatra was represented handing the victorious Octavius a list of her wealth. *Death of Cleopatra*: Following the defeat at Actium, Cleopatra refused to become

24. Nerocci de' Landi and Master of the Griselda Legend, *Claudia Quinta*
25. Master of the Saint Lucy Legend, *Mary, Queen of Heaven*

26. Antoine Dufour, *Cleopatra,* detail from *Vie des Femmes Celebres*

the slave of Octavius, so she committed suicide with the bite of a poisonous snake, often identified as an asp or a cobra and represented as hidden within a basket of figs. Especially popular in *baroque and *romantic art, representations of this topos followed the description found in Plutarch's *Lives* (44:86). The dying queen was either seated on her throne or reclining on her fabled golden bed as she held the asp to her naked breasts. A basket of figs, the reported vehicle for the snakes, was often present on Cleopatra's lap. She was portrayed as a beautiful queen in Egyptian, classical Greco-Roman, renaissance, baroque, and romantic art.

Clio. From the Greek for "she who praises." Greek muse of history. In classical Greco-Roman and *renaissance art, Clio was identified by her attributes of a *scroll and a trumpet (of fame).

Clitoris. From the Greek for "divine, famous, goddesslike." Source of sexual pleasure in a woman's body associated with goddesses and female aspects of love and sexuality in western religious art and mythology. With the advent of Christianity and the denial of female sexual pleasure, the clitoris was viewed as an instrument of evil.

Clitoridectomy. Surgical removal of the clitoris (so-called female circumcision), thereby the denial of female sexual pleasure. Clitoridectomy has been practiced within varied cultural traditions rarely with any religious significance but as a form of control over women, while many nineteenth- and twentieth-century physicians identified it as a possible "cure" for female hysteria, dementia, and catalepsy.

Cloak. A covering garment signifying protection or dignity and rank. Covering and protecting the *body, the cloak was also interpreted as a symbol of modesty. A cloak divided into halves by a *sword was an *attribute of Martin of Tours.

Cloelia. Roman noblewoman renowned for her courage. During the war between the Romans and the Etruscans, Cloelia was a hostage of the Etruscan king Porsenna. She escaped from his custody and fled across the Tiber River on horseback only to be returned to her captor by the Roman consuls who feared his reprisals. However, the Etruscan king was impressed with both her courage and her horsemanship, and so he freed her. A rare topic in classical Roman and *renaissance art, Cloelia was usually depicted as a proper Roman matron either being released by the Etruscan king or in the act of fleeing his camp on horseback.

Clorinda. Famed *Amazon warrior and legendary beloved of Tancred. The Italian poet, Tasso, built upon the legendary motif of the Amazon in his *Jerusalem Delivered*, his epic poem about the First Crusade. A beautiful Amazon warrior, Clorinda elected to fight with the Saracens against the invading crusaders despite the fact that she was in love with the knight, Tancred. Unknown to him in her armor, the two lovers entered into combat in which Clorinda was mortally wounded. Near death, the wounded warrior requested the rite of Christian *baptism, so Tancred removed his helmet as a container for the necessary water. As he removed the helmet of the wounded warrior he was about to baptize, Tancred recognized his beloved

Clorinda. A popular topic in *baroque and nineteenth-century art, Clorinda was depicted as a youthful but strong female figure dressed in medieval armor. The death-bed baptismal scene became the most common representation of her story as Tancred knelt over her prone body.

Clothing. Coverings for the body that simultaneously hid *nakedness and distinguished rank, social station, and sex. The elegance or poverty of clothing signified the economic and political status of an individual, and at the same time, served as a camouflage for the wearer. Significantly, the act of taking off one's clothes was interpreted as a removal of one's social or public persona, while the act of putting on one's clothes signified the wearing of a persona. With particular regard to female figures, the removal of clothing indicated preparation for seduction or sexual encounter.

Clotho. One of the *Moirai. As the daughter of Zeus and Themis, Clotho was the sister of *Atropos and *Lachesis. She was the "spinner" among the three sisters, the other two being the "measurer" and the "cutter" of the individual thread of life for each human being's destiny.

Clouds. Meteorological symbol for the omnipresence of God. The Divine Omnipotence of God was signified by a right *hand emerging from the clouds.

Clover. Dual symbol of good and of evil in western Christian art. A four-leaf clover was a sign of good luck, a five-leafed clover of bad luck. A three-leaf clover represented the Christian Trinity. The Irish clover, or shamrock, was an *attribute of Patrick and of Ireland.

Club. In classical Greco-Roman art and mythology, an attribute of *Melpomene, the *muse of tragedy, and of *Fortitude, one of the *Virtues.

Clytemnestra. Legendary Greek queen who was the sister of *Helen, Castor, and Pollux; wife of Agamemnon; and mother of *Electra, *Iphigenia, and Orestes. Clytemnestra was forced to marry Agamemnon after he murdered her first husband and their child. She bore Agamemnon three daughters and one son. In order to appease *Artemis, irate over the murder of one of her sacred stags, Agamemnon sacrificed his daughter Iphigenia. Almost immediately, the necessary winds appeared and the king-warrior and his army set sail for Troy. During the siege of Troy, Clytemnestra ruled Mycenae and took the youthful Aegisthus as her lover. Ten years later, Agamemnon returned to a royal welcome that turned into disaster when the queen and her lover killed the king in his bath. Revenged for the death of her two children, Clytemnestra ruled for seven more years until her son, Orestes, attained his maturity. Encouraged by his sister Electra, Orestes returned home, claimed his rightful throne, and avenged their father's murder with the death of Clytemnestra and her lover.

Clytie. Another female victim of unrequited love in Greek mythology. There were two variants to her story. In the one version, Apollo rejected Clytie in favor of Leucothoe. Angered by this denial, Clytie reported this liaison to her rival's unsuspecting father who buried his daughter alive. Despite all her efforts, Apollo continued to reject Clytie. In the other version, the ocean nymph's adoration of Apollo caused her to follow his daily course as the sun with steadfast attention until she faded away. Sympathetic to her plight, the other gods transformed her into the *sunflower (marigold), which watched the daily course of the sun with unwavering devotion.

Coat. *See* Cloak.

Coatlicue. From the Aztec for "serpent lady." Terrifying Aztec goddess of earth, fire, and fertility. Coatlicue was the mother of all the first gods and finally of the war god, Huitzilopochtli, who was conceived when she swallowed a ball of hummingbird feathers, and of the great god, Quetzalcoatyl, who was conceived when she swallowed an emerald. In Aztec art, she was portrayed wearing a skirt of *snakes, and a necklace of human heads and hearts. Coatlicue was decapitated by the just gods in revenge for conceiving Huitzilopochtli, and two snakes representing spurting blood replaced her head.

Cock. A worldwide avian symbol for the rising sun. In classical Greco-Roman art and mythology, the cock was associated with *Demeter (*Ceres) and *Prosperina (*Persephone), as signs of fertility and rising spring; and of *Athena (*Minerva) as an emblem of war. It also signified Vigilance, Lust and Gluttony, and Love in classical Greek art. In Shinto art, the cock was an attribute of *Amaterasu Omikami.

Colomba of Córdova, Saint (d. 853). Spanish virgin martyr and defender of *Christianity against *Islam. Although little was known of her childhood or early life, Colomba of Córdova resided with a community of nuns at Tabanos. Following the invasion of the Moors and the ensuing exile of this religious community of Christian women, she appeared publicly before the magistrate and in an act of open defiance denounced Mohammed as a prophet. Colomba was condemned to death, and later beheaded. A rare topic in western Christian art, she was included as beautiful but simply dressed young woman holding her severed head in the narrative cycles of the saints of Catholic Spain.

Colors, symbolism of. Signifiers of the identity of individuals, rankings in society, and emotional or personal characteristics. In Christian art, colors were interpreted on the two levels of inherent characteristics and emotional connotations. For example, because the inherent characteristic of *red was heat, the color red signified hot temperatures, hot tempers, and *fire; the emotional connotations of red were emotional and physical passion and suffering. The same color could have had opposite meanings that could only be clarified by the narrative or theological contexts; thus red signified both the divine love of John the Evangelist and the sensual sinfulness of the Devil.

Columbine. From the Latin for "dove-like" and "dove." A botanical symbol for the *Holy Spirit. However, the blue columbine was a symbol for sorrow, and so seven blue columbines signified the *Seven Sorrows of the Virgin Mary. The seven *flowers on the stalk of the columbine denoted the Seven Gifts of the Holy Spirit.

Column. In Egyptian art, the column represented the support of the heavens. In western Christian art, the column was a sign of the Passion, specifically of the Flagellation. A depiction of the *Madonna and Child with a column represented the foreknowledge that this child was born to suffer and die. Falling columns topped with idols were a sign of the *Flight into Egypt. The column was an *attribute of Samson and Simon Stylites.

Comb. The depiction of a woman combing her *hair was a worldwide signifier of vanity or a *toilet scene. An iron comb was an *attribute of Blaise in western Christian art.

Comma. Antique stone in the shape of a comma or claw, most often of jade, found in Japan and Korea. As necklaces, commas were a ritual offering to Shinto deities. As a central element to the Three Sacred Relics of Japan, the others being the sacred mirror and the sword, commas were an enticement for *Amaterasu Omikami to leave the cave of darkness.

Compass. An instrument of measurement and a symbol for judgment in religious art. In classical Greco-Roman and *renaissance art, the compass identified *Urania as the Muse of Astronomy; Astronomy and Geometry of the *Seven Liberal Arts; *Justice; and *Prudence.

Concord. Female personification of a minor virtue symbolic of peace, especially as an end to war. In classical Greco-Roman and *medieval art, Con-

cord was denoted by the *olive branch motif on her shield, while in *renaissance and nineteenth-century art, she held a *cornucopia, two *doves, a bundle of *arrows, or a sheaf of corn.

Concordia. Roman goddess and female personification of Harmony. Concordia was a popular topos on Roman coins. She was identified by her *attributes of the sacrificial bowl and the *cornucopia.

Concubine. In the Hebraic tradition, the concubine was a woman who was devoted to one man but was not formally married and thereby was not treated as a wife under Hebraic law. Following the *Old Testament, six of the tribes of Israel were descended from concubines and King Solomon was famed for his several hundred concubines. The social practice and tolerance of concubinage was discouraged from Rabbinic times.

Confucianism. Intellectual tradition of China founded by Confucius (551–479 B.C.E.). The foundation of Confucianism was a strict code of morals and rules of political conduct that formed the good society. Among these morals were the tenets of filial piety, ancestor worship, nature worship, and Heaven. Often critiqued as a moral tradition not a religion, Confucianism was the official religion of Imperial China.

Constancy. Female personification of a minor virtue symbolic of personal and civic loyalty and steadfastness. A popular topic on medals and funerary monuments, Constancy was characterized as a female figure in a military posture of alertness who held either a *sword or a spear.

Convent. The house of a religious community of women, such as the *Bridgettines or the *Poor Clares.

Convolvulus. Floral symbol of humility in western Christian art, and of love and marriage in Chinese art.

Copia. Roman goddess of wealth and abundance. Copia was a servant of *Fortuna. In classical Roman and *renaissance art, she was identified by her cornucopia, which was filled with food and drink.

Coptic Christianity. Ancient Christian tradition of Egypt. Traditionally established by the Apostle Mark in the first century, Coptic Christianity separated from the larger Christian world as a result of the *Council of Chalcedon (451). Committed to the theological teaching of monophysitism, Coptic Christianity interpreted the Chalcedonian formula as a triumph of the Greek culture and a defeat of the Egyptian. Nationalistic in its orientation, Coptic Christianity sought to affirm Egyptian culture by retaining Coptic as their liturgical language.

Coral. Alleged petrified seaweed created when Perseus rescued *Andromeda from the sea monster, Cetus, and laid down the severed head of *Medusa, which bled and turned it to a red color. Believed to have healing powers, coral was used by the classical Greeks and Romans to protect their children from the "evil eye." Coral was worn by the Japanese as a symbol of the power to disperse evil and by the Chinese as a sign of long life. In Christian art and spirituality, this light-red stone was used as an amulet or charm against evil,

witchcraft, or possession by the Devil. Worn by infants and small *children, a piece of coral or a *rosary of gold and coral beads as when held by the Christ Child was a sign of triumph over the Devil.

Core. *See* *Kore.

Corn. A worldwide symbol of fertility, harvest, and honor; the emblem of corn deities. Corn was an attribute of *Cybele, *Demeter (*Ceres), *Inanna, *Ishtar, *Isis, *Persephone (*Proserpina), and *Fides in classical Mediterranean and Near Eastern religious art. Ears of corn entwined in vines, perhaps held by the *Madonna and Child, signified the Eucharist. As the basic crop and nuturant of human life among Native American tribes, corn was a central metaphor for birth and the life cycle, and thereby signified the Earth Mother in her aspects as either the Corn Mother or the virginal Corn Maiden.

Cornelia (second century B.C.E.). Roman matron who was daughter of Scipio Africanus, wife of Gracchus, and mother of the Gracchi. A pious widow dedicated to the care of her children, Cornelia refused remarriage. She instilled in her children a sense of civic duty and a desire for glory. According to tradition, when a wealthy Roman matron bragged about her jewels, Cornelia responded by pointing to her sons who "are my jewels." She was a classical symbol of the devoted mother and of civic virtue. In classical Roman and *baroque art, Cornelia was portrayed as a pious Roman matron standing between her two sons and in the company of a richly attired and bejeweled matron who stands next to a table covered with jewelry.

Cornucopia. A symbol of fruitfulness and plenty, especially of the harvest. This horn filled with fruits and flowers signified varied gods and goddesses characterized by abundance and prosperity such as *Fortuna, *Almathea, *Demeter (*Ceres), the season of Autumn, Hospitality, and the Cimmerian *Sibyl in classical Greco-Roman, *renaissance, and *baroque art; or the Garden of Eden as the *Paradise Garden in Christian art.

Coronation of the Virgin Mary. Final legend in the narrative cycle of *Mary. When she was received by God the Father and her son into *heaven, Mary was enthroned and crowned as Queen of Heaven. This iconographic motif developed in thirteenth-century *cathedral *tympanums in which the seated Mary crowned by her son fulfilled the *Old Testament foretypes of Solomon and the *Queen of Sheba (1 Kgs 10:1–13), and of *Bathsheba seated at the right *hand of her enthroned son, Solomon (1 Kgs 2:19). A popular topic in *medieval, early *renaissance, and early southern *baroque art, the Coronation of the Virgin Mary illustrated the conflation of the temporal with the eternal as Mary was the intermediary both to heaven and the power of the secular queen. As *Mater Ecclesia* ("Mother Church"), Mary became a visual image for the enhanced power and authority of the Church in the medieval, early renaissance, and southern baroque worlds. In western Christian art, Mary was depicted dressed in elaborate royal *robes being assumed into heaven with the assistance of *angels and *clouds, or kneeling at the foot of her son's (and later jointly God's) throne, as a crown held jointly by Father and Son was placed upon her head. This image was replaced by the *iconography of the *Immaculate Conception in southern baroque art.

Coronis. Mythic Greek princess transformed into a crow by *Athena. A daughter of King Coroneus, Coronis caught the attention of Poseidon as she walked on the seashore. Infatuated with her, the sea god sought her affections but was rejected. He then chased her and as he was about to ravage her, Coronis cried out for divine assistance and the goddess Athena turned her into a crow which flew away from her suitor.

Council of Trent. The ecumenical council convened in Trent from 1545 to 1565 to examine, study, and promulgate official ecclesiastical decrees defining the Roman Catholic Church's position on all aspects of Christian life, religious practice, liturgy, and canon law. Directly responding to the attacks and critiques of the Protestant Reformers, the Council of Trent carefully defined *Roman Catholic orthodoxy and codified the practice and meaning of Roman Catholicism until the Second Vatican Council (1962–65). At its Twenty-Fifth Session in December 1563, the Council of Trent issued a decree "On the Invocation, Veneration, and Relics of Saints, and on Sacred Images," in which the accepted rules and regulations for art in the church were defined. Works of art as visual images of moral and religious pedagogy were to be welcomed into the church as long as they were appropriate to scripture and church teachings, and were not of a lascivious nature. The ultimate judge of the appropriateness of a work of art for the church was the local bishop.

Counter-Reformation. The Roman Catholic Church's formal response to the theological and critical attacks of the Reformers. This response was shaped by the *Council of Trent, the establishment of new religious orders including the Society of Jesus, and the new spirituality as advocated by *Teresa of Avila, John of the Cross, Vincent de Paul, and others. It clearly defined Roman Catholic identity and spirituality and led to the reinvigoration of religious *iconography, especially the development of new motifs that visually defended the church against the Reformers's criticisms, such as the motif of the penitential saints in defense of the sacrament of penance, and those of the *Immaculate Conception and *Assumption in defense of *Mary.

Cow. A worldwide symbol for the *mother goddess or *Great Goddess in religious art. In Sumerian art and mythology, the cow suckling her calf was the sign of *Ninhursag. In Egyptian art and mythology, the cow signified the "giver of milk" and thereby, hope for continued human existence. This animal was intimately connected to *Hathor who either took bovine form or a bovine head, or wore a bovine headdress. In classical Greco-Roman and *renaissance art, the cow represented *Hera (*Juno), *Demeter (*Ceres), and *Io. In Scandinavian mythology, the cow identified as Audhumbla, the first living being, originated from Gumungagap (Chaos). She licked the giant ancestor of the gods out of salty ice.

Cowrie shells. Worldwide symbol for the vulva of the Great Goddess and of rebirth. Cowrie shells have been used as amulets of healing and regenerative powers by ancient Egyptian women, classical Greco-Roman women, Japanese women, and Gypsy women. It was an *attribute of many goddesses or female personifications of fertility and sexuality such as *Astarte, *Demeter, and *Alma Mater.

Crab. Crustacean symbol for the fourth sign of the *Zodiac in the Greco-Roman astrological calendar, the month of June. In western Christian art, this crustacean that regularly shed its shell was a sign of the Resurrection of Jesus Christ.

Cranach, Lucas (1472–1553). One of the leading sixteenth-century German artists and a close friend and supporter of *Martin Luther. A talented engraver, etcher, and printmaker, Cranach was important in the initial development of the *iconography of the Reformation especially in terms of the image of woman. He painted *altarpieces and single panel paintings illustrating Luther's theology, and also produced a series of woodcuts to illustrate Luther's writings and his translation of the Bible into German in 1520. Along with his son, Lucas Cranach the Younger (1515–86), Cranach the Elder developed a series of iconographic types of women, such as the themes of woman as *femme fatale, seductress, and *witch, thereby transforming the fundamental characterizations of woman into images more appropriate to Luther's theology. With the development of the printing press, he was able to disseminate these new visual motifs of women widely and rapidly, and transforming the image of woman into evil creatures in western art. Cranach the Elder was also important for his depictions of biblical

27. Lucas Cranach the Elder, *The Nymph of the Spring*

28. *Cybele Enthroned on a Cart Drawn by Two Lions*

heroines, and helping to popularize the themes of the *Holy Kindred and *Blessing the Little Children.

Crane. In Chinese art and mythology, the crane symbolized longevity. As the avian servant and messenger of *Hsi Wang Mu, this bird carried the tablets inscribed with human fate to earth. In early Christian art, the crane was an avian symbol for loyalty, good works, vigilance, and order, especially in terms of the monastic life. According to legend, the cranes gathered every evening and formed a protective *circle around their king. One crane was selected as the watch for the evening; to insure that it remained, this crane had to balance itself on one leg, so that if it fell asleep it would fall to the ground and awaken immediately.

Crescent. Worldwide symbol of lunar deities and of feminine energies, especially of *Mother Goddesses, in religious art. In classical Mediterranean traditions, the crescent was the symbol of *Artemis (*Diana), *Io, *Ishtar, *Luna, and *Selene. This symbol of the purity of *Mary was assimilated into Christian art and symbolism from her association with the classical Greco-Roman virginal goddesses of the moon, Artemis (Diana) and Selene (Luna). In Spanish art, Mary was represented standing on an upside-down crescent *moon that signified the triumph of Spanish Christianity over *Islam. When placed within a *circle, the crescent represented the Kingdom of Heaven.

Crocodile. An animal symbol for hypocrisy. Insincere "crocodile tears" supposedly were shed by this animal after it had entrapped and eaten its human prey.

Reputed to have uncontrollable sexual urges, the crocodile was also a symbol of lust. In Egyptian art and mythology, the crocodile was a binary symbol of the demonic and the beneficent, and was an attribute of Osiris and Seth. Ammit the wailing demon known as the "devourer of the dead" was composed of a crocodile head, and the forelegs and mane of a lion. He was present at the weighing of the souls at judgment. The Egyptian god, Sebek, was worshiped at Crocodilopolis. In Christian art, the crocodile—like the *whale—was associated with *Hell because it slid through the mud into the *waters, and had large teeth like the "maws of Hell."

Crone. Worldwide fearsome aspect of the Triple Goddess. A crone was originally identified as the female embodiment of old age, death, winter, doomsday, and a waning moon. She was a metaphor for the necessary destruction and dissolution in preparation for regeneration. As such she was identified as *Kālī, *Cerridwen, or *Ereshkigal among other goddesses. However, as a female embodiment of wisdom, specifically that form of "blood wisdom" retained and regenerating postmenopausal or "old women," the crone was signified by "wise women" such as *Athena, *Minerva, and *Sophia.

Cross. An ancient, worldwide symbol of the conjunction of opposites with the vertical bar representing the positive forces of life and spirituality and the horizontal bar the negative forces of death and materialism. The cross also symbolized the meeting of *heaven and *earth. As the instrument of death, the cross became the primary emblem of

Christianity, signifying both the sacrifice of Jesus Christ and his victory over death through the Resurrection. In Christian legend and art, the cross became a sign of the *Tree of Life and the Tree of *Paradise. There were over four hundred varieties of the cross possible in Christian art and symbolism. The most commonly represented form was the Latin cross, in which the upper vertical bar and two horizontal bars were equal in size while the lower vertical bar was elongated. According to Christian tradition, Jesus was believed to have been crucified on a Latin cross, and therefore the Latin cross was a symbol of the Passion. The Greek cross, which was identified by its four equal arms, came to symbolize the *church and represented the basic floor plan for ecclesiastical buildings. An archiepiscopal cross used by bishops and patriarchs was a Latin cross with an additional shortened upper crossbar for the placement of the inscription. An Eastern Christian variant of the archiepiscopal cross included a slanted crossbar towards the bottom of the cross to suggest the *suppadaneum* ("footrest"). A Latin cross on a pedestal of three-graded steps was the Calvary cross, while the Papal cross was a Latin cross with three graduated, ascending bars. In remembrance of his crucifixion, *Andrew was identified with the X-shaped or saltire cross. The Old Testament cross that served as the sign of the Passover was also known as the T, *tau*, or Egyptian cross, and was an attribute of *Philip and *Anthony the Abbot. The Maltese cross—the sign of the Crusaders, Hospitalers, and Knights of Malta—was a Latin cross whose arms ended in inward-pointed

spearheads. A Celtic cross was elaborately carved with the stories of the Passion, Death, and Resurrection, and with a circle incised around its central crossing. A simple Latin cross was the sign of *Reparata and *Margaret, while one with loaves of *bread represented Philip. A Latin cross with a chalice suggested the Agony in the Garden, while with a *crown it denoted the reward of the faithful in heaven. *Catherine of Siena was signified by a Latin cross surmounted by a *lily or a heart, John the Baptist by a Latin cross with a reed, and *Helena by a Latin cross with a hammer and nails. The Church Triumphant was represented by a Latin cross surmounting an orb or the globe, while the Latin cross on an obelisk represented the Triumph of Christianity over Paganism. A red Latin cross on a white banner typified George of Cappadocia and Ursula. When the Christ Child held a cross it meant a prophecy of his destiny. In *renaissance art, the cross signified *Faith who also held a chalice, and several of the *Sibyls (Hellespoint, Phrygia, and Cimmeria).

Cross, Finding of the True. *See* Finding of the True Cross.

Crow. Sacred to Apollo, the white plumage of this bird was turned black when it told tales about *Coronis. An attribute of *Athena (*Minerva) as the patron of the arts and of oracles. In *Taoism, and *Shintoism, this avian symbol was the messenger of the sun as personified by the goddess *Amaterasu Omikami. In western Christian art, the crow was an avian symbol for solitude and the Devil blinding sinners, the crow was an *attribute of Vincent of Saragossa. In *renaissance art, the crow personified the virtue, *Hope.

Crown. A sign of distinction, royalty, and victory. In Egyptian art, a crown was the insignia of the deities and the Pharaohs, and a symbol of ruling powers. In Christian art, crowns denoted the royal lineage of a particular *saint or of *Mary, who was from the Royal House of *David. When worn by a martyr, a crown implied victory over human sinfulness and death. *Catherine of Alexandria wore a royal crown, as did Mary as Queen of Heaven. *Elizabeth of Hungary was signified by the triple crown of her royal birth, royal marriage, and royal status in *heaven. *Cecilia wore a crown of *lilies and *roses; Louis of France, *Catherine of Siena, *Veronica, and William of Norwich each a crown of thorns. Louis of Toulouse was illustrated standing on a crown and scepter. The crown of thorns and nails symbolized the Passion and Crucifixion. The crown of thorns was a symbolic reversal of the Roman Imperial Crown of Roses.

Cube. A geometric symbol for stability in religious art. As a polyhedron with more than six sides, the cube signified the Pythagorean doctrine that six was the basis of the universe in classical Greco-Roman art. In classical Greco-Roman, Christian, and *renaissance art, the cube was an *attribute of *Faith who rested her foot on the sign of stability as opposed to *Fortuna who favored the instability of the sphere.

Cuckoo. This bird was known as the "secret lover," and was a sign of unrequited love in Japanese art. An avian attribute of *Hera as herald of the spring and as a sign of Zeus as her lover in Greek art and mythology.

Culsu. Etruscan female demon standing at the entrance to the underworld. She was identified in Etruscan and Roman art by her *attributes, a burning torch and a pair of scissors.

Cundī. From the Sanskrit for "the pure." *Bodhisattva and a female emanation of *Avalokiteshvara. Originally identified as the solar deity, *Usas, Cundī became transformed into a *Bodhisattva and as the Japanese translation of *Durgā. In Buddhist art, Cundī was characterized as having as many as sixty-four arms but most regularly eighteen with which she formed *mudrās or held any of the following *attributes: a *sword, *rosary, *fruit, axe, elephant goad, *vajra, pendant, pilgrim's staff decorated with flames, *lotus, *vase, *rope, *ring, conch shell, or a box of sutras. She was either seated or stood upon a lotus. Cundī was dressed in a flowing robe that covered her shoulders and arms but exposed either or both of her *breasts, while her many arms were bedecked with bracelets and her head with a crown or conical tiara. In her Japanese form as Juntei Kannon Bosatsu, she was represented as a beautiful young woman seated on a lotus whose four principal hands formed mudrās of peace and enlightenment while she held a trident, rosary, fruit, *cintāmani, sword, lotus, Wheel of the Law, jar, and vase in her other hands. Juntei Kannon Bosatsu wore a long flowing skirt, covered her left shoulder with a celestial scarf, and was bedecked with jewels while her torso remained uncovered. As Juntei Kannon, she was the source of fertility, the facilitator of childbirth, and the protector of children.

Cunegunda, Saint (d. 1033) (*The Golden Legend*). Benefactress of the Benedictine Order. Wife and later widow of the Holy Roman Emperor Henry II, Cunegunda supported the Benedictines and with her husband assisted in the building of Bamberg Cathedral. Unjustly accused of infidelity with a knight, she walked barefoot over fifteen feet of red-hot plowshares without injury or pain, thereby affirming her innocence and her marital fidelity. Following the death of her husband, she retreated to the Benedictine Monastery at Kaufungen in Hesse and was eventually buried beside her husband in Bamberg Cathedral. A rare topic in western Christian art, Cunegunda was represented as a pious widow dressed in the habit of a Benedictine nun and held a model of Bamberg Cathedral. Her *attribute was a plowshare.

Cup. A sign for the Agony in the Garden (Mt 26:39). *See also* Chalice.

Cybele. Phrygian and Lydian *Great Mother and goddess of fertility associated with *Rhea and *Demeter. Her annual spring festival celebrated her love of the youthful and virile, Atys, with orgiastic rites and cultic practices. She was accompanied by a retinue of ecstatic dancers identified as the korybantes. In classical Mediterranean and *renaissance art, she was represented either in her chariot drawn by *lions and *panthers, and accompanied by dancing priests, dwarfs, and musicians; or enthroned between lions, wearing a towerlike crown as the guardian of cita-

dels and cities, and holding a ritual drum or cymbal. Cybele was portrayed wearing a green dress decorated with flowers. Her sacred animal was the lion, and her sacred trees were the oak and the pine. Her attributes included the *pomegranate, *mirror, key, drum, cymbals, flute, and horn.

Cyclamen. A symbol for voluptuousness, especially in relation to fertility goddesses, in classical Mediterranean and Near Eastern art. In western Christian art, a floral symbol whose red center signified the bleeding heart and sorrow of *Mary at the death of her son.

Cyhiraeth. Celtic goddess of rivers who was transformed into the spirit of brooks and whose wail predicted death. *See also* Banshee.

Cynthia. From the Greek for "she who comes from Mount Cynthus (on Delos)." Ancient Greek goddess of the moon who was assimilated into *Artemis (*Diana).

Cypress. A classical and widespread symbol for death and immortality. An evergreen *tree that was popular in cemeteries, the cypress took on its symbolic meaning because it never recovered from any pruning. Cypress branches were carried at funeral processions as a sign of death.

Cyprian of Carthage, Saint (c. 200–58). Biblical scholar and bishop. Cyprian was converted to Christianity after a career as a lawyer, rhetorician, and teacher. He turned his scholarly attention to the study of the scriptures and patristic texts. Cyprian wrote many significant theological treatises, including several on the definition of virginity and the role of women in the Christian church, and was instrumental in the establishment of Latin Christian literature.

D

ॐ

Daēnā. From the Persian for "that which has been revealed." Ancient Persian goddess who was the daughter of Ahura Mazda and Arinarti.

Daffodil. An attribute of David, the patron of Wales, in western Christian art.

Dagger. Weapon of destruction or justice in religious art. The dagger was an *attribute of *Kalī in Hindu and Buddhist art; of *Hecate, *Melpomene, and *Wrath in classical Greco-Roman and *renaissance western art; and of *Lucretia in classical Greco-Roman, medieval, renaissance, *baroque, and nineteenth-century western art. It also served as an attribute of those Christian martyrs who were stabbed to death, including *Lucy in western Christian art.

Daisy. A floral symbol for simplicity and innocence, particularly that of the Christ Child.

Dakini. From the Sanskrit for "sky walker." Tantric Buddhist priestess as female embodiment of Kālā Ma, the "angel of death." Most often an old woman (read postmenopausal), a dakini functioned as an empathetic attendant and helpmate of the dying or in her fiercest form as the provider of a tortured death agony.

Dākinīs. Lesser female deities of the Tantric Buddhist pantheon, and companions to higher deities whose invocation they signify. Within the Indian Buddhist tradition, the Dākinīs were characterized as dancing female figures each of whom held a *khatvānga*, or magic staff. Too numerous to identify individually, at least five major groupings of the Dākinīs were identifiable within Indian Buddhist art. *Buddha Dākinī* was denoted by her major *attribute, the Wheel of the Law. Represented as a naked female figure, she was an acolyte of Vajravārāhī, the Tibetan form of *Mārīcī. Buddha Dākinī was represented in a posture of *dancing as she crushed two persons, one red and one blue, under her left foot. She held a chopper, a magic staff, and a skull cup, and wore a garland of *skulls. *Vajradākinī* was distinguished by her attribute of the *vajra. Characterized as a dancer, she trampled a corpse with her left foot, and held a skull cup and magic staff in her hands. *Ratnadākinī* was connoted by the *cintāmani; *Padmadākinī* by a *lotus; and *Vishvadākinī* by a double vajra. There were also the *Karmadākinī*, who held swords, and the *Simhavaktrā*, who held a white lion's head. The only Dākinī venerated by the Japanese Buddhist traditions was *Dākinī-ten* who rode a fox and was the center of a Samurai cult. There were eight distinctive groups of the Dākinīs in Tibetan Buddhist art and mythology, and these were comparable to the "eight mothers." All of these lesser female deities were represented as beautiful young women, they were particularized by their symbolic colors and their attributes. *Lāsyā* (Sgeg-pa-ma) was a white female figure who regarded herself in the *mirror she held in her right hand. *Mālā* (Phreng-ba) held a *rosary and was yellow in color. *Gītā* (Glu-ma) was a red female figure who held a musical instrument. *Puspā* (Me-tog-ma) held a *flower and was red in color. *Dhupā* (Bdug-spos-ma) was a yellow female figure who held a bowl of incense. *Dīpā* (Snang-gsal-ma) held a lamp and was red in color. *Gandhā* (Dri-chab-ma) was a green colored female figure who held a flask of perfume.

Damgalnuna. Mesopotamian goddess associated with the Sumerian mother goddess *Ninhursanga. Damgalnuna was the wife of Enki and mother of Marduk. She was venerated with offerings of *fish and her sacred *animal was the *lion.

Damona. From the Gallic for "the big cow." Indigenous Gallic goddess who was wife to Burvu.

Dana. *Great Mother of the gods and goddesses in Danish, and later in Irish,

mythology. In her Irish form of Danu-Ana, or Dana-Anu, she was the leader of the *Morrigan.

Danaë. Only daughter of Acrisius, King of Argos, and Eurydice in Greek mythology. According to an ancient prophesy, her son would bring about the death of Acrisius. In an effort to protect himself, the *king had his daughter imprisoned in an ivory *tower. Nonetheless, the god Zeus came to her in the form of a shower of *gold, and she bore him a son, Perseus. Acrisius locked Danaë and her son in a chest, which was cast into the sea. After floating to the island of Seriphus, the chest was found by Dictys, a fisherman, who sheltered Danaë and Perseus. Dictys' brother, Polydectes, was of Seriphus. He fell in love with Danaë, who spurned his advances. In an attempt to garner her affection, Polydectes sent Perseus to capture the *head of the *Medusa. When he returned, Perseus recognized that his mother was being harassed, so Perseus displayed the Medusa's head at a banquet and the king and his companions were immediately turned into stone. Danaë was the Greco-Roman mythological foretype for several *Old Testament women including *Susanna and *Bathsheba. As a symbol of *chastity and miraculous conception, Danaë was a medieval foretype of the Virgin Annunciate.

Danann. Mother goddess of Celtic-Irish mythology. Danann was the ancestor of the supernatural "Tuatha Dé Danaan," or "the people of the goddess Danann," which was one of the early nations of Ireland.

Dance. Patterned movement of the body, signifying both joyous celebration and sexual seduction. According to the Lucian, the ancient Egyptians expressed their religious secrets through dance, especially in ritual processions and mortuary cult dances. Depictions of the celebratory dances of David and of *Miriam were found in *medieval art, while the representations of the Dance around the *Golden Calf signified licentious behavior and were modeled upon classical Greco-Roman images of the Dionysian reveleries and bacchanals. The Christian ambivalence towards dance as celebratory and seductive was evidenced in the history of the images of *Salome. In the apocryphal *Acts of Saint John*, the twelve apostles circled Jesus Christ. The celebratory circle dances and processions practiced in the early and medieval Christian liturgies were the sources for the medieval and renaissance depictions of the Dance of the Angels and the Dance of the Blessed in paintings of the Last Judgment.

Dance of Death. Medieval belief that the dead rose from their *tombs at midnight and danced before leaving the cemetery to claim "fresh" lives. The Dance of Death became confused (and conflated) with the *Danse Macabre. The most famous images of the Dance of Death were found in the series of woodcuts by *Albrecht Dürer and *Hans Holbein.

Dandelion. Bitter herb that the Israelites were ordered to eat at the Passover meal (Ex 12: 8). A symbol of suffering and grief, the dandelion signified the Passion of Jesus Christ and thereby placed in scenes of the Crucifixion, *Noli Me Tangere*, and *Veil of Veronica. In images of the *Madonna and Child, the dandelion implied his Pas-

sion, and their foreknowledge of the events to come. The medicinal qualities of this flower made it an *attribute of *Mary in *medieval art.

Danse Macabre. Visual allegory of death as a lively *skeleton or corpse who led all levels of humanity (popes, housewives, emperors, lords, knights, and *children) in a processional *dance in which both the living and the dead participated. Originating from fourteenth-century German morality plays, the Danse Macabre became very popular throughout the late Middle Ages, especially in those areas decimated by the Black Plague. The first depiction of the Danse Macabre was the stone relief in Holy Innocents Cemetery, Paris (1424/5). The Danse Macabre became confused (and conflated) with the *Dance of Death.

Dante Alighieri (1265–1321). Author of *The Divine Comedy* (*Divina Commedia*) among other epic poems first written in Italian. Divided into three parts, this narrative poem recounted the poet's journey through Hell and Purgatory, accompanied by Virgil, and into Paradise, accompanied by his ideal woman, *Beatrice. Dante's vivid descriptions of both the settings and the persons he saw on his journey were influential upon depictions of heaven and hell in late *medieval and *renaissance art. His daily conversations with *Giotto in Padua influenced in the latter's representation of the *Last Judgment*, in particular the image of the Devil as *blue in *color and frozen in ice in the deepest pit of Hell. Further his descriptions of his beloved *Beatrice as the ideal of feminine beauty and spirituality played a decisive role in the depiction of women in *renaissance and nineteenth-century art, including that by *Sandro Botticelli, *Raphael Sanzio, Eugene Delacroix, and *Dante Gabriel Rossetti.

Danu. Mother of the demons in Hindu mythology. In her aspect as Vritra, Danu was the enemy of Indra.

Daphne. From the Greek for "laurel tree." Mythological hunter who, like the virgin goddess *Artemis, rejected all suitors. Struck by one of Eros's lead arrows, Daphne fled from love. Apollo fell in love with her, but she sought refuge from his advances by praying to her father, the river god Peneus. Just as Apollo was about to embrace Daphne she was transformed into a *laurel tree. Binding his head with laurel leaves, Apollo promised that the laurel would always be green as a sign of his eternal love for Daphne. The *laurel wreath became the prize awarded to victors at the Pythian Games in Delphi, which were dedicated to Apollo. The laurel wreath became a symbol of both the champion and of victory, and was assimilated into early Christian art through the writings of those church fathers who described the early Christian martyrs as the *Athletes of God. The theme of Daphne and Apollo was popular in classical Greco-Roman, *renaissance, and *baroque art.

Da-shi-zhi. From the Chinese for "the strongest." Chinese female *bodhisattva who destroyed the rule of Karma through the power of love. Da-shi-zhi created the path for all those who wished to escape rebirth. She was portrayed as a beautiful woman dressed in a flowing garment who received souls in the shapes of *flowers in the heavenly *paradise.

Date. Emblems of fertility in Egyptian and Mesopotamian art.

Dawn. Sign of the coming of the new day, or the beginning of the day in religious art. Dawn was personified by a beautiful and youthful goddess such as *Aurora and *Eos. In western Christian art, the dawn represented Christ and eternal salvation. Jesus' act of shedding his *blood to redeem humanity was interpreted as a conquest of darkness and a triumph (return) of the *light. Thus, rosy color was associated with dawn in art and poetry. The Risen Christ wore rose-colored garments in scenes of the Resurrection to imply the dawn of eternal salvation.

Deaconess. From the Greek for "to serve" and "server." Pious women, usually widows, who cared for the sick, the poor, the elderly, and the imprisoned, and assisted in the *baptism of women and the catechizing of women in the early church. With the coming of the institutionalized church in the fourth century and the eventual decline of the practice of adult baptism, the office of deaconess faded and the title was retired in the tenth century. In 1861, the *Anglican Church reinstituted the office of deaconess. In early Christian art, deaconesses were depicted as women assisting in the care of the sick, the administration of the Eucharist of milk and honey, the anointing of female catechumens in preparation for baptism, and the baptismal rites of female catechumens.

Death. Personifications or symbols for the end of physical existence or human

29. *Veiled Dancer*

30. *Dancing Celestial Figure (Apsarās)*

31. Fra Angelico, *Dance of the Angels*, detail from *The Last Judgment*

life on earth. Personified by a *skeleton or mummified corpse, Death was garbed in *black *robes, and held either an *hourglass, which measured the passage of life, or a *scythe, which quickly cut off life. A creature of the night, Death was often fused with Time. In western Christian art, the common symbols for death were the *skull or death's head moth as *memento mori signifying the transitory nature of life; a skull with wings indicating death's swiftness; and an hourglass suggesting the passage of life. Scriptural sources for the imagery of Death were the meditation on the vanities of life (Eccl 3) and the description of the Four Horsemen of the Apocalypse in which Death rode a Pale Horse (Rv 6:8). The symbolism of Death was popular in *medieval art, especially during the era of the Black Plague.

Death Goddesses. Female deities who provided encouragement and succor to those engaged in the act of dying, protected their souls during this final rite of passage, and administered to the appropriate ritual ceremonies of death.

Death of the Virgin Mary. *See* Dormition of the Virgin Mary.

Deborah. From the Hebrew for "bee" (as in a sign of prophecy). Only female judge of Israel and thus in rabbinic tradition a successor of Moses and Joshua as the leader of the people of Israel, and a prophetess (Jgs 4:4). According to both tradition and scripture, Deborah sat under a *palm tree on Mount Ephraim as Jews of all ages and genders came to her for adjudication of differences, arguments, and problems. She was also a keeper of the lamp of tabernacle. "The Song of Deborah" is the oldest written biblical text. She directed the war against the Canaanite general, Sisera, and prophesied his death at the hand of a woman, the Kenite *Jael (Jgs 4:17–22). Representations of Deborah were rare in western Christian art; when they did exist, she was in the context of either the female worthies (classical and biblical women of valor including *Judith and *Lucretia) or *Old Testament foretypes of *Mary.

Deceit. Female embodiment of one of the *Seven Deadly Sins. Also identified as Fraud, Deceit was represented with a beautiful young face, a reptilian body, and lion feet. She held a honeycomb in one hand and her reptilian tail in the other. Alternatively she was signified by an old woman who wore the mask of a beautiful young woman.

Decuma. One of the three *Fates, or Parcae, of Roman mythology.

Deer. Symbol for longevity and wealth, and a divine messenger. Sacred to *Artemis (*Diana), the deer was represented either standing at her side or seated in her lap. The deer was an animal symbol for the Christian *soul thirsting for God (Ps 42:1). In association with a particular saint or martyr, the deer denoted either the moment of conversion, miraculous salvation, or martyrdom. A deer whose *head rested on a man's lap signified Giles, while a stag with a crucifix between its antlers was an *attribute of *Eustace and Hubert.

Deesis. From the Greek for "entreaty." The grouping of the Resurrected Christ enthroned in majesty with *Mary and John the Baptist, on either side. As the two intercessors, Mary and John typified the sacrifices of the flesh and the spirit. This motif was first developed in byzantine *iconography and transferred to northern *medieval art, as exemplified by *Hubert and Jan van Eyck's *Ghent Altarpiece*. By the High Renaissance, the deesis became the central grouping in depictions of the Last Judgment.

Deianira. Legendary wife of Herakles who brought about his death. Following the death of Meleager, Herakles descended into the underworld to capture Cerberus, the watchdog of the entrance. Herakles met the shadow of the valiant Meleager and promised to wed his sister, Deianira, upon Herakles' return to earth. This happy union resulted in five children, and Herakles' untimely demise. During a journey across a river, Deianira accepted a ride offered by Nessus, the centaur. However, he attempted to seduce at midstream when an angry Herakles responded with a poisoned arrow. The dying Nessus cautioned Deianira to retain some of his blood to use as a love charm should Herakles express martial disinterest. Following a fifteen-month absence for a series of battles, Herakles sent his concubine home for protection. A distraught Deianira rubbed the centaur's tainted blood on a robe she sent as a gift to the still absent Herakles. She noticed that a wool fragment from this robe smoldered, Deianira sent a herald to warn her husband. The messenger arrived too late to warn Herakles who put on the robe immediately upon receiving it and was burned to death. The grieving Deianira hanged herself.

Deirdre. Tragic heroine of tale of elopement in Celtic-Irish mythology. Deirdre was identified at birth by the prophecy that she would bring trouble to the men of Ulster.

Delia. Epithet of *Artemis (*Diana) who was reputed to have been born on Delos.

Delilah. From the Hebrew "to enfeeble." A woman from the Valley of Sorek who became Samson's lover (Jgs 13:5). After repeated goadings, she learned that the secret of Samson's strength lay in his unshorn locks. She betrayed him for eleven hundred silver shekels to the Philistines, who captured him in Delilah's bedroom before cutting off his *hair and blinding him. A favorite subject of northern artists including *Lucas Cranach I and *Rembrandt, Delilah became one of the great temptresses of western art. She was categorized along with Tomyris, *Judith, and *Salome as a headhuntress. In western Christian art, the story of Samson and Delilah was popular in manuscript *illuminations that depicted Delilah herself cutting Samson's hair. Delilah's betrayal of Samson for *silver shekels was a foretype of the *Betrayal by Judas for thirty pieces of silver.

Delphi. Preeminent *oracle of classical Greece. Located on the southernmost slope of Mount Parnassus, Delphi was the home of the *omphalos, the symbolic "navel of the earth." The oracle of Delphi symbolized by the prophetess *Pythia answered personal and public queries on political, social, religious, and futuristic concerns. Except for the winter months, Delphi was the site of the most important temple of Apollo.

According to tradition, this oracular locale was originally under the protection of Python, the *serpent son of *Gaia, whom the sun god killed with an *arrow when he took possession of Delphi. Apollo was required to undergo an eight-year period of purification and penance by the performance of menial tasks in order to return as patron of Delphi. Ritual reenactment of this ceremonial cleansing was performed every eighth year at the shrine to Apollo in Delphi. Seated on a golden *tripod, Pythia received her oracular divinations by inhaling the cold vapors from a cleft in the ground of the sanctuary. She entered into an ecstatic trance and uttered responses to the questions given her by a priest who in turn interpreted her sayings for the petitioners. Many of those who came to Delphi in search of the oracle's prophecies brought expensive gifts. When the hero Herakles was denied access to the oracle by Pythia, he became enraged and soon entered into combat with Apollo. Zeus intervened and the prophetess gave Herakles a response to his query and Apollo regained possession of the oracle. Renowned throughout the Hellenistic and Roman Imperial periods, the oracle of Delphi was plundered by Constantine in mid-fourth century and silenced by Theodosius II at the end of the fourth century. As the female personification of the oracle of Delphi, Pythia was represented as a veiled matron, often with her forehead resting on her hand, seated on a tripod and inhaling the vapors from a pot, signifying divine access, at her side.

Demeter. From the Greek for "the mother." The Greek goddess of the *earth, donor of the earth's abundance, and patron of agrarian civilizations whose most venerated role was a mother and goddess of women. Demeter was the daughter of *Rhea and Kronos, and the mother of *Persephone (*Kore) by Zeus. One of the strongest figures in Greek mythology, she was renowned for her aspect as the mourning mother. The abduction of her daughter by Hades, the god of the Underworld, was central to the worship of Demeter, especially through the *Eleusian Mysteries. In sorrow, Demeter abandoned Mount Olympus and walked the earth in the form of an elderly woman. The earth became bare and humanity was subject to famine and death. Despite all the entreaties by Zeus, Demeter demanded the return of Persephone. Hades agreed on the condition that Persephone spend six months of the year, equal to the number of *pomegranate seeds she had eaten in the underworld, with him. This story explained the cyclic patterns of the seasons, and the rhythm of the sowing and harvesting of crops. Her annual feast of the *Thesmophoria was a fertility ritual that excluded men, and during which phallic symbols such as *snakes, pine cones, and piglets, were offered to the goddess and thrown into her cave to enhance the earth's generative powers. Demeter was a classical Greco-Roman foretype for *Mary both as an earth mother and a sorrowing mother. Many of her physical characteristics and attributes were assimilated into the early and byzantine Christian images of Mary. In classical Greco-Roman and *renaissance art, Demeter was depicted as a mature woman, fully clothed with a *veil over her *head, and often accompanied by Persephone. Her *attributes were sheaves of *wheat or corn, or *baskets of *fruits and *flowers, denoting the earth's abundance;*poppies signifying sleep and death, and the *pomegranate, pig, and *snake as allusions to the fecundity of the earth.

Demons. From the Greek for "supernatural being, spirit." Among the ancient Egyptians, demons were recognized as a force to be reckoned with. As messengers of the goddess *Sekhmet as the embodiment of Evil, demons obeyed her commands and spread disease and pestilence all over the earth. In Mesopotamia, demons were associated with Lamaštu and played a role in incantations against her evil presence. Although rare in Mesopotamian art as they were perceived as an image of endangerment, demons were depicted as upright human-bodied hybrid creatures. Among the *Hebrews, demons were believed to have been created upon the eve of Creation and thereby had no bodies as the Sabbath approached. As disembodied spirits, then, they had no shadows or thumbs, and were capable of flight, knowledge of the future, and mortality. Demons surrounded human beings on all sides in order to wear out clothing and to spread disease, unless warded off by amulets or incantations. They haunted trees, ruins, and toilets; and were believed to attack those Hebrews who slept alone, went out at night, or did things in pairs. According to Hebrew tradition, it was dangerous to drink water at certain times as it was contaminated with the menstrual blood of a female demon, that is, Agrat Bat Mahalt, or *Lilith. Demons were identified as the "fallen angels" who accompanied the Devil (Satan, Lucifer) in his rebellion against God, and who served in Hell as tormentors of the damned.

Demons were identified by their dark color, usually *black, and sinister gestures in *medieval and *renaissance art, especially in depictions of the Last Judgment.

Deposition (Mt 28:58–60; Mk 15:46; Lk 23:53; Jn 19:38–40). Scriptural event signifying the removal of the body of Jesus from the cross. Following Jewish law, bodies could not hang on the gallows or the cross after sunset, and the burial of the body was an act of Jewish piety. According to all four Gospels, Joseph of Arimathea received permission from Pontius Pilate to remove the body from the cross. In the earliest depictions of the Deposition, also identified as the Descent from the Cross, Joseph acted alone to remove the body from the cross. In the ninth century, the figure of Nicodemus entered this scene, either assisting Joseph with the body of Jesus or removing the *nails from the body. In tenth-century byzantine icons of this theme, *Mary and John the Evangelist watched as Joseph and Nicodemus removed the body. By the thirteenth century, the *iconography of the Deposition expanded to include a larger group of mourners, including *Mary Magdalene, and more dramatic action, no doubt in tandem with the development of liturgical drama and devotional practices. From the late medieval into the baroque periods, the characters and symbolic objects become more exaggerated. The expressions of grief, most especially Mary Magdalene's, became heightened as this scene became the moment in which the followers recognized what they believed to be the death of Jesus. As Joseph of Arimathea was a man of wealth and social status, he became the scriptural basis for the late medieval and renaissance inclusion of the portraits of wealthy *donors into this scene. The *Three Marys were included in the background of this scene to indicate the anointing of the body prior to the Entombment. The Lamentation, a variant of this theme, denoted the mourning and grief of the gathered followers over the crucified body that had been removed from the cross. A popular variant, the Pietà, was developed in medieval German art and depicted only *Mary mourning her dead son. In the course of Christian art, the Deposition and its variants became conflated with the Entombment.

Descent from the Cross. *See* Deposition.

Desert. Ambiguous symbol for desolation or contemplation. In the *Old Testament, the desert typified separation from God and the place of his special intense presence. In the *New Testament, it was the place of retreat and of trial for both Jesus and John the Baptist. Hermit saints and the famed desert fathers of earliest Christianity withdrew to the desert in order to meditate, be close to God, and be free of temptations.

Desert Mothers. Early Christian female solitaries who lived in the deserts and outlands of ancient Egypt, Palestine, and Syria between the third and the sixth century. The Desert Mothers were characterized as emaciated, haggard, and shriveled images of woman ranging in age from sixteen to eighty. Some believers claimed that these women were graced with exceptionally long and full hair, oftentimes gray with age, as a natural form of protection of their bodies and thereby of their chastity. Sarah

(Sara), Syncletia, and Theodora were among the most well-known of the Desert Mothers.

Despoina. From the Greek for "miss, mistress." Arcadian fertility goddess and daughter of *Demeter in Greek mythology. Despoina was also an epithet used for any goddess or female divinity.

Devana. From the Slavonic for "Diana." Central Slavonic goddess of the hunt. Like her counterparts *Artemis and *Diana, Devana was represented in the midst of the hunt, most often riding to the hounds through heavily forested areas.

Devi. General designation of female deities, incarnations of natural phenomena, and the spouse of Shiva in Hindu mythology. As the *Mahadevi, or *Great Goddess, Devi was descended from the pre-Hindu cults and indigenous traditions of India. Her own story included her transformation into an independent goddess who was known under many names including *Durgā, *Kali, *Lakshmi, *Mahadevi, *Pārvātī, and *Sati.

Devil. From the Sanskrit *devi* for "god, deity" as transformed by *Zoroastrianism into "evil being." Symbol for evil personified. The *Devil was also identified as Satan (from the Hebrew for "adversary" and possibly an ancient desert deity) and Lucifer ("the morning star"). The devils were the *angels who fell with Lucifer in his unsuccessful rebellion against God. In Christian art, these devils were usually depicted as evil angels, that is, formed like angels but covered from *head to toe in *black. As the tormentors of *souls in *Hell and the tempters of *saints, these devils came to be imaged as small *animals, especially as *cats or *monkeys, or in horrific shapes, and were seen whispering in the ears of those being tempted. In certain depictions of the temptations of saints, especially those of Anthony the Abbot, the devil adopted the guise of a beautiful woman. Devils were popular elements in depictions of the Last Judgment and the temptations of saints in *medieval and *renaissance art.

Devil's Gateway. Phrase associated with *Martin Luther and used to signify both the vagina, perhaps as a *vagina dentata, and the role of female sexuality as the downfall of moral Christian men.

Devotio Moderna. Latin for "Modern Devotion." Popular spiritual movement in medieval Christianity, especially in the north of Europe, which deepened the religious life of the laity and the clergy. The Devotio Moderna was contemporary to another lay spiritual movement, the Brotherhood of the Common Life; together these movements supported popular literacy, even among women, and the role of women in the spiritual life. Significant and identifiable changes in the iconography of women in the Christian art produced by northern European artists such as *Rogier van der Weyden were effected by the Devotio Moderna.

Dew. Symbol of purity and the new beginning of each new day. *Eos (*Aurora) was characterized as sprinkling the dew from a *vase as she announced the rising of the dawn in classical Greco-Roman and *renaissance art. The dew on Gideon's Fleece was an *Old Testament foretype of the *Virginal Conception and

thereby, of the *Annunciation of Mary. Drops of moisture on plant leaves or flower petals denoted the vitality of human life in *still-life paintings, especially seventeenth-century Dutch flower paintings.

Diana. From the Latin for "the shining (female) one." Virginal Roman goddess of the *moon, the forest, and the hunt, and the protector of chastity, women, and childbirth. Diana was identified with *Artemis, *Hecate, *Luna, and *Semele. The twin sister of the sun god, Apollo, she was the female personification of the cycles of feminine fertility as symbolized by the phases of the moon. *Diana the Huntress*: Most popular motif of this goddess in all periods of western art styles. Concentrating on the depiction of Diana as the exemplary huntress, this motif was characterized as the presentation of a beautiful but physically powerful young woman who wore a knee-length tunic bound at the waist by a *girdle, and whose hair was tied back or up with a decorative crescent moon pin. With one hand she held her *bow as she drew an *arrow from the quiver that was either on her back or the ground. Her companions were either her favored hunting hounds or stags, or occasionally *nymphs or satyrs. If Diana the Huntress was not in the posture described, then she stood astride as she held her bow with one hand and her hunted booty of birds or small animals with the other. *Diana Bathing* (*Diana at the Bath*): Naked except for the crescent moon pin in her hair, Diana was depicted as she sat or stood near a pool of water located in either a shady grotto or woodland grove. Her clothes were held by her companion nymphs, one of whom may be in the posture of washing or wiping the goddess's feet. *Diana and Actaeon* (*Metamorphosis* 3:138–253): According to this legend, while on a hunt the youthful prince, Actaeon, espied the beautiful goddess as she bathed. As his punishment for this vision of divine nudity, he was transformed into a stag that was torn to pieces by the goddess's hounds. In classical Greco-Roman, *renaissance, and *baroque art, this motif had two distinct presentations: Actaeon's discovery of the bathing goddess or his transformation and death. *Diana and Her Nymphs Surprised by the Satyrs*: This legendary theme was transformed into a symbolic motif of the triumph of *Chastity over *Lust in classical Greco-Roman, *medieval, and *renaissance art. As the goddess's dogs responded in postures of attack and defense, the Satyrs approached the place in the woodlands where a naked Diana and her nymphs bathed in supposed privacy and serenity. Oftentimes, a naked goddess was depicted with her spear raised in defense of herself and her nymphs. *Diana and Endymion*: Trapped in an eternal sleep, the handsome Endymion was visited nightly by the besotted goddess in the form of moonlight. As she bathed him with the embrace of the moon's light, Diana retained her chastity despite her passion for this youth. A rare topic in classical Greco-Roman art, the theme of Diana and Endymion garnered popularity in *renaissance and *baroque art when it was characterized by the sleeping form of the handsome but naked male youth bathed in the glow of moonlight. *See also* Callisto. Diana's most celebrated shrine was in Ephesus, which was visited by those who saw her as the Great Mother. Her annual feast was celebrated on August 13th. She was a foretype of *Mary, whose imagery assimilated many of Diana's attributes including the *crescent moon. The *Council of Ephesus (431) decreed Mary as *Theotokos ("God-bearer") and defined her role in the Christian mysteries. The site of this council was carefully selected to signify that Mary fulfilled and superseded the place of the virgin goddess of the moon and the hunt. In classical Greco-Roman, early Christian, and *renaissance art, Diana was represented as a beautiful young woman clad in a short tunic with a crescent moon in her hair who carried a *bow and arrow over her shoulder and was accompanied by either her faithful hounds or stags, a bear, or her attendant nymphs.

Diana of Ephesus. Ancient Asiatic female personification of the fertility of nature who was incorporated into the classical Greek *Artemis and the classical Roman *Diana. Her temple at Ephesus was one of the Seven Wonders of the Ancient World, and was the site of the *Council of Ephesus (431), which declared *Mary to be *Theotokos. In classical Near Eastern, Greco-Roman, and *renaissance art, Diana of Ephesus was depicted as a beautiful woman with multiple breasts placed between her neck and her waist, while her lower body was covered by a tight sheath covered with symbolic figures. She wore a flat-topped high crown and held *snakes in both hands.

Dido (*Aeneid* 4). From the Phoenician for *Astarte (*Artemis). Literary name of the legendary Roman princess Elissa, daughter of the king of Tyre. Her wealthy husband, Sychaeus, was killed by Pygmalion, her brother. She escaped

32. *Demeter of Cnidus*

33. *Diana the Huntress*

34. *Diana of Ephesus*
35. *Durgā as the Slayer of the Buffalo Demon*

to north Africa where she was permitted to purchase as much land as she could encompass within the hide of a *bull. Elissa cut the skins into narrow strips which set off an extraordinary amount of territory on which she established the city of Carthage. According to Virgil, this heroic queen's name was Dido and she symbolized the ideal pious widow. Following a storm at sea, the Trojan hero, Aeneas, and his ship were forced upon the shores of Carthage where Dido's soldiers rescued them. Empowered by *Venus, the widowed queen fell passionately in love with the stranded hero, and they became lovers. However after a one-year sojourn, Aeneas was ordered to depart Carthage in order to complete his journey to establish Rome. A desperate and grieving Dido cursed the Trojans, prayed for eternal enmity between Carthage and Troy (later Rome), and as she prepared a ritual funeral pyre for all of Aeneid's things, including their marriage bed, she fell upon his *sword and died. Her shadow was consigned to the region of unhappy love and when Aeneas visited the underworld he was shunned by Dido's shadow.

Dimu. From the Chinese for "earth mother." Female partner in the primordial couple who brought forth humanity and all other created beings as a result of their sexual union in Chinese mythology.

Dinah. Seventh child and only daughter of *Leah and Jacob. Just prior to this birth, Leah prayed for a daughter as Jacob was destined to have twelve sons in order to establish the Twelve Tribes of Israel. As he had sired five sons with his concubines, and six with Leah, she asked for a daughter that Jacob would also sire a son with her sister, *Rachel.

Discordia. Goddess of conflict in Greek mythology. Discordia was the daughter of *Hera and Zeus, and the twin sister of Ares, the god of war.

Dish. A symbol or *attribute for certain biblical events or persons. A paten, or shallow dish, signified the Last Supper, and often contained a *fish or *bread. A dish with bread and fish typified the miracle of the Multiplication of Loaves and Fishes. A dish with a man's *head was an attribute of John the Baptist. A dish with an *eye or eyes symbolized *Lucy, while a dish with *roses represented *Dorothea. A dish with female *breasts denoted *Agatha, and a dish with a bag of money signified Laurence.

Disir. Collective appellation for female deities or supernatural female beings associated with fertility and destiny, especially those functioning as midwives, in Germanic and Norse mythology. *See* Norns, Valkyries.

Distaff (Prov 31:19). Emblem of women's activity. The distaff or spindle signifying weaving, and by extension gestation of an idea or new life, was an *attribute of *Athena, *Clotho, and *Omphale in classical Greco-Roman and *renaissance art, and *Eve, *Mary, and *Geneviève in Christian art.

Divine Comedy. Renowned narrative poem written by *Dante Alighieri. *The Divine Comedy* was divided into three parts, or volumes, in which the poet described his journey through Hell (Inferno), Purgatory (Purgatorio), and

Paradise (Paradiso). Symbolizing the spiritual journey of every human being, Dante began his spiritual journey on the dawn of Good Friday and concluded it on Easter morning. He was accompanied by spiritual guides, the classical poet, Virgil, in Hell and Purgatory, and his beloved *Beatrice in Paradise. His depiction of Beatrice symbolized both ideal love and the spirituality of the feminine. Representations of scenes from *The Divine Comedy* were popular in *medieval, *renaissance, and nineteenth-century art, while Dante's vivid descriptions of the levels of Hell inspired transformations in the iconography of the Last Judgment beginning with that of his friend, *Giotto. Additionally, the poet's descriptive and thematic characterizations of Beatrice influenced future artists' portrayals of both the ideal feminine figure and of their beloveds. The nineteenth-century revival of interest in *The Divine Comedy* resulted in the retrieval of Beatrice as the idealization of feminine grace and love.

Djata. Ngadju-Dayak goddess. Originally the water snake identified as Tambon, Djata resided in the underworld and ruled over the *crocodiles.

Doctors of the Church. These Christian theologians were distinguished for their *wisdom, sanctity, and theological learning. Originally this term signified the Four Western Church Fathers: Gregory the Great, Ambrose, *Augustine, and *Jerome; and the Four Eastern Church Fathers: Basil the Great, Athanasius, Gregory Nazianzus, and John Chrysostom. As an honorific title, Doctor of the Church was expanded to a group of about thirty in-

cluding *Thomas Aquinas and John of the Cross, but only two women—*Catherine of Siena and *Teresa of Avila. In western Christian art, the title normally signified the Four Western Church Fathers who were each depicted with a *book inscribed with the title(s) of their works. Ambrose and Augustine were identified by bishop's *robes and *miters; Gregory by the papal robe and *tiara; and Jerome by the cardinal's robe and *hat.

Dog. Worldwide animal symbol for faithfulness, companionship, and healing. Ancient Mesopotamia recognized the dog as a divine symbol of the goddess of healing, *Gula. Her dogs sat on either side of the enthroned goddess and were further identified by the crooks they held in their mouths. Eventually, the dog was recognized as an emblem of protection from wolves or jackals. The Assyrian goddess, Gula, was represented as a dog suckling her puppies; however if the goddess was represented anthropomorphically then she was accompanied by a dog. In classical Greco-Roman art and mythology, the dog was a symbol of faithfulness, companionship, and a divine messenger. However, a black dog was an *attribute of *Hecate. The dog was an ambiguous *animal symbol in Christian art denoting either fidelity or evil. When the negative aspects of the dog's nature was emphasized, the dog was an abusive and reprehensible figure (Rv 22:15; Phil 3:2). It was a sign of evil as "the hound of Hell" or the *Devil; *black dogs were the companions of *witches; a lascivious female was referred to as a "bitch" (female dogs were associated with the goddesses *Cybele and *Artemis); the howling of the dog was an omen of death; and anal copulation was typified as "dog style" and interpreted as bestial. In *medieval art, dark dogs symbolized disbelief and/or the heathens. However a dog could also be a symbol of fidelity, devotion, courage, and watchfulness (Jb 30:1; Is 56:10). The dog was the first animal to be domesticated, and therefore a sign of human dominion over animals. When a dog was at the *feet of or stood between a man and woman, it signified the fidelity of marriage. In medieval times, a dog placed at the feet or on the lap of a recumbent female figure on a *tomb sculpture indicated faithfulness unto death. The dog was sometimes used as a symbol for the priest who protected and guided his human flock to eternal salvation. Tobias's dog was his faithful companion on his travels (Tb 6:2). Generally, the dog played an important and positive role in Christian hagiography and *iconography. Roch was nurtured by the *bread brought to him by his dog. Vitus was accompanied by his faithful dog on his *pilgrimages. A dog carrying a torch signified Dominic's attempts to spread the gospel. The mothers of Bernard of Clairvaux and Dominic dreamt of dogs before the births of their sons, and these dreams were interpreted as prophetic of the sons becoming propagators of Christianity. Black and white dogs denoted the Dominican Order in a visual pun on the colors of the Dominican habit, and as a verbal pun, the faithfulness and devotion of the dog is part of the pun that the "Domini canes" were the dogs of the Lord.

Dolphin. Sacred to *Aphrodite (*Venus) as goddess of the deep sea in classical Greco-Roman art. The dolphin denoted maritime power and was asso-

ciated with the *nereids, especially with *Galatea and *Thetis. The dolphin was a symbol for *resurrection and salvation in Christian art. Represented more often than any other form of *fish, the dolphin was an elegant and friendly *animal. When depicted by itself, the dolphin as the swiftest of all animals transported the *souls of the dead to the next life. A dolphin with an *anchor signified the Christian traveling to salvation or the *church being guided to salvation by Jesus Christ. A dolphin with a trident represented the Crucifixion. Occasionally, the dolphin substituted for the sea monster in early Christian depictions of the story of Jonah, whereby the dolphin became a symbol of resurrection and of Christ. In *renaissance art, the dolphin was an attribute of *Fortune.

Dominations. *See* Angels.

Dominic, Saint (1170–1221). A Spanish mendicant and theologian renowned for his intellectual learning and his successful campaigns against the Albigensian heresy. Originally a Benedictine monk, he established the Dominican Order of Preachers (1215), which was dedicated to the harmonizing of intellectual life with popular devotion. He was reputed to have initiated the use of the *rosary, a special sequence of prayers dedicated to *Mary, as an aide to devotion for the illiterate. Throughout his monastic life, Dominic placed an important emphasis on the role played by women in the church, even to the installation of an order of nuns at San Sisto in Rome. In western Christian art, Dominic was depicted in the black-and-white robes of the Dominican Order. A popular motif was the scene in which he knelt before a vision of Mary either to receive the rosary or the infant Christ from her. A *star over his chest referred to the legend that at the moment of his *baptism, a star shone over his *head. He was occasionally accompanied by a *dog with a *torch in its mouth, denoting his pregnant mother's dream that she had given birth to a dog carrying a flaming torch that would light the world and which was interpreted as a prophecy of his own and his order's missionary activities. His *attributes included the *lily and *rosary.

Dominicans. The Order of Preachers established by *Dominic between 1215 and 1221 to preach and teach the faith, and to combat the heresy of Catharism. A highly influential group of teachers and preachers in the intellectual life of late medieval Europe, the Dominicans were mendicants dedicated to the study and preaching of the *Gospel and to poverty. They were entrusted with the tribunal of the Inquisition. They were also known as the Black Friars because their *habits that consisted of a long *white garment with a black-hooded *cloak (signifying the death of *Mary).

Dominions. *See* Angels.

Donatello (c. 1386–1466). The greatest Florentine sculptor and the most influential individual artist of the Early Renaissance. His development of heroic types, religious emotion, and measurable space influenced painters in late fifteenth-century Florence and Padua as well as *Andrea Mantegna and *Giovanni Bellini. Influenced by classical Hellenistic and early Christian art, figures such as Donatello's *Judith* exemplified a new humanity—slightly larger-

than-life, with those qualities of valor and will so highly admired in the Early Renaissance. In his later works, such as the *Repentant Magdalene*, he emphasized the dramatic impact of extreme ugliness through the distorted expression of religious emotions in the gestures and poses of the human *body.

Donkey. *See* Ass.

Donors. Commissioners of a votive work of art, usually an *altarpiece for a *church. The donor was identified as the figure kneeling in prayer with his or her attention focused upon the central theme of the altarpiece, notably the *Madonna and Child or the Crucifixion. If the donor was a man, he was accompanied by his wife and/or family. The donor was immediately identifiable as being smaller in scale than the other figures in the painting or sculpture. This practice of including the donor's portrait within the work of art began in northern European painting. By the fifteenth century, the inclusion of donor portraits had three advantages: the donor earned indulgences or spiritual merit for the gift of the work of art to the Church, the incorporation of the donor's portrait into the same frame as that of the Madonna and Child rendered social prestige, and artistic immortality was offered to the donor by the portrait.

Door. A symbol of entry. In works of art dedicated to the theme of the *Annunciation, the door signified a feminine symbol of entry. A door placed by the figure of Jesus Christ referred to the pronouncement that he was the entry to eternal salvation (Jn 10:7–9). The *three doors on the facade of medieval *cathedrals were interpreted as signs of *faith, *hope, and *charity.

Dormition of the Virgin Mary. From the Greek for "sleep" (apocryphal *Gospel of the Assumption of the Virgin* and *The Golden Legend* 119). Legendary event signifying the "falling asleep" of *Mary at the end of her earthly life. Following the Ascension, Mary reportedly went to live in Ephesus with John the Evangelist and *Mary Magdalene. After some time, she prayed to be released from this life. Michael the Archangel appeared and presented her with a palm branch as a sign that her request was granted by God. According to pious legend, she "fell asleep" in Jerusalem with all the apostles present, except for Thomas. In Christian art, the *Dormition and the *Assumption were divided into a series of events starting with the *Annunciation of the Death of Mary and ending with her being assumed into *heaven with the assistance of *angels. In the *Eastern Orthodox Church and byzantine *iconography, there was a pious belief that after Mary fell asleep, Christ carried her *soul to heaven. A vivid and lengthy description of the Dormition of the Virgin Mary in *The Golden Legend* influenced the many medieval paintings on this theme. The Annunciation of the Death of Mary was rarely represented in western Christian art, while scenes of her Dormition were popular in the byzantine, medieval, and renaissance periods. In late *renaissance and *baroque art, this theme was misidentified as the Death of the Virgin.

Dorothea of Cappadocia, Saint (d. 303). Virgin *martyr from Caesarea who died during the Diocletian persecutions. Esteemed for her beauty, she was accosted by two apostate women who attempted to defile her. Instead, Dorothea's piety brought them back to the Christian faith. She refused to worship idols and to marry a pagan. Condemned to death, she was taunted by the Roman lawyer, Theophilus, to send him *flowers from *paradise, where *fruits and flowers were believed to be eternally in bloom. Immediately upon Dorothea's decapitation in midwinter, an *angel presented Theophilus with a *basket of *apples and *roses. Stunned, he converted to Christianity and was martyred. Dorothea was the patron of florists, brides, brewers, and midwives. In western Christian art, she was depicted as a beautiful and elegantly garbed young woman with roses in her *hand or on her *head, or with a basket of apples and roses; sometimes confronted with a vision of the Madonna and Child in a garden setting.

Dove. An avian symbol for the *soul in religious art, and particularly for the Holy Spirit in Christian art. By nature, the dove was characterized by gentle affection and simplicity. The dove was an *attribute of the mother goddess, especially those in the Near East such as *Astarte and *Ishtar. In classical Greco-Roman art, the dove signified purity and peace, and was an *attribute of *Aphrodite and *Fides. The Hebrew tradition recognized the dove as a symbol of peace and innocence. According to the Talmud, the dove denoted Israel and the Divine Presence of the *Shekinah. Following prevalent customs, Judaism advocated that the dove was the only appropriate *bird offering for Temple rituals. In Christian art, it became the symbol for the Holy Spirit (Jn 1:32). In the *Old Testament, the dove typified both peace and ritual purity. The dove that Noah sent forth from the ark in search of dry land returned with an *olive branch (Gn 8:11). Under the law of Moses, the offering for the purification of a newborn child was the sacrifice of a dove. Seven doves indicated the seven gifts of God's grace (Hos 11:11). In the New Testament, Joseph (of Nazareth) carried two white doves in a *basket as an offering when the infant Jesus was brought to the temple to be purified along with his mother (Lk 2:24). The dove perched upon Joseph's blossoming staff symbolized Mary's purity. The dove denoted the Holy Spirit in scenes of the *Annunciation to Mary and the Pentecost. Twelve doves implied either the Twelve Fruits of the Holy Spirit (Gal 5:22–23) or the twelve apostles. The imagery of the dove departing the *body of Mary or the lips of any of the *saints suggested the departure of the soul at death. Doves shown pecking at *bread or drinking from a *fountain denoted the Christian soul being nourished by the Eucharist. As an *attribute of any of the Apostles or Christian saints, the dove typified divine inspiration. *Catherine of Siena had a dove perched on her *head when she prayed as a *child; and according to a medieval legend, the Holy Spirit in the form of a dove dictated theological treatises to Gregory. The dove was an attribute of *Eulalia, *Thomas Aquinas, and *Scholastica.

Dragon. From the Greek for "serpent." Among the eastern traditions, the dragon was a beneficent creature connoting power and enlightenment. Mesopotamian mythology characterized the dragon as a terrifying monster simultaneously combining beneficent and ma-

levolent natures. A prevalent symbol for the mother goddess, the dragon was an *attribute of *Cybele and *Demeter (*Ceres). The dragon was a symbol of the Devil or evil in Christian art. The dragon typified primal powers that were hostile to God and thereby had to be overcome. This legendary *animal was imaged as a ferocious winged beast with *lion's claws, *eagle's *wings, a *serpent's tail, scaly skin, and fiery breath. The dragon's tail was its greatest weapon; it killed either by engulfing a person or by swift and violent blows. This enemy of God symbolized heresy in *medieval art and theology (Rv 12:7–9). The dragon's mouth was the model for the mouth of Hell devouring the souls of the damned as the dragon devoured beautiful princesses or chivalrous knights. As a sign of their victories over the Devil (evil), the Resurrected Christ, *Mary (Rv 12:1–6), and the Archangel Michael (Rv 12:7–9) were depicted with a dragon crushed by their *feet. George of Cappadocia, *Martha of Bethany, and *Margaret of Antioch were all shown with the dragons they fought and vanquished; these images were interpreted as fulfillments of *Old Testament prophecy (Ps 91:3).

Dress. *See* Clothing.

Druden. From the old Norse for "to tread, push." Female demons in southern German and Austrian mythology. The Druden harried one's sleep, interrupted dreams, and cast evil spells over human beings. According to tradition, the pentagram was a protective charm against the evil actions of the Druden.

Druids. From the Celtic for "very wise" or the Greek for "oak:" Celtic priests and *priestesses with "oak" knowledge, that is, great wisdom. The Druids were an extraordinary group of religious officials who garnered positions of social power; led sacrificial, prophetic, and religious rites; and served as advisers, judges, healers, teachers, and ambassadors. Julius Caesar reported that all Druids undergo a rigorous twenty-year training period that resulted in their individual knowledge of secular and canon law, philosophy, science, and religion. Under the covenant of international and tribal law, the council of the Druids could offset decrees of war, and pronounce secular and religious verdicts with both moral and legal authority. The roles and offices of the Druids were analyzed in the Irish texts, *Dinnsenchas*, which were written by Christian monks. The Druids were interpreted as foretypes of Christian saints. They were depicted in religious art as garbed in dark hooded garments that both covered their bodies and hid their sex. Their *attribute was the oak tree.

Drum. Musical instrument featured in ceremonial rites and orgiastic festivals. The drum was an *attribute of *Cybele and the *Maenads.

Dryads. From the Greek for "oak tree." Female nature spirits resident in *trees. The fate of the Dryad was identical to that of her tree. In classical Greco-Roman and *renaissance art, the Dryad was signified by an inscribed female face or torso on the trunk of a tree.

Duccio di Buoninsegna (c. 1255/60–1315/18). The first major Sienese painter and an iconographic innovator, especially in terms of his images of *Mary. His art was categorized as Italo-Byzantine in style; that is, incorporating both the austerity and severity of byzantine icons with a growing interest in human emotions, a product of Dominican and Franciscan spirituality. An artistic innovator of the highest order, Duccio was also an effective storyteller and a master of traditional *iconography. His masterpiece was the *Maestà*, created for the Cathedral of Siena in 1311. Dedicated to Mary, the *Maestà* was an enormous *triptych whose central front panel featured the *Madonna and Child enthroned in majesty and surrounded by all orders of *angels and *saints. The other panels were filled with depictions of the life of Mary. The center back panel was filled with twenty-six scenes of the Passion, while the side panels depicted the events in the life of Jesus Christ. In his *Maestà*, Duccio fused the contemplative and devotional aspects of the icon with the narrative cycles of the humanity of Mary and Christ.

Duck. Avian symbol of partnership and faithfulness in marriage. Depictions of ducks were popular in Oriental art.

Duillae. Ancient Hispanic goddesses and protectors of vegetation.

Dumuziabzu. From the Sumerian for "true child of Abzu [Apsu]." A Mesopotamian goddess, Dumuziabzu was the tutelary goddess of Kinirsa.

Dürer, Albrecht (1471–1528). One of the leading German artists of the sixteenth century. Dürer brought renaissance art forms and ideas to the northern parts of Europe through his own works of art and his books, including his treatises on measurement (1525) and on proportion and artistic theory (1528). Dürer sought to combine the renaissance concept of individualism with the Gothic tradition through his emphasis on vivid imagery, technical refinement, draftsmanship, and complex *iconography. From 1490 to 1494, Dürer went to Strasbourg, Basle, Colmar, and Venice. He made a second trip to Italy in 1505 to study the works of *Leonardo and *Mantegna; during his two-year stay he also came to know *Giovanni Bellini. He was appointed Court Painter to the Emperor Maximilian I in 1512 and to the Emperor Charles V in 1520. Dürer admired the works of *Martin Luther and Erasmus, and was a friend of Melanchthon. His greatest legacy to the history of Christian art were his woodcuts, for books including the *Apocalypse* (1498), *Great Passion* (1498–1510), *Little Passion* (1509–11), and *Life of the Virgin* (1501–11); and his individual prints, engravings, and plates that later accompanied the writings of Reformed theologians, including Luther and Melanchthon.

Durgā. From the Sanskrit for "she who is difficult of access." Great Mother of Hindu mythology, and a manifestation of *Pārvāti as *Kālī. Durgā earned her name from that of the giant whose severed head she carried in her left hand. She was the fierce form of the wife of Shiva. According to tradition, Durgā like her Greek counterpart *Athena was born fully formed. When identified with the epithet, annapurna, Durgā was identified as the giver of food and images with a rice bowl and a spoon. However in her fearsome form, or *Candī, from the Sanskrit for "the cruel one," she became Kālī, from the Sanskrit for "she who is black." Durgā became associated with the Buddhist Tārā, from the Sanskrit for "she who sets free," and was merged in Hindu art and cultic practice with *Pārvāti. Durgā's annual feast was the Durgapujā and was celebrated in the autumn months.

E

❧

Eagle. A symbol of solar and sky deities, and of the soaring spirit, justice, generosity, and the virtues of courage, faith, and contemplation. This avian symbol was characterized by the qualities of strength, endurance, and heavenward flight. In classical Greek art, the eagle signified Zeus and served as his messenger, especially in making the divine will known to humanity. The eagle, according to Aristotle, could look directly into the *sun and trained its young to do the same; those offspring incapable of staring into the sun were discarded. The eagle thus symbolized Jesus Christ, whose Ascension was a soaring upwards and who could look directly at God without blinking. The *Physiologus* characterized the eagle like the *phoenix that in old age, after finding a *fountain, would fly very close to the sun to burn off its aging *wings and dimming eyes, and then plunged into the fountain three times. These birds thereby typified the new life available through the ritual cleansing of *baptism and of the rebirth of the Resurrection (Ps 103:5). The eagle was an *attribute of John the Evangelist because his gospel's philosophical nature allowed it to soar about

the other three gospels. Lecterns were shaped like winged eagles as a sign of the inspiration of the gospels. As a motif on the baptismal font, the eagle represented new life (Is 40:31). As a bird of prey, however, the eagle typified the ambiguity of generosity (leaving part of its prey for others) and evil (ravishing life). It also denoted Sight and Pride in *renaissance art.

Ear. Symbol for hearing, communication, and obedience. In Christian art, the ear was a symbol of the *Annunciation, according to the medieval belief that *Mary conceived the Word of God through her ear.

Earth. The solid element offering humanity sustenance through its production of *flowers, vegetation, and *trees, and by providing sites for habitation. The earth symbolized the *church as a provider of spiritual nourishment and shelter. In Christian art, the earth was represented by the *globe or a human being, such as Atlas, supporting a heavy weight.

East. One of the four cardinal points, the east signified the sunrise; the Christian tradition, it was a sign of Jesus Christ as the "sun of righteousness" in western Christian art. The east was the source of light and truth. The *altars of Christian churches were "oriented" towards the rising sun in anticipation of the Second Coming of Jesus Christ.

Eastern Orthodoxy. From the Greek for "right believing." Christian federation of the "one holy catholic and apostolic church" of the Seven Ecumenical Councils—Nicaea (325), Constantinople (381), Ephesus (431), Chalcedon (451), Constantinople (553), Constantinople (680–681), and Nicaea (787)—and patristic spirituality. This fellowship of autocephalous churches gathered under the patriarchates of Alexandria, Antioch, Jerusalem, and Moscow advocated the authority of the Ecumenical Patriarch of Constantinople as the "first among equals." The Seven Ecumenical Councils attested to the highest authority of the church on earth; condemned heresies, defined Christology, the Trinity, and Mary as *Theotokos*; and formulated the creeds. Between the eighth and ninth centuries, the Iconoclastic Controversy occurred throughout the eastern churches and ultimately resulted in the conciliar decrees that defined the appropriate and necessary role of the *icon within Christian faith and religious practice. The Great Schism of 1054 was premised as much on economic, political, and cultural issues as upon the overt theological differences of papal supremacy, the filioque clause, ecclesial celibacy, fasting regulations, and the liturgical use of leavened bread that divided the eastern and western Christian churches. Eastern Orthodoxy defined the three sources of Christianity as the *Bible, the *Ecumenical Councils, and the creeds; and expressed Christian faith through words, actions, gestures, and art. The central focus of Eastern Orthodox religious life was the liturgy and the Seven Sacraments. The hierarchy of the eastern church, that is, the episcopacy and the priesthood, was grounded in Apostolic Succession.

Ecce Ancilla Domini (Lk 1:38). Latin for "Behold the Handmaid of the Lord." The proclamation of *Mary in accepting the role God ordained for her. In depictions of the *Annunciation in Christian art, especially in *medieval art, this phrase was found on a *scroll or *book that was either held by Mary or placed on a table or *prie-dieu near her.

Ecce virgo concipiet (Is 7:14). Latin for "Behold, a virgin shall conceive." The prophecy of Isaiah, taken as a foretype for the *Annunciation. In depictions of the Annunciation and the Nativity in Christian art, especially in northern *medieval art, this phrase was written on a *scroll or *banner held by Isaiah.

Ecclesia. From the Greek for "assembly" or "gathering." The name given to the gatherings of Christians, eventually identified as the *church. In Christian art, Ecclesia was depicted as a young woman with a *crown of *flames, and was wide-eyed in contrast to the blindfolded *Synagoga. In *medieval art, Ecclesia's size was dependent upon the narrative context in which she was represented; in scenes of the *Nativity she would be diminutive as the church was just being born.

Echo. Legendary mountain *nymph enamored of Narcissus. A daughter of

*Gaea, Echo encountered the wrath of *Hera when her idle chattering prevented the goddess's discovery of her consort's infidelity with several nymphs. The irate goddess silenced the nymph and only permitted her the sound of the most recent words spoken to her. Echo was infatuated with the handsome youth, Narcissus, who rejected the nymph and in her grief she faded away into the sound of her own voice. One variation of her story indicated that Echo was a companion of Hera and was pursued romantically by Pan. When she rejected his advances, he commanded a group of mad shepherds to tear Echo into pieces leaving only her voice behind. In classical Greco-Roman and *renaissance art, Echo was characterized as a beautiful young nymph who gazed wistfully at Narcissus as he admired his own reflection in a pond.

Eden (Gn 2). The site of the original *paradise created by God. Located somewhere in the "east," it was filled with an abundance of every kind of fruit, flower, and tree. As the first home of human beings, from which Adam and *Eve were expelled, the *Garden of Eden became the image for that perfect, peaceful, and idyllic setting to which all human beings seek to return. In western Christian art, it was represented as a lush and lovely garden filled with blooming flowers, fruit-laden trees, sparkling *waters, and all kinds of *animals. The Garden of Eden was typified by the *Enclosed Garden in representations of the *Madonna and Child, and was also signified by a *rose without *thorns.

Ecumenical Councils. Historically those meetings of all the bishops of the Christian Church to discuss and decide on the issues of Christian doctrine and morality. The decrees of these councils were defined as normative for Christian belief. The term "ecumenical council" signified especially the seven earliest church councils which convened prior to the Schism of 1054 which resulted in the separation between the Church of Rome and *Eastern Orthodoxy. *Council of Nicaea I* (325). First of the seven ecumenical councils of early Christianity. Convened to discuss Christology, the first Council of Nicaea condemned Arianism, affirmed the divinity of Jesus Christ, and pronounced the Nicene Creed. *Council of Constantinople* (381). Second of the seven ecumenical councils of early Christianity. Convened in order to discuss the continuing debate over Christology, the Council of Constantinople condemned Apollinarianism, affirmed the *Council of Nicaea and the humanity of Jesus Christ thereby emphasizing *Mary's role as Mother. *Council of Ephesus* (431). Third of the seven ecumenical councils of early Christianity. Convened in order to discuss *Mary's role, the Council of Ephesus defined her as *Theotokos*, thereby identifying her as the Mother of God or God-bearer. Significantly, this ecumenical council was held at the site of the major worship center of *Diana of Ephesus. *See also Theotokos. Council of Chalcedon* (451). Fourth of the seven ecumenical councils of early Christianity. Convened in order to discuss the continuing debate over Christology, the Council of Chalcedon condemned Monophysitism, that is, the interpretation that Jesus as the Christ was one person in one nature, and defined the "Chalcedonian formula" that he was one person in two natures, being simultaneously human and divine. This theological position affirmed the decree of the Council of Ephesus that Mary was Theotokos. *Council of Nicaea II* (787). Last of the seven ecumenical councils of early Christianity. Convened to discuss the iconoclastic controversy, the second Council of Nicaea affirmed and clarified the role of *icons in the spirituality and liturgy of the Christian Church.

Education of the Virgin Mary (*The Golden Legend*). Legendary instruction of *Mary in reading and needlework by the angels or her mother, *Anne, at home, not within the Temple. According to tradition, the youthful Mary pricked her finger with a needle as an omen of the *Sorrows of the Virgin Mary. The motif of Anne Teaching the Virgin to Read (to Sew) was popular in *medieval and *baroque art.

Egeria (legendary). Roman *nymph associated with springs and wells, and a goddess of childbirth. According to legend, a counselor of King Numa Pompilius visited the well in the evenings to reveal the will of the gods.

Egeria (late fourth century). Consecrated Christian virgin pilgrim to the Holy Land. According to tradition, Egeria lived in a Christian convent in either Spain or southern France. She wrote a detailed journal of her pilgrimage to the Holy Land, *Diary of a Pilgrimage*, in which she carefully described all the holy sites and liturgical ceremonies. A rare topic in western Christian art, Egeria was represented in a nun's habit either in the posture of writing her journal or holding the finished book.

Egg. Worldwide symbol for the source of life, or the womb. According to ancient Egyptian mythology, the creation myth began with the episode of the first deity who was hatched from the cosmic egg. In Egyptian cultic practice, the egg was placed in the innermost coffin next to the mummified body as an emblem of hope in the afterlife. For the ancient *Hebrews, the egg connoted mourning as its round shape affirmed the cycle of birth, life, and death. In classical Greek mythology after Zeus transformed himself into a *swan in order to seduce *Leda, she laid two eggs from which emerged their daughters, *Clytemnestra and *Helen of Troy. In Christian art, the egg was a dual symbol, first for *hope and *resurrection as the chick broke out of the egg at birth; and second for chastity and purity like the innocence of the newborn chick. Ostrich eggs signified the *Virgin Birth as the ostrich laid her eggs on the ground and allowed them to hatch independently of her (Jb 39:13–14).

Egyptian art. The art created over a period of four-thousand years by the ancient Egyptians which narrated their history and preserved their religious values. Although stylistic distinctions existed between the varied eras of Ancient Egypt which spanned the predynastic period to the Old Kingdom, Middle Kingdom, and the New Kingdom to the Amarna period and down to the Ptolemaic period, there are identifiable characteristics to the more generic category of Egyptian art including the representation of the human figure with a profiled head, frontal eye and shoulder, and pelvis, legs, and feet in profile; minimal, if no, spatial illusion; no linear perspective; and flat tonal colors. Thematically, Egyptian art incorporated both the narration of its monumental history and a visualization of its extraordinary mythology. The legacy of Egyptian art included its widespread influence on the sacred and secular iconography of western art.

Egyptian religion. Complex and multi-layered indigenous belief system of Ancient Egypt. Numerous local deities coexisted with the predominant national gods and goddesses, often appearing to be more or less identical in cosmogony and/or duties, while multiple myths characterized the creation of the world and the natural order. Nonetheless, throughout its almost four-thousand year history, Egyptian religion was committed to the enduring affirmations of the rising of the sun as the sign of ultimate immortality, the power of the Nile River, and the reality of the Afterlife. Most probably beginning with tribal rituals and ceremonials premised upon animal worship, Egyptian religion evolved into an elaborate veneration of a complex cosmology of deities who were inherent in nature and who enabled the correlation of human, natural, and divine life. With the eventual establishment of a coherent and powerful nation state, Egyptian religion affirmed the relationship between the divine and the human, and the monumental and sacred character of the nation, especially through the development of complex religious iconography and sacred architecture.

Eight. A symbol of rejuvenation, purification, eternity, and the Resurrection, for Christ rose from his tomb on the eighth day after his entry into Jerusalem, eight persons were saved in Noah's Ark, and Jesus was circumcised and named on his eighth day of life. Thus, the octagon became the favored form for both baptismal fonts and early Christian basilicas.

Eileithyia. From the Greek for "she who comes to help." Greek goddess of women and childbirth. Eileithyia was identified with the Roman *Lucine, and was merged with *Artemis.

Eirene. From the Greek for "peace." Greek goddess of peace. One of the *Horae, Eirene was venerated as a goddess of wealth and identified with the Roman goddess, *Pax. She was characterized as a beautiful young woman in a long flowing garment holding the infant Pluto, god of riches, in classical Greek and *renaissance art. Eirene's *attributes included an *olive branch, ears of corn, *caduceus, and *cornucopia.

Ekajatā. From the Sanskrit for "she who has but one shock of hair." Terrifying Buddhist female deity feared by men. In Buddhist art, Ekajatā was depicted as being blue in color and having one head with three *eyes and a facial expression distorted by rage. She had six arms, the first two held her *attributes including serrated knives and skulls, and the other four held a *sword and *arrows on the right side, and a *bow and skulls on the left. Ekajatā's loins were covered with tiger skins.

Elaine. Feminine embodiment of unrequited love in the Arthurian romances. This beautiful daughter of the Fisher King came to an untimely death because of her love for Lancelot (of the Lake). According to legend, Lancelot, infatuated with *Guinevire, mistook Elaine for his beloved and lay with her. As a result of this one-time encounter, Elaine gave birth to Galahad, the famed ideal Christian knight. She requested that after her death, her body be placed on a barge and sent back to Camelot. She was to hold a white lily in one hand and a letter describing her tragic love in the other. A popular topic in medieval and nineteenth-century art, Elaine was depicted as a beautiful young woman regally dressed and with long flowing hair. Most often, she was represented on her death barge.

Electra. Legendary ideal of filial piety and devotion in Greek mythology. Daughter of Agamemnon and *Clytemnestra, Electra was the sister of *Iphigenia, Chrysothemis, and Orestes. Following her father's triumphant return from Troy, she watched in horror as her mother and Aegisthus, her mother's lover, murdered Agamemnon. Electra rescued her brother from the murderous duo and helped him escape to Phocis. For the ensuing eight years, she remained as a slave in Mycenae and awaited the appropriate moment to avenge her father's murder. When Orestes and his companion Pylades were reunited with her in Mycenae, she supported the two youths in the murder of Clytemnestra and Aegisthus. Eventually, she and Pylades married and had two sons.

Elements, Four. *See* Four Elements.

Elephant. An animal symbol for sovereignty, royal wisdom, and moral and spiritual strength in eastern religious art. The mother of the Buddha conceived miraculously when she dreamt that a white elephant entered her side. Following the defeat of Hannibal, the elephant became a symbol of military victory in classical Roman art and culture. The elephant was an animal symbol for modesty and chastity, especially of Adam and *Eve before the *Fall in western Christian art. According to the *Physiologus*, the elephant's sexual organs were reversed because it was a shy and modest creature. Further, the elephant's supposed practices of monogamy, low sex drive, and copulation only for reproduction allowed it to become a metaphor for the ideal Christian marriage. As a trampler of *serpents, it also signified Christ trampling on the Devil. While in *renaissance art, the elephant connoted Africa.

Eleusian Mysteries. Preeminent religious mysteries of ancient Greece celebrated in honor of *Demeter and *Persephone. Known as the Greater and Lesser Eleusinia, these mysteries were held in Eleusis, and celebrated between the times of harvest in September and the next planting. The ceremonial rites included processions, sea bathing, sacrifices, libations, fasts, torch ceremonies, and religious dramas as they signified the descent of Persephone into the underworld and her return to her mother. Initially restricted to Greeks, the Eleusian mysteries were eventually opened to Romans. These secret rituals affirmed the cycle of life and the rewards and punishments of the afterlife. Contemporary commentators interpreted the Eleusian mysteries as influential upon morality and ethical behavior. Practiced into the early Christian period, the Eleusian mysteries were abolished by Theodosius II at the end of the fourth century.

Elisheba (Ex 6:23). From the Hebrew for "God her oath." Wife of Aaron, the high priest and brother of Moses. A daughter of Amminadab, a leader of the tribe of Judah, Elisheba was a rare topic in western Christian art, and if depicted, was characterized as an appropriate matron in either the narrative cycles of Aaron or Moses.

Elizabeth, Saint (first century). Cousin of *Mary, and mother of John the Baptist. Elizabeth was present in representations of the Nativity of John the Baptist, and with her young son was included in representations of the *Madonna and Child. The most important presentation of Elizabeth in Christian art was that of the *Visitation, the encounter between the then pregnant Mary and her pregnant cousin (Lk 1:39–55). In Christian art, Elizabeth was depicted as an elderly woman who offered through her gestures both affection and respect to Mary. She has no identifiable *attributes.

Elizabeth of Hungary, Saint (1207–31). Also identified as Elizabeth of Thuringia, a model of Christian piety and *charity. This daughter of King Andreas II of Hungary was betrothed as an infant to Louis (Ludwig) II of Thuringia. During her childhood when she lived with her future husband's family Elizabeth was reportedly maltreated. In her loneliness, she turned to religion, devoting her time to charitable activities, especially feeding the hungry. Once, when she was smuggling *bread in her *apron, her suspicious husband confronted her only to find her apron filled with *roses. As a young widow expelled from the castle by her greedy brother-in-law, Elizabeth was forced to abandon her *children. She joined the Order of Saint Francis in 1228 in Marburg, where she continued her work for the poor. Elizabeth was the patron of beggars, bakers, lace makers, queens, Catholic Charities, and the Third Order of Franciscans, and was invoked against toothache. In western Christian art, Elizabeth was depicted as a beautiful young woman dressed in a Franciscan *habit and wearing either a *crown or a triple crown as she was a queen by birth, marriage, and glorification in *heaven. Her *attributes were a *basket of roses or an apronful of roses.

Elm. A tree symbol of the dignity of life. The breadth of its growth and the span of its branches in all directions typified the stability and strength that derived from Christian faith.

Elves. From the old German for "friendly female spirits." These supernatural female spirits were fond of dancing and music, and were well disposed to humanity.

Embla (*The Prose Edda*). First woman in Scandinavian mythology. The three gods—Odin, Vile, and Ve—walked along the seashore and found two trees from which they created the primordial couple. Each of the gods gave them a gift: the first spirit and life, the second understanding and movement, and the third speech, hearing, and sight. Then they clothed and named them Embla and Ask. In time, they became the parents of the races of humanity who lived in Midgard.

Empung Luminuut. Minahasan female deity who arose from the earth or was sweated out of a stone. Empung Luminuut was impregnated by the west wind, and gave birth to a sun god, Toar. According to tradition, the mother and son were separated, and when they were reunited, Toar and Empung Luminuut did not recognize each other. Unknowingly they married and conceived the race of the deities and humanity as a result of their incest.

Empusa. Female phantom and companion of *Hecate in Greek mythology. Empusa was empowered with transformative powers to become an animal or a beautiful mortal maiden. She was sent by Hecate to those who invoked her name as they faced a crossroad with anxiety and/or terror.

Enchantress. From the Latin for "to say or chant a charm" or "to bewitch." Female magician. The term enchantress originally associated with magical forms of power and seduction has been transformed to mean a delightful, charming, and thereby bewitching woman. *See* Circe, Medea, Morgan Le Fay.

Enclosed Garden (*Hortus Conclusus*). A characteristic of the beloved bride (Song 4:12), and a symbol for the perpetual virginity of *Mary. In northern *medieval art, the Enclosed Garden became the setting for the *Madonna and Child, and signified both the restoration of *paradise through the Passion, Death, and Resurrection of Jesus Christ, and Mary's foreknowledge that her son was born to die. In *medieval and *renaissance art, it was the locale for the depiction of the *Annunciation (to the Virgin Mary), and occasionally for the *Nativity of Jesus Christ; and for the *Immaculate Conception and the *Assumption of the Virgin Mary in *baroque art.

Ende (fl. c.975). Spanish woman manuscript illuminator. Next to nothing is known of the biography of the woman artist identified as Ende. Most probably a nun, she was renowned for her work on the Spanish romanesque manuscript identified the *Beatus Apocalypse*, or the *Gerona Apocalypse*, which has been acclaimed as the finest example of Mozarabic book ornamentation and illustrations. Ende was clearly the artist of this work as her name preceded that of a man, Brother Emeterius Presbiter, in the signature inscription; a fact that distinguished her from other woman artists of her day.

Enodia. From the Greek for "goddess of the ways." An epithet of *Hecate.

Envy (*Metamorphosis* 2:760–90). Female personification of one of the *Seven Deadly Sins. Envy was represented as a pale woman with a sickly wasted body, squinty eyes, and rotten teeth. She had a venomous tongue and blue-green breasts that oozed poison. Envy fed on *snakes and her staff was entwined with thorny briars.

Enyo. Minor Greek war goddess. Enyo was the daughter of Ares and his battle companion. She became fused with the Roman *Bellona.

Eos. Female personification of the dawn in Greek mythology. The daughter of Hyperion and Theia, Eos was the sister of Helios, the sun, and *Selene, the moon. As the wife of Tithonus, she begged Zeus to make her beloved husband immortal but omitted the request for eternal youth. Zeus transformed Tithonus into an immortal—but one who aged. She was mother to the winds:

Zephyrus (west), Boreas (north), Nortus (south), and Eurus (east); and also all the *stars, including Heosphorus, the morning star, and Hesperus, the evening star. According to legend, Eos awoke each morning and rode her golden chariot, drawn by four white horses, from her bed on the eastern ocean to proclaim the arrival of day to her brother, Helios. She was identified with the Roman *Aurora. Eos was portrayed as a beautiful winged woman with rosy arms and fingers who wore a saffron mantle and a chiton in classical Greek, *renaissance, and *baroque art. She was depicted in her chariot as she rode across the sky sprinkling morning dew from a vase or holding a torch before her beloved Ares (Mars). Eos was infatuated with several mortal lovers including Orion, Cephalus, Ganymede, and Tithonous; and episodes of her amorous adventures were popular in renaissance and baroque art.

Eostre. Classical Teutonic goddess of the dawn, associated with *Ishtar, whose spring festival was assimilated into the Christian feast of Easter.

Epona. From the Celtic for "the big mare." Celtic tribal female deity associated with fertility, and a protector of *horses, *donkeys, and *mules, and of riders and grooms. Reputed to be the daughter of a mare and a mortal male, Epona was also venerated as a goddess of fertility and of the underworld. She was identified by either her *attribute of a horse totem, a *cornucopia, or a bowl of *fruit. Epona was the patron of riding and of the Roman calvary. She was identified in the visual arts either as a female rider or as a strong woman feeding her horse(s).

Erato. *Muse of lyric and amorous poetry in Greek mythology. A daughter of Zeus and *Mnemosyne, Erato was identified as a beautiful maiden in a long flowing garment who held her *attribute, the *lyre, in classical Greek and *renaissance art.

Ereshkigal. From the Sumerian for "queen of the great below." Sumerian goddess of the underworld, and a sister of *Inanna and *Ishtar.

Erinyes. From the Greek for "the mad ones." Trio of sinister subterranean female avengers who were also known as the three *Furies in Greek mythology. Usually a private triad, the Erinyes consisted of Allekto or "the unremitting one," Megaira or "the envious one," and Tisiphone, or "the avenger of murder." Daughters of *Gaea, these ancient female deities were believed to be older than the Olympian divinities. Residents of Erebus in the underworld, the Erinyes were the frenzied avengers of evil doers. Following their successful pursuit of the guilty, these three sisters drove them to madness and continued to torment them in Hades. Famed for their pursuit of Orestes for his act of matricide in killing *Clytemnestra, the irate Erinyes were persuaded by *Athena in the mode of the goddess of order and wisdom in her defense of Orestes to transform themselves into the Eumenides, or "the kindly," who brought about well-being by destroying evil, and to reside with her on the Acropolis. As a result of this transformation, the citizens of Athens honored the Erinyes with the epithet of the "Solemn Ones." The three Erinyes were portrayed as hideous women with *snakes in their hair, thereby similar to the *Medusa, or with *dog heads, and holding *scourges in both hands.

Eris. From the Greek for "strife." Goddess of discord in Greek mythology. The daughter of *Nyx, or of Zeus and *Hera, Eris was identified as the twin sister of Ares, the god of war. Angered when she was not invited to attend the wedding ceremony or feast of Peleus and *Thetis, Eris became renowned for her act of tossing the Apple of Discord, better known as the golden apple, inscribed with the fateful phrase "to the fairest," into the wedding feast. The immediate result of Eris's action was the *Judgment of Paris, and eventually the Trojan War and the death of Achilles, the son of Peleus and Thetis. She was identified with the Roman goddess, *Discordia.

Ermine. An *animal symbol for chastity, innocent, incorruptibility, and purity. According to the medieval *bestiaries, this small animal was so concerned about its *white fur that it would allow itself to be captured by hunters rather than run through or hide in mud. Thus, the ermine became associated with the motto, "Better death than dishonor." A symbol for the miraculous conception of Jesus Christ and of *Mary's perpetual virginity, the ermine, according to the *Physiologus, conceived through its *ear, paralleling the medieval belief that Mary conceived the Word of God through her ear.

Erminia. Saracen princess hopelessly enamored of the Christian knight Tancred in Tasso's romantic epic of the First Crusade, *Jerusalem Delivered*. The beautiful young princess, Erminia, fell hopelessly in love with a Christian knight who himself was in love with the Amazonian warrior, *Clorinda. Several scenes from this popular poem became popular in *baroque and nineteenth-century romantic art. *Erminia's Search for the Lost Tancred* (7:6ff): The feminine princess put on Clorinda's armor in an effort to locate her beloved who was lost in battle and feared dead. As she searched for Tancred, Erminia encountered an aged shepherd who extolled the virtues of the serenity of the pastoral life as opposed to the violence and activity of war. *Erminia Nursing the Wounded Tancred* (19:103–14): Badly wounded from combat with the Egyptian general, Argantes, Tancred was nursed back to health by Erminia who used her beloved's own sword to cut off her beautiful long hair to use as bindings for his bandages.

Estanathlehi. Navaho female deity of creation. Estanathlehi was the ruler of the underworld.

Esther (Book of Esther). From the Hebrew for "star." A Jewish heroine, one of the female Worthies (classical and biblical models of ideal womanhood, including *Jael and *Lucretia), and a fore-type of *Mary. Following the Hebraic tradition, Esther was forty years of age but continued to look youthful and beautiful. The adopted daughter of the king's minister, Mordecai, Esther became the Persian Ahaseurus's Queen, while her Jewish heritage was hidden from him. On the counsel of his chief minister, Haman, the King issued a decree that all the *Hebrews were to be killed and their property reverted to the state. In a daring action, Esther made an unsummoned appearance before the king to announce her Jewish heritage and to plead for her people. Under threat of imminent death, Esther was saved by the touch of Ahaseurus's *scepter. Moved by Esther's beauty and intelligence as well as her courage, Ahaseurus canceled the edict against the Hebrews; Haman was revealed as a traitor and hanged. The Jewish festival of Purim commemorated Esther's successful intervention on behalf of her people (Est 9:19). Esther's coronation as queen by Ahaseurus prefigured the *Coronation of the Virgin Mary as Queen of Heaven, while Esther's act of intercession prefigured Mary's intercession at the Last Judgment. In western Christian art, Esther was depicted as a beautiful richly dressed woman wearing a *crown either in the company of the Worthies, the foretypes of Mary, or *Old Testament heroines; or in a narrative depiction of Esther swooning (fainting) before Ahaseurus.

Eudocia of Constantinople (400–60). Empress and Christian poet. As the Christian wife of the Emperor, Theodosius II, Eudocia was renowned for her poetry, and her eloquent letters, especially those on behalf of Christians, to Popes and Emperors. A very rare topic in early Christian art, Eudocia was depicted as an Empress either in the act of writing or standing as she held her writing instruments in one hand and a cross in the other.

Eugenia, Saint (third century). Early Christian virgin martyr. Although historical evidence affirmed the martyrdom in Rome and burial in the Apronian on the Via Latina, there were varied interpretations of her life. According to *The Golden Legend*, Eugenia was famed for her erudition and for her desire to lead an exemplary ascetic life of prayer. She wore male dress, entered a monastic community, and eventually became abbot of that Egyptian monastery. When she was unjustly accused of sexual misconduct, a disguised Eugenia was brought for judgment to Duke Philip of Alexandria, who was her father. Following revelation of her true sex, she was released. Eugenia traveled to Rome where she was brought to judgment before the Emperor Severus for her Christian faith and beheaded. Her popularity among early Christians was witnessed by the many legends attached to her story.

Eumenides. From the Greek for "the kindly" or "well intentioned." Group of female spirits also known as the *Furies. The Eumenides were commanded to punish those crimes of a violent nature against one's own family. In classical Greco-Roman and *renaissance art, the Eumenides were represented by three old and ugly dog-faced women who haunt those who will not face them. When they are identified as the Fairies, they were beneficent deities. *See also* Erinyes.

Eunice. From the Greek for "conquering well." Mother of Timothy, the companion of Paul. A Jewish woman married to a Greek, Eunice was converted by Paul in Lystra (Acts 16:1). Praised as an exemplary mother, she and her mother, *Lois, were credited with providing Timothy, the future bishop of Ephesus, with an excellent knowledge of the Jewish faith and the *Hebrew Scriptures (2 Tim 1:5; 2 Tim 3:14–15). A rare topic in western Christian art, Eunice was represented as a proper Jewish matron in the company of her mother and her son in the narrative cycles of Paul.

Euodia. From the Greek for "prosperous journey" or "fragrance." One of the two Christian women cited in Paul's Letter to the Phillipians (4:2,3). Euodia and *Syntyche were reported to be engaged in a bitter dispute. They were ordered to stop this quarreling by Paul. A rare topic in western Christian art, Euodia was represented with Syntyche dressed as two proper matrons and in postures of verbal dispute in the narrative cycles of Paul.

Euphemia, Saint (d. c. 307). One of the most famous female saints of the *Eastern Orthodox Church. According to legend, she was persecuted for her Christian faith by being condemned to death by *fire. When that form of martyrdom failed, she was offered to *lions or the *bears who refused to devour her. Eventually, she was beheaded. In eastern Christian art, Euphemia was depicted as a beautiful young woman holding either the *palm of victory or the *sword of her martyrdom. Her other *attributes included the *lily, the lion, and the bear.

Euphrosyne. One of the *Charites, or *Graces, of Greek mythology. Euphrosyne was the female personification of joy.

Europa. Phoenician princess raped by Zeus in the form of a white *bull in Greek mythology. A daughter of Phoenix of the Phoenician king. Europa's beauty attracted the ever-roaming eye of Zeus who sent Hermes as his messenger to entice her and her maiden friends to the seashore. Transforming himself into a magnificent white bull with golden horns, Zeus emerged from the sea and lured the naive Europa to ride his back. Then he turned and plunged into the sea, and abducted the maiden princess to Crete where she eventually bore him two sons. Following Zeus's abandonment of her, Europa married Asterius, king of Crete, who adopted her sons as his heirs. Revered as the "Hellotis" by the Cretans, Europa was honored at the annual festival of the Hellotia. She was portrayed as a beautiful maiden in varying states of undress but covered with *flowers including a crown or garland of flowers, and riding on the back of a golden-horned white bull in classical Greco-Roman, *renaissance, and *baroque art.

Eurydice. Beloved wife of Orpheus in Greek mythology. Infatuated with the beautiful Eurydice, the beekeeper, Aristaeus, attempted a seduction that resulted in Eurydice's death. Fleeing her seducer, she stepped on a poisonous snake and died from its bite. The gods punished Aristaeus by killing all his bees. The distraught Orpheus risked the descent into the underworld in order to beg for the return of his beloved wife from Hades and *Persephone. Accompanied by Hermes, the legendary musician's tragic lament so touched Persephone's heart that she agreed to return Eurydice to the earth on one condition: that during the journey back to earth Orpheus must be in the lead and he was forbidden to look back at Eurydice until the first sight of daylight. Sadly, the eager husband could not resist his wife's constant calls for his attention. Orpheus looked back and as Persephone commanded, Eurydice's shade immediately returned to the underworld. An eternally grieving Orpheus returned to earth where his songs became perpetual laments for his lost wife. Following his death, the lovers were reunited in the Elysian Fields. In classical Greco-Roman and *renaissance art, Eurydice was portrayed as a beautiful young woman walking behind her husband in the scene of their journey from the underworld. In Christian art, Orpheus's descent into the underworld to retrieve Eurydice was interpreted as a classical foretype of Christ's Descent into Limbo to retrieve the souls of the dead.

Eurynome. Mother by Zeus of the three *Charites or Graces in Greek mythology. Eurynome reputedly joined *Thetis in the rescue of Hephaestus when he was thrown from heaven by his mother, *Hera.

Eustochium. *See* Paula.

Euterpe. *Muse of music in Greek mythology. A daughter of Zeus and *Mnemosyne, Euterpe was the patron of flute players, and the inventor of joy and pleasure. In classical Greek and *renaissance art, she was depicted as a beautiful young woman dressed in a flowing garment and holding a *lute in her hand. Euterpe was identified by her *attributes of varied musical instruments either placed around her or as decorative motifs on her garments.

Eve. According to biblical etymology "the Mother of All Living," but linguistically rooted in the Aramaic for "serpent." The first woman and wife of Adam in the *Old Testament. Eve was created from Adam's rib (Gn 2:21–23). Tempted by the *serpent in the *garden,

she ate of the Tree of Knowledge and then offered the forbidden *fruit to Adam, an act of disobedience for which they were expelled from the *Garden of Eden (Gn 3:1–24); and, condemned to die; Eve was also to suffer pain in childbirth (Gn 3:16). She was the mother of Cain and Abel (Gn 4:1–2), and Seth (Gn 4:25). According to *Hebrew tradition, Adam was an *androgyne and Eve was his female half. Although Cain was conceived from the sexual union of Adam and Eve, Abel was Adam's child. According to Christian doctrine, sin entered the world through the disobedience of Adam and Eve, but by the medieval period, the blame for the entry of sin into the world was directed solely upon Eve. The early church fathers beginning with Justin followed *Paul's lead in characterizing *Mary as the Second Eve—as the First Eve's disobedience brought sin into the world, the Second Eve's obedience enabled human salvation. Eve became a foretype of *Mary and the *church; thus the Creation of Eve from Adam's side paralleled the Creation of the Church from the wounded side of the Crucified Christ. A popular topic in Christian art, Eve was depicted first on the sarcophagi and *frescoes of the early Christian *catacombs as a beautiful nude young woman with long *hair who held an *apple as the sign of her disobedience. She was presented with Adam in scenes of the Temptation and *Fall. In *medieval art, Eve became an independent topic and began to be included in depictions of the *Madonna and Child, or as a visual comparison between herself as the First Eve and Mary as the Second Eve.

Ewer and Basin. Sign of the act of cleansing the *body, especially the ritual

36. Jean Cousin the Elder, *Eva Prima Pandora*

washing of *hands or *feet. In the classical Greco-Roman world, the act of washing one's hands was a symbolic act of innocence and purity as in *Pontius Pilate washing his hands (Mt 27:24). In scenes of the *Annunciation, especially in northern *medieval art, the ewer and basin symbolized the spiritual and physical purity of *Mary. The ewer and basin were also liturgical vessels and were used when the celebrant washed his hands during the preparation for the *sacrament of *Eucharist.

Eyck, Hubert (d. 1426) and **Jan van** (d. 1441). Netherlandish traditionally credited with the invention of oil painting, and best known for the *Ghent Altarpiece*. This large polyptych featured a complex *iconography of judgment and salvation with its central upper register depicting the first western presentation of the *deesis while the lower center panel represented the Adoration of the Lamb. Jan van Eyck created many iconographically complex images of *Mary that reflected the Marian devotions then popular among the laity. He was also well-known for his intricate combinations of sacred *iconography within the context of a secular theme, such as *The Arnolfini Wedding Portrait*, which was prophetic of the fusion of sacred and secular that dominated sixteenth- and seventeenth-century Netherlandish *still-life and *vanitas paintings.

Eyck, Margaretha van (fl. 1406). Miniaturist and manuscript illuminator. The sister of Hubert and Jan van *Eyck, Margaretha was esteemed as an artist in her own lifetime. Whether she had any involvement in her brothers' works remains unclear. However, it would not have been uncommon practice for the times, if she had worked on the *Ghent Altarpiece* for example, that she would have been given minimal if no credit. Margaretha van Eyck was credited with the excellent illuminations in the Missal of the Duke of Bedford.

Eye. A symbol for the omniscience, vigilance, and omnipresence of god in religious art. Among the ancient Egyptians, the eye was the most important organ as it permitted the composite of light, color, and magic to make images. It was also a sign of authority and of fire, as in the "place of the eye" as a metaphor for Osiris. The Eye of Horus was the sun, the moon his second eye. Enclosed in a *triangle, the Eye of God denoted the Trinity in Christian art; whereas this same symbol enclosed in a *circle and radiating rays of lights signified the infinite holiness of the Triune God (1 Pt 3:12; Prv 22:12). The *cherubim and *seraphim, two of the highest orders of *angels, had winged bodies that were covered with eyes. When carried on a platter or held in a *hand, eyes were an *attribute of *Lucy.

F

⁂

Fabulous Beasts. *See* Mythical Beasts.

Fairy. From the Latin for "(female) seer" and "fate, destiny." Lowest order of nature spirit in myths and legends. Dwelling in springs, forest, and caves, fairies were capable of being present at any moment. Although favorably disposed towards human beings, they were capable of punishing the ungrateful and of being demonic. In classical Greco-Roman myths and legends, fairies were associated with the *Moirai and the *Parcae, and were later identified as elves in German mythology. Fairies were portrayed as beautiful winged female figures with long flowing garments and garlands of leaves in their long hair. They were often characterized as being very small, almost minuscule, in size.

Faith. One of the three theological virtues of faith, *hope, and *charity. Also one of the *Seven Virtues, faith was represented as a woman who held a *cross and *chalice, and was seated in a place of honor at the right of Christ in *medieval art. In *baroque art, she held an open *Bible with a cross. Additional attributes included the font, *candle, and *helmet.

Faith, Saint (second century). Female personification of the cult of Divine Wisdom (Sophia) in the eastern Mediterranean. According to this tradition the Roman widow *Sophia had *three daughters—Faith, *Hope, and *Charity. The mother and her daughters were tortured and beheaded under the Emperor Hadrian.

Falcon. An avian symbol associated with solar deities in classical cultures, and later an ambiguous symbol for evil or for righteousness in Christian art. Among the ancient Egyptians, the falcon was characterized by its soaring flight and aggressive nature, thereby its general use as a sign for deity in Egyptian hieroglyphs, especially the god Horus, the son of *Isis and Osiris. It was the sacred animal of several solar deities including *Hathor in Egyptian art. The wild falcon personified evil thought or action, while the domesticated falcon denoted the righteous or the pagan converted to Christianity. A favored hunting bird, the domesticated falcon was included in renaissance depictions of the *Adoration of the Magi.

Fall of Adam and Eve (Gn 3). Scriptural event signifying the fall of humanity and the entry of sin into the world. Adam and *Eve's sin was in disobeying God's command and eating of the forbidden *fruit of the Tree of Knowledge in the *Garden of Eden. Eve was tempted by the *serpent, sometimes represented in late *medieval and *renaissance art as having the *head and torso of a woman. Eve then tempted Adam by offering him the forbidden fruit. The *apple became the forbidden fruit due as much to the pun of *malum* (Latin for "apple") and *malus* (Latin for "evil") as to mispronunciation. Having eaten of the apple, Adam and Eve "knew they were naked" and tried to hide from God. They attempted to cover themselves with garments made from *fig leaves. As punishment for their act of disobedience, Adam and Eve, and all their descendants, were condemned to die; further, during their lives men were to labor in the fields and women to suffer in childbirth.

Falling Asleep of the Virgin Mary. From the Greek for "the dormition of the Theotokos." Title of the feast commemorating the Dormition of the Virgin Mary in the *Eastern Orthodox and *Anglican Churches. *See also* Dormition of the Virgin Mary, Koimesis of the Virgin Mary.

Fama. Roman female personification of rumor in classical Latin literature and art. Fama was portrayed as a woman with an extraordinarily large and open mouth as in Virgil's description of her as a horrible creature with several babbling tongues.

Fame. Female personification of the heroic in deed and in person. In classical Greco-Roman art, Fame was depicted as a winged female figure; while she acquired a golden trumpet and/or wooden recorder in *renaissance art.

Fata Morgana. *See* Morgan Le Fay.

Fates. Three goddesses of human destiny in Roman mythology. Identified with the Greek *Moirai, the Fates foretold the course of individual human existences at the moment of birth. These three sisters were individually identified as *Clotho who wove the thread of life and held the spindle in her left hand; *Lachesis who measured the length of each individual thread of life; and *Atropos who severed the thread with the shears she held in her right hand. In classical Greco-Roman and *renaissance art, the Fates were represented as three gray-headed matrons identified by their individual *attributes of the spindle, thread, and shears. *See also* Fatit.

Fatima (legendary). Indigenous Arabian moon goddess. A form or manifestation of the preexistent Great Goddess, Fatima was variously identified as a mother goddess, an earth goddess, and a sun goddess. However she was most regularly associated with the moon, thereby a foretype of *Artemis (*Diana) and later of *Mary. According to pious legends, her characteristics and attributes were assimilated into *Fatima, the daughter of the prophet Muhammad.

Fatima (c. 605–33). Religious figure revered by Muslims for her religious fervor and as the daughter of the prophet Muhammad. Fatima was esteemed as one of "four perfect women," the others being Khadija, her mother; *Mary; and

Asiyah, the wife of the Pharaoh who drowned while pursuing Moses and the Israelites. As her father's companion throughout his years of persecution, Fatima traveled with him on the Hijrah, his dramatic escape from Mecca to Medina in 622. She married his nephew and devoted discipline, 'Alī, and was dedicated to their children, three sons and two daughters. She survived her husband's infidelities and cruelties to become revered as the "model wife and mother." According to tradition, she was characterized as being "bright blooming" to signify that she never menstruated and was thereby perpetually virginal. Fatima attended her father throughout his final illness but separated herself from family following the selection of Abuū Bakr instead of 'Alī as Muhammad's successor. Revered by all Muslims, Fatima received special accord from the Shi'ite Muslims because of her lineage. *See also* Hand-of-Fatimah, Islam.

Fatima al-Ma'sumah (d. c. 816–17). Sister of the eighth Shi'ite imam Riza. Fatima al-Ma'suma fell ill her during her journey to visit her brother in Tus. When she became ill at Sava, a Sunni town, she requested transfer to Qum where she died and was buried. During the Safavid Dynasty (fl. 1501–1732), Shi'ism was adopted as the state religion of Iran, and Fatima's tomb gained spiritual importance. In an attempt to attract pilgrims to the Shi'ite shrines of Iran, the early seventeenth-century ruler 'Abbas I renovated and expanded the site of her tomb. The shrine of Fatima al-Ma'sumah is the only major shrine in Iran dedicated to a woman.

Fátima, Our Lady of the Rosary of. Shrine erected on the site of six appearances of *Mary to four Portuguese peasant children between May 13 to October 13, 1917. According to these children, they were directed to pray the *rosary, observe the sacrament of penance, and participate in processions as homage to the *Immaculate Conception. A reputed 70,000 persons observed the darkening of the sun on Mary's last appearance to the children on October 13, 1917. Following these appearances, a cathedral with a large piazza and a shrine were built both to commemorate these appearances and to honor Mary. Our Lady of the Rosary of Fátima was visited by Pope Paul VI in 1967, and Pope John Paul II in 1982.

Fatit. Supernatural female beings who determine individual destiny in Albanian popular folklore. According to tradition, the three Fatit approach the newborn's cradle on the third day of life and determine its future. They were represented in Albanian folk art as three miniature female figures each riding on a *butterfly. *See also* Fates, Moirai, Parcae.

Fauna. Ancient Roman goddess of livestock, fields, and forest. The female counterpart of Faunus, Fauna was identified with *Bona Dea and venerated with her.

Feast in the House of Simon (Mt 26:6–13; Mk 14:3–9; Lk 7:36–50; Jn 12:1–8). Scriptural event signifying the forgiveness of sins. In this variant of the *Anointing at Bethany, Jesus came to the house of Simon the Leper to dine. An unknown woman entered with an alabaster box of precious ointments, she broke the box and anointed Jesus' *head. Many were angered by this extravagance, but Jesus rebuked them in a manner similar to the Anointing at Bethany. In the Western Christian Church since *Augustine, this unnamed woman was conflated with several other anonymous women into the person identified as *Mary Magdalene. As she participated in other anointing (and attempted anointing) scenes, and was identified as the Repentant Sinner, this conflation was appropriate. Occasionally depicted in western Christian art, the Feast in the House of Simon was distinguishable from other "meal scenes" by the presence of the female figure anointing Jesus's feet.

Feather. The light weight and ephemeral nature of the feather made it the appropriate *attribute of *Maat, the goddess of truth, justice, order, and morality, in ancient Egypt. She was portrayed with an ostrich feather on her head or in her right hand as a sign of truth in testimony, and also used this feather as the measure of truth when weighing the soul of the dead. The ancient goddess of the Nile cataracts, *Anukis, wore a crown with four ostrich feathers. The feather was a sign of faith and contemplation or as the quill of a *pen, the Word of God in Christian art. The *peacock feather was an *attribute of *Barbara. In *renaissance art, the feather was an *attribute of America.

Felicitas. Roman female personification of happiness.

Felicity. *See* Perpetua and Felicity.

Felicity, Saint (d. 165). Roman noblewoman martyred with her children for their Christian faith. A widowed convert to Christianity, Felicity refused to worship pagan idols on the command of the Roman Consuls. She was condemned to watch as her seven sons were martyred for their faith, and then she was martyred either by decapitation or being boiled in oil. A rare topic in early Christian art, Felicity was depicted as a Roman matron or a *nun who was surrounded by her children all holding *palm branches.

Femme Fatale. Female embodiment of seduction and destruction. Believed to be an extension of the late nineteenth-century's fixation on evil seductresses in the arts of the Symbolists like Gustave Moreau, the femme fatale was in fact an ancient visual and literary motif. Characterized as exemplars of feminine beauty, extraordinary sexual energies, and heightened eroticism, the femme fatales were also evil destroyers of men; their goal being simply seduction only to bring about destruction. *Circe, *Cleopatra, *Siren, *Salome, and *Thaïs were among the most popular femme fatales in classical Greco-Roman and early Christian art. *See also* Lucas Cranach.

Feng Po. "Mrs. Wind" in Chinese mythology. Feng Po was the old woman who stored the winds in her goatskin bag. She determined when to release the winds, and whether to release a beneficent or an angry wind. She was depicted in Chinese art as an old woman usually seated or stooped over, with an enormous bag at her side.

Fern. A symbol for humility, sincerity, and frankness. The fern concealed its graceful elegance and delicacy in the shadow of larger plants.

Feronia. Etruscan goddess of fertility and fire.

Fertility Goddesses. Female deities who provided fecundity to barren women and barren land, protected pregnant women during the period of gestation and the land during the time of growth, and administered the appropriate ceremonial rituals for conception and childbirth, and for planting and harvest.

Fides (as a goddess). Roman goddess of oaths and loyalty. In classical Greco-Roman and *renaissance art, Fides was distinguished as a young woman with her hands interlaced.

Fides (as a metaphorical action). From the Latin for "faith." Female personification of fidelity or faith in Roman mythology. During sacrificial ceremonies, the petitioner bound his or her right hand with white cloth as a sign that honor resided in the right hand. In classical Greco-Roman and *renaissance art, Fides was depicted as a respectable matron dressed in a long flowing garment who wore a *wreath of *laurel or *olive leaves on her head, and carried a *basket of *fruit or ears of corn.

Fifteen. Number sacred to *Mary in western Christian art. Originally a numerical symbol of progress, fifteen was associated with the number of steps ascended by the young Mary when she left her parents' home and was dedicated to the service of the Temple.

Fig. As the patron of the fig tree to Attica, *Demeter had the many-seeded brown-skinned fruit as one of her *attributes in classical Greek art. In Christian art, the fig was a symbol for fertility, fecundity, and good works because of its many seeds. In relation to Adam and *Eve, the fig, fig tree, and fig leaves symbolize lust.

Fina, Saint (c. 1238–53). Youthful Christian visionary. As a sickly young child in San Gimignano, Fina dedicated herself to God and a Christian life of good works. Despite many serious illnesses, she devoted herself to easing the suffering of the poor. She lived an austere life even to sleeping on a bare bedboard in a room infested with rats. Prior to her death, she had a vision of Gregory the Great. Immediately following her death, white *violets reportedly sprung up around her bed. A rare topic in western Christian art, Fina was identified by either the depiction of Gregory the Great standing by her deathbed or by her *attributes of the white violet and the rat.

Finding of the True Cross. According to medieval legends and pious traditions, *Helena, the mother of the emperor Constantine, began a new journey following her son's order that Christians not be fed to the *lions. Helena dedicated her life to good works and founded churches in the Holy Land. According to legend, Helena located *three crosses but needed to discover which one was used for Jesus, so she ordered that a corpse be laid on all three crosses. The *cross that was identified as "giving life" was taken by her back to her son's new capital city of Constantinople (Istanbul).

Fir Tree. Symbol for penitence, or the virtuous aspirations of the elect in *heaven in western Christian art.

Fire. Ambiguous symbol of destructive and of beneficent energies. Among the ancient Egyptians, fire denoted both the purification of goodness and the destruction of evil; and was an *attribute of the goddess *Taweret. Fire signified of religious fervor and martyrdom, or the torments of *Hell in Christian art. In the *Old Testament, fire was used as a metaphor for God—a column of fire and the *burning bush. Tongues of fire appearing above the *heads of the twelve apostles at the Pentecost symbolized the gift of tongues, that is, the ability to speak in all languages.

Fish. Marine symbol of fertility and simultaneously impurity, and a prevalent sacrificial offering in the classical world. Among the ancient Egyptians, the fish had multiple meanings as in a sign of evil and impurity in relation to Seth, a symbol of procreation as the lost penis of Osiris, and a signifier of fertility, procreation, and female health in association with mother goddesses, such as *Hathor, *Hatmehit, and *Neith. The fish was the primary early Christian symbol for Jesus Christ and signifier of *baptism, the Eucharist, the Last Supper, the Resurrection, and immortality. As the *cross denoted the ever-present danger of persecution until the middle of the fourth century, the fish identified individuals as Christians. The initial use of the symbol of the fish was related to the acrostic formed by the Greek word, *icthys*, for fish, which was understood to refer to the words, "Jesus [*i*] Christ [*ch*] God's [*t*] Son [*y*], Savior [*s*]. The fish typified baptism, for just as the fish cannot live without *water, neither can the Christian survive without baptism. One of the earliest metaphors for Jesus and his apostles was that of the fish-

ermen who were in fact fishers of souls. The robe of Philosophy was decorated with a motif of fish signifying wisdom and creativity in *renaissance art.

Five. Symbol for the number of the *wounds of the Crucified Jesus, and of the Wise Virgins or Bridesmaids.

Fjörgyn. Old northern German goddess of mountains, forests, and fertility.

Flag. A sign of military victory adopted by Christians in the fourth century as a symbol of Christ's victory over death. The *white flag with a *red *cross was commonly found in depictions of the Resurrection, or held by the Resurrected Christ. In *renaissance and *baroque art, Christ descended into *Hell holding his flag of victory. The flag was an *attribute of all military *saints, including *Ursula and *Joan of Arc, and also of the *Sibyl of Phrygia.

Flames. Symbol for religious zeal and martyrdom as well as for the torments of *Hell. Flames were an *attribute of *Agnes. Flames over the *heads of *Mary and the twelve apostles at Pentecost represented the gift of tongues; that is, the ability to speak all languages.

Fleur-de-Lis. Symbol for the Trinity in western Christian art. Chosen by King Clovis as a sign of his purification, the fleur-de-lis became an emblem of French royalty and as such the attribute of the monarchs, and of *Mary as Queen of Heaven.

Flidhais. Celtic goddess of the woods. Flidhais was characterized as a great adventuress and nurturer of heroes. She was depicted as a physically strong young woman often dressed as a huntress and accompanied by her animal *attributes of a hind or a doe. She was often identified as the Celtic *Diana.

Flight into Egypt (Mt 2:13–15). Scriptural event signifying the necessary journey of the *Holy Family so that like Joseph and Moses, Jesus would be called from Egypt by God, thus fulfilling the *Old Testament prophecy (Hos 11:1). Following Joseph's (of Nazareth) second dream in which the Archangel Gabriel warned of the Massacre of the Innocents, *Mary and the infant Jesus left with him to seek shelter in Egypt. A popular theme throughout the history of Christian art, the imagery and *iconography of the Flight into Egypt was dependent upon apocryphal and legendary texts. In the Arabian *Gospel of the Childhood of Christ* as well as the apocryphal *Gospel of Pseudo-Matthew*, the episode of the "falling idols" at the Temple in Heliopolis signified the fulfillment of the Old Testament prophecies (Is 19:1 and Jer 43:13), and affirmed the divinity of Christ and the superiority of Christianity over all forms of idolatry. The story of the Flight into Egypt was also interpreted as a sign of the revelation of Jesus as the Christ to the heathens. Representations of the Flight into Egypt included one or all of these symbols and legendary attributes, including the signs of the victorious *palm, falling idols, and images of Joseph or Moses in an oasis setting of palm trees, watering hole, and flowering shrubs. Mary and the Child were posed either sitting in the oasis (a motif of the *paradise or *Enclosed Garden) or riding astride the *donkey. Joseph was either attempting to gather *fruit or *water for his family with the assistance of *angels, or walking before the donkey. The use of the palm and the palm

trees prefigured the Entry into Jerusalem. *Baroque artists represented the Flight into Egypt as a night scene, while later artists with their growing interest in the *landscape expanded the naturalistic setting of the event and minimized the figures and symbolism.

Flight into Egypt, Rest on the (Mt 2:13–15). A separate motif from the *Flight into Egypt in the late fourteenth century, and as such a popular theme of northern late *medieval art. Without scriptural authority, this event naturally evolved in Christian art and devotional texts in the medieval period. In early fifteenth-century representations, *Mary breasted her son. Following contemporary representations of the *Nativity, the *Madonna and Child loomed large while Joseph all but disappeared from the scene. The intricate and complex symbolism of the flowering shrubs and other vegetation at the "rest stops" were directly related to late medieval Marian devotions. A popular motif in *medieval and *baroque art, the Rest on the Flight into Egypt continued to fascinate artists into the late nineteenth century because of the *landscape setting.

Flora. Ancient Sabine female deity later transformed into the Roman goddess of the flower of youth and its pleasures, including love and fecundity. As the patron of flowers and of the spring, Flora was identified with the Greek *Chloris; while as a goddess of corn, flowers, and green gardens she was related to *Ceres (*Demeter). She was honored at the annual festival of Floralia held in early May and characterized by theatrical events, games, and licentious behavior as symbolic of fertility. A popular motif for female portraiture, Flora was depicted as a youthful and beautiful maiden bedecked with flowers—wreaths, garlands, and bouquets—in classical Greco-Roman, *renaissance, and *baroque art.

Flora, Saint (d. 851). Christian virgin martyr. Daughter of a Muslim father and a Christian mother, Flora was secretly reared as a Christian. As a young woman, she was identified as a Christian by her Muslim brother into whose legal care she was placed. In an effort to force her to recant her Christian faith and to turn to *Islam, he had her tortured. Later she fled his estates and was befriended by another Christian woman, Mary, whose brother had been martyred. The two women publicly identified themselves as Christians and were condemned to a brothel by the local magistrate. They received divine protection and their chastity was preserved. Eventually, Flora and Mary were beheaded. A rare topic in western Christian art, Flora was occasionally depicted either with Mary, each of them holding the martyr's *attribute of a *palm branch, or by herself with the symbols of her martyrdom.

Flowering Staff. A common symbol for divine providence, especially in relation to *Mary, in Christian art. There were three interrelated references to the flowering staff and Mary in scriptural and Christian legendary sources. *Aaron's Staff* (Nm 17:5–11): Following God's command, Moses ordered that each of the twelve tribes place an identifying staff before the Ark of the Covenant. Only Aaron's staff blossomed and brought forth *almonds as a sign of his divine selection to exercise priestly of-

fice and as a sign that the honor of the priesthood belonged to the tribe of Levi. This motif was the *Old Testament foretype of the flowering of Joseph of Nazareth's staff as a sign of his divine selection as Mary's earthly bridegroom. *Betrothal of Mary* (*Protoevangelium of James*): The High Priest Zacharias, father of John the Baptist, supervised the search for a proper husband for the young Mary. He summoned all the local widowers, including Joseph of Nazareth, to bring their walking staffs to the temple and to leave them overnight so that God could identify the appropriate spouse. In the morning, Joseph's staff was identified as the one that had blossomed into *flower, while a *dove hovered over his head. According to pious legends, and as a wordgame on the Latin for "branch" (*virga*) as opposed to "virgin" (*virgo*), any staff that burst into bloom, especially of *lilies, signified Mary.

Flowers, symbolism of. The botanical cycle of life, death, and resurrection in the fullness of the four seasons. As the blossoms of the earth, flowers like *fruits and *vegetables contained the seeds for each new and successive generation. As a generic symbol, a flower indicated the beauty of the *earth, fertility, and earthly desires associated with fecundity and creation of new life. More often than not, flower deities were the female descendants of ancient fertility goddesses, such as the Taoist *Hua Hsien and *Hsi Wang Mu, or the Shinto *Sengen, the Hindu *Saravastī, the Roman *Flora, and the Greek *Eos (*Aurora). Among the ancient Egyptians, flowers signified life and thereby had an important role in the Cult of the Dead. The *lotus was identified as the journey

37. Rembrandt van Rijn, *Flora*

for purification and of rebirth as the plant struggled through the primeval waters to bring to bloom a pure white flower. In classical Greco-Roman art, flowers signified Flora, while specific flowers such as the *rose symbolized *Aphrodite or *Venus. In Christian art, flowers were purely decorative while a specific flower was an integral element of the theological intent of the image; for example, *violets signified *Mary's humility while the *iris represented her sorrow. A *basket of *roses was an *attribute of *Dorothea. *See also* Almond, Anemone, Blancheflor, Blodeuwedd, Bluebell, Carnation, Cherry, Columbine, Convolvulus, Cyclamen, Daffodil, Daisy, Dandelion, Flora, Forget-me-not, Hyacinth, Iris, Jasmine, Lady's Bed Straw, Lady's Mantle, Lady's Slipper, Lavender, Lily, Lily-of-the-Valley, Lotus, Marigold, Myrtle, Narcissus, Pansy, Peony, Periwinkle, Poppy, Primrose, Rose, Snowdrop, Sunflower, Sword Lily, and Violet.

Flute. Reed instrument symbolic of music and frivolity in classical Greco-Roman and *renaissance art. The reed was the identifying *attribute of Dionysus, the *Maenads, *Euterpe, and *Cybele.

Fly. Ambiguous symbol for courage or evil. In Egyptian art and cultic practice, the image of the fly signified bravery and a curative amulet for disease. As a bearer of bad tidings, evil, and pestilence, the fly was a symbol for sin in western Christian art. In depictions of the *Madonna and Child, the fly represented the sin that the child conquered. As a symbol of the plague, the fly was accompanied by the *goldfinch as a protector against the plague.

Fontana, Lavinia (1552–1614). First woman artist named official painter to the Papal Court. Daughter of the Bolognese painter, Prospero Fontana, Lavinia studied the discipline and craft of painting in her father's studio. The Fontana home was a center of artistic and intellectual life in sixteenth-century Bologna, so she became well versed in the literary, philosophical, and religious issues of her day. By the age of eighteen, Lavinia was established as an independent artist and her commissions included portraits and history paintings. Her marriage to the Luccan painter, Gian Paolo Zappi, produced eleven children. Her artistry garnered the attention, and later the patronage, of several popes. She was named official painter to the Papal Court by Clement VIII, and elected a member of the Rome Academy. Although not an iconographic innovator, she created religious works such as her *Noli Me Tangere* (1571) and her *Holy Family with Sleeping Christ Child* (1590s), which displayed both fine technical skill and subtle emotion, especially in terms of her depictions of women. Although she moved to Rome as an independent painter, her popularity continued to earn her sufficient commissions to operate workshops in both Rome and Bologna. Lavinia successfully completed major commissions for *altarpieces, including one for Saint Paul's Outside the Walls on the theme of *The Stoning of Stephen*. Her financial and critical success made her a role model for younger women artists even into the nineteenth century.

Foot. A bodily symbol of humility and willing service touching the "dust of the earth" in Christian art. In a ritual of penitence and humility, an unknown woman washed the *feet of Jesus with her tears (Lk 7:38). In an action of humble service and of hospitality, Jesus washed the feet of the apostles at the Last Supper (Jn 13:5). As a symbol of both humility and bondage, certain religious orders of male and female monastics either went barefoot or wore only sandals.

Forest. Symbol for the dangerous, uncontrollable power of nature and the wilderness.

Forget-me-not. Floral symbol for fidelity in love.

Fortitude. One of the *Seven Virtues. Fortitude was personified as a female figure with a *sword, *shield, *club, *globe, *lion's skin, or *column, all in allusion to Samson's destruction of the pagan temple in Christian and *renaissance art. Samson rested at her feet.

Fortress. A sign of refuge in God or faith in Christian art. A fortress was protection against *demons.

Fortuna. Goddess of good luck and fortune in Roman mythology. Originally an old Roman goddess of women and fertility, thereby the center of an oracular cult, Fortuna was transformed into the divine female personification of public and private fortune. Identified with the Greek *Tyché, Fortuna was venerated as the patron of women, of brides, and of male virility. She was represented as bestower of blessing as signified by a *cornucopia in classical Roman and *renaissance art. Fortuna's *attributes included *wings, a *globe, a *wheel, and a *ball as a sign of the wheel of fortune, the new year, and chance; a *shell, *dol-

phin, blindfold, and dice, and a rudder as the pilot of destiny.

Forty. The number associated with trials or probation, as exemplified by the forty years the Israelites spent in the wilderness and in bondage to the Philistines, the forty days and forty nights of the Flood, and the forty days that Moses stayed on Mount Sinai. Jesus spent forty days of prayer and fasting in the wilderness. The Christian fast of Lent in preparation for Easter lasted for forty days.

Fountain. Symbol for cleansing, purification, and salvation as Jesus was the "fountain of life." As a closed container of *water, the fountain related to *Mary (Ps 36:9; Song 4:12). *See* Well.

Four. A number of completion and fulfillment, as in the four Christian Evangelists, the four corners of the earth, the four *rivers of *paradise, the four elements, the four seasons, the four *Horsemen of the Apocalypse, the four Christian gospels, and the four ages of man.

Four Elements. Alchemical practice of contrasting pairs, in this instance contrasting pairs of the fundamental components of daily life and of the earth. The Four Elements were related to the four seasons and the symbolic animals. In *renaissance art, they were characterized by specific classical deities. *Earth* was signified by the old fertility goddesses and their identifiable *attributes of the *cornucopia, *snake, *scorpion, and turreted crown. Most often, the symbolic agricultural motif of a mother suckling one or two of her children denoted the earth. *Air* was characterized as a *chameleon, and represented by *Hera (*Juno) along with her attribute of the *peacock. In western art, *Air* was symbolized by the depiction of children with either windmills or in the act of blowing bubbles. *Fire* was the *salamander, thunderbolt, flaming head, and the phoenix headdress. It was represented by Hephaestus (Vulcan). *Water* was imaged as a river god holding an urn, and symbolized by Poseidon (Neptune).

Fourteen. A number of goodness and mercy, as it was comprised of a double seven.

Fourteen Holy Helpers. A group of Christian *saints whose identities varied, but who were quick in their responses to prayers for recovery from disease or for a good death. Both the *iconography and cult of the Fourteen Holy Helpers was popular during the Black Plague.

Fox. Symbol for cunning, guile, heretics, and the *Devil.

Francesca Romana, Saint (1384–1440). Exemplary Christian noblewoman and visionary. Francesca Romana committed herself to a life of Christian *charity, especially the care of those afflicted by the plague. She established the community of the Oblates of Tor de'Speechi for women dedicated as she was. These religious women worked with the Benedictine community of Monte Olivieto. A popular topic in *renaissance and *baroque Christian art, Francesca Romana was depicted as a mature woman dressed in the black habit and white hood of the Olivetan Oblates and seated with the book on her lap open to Psalm

73:23–24. If postured as kneeling, she was either in prayer among those dead and dying from the plague, or gifted with a vision of *Mary who offered her a broken arrow as an emblem of the conquest of the plague.

Francis of Assisi, Saint (c. 1181–1226). Founder of the Franciscan Order. Although he was frivolous as a young man, his experiences as a prisoner of war and a serious illness caused him to empathize with the situation of the poor and underprivileged. Following his conversion experience before the Crucifix in the Church of San Damiano, the young Francis dedicated himself to a life of service to the meek and the poor. He was famed for his love of and devotion to *animals and *birds. His example of humility, simplicity, lowliness, and evangelical freedom was enhanced by his spiritual marriage to Lady Poverty to create a spiritual fervor of the highest order. With *Clare, he established the first community of Poor Ladies in 1212, one year after the Order of Minor (Lesser) Friars was accepted by Pope Innocent III. During a period of intense prayer and silent contemplation in 1224, Francis received the *stigmata, or the wounds of the crucified Jesus. A popular figure in western Christian art, Francis was depicted as a lean, young man who wore the *brown *habit of the Franciscan Order. Usually accompanied by animals and birds, the most popular image of Francis was that of his preaching to the birds. Episodes from the life of Francis were popular in late *medieval, *renaissance, and *baroque art, including his denunciation of family wealth, his cure of lepers, and his receipt of the stigmata. Often depicted in prayer, he was identified by his many

*attributes, including a *skull, *cru-
cifix, *lily, *lamb, or *wolf. He was
also represented symbolically marrying
Lady Poverty or being handed the
Christ Child by *Mary. Francis's influence on western Christian art was
apparent in the development of devotionalism and humanistic themes by artists from the late medieval period into
the baroque period.

Franciscans. A monastic order established by *Francis of Assisi between
1209 and 1211. Committed to issues of
social justice and charitable service to
the poor, Franciscans were also dedicated to popular spirituality and devotionalism, especially of the *Madonna
and Child. They encouraged the popular devotions of the Stations of the
Cross, the *Nativity creche, and the An-
gelus, as well as fostering the development of the Marian doctrine of the
*Immaculate Conception.

Fravaši. From the Persian for "she who
confesses" or "she who is chosen." Ancient Persian spiritual preexistence of
believers. The Fravaši were characterized as protective female spirits who
watched over human beings, assisted
Ahura Mazda in the creation of the
world, fostered the growth of vegetation, and served as armed female warriors in defense of the gates of heaven.

Fresco. Wall painting on plaster. In its
best form ("buon fresco"), this art medium developed in the thirteenth century and was perfected in the sixteenth
century. The artist prepared the surface
to be painted with rough plaster upon
which a cartoon (model) was drawn.
The actual working area was then covered with a final layer of plaster, which
was painted while still damp. The careful preparation of the fresco's surface
and the proper combination of the
damp plaster, paint pigments, and lime
water resulted in a work of art that
lasted through the centuries, such as Michelangelo's frescoes for the Sistine
Chapel ceiling. An improperly prepared
surface or improper combination of
damp plaster, paint pigments, and lime
water could result in premature peeling
or fading, as in the instance of Leonardo's *Last Supper.*

Freya. From the old Norse for "mistress, lady." Most powerful goddess of
ancient Scandinavians, and composite
mother goddess of Scandinavian and
Teutonic mythology who embodied female sensuality and maternal power.
Freya was the goddess of fertility, love,
marriage, ecstasy, shamanism, death,
and war. In her northern Germanic
form of Freya, she was goddess of love,
fertility, and peace who assisted women
in childbirth. As a goddess of fertility
and love, she was reputed to have many
lovers including the four dwarfs who
forged the *Brisingamen, a solar *necklace of great beauty and power, in return
for four nights of love. According to
The Prose Edda, she wept golden tears
during the absences of her beloved husband, Od. Freya was described as a mature woman, often pregnant, who either
rode a golden boar or drove a chariot
drawn by *cats. She owned the Valhamar, a fabled cloak of falcon feather;
and the Brisingamen. Her animal *attributes included the cat and the pig.

Frog. Amphibian symbol for fertility
and procreation in classical cultures,
and for repulsive sin, worldly pleasures,
and heretics in Christianity. A chthonic

animal, the frog was believed to be involved in the forces that brought life into being. *Heket, the Egyptian goddess of birth and protector of women in childbirth, was represented with a woman's body and a frog's head. The frog was also a sign of the Resurrection as it hibernated during the winter and awakened in the spring.

Fruits, symbolism of. Symbols for the cycle of life, death, and resurrection in the fullness of the *four seasons. As the produce of the *earth, fruits—like *flowers and *vegetables—contained the seeds for each new and successive generation. As a generic symbol, fruit indicated the abundance of harvest, fertility, and earthly desires (as associated with fecundity and creation of new life). In classical Greco-Roman and *renaissance art, fruit denoted *Demeter (*Ceres) and *Fides. In Christian art, a specific fruit was an integral element of the theological intent of the image; for example, the combination of *peaches, *pears, and *cucumbers represented good works, while the *apple referred to the Temptation and *Fall. A variety of fruit signified the twelve fruits of the spirit: peace, love, joy, faith, gentleness, goodness, patience, modesty, meekness, chastity, temperance, and long suffering. Fruit in a *basket was an *attribute of *Dorothea. *See also* Apple, Apples of the Hesperides, Cherry, Date, Fig, Grapes, Lemon, Orange, Peach, Pear, Plum, Pomegranate, Quince, and Strawberry.

Fugora. Roman goddess of lightning. Fugora was invoked against thunderstorms and inclement weather. Her images were used as amulets against thunder and lightning.

Furies. Adaptation of the *Erinyes into Roman art and mythology. In classical Roman art, the Furies were depicted as driving the guilty to earthly insanity or tormenting them in the underworld.

Fylgir. From the old Norse for "female attendants." Legendary protective female spirits. According to Germanic tradition, the Flygir appeared if visualized by an individual in need of their help. They were represented as being either human females changing shape into animals or female animals, often miniature in size, and winged.

G

❦

Gabija. Lithuanian feminine spirit of fire. Venerated as the "mistress of the holy fire," Gabija received homage when a devotee threw salt upon the fire and chanted "Holy Gabija, be thou satisfied."

Gabjauja. Lithuanian corn goddess. Gabjauja was invoked for riches and prosperity. With the advent of Christianity in Lithuania, this beneficent female deity was transformed into an evil spirit.

Gaea. From the Greek for "earth." Most ancient Greek goddess and mother earth. The daughter of Chaos, Gaea was the mother of Uranus, Pontus, the mountains, and several monstrous beings including the cyclops and the giants. She was characterized by prophetic and visionary powers as witnessed by the first oracles of Olympia and Delphi. Invoked with Zeus as the witness to oaths and vows of truthfulness, fidelity, and loyalty, Gaea was venerated by many cultic groups. Gaea played a significant metaphorical role in classical Greek philosophy and cosmological literature. According to tradition, she was instrumental in the downfall of Kronos and later supported the Titans and the Giants in their battle against Zeus. Once Zeus was declared the victor, Gaea recognized him as the most powerful Olympian deity. She was identified with the Roman goddess *Tellus. In classical Greek and *renaissance art, Gaea was portrayed as a powerful and veiled matron who was identified by her *attributes, a black lamb, which was her favored sacrifice, and the *cornucopia and *fruits of the earth as signs of beneficence and fecundity.

Galatea. From the Greek for "she who is milk white." Legendary maiden sculpted by Pygmalion. According to Greek mythology, Galatea was a *nereid who was courted by Polyphemus. In one variant of the story, she bore Polyphemus a son while in another she rejected his courtship. A popular subject in Hellenistic art, Galatea was portrayed as a beautiful maiden dressed in a long flowing garment.

Galaxy. *See* Milky Way.

Galizia, Fede (1578–1630). Internationally renowned woman artist from

Trento. A daughter of the miniaturist Nunzio Galizia, Fede was a child prodigy who garnered not simply public but international recognition for her skills as a portrait painter by the time she was sixteen. She was also recognized for her public commissions for churches. Like her female contemporaries, she painted the story of *Judith. However Galizia's *Judith and Her Handmaiden* was more or less a traditional interpretation of this scene as a refined portrait with an implicit moral message.

Galla. Seven female companions of *Inanna in Mesopotamian art and mythology. The Galla were the underworld demons responsible for the journeys of human beings to the underworld.

Galla Placidia (c. 390–450). Christian noblewoman and patron of the arts. The daughter of Theodosius the Great, Gala Placidia lived a politically complex existence. Initially part of the booty that Alaric claimed for his successful sacking of Rome, Galla Placidia married his brother, Ataulf. Following the deaths of her husband and their son in Spain, she returned to Rome under the claim of Constantius whom she was forced to marry in 417. Once she was declared "Augusta," her husband immediately earned the title of "Augustus." Following Constantius's death in 421, she angered her brother with her political intrigues and he exiled Galla Placidia to Constantinople until the time that her son, Valentian, became Emperor, when she returned to Rome. A regular and generous patron of Christian artists, Galla Placidia was best remembered for her exquisite mausoleum in Ravenna, which is a landmark in the history of Christian art.

Ganga. Hindu goddess of the Ganges River, thereby of healing. As the female personification of the most sacred of all rivers, Ganga was the subject of veneration and adoration. In Indian art she was characterized as a lithesome nude young woman with full breasts and with a *snake flowing like the river from her head into her right hand.

Garden. A common symbol for *Paradise in eastern and western religious art, ancient and modern. The representations of a "heavenly garden" as the eternal residence of the dead was found in Egyptian art and hieroglyphics, in Sumerian and Babylonian art and mythology, and in Buddhist and Taoist art and philosophy. For example, *Hsi Wang Mu nurtured and protected her *peaches of immortality in the gardens of the Taoist Paradise. In classical Greco-Roman art and mythology, the garden of the *Hesperides was home to the sacred *tree bearing the golden *apples while the paradisiac gardens of *Flora were blessed by Zephyr, the west wind. The garden was a symbol for disciplined and controlled nature as opposed to the unruliness and power of the wilderness in western religious art. As the opposite of the city, the garden was the primal sin-free condition of humanity. In Christian art, the garden abundant with *flowers and *fruits signified Paradise. In northern *medieval art, the motif of the *Madonna and Child in the Enclosed (Rose) Garden represented the belief that through *Mary's current action and the Child's future sacrifice, humanity would be able to return to the *Garden of Paradise. The *enclosed, or walled, garden (*hortus conclusus*) was a biblical metaphor (Song 4:12) for Mary's perpetual virginity, and was included in medieval and renaissance depictions of the *Annunciation, *Nativity, Madonna and Child, and in baroque presentations of the *Immaculate Conception and the *Assumption of the Virgin Mary.

Garden of Eden (Gn 2). Paradisiacal first home of humanity. A fertile place abundant with *fruits and *flowers, crystal-clear *waters and tamed *animals, the Garden of Eden was an idyllic place where no one went hungry, thirsty, loveless, or suffered illness or death. God the Father not only placed Adam and *Eve but the Tree of Knowledge and the *Tree of Life there. Eve, in her innocence, was beguiled by a *snake or *serpent to disobey God's single command not to eat of the fruit of the Tree of Knowledge. She then tempted Adam also to disobey God, and the result of their actions was that they became aware of their bodily nature, which they described as a state of nakedness. God learned of their disobedience when he found them covering themselves with *fig leaves. He cursed the snake (serpent) commanding that it should crawl on its belly for all eternity and be the enemy of humanity. Adam and Eve were expelled into the world where they and all their descendants would suffer death, where Adam and all men would have to labor, and Eve and all women would suffer pain at the birth of their *children. In Christian art, the Garden of Eden was depicted as a lush, lovely green place covered with beautiful flowers, trees, and bushes, and in which wild animals lay peacefully together. The Garden of Eden was included in depictions of the Creation of Adam, the Creation of Eve, the Marriage of Adam and Eve, the Temptation and the *Fall,

and the *Annunciation to the Virgin Mary. The iconography of Mary in the Rose Garden in northern medieval art was directly related to the medieval legend that in the Garden of Eden roses grew without thorns, for thorns like death and labor pains were the result of *Original Sin. The Garden of Eden prefigured *heaven and *paradise.

Garden, Enclosed. *See* Enclosed Garden.

Garden of the Hesperides. Holy garden of deities protected by the *Hesperides and the dragon, Ladon, in Greek mythology. These guardians were specifically charged with the custody of the tree bearing golden apples that *Gaea gave Zeus and *Hera as a wedding gift.

Garlic. An aphrodisiac. According to the Talmud, garlic aroused the passions and multiplied a man's production of semen. Therefore, a couple was advised to eat garlic prior to engaging in sexual intercourse to help insure the conception of a child, preferably a male child.

Gate. Symbol for multiple and ambiguous meanings as both exit and entrance. The gate into the *Garden of Eden as *Paradise was the same gate through which Adam and *Eve were expelled, and was an *attribute of *Mary as the symbolic gate of reentry into Paradise. The gate separated the damned from the saved in depictions of the Last Judgment, and the gate broken open signified the Descent into Hell (Harrowing of Hell). The closed gate denoted the perpetual virginity of Mary (Ez 44:1–3).

Gatumdu. Sumerian mother goddess of Lagas.

Gaurī. From the Sanskrit for "the white one." Beneficent and empathetic manifestation of the *mother goddess in Hindu art and mythology. Gaurī was the complement to *Kālī, thereby she was portrayed as a white goddess dressed in white garments in Hindu art.

Gazelle. Animal symbol for a goddess, especially those related to the hunt like *Artemis (*Diana). It was also the sacred animal of *Anukis, the goddess of the Nile cataracts. In western Christian art, the gazelle's acute vision symbolized penetrating spiritual insight. The gazelle's natural speed, which allowed it to escape its predators, represented Christians fleeing from earthly passion.

Gefjon. From the German for "to give." Indigenous German goddess of fertility, prosperity, and good fortune. Although eventually associated with *Freyja, Gefjon was identified by her *attribute, the plow.

Gender. Those modes of behavior, cultural attitudes, and manners into which one is socialized as either a man or a woman and which thereby define one as being simultaneously a member of and either male or female within that culture. Gender is distinguished from sex, which is the physical identification of a man or a woman according to the appropriate body parts.

Geneviève, Saint (c. 420–500). Renowned for her charitable works, mystical visions, and prayer. Devout from childhood, she became a *nun at fifteen due in part to the efforts of Germanus, bishop of Auxerre. According to pious legend, her mother, distraught at her daughter's decision to become a "bride of Christ," slapped her, and was blinded. Geneviève restored her mother's sight as a sign of her faith and as an omen of her gift to light her candle without fire or flint, and despite the interference of the Devil. Geneviève alleviated the starvation of Paris when she led wagonloads of food through the Frankish blockade. Eventually she persuaded King Clovis to release the prisoners of war. Her prayers saved Paris from an attack by Attila the Hun in 451. At another time, she prayed for assistance to find the lime necessary to build a church dedicated to the care and protection of the remains of Denis. The patron of Paris, Geneviève miraculously intervened against the plague and several invasions of the city. In western Christian art, she was depicted as a young woman dressed either as a shepherdess or as a *nun with the *keys to the city of Paris either in her *hand or attached to her *belt.

Genii (plural of genius). Ancient protective spirits who guided human beings in moral activities. Genii were represented as naked winged youths in Etruscan and Roman art, and as clothed winged male and female figures in seventeenth-century western art. These same genii were characterized as hybrid figures with the bodies of human beings and the heads of *birds in Asian art.

Genre. Depictions of scenes from daily life. Typically associated with the development of seventeenth-century Dutch art, genre scenes represented the activities of average persons engaged in everyday situations. Occasionally, such works contained an implicit religious subject or taught a moral lesson.

Gentileschi, Artemisia (1593–1652/3). Significant Caravaggesque painter and a woman of formidable personality. The daughter of the painter, Orazio Gentileschi, Artemisia received her initial training as an artist in his studio. As famed for her artistic skills as for her bravado in confronting her former teacher, Agostini Tassi, on the charge of rape, she lived a life of independence and artistic vocation rare for her time. Artemisia was the first woman artist to select women as the subject matter for her paintings in which she depicted strong, powerful heroines. Her renditions of the stories of the scriptural heroine, *Judith, were renowned for their brutality and for her ability to render technically the fierce intensity within the style of *baroque painting. She painted secular as well as religious subjects, but her development of a female perspective transformed the iconography of such scriptural figures as Judith, *Susanna, and *Mary Magdalene.

Gerd. Scandinavian giantess of great beauty with whom Freyr fell in love with, wooed, and eventually married.

Gertrude, Saint (d. 659). *Abbess, foundress of hospices, and patron of travelers. Renowned for her works of Christian charity, Gertrude was reported to have died at the age of thirty as abbess of the convent at Nivelles. According to pious legend, she cared for Christian souls during the first night of their three-day journey to heaven. A mature woman garbed as an abbess, Gertrude was identified in western Christian art by her role as protector of mice and rats that surrounded her, ran around her *distaff as she spun, or gathered around her pastoral *staff.

Gertrude the Great (1256–1302). Christian visionary and mystical writer. Entrusted into the care of the Benedictine nuns of Helfta as a five-year-old child, Gertrude had her first vision of Christ when she was twenty-five. Although originally committed to a life of the mind she turned her attention from her studies of Latin and philosophy towards the writing of mystical texts, including those of her friend, Mechtild of Hackeborn. Gertrude carefully studied the writings of *Augustine, Gregory, and Bernard of Clairvaux. She became the author of a series of influential books such as *Exercitia spiritualia septem* (*Seven Spiritual Exercises*) and the *Legatio divinae pietatis* (*Study of Divine Compassion*), and recorded the visions of Mechtild in the *Liber specialis gratiae* (*Book of Extraordinary Grace*). Gertrude and Mechtild collaborated on a collection of devotional prayers that helped them establish the cult of the adoration of the Sacred Heart. Patron of the West Indies, Gertrude the Great was a rare topic in western Christian art but when represented she was characterized as a mature woman dressed in the habit of her order who held a *book and a *quill as *attributes of her authorship. Her significance to the development of the iconography of women in Christian art was due to the widespread influence of her mystical texts, including the visions of Mechtild.

Geštinana. From the Sumerian for "old woman, interpreter of dreams."

Gestinanna. From the Sumerian for "vine of heaven." Mesopotamian goddess of the netherworld. According to tradition, Dumuzi, the brother of Gestinanna and the husband of *Inanna, substituted himself for his wife in prison in the netherworld. When the irate Pallas sought Dumuzi, his sister would not reveal her brother's hiding place and sent the irate Pallas off on a wild goose chase. The variant to this episode reported that despite torture, Gestinanna would not reveal her brother's secret location. When he was discovered by demons, his sister sang a death lament. As the traditional explanation of the cycle of the seasons, Gestinanna and Dumuzi resided during alternate six-month periods in the netherworld. During her six-month stay, Gestinanna was the scribe, or secretary, to *Ereshkigal.

Gilitine. From the Lithuanian for "to sting, to harm." Lithuanian goddess of death. Gilitine was depicted as tall and slender female figure clad in white for her visits to the houses of the sick whom she reportedly strangled or suffocated.

Giotto (1266/7–1337). The acknowledged founder of modern painting and an innovator infusing human emotions into western Christian art. A Florentine by birth, Giotto trained under Cimabue from whom he learned the traditional manner of painting, perception of form, and *iconography. In his great *frescoes at the Scrovegni Chapel in Padua and the Basilica of San Francesco in Assisi, he broke with the Italo-Byzantine tradition and instilled solidity and naturalism to his figures, and spatial perceptive. Using nature as his foundation, Giotto turned his attention to a careful rendering of shapes and forms, and naturalistic background. In keeping with this emphasis on naturalism, Giotto also instilled his human figures with the expression of human emotions and passions through gestures, facial expressions, and body postures. In his narrative cycles of the life of *Mary and Jesus Christ for the Scrovegni Chapel, Giotto emphasized the humanity of their experiences, from the touching gestures of the *Anne and Joachim at the Golden Gate to the tortured, sorrowing *angels of the *Lamentation. His interpretation of the Last Judgment based on his conversations with his friend, the poet *Dante, transformed the iconography of this theme, specifically in terms of the illustration of the *Devil as a motionless *blue monster trapped in ice and of the torments of *Hell. In his frescoes for the Basilica of San Francesco in Assisi, Giotto imbued the visual image with the humanity and spirituality of *Francis of Assisi, as witnessed by his representations of *Mary Magdalene for the Magdalene Chapel in the lower church.

Giraffe. A strange-looking and rare creature, and a popular *animal in *renaissance art. Included in the *Nativity and the *Adoration of the Magi, the giraffe had no specific symbolic referent in Christian art.

Girdle. Worn over one's clothing as an item of protection, ornamentation, and purse in the classical Greco-Roman world. Young girls received an ornamental girdle from their parents at puberty as a symbol of their womanhood and their chastity. This girdle was replaced at marriage with one given by her husband as a sign of marital fidelity; thereby it was an *attribute of *Hera (*Juno). The girdle of *Aphrodite (*Venus), however, endowed the wearer with sexual energy and power. In Christian art, the girdle signified obedience and chastity (Lk 12:35 DR; Eph 6:14). A

38. Fede Galizia, *Judith with the Head of Holofernes*
39. Artemisia Gentileschi, *Susanna and the Elders*

40. Giotto di Bondone, *The Meeting of Joachim and Anne at the Golden Gate*

girdle of cords represented Jesus at the Flagellation. In the *Old Testament, prophets wore leather girdles as a sign of their humility and contempt for the world, while the monastic girdle symbolized the vows of poverty, chastity, and obedience. In byzantine and baroque depictions of the *Assumption of the Virgin Mary, she dropped her girdle on the *head of Thomas, who doubted her death and assumption.

Girdle of Venus. According to classical Roman tradition, the Girdle of Venus endowed its wearer, whether a mortal or immortal woman, with heightened sexual appeal and commensurately with extraordinary sexual energy.

Glass. Symbol with multiple meanings including purity and the *Incarnation. In its clarity and transparency, glass signified the purity of *Mary, and was included in representations of the *Annunciation and the *Immaculate Conception. Glass also typified the Virgin Birth, following the medieval understanding that just as light penetrated glass but did not shatter it, so *Mary conceived and bore Jesus but her virginity was not impaired.

Glispa. According to Navajo tradition, Glispa visited the otherworld and learned the great chants of her tribe. Following her return to this world, she taught these chants to her brother and later bequeathed them to the tribe. She was invoked during the chants of the cultural ritual that accompanied the creation of sand paintings.

Globe. A symbol for the *earth, and thus of terrestrial power and sovereignty. The globe was an *attribute of God the Father, Christ as King, and monarch saints such as Louis of France and Charlemagne in eastern and western Christian art. A globe surmounted by a *cross represented the universal Triumph of Christianity. It was also the emblem of *Abundance, *Fortune, *Justice, *Lachesis, and *Philosophy in classical Greco-Roman, *medieval, and *renaissance western art.

Glory. From the Latin for "splendor." A luminous glow surrounding the head and the body of either God the Father or Jesus Christ in Christian art. The emission of light around the entire body was a sign of the most elevated divine state. The glory was bright *white or soft *gold or *yellow in *color. The glory was to be distinguished from an *aureole, which only surrounded the body and was *blue, rainbow-hued, gold, or white in color, and from the *nimbus or *halo, which only encircled the head.

Gnosticism. From the Greek for "secret knowledge." Late Antique sect that advocated the imperfection of the material and sought to return the pure spirit to Light. For the Gnostics, the self was defined as a spark of light that could only be released from the material darkness by gnosis, that is, the secret knowledge dispensed by a savior. Various strains of Gnosticism survived well into the Christian world even unto the formation of Christian Gnosticism in which the salvific female figure known as *Sophia played a critical role. For some Christian Gnostics, Sophia was the world soul, while for others she was a *Great Mother figure. Within the context of Gnostic literature, she was a full-fledged cosmic parent who created the universe and its laws, and was a ruler of Nature, Fate, Time, Eternity, Truth, Wisdom, Justice, Love, Birth, and Death. She was characterized as a deity who infused all creation with the vital blood of life. Further the regular presence of female imagery in the sect and the possibility that several of the anonymous authors of Gnostic texts might be women indicate the major roles for women in this variant form of Christianity. The Church Fathers were offended further by this gnostic propensity to admit women into ecclesiastical positions and rank. Strains of Gnostic Christianity survived into the medieval world, one that advocated that true revelation could only be made available through a woman, and another that fused into the cathari heresy later identified as Albigensianism. Christian Gnosticism was influential upon the development and later the medieval transformations of the *iconography of women in Christian art. *See also Gospel of Mary*, Pistis Sophia, Sophia.

Goat. Embodiment of fertility, especially as male sexuality, and a common sacrificial animal of the classical Mediterranean cultures. As an ancient Egyptian symbol of fertility, thereby of procreation, the goat was a significant amulet for barren women. The goat signified *Hera, *Juno, *Amalthea, and *Aphrodite in classical Greco-Roman and *renaissance art.

Goblet. An *attribute of several *saints including Donatus and Benedict of Nursia, who each miraculously restored a smashed communion *cup, in Christian art. A goblet with a *serpent was an attribute of John the Evangelist and Benedict of Nursia.

Goddess. From the Sanskrit for "the called-upon" gatha. Female deity or divinity. According to popular legend and tradition, magic and power resided within the body of a goddess, and she was thereby capable of transforming the world even unto the great mystery of creation and birth of a child. *See also* Great Goddess.

Goddesses. The female personifications of the mythological figures of classical cultures, especially of Egypt, Greece, and Rome. The presentations of these goddesses in human forms in literature and art influenced the development of Christian art and legend. The positive attributes or characteristics of these goddesses, particularly of the most powerful ones, were assimilated into the iconographies of the indigenous religious traditions and later transferred to succeeding religious traditions, for example, classical Greek and Roman into Christian.

Gohei. Ritual object signifying separation and power. A gohei was composed of strips of paper or metal suspended from a frame, and located in Shinto temples. Ostensibly the gohei attracted the attention of the deities who responded to the offerings and petitions on the strips of paper, or who granted rain in a time of drought. According to tradition, the gohei was among the sacred objects that lured *Amaterasu Omikami from her cave refuge.

Gold (as a color). A color signifying solar deities, wealth, power, divine energy, and light in religious art.

Gold (as an element). An element signifying precious offering, divinity, monarchy, and the ambiguity of material wealth. Gold was the divine metal, thereby gift, of the sun god and its immutability symbolized survival after death in ancient Egypt. It was the gift offered to the newborn Christ Child as a sign of kingship by Caspar, one of the Magi. Liturgical vessels and vesture, religious objects, and religious art have been encrusted with or formed from gold as a sign of offering only the best and most precious to God. The *Old Testament story of the Golden Calf indicated wealth and power gone astray and offered not to God but to an idol.

Golden Calf. *See* Calf, Golden.

Golden Legend. A thirteenth-century compilation of legends, lore, verses from scripture, and Christian theology about the saints arranged according to the Church Year by *Jacobus de Voragine (1230–1298), a Dominican friar and confessor to a *Dominican convent. According to tradition, he prepared this text as appropriate readings for the Dominican *nuns. *The Golden Legend* was an influential sourcebook for Christian *iconography.

Goldfinch. A *bird that fed on *thorns and thistles, thereby symbolizing the Passion. When held by the Christ Child, the goldfinch signified that this *child was born to die and had foreknowledge of his sacrificial death. If held by *Mary, whether or not her son was present, the goldfinch denoted her foreknowledge of this sorrowful event. According to medieval legend, the goldfinch was characterized as a "savior" because of its connection to the Passion, and thereby became an amulet against the plague.

Gomer (Hos 1:3). From the Hebrew for "ember." Unfaithful wife of the prophet Hosea. The daughter of Diblaim, Gomer was the beloved but unfaithful wife of Hosea who named their three children with terms of bitter rejection. Although her infidelities and immoralities, led the prophet to divorce Gomer, they were reunited. The marriage of Gomer and Hosea, colored by her infidelities and his forgiveness, symbolized the relationship between God and Israel. A rare topic in western Christian art, Gomer was included in the narrative cycles of the lives of the prophets as a beautiful woman of loose moral character as signified by her elegant upswept hairstyle and her provocative clothes.

Goose. This avian symbol for intelligence, knowledge, and marital bliss was popular throughout the religious art of Asia. In ancient Egypt, the goose was identified by its epithet, "the great cackler," which was responsible for the egg of the creation myth. The goose was a classical Greco-Roman sign of providence and vigilance, thereby a guardian of the city. The goose was sacred to *Hera and *Juno as an emblem of feminine fertility and fecundity in marriage. In western Christian art, the goose was an *attribute of *Werburga. In *medieval art, a gaggle of geese listening to a *fox was a metaphor for innocent Christians confused by false preachers.

Gopīs. Herdswomen among whom the youthful Hindu god Krishna lived. As part of their daily rituals, the gopīs left their husbands, children, and homes to flirt with Krishna on the banks of the Yamunā River. They were characterized as participants in a sacred circular dance

41. *Cycladic Idol*

42. *Etruscan Mother Goddess (Mater Matuta)*

43. *Three Goddesses from East Pediment of the Parthenon:*
Hestia, Dione, and Aphrodite or *Hestia, Thalassa, and Gaea*

in which each gopī held Krishna's hand (*Vishnu Purāna* 5:13). According to the *Bhāgavata Purāna,* the young god mutilated himself so that he could dance between each pair of gopīs. As female embodiments of fertility, the gopīs, who participated in the idyllic dance with Krishna, signified the ideal relationship between the deity and his devotees. One of the most famous gopīs was Rādha, who, although she was the wife of Ayanaghosa, symbolized the female principle necessary for divine duality. The love story of Rādha and Krishna was related in the *Gitāgovinda.* In Tantric Buddhism, Rādha embodied the infinite love that constituted the essence of Krishna.

Gorgons, Three. Legendary maidens transformed into terrifying monsters in Greek art and mythology. These three daughters of Phorcys and Ceto were named Euryale, Sthenno, and *Medusa. Characterized as ghastly monsters with *snakes in their hair and wrapped around their waists, wings, talons for hands and feet, and huge teeth, the gorgons resided in the western ocean. The sight of any one of them was so horrific that mortals were instantly turned into stone. Although immortality was granted to two of the gorgons, the third being the mortal *Medusa, they signified the awful aspects of the numinous. In classical Greek and *renaissance art, the gorgons were characterized as winged female figures who had claws for hands and feet, and reptilian tresses on their heads.

Gorgoneion. Severed head of *Medusa. The Gorgoneion was a grotesque and horrifying image of Medusa with a frothing open mouth and extended tongue, and dishelved reptilian hair. This emblem of terrifying divine powers was placed on the shield of *Athena.

Gospel. From an Anglo-Saxon compound word for "good news." The collection of texts by the four evangelists, which narrated the events in the life of Jesus Christ. Understood to be "glad tidings" or the "good news," these accounts were the scriptural foundation of all forms of Christianity. The first four books of the *New Testament—Matthew, Mark, Luke, and John—were characterized as both divinely inspired and as eyewitness narrations of events and teachings of Jesus Christ. In Christian art, the gospel was denoted by a large *book on the cover of which was incised the tetramorphs (signs of the four evangelists) or an image of Christ.

Gospel of Mary (second or third century). Gnostic text emphasizing the role of *Mary Magdalene. The *Gospel of Mary* exists in a fifth-century Egyptian version of the Greek original. In the first part of the text, there are fragments of conversations between the Risen Christ and his disciples, including his positions on the relationship between matter and sin, and the preaching of the *Gospel to heathens. The second part of the *Gospel of Mary* significantly negated a traditional antifeminist posture as Mary Magdalene intervened and comforted the disciples who begged her to reveal the secrets of redemption that the Risen Christ had confided to her. In an extraordinary exchange between the Magdalene and Peter, Levi defended her role as a disciple and rebuked Peter.

Gothic art. From the architectural style of the twelfth to the sixteenth centuries, the great age of cathedral building, a style of visual art predicated upon verticality, spaciousness, and a fascination with light. The elegant figures of Gothic art were characterized by the S-shaped curve of their bodies, which gave a sense of elegance, movement, and grace. This was the idealized art style of the medieval synthesis as evidenced in *altarpieces, tapestries, cathedral carvings, sculptures, and manuscript *illuminations.

Gourds. A vegetable symbol with multiple meanings, including brevity and frailty of life, *pilgrimage, and resurrection in religious art. As the sign of *pilgrims and pilgrimage, dried and hollowed-out gourds were used as drinking flasks for *water. The formation of two gourds, one placed on top of the other, or the *hu-lu*, "double gourd," of ancient Chinese art and mythology signified good omens, and the union of heaven and earth, and of *yin and yang. Gourds used as water bottles were an *attribute of several Christian pilgrims including James Major, the two disciples with the Risen Christ on the Road to Emmaus, and the Archangel Raphael. Gourds also signified the Resurrection as Jonah refreshed and renewed himself under an arbor of gourds after having been spewn out of the great *whale. In the *hand of the Christ Child, or in *Mary's hand as she held her son on her lap, the gourd denoted the Resurrection. When placed near each other in a work of western Christian art, the gourd canceled out the evil and death signified by an *apple. In western Christian art, the gourd resembled in shape and *color the cucumber.

Graces. From the Latin for "grace, charm." Three Roman goddesses embodying feminine beauty, charm, and joie de vivre. As the attendants of *Venus (*Aphrodite), they were known as Aglaia, Euphrosyne, and Thalia. Identified with the Greek *Charites, the three Graces were portrayed in classical Greco-Roman and *renaissance art as the idealizations of feminine beauty in their faces, bodies, and actions. They were depicted as beautiful young maidens either naked or garbed in long flowing garments covered with a floral motif. The Graces were adorned with floral *wreaths and garlands.

Graeae. From the Greek for "the gray ones." These three elder daughters of Phrocys and Ceto were the guardians of their younger sisters, the *Gorgons. Identified as Pemphredo, Enyo, and Dino, the Graeae were reportedly born with gray hair and acted as old women from the moment of birth. They shared one eye and one tooth, which legend claimed they rotated. The Graeae were characterized as three aged and ugly hags with long gray hair and wearing gray garments in classical *Greek and *renaissance art.

Grail, The Holy. The legendary *chalice used by Jesus at the Last Supper. According to the apocryphal *Gospel of Nicodemus*, Joseph of Arimathea preserved both the grail and several drops of the precious *blood that fell from the crucified *body. He brought them to England, ostensibly to Glastonbury, and buried them in a soon-to-be forgotten site. The quest for the Holy Grail became the focus of many medieval—especially English legends—including the Arthurian tales of the Knights of the

Round Table. It was believed that if any impure person approached the Holy Grail, it would disappear; therefore only the purest of Christian *knights could retrieve it. The honor of England depended upon the safe recovery and continued preservation of the Holy Grail. The theme of the "quest for the Holy Grail" or the pure knight with the Holy Grail was popular in the decorative motifs of medieval cathedral carvings.

Grain. A sign for *bread, and thereby human sustenance. In Christian art, grain signified the humanity of Jesus Christ (Jn 12:24). Representations of ears of grain and bunches of *grapes represented the bread and wine of the Eucharist.

Grammar. Female personification of one of the *Seven Liberal Arts. Grammar was represented as a female figure dressed as a sage or teacher who held a whip as a sign of discipline.

Grapes. Fruit symbol with multiple meanings in Christian art, including the *blood of Jesus, the Eucharist, or Jesus Christ as the "true vine" from the *parable of the laborers in the vineyards. In the *hands of the Christ Child, or of *Mary as she held him, the reference was to both his future sacrificial death and the sacrament of the Eucharist. In *medieval art, the depiction of two men laboring with their burden of enormous bunches of grapes was very popular as a sign of the Promised Land (Nm 13:23).

Grapevine. Symbol of abundant life. In the *Old Testament, the grapevine was a sacred plant signifying Israel and the Messiah; while in the *New Testament,

it represented Jesus Christ as the "true vine."

Grasshopper. A general identification for crickets and locusts. The grasshopper was a sign of happiness in the Egyptian *Book of the Dead, but also was depicted as an enemy of *Maat as the goddess of cosmic law and order in Egyptian art. In the *Old Testament, grasshoppers were one of the plagues God sent to Egypt when Pharaoh continued to deny the *Hebrews freedom to leave (Ex 10:14). According to legend, John the Baptist fed on grasshoppers during his time in the wilderness. In the *hands of the Christ Child, the grasshopper denoted the evangelization of the pagan nations in western Christian art.

Gray. The color of ashes, mourning, and humility. In western Christian art, Jesus was often dressed in gray garments as a sign of his humility, and in relation to the Passion it typified his eminent death. The Vallombrosian Order of the *Benedictines wore gray *habits.

Great Goddess. Worldwide concept of the female cosmic maker who created the universe with laws, was ruler of nature, guardian of truth and justice, giver of life and death, and protector of love and wisdom. The Great Goddess was the main participant in the formation or creation of the universe among many preliterate and/or archaic cultures. The evolution of the Great Goddess into the goddesses, *heroines, and prophetesses of world religions followed the structure of a primeval Great Goddess in the form of a *hermaphrodite who impregnated herself to the eventual division into a god and goddess with the latter becoming the Triple Goddess of mother, sister-wife, and daughter who becomes the Virgin Mother renewed monthly by the lunar cycles and whose central characteristics were fertility, the sky, and the moon, and ultimately devolved into the multiple goddesses, heroines, and prophetesses whose manifestations in world mythologies, sacred scriptures, and religious art represented the energies of the Great Goddess. *See also* Primordial goddess, religions; Primordial goddess, symbolism.

Great Mother. Worldwide concept of female powers of fertility, fecundity, and birth common among many religious and cultural traditions.

Greco, El (Domenikos Theotocopoulos) (1541–1614). A leading painter of the Spanish baroque style, originally trained in the byzantine iconic tradition on his native Crete. El Greco traveled to Venice to study the late renaissance master, Titian, and went to Rome in 1566, where he studied *Mannerism. His personalized ecstatic and passionate style of painting was a fusion of these three artistic traditions—byzantine icons, Venetian renaissance, and Mannerism. He relocated to Spain in 1572, where he was influenced by the *Counter-Reformation, in particular the spirituality and immediacy of religious experience advocated by both *Ignatius of Loyola and *John of the Cross. El Greco created a style of western Christian art that advocated the Tridentine position. His elongation of the human figure combined with the contortions of perspective and space to create an aura of nervous tension in his paintings. His use of color was a study in sharp contrasts and heightened the emotional intensity of his work. His extraordinary ability to represent air, especially in the billowing drapery of his garments, permitted a spiritual sensuality to permeate his work. In his paintings, El Greco transformed mystical experience into spiritual catharsis. His floating, elongated, pinhead figures closely resembled the shapes of *candle *flames, and signified a conflation of both the byzantine tradition of divinization and Spanish mysticism, creating a vision of spiritual energy and ecstasy.

Greek art. Complex and delicate art forms created by the indigenous peoples of the Aegean basin, later identified as Greece, over a span of more than two thousand years. Although stylistic distinctions existed between the varied eras of classical Greece from the Aegean, Minoan, and Mycenaean civilizations to the geometric, archaic, and classical periods, there are identifiable characteristics to the more generic category of classical Greek art including the confirmation of the human figure as a visualization of the divine, idealization, graceful beauty, elegant proportion, linear perspective, expression of human emotions, abstract harmony of forms, and respect for the individual. The tenets and styles of classical Greek art were assimilated into western European art, especially in Christian iconography and *renaissance art.

Greek religion. Indigenous belief system of the Aegean basin, later identified as Greece. This idiosyncratic and flexible organization of local and national ceremonies, rituals, festivals, and myths characterized classical Greek religion. As with other religious traditions, classical Greek religion integrated the local with the national, the individual with the communal, the sacred with the secular, and defied rational definition. Among the common identifiable characteristics of classical Greek religion were the Olympian gods and goddesses; the *oracles, especially at Delphi; the essential religious ritual of animal sacrifice; the sacred sanctuaries; the stories of the heroes; and the spirituality of the polis (the city state). The legacy of classical Greek religion shaped the cultural and philosophic attitudes of "the west," that is, Europe and North America.

Green. A symbol of fertility, regeneration, and hope. The color of spring vegetation, green represented the restoration of nature's bounty over the barrenness of winter. In Egyptian art and culture, green signified plant life and the resurrection of Osiris. As a fusion of the two primary colors, *yellow and *blue, green denoted the regeneration of the *soul brought about through acts of *charity in Christian art. As the signs of victory over death, especially of a martyr's death, the *palm branch and the *laurel wreath were composed of evergreen leaves. Green was the color worn during pagan rites of initiation, and was associated in classical Greco-Roman culture with *water. In Christian art, John the Baptist wore a green mantle over his hair shirt to indicate the Christian ritual of *baptism as a spiritual initiation and the promise of new life through the Resurrection.

Grey. *See* Gray.

Griffin. A mythical beast with a crested head, wings, and feet of an eagle, and the body of a lion that originated in Syrian art in the second century B.C.E.

As a human-bodied figure with a bird's head and wings, the griffin was both the sign of a demon and in representations of the Seven Sages of Babylon as a guardian of homes and palaces. In Egyptian art, the griffin was interpreted as a leonine manifestation of Pharaoh and the falcon form of Horus, thereby a sign of the victorious ruler. It also came to signify the mightiest of animals and the retribution of Justice. The classical Greek version of the griffin included large donkeylike eyes, a beak with an extended curling tongue, and spiraling curls like a mane. An ambiguous emblem for vengeance and retribution, or for vigilance and strength, the griffin was an *attribute of *Athena (*Minerva) and *Nemesis in classical Greco-Roman and *renaissance art. A popular motif in western *medieval art, the griffin signified heroes and great knights renowned for their valor and magnanimity. Nemesis's chariot was drawn by griffins. Reputed to walk on four *feet, it was identified as an unclean animal (Lv 11:20–23) and came to typify the *Devil or the Antichrist. The griffin, paradoxically, also denoted Jesus Christ in Christian art and in the writings of *Dante.

Griselda. Female personification of appropriate wifely devotion, humility, and obedience in western Christian art. According to legend, this "ideal" woman accepted marriage to a man of higher social status and silently withstood all his forms of emotional, physical, and/ or sexual abuse. A model of Christian virtues, especially patience, Griselda's endurance of all her sufferings resulted in her husband's conversion both to Christianity and to a loving partner.

Grünewald, Mathias (c. 1470/80–1528). A sixteenth-century German artist about whom little biographical information was known. His masterpiece, *The Isenheim Altarpiece*, was well known to students of western Christian art. Grünewald employed a complex iconographic scheme for this *polyptych, which integrated medieval legend and symbolism with a recognition of renaissance perspective and presentation of spatial relationships. His use of exaggerated gestures and bodily forms heightened the emotional impact of his paintings.

Gryphon. *See* Griffin.

Guda (twelfth century). Medieval woman artist. Ostensibly a *nun, Guda was renowned for her excellent illuminations of liturgical books. Although little, if nothing, is known of her life, her existence and personal pride in her art was evident by her signature on her illuminations. In her most famed illumination, Guda included her self-portrait and clung to an initial in a homeliary.

Guinevere. From the German Cunneware for "female wisdom" and the Welsh Gwenhwyfar for "the first lady of these islands" identified as a Triple Goddess. Legendary wife of King Arthur and beloved of Lancelot. According to tradition, Guinevere was the female embodiment of Britain, and thereby the necessary companion to anyone who would rule Britain. He who lost Guinevere lost his crown. This tale of beauty and abduction leading to betrayal, war, and disaster was a medieval Christian cognate of the classical Greek legend of *Helen of Troy. A popular topic in medieval and nineteenth-century art, Guinevere was represented as a beautiful and youthful queen often within the narrative episodes of the Arthurian Legends. *See also* Holy Grail.

Gula. From the Sumerian for "the great one." Mesopotamian goddess of healing and patron of physicians. Gula was represented as a physically powerful matron with both hands raised and enthroned between *dogs, which were her *attribute.

Gullveig. From the Norse for "gold branch." One of the *Vanir in Norse mythology. A sorcerer and a giant, Gullveig was speared and tortured with fire by Aesir. Gullveig was also identified with the *völva*, or *sibyl, for whom the epic *Völuspa* was named.

Gul-šeš. From the Hittite for "scribes" or "[female] determinators of fate." Hittite goddess of fate. Corresponding to the *Moirai, Gul-šeš dispensed good and evil, and life and death.

H

⚜

Habit. The distinctive garb worn by religious orders of *nuns and monks. Each order was identified by their particular style of garment with the basic variations being in *colors and cloth. The basic items of the nun's habit consisted of a tunic, *girdle, *wimple, and the *veil.

Hadewijch (thirteenth century). Flemish *Beguine. Hadewijch was known only by her writings—poetry, letters, and reports of her visions—which reflected her life of Christian prayer, good works, and love. Although herself not a topic in western Christian art, she influenced artistic and religious attitudes towards the iconography of women.

Hag. From the Egyptian language for "the matriarchal ruler who knew the words of power." Female embodiment of the wisdom that accompanied age and death. The hag was a prevalent image in religious art. She was transformed from the Egyptian image of the wise woman to the Greco-Roman *Hecate and the Scandinavian Hag of the Iron Wood. By the Renaissance, the status of the hag had been demeaned to that of

a *harpy. In her role as wise woman or a goddess of death, the hag was depicted as a matronly figure whose face was veiled to signify the unrevealed mystery of each individual death. Whereas in her lesser and demeaned form, she was depicted as a supernaturally ugly and withered witchlike figure.

Hagar (Gn 16:1–15; 21:8–21). The Egyptian maidservant given to Abraham by his barren wife *Sarah as was the custom of the time. Abraham fathered Hagar's son who was called Ishmael. Following the birth of Sarah's own son, Isaac, much jealousy arose between the two women. Eventually Sarah forced her husband to expel the maidservant and her son with only minimal *bread and *water into the *desert. Miraculously, Hagar and Ishmael survived as God intervened by sending an *angel with water. Ishmael was identified as the father of the Arab nations. In western Christian art, the topos of the Expulsion of Hagar and Ishmael was interpreted as a foretype of the Cleansing of the Temple.

Hainuwele. Divine maiden responsible for human mortality in the mythology of the Moluccan peoples. Hainuwele arose from a coconut and was slain by men during the primeval period. Her dismembered parts were buried throughout Polynesia and from them grew up the first *fruits of the *earth. As a result of their guilt in the untimely death of this innocent maiden, human beings were condemned to mortality.

Hair. Symbol of energy and power premised upon its connections to the hair that covered the bodies of *animals as both protection and decoration. Among the ancient Egyptians, hair signified the receptacle of physical, if not secret, power. *Isis cut off a lock of her hair as an emblem of her mourning for the death of Osiris. The symbolic gesture for mourning became the "sacrifice" of three locks of hair. The Egyptian hieroglyph for "child" was the image of a lock of hair. In classical Mediterranean culture, young unmarried women wore their hair loose and flowing, respectable matrons covered their hair with *veils and mantles, and prostitutes piled their hair upon their *heads. Samson's strength was directly related to his unshorn hair. Loose, flowing hair became associated with penitence as the woman who anointed the *feet of Jesus during the *Feast in the House of Simon used her long hair to wipe his feet with her tears. This woman became identified with *Mary Magdalene, one of whose *attributes was her long, flowing hair that denoted spiritual regeneration. The male and female hermit *saints were characterized by their long, flowing hair that covered their bodies and protected them. The sacrifice of hair—a sign of devotion and allegiance or penance—was the basis of the tonsure of *nuns and women religious.

Halo. From the Latin for "cloud." A circle of light surrounding the *head of a divine or sacred person. An *attribute of sanctity, the shape of the halo was its distinguishing characteristic. The triangular halo was reserved for God the Father, and the cruciform halo for the Resurrected Christ. Square haloes identified persons who were alive when a work of art was made, circular haloes were reserved for *Mary, *saints, and *angels, and hexagonal haloes for allegorical or legendary persons. In Christian art, the halo was initially employed to denote the *Trinity and angels; however, by the byzantine and throughout the medieval period, use of the halo spread to Christ, Mary, and the saints. The growing renaissance interest in the human resulted in the diminished use of the halo. *See also* Aureole, Glory, and Nimbus.

Hamadryad. Wood nymphs of Greek mythology. According to legend, each hamadryad partook of the joys and sorrows of her *tree. She began and ended her existence with the life of her tree. Characterized as the "spirit of the tree," the hamadryads were represented in classical Greco-Roman and *renaissance art as the feminine figures within a tree or by the feminine anthropomorphization of a tree, for example, with a feminine face or torso inscribed on the tree's trunk.

Hammer. An Instrument of the Passion and a symbol of the Crucifixion. A hammer with nails was an attribute of *Helena who according to legend directed the excavations of the True Cross.

Hand. A symbol for creativity, judgment, anger, power, and affection. An open raised right hand was a sign of salutation and of blessing. The clasping of hands signified the solemnity of a vow, such as betrothal, marriage, or friendship. Among the ancient Egyptians, the hand connoted creative power. According to the creation myth of the Heliopolitan cosmogony, the first creatures—Shu and Tefnut—arose from the semen that the primeval god produced by his own hand, thereby the feminine element in this original creation was the so-called wife of Amun, or the hand of the god. In Mesopotamia, a hand denoted control or seizure, and was a dispenser of disease. Amulets in the shape of a hand were sacred protections against psychological and emotional illnesses. The most ancient and common symbol for God the Father was a right hand issuing from *clouds, perhaps holding thunderbolts or rays of light in Christian art. Hand gestures were an important form of communication in both the visual arts and drama, as well as in everyday life. In Christian art, a raised right hand with the palm extended connoted the act of blessing, an open palm reaching outward to a person friendship or assistance. Hands clasped between a man and a woman implied intimacy and affection. An upright open hand with either three fingers raised or the thumb and first two fingers raised typified the Trinity. The Betrayal by Judas was denoted by pouring *coins from one hand into another. The washing of hands suggested cleanliness, ritual purification, and the act of Pontius Pilate who "cleansed" himself from responsibility in the Crucifixion of Jesus.

Hand-of-Fatima. From the Arabic for "five" and the name Fatima. Artistic representation of a human hand, most often as a piece of jewelry. The Hand-of-Fatima was an amulet defense against the evil eye, and was especially popular in North Africa. This image was associated, albeit ahistorically, to *Fatima, the daughter of the prophet Muhammad.

Hand-of-Ishtar. From the Sumerian, Qāt Ištar, for "hand of Ishtar." Amulet of the goddess's hand as a protection against psychological or spiritual illness. Archaeological discoveries in Mesopotamia and Babylonia revealed the prevalence of these clay images or decorative wall motifs of a clenched first as a magical emblem against evil or disease entering a room or building.

Hannah (I Sm 1:1–28). *Old Testament foretype of *Anne, especially her miraculous conception of *Mary following years of barrenness. Beloved wife of Elkanah, Hannah was barren until past the normal age of childbearing. Following her solemn vow of dedication of her son to God, she miraculously conceived at the sanctuary of Shiloh while deep in prayer. Hannah gave birth to the prophet Samuel. An Old Testament prophetess, Hannah was among the matriarchs of Israel and female exemplar of prayer. In western Christian art, she was portrayed as an old woman—with a matronly figure and gray hair—in the posture of devout prayer, or with her newborn son.

Hannahanna. From the Hittite for "grandmother." Hannahanna was the Hittite mother goddess and protector of birth. In ancient Near Eastern art, she was portrayed as a matron identified both by her *attribute of the *bee and by her act of searching for a vanished god.

Hanwašuit. Tutelary goddess of Hittite monarchy and the throne. Hanwašuit gave each Hittite monarch a mandate upon ascension to the throne. In ancient Near Eastern art, she was characterized as a physically powerful female figure who either held a throne, wore a crown surmounted by a throne, or wore a garment with the decorative motif of the throne.

Har. Manifestation of *Ishtar. As the *Great Goddess Har, Ishtar was the protector and patron of those among her priestesses identified as the *harines* or temple prostitutes. As part of the annual ritual for the renewal of both the fertility of the land and the right to kingship, a king proved his virility, thereby his right to rule, by impregnating a harine. *See also* Prostitute, Temple Prostitution.

Harbor. A sign of safety and eternal life. As ships sought harbor, so the Christian *soul sought *Heaven.

Hare. An ambiguous symbol for longevity and passivity or fertility and lust. Among the religious traditions of Asia and the Middle East, the hare symbolized the lunar deities such as *Heng-O. Among the ancient Egyptians, the hare was the sacred animal of the goddess *Wenet who wore a standard of a recumbent hare on her *head. According to Plutarch, the hare connoted the divine qualities of swiftness and acute senses. As a sign of lust and fecundity, the hare was an *attribute of *Aphrodite (*Venus) in classical Greco-Roman and *renaissance art. In its meekness and passivity, the hare was defenseless against larger *animals, so it relied upon its *wisdom for survival. Thereby, the

hare signified the Passion and those Christians who placed their hopes of salvation in Jesus Christ. Its fecundity and rapidity of movement also categorized the hare as a symbol of lust. In the *hands of either the Christ Child or *Mary, however, a *white hare represented the triumph of chastity over lust. According to legend, this animal was believed capable of reproduction by parthenogenesis, and thereby was an emblem of the Virgin Birth. The hare was the emblem of Lust in renaissance art.

Hāriti. Famed for devouring *children, the demon Hāriti was transformed by Buddha into a protector of children and the goddess who blessed married couples with children. She was identified in Buddhist art by her *attribute, the *pomegranate as an emblem of fertility.

Harlot. From the Old French or Old Spanish for "vagabond." Originally identified as foreign-born prostitutes, harlots came to be identified as "idol worshipers" in Jewish literature and Christian art and legend.

Harmonia. Legendary maiden whose bridal jewelry initiated bloodshed and destruction. A daughter of Ares and *Aphrodite, Harmonia's marriage to Cadmus was celebrated by all the Olympian deities with festivities and magnificent gifts. Hephaestus made her an extraordinary *necklace and robe that brought misfortune—strife and death—to all who wore them. These objects were involved in the mythic episodes of the Seven against Thebes and the Epigoni, and ultimately were placed under the protection of Apollo in his sanctuary at Delphi. According to tradition, Harmonia and Cadmus were transformed into *serpents in the *paradise of the Elysian Fields.

Harp. Stringed musical instrument common throughout eastern and western, and ancient and modern cultures. The principal musical instrument of Egypt, the harp was an emblem of Bes as patron of music and dance in Egyptian art and mythology. It was the *attribute of *Terpsichore in classical Greco-Roman, *medieval, *renaissance, and *baroque art. The harp signified celestial music and the glorification of God in western Christian art, and was an attribute of *Cecilia.

Harpy. From the Greek for "snatchers." Legendary beautiful winged female monsters in Greek mythology. Characterized as lustful, rapacious, and sordid, the harpies were the vindictive female emissaries of the deities, and most often were involved with the torment or punishment of evildoers and the dead. They brought painful death by starvation as they "snatched" the food from the table and befouled any remains. The harpies were the messengers of death who carried the souls of the dead to the underworld. As female personifications of whirlwinds and storms, they were perceived as agents of destruction, and confused with the *Sirens. A prevalent motif in funerary art, the harpies were first represented in classical art as beautiful winged goddesses who were eventually transformed into hideous gigantic birds with haglike female faces. They were depicted in classical Greco-Roman and *renaissance art as having the head and torso of a woman combined with the wings and clawed feet of a bird of prey.

Hart. Symbol for the faithful Christian who longed for God (Ps 42:1). The hart was an *attribute of Eustace, Giles, and Hubert.

Harvest. A symbol for fulfillment, completion, *Last Judgment, *Ruth, and the *Flight into Egypt in western Christian art.

Hathor. From the Egyptian language for "house of Horus." Egyptian goddess of the sky, of love and beauty, and of music and dance. As a guardian of the dead, Hathor was venerated as a mortuary goddess in Thebes. One of the oldest of all Egyptian goddesses, she was recognized as a great mother or cosmic goddess who conceived, brought forth, and sustained all forms of life. Hathor nourished the living with her milk and supplied celestial food for the dead in Tuat, or the underworld. According to ancient tradition, she was the mother cow who stood on the earth so that her four legs became the pillars of the sky and her belly the firmament. As the divine mother of the pharaoh, she took the form of the cow to suckle him. Every evening Horus as a solar deity took the form of a *hawk and entered Hathor's mouth in order to be reborn as her son and husband in the morning. Her destructive aspect was manifested following the instigation of an aged and angry sun god who urged her to slay humanity. During this act of slaughter, Hathor came to revel in her actions and the other deities supported her by plying her with an intoxicating drink so that she could not see human beings as anything other than objects to be destroyed. Hathor was originally venerated as a *mother goddess, but eventually became associated with *Sekhmet and

*Isis. The center of her cult was located at Dendera where annual new year festivals commemorated her symbolic birth with drunken orgies in honor of the mistress of merriment and dance, and the goddess of love. She was associated with *Isis, *Aphrodite, and *Venus, and later in Christian art, with Mary. In Egyptian art, Hathor was portrayed as a female figure with either a cow's head or a headdress of a cow's head or of a solar disk encased in bovine *horns. She was also signified by a cow walking out of a funeral mountain or by her cult symbol of a round pillar surmounted by two cow's heads or female heads. Her *attributes included the *menat, the *sistrum, the cow, and the solar eye. *See also* Toilet, Toilet Scenes.

Hat-mehit. Minor fish goddess of Mendes in Egyptian mythology. Hat-mehit was characterized as a woman with a *fish on her head or as a *dolphin in Egyptian art.

Hatshepsut (1503–1482 B.C.E.). From the Egyptian language for "foremost in nobility." Most significant woman pharaoh and one of the greatest rulers of ancient Egypt. According to tradition, Hatshepsut was the special child conceived by Queen Akmet and the god Amun disguised in the form of the pharaoh Thutmose I. The Hathors attended the mother during the childbirth, and according to tradition, the goddess *Hathor nursed the newborn infant girl. Married to her half-brother, Thutmose II, she eventually took on the title of pharaoh. Hatshepsut became regent for her stepson, Thutmose III, who would eventually succeed to the throne upon her death. Famed for her administrative and military skills that resulted in a reign

identified with peace and prosperity, this woman pharaoh was venerated at her tomb-temple at Deir el-Bahri in the Valley of the Kings in West Thebes. Hatshepsut was depicted as either ruler with her stepson or as a male figure wearing the beard and garments of kingship including the double crown, but with hieroglyphic inscriptions noting her female sex. Her life story including her miraculous conception and birth, her military achievements, and the prosperity of her reign were represented on the walls of her mortuary temple. Unfortunately, these images form the visual history of Hatshepsut who instilled such animosity in her stepson that he had most of her statues destroyed, inscriptions and references to her name erased, and her tomb uncompleted after her death and his ascent to the throne in his own right.

Haumea. First woman of Hawaiian mythology. Haumea was patron of childbirth and protector of women in labor.

Hawk. A solar *bird like the *eagle and a symbol for death in western *medieval art.

Hawthorn. An ambiguous symbol used either to represent *chastity and *virginity or the Crown of Thorns in western Christian art. The hawthorn signified caution and hope in western *medieval art.

Hay. A scriptural symbol for the transitoriness of life and of the world in western Christian art.

Hazel. Food source for female wisdom and sacred to *witches. According to legend, the hazel was sacred to the

*Great Goddess, and it was believed that those who ate hazelnuts partook of "the goddess as instructor." The wood of the hazel tree became associated with witches, especially given its use for divining rods, and thereby "witch's hazel" was believed to have magical therapeutic powers.

Head. Uppermost part of the human *body, and site of the life force, the brain, and the soul in the ancient world. As the part of the body closest to *heaven, the head signified spiritual nature. Decapitation was considered the most vicious punishment as the severed head would be buried apart from the decapitated body, so that the dead would know no rest. Multiple heads were a common characteristic of sacred personages in eastern religious art. For example, Brahma had four heads while Shiva had three. *Kālī wore a necklace composed of the heads of her victims. In classical Mediterranean art, *Hecate had three heads. In Christian art, the severed head was the *attribute of many *saints who were beheaded, including John the Baptist and Denis. Following the classical Greco-Roman foretype of Perseus holding the severed head of *Medusa, the biblical hero David was represented as a young man holding a severed head; and the apocryphal heroine *Judith also held a man's head in her right hand. A man's head on a platter signified John the Baptist while the woman holding the platter was *Salome, and one on a Bible suggested Denis. A woman holding a cloth inscribed with a man's head denoted *Veronica.

Healing of Peter's Mother-in-law (Mt 8:14–15; Mk 1:30–31; Lk 4:38–39).

When Jesus entered Peter's house, he saw that Peter's mother-in-law was sick with fever. After he touched her *hand, the fever disappeared and she left her sickbed to prepare a meal. This event was rarely depicted in western Christian art. It was however distinguished from the healing of *Jairus's daughter because no one else was present in the room when Jesus raised the young girl from her sleep.

Heart. A symbol for understanding, love, courage, devotion, sorrow, piety, happiness, and joy. The central organ of the human *body coordinated the intellect and the emotions. The ancient Egyptian emblem of life, the deceased's heart was weighed against *Maat's ostrich feather on the scales of justice in the Hall of Judgment. The Chinese *hsin*, or heart, was one of the Eight Precious Organs or Treasures of the Buddha, and signified the location of the emotions and intelligence. Religious fervor was typified by a flaming heart, while contrition, repentance, and devotion under trial were represented by a heart pierced by an *arrow in Christian art. A heart with a *cross was an *attribute of *Catherine of Siena, a simple heart of Bernardino of Siena, and a flaming heart or one pierced by an arrow represented *Augustine and Anthony of Padua. The *Sacred Heart of Jesus, as described in the mystical vision of *Margaret Mary Alacoque (1647–90), was the image of a flaming heart surmounted by a cross and enclosed in a *crown of thorns. A heart pierced by seven arrows represented the *Seven Sorrows of Mary, and a heart transfixed by a *sword and encircled by a *wreath of *roses represented *Mary. The heart crowned with

44. *The Goddess Hathor and Pharaoh Seti I*
45. *Hatshepsut Enthroned* from the Valley Temple
of Hatshepsut at Deir-el-Bahri, Thebes

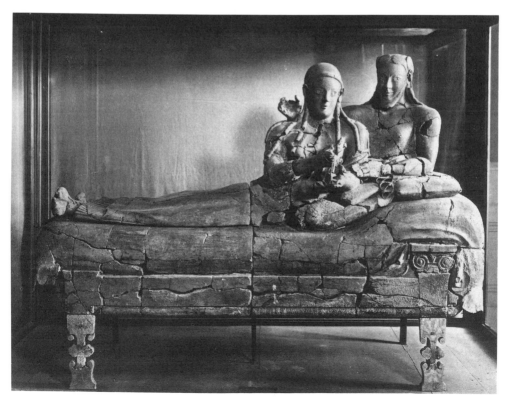

46. *Hieros Gamos*

thorns was an emblem of the *Jesuits and an attribute of *Ignatius of Loyola.

Heaven. The peaceful and bountiful kingdom in which God the Father reigned in love and justice. It was believed to be located in the highest celestial region and to be populated with the *souls of blessed. Heaven was also called the Holy City, *paradise, New Jerusalem, and the Garden of Paradise. In western Christian art, heaven was depicted as either a verdant, lush garden filled with beautiful *flowers and *fruits, and *angels, or a light-filled glorious *cloud inhabited by the choirs of holy *angels, the blessed, God the Father, the Resurrected Christ, and *Mary.

Hebat. Chief goddess of Hurrians and identified as the "queen of heaven." In the Hittite pantheon, Hebat was known as Arinna, the goddess of the sun. In ancient Near Eastern art, Hebat was represented wearing a pointed regal cap and as standing on either a *lion or a *panther, or as seated on a royal throne.

Hebe. From the Greek for "freshness of youth." Goddess of eternal youth and spring in Greek mythology. The daughter of *Hera and Zeus, Hebe was the original cupbearer on Mount Olympus until she was replaced by Ganymede. Gifted with the power of revitalization, she was venerated by those who sought a restoration of youthful energy and vigor. Hebe became identified as *Dia when she married the deified Herakles, and they were worshiped as a celestial married couple. Her classical Roman counterpart was *Iuventas (Juventas). In classical Greek and *renaissance art, Hebe was portrayed as a youthful female figure often dressed in a chiton

and carrying the cup of the Olympian divinities. She was also depicted as a beautiful woman dressed in a long flowing garment and crowned with a *wreath of spring flowers, as she accompanied her husband.

Hebrew Scriptures. *See* Old Testament.

Hebrews. Traditional designation for the Israelites starting with the patriarchs—*Abraham, Isaac, and Jacob—through the *Old Testament period embracing the twelve tribes, the era of development of the Kingdom of Israel, and the division of the kingdom into the Northern and Southern kingdoms. Following the Babylonian Captivity, the designation *Jews identifying the peoples of the Kingdom and province of Judea who practiced the monotheistic religion of Judaism became the common usage. In western Christian art, the Hebrews and the Jews were commonly misidentified as one and the same.

Hecate. Originally from the Egyptian *heka* for "magic" as personified by Hekat, a goddess, and then transformed into the Greek for "she who encounters you." Female personification of divine power and goddess of "the way," that is the crossroads, the night, the earth, and the underworld in Greek mythology. Invoked at the beginning of all ritual sacrifices, Hecate was associated with witchcraft, witches, necromancy, and the restless souls of the dead who roamed the earth in the dark of night. A chthonic deity, she was venerated by the common folk as Hecate Enodia, or the "guardian of the ways" whenever they came to a crossroad on a journey, and thereby corresponded to the Roman goddess *Trivia. Hecate manifested herself in a triple formula: with *Artemis, she was goddess of women in childbirth; with *Persephone, she was goddess of the underworld; and by herself, she was a moon goddess. In classical Greco-Roman and *renaissance art, Hecate was represented as either a triple-figured goddess whose three bodies stood united in a back-to-back formation, and were most often nude or in a state of partial undress; or as a triple-headed goddess whose three faces signified her triple form as Artemis, Persephone, and Hecate. Her destructive aspect was symbolized by the *snakes in her *hair and her brandishing of a torch and a whip. Characterized as invisible when she flew through the night in the company of her faithful hounds, Hecate was identified by her *attributes of *keys, daggers, and torches, or her common animals, *snakes and *dogs (hounds).

Hecuba. Queen of Troy, and mother of *Cassandra, Paris, and Hector. Faithful and devoted wife of the Trojan king Priam, Hecuba reportedly bore him nineteen sons and twelve daughters. When she was pregnant with Paris, she had a fearful vision of death and destruction as she slept one night. From the moment of his birth, Hecuba sent the infant to a group of shepherds who were to kill him as he slept. Defying their queen, the shepherds rescued the infant prince, raised him, and one fateful afternoon the young shepherd-prince was sought out by Zeus to render the famed *Judgment of Paris that began the Trojan War. Following the fall of Troy and the death of her husband and sons, Hecuba was indentured to Odysseus. Avenging the death of her son Polydorus by blinding his murderer, Polymnestor, and killing his two sons, Hecuba was changed into a *dog and drowned herself in the sea. A classical symbol of wifely devotion and maternal grief, Hecuba was depicted in classical Greco-Roman art as a regal matron often garbed in royal robes and the regalia of Troy.

Hedetet. Scorpion goddess identified in the Egyptian *Book of the Dead*. Hedetet became assimilated with *Isis in ancient Egyptian art and mythology.

Hedgehog. An *animal hunter of *serpents, thereby a symbol of opponents. According to the *Physiologus*, the hedgehog robbed the vine of its *grapes and thereby signified the *Devil in who took human *souls.

Heket. Ancient Egyptian tutelary goddess of conception and of childbirth. As a goddess of fertility, Heket became associated with the appearance of the *frogs two or three days before the Nile rose, which was a sign of new life and regeneration; thereby the frog symbolized life and fertility. She assisted *Isis in her search for Osiris, his ensuing resurrection, and the conception of Horus. Heket was characterized as either having the physical form of a *frog or of a woman with the head of a frog in Egyptian art.

Hel. Norse goddess of the dead and of the underworld. A daughter of Loki and Angrboda, Hel claimed dominion over all those who died in peace and not in battle. The realm of the dead over which she ruled became the opposite of Valhalla. Although unpleasant in appearance, Hel was characterized as a *sibyl who resided in a cave and possessed oracular powers.

Helen of Troy. Tragically beautiful woman responsible for the Trojan War in Greek mythology. As the daughter of Zeus and *Leda, Helen was the twin sister of Polydeuces, and the sister of Castor and *Clytemnestra. Originally a vegetation goddess, she was transformed into the mortal heroine known as "the most beautiful woman in the world." Characterized as a beauty even as a young girl, she was kidnapped by Theseus, king of Athens, only to be rescued by her brothers. Upon her return to Sparta, she was courted by many men renowned for their political or military powers. To ensure a peaceful marriage for their sister, Helen's brothers negotiated an agreement among her suitors that they would stand together once she made her choice of a husband and later support him if she were ever abducted. As decreed by the Fates, Helen married Menelaus, king of Sparta. Following the *Judgment of Paris, *Aphrodite fulfilled her promise of "the most beautiful woman in the world" by presenting Helen. The youthful shepherd-prince and the beautiful queen became lovers, and Paris carried her off to Troy in the proverbial middle of the night when Menelaus was away in Crete. Thereby, Helen was the cause of the Trojan War. Initially happy in Troy with Paris, Helen eventually rued her behavior, and was reunited with Menelaus after Troy fell. In classical Greco-Roman, *renaissance, *baroque, and nineteenth-century art, Helen was portrayed as a physically beautiful, in face and body, woman often in a state of partial nudity, and usually in a scene of her abduction by Paris or her recovery by Menelaus.

The plane tree, under which the *Judgment of Paris occurred, was sacred to her.

Helena, Saint (255–330). The Christian mother of Emperor Constantine. A great *church builder distinguished for her *charity, Helena went on a *pilgrimage in quest of the True Cross, which she believed she found when a sick or dead man—depending on which legendary account is used—was restored by touching it. She also located the *nails, and the site of the *Garden of Gethsemane and the *tomb of Jesus. She had the Basilica Church of the Holy Sepulcher built on the site of the tomb, and a golden cross erected on the site of the True Cross. She took the True Cross and the nails back with her to her son's capital, Byzantium. Helena was the patron of dyers. In Christian art, she was depicted as an elderly woman dressed in regal garments with an imperial *crown. Her *attributes included a golden *cross, the model of the Holy Sepulcher, *hammer, and nails. The *iconography of "The Invention of the Cross" celebrated her discovery of the True Cross. See also Finding of the True Cross.

Helfta, Convent at. Exceptional medieval female monastic community singular for its intellectual and spiritual life. During the tenure of Gertrude of Hackeborn as abbess (1251–92), Helfta was the center of Christian mysticism in Germany as it prospered and developed an excellent scriptorium, choir, and liturgical life. Initially influenced by the Cistercian reform of Benedictine monasticism, this community fell under the sway of the Dominican Order after 1271. The leading authors of Helfta—

Mechthild of Hackeborn, *Gertrude the Great, and *Mechthild of Magdeburg—were effective in their support of the intellectual and spiritual life of medieval women. This community provided an outstanding refuge and center for medieval women to receive training as scholars, mystics, and craftswomen, especially in the arts of making books.

Hell. The place of eternal punishment and damnation. As the opposite of *heaven, hell was perceived to be in the lowest regions of the *earth. Biblical references to hell suggested a place of perpetual *fires where sinners were tortured by the constant *flames and heat. Until *Dante revised this description of hell, western Christian artists depicted it as a flame-filled place in which the damned suffered physical tortures and indignities. In this vision of hell, the *demons and the *Devil were represented as evil creatures blackened from the fires and the *smoke. In accordance with the medieval thinking about God as light, Dante conceived of hell as a cold and dark place deprived of the warmth and the light of God. In the lowest region of Dante's Inferno, Satan was an ice-blue creature trapped forever in a frozen lake. Dante's description of hell was represented by *Giotto, the poet's friend and companion in Padua, in his frescoes for the Scrovegni Chapel.

Helle. Legendary stepdaughter of *Io for whom the Hellespoint was named. The daughter of Athamas of Thebes and his first wife, Nephele, Helle was the sister of Phrixus. Following their father's marriage to Io, the stepmother tried to sacrifice Helle and Phrixus. Their mother intervened and whisked them away to Colchis by means of the

Golden Fleece. However during this rescue, the brother landed safely but Helle fell into the Dardanelles and drowned by the place identified as the Hellespoint in remembrance of her.

Helmet. A piece of military *armor that protected the *head, thereby a sign of spiritual protection.

Héloïse (1101–65). Beloved of Abélard, female personification of ideal love, and famed medieval *abbess. As the orphaned niece of Canon Fulbert of Notre-Dame de Paris, the lively and intelligent young Héloïse resided in the same house as her guardian and his colleagues. Canon Fulbert hired one of these young men, Peter Abélard, to be his niece's tutor with tragic consequences. Student and tutor became lovers, and were reputed to have a secret alliance following the birth of a child. The enraged and humiliated guardian separated the couple, and employed several ruffians to castrate Abélard. A sorrowful Héloïse entered a convent but continued a correspondence with her former lover. Originally written in Latin, the surviving letters of Héloïse and Abélard have been embellished over the centuries, but provide a window into the medieval concepts of love and the role of the abbess. Abélard established the Convent of the Holy Paraclete on his beloved's behalf, and of which she eventually became abbess. According to tradition, the two lovers were buried together in the Cemetery of Père Lachaise in Paris. Varied episodes in the romantic liaisons of Héloïse and Abélard were depicted in *medieval, *renaissance, *baroque, and nineteenth-century art; while Héloïse was portrayed as an abbess holding a model of her convent in medieval and renaissance western Christian art.

Hemessen, Caterina van (1528–87). First Flemish woman artist. A daughter of Jan Sanders van Hemessen. Caterina garnered her early artistic training at his studio. She was famed for her simple yet subdued style of half-length portraiture and religious subjects, such as her *Christ and Veronica* and *Rest on the Flight into Egypt*. Caterina married the organist, Christian de Morien, and they lived together under the patronage of Queen Mary of Hungary in Spain.

Hemlock. Botanical symbol for death in western religious art. Hemlock was an *attribute of the personifications of Death and Treason.

Hemorrhissa. *See* Woman with the Issue of Blood.

Hemsut. Ancient Egyptian goddesses of fate and protectors of newborn children. The Hemsut were famed for their role as the guardian spirits of newborn infants whom they protected by holding in their arms. They were identified by their distinctive headdress of a shield transfixed by two *arrows in Egyptian art.

Hen with chicks. Symbol for Jesus Christ with a flock of Christians.

Heng-O. Goddess of the moon in classical Chinese mythology. According to tradition, Heng-O stole the pill of immortality from her husband, the sun god Shen Yi. She then escaped to live forever as a *toad on the *moon. She was venerated as the female personification of the *yin, that is, the cold dark female principle. Heng-O was depicted as a beautiful woman dressed in regal garments and holding the disk of the moon in her right hand.

Hera. Queen of the Greek *gods and goddesses, the lawful wife of Zeus, and the female personification of the feminine aspects of all natural forces. She was the goddess of woman and childbirth, as well as the protector of marriage and domestic harmony. Her sexual union with Zeus signified the fusion of the native energies of the feminine with the active dynamism of the atmosphere. As both the patron of marital fidelity and as a devoted wife, Hera was the stern and jealous protector of her own marriage, the only proper one on Mount Olympus, to Zeus who was famed for his infidelities. Greek mythology was replete with tales of Hera's revenge upon unsuspecting mortal and divine women who were the momentary object of Zeus's affections. She was the mother of *Hebe and Hephaestus. Hera was the classical Greco-Roman foretype for both *Anne and *Mary. In classical Greco-Roman and *renaissance art, Hera was depicted as a large, matronly woman fully clad in soft, flowing garments cinched with her magic *girdle and with a *crown or diadem and *veil on her *head and a *scepter in her *hand. Hera's chariot was drawn by *peacocks. Her *attributes included the *cuckoo, *crow, peacock, and *pomegranate. *See also* Breast, Galaxy, Hieros Gamos, and Milky Way.

Hermaphrodite (*Metamorphosis* 4:274–388). From the Greek for "Hermes-Aphrodite," often translated as "exceptional beauty." Hybrid divinity of classical Greek mythology. As the son of

*Aphrodite and Hermes, Hermaphroditus was a youth of exceptional male beauty. The water *nymph, Salmacis, became infatuated with him but the youth rejected her. Nonetheless, she begged the Olympian deities to take pity on her and to unite their bodies forever. Thereby arose the prevalent belief that anyone who bathed in the spring of Salmacis became a hermaphrodite.

Hero and Leander (*Heroids* 18–19). Tragic symbols of ideal love in Greek mythology. A priestess of *Aphrodite at Sestos, Hero was in love with Leander who lived in Abydos. Their parents objected to the young lovers's relationship so they met in secrecy every night. The youthful lover swam the dangerous waters of the Hellespoint every night to visit his beloved guided by the light of her *tower. During a stormy, thereby dark and windy, night, the tower light was extinguished and Leander was lost in the perilous waters. When the grief-stricken Hero found her lover's lifeless body on the shore, she was inconsolable. She ascended to the heights of her tower, and flung herself into the Hellespoint in order to join Leander in a watery death.

Herodias (first century). Granddaughter of Herod the Great, she first married Herod Philip and then his brother, Herod Antipas, the Tetrarch of Galilee. Her adulterous union was condemned by John the Baptist, who she both feared and despised. She persuaded her unnamed young daughter to dance at her stepfather's banquet, and when he was pleased enough to offer the dancer a prize, she consulted with her mother, who demanded the *head of the Baptist

on a platter. In Christian art, Herodias was depicted as a royal but lascivious woman who was regally dressed and wore a *crown. She was distinguished from her daughter—later identified as *Salome by *Flavius Josephus—by her larger physical stature and by her legendary action of piercing the decapitated Baptist's tongue with a fork. By the High Renaissance, the figures of Herodias and Salome become conflated into that of one woman.

Heroine. From the Latin for "female hero." Female intermediary between woman and goddess, thereby a "demi-goddess." The heroine was transformed into a woman distinguished by singular courage, fortitude, or achievement. A popular motif in religious art and literature, the heroine was distinguished by her extraordinary action, usually on behalf of her people or her nation, as in the apocryphal story of *Judith or the medieval history of *Joan of Arc.

Heron. A solar *bird like the *stork and the *crane, and a symbol of vigilance and quietude. As a destroyer of *serpents, the heron signified Christ. According to Pliny, the heron's tears of pain foretold the tears Jesus shed at the Agony in the Garden. The *gray heron typified penance.

Herrade of Landsburg (1125-d. 1195). *Abbess and Christian artist. Herrade of Landsburg was renowned for her 636 illustrations for the *Hortus Deliciarum, a pictorial encyclopedia, which was written between 1160 and 1170, but not finally produced until shortly after her death. Developed for the education of her *nuns, this religious compilation by a religious woman is ranked with *Hildegard of Bingen's *Scivias* for its significance to women's spirituality. Herrade was elected abbess of the convent in Hohenburg where she served until her death. A rare topic in western Christian art, Herrade of Landsburg was depicted as an abbess often in the act of creating an illuminated page.

Hesperides. Daughters of Atlas and guardians of the Golden Apples. These three beautiful sisters were responsible for the care and protection of the tree that bore golden apples that *Gaea gave *Hera as a wedding present. For its safety as well as its regular bearing of fruit, this tree was planted in the far west. A *dragon assisted the Hesperides in their protective duties, but was eventually killed by Herakles who sought the golden apples for his eleventh labor.

Hestia. Greek virgin goddess of the hearth and household. A daughter of *Rhea and Cronos, Hestia swore a vow of *chastity. Although pursued by Apollo and Poseidon, she rejected both gods and sought never to leave Mount Olympus as a sign of her duty as goddess of the domestic realm. As protector of the center of cities, states, and colonies as symbolic hearths, Hestia was worshiped at the beginning and end of every ritual sacrifice and entertainment. In classical Greco-Roman and *renaissance art, Hestia was depicted as a serious but gentle woman in simple, flowing drapery with unadorned *hair who held a *scepter. She was a classical Greco-Roman foretype of *Mary.

Hetaera. From the Greek for "companion." Honorific of the courtesan in classical Greece. The hetaera retained full legal equality with men, that is, the right

to own property, to handle business affairs, the right to an education, and freedom of movement. A woman relinquished all rights upon marriage. Hetaera were characterized as women of extraordinary physical beauty and sexual skills in classical Greek art. They were often represented in the nude and in the midst of a sexual encounter.

Hexagonal Halo. A sign of an allegorical or legendary person such as the Virtues.

Hieronymus, Saint. *See* Jerome, Saint.

Hieros Gamos. From the Greek for "sacred marriage." Omnipresent motif of ritual marriage between a god and goddess, or between the earthly surrogates of the god and goddess, in world mythologies and religious art. The sacred marriage of either the primordial earth mother to the sky god, or that between the gods and goddesses of the mythological pantheon was a prefiguration of the earthly marriage of men and women. The primordial hieros gamos of the earth mother and the sky father explained the creation and the fertility of the earth, and thereby the sustenance of human life. Among the ancient Mediterranean cultures, there were two forms of the *hieros gamos*, or sacred marriage of the deities. First there was the ritual ceremony in which the cult images of a god and goddess were united on an annual basis as a symbolic explanation of creation, as in the annual reunion of *Hera and Zeus following the ritual bath that restored her virginity. Secondly, there was the ritual reenactment of the lovemaking, or sexual encounter, between the deities as performed by their earthly surrogates, ostensibly a king and a priestess, as a form of ritual and sympathetic magic that insured the fertility of vegetation, animals, and humanity.

Hildegard of Bingen, Saint (1098–1178/9). Artist, musician, abbess, and Christian visionary. Sickly as a child, Hildegard entered a Benedictine convent around the age of seven and was professed by age fourteen. An able administrator for her order, Hildegard supported the growth of her community by moving it to Rupertsburg near Bingen, and established other convents. She served as counselor to Pope Eugenius III, King Henry III, and Frederick Barbarossa; and with Bernard of Clairvaux, she called for the Second Crusade. She was the first Christian thinker to consider seriously and positively the idea of the feminine, especially in relation to *Eve, *Mary, and *Ecclesia. Central to her unique and innovative female spirituality was *Sapientia and *Caritas as visionary and female forms of Holy Wisdom and Divine Love. Hildegard was the first Christian writer to personify Divine Love as a beautiful woman. Hers was a form of Christian though that centered on the role of Holy Wisdom in creation and redemption, especially as manifested in the female aspects of God, the Church, and the Cosmos. One of her most significant roles was in her support of the reforms to rid the Church of corruption and materialism. However, she was also an influential mystical writer who extended her gifts into the realms of the visual arts and music. Hildegard began to have visions at the age of forty-three and related these visions through her writings. She illustrated her books of mystical visions, *Scivias (c. 1165); and

authored poetry, liturgical dramas, liturgical music, and hymns as well as biblical commentary, hagiography, theological analyses, and compendia of science and the healing arts. Well-versed in scientific studies, including medicine, biology, geology, and botany, Hildegard earned the appellation of "the *Sibyl of the Rhine." Although herself a rare individual topic in western Christian art, it was Hildegard's own artistic renderings, or at the very least her careful directions for the illustrations for her books, and her writings that influenced the development of the iconography of women in western Christian art. Occasionally, she was represented dressed as a Benedictine abbess seated at her desk either writing or illuminating a page.

Hina. Mother goddess of Polynesian mythology. As the female embodiment of the *moon, she was both virgin and mother. Hina was simultaneously the first woman and embodied in every woman. According to tradition, she was the mother of all the deities and of the human race.

Hind. Animal sacred to *Artemis (*Diana) as goddess of the hunt in Greek art and mythology. *See also* Hart.

Hindu art. Complex iconography and art forms created by adherents of Hinduism. Characterized by regional differences in presentation and stylization throughout its religious history, Hindu art was premised upon the indigenous Indian and formal Hindu textual commitment to image worship as the visualization of the living quality of nature which mediates life by the breath (*praña*) and the pulsation of sap (*rāsā*). The image, then, is a bridge between the devotee and the sacred. Hindu art can be characterized by its sensuous representations of the human body, the intricate patterns of design, a dynamic sense of movement, and an elaborate iconography which visualized its mythology.

Hinduism. From the Sanskrit *sindhu* for "river," especially the Indus River, and eventually characterized as "one living near the Indus River." Generic term for the diverse collection of the religious traditions of India premised on the teaching of eternal *dharma*, from the Sanskrit for "eternal principle," which affirmed the *Vedas* as authoritative texts, the teachings on Atman-Brahman, *karma* (law of moral causation), transmigration, social caste system, a pattern of life stages including renunciation, and the achievement of moksha as liberation. As Hinduism spread throughout the Indian subcontinent, it assimilated indigenous cultic practices and deities.

Hine-ahuone. From the Maori for "earth-formed maiden." First woman of the human race in Maori mythology. Hine-ahuone was created when Tane modeled red earth into a figure form and breathed life into it. Later they mated and conceived a daughter, *Hine-titama. In Maori art, Hine-ahuone was portrayed as a physically powerful demon.

Hine-nui-te-po. From the Maori for "lady of darkness." Maori goddess of death, and protector of the dead. *See* Hine-titama.

Hine-rau-wharangi. The daughter of Tane and *Hine-titama in Maori my-

thology. Hine-rau-wharangi was the female personification of the growth of vegetation.

Hine-titama. From the Maori for "dawn maid." Female deity associated simultaneously with natural growth, and with thunder and lightning in Maori mythology. The daughter of *Hine-ahuone and Tane, Hine-titama eventually mated with her father and bore him a daughter, *Hine-rau-wharangi. Following the birth of this child, she accompanied her husband/father to dwell eternally in the underworld where she became one with *Hine-nui-te-po.

Hintubuhet. From the Melanesian for "woman." Androgynous supreme being of Melanesian mythology. Hintubuhet was composed of Talmago, the male personification of the *sun and the *butterfly, and *Heba, the female personification of the *moon and the *butterfly.

Hippocampus. Fantastic monster in Greek mythology. The hippocampus had a composite body of the foreparts of a *horse and the tail and finlike wings of a *fish. It was associated with minor sea deities and drew the chariot of *Galatea in classical Greek and *renaissance art.

Hippolyta. Legendary queen of the *Amazons in Greek mythology. The daughter of Ares and Otera, Hippolyta wore an extraordinary *girdle given to her by her parents. She married Theseus and bore him a son, Hippolytus. For his ninth labor, Herakles was required to retrieve Hippolyta's girdle for Eurystheus. Although willing to surrender her girdle to the hero, Hippolyta was pro-

47. Hildegard of Bingen, Manuscript Illumination from *The Seasons*
48. *Hygeia*

49. Lucas Cranach the Elder, *The Holy Kindred*

tected by her army of Amazons who unaware of their queen's decision prepared to attack Herakles. Fearful of a trap, Herakles defeated the Amazons in battle, slew Hippolyta, and garnered her girdle as his booty.

Hippopotamus. In Egyptian art, the goddesses *Taweret, and *Thoeris, protectors of women in childbirth, were represented with the body of a woman and the head of a hippopotamus. This animal was a scriptural symbol for the brutal power that only God can subdue in western Christian art.

Historia Animalium. One of Aristotle's books on the natural sciences, in which he compiled and systematized all that was then known about *animals. An early precursor of the medieval *bestiary, the *Historia Animalium* was influential upon early Christian and *medieval art.

History. Female personification of recorded time past. In classical Greco-Roman and *renaissance art, History was a winged female figure dressed in a flowing white robe who was seated as she wrote in a *book or on a tablet supported by Father Time. One of her feet rested on a solid cube as an emblem of the factual foundation of her texts.

Hive. A sign of motherhood and industry. The hive was an *attribute of *Hope, and of Bernard of Clairvaux who compared the ordered, cloistered community to a hive. *See also* Beehive.

Hlodyn. Goddess of fertility and of the earth in Icelandic mythology.

Hog. Sign of the *demon of sensuality and gluttony. The hog was an *attribute

of Anthony the Abbot, who triumphed over these temptations.

Hoglah (Num 26:33, 27:1, 36:11; Josh 17:3). From the Hebrew for "partridge." One of the five daughters of Zelophehad who plead the case for their patrimony before Moses. As there were no male heirs, the daughters were each awarded one-fifth of their father's estate.

Hokmah. From the Hebrew for "wisdom." A manifestation of the Great Mother as wisdom in the *Old Testament (Prvbs 8). Identified with *Sophia and *Sapientia, Hokmah was signified by the *dove, and according to tradition was the inspiration for the Wisdom Literature of the Old Testament.

Holbein the Younger, Hans (1497/8–1543). Most technically accomplished and realistic portrait painter of the northern *renaissance art. A friend of Erasmus, the great humanist, Holbein was also a book illustrator who designed illustrations for *Martin Luther's translation of the Bible into German, as well as two major series of prints on the *Dance of Death* (1523/4) and the *Alphabet of Death* (1524). In accordance with the reformist tendencies in northern Europe, Holbein's religious-theme paintings, especially his paintings of the *Madonna and Child*, were restrained and almost grimly realistic, verging more on the decorative than on the devotional.

Holle. From the Teutonic for "priestess of the lunar cult." Ancient lunar goddess of *witches and the *witches's sabbath in Germanic mythology. Holle was characterized as a mature woman bathing in the forest, or the impish figure who shook the snow off *trees.

Holly. Evergreen tree with prickly leaves that symbolized the Crown of Thorns. According to legend, the holly was the only *tree that did not splinter under the *ax, and therefore was used for the *cross of Jesus. The *red berries of the holly signified the suffering and sacrificial *blood of Jesus. In representations of *Jerome, the holly represented his meditations on the Passion; while in depictions of John the Baptist it symbolized the Passion of Christ. As it was a Roman custom to distribute gifts of holly as a sign of good fortune for the new year, it became associated with the traditions of Christmas. The holly was also identified by its Latin name, *ilex.*

Holy Family. Title given to a variety of domestic scenes in which the *Madonna and Child were accompanied by other family members, including *Anne, Joseph (of Nazareth), and/or John the Baptist in western Christian art. In these images, Joseph taught Jesus about carpentry; or *Mary or Anne taught the *child to read; or either or both parents taught him to walk. The *Sacra Conversazione* (Holy Conversation) in which saints were included in teaching, reading, or conversing with the Christ Child in the presence of his parents, was a variant on the theme of the Holy Family.

Holy Kindred. Title given to the depiction of the three husbands, three daughters, and several grandchildren of *Anne in western Christian art. A popular theme in northern *medieval art, the Holy Kindred became popular during the Reformation when the cult of Mary

was being silenced. As the Holy Kindred signified that Anne had three husbands and three daughters (one child by each husband) the uniqueness of Mary's conception and birth were diminished.

Holy Women. The Three *Marys in Christian art.

Honey. As the sacred fluid excreted with the tears of Ra, honey denoted resurrection and eternal life to the ancient Egyptians. Honey was a sign for sweetness and purity, and a symbol of Jesus Christ's *ministry on *earth. It also represented *paradise, "the land flowing with milk and honey," which was the biblical basis for the early Christian Eucharist of milk and honey offered to children, the aged, the sick, and pregnant women.

Hope. Single element retained in the *box opened by *Pandora in Greek mythology. Hope was one of the three theological virtues of *faith, hope, and *charity in Christian art and spirituality. The symbol of hope was the *anchor. When personified as one of the *Seven Virtues, Hope had *wings that allowed her to soar towards *heaven. She was represented as reaching heavenward for a crown as a *basket of *flowers, James Major, and an anchor rested at her *feet in western Christian art.

Hope, Saint (second century). The female personification of the cult of Divine Wisdom (Sophia) in the eastern Mediterranean. According to tradition, the Roman widow, *Sophia, had three daughters—*Faith, Hope, and *Charity. The mother and her daughters were tortured and beheaded under the Emperor Hadrian.

Horae. Female guardians of social and political order, and goddesses of the seasons in Greek mythology. The three daughters of *Themis and Zeus—Thallo, from the Greek for "blossom," Auxo, from the Greek for "growth," and Karpo, from the Greek for "ripe fruit"—the Horae were the guardians of the gates of Mount Olympus, controllers of the weather, regulators of the power of nature, and supervisors of the changing of the seasons. According to Hesiod, these three sisters were transformed from nature deities to the ethical guardians of the social order, and became individually identified as Eunomia, from the Greek for "good order;" Dike, from the Greek for "justice;" and Eirene, from the Greek for "peace." The Horae were depicted as three beautiful winged maidens wearing wreaths of appropriate botanical products, such as tulips and roses for spring, or bunches of grapes for the fall, in classical Greco-Roman and *renaissance art. Representations of the "dance of the Horae," or the circle dance of the three sisters, signified the passage of the seasons.

Horn. Ambiguous symbol for power and strength, especially as exhibited in horned animals, in religious art. In ancient Near Eastern art, especially that of Mesopotamia, the "horned cap" consisting of seven superimposed pairs of horns on a cap denoted divinity. This headdress was later transformed into the symbolism of the *fleur-de-lis, the dome, and knot. Among the ancient Egyptians, horns were simultaneously a solar and a lunar symbol through the daily passage of the solar disk through the sacred body of the cow goddess, personified as either *Hathor or *Isis, who swallowed the sun each evening, allowed its nocturnal rest, and then forced its emergence each morning. Thus the connection between these goddesses and their sacred headdress of the solar disk encased within bovine horns. As a symbol of creative power and energy, the horn signified the mother goddesses, especially those of the ancient Near East such as *Astarte, *Inanna, and *Ishtar. The phallic imagery of the horn connoted male sexuality and power, and when fused visually with the solar disk procreation. As a lunar symbol, the horn implied the passage of the lunar cycle at both its beginning and its end in the form of the crescent moon. In classical Greco-Roman art, the horn was associated with Pan and the satyrs; while it was an *attribute of David in western Christian art. As a musical instrument, the horn was an emblem of *Melpomene in classical Greco-Roman and *renaissance art.

Horn of Plenty. *See* Cornucopia.

Horse. A solar and marine symbol of courage, generosity, virility, strength, speed, and lust in religious art. According to legend, the horse was the only *animal that displayed emotion when it wept for its master. As a symbol of mourning and of death, the horse was the carrier of the soul to the afterlife, and became a prevalent motif on funerary art. Several goddesses were associated with the horse including *Epona, the Celtic horse goddess, and Kassite (Mirizir), the Mesopotamian goddess of horse breeding. In classical Greco-Roman art and mythology, the winged horse, Pegasus, as the son of *Medusa and Poseidon (Neptune) was a popular image and came to denote

Fame in *renaissance art. The horse was associated with *Europa, especially in *renaissance art. Another legend related that if the horse's mane was cut, the animal lost its sexual prowess. The rider who controlled the strength and power of the horse was the ideal of control and moral virtue as symbolized by Donatello's portrayal of *Judith. George of Cappadocia, James Major, and Martin of Tours were represented on horseback in western Christian art. See also Four Horsemen of the Apocalypse, Unicorn.

Hortus Conclusus. See Garden Enclosed.

Hortus Deliciarum. Compendium of medieval learning created by *Herrade of Landsburg between 1160 and 1170. The Hortus Deliciarum, or The Garden of Delights, was a varied collection of information on a myriad of topics ranging from a practical guide to gardening to prayerful devotions. Produced to assist in the education of *nuns, this text consisted of 324 parchment sheets, approximately 636 illustrations, and over 1,200 texts by various authors including Herrade's own poetry. This comprehensive history of humankind and of natural history had an enormous influence on the development of women's spirituality, perhaps second only to the *Scivias of *Hildegard of Bingen. Among the illustrations Herrade designed for the Hortus Deliciarum were the *Seven Liberal Arts, the Last Judgment, and the *Seven Deadly Sins and the *Seven Virtues.

Hourbout, Susannah (1503–after 1567). Flemish woman artist. A daughter of Master Gerhard, Susannah Hourbout received her training as an illuminator and miniaturist in his studio. The only historical record of her existence was *Albrecht Dürer's notation of praise for her work and of his purchase of her drawing of a "Salvator" for one florin.

Hourglass. A sign of the passage of *time, and thereby the transitoriness of human life in religious art. The *hourglass was an *attribute of Time, Death, and the penitential *saints, especially *Jerome and *Mary Magdalene in western Christian art. The hourglass was a common element in *vanitas and *momento mori paintings.

Houri. Youthful servant maidens in the Muslim paradise, Dar al-jannah.

Hsi Wang Mu. Royal Mother of the Western Paradise in classical Chinese mythology. Originally a terrifying demon, Hsi Wang Mu became a beneficent and beautiful goddess who protected the herbs of immortality in Taoist mythology. The sacred *peach tree from which fruit was harvested only once every three years was placed in her care. With her attendants, Hsi Wang Mu guarded it jealously because this delicious fruit granted immortality to those who ate it. She was portrayed as a beautiful young woman garbed in elegant royal robes and seated on either a *peacock or a *crane. Hsi Wang Mu had two female attendants, one held a basket or dish of peaches, and the other a fan. Blue-winged birds served as her messengers, and her *attributes included bamboo, *gourds, and baskets of *flowers, especially peach blossoms.

Huitaca. Columbian Indian goddess. Huitaca was characterized as a beautiful but debauched woman in Columbian Indian art and mythology.

Huixtocihuatl. Goddess of salt in Aztec mythology.

Huldah (I Kgs 22:15). From the Hebrew for "weasel." Hebrew prophetess. Huldah was famed for her admonition to King Josiah that being a woman she was more compassionate about the weaknesses of the Israelites than any man could be. She reportedly taught the oral Torah to the elders in the Yeshiva of Jerusalem. Huldah was the only "nonroyal" buried within the walls of Jerusalem, and was responsible for the women's sections of Paradise. A rare topic in western Christian art, scriptural episodes related either to Huldah and King Josiah, or her teaching the Torah, were included in narrative cycles of the *Old Testament in *byzantine and *medieval art.

Human Body. The physical symbol of the microcosm to the macrocosm that was the *earth or the universe. The human body had symbolic properties both as a whole, and in its individual parts. *See also* Breast, Eye, Foot, Hand, Head, Heart, Skeleton, Skull, and Teeth.

Humility. Rare but significant virtue personified by a woman in religious art. Humility was signified by a woman whose downcast eyes symbolized her modesty, the crown at her feet the rejection of materialism, the globe universality, and the lamb in her arms innocence. *See also* Seven Virtues.

Humility, Saint (1226–1310). Founder of the Benedictine Order of Vallombrosan nuns. A wealthy young woman from Faenza, Rosana married a nobleman, Ugoletto. Following the tragedies of the deaths of their two infant children and Ugoletto's own near-fatal illness, Rosana persuaded her husband that they should enter the religious life: she as a nun named Humility in the Order of the *Poor Clares, and he as a lay brother at the monastery of St. Perpetua near Faenza. Despite her illiteracy, Humility read aloud to her religious sisters in the refectory as she was empowered by the Holy Spirit which, as a *dove, rested on her shoulder and whispered the textual passages into her ear. Famed for her visions, she claimed to be ordered by an *angel to enter the Convent of Saint Clare of Assisi. Identified as a miracle worker, Humility was reputed to have walked over the River Lamone, to have cured the gangerous limb of a monk with the sign of the cross, to have revived a dead child, and to have stilled a nun's hemorrhage. She lived an austere and spiritual life in her monastic cell adjoining the Vallambrosan Abbey of Saint Crispin. Influenced by the Abbot General of this monastic order dedicated to the primitive rule of Saint Benedict, to charity and poverty, to the support of the poor, to the defeat of simony, and to the admission of lay brothers, Humility established the Convent of Santa Maria Novella alla Malta, thereafter the motherhouse of Vallambrosan nuns, and later a second convent in Florence. She assisted in the building of her two convents, and also miraculously guided her nuns to a well filled with ice in mid-August, which eased Humility's suffering in her final illness. A rare topic in western Christian art, Humility was portrayed as a mature woman dressed in the black Benedictine *habit of an *abbess and either holding a model of one of her convents or loading bricks on an *ass to assist in their construction.

Hundred. A numerical symbol for heavenly bliss.

Hunt. Symbol for the *soul's quest for God or the striving for spiritual goals.

Hyacinth. A floral symbol for prudence, peace of mind, and desire for heaven. According to the classical Greco-Roman myth, Hyacinth was a handsome youth who was accidently killed by Apollo and from whose *blood sprang the *flower named in his honor. As an aromatic spring flower, the hyacinth signified the Resurrection.

Hyades. Sisters of the *Pleiades and the *Hesperides in Greek mythology. The daughters of Atlas and Pleione, these five or seven sisters were reputed to have been the nurses of the infant Dionysus. The Hyades committed suicide as a result of their grief at the death of their beloved brother, Hyas. Zeus transformed them into stars forming the constellation Hyades.

Hyena. A medieval symbol for greed, and for the *Devil feeding on the damned in Christian art.

Hygeia. Greek goddess of health. As either the daughter or the wife of Asklepios, he and Hygeia were worshiped together. She was portrayed as a mature woman who held a *snake in her right hand and a pot filled with healing potions in her left.

Hyssop. A small *white or *blue blossomed labiate herb with white spicy leaves and with diuretic properties. Hyssop was used in the Jewish and Christian ritual of sprinkling the *blood of sacrificial animal or holy *water. By its natural characteristics, hyssop represented penitence and humility, and by its medicinal powers, *baptism (Ps 51:7) and *Mary.

I

"I." Goddess of water in Mayan mythology. "I" was portrayed as holding the earthenware vessel overflowing with water. She was associated with *Chalchihuitlicue.

Ibis. Species of wading *birds popular in Egyptian art.

Icon. From the Greek for "image." Traditionally, a religious picture of Jesus Christ, *Mary, or a *saint in Christian art which was limited in subject matter and restricted in form, that is, emphasizing frontality, flatness, statis, and shadowlessness. In *Eastern Orthodoxy, icons were understood to be windows to the meaning of the event being depicted, not a realistic renderings of persons, places, or events. In western Christian art, icon came to signify a "holy picture," while the term "iconic" denoted either a stylized depiction of the human form of holy persons, or as having the characteristics of a holy picture. The term "icon" has become associated with the presentation or representation of divine or holy persons in the art of the world's religions. *See also* Aniconism; Ecumenical Councils

(Council of Nicaea II); Iconoclasm; Iconography.

Iconoclasm. From the Greek for "image breaking." Destruction of images premised upon the conviction that all images are idolatrous. In the *Eastern Orthodox Church, the Iconoclastic Controversies raged from about 726 until 842, when the veneration and liturgical use of *icons was restored. In western Christianity, there was a brief eruption of iconoclastic impulse under Charlemagne, while the major wave of Protestant iconoclasm was precipitated by the Reformation. In terms of world religious art, those traditions which deny or downgrade the visual arts, such as *Judaism and *Islam, are characterized as being iconoclastic.

Iconography. The study of the meanings attached to pictorial representations, including signs, symbols, *attributes, and emblems.

Iconostasis. The screen dividing the sanctuary from the laity in Eastern Orthodox Churches. This screen was covered with *icons beginning with the

ILLUSTRATION · 185

*Annunciation on the central doors ("Gates of Paradise"); to the left of the doors was an icon of the *Theotokos, to the right of the doors was an icon of Jesus Christ as King and Judge, and immediately to the right another icon of the *saint to whom the *church was dedicated. The iconostasis was the foundation for the development of the rood screen in medieval *cathedrals.

Ida. From the Sanskrit for "libation." Simultaneously the ceremonial sacrifice of milk and butter in Hindu rituals, and the mythic goddess of prayer and devotion. Although she was the daughter of Manu and the wife of Buddha, Ida was transformed from a masculine figure into a woman when she entered the sacred enclosure where Shiva rested in his female disguise.

Idun. From the Icelandic for "she who renews, makes young." Ancient Germanic goddess whose abduction and return signified the cycle of life and death. Idun was kidnapped by the giant Thiassi and during her captivity the deities were denied her golden apples and thereby took on the characteristics of age and infirmities. Loki rescued her and upon Idun's return the deities were rejuvenated by eating her golden apples. Idun was a common figure in Scandinavian and Germanic mythologies. She was represented as a beautiful and youthful maiden who held her life-giving *fruits, especially the golden apples, either in her hands or in a *basket in northern European art.

Ignorance. Female personification of one of the *Seven Deadly Sins. Ignorance was characterized as an obese and blind, or blindfolded, female or *her-maphrodite figure who wore a crown. Her representation was derived from that of Hades, the classical Greek god of the underworld and of wealth.

Ilamatecuhtli. From the Aztec for "old princess." Fertility goddess of Aztec mythology. Ilamatecuhtli was associated with the *Milky Way and ruled over the thirteenth hour of the day.

Ilazki. From the Basque for "grandmother, holy grandmother." Female personification of the *moon in Basque art and mythology. When identified as Illarqui, or "light of the dead," Ilazki was characterized as the nocturnal light illuminating the path for the souls of the dead. Ilazki was signified by a female face inscribed on the moon in Basque art.

Ildefonso, Saint (c. 606–67). A *Doctor of the Church, a Spanish abbot, and archbishop of Toledo. Devoted to *Mary, Ildefonso was a distinguished musician, mystic, and writer who prepared a treatise on the perpetual virginity of Mary. The patron of Toledo, Ildefonso was credited with establishing the cult of Mary in Spain. In western Christian art, especially in Spain, he was depicted receiving his *chasuble from *Mary.

Ilex. *See* Holly.

Illumination. From the Latin for "light." The more elaborate depictions of a letter or image with richly colored paints, *gold leaf backgrounds, and elegant borders in medieval manuscripts.

Illustration. From the Latin for "clarity." The simple rendering or depiction of a story with colored inks or paints in medieval manuscripts. Illustrations contained no *gold leaf backgrounds or elaborate borders.

Immaculate Conception. The Roman Catholic dogma that *Mary had been especially graced and kept free from the stain of *Original Sin from the moment of her conception by *Anne and *Joachim. Mary's unique purity from sin was granted in view of her destined role as the future mother of Christ who as God's *child would be born sinless through a sinless mother. A teaching of unfolding revelation, the Immaculate Conception created much dissension between the *Franciscans and the *Dominicans in the thirteenth and fourteenth centuries. Pope Pius IX officially defined the Immaculate Conception as a dogma of the faith in 1854. The Immaculate Conception became a major devotional theme in southern *baroque art as a part of the new *iconography of Mary that defended her position against the attacks of the Reformers. The symbols and images associated with the Immaculate Conception were derived from both the Song of Songs and the Book of Revelation. The most common *attributes of the Immaculate Conception were the *blue and *white dress, twelve *star *crown, and Mary's *feet resting on a *crescent *moon. Mary floated on *clouds and was surrounded by *cherubs holding *roses of sharon, *lilies, *mirror, and *column.

Inanna. Sumerian goddess of love and war. As the principal female deity of Mesopotamia, Inanna was also identified as Ninanna, or "Queen of Heaven," and Ninsianna, "Goddess of Venus." She had no permanent male partner and played her role as goddess of love with

masculine independence. An ancestor of *Aphrodite (*Venus), Inanna was assimilated into *Ishtar. According to myth and legend, Inanna had three aspects or natures. Her primary role was as goddess of love and sexual behavior, especially in terms of extramarital sexuality. She was neither a protector or patron of marriage. Her secondary role was as a warlike goddess fond of battle. This was Inanna as a violent being who lusted after power. Her tertiary role was as the planet Venus, that is, as the morning and evening star. Traditionally in ancient Near Eastern art, Inanna was depicted in two forms: as the winged warrior goddess protected by armor or surrounded by an astral *nimbus, and as the goddess of love characterized by her wings, horned cap, and total or partial nudity. Her *attributes included the *lion, *star, rosette, and a reed bundle.

Incarnation. From the Latin for "take on flesh." The Christian dogma that the Logos, the Word of God, took on human flesh and nature in the historic person of Jesus. The moment of this "enfleshment" was the *Annunciation to Mary when the Holy Spirit descended upon her and she conceived miraculously.

Incense. Incendiary and aromatic form of divination or adoration used in religious rituals. Incense was a fragrant smoke element to religious ceremonies and sacrificial offerings in ancient Mesopotamia, Egypt, Babylonia, Greece, and Rome. Assimilated into Christianity from the court ceremonial of the Roman Empire, incense became a sign of the ascent of prayers and petitions to God the Father. In Christian art, incense was represented by a priest, apostle, or holy person holding a censer.

Inez, Saint. *See* Agnes, Saint.

Initials. Monograms and abbreviations that served as both decorative devices and/or identifications. The most common initials in Christian art were Alpha and Omega, the first and last letters of the Greek alphabet that signified the eternity of God (Rv 1:8) and were incorporated into portraits of Jesus Christ; IC, the first letters of Jesus Christ in Latin, which were *the* sacred monogram; *MA, the first two Greek letters in *Mary; and *M with a crown as a monogram of Mary as the Virgin Mother.

Innocence. Female personification of one of the minor virtues in religious and secular allegories. Innocence was depicted as a young woman who held a *lamb, washed her hands, or was being rescued by *Justice from the vices symbolized by animals such as the *wolf (gluttony), *lion (wrath), or the *snake (deceit).

Ino. Legendary daughter of Cadmus and *Harmonia in Greek mythology. Initially a mother figure, Ino was famed for rearing Dionysus as well as her own children Athamas, Learchus, and Melicertes, and her stepchildren Helle and Phripus. She was doomed when she entered into a conspiracy to murder her stepchildren. In the midst of this plan, Athamas killed Learchus, and as a result a distraught Ino leapt into the sea with Melicertes. She was transformed into the sea goddess, Leucothea (*Magna Matuta).

Inquisition. An ecclesiastical tribunal first appointed by Pope Gregory IX in 1231 to root out heresy and prevent its spread. Administered by the *Dominicans and the *Franciscans, the Inquisition was granted permission to employ torture to force confessions in 1252 as a means to halt the Catharist heresy. The Spanish Inquisition was established in 1478 to detect the apostasy of apparent Jewish, Moorish, and later Protestant converts to the Church of Rome.

Inspiration. Female personification of the creative force that births ideas into reality. Inspiration took on a myriad of symbolic and emblematic forms in western religious art from the *Muses of classical Greco-Roman and *renaissance art to the *dove of the Holy Spirit in Christian art. In almost all cases, no matter what the form, inspiration was characterized and understood to be female. So for example, the Muses were believed to instill inspiration through their breast milk (*Purgatory* 22:101). The verbal and visual metaphor of full breasts signified the fruitfulness of ideas waiting to be expressed. In classical Greco-Roman and *renaissance art, inspiration was indicated by the image of one of the Muses lactating upon either a blank book page, empty canvas, or *musical instrument.

International Gothic. The style of art identified with the late fourteenth-century Franco-Burgundian courts that developed a realistic approach to details, especially of *landscape, *animals, and costumes. The International Gothic style spread from France into Italy, Germany, and Bohemia.

Io. Legendary priestess of *Hera and beloved of Zeus. A daughter of Inachus and Melis, Io was transformed by Zeus into a white cow that was demanded as a gift by a jealous Hera. In this guise, Io was guarded by Argos Panoptes and eventually freed by Hermes. She was then pursued by Hera's gadfly throughout Europe until her human form was restored in Egypt where Io bore Zeus a son, Epaphus, who became the king who built Memphis. The Bosporus, from the Greek for "cattle ford," was named in Io's honor.

Iphigenia. Female sacrifice required by *Artemis to permit Agamemnon's departure for the Trojan War. The daughter of *Clytemnestra and Agamemnon, Iphigenia was the sister of *Electra and Orestes. After her father had insulted Artemis by killing one of her sacred *stags, the winds necessary for his disembarkation to Troy disappeared. On the pretense that he was about to present his daughter in marriage to the hero, Achilles, Agamemnon sent for Iphigenia. Delighted at the prospect of such a heroic son-in-law, Clytemnestra sent her daughter to Aulis to meet her father. Just as the sacrificial offering was to be made on her sacred altar, Artemis intervened and rescued the unsuspecting princess. Iphigenia became a priestess of Artemis at her temple in Tauris where shipwrecked strangers were sacrificed to the goddess. Many years after the fall of Troy, Orestes came to Tauris in order to capture Artemis's sacred image and bring it to Attica. He was rescued from being a ritual sacrifice by his priestess sister, who brought the divine image with her when they returned home.

Irene, Saint (third century). Legendary widow of Castulus and nurse of the wounded Sebastian. According to tradi-tion, the pious widow Irene and her companion holy women found Sebastian following his torture, removed the arrows from his body, treated his wounds, and nursed him back to health. Irene was the patron of nurses. In western Christian art, she was represented as a mature matron in the companion of two or three other women all engaged in the act of removing the arrows from the body of Sebastian or holding the lit torches so that medical treatment could be administered to him. Her *attribute was a *vase of medicinal ointments.

Irene, Saint (d. 304). Learned Christian virgin martyr. With her sisters, *Agape and *Chiona, Irene refused to eat foods sacrificed to pagan idols, and the Christian trio were sentenced to death by the governor of Macedonia. However given her erudition, Irene was initially spared from martyrdom by fire so that the governor could reexamine her. Following the issuance of a degree against the possession of Christian books, she escaped to the mountains but was eventually captured and incarcerated without clothes in a brothel. Divine intervention shielded Irene from molestation and allowed her to preserve her vow of chastity. She was retried for treason and condemned to death in the same fire in which her books were to be burnt. A rare topic in eastern and western Christian art, Irene was identified by her *attribute of *books and flames, or by her two sister companions.

Iris (as a flower). From the Greek for "rainbow." A floral symbol for *Mary, and a sign of reconciliation between God and humanity. Since its leaves had a shape similar to that of *swords, the iris was also known as the "sword lily"

50. *Inanna-Ishtar, crowned with a star and holding a bow,
with the Image of Sirius and the Tree of Life*

51. *Pectoral in the form of Winged Isis*

and represented the *Seven Sorrows of Mary and her suffering during the Passion. In medieval Flemish painting, the iris replaced the *lily as Mary's botanical emblem. Spanish artists adopted the iris as an *attribute of Mary, especially in representations of the *Immaculate Conception.

Iris (as a goddess). From the Greek for "rainbow." Goddess of the *rainbow in Greek mythology. A daughter of Electra and Thaumus, Iris was sister to the *Harpies. She was a messenger of the Olympian deities and travelled along the rainbow to the underworld and the ends of the earth. In classical Greco-Roman and *renaissance art, Iris was portrayed as a golden-winged maiden dressed in a long flowing garment, often colored like the rainbow, and identified by her *attribute of the *caduceus as a divine messenger.

Išduštaya and Papaya. Ancient goddesses of fate in Asia Minor. These two sisters controlled the *spindle and the *mirror that determine each human's destiny at the moment of their birth. *See also* Fates, Moirai.

Išhara. From the Mesopotamian for "queen of the judgment seat and of sacrificial display." Mesopotamian goddess of love and war, and guarantor of oaths. In her Hittite form, she was known as the "queen of the mountains," while she signified sexual potency in Syria. Išhara was identified by her *attributes, *snake and *scorpion, in ancient Near Eastern art. She was assimilated into *Inanna.

Ishtar. Principal mother goddess of Akkadian, Assyrian, and Babylonian mythology. According to tradition, Ishtar had many lovers but always remained virginal. Like her Sumerian counterpart *Inanna and her Syrian counterpart *Astarte, Ishtar was characterized as erotic, belligerent, and astral. One of her emblems was Venus as the morning and the evening star. To ensure the fertility of the crops, the *hieros gamos of Ishtar and Tammuz was celebrated by the king and a priestess each New Year festival. Ishtar journeyed to the underworld where she performed the customary rites including the removal of all her clothes and jewels, and the initiatory tests of afflictions of disease and bodily tortures by *Allatu. All this Ishtar suffered in order to revive her dead husband, Tammuz, as god of vegetation, in the annual cycle of the seasons. In this mythic love journey and fertility ritual, she was associated with *Isis seeking Osiris, *Aphrodite seeking Adonis, and *Cybele seeking Attis. In the art of the ancient Near East, Ishtar was represented as an eight-pointed star or *rosette. She was also portrayed as a beautiful nude female figure who wore either a crescent moon or astral crown, or bull's horns or a horned cap, and drove a horse-drawn chariot. Or like *Athena, Ishtar was represented as a female warrior dressed for battle with her full armor including her bow, arrow, and quiver, and accompanied by her lions.

Isis. From the Egyptian language ostensibly for "seat, throne," but more probably meaning "place." Principal mother goddess and "ruler goddess" of ancient Egypt. Isis as the goddess of magical wisdom was characterized as the female personification of feminine creative power, and the throne. She was described as the love that pervaded heaven, earth, and the underworld. As sister and wife to Osiris, Isis's search for her beloved husband's body following his murder by Seth was the model of unswerving conjugal fidelity and the prototype of an ideal wife. As the wife of Osiris and the mother of Horus, she was the noblest example of a faithful and loving wife and mother. Although her main myth was her search for and restoration of the body of Osiris, Isis was involved in many myths including those dealing with the deadly sting of a *scorpion, poisonous *snakes, miraculous births, and the restoration of a dead child to life. Her epithet, "great of magic," signified her role as protector of her son, Horus, and thereby of all children. As protector of seamen, she was identified by the *rudder as her *attribute. Originally a goddess of the *moon, she was later venerated as a goddess of nature and of vegetation. In the Hellenistic syncretism of the Ptolemaic period, Isis was identified with *Aphrodite (*Venus), *Selene (*Luna), *Demeter (*Ceres), *Io, *Persephone, *Thetis, and *Venus, and was a classical foretype of *Mary. In classical Egyptian art, Isis was portrayed as a female figure often with a *vulture headdress and holding a papyrus scepter in one hand and an *ankh in the other. Her symbol was the *thet, or knot of Isis, signifying the blood of life. From her association with *Hathor, Isis also wore a crown composed of the solar disk encased in bovine *horns which was surmounted on a throne or decorated with plumes, and carried a *sistrum and wore a *menat. She might also have worn the united crown of Upper and Lower Egypt with the *feather of *Maat at the back. The most regular representation of Isis in Egyptian art was in the act of suckling

her infant son, Horus. The goddess could be either seated or standing as she held her infant son at her breast. These images, which were popular motifs on the walls and the altar of the *mammisi, prefigured images of Mary with the Christ Child. Isis was also depicted as the ideal eternal mourner with her sister, *Nephthys. Their lament at Osiris's death became the official funerary dirge of ancient Egypt. They were often symbolized as two *birds of prey, usually kites. Whether anthropomorphic or avian in form, these two sisterly mourners stood at the sides of the coffin with their outstretched wings protecting the deceased and empowering him or her with the afterlife. Isis and Nephthys also took the form of two snakes in the posture of rearing up in the bow of a solar barque facing the direction of the journey to the afterlife. Her *attributes included the *crescent moon, the *cow, and bovine *horns. As the female personification of the fertility of the lands flooded by the Nile, Isis was characterized as being black in coloration. As her cult survived into the early Christian world and throughout the Mediterranean, she became the classical foretype of the *Black Madonna.

Islam. From the Arabic root *s-l-m* for "submission" or "peace." Monotheistic religious tradition predicated upon surrender to God's will or law, thereby achieving peace within oneself and with God. Although part of the Middle Eastern heritage of prophetic religions, Islam is distinguished by its commitment to the doctrine of uncompromising monotheism which dominates both belief and practice. Muslims believe in God's revelation, the prophets, an ethics of personal responsibility and accountability, and a Day of Judgment. As members of a global faith community, Muslims share an individual and corporate religious identity premised upon their responsibility to implement God's will in personal and social life. The Five Pillars—profession of faith, daily prayer or worship, almsgiving, fasting, and pilgrimage to Mecca—unify global Islamic practice. As a religion which emphasizes law over theology and practice over belief, Islam is characterized by its singular commitment to religious discipline, and by Islamic law as the definitive norm for an Islamic lifestyle.

Between 160–632, the prophet Muhammad received the revelations of Allah through his angel-messenger, Gabriel. These revelations were collected and recorded in the *Qur'ān. Muhammad taught God's mesage of a new moral order dedicated to God's will, and established the first Islamic community in Medina following the Hijrah (emigration of Muslims from Mecca to Medina in 622). After the death of the prophet Muhammad, a debate over the process of succession divided Sunnis from Shi'ites. Sunnis advocated a caliphate in which the elders elected their political ruler of caliph ("successor" to Muhammad), whereas Shi'ites were committed to the familial succession of the imamate (from the Arabic *imam* for "leader"), that is, religio-political leadership and authority inherited by descendants of 'Ali, son-in-law of Muhammad. From the eighth century, Sufi mysticism developed emphasizing asceticism and love of God, often expressed through song, dance, and poetry. *See also* Fatima (c. 605–33), Fatima al 'Masumah, and Hand-of-Fatimah.

Islamic art. Architectural, manuscript, and decorative arts created either by Muslims or within an Islamic culture. Faithful to the teaching that God alone is the Creator and the Artist, Muslim craftsmen and architects have worked anonymously and emphasized tradition and conformity. They have excelled in the ornamental arts of calligraphy, arabesque, and geometric design as well as color symbolism. Islamic art has been characterized by serene elegance of design, clarity of line, and intellectual stability. It has traditionally rejected the use of religious *iconography, and the creation of representational images to propagate the faith or to instill devotion or meditation during prayer.

Itzpapaloyl. From the Aztec for "obsidian butterfly." Aztec fire goddess. Itzpapalotyl was an astral goddess who was represented in Aztec art as either a *butterfly or a *deer.

Iusas and Nehbet Hotep. Female aspects of the god Tem in Egyptian mythology. This set of doubles signified the "mistress of the gods." Iusas was depicted as a beautiful woman holding a scepter in her right hand and an *ankh in her left, and wearing a vulture headdress surmounted by the *uraeus and a solar disk encased in bovine horns.

Iustitia. Female personification of justice in Roman art and mythology. When identified as "Iustitia Augusta," she signified the virtue of the Emperor. Comparable to the Greek *Dike, Iustitia was portrayed as a seated woman who was blindfolded and who held a sword in her right hand and the scales of justice in her left hand.

Ivory. Symbol of purity and moral fortitude. In *medieval art, ivory typified

Jesus as the Christ as its *white *color and firm texture reflected his incorruptible *body, which lay in the *tomb for three days.

Ivory Tower. A symbol for incorruptibility, moral strength, and ascetic distance from the world. The ivory tower was an *attribute of *Mary and *Barbara.

Ivy. A green vine that clung tightly to its support and had multiple meanings: death and immortality, as well as fidelity and unceasing affections.

Ixazalvah. Mayan goddess of weaving.

Ix Chel. From the Mayan for "rainbow lady." Goddess of the *moon, and protector of women in childbirth and of weaving in Mayan mythology. She was characterized by her concerns for the female marital role, including childbirth and sexuality; and of weaving and the healing arts. Ix Chel was depicted as an old woman with clawed hands and feet. She was assimilated into the Aztec goddess *Coatlicue.

Ix Chiup. From the Mayan for "the woman." Goddess of the *moon in Mayan mythology.

Ixtab. Mayan goddess of suicides, and death by hanging.

Izanami-No-Mikoto. From the Japanese for "she who invites you to enter." Principal primeval goddess of Japanese religion and later of *Shintoism. Izanami-No-Mikoto was the embodiment of the mother goddess who died in childbirth and ruled the underworld after her death. She was portrayed as a beautiful woman garbed in a regal kimono often standing on the water and always gesturing welcome in Japanese art.

J

❦

Jacobus de Voragine (c. 1230–98). A Dominican monk and Archbishop of Genoa. Famed for his learning and piety, Jacobus de Voragine was the author of *The Golden Legend* (*Legenda Aurea*), the thirteenth-century text that became a major sourcebook for western Christian art.

Jael (Jgs 4:17–22). Kenite woman who fulfilled *Deborah's prophecy that Israel's enemy, the Canaanite General, Sisera, would die an ignominious death at a woman's hands (Jgs 4:9). Following defeat in battle against Deborah and Barak, Sisera sought refuge with Heber and his wife Jael. Having been offered hospitality, Sisera was offered *milk to drink and a place to rest inside Heber and Jael's tent. Contrary to all the laws of hospitality, Jael murdered him as he slept by driving a tent peg through his *head (often depicted as in his *ear or on his temple). Later, Jael displayed Sisera's corpse to Barak. In Deborah's song of victory, Jael was credited with slaying Sisera near the entrance to her tent. Although she was not Israelite, Jael was listed among the heroines of Israel. In western Christian art, she was depicted as a beautiful woman holding a *hammer and a tent peg. Sisera's body was located nearby with the tent peg visible in his head. Representations of Jael were rare in western Christian art except during the medieval and early renaissance when her action of killing Sisera was interpreted as a foretype of *Mary's crushing the head of the *serpent, especially in terms of Deborah's prophecy that "Blessed above women shall Jael be" (Jgs 5:24).

Jainism. From the Sanskrit for "followers of the victor." Indian religion established in the sixth century B.C.E. by Vardhamma Mahavira. Premised upon a reinterpretation of *Hinduism, Jainism rejected the authority of the Vedas and the rule of the caste system. This new religious tradition advocated that the fundamental law of karma resulted in either condemnation to the endless cycle of birth-death-rebirth as a process of purification for those individuals laden with the heavy karma of demeritorious deeds or *moskha,* "liberation," for those with the lighter karma of meritorious actions. The Jain interpretation of the teaching of ahimsa, or non-injury, extended beyond human relationships to the preservation of all living things from physical and psychological pain, and supported an ethic of restraint. Jainism was divided into two groups—Digambara (or the "sky-clad") and the Shvetambara (or the "white-clad")—in the first century during an interpretative dispute over the necessity of nudity as an element of the ascetic life.

Jain art Originally premised upon the symbolism and aesthetics of the Hindu tradition, Jain art eventually was characterized by a rigid symmetry and immobility in the representation of Mahavira or any of the twenty-four Tirthankaras. This stylization of the human figure was a symbolic expression of the spiritual aloofness that transcends the human body of a holy man. Jain art assimilated the symbolic iconography—*lotus, stupa, and the *mudras—of *Buddhist art.

Jairus's Daughter (Mt 9:18, 23–25; Mk 5:22–24, 35–42; Lk 8:41–42, 49–56). An elder of the *synagogue, Jairus asked Jesus to restore his daughter's life. Jesus accompanied Jairus to his house where mourners scorned Jesus's claim that the girl was merely asleep. Ordering everyone out of the house, Jesus placed his *hand on the young girl's hand and she rose from her bed. In western Christian art, representations of Jairus's Daughter were rare except for those within the byzantine and medieval life cycles of Jesus Christ. This episode was distinguished from the *Healing of Peter's Mother-in-law, in which story the crowd remained to witness the cure brought about when Jesus laid his hand on that of the sick woman.

Jameson, Anna Brownell Murphy (1794–1860). First woman author of texts on the history of Christian art, a feminist writer, and an advocate of women's education. Daughter of an Irish miniaturist, Anna Murphy was trained as an artist in her father's studio following the family's migration from Dublin to London. Self-educated, she became a governess at the age of sixteen to the children of the Marquis of Winchester. Her own curiosity and native intelligence were piqued by the travels made with this family, and she began to write what would become her successful and popular *Diary of an Ennuyée* (1826). She suffered through an unhappy marriage and her duty as the financial support of her parents and younger sisters. As her books on travel, including guides to a variety of museums throughout Europe, garnered her a popular audience, Mrs. Jameson established herself as an expert on culture and became associated with leading artists, writers, and successful independent women in England, France, Germany, and the United States. While she continued her lifelong interest in women's rights and education with books such as her two volume, *Characteristics of Women* (1832), she began a multivolume project entitled *Sacred and Legendary Art*. These texts including her two volume, *The History of Our Lord, as Exemplified in Works of Art* (1864), and *Legends of the Monastic Orders* (1850), were the first books on the history of Christian art, or of the *iconography of Christian art, written by a woman. Her *Legends of the Madonna* remains as the most comprehensive one-volume study of the symbolism of Mary in Christian art.

Jasmine. A floral symbol for Jesus Christ because of the purity of its whiteness and the sweetness of its scent. A flower of grace, elegance, and amiability, the jasmine also signified *Mary.

Jecoliah (2 Kgs 15:2; 2 Chr 26:3). From the Hebrew for "God is mighty." Wife of Amaziah, king of Judah, and mother of Uzziah. A rare topic in western Christian art, Jecoliah was represented as a proper Jewish matron in the narrative cycles of the royal line of Israel or the ancestors of Jesus Christ.

Jehosheba (2 Kgs 11:2; 2 Chr 22:11). From the Hebrew for "oath of God." The daughter of Joram, king of Judah, Jehosheba provided haven for her nephew Joash when his grandmother Athaliah sought to murder so she could seize the throne and ostensibly then murder all her other grandchildren who had a rightful claim to the throne. A rare topic in western Christian art, Jehosheba was represented as a proper Jewish matron whose flowing garments or cloak hid a male child and included in the cycles of the *heroines of Israel.

Jemimah (Job 42:14). From the Hebrew for "dove." First daughter born to Job following the end of his trials and tribulations with God, and signifying his new life. A rare topic in western Christian art, Jemimah was represented as either an infant or a small girl in the narrative cycles of Job.

Jephthah's Daughter (Jgs 11:30–40). On the eve of a major battle with the Ammonites in defense of Gilead, the Israelite general, Jephthah, made a victory pact with God to sacrifice the first living creature exiting his home to greet his victorious return. Jephthah was to forfeit the life of his only child, a beloved daughter, who came to meet him with tambourines and *dances. When the grief-stricken father confessed his vow to his daughter, she maintained that the promise be kept. After a two-month period of lamentation over her virginity, the daughter returned home from the mountains and was sacrificed by her father. She was an *Old Testament foretype of *Mary, especially of the medieval and baroque themes of the Education of the Virgin. A rare theme in western Christian art, the story of Jephthah's daughter was an occasional element in the *Old Testament narrative cycles. It was a popular motif in French baroque painting in two thematic arrangements as either the victorious warrior rent his garments in grief as his daughter exited the house, or the daughter knelt beside an *altar as her father gestured her execution with his *sword.

Jerome, Saint (c. 342–420). One of the Four *Fathers of the Western Church, he revised and translated the Bible from its Greek and Hebrew sources into the Latin Vulgate (a revision of which was declared normative for Roman Catholicism at the *Council of Trent). Born of Christian parents in Dalmatia, he traveled to Antioch in 374 to study. Reprimanded by Christ in a vision for his study of pagan literature, Jerome took refuge in the *desert for four years and studied Hebrew. Following his ordination to the priesthood in Antioch in 378, Jerome lived briefly in Rome where his criticism of the clergy and of clerical abuses won him few friends. He established a monastery and the Jeronymite (Hieronymite) Order in Bethlehem, and benefited from the financial patronage of a wealthy woman and her daughter, who were later identified as Paula and Eustochium. He became the latter's spiritual director and wrote her a series of famous texts, including the *Letter to Eustochium* and his treatise, *De Virginitate* (*Concerning the Keeping of Virginity*), in honor of the event of her vow and receipt of the *veil of perpetual virginity in 384. These texts contained influential admonitions about the appropriate behavior, styles of dress, manners, and reading for a proper Christian woman that have survived well past Jerome's own lifetime, including his encouragement of women's literacy as a mode of teaching the *Bible to their children, a defense of female celibacy, and a definition of the perpetual virginity of *Mary (*Ad Helvidius*). Jerome established the church's policy towards female *nakedness as a state of shamefulness of the female body that incurred embarrassment to the proper Christian who blushed at the sight of her body and thereby never bathed so as to protect herself from female nakedness. A popular figure in western Christian art and legend, Jerome's story was retold and embellished in several medieval texts including *The Golden Legend*. Among those episodes was the story in which Jerome appeared in *church garbed in female dress after his spiteful fellow students stole his clothes while he slept. Jerome was the patron of students. In western Christian art, he was depicted as a bearded, ascetic elderly man who was accompanied by a *lion. The two most popular motifs of Jerome were either reading or writing in his study, or as the repentant hermit in the *desert who beat his chest with a stone to signify both his repentance and the mortification of the flesh. His *attributes included the *cardinal's hat, *crucifix, *skull, lion, and *owl.

Jesse, Tree of. A botanical symbol for the royal "House of David" from which the *Messiah would come (Is 11:1–2). In western Christian art, depictions of the Tree of Jesse included the aged Jesse seated or recumbent at the base of the *tree (bush) that arose from his genital area blossomed with the *fruits or *flowers that signified the ancestors of Jesus. In some presentations, the ancestors were identified by *scrolls inscribed with their names or a biblical verse with which they were associated. The *iconography of the Tree of Jesse was established by the Abbot Suger in the designs for a stained-glass window for the twelfth-century Abbey Church of Saint Denis in Paris. A popular topic in late *medieval art and Netherlandish *renaissance art, the Tree of Jesse became an important Mariological symbol, and often had an image of the *Madonna and Child crowning the tree. Such Mariological presentations of the Tree of Jesse were a reversal of *Eve's act of disobedience at the Tree of Knowledge.

Jewels/Jewelry. Characteristic symbols and *attributes of significant historical persons and deities in eastern religious art. Multiplication of jewelry on a single figure, such as necklaces, earrings, bracelets, anklets, armbands, and rings, was more significant in identifying Hindu deities such as *Pārvati, *shaktis, *apsarāses, and *Gaṅgā than the material value or nature of the jewels. Similarly in Buddhist art, appreciably bejeweled figures connoted *bodhisattvas such as *Kuan-yin as opposed to the simplicity of an unadorned Buddha. Specific jewels were attributes of particular goddesses such as the flaming pearl of *Avalokiteshvara. Similarly, jewels were linguistic metaphors for spiritual values as in the Tibetan Buddhist incantation of *"om mani padme hum"* ("the jewel in the Lotus"). Jewels and jewelry functioned as binary symbols for the transience of material objects as opposed to the eternality of moral virtues, and for the personifications and human characteristics credited in *alchemy and other healing arts traditions, in western religious art. Opulent jewelry connoted wealth and *Vanity personified. The motif of a woman casting off jewelry as a sign of her moral tenor began with the classical Roman heroine, *Claudia, and was also a sign of religious conversion for *Mary Magdalene. Bejeweled female figures denoted either wealth and beauty as in images of queens and goddesses, or materialism and lasciviousness as in depictions of demons, seductresses, and *femmes fatales. See also* Brisingamen, Cintāmani, Comma, Coral, Cowrie Shells, Crown, Gold, Hand-of-Fatima, Hand-of-Ishtar, Menat, Necklace, Pearl, Silver, and Tiara.

Jewish art. Ambivalent identification of any of the following: works of art created by Jews whether or not the theme or function was religious in nature; works of art created by Jews for ritual or ceremonial purposes; or works of art with a Jewish theme, religious or secular, created by non-Jewish artists. Traditionally, Judaism has supported the arts of poetry and music, and downplayed the visual arts in accordance with the second commandment (Ex 20:2–3). However, archaeological excavations have revealed that there was a tradition of the visual arts with pedagogical and ceremonial purposes such as the frescoes found at Dura-Europos. The use of the term "Jewish art" requires careful definition and future study. See also Ketubbah.

Jews. Originally identified as the people of the tribes of Judah and Benjamin, and later those from the Roman Province of Judaea who professed the monotheistic tradition known as Judaism. These are the descendants of Abraham, Isaac, and Jacob who were constituted as a unique people by the Mosaic covenant with Yahweh. According to both biblical texts and their own self-description, the Jews were the "chosen people" of God who after the Babylonian destruction of the Kingdom of Judah awaited the coming of the Messiah to free them from all forms of bondage and to reestablish the Kingdom of David. From the earliest beginnings of Christianity, Jews who continued in the tradition of Judaism were seen in conflict with the new religion. Innumerable historic disputes occurred in which the early Christians were denounced as polluting or debasing the Hebraic tradition, while the Jews were characterized as the "Christ killers." This mutual religious intolerance led to multiple persecutions and injustices as Christianity became the dominant religious and sociopolitical power throughout western culture. In western Christian art, the heroes and heroines, *prophets and prophetesses of the *Old Testament were depicted with sincerity and respect. However, "the Jews" became characterized as evil and villainous figures who had *red *hair and large noses, and wore conical hats and *yellow badges—all of which signified that they were outcasts, and possibly the *children of the *Devil (in which case, the Jews had cloven hoofs for feet and a tail). *Medieval and *renaissance art was replete with anti-Semitic signs, symbols, and depictions of the Jews. In western Christian art, the *Hebrews and the Jews were commonly identified as one and the same.

Jezebel (I Kgs 18). Renowned symbol of female wickedness, loose morals, scheming, and wanton sexual intrigues. The foreign-born princess from Tyre and dominating wife of King Ahab, Jezebel threatened to punish any Hebrew prophet or elder who opposed her initiation of Baal worship into the Hebrew religion. Fearing God more than this powerful queen, the prophet Elijah persuaded the people to repent their idolatry and repudiate this evil woman. Despite her wickedness, Jezebel was characterized in the *Old Testament as compassionate because she never permitted a funeral procession to pass without walking herself behind the bier, and clapping her hands as a sign of respect and wailing with the mourners; and she accompanied nervous bridegrooms to their wedding feasts and participated in their public joy. Thrown from the palace balcony, Jezebel was killed and her lifeless body was left for the *dogs. However, her *head, *hands, and *feet were not eaten by the animals, and since these were the instruments of her good deeds they were honored with proper burial. A rare topic in western Christian art, Jezebel was depicted as a beautiful woman of loose morals, signified by her style of dress and hairdo, and her heavy facial makeup. The phrase "a painted Jezebel" referenced her immoral action of painting her face in preparation for seduction and wanton lust.

Jian Lao. From the Chinese for "the stable one." Buddhist goddess of the earth and of permanence. Jian Lao was identified in Buddhist art by either the gesture of hands placed together or her *attribute of an ear of grain.

Jingo. According to Japanese tradition, Jingo was the widowed Empress who magically invaded Korea following her husband's death. Throughout this three-year conquest, she was pregnant with their son, Ojin. In Japanese art, Jingo was represented as either a woman warrior or a pregnant woman garbed in Imperial robes.

Joan of Arc, Saint (c. 1412–31). A thirteen-year-old French peasant girl who began to hear "inner voices" calling her to save France from the English and Burgundian invaders. Following several audiences with the dauphin, she persuaded him to be crowned as Charles VII in Rheims. Provided with a suit of *armor, Joan led the French army to victory at Orléans, Patay, and Troyes. She was captured by the Burgundians in Compiègne and sold to the English. Following brutal maltreatment, she was confined and ridiculed by the English soldiers and priests. She was tried by an English-allied Burgundian ecclesiastical tribunal on charges of witchcraft and heresy, and found guilty. At the age of nineteen, Joan of Arc was burned at the stake in the marketplace of Rouen. A patron of France and of the radio, Joan of Arc was a symbol of inspiring female leadership and was prefigured by other female warriors like *Athena, *Minerva, and *Judith. In western Christian art, she was depicted as a young woman dressed in a suit of armor, often on horseback, who held a *banner of victory inscribed with the *fleur-de-lis and a *palm. She was also represented as a young woman in peasant dress who knelt in prayer as she heard "her voices."

Joan, Popess (d. 858 or d. 1103). Legendary ninth- or eleventh-century woman who masqueraded as a man and was elected pope. Although not mentioned in the historical *Liber Pontificalis*, or *Papal Book*, it was reputed that the person elected as John VIII in 855 was actually a woman who served as pope until 858, but according to historical records Benedict III succeeded Leo IV in 855. Originally identified as a woman named Agnes or Gilberta, the story of Popess Joan was first given credence in the writings of the Dominican chronicler, Jean de Mailly, in the thirteenth century. Another version of her story was recounted in the thirteenth-century chronicles of Martin of Troppau (d. 1278); and a more colorful version in the thirteenth-century *De septem donis Spiritu Sancti* (*Seven Gifts of the Holy Spirit*) by the Dominican Stephen of Bourbon who identified Joan as a gifted scribe and notary, cited her election as being in 1100, her birthing of a child in the midst of a procession on the way to the Lateran, and finally her exile from Rome and her death by stoning. As a result, successive popes have changed the procession route to the Lateran thereby avoiding the street upon which Joan was alleged to have given birth. The thirteenth-century Dominican known as Johannes Angelicus reported that Joan was born of English parents in Mainz, followed her beloved to Athens where she studied philosophy and theology, and was elected pope in 855. In an earlier ninth-century version of

Popess Joan's story, and thereby one contemporary with her possible papacy, she was reputed to be in love with a Benedictine monk and so masqueraded as a man in order to be with her beloved, becoming famed for her learning and eventually becoming both cardinal and pope. The legend of Popess Joan experienced widespread popularity throughout western Europe during the fifteenth-century debates over papal power, and was revived by the Protestant Reformers during the sixteenth and seventeenth centuries; however, by the eighteenth century, general interest in Popess Joan had disappeared. Scholars believed that hers was either a modification or medieval Christian revision of the Roman folk legend about a priest of Mithra or the female Roman Senator Marazia. In western Christian art, Popess Joan was depicted as matronly figure dressed in the regalia of the Pope, holding the *attributes of the papal office, and enthroned in majesty.

Joanna (Luke 8:3, 24:10). Among the faithful women who supported Jesus of Nazareth and witnessed the empty tomb. Joanna was the wife of Chiza, the domestic administrator and wine steward in the household of Herod Agrippa. She heard the sermons of Jesus, supported his mission financially, and was counted among the holy women present at the empty tomb. A rare topic in western Christian art, Joanna may be included among the anonymous holy women at the Sermon on the Mount, at the foot of the cross, and at the empty tomb.

Jörd. From the Icelandic for "earth." Indigenous northern Germanic *mother goddess.

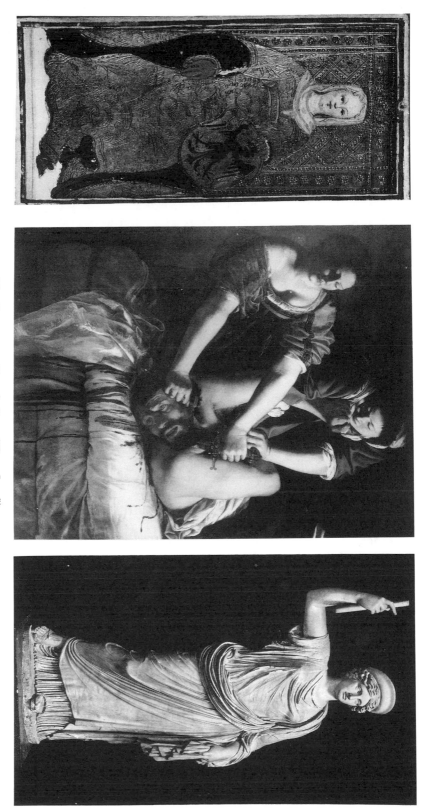

52. *The Priestess or Female Pope* ("Pope Joan")
53. Artemisia Gentileschi, *Judith*
54. *Juno*

Josephus, Flavius (c. 37–d. early second century). Jewish historian and Pharisee who had close associations with both the Roman Imperium and apparently the Essene Community. His significance to Christian art and legend was his many texts, particularly *History of the Jewish War* and *Jewish Antiquities*. In these, Josephus sought both to record the history of his people and also to rehabilitate their position with Rome, especially following the revolt in 66 C.E. As an "objective" source, his texts historically verified the existence of John the Baptist (*Antiquities* 18:166) and James Minor (*Antiquities* 18:200), and his *History of the Jewish War* contained a passage that was a reference to the ministry, passion, death, and resurrection of Jesus Christ. He identified the unnamed daughter of *Herodias as "*Salome," but made no mention of her dancing, and placed the blame for the execution of John the Baptist on Herod.

Judaism. The form of religious monotheism practiced by the Jews of the post-second century Rabbinic tradition. The historic religion could be traced back to the prophetic ministry of Moses, who received the Covenant and Torah from God on Mount Sinai during the forty years of wandering in the *desert, and the teachings of the *Old Testament *prophets. Both Rabbinic Judaism and Christianity were rooted in the tradition of biblical Israel as recorded in the Old Testament. As the Christ, or Messiah, Jesus was interpreted by the post-Jewish Christians as the fulfillment of the prophecies and promises of the Old Testament. In western Christian art, Rabbinic Judaism was represented by a series of symbols and images that affirmed it as a preparation for Christianity; for example, the foundation level of a building was represented as an antique (older) architectural style such as the romanesque while the building was represented in the modern (newer) style such as the gothic. There were also derogatory (anti-Semitic) images throughout the history of western Christian art, including the ass, the scapegoat, the blinded *Synagoga, and the chamber pot; individual Jews were identified by their conical hats, yellow badges, large noses, red hair, and *horns. *See also* Hebrews, Jews.

Judgment of Paris. Mythological basis for the Trojan War. Unhappy at not being invited to attend the wedding of Peleus and *Thetis, *Eris tossed a golden apple into the crowd at the wedding banquet. As this fruit was engraved with the phrase, "to the most beautiful," it was sought by each of the goddesses. In a moment of extraordinary sagacity, Zeus (Jupiter) claimed that he could only narrow the group of candidates to three—*Aphrodite (*Venus), *Athena (*Minerva), and *Hera (*Juno)—and was unable to make a final selection. After some deliberation, the handsome Paris, prince of Troy, was asked to make the final selection among the three worthy goddesses. In an effort to earn the desired award, each goddess suggested her worth in the form of a promise to Paris: Aphrodite promised him the love of the most beautiful woman in the world; Athena victory in battle and wisdom in life; and Hera a happy and successful marriage. Paris opted for Aphrodite who rewarded him with the love of *Helen, wife of King Melaneus. Following the goddess's directive, the erstwhile prince-lover abducted his beloved queen, and unwittingly began the Trojan War.

Judgment of Solomon (1 Kgs 3:16–28). The story of the two women, ostensibly prostitutes, who lived in the same house and who each bore a son on the same day. One of the infants died, and each claimed the living *child as her own. Brought before Solomon for judgment, the two women each made an emotional appeal for the living child. Solomon ordered that the healthy child be cut in two with a half given to each woman. One woman agreed to this act, but the true mother of the child relinquished her claim so that the child might live. Solomon then granted this mother her child. In western Christian art, depictions of the Judgment of Solomon signified both the *wisdom of the king, and prefigured the Last Judgment.

Judith. An apocryphal heroine and one of the Female Worthies (models of ideal womanhood such as *Susanna, *Lucretia, and *Jael). The widow of Manasseh, Judith came out of her seclusion to save Israel from Nebuchadnezzar. The city of Bethulia was besieged by the Assyrian army and its general, Holofernes. As the elders of the city led by the high priest Ozias prepared to surrender, Judith upbraided them and declared that God would save the city. She returned to her home, praying to God for inspiration and help, took off her widow's weeds, bathed and anointed her body, dressed in her finest clothes and *jewels, and gathered a sack of ritual foods. She and her maid, *Abra, then departed for the camp of Holofernes. She met Holofernes and declared that she could lead him to victory at the cost of only one life. For three days and nights she stayed

at his camp, but was allowed free access to the river each night to bathe and eat her ritual foods. Captivated by her beauty, Holofernes rejoiced when Judith informed him that she would eat with him on the fourth day of her visit. He prepared a lavish feast for her, hoping to seduce her. At the appropriate moment, his commanders and soldiers withdrew from the tent, and Judith and Holofernes were alone. Already drunk into a state of semiconsciousness, Judith seized his *sword and with two blows decapitated him. She placed his severed *head in her food sack, and with her maid left the enemy camp without arousing any suspicion. When she displayed the severed head upon the ramparts of Bethulia, the Israelites vanquished the stunned Assyrians, and Judith was declared a heroine of her people. In western Christian art, Judith was interpreted as a foretype of *Mary as the Second *Eve (crushing the *head of the *serpent). Judith was represented as a chaste but beautiful widow who holds the severed head of Holofernes by the *hair. In *medieval art, she was the virtuous foretype of *Mary, a descendent of *Athena Nike, and an ancestor of the female warrior *saints like *Joan of Arc. Judith was sometimes depicted in the act of slaying Holofernes, but more often shown with his head in her hand. During the Renaissance, she became fused with the female personification of democracy and the city, and prefigured Ladies Liberty and Democracy. From the *Counter-Reformation period forward, Judith was represented as a seductive femme fatale who rejoiced in the dreadful deed she had committed.

Judith's maidservant. *See* Abra.

Jugumishanta. Female creator of humanity, giver of the established order and the form of the land. Jugumishanta was the *mother goddess of the eastern highlands tribe of Papua, New Guinea.

Ju-i. From the Chinese for "as you may desire." Jade or wooden s-shaped blade signifying good wishes and beneficence. In Chinese and Japanese Buddhist art, the ju-i denoted the *lotus, thereby symbolizing the Buddha and his teachings. It was an *attribute of *Kuan-yin and other *bodhisattvas.

Julia (Rom 16:15). Otherwise anonymous Christian woman who with her husband, Philologus, were greeted by Paul in his letter to the Church of Rome. Their names—Lois and Philologus—were common slave names at the time of Jesus of Nazareth.

Julian of Norwich (1342–after 1413). Christian visionary and mystical writer. Famed *anchoress residing outside the walls of Saint Julian's Church in Norwich, Julian experienced a severe illness in 1373 that ended with a two-day episode of sixteen revelations on the Passion of Christ and the Virgin Mary. For the following twenty years, she meditated upon these ecstatic visions and ultimately wrote her *Revelations of Divine Love*, which was influential upon both medieval spirituality and Christian art, especially in terms of her use of feminine imagery for God. A rare independent topic in western Christian art, the visions of Julian of Norwich played a significant role in the *iconography of women, particularly of *Mary, in western Christian art.

Junit. Egyptian goddess of Tuphium and the female personification of the sacred pillar.

Juno. From the Latin for "vitality of a young woman." The Roman goddess of womanhood identified with the Greek *Hera. As the queen of the gods and goddesses, Juno symbolized the ideals and honor of womanhood. She was the protector of marriage, and of women in childbirth (*gold *coins were offered to her following the safe delivery of a male *child). In classical Greco-Roman and *renaissance art, Juno was represented as a full-bodied, properly dressed matron who held either an infant in swaddling clothes in her left *hand and a *flower in her right, or a *shield and a *spear, and was accompanied by a *serpent. She might be represented wearing the *girdle of Venus. Her *attributes included the *peacock, *girdle, *goat, *fig, and *pomegranate. She was a classical Greco-Roman foretype for both *Anne and *Mary. *See also* Hieros Gamos.

Juno Lucina. From the Latin for "vital young woman who brings children into the light of the world." Manifestation of *Juno as the protector of women in childbirth.

Juno Regina. Manifestation of *Juno as the feminine guardian of Rome and of the Empire.

Justa and Rufina. Legendary Spanish martyrs and defenders of *Christianity against pagan traditions and folk religion in Spain. The daughters of an impoverished potter in Seville, Justa and Rufina opposed the sale of any of his goods for use in any pagan ritual or temple, especially those dedicated to *Venus. Following a series of disputes with potential customers, the two sisters were brought before the Roman governor of Seville. In an act of defiance, they smashed an image of Venus during their civil trial, and were found guilty of sacrilege and commanded to death. They were the patrons of Seville. A rare topic in western Christian art, Justa and Rufina were a popular subject in Spanish *baroque art. Their attributes included earthenware pots and *palm branches.

Justice. One of the Four Cardinal Virtues (and one of the *Seven Virtues). Usually personified as a female, Justice was represented in ancient Egyptian art by *Maat, and in western Christian art as blindfolded (impartial) and holding a *sword (temporal power) and *scales (a weighing of arguments and evidence for and against). In *medieval and *renaissance art, Justice was identified by the scales and sword she held, and the representation of Emperor Trajan at her *feet. As a female figure, *Justitia was a metaphorical foretype for *Athena, *Minerva, *Judith, *Mary as the female personification of *wisdom, and *Sophia.

Justina of Antioch, Saint (early fourth century). A virtuous and beautiful young woman whose commitment to Christianity brought about the conversion of the pagan magician, Cyprian. Although he conspired with her pagan suitor, Aglaides, to destroy Justina's virtue, Cyprian came not only to lust for her but to admire and respect her ability to deny the temptations of the Devil. They were tortured in a *cauldron of boiling pitch, and then transferred to Nicodemia and beheaded under the orders of Diocletian. In eastern and western Christian art, Justina of Antioch was depicted as a beautiful young woman who was identified by her *attribute, the *unicorn.

Justina of Padua, Saint (early fourth century). Daughter of the pagan King Vitalcino of Padua, and raised a Christian by Prosdochimus, the first bishop of Padua. The imprint of her knees were visible on the bridge over the Po River where she was seized by Roman soldiers and knelt to pray for strength. She was martyred by a *sword thrust into her side. Justina was a patron of Padua and Venice. In western Christian art, she was depicted as a beautiful, regally dressed young woman. Her *attributes included a *sword, *crown, *palm, and *unicorn (hence the confusion with *Justina of Antioch).

Justitia. *See* Iustitia.

Juturna. Roman goddess of healing springs, and of wells in times of drought. Juturna was originally an Etruscan goddess who was assimilated into the Roman pantheon.

Juventas. Roman goddess of eternal youth. Juventas was the special guardian of Roman youths and corresponded to the Greek goddess *Hebe. A special sacrifice was made to Juventas when a young boy first wore a toga or when a young girl first menstruated.

K

✿

Kabbalah. From the Hebrew for "received tradition." This mystical tradition of esoteric teachings was popular since thirteenth-century southern France and Spain, and continues today especially in some branches of Hasidism. The teachings of Kabbalah were reputed to have been given originally with the Torah to Moses on Mount Sinai. This specialized category of spiritual enlightenment was developed from the earlier mystical tradition of Maashen Bereshit and Maasheh Merkavan, and based on the *Sefer Habahir* (*Book of Brightness*). The *Sefer Yetzirah* (*Book of Essences*) and the *Zohar*, from the Hebrew for "splendor," were the main texts of Kabbalah.

Kadeš. Canaanite goddess of love and female sexuality. In classical Near Eastern art, Kadeš was portrayed naked as she stood on a *lion and held a *snake in both her hands.

Kadi. Babylonian goddess. Kadi was the virgin bride of the gods, and thereby signified the practice of temple *prostitution. She was represented as a *serpent having a woman's head and breasts, and thereby was the Near Eastern foretype of *Lilith and the serpent temptress of *medieval and *renaissance art.

Kala-Nath. Epithet of *Kālī as the cosmic womb of creation or the primordial abyss.

Kālī. From the Sanskrit for "she who is black." Menacing *great goddess and wife of Shiva in the Hindu pantheon. As the goddess of time and the mystery of life and death, Kālī was portrayed dancing through space, garbed in a garment decorated with *skulls, and having four arms. She held a *sword in one hand and a severed *head in another hand, as she gestured the mudrās for "peace" and for "grasping for power" respectively with each of the other two hands. Kālī was the terrifying, if not menacing, aspect of *Durgā. In her manifestation of Kālaratri, or the "black night," Kālī was the mythic embodiment of the natural force that veils everything at the time of either the creation or destruction of the world. In Hindu art, Kālī was depicted as black in color with a bright red tongue that protruded from her wide-open mouth, and bejeweled with an elaborate necklace of skulls. She was postured either standing upon her husband Shiva or as placing her left foot upon him in a gesture of dominance, or seated or mounted on a *lion.

Kalteš .Western Siberian goddess of childbirth and human destiny. The birch tree was her *attribute while the *goose and the *hare were Kalteš's sacred *animals.

Kāmākśī. From the Sanskrit for "she who ogles." Benign goddess of southern India. In Indian art, Kāmākśī had four arms and was seated on a *lotus.

Kaménae. Ancient Italic goddess of springs and wells. According to tradition, the *Vestal Virgins drew their sacred waters daily from the well at the shrine of Kaménae in Rome. In later classical poetry, Kaménae was assimilated into the *Muses.

Kamrušpa. Hittite goddess of healing.

Karpo. Greek goddess of ripe fruit and one of the *Horae. Karpo was the daughter of Zeus and *Themis, and sister of *Auxo and *Thalia.

Kassiane (ninth century). Eastern Christian nun and renowned hymnographer. A defender of icons during the final iconoclastic controversy, Kassiane was known for her singular secular poetry and liturgical music. She wrote *The Troparion of Kassiane* with its special mentions of *Mary Magdalene for the Holy Wednesday Liturgy. A rare topic in eastern Christian art, Kassiane was depicted as a nun who held sheet music in both her hands.

Kauri. From the Sanskrit for "brilliant one." Epithet of the *Great Goddess as the giver of compassion (*karuna*). Simultaneously, kauri also signified the *yoni and thereby was symbolized by the *cowrie shell.

Kebechet. Egyptian goddess dedicated to the purification of sacrificial waters. The daughter of Anubis, Kebechet was the means of revitalization for the cult of the dead. She was identified by her *attribute the snake in Egyptian art.

Kekhet. Epithet of *Isis as the goddess of cultivated land and fields.

Kelle. From the Celtic for "spirit of Kele." Honorific for the priestess or priest of the indigenous Druid practices of Ireland. Etymologically, if not pragmatically, associated with ancient veneration of *Kālī. Kelle was a manifestation of the Triple Goddess who controlled the powers of creation, preservation, and destruction. She was the ancestor of *Brigit, and thereby a classical Celtic foretype of *Mary, as well as the patron of a major shrine in Kildare.

Ketubbah. From the Hebrew for "document." Aramaic marriage document given by groom to the bride. In a Ketubbah, the new husband details his responsibilities and guarantees his new wife financial support. Throughout the centuries, ketubbahs have become elaborately decorated and/or illuminated with floral, geometric, and figural designs. *See also* Jewish art.

Keys. Symbol of authority and ownership. Keys were an *attribute of *Cybele in classical Greco-Roman art, and of

*Benten in Japanese Buddhist art. As the guardian of the *gate of *heaven, Peter (and all his successors on the papal throne) were typified by two or three crossed keys (Mt 16:19) in Christian art. Keys on a woman's *girdle or *belt denoted *Martha of Bethany, while keys in a woman's *hand were an attribute of *Geneviève.

Keziah (Job 42:14). From the Hebrew for "cassia." Second daughter born to Job after his sorrowful confrontation with God as a sign of his new life. A rare topic in western Christian art, Keziah was represented as an infant or small girl in the narrative cycles of Job.

Khut. Epithet of *Isis as the light giver.

Ki. From the Sumerian for "earth." Sumerian earth goddess who mated with the sky god to produce air.

Kilya. Incan goddess of the moon and of matrimony. In Incan art, Kilya was portrayed as a silver disk inscribed with a human face.

Kišar and Anšar. Primordial Mesopotamian couple.

Kiss. A sign of physical and spiritual love. This act of physical intimacy was interpreted as a moment of bodily union and pleasure that prophesied the fuller ecstasy of the union with the deity. In Christian art, a kiss denoted the *sacrament of marriage, whether of an earthly or mystical nature. A kiss also typified the veneration of a sacred person, relic, or object by the pious believer. It was also a sign of respect, loyalty, and humility, as exemplified by the eldest of the three *Magi, who kissed the *foot of the Christ Child. The Christian liturgical gesture of the kiss of peace indicated fellowship. The Betrayal of Jesus by Judas's kiss was therefore a complete reversal of the symbol of the kiss, and thereby a despicable betrayal of all the meanings associated with this gesture of love, loyalty, respect, veneration, and fellowship.

Kitchen utensils. *Attributes of *Martha of Bethany.

Knife. Symbol of sacrifice, vengeance, and death. In Tantric Buddhist art, the knife was an *attribute of female deities in their fierce aspect, such as the *shaktis, *Dakīnīs, and *Dharmapalas; and *Avalokiteshvara in all her manifestations. In western Christian art, the knife was both an *attribute of *Abraham (alluding to circumcision as a sign of entry into the community of the covenant and the Sacrifice of *Isaac) and a sign of the Circumcision of Jesus Christ. In relation to Christian *saints, a knife signified the instrument of their martyrdom. Thus, Bartholomew held both a knife and a flayed human skin, while Peter Martyr held both a knife and his *head or *hand, and Edwin Martyr a knife and a *cross.

Koimesis. From the Greek, for the "falling asleep (of Mary)." *See also* Dormition.

Koran. *See* Qur'ān.

Kore. From the Greek for "core maiden." In classical Greek mythology, Kore was the cultic name given to *Persephone. In classical Greco-Roman art, a kore was a statue of a maiden.

55. *Kālī Slaying the Demon Generals Chaṇḍ and Muṇḍa.*
In the background she presents their severed head to the goddess Chaṇḍī.

Kore-Aresthusa. Composite Greek goddess who assimilated characteristics of *Kore as *Persephone, and *Aresthusa, the ancient Greek goddess of wells and springs. In classical Greek art, Kore-Aresthusa was identified as a nymph with ears of *corn adorning her head.

Korrawi. Tamil goddess of battle and victory. The temples of Korrawi located in the forest were guarded by corpses, demons, and spirits. In her aspect as Kātukilal, Korrawi was known as "the lady of the jungle."

Korybantes. Demonic companions of the ancient Phrygian mother goddess, *Cybele. The korybantes were famed for their orgiastic dances performed to the raucous music of percussion and wind instruments. According to legend, they were the progeny of Zeus who impregnated the earth when his sperm fell like raindrops.

Kuan-yin. Chinese Buddhist *bodhisattva derived from the Indian masculine bodhisattva identified as *Avalokiteshvara who was eventually transformed into the goddess of compassion as this characteristic became categorized as feminine. Kuan-yin dispensed blessings on children, and aided devotees in attaining enlightenment. According to tradition, she introduced human beings to the cultivation of rice which Kuanyin made wholesome by filling it with her milk. Among Chinese Buddhists, she was venerated as the "lady giver of children," the model of feminine beauty, and the patron of sailors. In Chinese Buddhist art, Kuan-yin was portrayed as a genteel woman dressed in a long flowing garment and either enthroned on a mountain or the island of the Eastern Sea. She was postured either in a pose of meditation, often by the seashore; or standing with a child in her arms.

Kubaba. Ancient Mesopotamian mother goddess. Kubaba corresponded to the Hurrian goddess of love, Sauška, and the Phrygian mother goddess, *Cybele. In Near Eastern art, Kubaba was identified by her *attributes of the *mirror and *pomegranate.

Kurukullā. Tibetan Buddhist goddess of love and of wealth. One of the most popular goddesses of Tibetan Buddhism, Kurukullā cast lovespells on men and woman in order to inveigle their services. In Tibetan Buddhist art, she was identified by her *attributes of the red lotus, and a *bow with *arrows. Kurukullā was portrayed in the lotus position with Kama, the god of love, and his partner underneath. *See also* Tārā.

Kwannon. Japanese Buddhist goddess of mercy and compassion. As the protector of children and of women, Kwannon was identified as the "lady giver of children." This compassionate female savior was derived from the Indian masculine *bodhisattva *Avalokiteshvara and the Chinese feminine *Kuan-yin. This Japanese manifestation of mercy and compassion was fully female in character, body, and postures. In Japanese Buddhist art, Kwannon was a beautiful woman garbed in an elegant kimono with either a *lotus and/or *children as her *attribute.

L

⚜

Labyrinth. A maze constructed in such a complicated and intricate fashion that it was too difficult to clearly define one's path. In classical Mediterranean mythology, a great labyrinth was created by Daedalus for King Minos, who sought to restrain the Minotaur inside it. When the princess Ariadne was to be sacrificed to the Minotaur, she helped Theseus rescue her by dropping string from her web as the Minotaur carried her into the depths of the labyrinth. Theseus killed the Minotaur, rescued Ariadne, and freed the Cretan people from the curse of this monster. In medieval Christian liturgical and devotional practice, a labyrinth was constructed on the pavement of the *nave in *cathedrals such as Chartres, and served as the ritual area for the liturgical *dance of the labyrinth, which was derived from the mystery cults. The dancers sought to journey to the center of the labyrinth and back out again as a metaphor for their spiritual journey with Christ. According to legend, the labyrinth was also a symbol for *Jerusalem; *pilgrims could try to travel to its center as a form of spiritual pilgrimage to the Holy City without leaving the confines of their own cathedral.

Lachesis. One of the *Moirai (*Fates). This daughter of Zeus and *Themis worked in unison with her sisters, *Atropos and *Clotho, in the allocation of each person's individual fate.

Ladder. A sign of the Passion of Jesus Christ, especially of the Deposition, in Christian art. In the *Old Testament, Jacob dreamed of a ladder upon which *angels ascended to heaven and descended to *earth, and at the top of which stood God proclaiming Jacob's family the Chosen People. The ladder was an *attribute of Andrew, Romauld, and John Climacus.

Ladle. An *attribute of *Martha of Bethany.

Ladybug. Insect symbol for good fortune and fecundity. Especially associated with agrarian cultures, the appearance of a ladybug was interpreted as a good omen forecasting an abundant harvest; however, the death of a ladybug was an ill omen. According to popular lore in Germany, the ladybug was "the bringer of babies," not the *stork. In medieval Christian art and legend, the ladybug was associated with *Mary.

Lady's Bedstraw. A floral symbol both for the *Nativity and for the humility of *Mary and her son in western Christian art. A wildflower that grew low to the ground, lady's bedstraw was traditionally believed to have been mixed with the straw that Joseph (of Nazareth) laid in the manger for the newborn child.

Lady's Mantle. An herbal symbol for *Mary in medieval Christian art.

Lady's Slipper. A variety of orchid associated with *Mary in *medieval Christian art.

Lahar. Sumerian mother goddess of herds. According to tradition, Lahar taught human beings how to breed and rear cattle.

Laima. From the Latvian for "material fortune." Latvian goddess of fate, fertility, and good fortune, and a protector of cattle. With a sympathetic interest in women in childbirth, Laima was characterized as a creator of humanity who participated in birth, marriage, and death. According to legend and tradition, she set a child's fate at birth, selected a husband for each female infant, and decided the time of death.

Laka. Hawaiian goddess of song and dance. Laka was devoted to pleasure.

Lakshmī. From the Sanskrit for "fortune." Hindu goddess of good fortune and prosperity, and the female personification of feminine beauty. According to tradition, this wife of Vishnu was cre-

ated during the churning of the ocean of milk from which the gods derived the elixir of immortality. Gifted with transformative powers, Lakshmī took on the personalities, if not the personae, of all the wives of Vishnu's avatars. She was known in Japan as Kichijo-ten, and in China as Gong-De-Tian. In Hindu art, this golden-hued goddess was depicted either standing or sitting on an open lotus; or holding a lotus and flanked by *elephants.

Lalita Tripurasundarī. Tantric Buddhist goddess symbolic of cosmic energy and secret ruler of the world. Lalita Tripurasundarī was a dynamic *Shakti whose union with Shiva as the male static principle generated the transitory world of deception characterized as *māyā*.

Lama. Sumerian beneficent protective female deity, usually anonymous. In Mesopotamian art, Lama was depicted as introducing worshipers to important deities. Lama was garbed in long, often flounced, skirts and horned cap with hands raised in the posture of supplication.

Lamaštu. Akkadian demon who performed evil simply for her own sake not under direction of a major deity. Lamaštu was principally concerned with unborn or newly born infants. Miscarriage and cat deaths were attributed to this demon who reportedly stole into a home either to touch a pregnant woman's belly the required seven times to induce a miscarriage, or to steal a newborn from its wet nurse. As both a thief of babies and a bringer of disease, Lamaštu's powers were debilitated, if not destroyed, by bronze amulets of the Pazuzu, the god who pushed the demon

56. *Vishnu and Lakshmi Riding on Garuda*

back into the underworld. In Near Eastern art, Lamaštu was depicted with the
head of *lion, the teeth of a *donkey,
and a hairy body with naked *breasts.
She had donkey ears, blood-stained
hands with long fingers and nails, and
the talons of a bird for feet. A piglet
may suck at her breast as she held a
*snake in each hand. Her *attributes
were a *donkey and a *boat.

Lamb. A symbol of innocence, purity,
meekness, humility, and docility. The
lamb was both a sign of sacrifice and
initiation. A popular symbol in Christian art, the lamb denoted Jesus Christ
as prefigured by the *Old Testament
references to the "lamb of God" (for
example, Ex 12). Depending upon its
bodily posture and *attributes, the lamb
implied multiple meanings within the
context of Christian spirituality and theology. Whenever the lamb was identified by John the Baptist, either through
a gesture or an inscription, it denoted
the sacrifice of Jesus on the *cross as
the fulfillment of the Old Testament
prophecies (Is 53:7; Ex 12). A upright
lamb with a *staff and a *banner inscribed with the cross connoted the Resurrection and Christ as the Redeemer
(Jn 1:29). A standing lamb with a cross
and *blood flowing from its wounded
side was the Lamb of God (*Agnus
Dei*)—a symbol for the Crucified Christ
and the Eucharist. In early Christian art,
a recumbent lamb implied the wounded
flesh of Jesus, while the upright lamb
was the Church Triumphant on earth. A
standing lamb with a cruciform nimbus
indicated the Resurrected Christ. When
the lamb stood on a *mountain from
which four *rivers flowed, it referred to
the Resurrected Christ who stood atop
the church as the four Gospels or Rivers

of Paradise flowed to evangelize and
nurture the world. A lamb seated on a
*book with seven seals was the Lamb of
the Apocalypse (Rv 5:12); while twelve
lambs represented the twelve apostles.
The lamb also typified sinful humanity
being rescued by Christ as the Good
Shepherd (Lk 15:1–7). In early Christian art (pre-fourth century) when the
anthropomorphic image of Jesus on the
Cross was considered a sacrilege, the
lamb was substituted. Such artistic use
of the lamb on the cross was forbidden
by the Council of Trullo (692). The lamb
was an *attribute of Joachim, Clement
of Rome, *Geneviève, *Agnes, and
*Francis of Assisi.

Lamentation. A variant of the Crucifixion narrative in Christian art and spirituality. Following the *Deposition or
Descent from the Cross, the body of
the crucified Jesus was received by his
mother, who was joined in her mourning and grief by John the Evangelist,
*Mary Magdalene, Joseph of Arima-
thea, Nicodemus, the *Holy Women,
and other followers. This scene was distinguished from the *Pietà by the presence of mourners other than *Mary, and
from the Deposition as the body was
completely removed from the *cross.
The Lamentation preceded the scenes
of the anointing and burial of the body
of Jesus. Ostensibly derived from the
byzantine liturgical *icon of the *threnos*,
the Lamentation developed in the narrative art of the medieval period, and
reached its zenith in the Renaissance. It
was sometimes conflated with the
Deposition and the *Entombment.

Lamia. From the Greek for "she who
swallows up." Mythic daughter of Belus
and Libya driven to madness by a jeal-

ous *Hera. Lamia was a beautiful young woman beloved by Zeus and impregnated by him. His irate wife inflicted madness upon Lamia who proceeded to swallow her own children. According to legend, Lamia was a horrible ghost who stole *children and sucked their *blood. This vampirelike creature was difficult to identify and to protect against as Zeus gave her the faculty of metamorphosis in order to defend herself against Hera. Lamia was associated with the Hebrew *Lilith and the Roman Lemures.

Lamp. A source of light signifying enlightenment, intelligence, and piety. In classical Greco-Roman and *renaissance art, a lamp denoted *Lucia, the *Sibyl of Persia, *Vigilance, *Night, and *Psyche when she sought to "uncover" her lover. In eastern and western Christian art and spirituality, the Word of God was characterized as a "lamp unto the faithful." Depictions of the *parable of the *Ten Bridesmaids (Wise and Foolish Virgins in DR) emphasized the lighted lamps of five bridesmaids, and downturned dark lamps of the other five bridesmaids. The lamp was an *attribute of *Lucy.

Landscape. A background element in paintings used to signify location or place of an event. Beginning with the Renaissance, the landscape reinforced the moral or Christian allegory of a painting; for example the inclusion of an ecclesiastical building to represent holy ground or secular persons to designate the separation of the sacred and the profane.

Lantern. As a source of light, a symbol for piety, *wisdom, and intelligence. In western Christian art, the lantern was an *attribute of Christopher, the *Ten Bridesmaids, and several of the *Sibyls.

Lark. A sign of a good priest, as this bird only sang as it flew upwards to *heaven in western Christian art.

Larunda. From the Latin for "may she cause (the earth) to turn green." Sabine goddess of the earth and of fertility.

Lasas. Etruscan supernatural female beings in the retinue of Turan, the goddess of love. In classical Etruscan and Roman art, Lasas were depicted as winged female figures who were richly adorned with jewels. Their *attributes were *wreaths of flowers and *mirrors.

Lat. From the Latin for "milk." Female embodiment of the *moon as the omnipresent source of nourishment, that is, as the celestial *breast and mother of the *Milky Way. Identified with *Latona, *Leto, and *al-Lāt, Lat was the descendent of the ancient goddess, Lat, who not only gave milk but all fluids from water to blood to semen. According to legends, she was the source behind the indigenous matriarchal culture of Rome.

Latona. Titan, and mother of Apollo and *Diana in Roman mythology. *See* Leto.

Lauka-māte. From the Latvian for "mother of the plowed lands." Latvian goddess of fields and fertility.

Laumé. A popular Lithuanian female fairy. Laumé was famed for her aide to the poor and her protection of orphans. In folk tradition, she merged with *Laima, the goddess of fate. In northern

European art, Laumé was portrayed as a naked nymph engaged in one of her two favorite activities of *bathing or spinning and weaving.

Laurel. A sign of immortality, triumph, and chastity. Although the Greek nymph *Daphne rejected the love of Apollo, he continued to pursue her until her river god father transformed her into a laurel tree. Sacred to the *Vestal Virgins and to Apollo, laurel was assimilated into Christian art and practice as a sign of the chastity and the victory of Christian faith over death. *See also* Daphne.

Laurel Tree. An evergreen *tree signifying eternity, and sacred to Apollo. *See also* Daphne.

Laurel Wreath. A symbol of virtue and victory. Originally, the sign of the champion at the Delphic and Olympic games, as well as the annual Drama and Poetry Contests that were dedicated to Apollo, the laurel wreath became a Roman symbol of both triumph (athletic, cultural, or military) and virtue (consecrated to the *Vestal Virgins). The laurel wreath was an *attribute of *Calliope, *Clio, *Fame, and *Truth in classical Greco-Roman and *renaissance art. It was assimilated into Christian art and practice as a sign of Christ's victory over death, and the spiritual virtue of Christian *martyrs (1 Cor 9:24–27). The laurel wreath was a common symbol on the *sarcophagi and *frescoes of the Christian *catacombs, and one of the earliest symbols for the body of Jesus on the cross.

Lavender. Fragrant labiate flower whose medicinal properties signified *Mary in medieval Christian art.

Laverna. Ancient Roman goddess of thieves and vagabonds, and queen of the underworld. Laverna was identified in classical Roman art by her ritual gesture of libation with her left hand, a sign of the underworld.

Leah. A matriarch of Israel and the elder daughter of Laban, Jacob's first wife substituted for her younger sister, *Rachel. In order to marry Rachel, Jacob was forced to serve Laban for an additional seven years. Leah bore Jacob ten sons and a daughter (Gn 29). In western Christian art, Leah was depicted as a matronly woman in contrast to her lithesome, beautiful sister Rachel.

Lectern. A reading desk upon which ecclesial, biblical, or sacramental *books, or *Books of Hours, were placed in Christian art, especially in depictions of the Evangelists, *Doctors of the Churches, Theologians, and the *Annunciation to Mary. Originally simple in design and functional in purpose, the lectern became more ornate and multipurpose as the Christian liturgy evolved. The relationship between these liturgical developments and the importance of the "Word of God" can be studied through the *iconography of the lectern.

Leda. From the Lycian for "woman." Mother of *Helen, *Clytemnestra, Castor, and Polydeuces in Greek mythology. The beautiful wife of Tyndareus of Sparta attracted the attention of Zeus. The god transformed himself into a *swan and seduced Leda. According to variations of this story, she bore either one egg containing Helen and Polydeuces, and conceived her other two children from her husband; or two eggs containing her four children. In classical Greco-Roman, *renaissance, and *baroque art, Leda was represented as a beautiful young woman, often in the nude, either covered or embraced by a swan.

Legenda Aurea. See The Golden Legend.

Lei-zi. Chinese goddess of thunder and originator of silkworms.

Lemon. A sign of fidelity in love. In medieval art, the lemon signified the purity of *Mary; it was also a symbol of life and protection against hostile forces such as poison, magic, and the plague.

Leocritia, Saint. *See* Lucretia, Saint.

Leonardo da Vinci (1452–1519). A Renaissance man well versed in the arts, science, philosophy, and military engineering. Trained as an artist under Verrocchio, Leonardo was one of the three great artists of the High Renaissance (along with *Michelangelo and *Raphael). His studies of human anatomy and of the scientific properties of light and color led to the refinement of the renaissance concepts of pyramidal composition, natural lighting, and one-point perspective. In terms of both *renaissance art generally, and western Christian art specifically, Leonardo was distinguished by his ability to concentrate upon the psychology of his subjects and the tension of the dramatic moment, as in his *Mona Lisa* and *Leda.* His most famous work on a Christian theme, *Last Supper*, was the first depiction of this theme to focus on the moment of Jesus' announcement that one

of his *apostles would betray him and the reaction of the apostles.

Leopard. An animal with ambiguous meaning, perhaps stemming from the belief that it was the result of the union of a *lion and a *panther or pard. The leopard connoted a sign of protection, of a safe journey, survival after death, and bravery in war. In Egyptian art and mythology, the leopard signified *Mafdet, the leopard-goddess who destroyed *snakes and *scorpions. The leopard signified cruelty, sin, the Devil, and the Antichrist (Rv 13:2) in western Christian art. It also typified the Incarnation as the fusion of the humanity and divinity of Jesus Christ. Therefore, the leopard appeared in representations of the *Adoration of the Magi.

Lesbia. Historical beloved of the Latin poet, Catullus (c. 84–c. 54 B.C.E.), and famed for her pet sparrow.

Lesbos. Greek island ruled by the *Amazons and home of the sacred colony dedicated to the veneration of the principles of female energy and power. During the historical period of classical Greece, female devotees of *Artemis and *Aphrodite ruled Lesbos, and eventually it became renowned as the home of the Greek woman poet, *Sappho. Sadly only a few fragments of her oeuvre survived the early Christian persecutions of "pagan" literature, let alone the works of a woman and an avowed Lesbian. The term, Lesbian, was derived from the history of being a citizen of Lesbos.

Lethe. From the Greek for "forgetfulness." One of the principal rivers of the Underworld in classical Greek mythology. The first temptation of a newly dead soul was to ease its thirst by drinking the waters of Lethe, which then condemned that soul to "no memory" of its previous life. This was in contrast to the springs of *Mnemosyne, or Memory. Both of these conditions of the human mind were personified as females and depicted as such in classical Greek art.

Leto. From the Lycian for "woman, wife." Mother of Apollo and *Artemis in Greek mythology. Infatuated with the beautiful and youthful Leto, Zeus transformed himself and her into *quails, and then seduced her. In this disguised form, he hoped to avoid discovery by his ever-jealous wife, *Hera. In her anger, the spurned wife set a python in pursuit of Leto, still in the form of a quail. However the young and now pregnant maiden was rescued either by a *dolphin or the south wind, and taken to Ortygia where she gave birth to Artemis. With her newly born goddess-daughter's assistance, Leto traveled to Delos where she gave birth to Apollo. Continuing her pursuit of her husband's mistress, Hera forced Leto to depart Delos and begin a life of wandering. Once a thirsty Leto sought to drink from a lake but the waters were muddied by the peasants whom Hera turned into *frogs. Finally, Apollo killed Hera's python; and thereby as the mother of two deities, Leto began life on Mount Olympus. Her devoted children acted with alacrity when a foolhardy *Niobe pronounced that she and her beautiful children were more worthy of worship than Leto. Worshiped in conjunction with Apollo and Artemis, Leto was portrayed in classical Greco-Roman and *renaissance art as a matron accompanied by either or both of her children; or with her children escaping from the python. Her *attribute was the quail.

Leucothea. *See* Ino.

Lewis, [Mary] Edmonia (1843 or 1845–after 1909). African-American sculptor. The daughter of an African-American father and a Chippewa Indian mother, Edmonia Lewis was born in either New York or Ohio. Determined to become a sculptor, she relocated to Boston where she made and sold portrait medallions and busts of abolitionists between 1863 and 1865. After earning sufficient monies to finance a trip to Europe, Lewis lived in Rome from 1865 until her death. After establishing a studio for her sculptures, she garnered an international reputation for her neoclassical depictions of heroic women including *Hagar* and *Cleopatra*. Following her death, Lewis and her sculptures fell into anonymity as a result of both her gender and mixed racial heritage, and the disregard for the neoclassic style.

Leyster, Judith (1609–60). Dutch woman artist, a student of Frans Hals, famed for her *genre scenes, stilllives, and portraits.

Lhamo. From the Tibetan for "goddess." Protective female deity who aided earnest devotees. In Tibetan Buddhist art, Lhamo was characterized with flowing locks with fiercely protruding eyes, ten arms, and enveloped in flames.

Libera. Roman goddess of the *vine and of fertility. Libera and her male companion Libera were identified with the Greek *Persephone and Dionysius.

Liberal Arts. A classical Greco-Roman convention in learning and art that often accompanied the *Seven Virtues in *medieval and *renaissance art. The established course of studies in medieval education, the Liberal Arts were grammar, rhetoric, dialectic, arithmetic, music, geometry, and astronomy. Usually personified as female figures, the Liberal Arts were distinguished by their *attributes: writing instruments, a fountain of scholarly waters, a rod of chastisement, and two pupils reading *books were placed at Grammar's *feet; Dialectic held a *snake, *scorpion, *lizard, *flowers, or *scales; Rhetoric held either a *scroll, book, *sword, or *shield; Geometry held a compass, terrestrial *globe, triangle, or *ruler; Arithmetic held a tablet, abacus, or ruler; Astronomy held a celestial globe, compass, sextant, or sphere; and Music held an instrument such as a *triangle, *lute, viol, small *organ, or bells.

Libertas. Ancient Roman goddess personifying the freedom of the Roman people. A popular topic on Roman coins, Libertas was characterized by the *pilleus*, or "freedom hat," which slaves were given in the ritual of manumission, and by a scepter or *lance.

Libitina. Ancient Roman goddess of burial and female personification of death.

Libya. A *lamia who was wife to Triton, and mother to Belus and Aginox.

Light. A sign of spiritual and intellectual brilliance. As the direct source of clarity, light typified divine power and holiness, and became a symbol for both Jesus Christ and the Holy Spirit in Christian art. An unlit or smoking candle was a popular medieval device to indicate the presence of either Christ or the Holy Spirit. As a sign for goodness and wisdom, light was a positive force in contrast to the evil and ignorance of the darkness.

Light Rays. Sign for the presence of the *Holy Spirit.

Lilith (Is 34:14). From the Hebrew for "she of the night." Demon queen of the night in Jewish tradition. According to the Talmud, Lilith was Adam's first wife, created before *Eve, who sought equality with Adam and then fled Paradise crying out in despair that her request was denied (Gn 1:27). Three *angels— Sanvi, Sansanvi, and Samangelaf—were sent by God to retrieve her on Adam's complaint. Having tasted freedom, Lilith refused to return but promised no harm to anyone who showed her the angels' names. She then married Samael, the king of the demons. Lilith became a screech *owl, a demonic creature with long hair who visited lonely husbands forcing nocturnal emissions to conceive demon children with, frightened pregnant women into miscarriage, and stole male *children less than seven days old in the middle of the night. Even the pronouncement of her name conjured Lilith's presence and struck fear in the hearts of Jewish and Christian women. Jewish women, especially those who were pregnant or in labor, had amulets inscribed with the names "Adam and Eve" hung on the walls. In birthing rooms, the names of the three angels were inscribed on the doorways. According to Jewish tradition, on the eve of Shabbat or the new moon, any child who smiles when playing was feared to be with Lilith, and had to be tapped on the nose three times as incantations were chanted. During the medieval era, no water could be drawn from wells during equinoxes or solstices as it was believed to be polluted with Lilith's menstrual blood. According to legend, Lilith took on the guise of the *Queen of Sheba before Solomon, but he suspected a ruse and so he forced the queen to lift up her skirts and the demon was revealed by her hairy legs. In western Christian art, Lilith was depicted as a female *head and/or torso on a serpentine *body rendered within the context either of the Temptation and the *Fall, or the *Madonna and Child. By the High Middle Ages, Lilith was conflated with the *serpent in the *Garden of Eden, as the cultural evidence suggested that a naive Eve would have trusted another woman not a serpent. Lilith was found at the base of images of the Madonna and Child, where she signified the serpent whose head was crushed by *Mary. The inclusion of the image of Lilith in western Christian art corresponded to the development of and interest in the esotericism of the *Kabbalah.

Lilītu. Family group of demons, the male being Lilū and the female Lilītu, who haunted deserts and countrysides in search of pregnant women and very young children. According to legend, Lilītu was a frustrated bride who was incapable of normal sexual activity. She compensated for her weakness with aggressive sexual activities with young men in a manner similar to *Lilith. As such, she was believed to be the source of both male impotence and female sterility. In classical Near Eastern art, Lilītu was depicted as a she wolf with a scor-

pion tail who was about to devour a young girl.

Lily. A floral symbol with the multiple meanings of purity, innocence, rebirth, and royalty as well as pleasure to the senses through its fragrance, and thereby sacred to the virgin and mother goddesses of the Mediterranean world. The lily was an *attribute of the *Sibyl of Erythraea in classical Greco-Roman and *renaissance art. In early Christian art, the *white *lily identified as the "Easter Lily" was a symbol for the Resurrection of Christ and the early virgin *martyrs. By the medieval period, this same flower signified *Mary, especially in the context of the *Annunciation. This transformation from a symbol of Christ to one of Mary, especially to the Virgin Annunciate, had as much to do with the rising *Mariology of medieval theology as to the simple fact that this *flower bloomed around the time of the feast of the Annunciation, and had the shape of a trumpet, which announced the birth (and hence also the death and resurrection) of Jesus Christ. According to tradition, the lily sprang from the tears of the repentant *Eve as she departed the *Garden of Eden. As Mary became the "Second Eve" in Christian art and theology, this flower was reclaimed for her as she became our entryway into *paradise. Generally, the lily typified Mary's perpetual virginity and purity, while a lily enframed by *thorns implied the *Immaculate Conception. The lily was an *attribute of the Archangel Gabriel, the infant Jesus, Joseph (of Nazareth), *Dominic, *Francis of Assisi, Anthony of Padua, *Catherine of Siena, *Clare of Assisi, *Euphemia, *Scholastica, Francis Xavier, Louis of France, Philip Neri,

*Thomas Aquinas, and Louis of Toulouse. The *fleur-de-lis, a variant of the lily, was selected by King Clovis of France to represent both the purification of Christian *baptism and the Christianization of France. As an attribute of royalty, the fleur-de-lis was depicted on the *crowns or *scepters of royal *saints, and of Mary as the Queen of Heaven.

Lily of the Valley. One of the earliest of all spring *flowers, and a sign of humility, virginity, and sweetness. In western Christian art, the lily of the valley was a symbol for the *Immaculate Conception (Song 2:1) and of the promise of new life through Jesus Christ. In its pure *white color and sweet aroma, the lily of the valley was an *attribute of *Mary, especially as a sign of Advent. According to medieval legend, the lily of the valley identified as "Our Lady's Tears" were believed to have sprung up from Mary's tears.

Limbo. From the Latin for "lip." A medieval theological idea never designated as a formal Catholic dogma. The place between *heaven and *hell reserved for those righteous people who died before the coming of Jesus Christ, and for unbaptized infants. It was traditionally divided into the *Limbus Patrum* (for righteous adults) and the *Limbus Infantum* (for unbaptized infants) who were awaiting the Judgment Day (Last Judgment). Limbo was a place of "no pain or suffering" but of undifferentiated waiting. It was distinguished from purgatory, which was the place where *souls in need of cleansing were purged of their sins in order to achieve the Beatific Vision. According to Christian art and legend, the Resurrected Christ de-

scended into Limbo to release all the souls of the righteous before he ascended into Heaven.

Lion. An ambiguous and multivalent animal solar symbol for strength, courage, majesty, fortitude, pride, wrath, and brute force. The lion was a symbolic guardian of temples, palaces, and tombs in religious art. According to the *Physiologus*, the lion cub was born dead and kept warm by its mother for three days, at which time its father breathed upon it and gave it life. The lion was the sacred *animal of *Cybele, the Phrygian mother goddess who was flanked by lions on her throne; while the Akkadian goddess *Ishtar rode lions into battle. The Hindu great goddess, *Durgā (*Devi), rode a lion in her battle against the Buffalo Demon. In Egyptian art and mythology, the lion characterized several goddesses: the lion-headed goddess, *Sekhmet, was the daughter of the sun god, Ra; the lion-headed goddess, *Mut, was tutelary of Thebes and protector of the Pharaoh in battle; and as protector of women in childbirth, *Bast had either leonine features or word a lion's pelt. Classical Greco-Roman mythology had the wild lion tamed by Androcles, who removed a prickly *thorn from its paw and became its lifelong companion. The medieval *bestiaries recorded that the lion slept with its eyes open as a sign of watchfulness and vigilant protection of its family. Legends recounted the lion as the "King of the Beasts," a sign of majesty, *wisdom, and valor. In the *Old Testament, the lion was the emblem of the tribe of Judah (Gn 49:9), the enemy destroyed by Samson (1 Sm 14:5–7), the intended executioner of Daniel (Dn 6:7), and a sign of the Devil (Ps 91:13). In the *New

Testament, the lion was the earthly counterpart of the *eagle (Rv 5:5) and a metaphor for Christ's ability to convert the heathen and bring peace. From the classical Greco-Roman and Hebraic foretypes, the lion became a symbol for Jesus Christ, especially for the Resurrection. The lion was an *attribute of *Jerome, *Mary of Egypt, *Euphemia, *Natalia, and *Thecla. The winged lion was the attribute of Mark the Evangelist and of his patronal city, Venice. In *renaissance art, the lion signified Africa, *Fortitude, *Choler, *Pride, and *Wrath.

Lizard. A sign of old age, evil, or the Devil in western Christian art. According to the *Physiologus, the aged lizard was as blind as the Christian *soul who sought out Christ as the Light of the World. The lizard's annual molting signified the Resurrection. In classical Greco-Roman and *renaissance art, the lizard was an *attribute of logic, one of the seven *Liberal Arts.

Ljubi. Legendary Albanian female folk demon. Ljubi was reputed to dwell in vegetable gardens and to shrivel up into a ball of evil, unless a virgin was sacrificed and her blood irrigated the garden.

Locana. From the Sanskrit for "eye." Tantric Buddhist goddess and consort of Vairocana or Aksobhya. In Tibetan Buddhist art, Locana was portrayed as a white spirit of peace who held her *attribute, the *wheel.

Lois (2 Tim 1:5, 3:14–15). Grandmother of Timothy and mother of *Eunice. Converted to Christianity by Paul at Lystra, Lois was praised in unison with her daughter for their model ful-fillment of the matriarchal duty of instilling knowledge of the Jewish faith and the *Hebrew Scriptures in Timothy, the future bishop of Ephesus. A rare topic in western Christian art, Lois was represented as a proper Jewish matron in the company of her daughter and grandson in the narrative cycles of Paul.

Longhi, Barbara (1552–1638). Woman artist from Ravenna. The daughter of the mannerist painter, Luca Longhi, Barbara received her early training in his studio but simplified his style. She was renowned in her own lifetime for her portraits and religious works such as her *Madonna Adoring the Child*.

Loom. Machine used in the weaving of cloth from spindles of woolen or silk threads. In classical Greco-Roman and *renaissance art, a woman weaving at a loom in the presence of *Athena (*Minerva) was *Arachne, while a woman weaving at a loom in the presence of young men was *Penelope.

Lo-ruhamah (Hos 1:9). From the Hebrew for "not pitied." Daughter of *Gomer and Hosea in the *Old Testament. Lo-ruhamah was named by a father as a sign of God's rejection of Israel for her sinfulness. A rare independent topic in western Christian art, Lo-ruhamah was represented as a young girl in the company of her father or both of her parents in the narrative cycles of Hosea and/or of the *prophets of Israel.

Lot's Daughters. *Lot and His Daughters* (Gn 19:30–38). After fleeing Sodom, Lot's daughters were convinced that there were no other human beings left alive, including their husbands. The two daughters intoxicated their father with

57. School of Leonardo da Vinci, *Leda and the Swan*
58. Edmonia Lewis, *Hagar*

59. Barbara Longhi, *Madonna Adoring the Child*
60. Guido Reni, *Lucretia*

wine, and lay with him in order to perpetuate the human race. Ammon and Moab, two male children, were the immediate results of these incestuous unions; their descendants were the Moabites and the Ammonites. These two narrative events in the life of Lot were popular themes in *medieval and *renaissance art.

Lot's Wife. *Destruction of Sodom and Gomorrah* (Gn 19:1–29): Lot offered hospitality to two traveling *angels. In the middle of the night, his house was disturbed by local men who wanted to violate the angels. In the name of hospitality, Lot offered these men his daughters in place of his guests. God struck the offenders blind for their perversity, and saved the angels, Lot, and his daughters. God warned Lot that Sodom would be destroyed along with the neighboring city of Gomorrah. Lot fled with his wife and daughters from the burning *ruins of Sodom; but against the direct instructions of God's angel, Lot's wife looked back and was instantly turned into salt. The story of the Destruction of Sodom and Gomorrah was a foretype for the Last Judgment.

Lotus. A common floral symbol of divinity, solar deities, and salvation. In Egyptian art, the lotus symbolized the solar deities, thereby rebirth, Upper Egypt, and *Hathor. The lotus denoted the creative powers and energies of goddesses in Phoenician, Assyrian, and Persian art. In Buddhist art and religious practice, the lotus denoted purity and spontaneous generation, thereby, divine birth. The different colors of lotus flowers distinguished their symbolic references in Buddhist art. The White Lotus (pundarīkā, byakurgene) connoted bodhī or the state of intellectual purity and spiritual perfection otherwise identified as enlightenment. It was the emblem of all the Buddhas. The Red Lotus (kamala, gurente) signified love, passion, and compassion; and was the emblem of *Avalokiteshvara. The Blue Lotus (utpala, nīlotpala, seirenge, shōrenge) symbolized victory over the senses, thereby attainment of wisdom, intelligence, and knowledge. A partially opened flower was the *attribute of *Prajñāpāramitā and the emblem of Mañjushrī. The Pink Lotus (padma, renge, lianhua) was the supreme lotus and symbol of the highest deity. This was the emblem of Gautama, the historical Buddha. The Purple Lotus (shirenge) denoted the mysticism of varied Buddhist esoteric sects. The floral symbol of the cosmic womb, the lotus signified the *mother goddess in classical Indian art and mythology, and was transferred to *Lakshmī, *Padmpani, *Pārvāti, and *Shakti in Hinduism and to *Prajñapāramitā in Buddhism. Female river deities were often posed seated or lying upon an open lotus in Hindu and Buddhist art. Within Tantrism, the lotus was the symbol of the feminine principle, and in Shaktism signified female genitalia and sex.

Lua. Ancient Roman goddess of religious purification. Lua was assimilated into *Rhea.

Lucia, Saint. *See* Lucy, Saint.

Lucina. Ancient Latin goddess of birth. Lucina was associated with *Juno as *Juno Lucina, and corresponded to the Greek goddess, *Eilcithyia, a daughter of Zeus and *Hera.

Lucrece. *See* Lucretia.

Lucretia. One of the nine Female Worthies (along with *Jael and *Judith), and the model of wifely and womanly virtue in classical Rome. Lucretia played a significant role in the depiction of women in western Christian art. According to tradition, Lucretia was instrumental in the establishment of the Republic of Rome, and her story was recounted in Livy's *History of Rome* (1:57–9), and Ovid's *Fasti* (2:721–853). Lucretia, the virtuous wife of Lucius Tarquinias Collatinus, was accosted by Sextus Tarquinias in her bedroom while her husband was away. He threatened to rape and murder her, and then lay a dead body next to her and tell her husband and father that he had caught her in an act of adultery. Lucretia submitted to his sexual lust. When her husband returned, she confessed her violation to both her husband and her father, then killed herself. Junius Brutus then organized a rebellion against the rule of the Tarquins, and the Roman Republic was established in 510 B.C.E. Two episodes in Lucretia's story—the Rape of Lucretia and the Death of Lucretia—were popular in classical Greco-Roman, *renaissance, and *baroque art. By the fourth century, Lucretia was contrasted to the chaste *Susanna by *Augustine in *The City of God* (1:16–19). He found Susanna the more admirable woman because she trusted in God when the elders sought to vanquish her and unjustly accused her of adultery. Lucretia, Augustine advised, was found wanting, as her suicide was an act of hubris and guilt (for having enjoyed physical pleasure with Tarquinias Sextus). Representations of Lucretia found their way into western Christian art as a classical Greco-Roman foretype of Susanna. In northern and southern baroque art, Lucretia was included within the topics of the moralizing prints that were created as a form of moral pedagogy for young, unmarried women.

Lucretia, Saint (d. 859). A beautiful young woman of Spanish Muslim descent whose secret conversion to Christianity caused her expulsion from her parents' home. After a period of seclusion and hiding, she was martyred with Eulogius. In western Christian art, Lucretia was depicted as a beautiful young woman holding a *scourge and a *palm.

Lucy, Saint (d. c. 304). A beautiful young woman from Syracuse who converted to Christianity following the miraculous healing of her blind mother at the shrine of the Christian virgin *martyr *Agatha. Lucy gave all her wealth to the poor, which angered her fiancee. He identified her as a Christian to the Roman authorities. At first condemned to a brothel, Lucy survived to suffer other indignities, including a variety of tortures—being burned in boiling *oil; having her *breasts shorn; her *teeth pulled; and flagellation. According to legend, she tore out her own *eyes and handed them to a suitor who admired them too much. Another legend recounted that a part of her martyrdom included having her eyes plucked out. In any case, she escaped all these tortures, was healed miraculously of all her *wounds, and ultimately was stabbed to death. The connection between the conversion experience and the metaphor of sight was central to her story, for in Latin her name meant "light." The patron of ophthamologists, optometrists, the blind, and those with eye diseases, Lucy was invoked against diseases of the eyes and throat. In western Christian art, she was depicted as a beautiful young woman who held her eyes or a plate with her eyes. Her *attributes included a *lamp, *sword, *dagger in the neck, *palm, and a pair of eyes.

Luna. From the Latin for "moon." Roman moon goddess associated with *Selene, *Diana, and *Hecate. Luna was the protector of charioteers in the circus ring. In classical Roman and *renaissance art, Luna was portrayed in a manner identical to *Diana except that her chariot was drawn by either two nymphs or two *horses, a white one signifying day and a black one night.

Luonnotar. Finnish mythic female creator of the world from her preexistent self. Luonnotar was floating on the cosmic waters when a duck laid an egg upon her knee. She hatched this egg in order to produce the earth and all the celestial bodies.

Lupa. Legendary she wolf who nourished and then nurtured the abandoned twins, Romulus and Remus, the founders of Rome. Associated with female fecundity, Lupa was venerated annually at the Lupercalia a series of orgiastic rites celebrated at the Grotto of the She Wolf. She was represented in classical Roman and *renaissance art as an enormous she wolf with engorged nipples, often standing over the suckling twins.

Luperca. Ancient Roman goddess of herds and fruitfulness.

Lur. From the Basque for "earth." Earth goddess and mother of the sun and the moon for the indigenous religious traditions of the Basques.

Lust. Infamous *Seventh Deadly Sin particular to women. Lust was signified by the image of a naked woman whose *breasts and genitals were being eaten or sucked on by *toads and/or *serpents. A popular motif in *medieval art and derived from the classical Roman image of *Tellus Mater, Lust was transformed both visually and philosophically in the Renaissance to the sensual gratification of Love, especially in terms of *Venus. Thereby, Lust became denoted by Venus when accompanied by a virile male animal such as a he goat, boar, cock, or pig; or by the depiction of an *ape looking at its reflection in a *mirror.

Lute. A stringed musical instrument employed in ritual ceremonies and signifying celestial music. The lute was an *attribute of the Shinto *Benten. In classical Greco-Roman and *renaissance art, the lute was the *attribute of *Euterpe, Hearing, *Polyhymnia, and a concert of *angels. In northern *medieval art, the lute was an *attribute of *Mary Magdalene. In *renaissance art, the lute typified music as one of the seven *Liberal Arts, and replaced the original *lyre of Apollo and Orpheus.

Luther, Martin (1483–1546). A former Augustinian *monk distinguished as the "Father of the Reformation." His recognition of the need for church reform following a visit to Rome (1510–11), and a dramatic personal conversion experience led him to challenge the traditional teachings on the relationship between faith and meritorious works, the authority of scripture, and the mediatorial priesthood. Luther's personal conversion experience led him to advocate that "justification [was] by faith alone" (*sola fides*), that grace was freely given by God even to the unworthy, and the Bible alone was the final authority. His initial academic challenge on the question of indulgences, issued at the University of Wittenberg on October 31, 1517, led to a religious, social, cultural, political, and economic revolt against the Church of Rome that has been identified as the Reformation. In terms of Christian art, Luther's own position was more of a *via media* than outright *iconoclasm. In his 1525 sermon, "Against the Heavenly Prophets," Luther decried iconoclasm but supported the traditional Christian position on the role of images as a form of religious pedagogy and even developed a list of the "appropriate" images that could be used as text illustrations or wall decoration. A close friend of the artist, *Lucas Cranach I, Luther included illustrations (woodcuts) by Cranach and *Albrecht Dürer in his German translations of the New Testament (1522) and the Old Testament (1524) as well as in the many pamphlets printed of his sermons and public letters. As to his theological position on the role of women, Luther was influenced by *Augustine, especially in terms of the fault of *Eve as the cause of the *Fall, which he acknowledged to be the result of a woman's uncontrollable sexual lust. He has been credited with the phrase "the devil's gateway" as a metaphor for the vagina. Although Lutheranism and the Reformed Traditions publicly espoused a posture supportive of women's literacy, especially as the ability to read the bible was deemed a necessary element to being a good mother, literacy studies have indicated that the reality was a lower rate of female literacy than in the preceding century. Additionally, those countries that affirmed Lutheranism and the Reformed Traditions closed monasteries and convents, and by doing so eliminated a young girl's choice for her future as she was now limited to being a wife and mother. *See also* Devil's Gateway.

Lutheranism. Properly denominated "The Evangelical Church," Lutheranism was the first of the Reformed traditions. Dedicated to the primacy of faith over works, Lutheranism accepted the authority of the Bible over ecclesiastical councils or hierarchical offices, and affirmed the sovereignty of God including his freedom to dispense grace and redemption through Christ. Liturgically the strongest of all the Reformed traditions, Lutheranism spread through northern Germany into Scandinavia and eventually into the American colonies.

Lydia (Acts 16:14, 40). Wealthy tradeswoman baptized by Paul. Engaged in the purple dye trade, thereby characterized as wealthy, Lydia heard the sermons of Paul and become a Christian convert. Hers became the first household in Europe to be baptized by Paul, who then accepted Lydia's offer of hospitality for himself and his companions, Timothy and Silas. She was instrumental in the establishment of the Christian community in Philippi. A rare topic in western Christian art, Lydia was represented as a noble matron garbed in a purple cloak in the narrative cycles of Paul.

Lynx. Wild cat with sharp eyes embodying watchful alertness. In classical Greco-Roman and *renaissance art, the lynx was an *attribute of the sense, Sight, which was reputedly able to see through a stone wall. The lynx signified the Devil in medieval Christian art.

Lyre. A stringed instrument from classical Greece that tradition identified as being created by Mercury for Apollo as the patron of music, poetry, and the *Muses in classical Greco-Roman and *renaissance art. It also identified *Erato, the Muse of lyric poetry; *Terpsichore, the Muse of music and dance; and Orpheus, especially in his role as the *good shepherd who charmed the wild *animals. In early Christian art, the lyre was an *attribute of Jesus Christ, whose words were as lilting and melodious as the music of Orpheus and capable of charming wild *animals. Orpheus was also the mythological figure who with his music charmed the god of the dead, Pluto, into allowing the return of his recently deceased wife, *Eurydice. Unfortunately, the condition for Eurydice's return to the world was that Orpheus not look back at her as she followed him during their journey from Hades. The loving husband could not resist the sound of his wife's voice and he looked back at her, whereupon she vanished forever, thereby prefiguring Lot's wife. The lyre was also an attribute of *Cecilia as patron of music. *See also* Harp, Lute.

M

M with a crown. This monogram of *Mary as the Virgin Mother was incorporated either into representations of her in Christian art, or within the symbolic and decorative design of liturgical vesture.

MA. This monogram of *Mary as the Virgin Mother was incorporated either into representations of her in Christian art, or within the symbolic and decorative design of liturgical vesture.

Ma. Cappadocian mother goddess. The female personification of fertile nature, Ma incorporated aspects of *Cybele as an earth mother and of *Bellona as a female warrior.

Maat. From the Egyptian language for "straight" as in steadfast and unalterable. Egyptian female embodiment of law, truth, and world order. As the goddess of the physical and moral laws of the universe, Maat was identified as the "lady of heaven," "queen of the earth," and the "mistress of the underworld." The daughter of the sun god, Ra, Maat was the female counterpart of Thoth, and assisted in the creation of the world.

As the symbol of moral power, she was revered as the greatest of Egyptian goddesses. In the *Book of the Dead*, she was identified as a form of Maati in two important roles. Maat stood with the Forty-two Assessors (Judges) who heard the confession of the dead in the Judgment Hall and their obligatory recitation of the Negative Confession, or denial to the list of various sins. She also participated in the Weighing of the Heart when the heart of the dead was balanced on the scales of justice against Maat's *feather, the symbol for Truth. With her role as the female personification of justice, Maat's shrines were the sites of judicial hearings. In her embodiment of justice, of general equilibrium, and of the stability of the social order, Maat was a protector of the Pharaoh who was recognized as "he who lives through her (Maat's) laws." In Egyptian art, she was characterized as a female figure who either wore a headdress of an *ostrich feather, or held an ostrich feather in her hand.

Mab. From the Celtic for "Son." Midwife of the *fairies. According to the mythological traditions of British and

Irish mythology, Mab facilitated in initiating dreams that were the progeny of the fairies.

Machas. The group of the three goddesses of motherliness, agriculture, and war in Irish mythology.

Macrina, Saint (c. 327–79). Dedicated Christian woman and elder sister of Basil the Great, Gregory of Nyssa, and Peter of Sebastea. Following her fiancee's death, Macrina committed herself to the care of her family, which included her three younger brothers and their mother, Emmelia. She influenced her brother Basil in his decision to abandon his secular career and to become a monk. Later she succeeded her mother as leader of a religious community of women in Pontus dedicated to a life of Christian prayer and meditation. Macrina's life including conversations and her deathbed visions were recorded by her brother, Gregory of Nyssa, in his *Life of Saint Macrina*. A rare topic in eastern Christian art, she was occasionally represented as a veiled matron in the company of one or more her saintly brothers in *Byzantine art.

Madonna. From the Italian for "my lady." Appropriate to medieval etiquette, this honorific term was initially associated with idealized representations of *Mary with the Christ Child in western Christian art. By the *Renaissance, the term became synonymous with Mary.

Madonna and Child. One of the most popular topics in Christian art and one that had no direct scriptural basis. The bodily postures and gestures of the Madonna and the Child as well as the sym-

bolism of the objects he held were the clues to the devotional or theological message. The Madonna and Child were depicted by themselves, or in the company of *angels, *saints, or *donors; in fact, the faces of the Madonna and Child were in some instances portraits of the donor's wife and son. The basic rules for the symbolic types of the Madonna and Child were developed in byzantine art following the decree of the Council of Ephesus (431) that Mary was *Theotokos ("God-bearer") and was to be venerated in that role—that is, with the Child. In *medieval and *renaissance art, the inclusion of symbolic objects such as the *apple (as a *fruit of salvation) or the *egg (as a sign of *resurrection) became a common and recognizable visual vocabulary of Christian art. *See* entries on specific animals, birds, flowers, fruits, objects, plants, and vegetables held by either the Madonna or Child for their symbolic value.

Maenads. From the Greek for "raving ones." Ecstatic women in the retinue of Dionysus. According to Greek mythology, the maenads and their male counterparts, the satyrs, were characterized as frenzied creatures who shouted wildly and incoherently as they moved in ritual processions accompanied by *serpents through the woods. They carried daggers or thyrsos stalks that they used to dismember animals, and were reputed for eating raw flesh and/or laurel leaves. A favored theme of the classical Greek vase painters, the Maenads were depicted as contorted female figures often in states of nudity or partially garbed with faun skins and in boisterous processions with the satyrs in classical *Greco-Roman and *renaissance art.

61. *Maat*

62. *Maenad Leaning on her Thyrsos*

Maestà. From the Italian for "majesty." Title given to representations of the *Madonna and Child Enthroned in Majesty surrounded by *angels, *saints, devotees, and/or *donors in western Christian art. Popular in twelfth and thirteenth-century Italian art, this theme was a part of the glorification of Mary in *medieval art and theology. One of the finest examples of a *Maestà* was the altarpiece created by Duccio for the High Altar of the Cathedral of Siena.

Mafdet. Egyptian goddess invoked for protection against *snakes and identified by the epithet, "Lady of the Castle of Life." In Egyptian art, Mafdet was characterized as a *cat, often with the *attribute of the *snake.

Magna Mater. From the Latin for "Great Mother." Roman identification for the Phrygian mother goddess, *Cybele, in the third-century Roman art and mythology. In the twentieth century, the term *magna mater* signifies the Jungian archetype of universal motherhood resident in the collective unconscious.

Magnificat. From the Latin for "My soul doth magnify the Lord." The response of Mary to the greeting of her cousin *Elizabeth at the *Visitation (Lk 1:46–55 DR).

Magnolia. Floral symbol for perseverance, beauty, love, and Nature.

Magpie. This *bird symbolized either evil, persecution, early death, vanity or the *devil in medieval Christian art.

Mahadevi. From the Sanskrit for the "Great Goddess." Manifestations of female energy among the Hindu goddesses. As a title, Mahadevi, was associated with Shiva's *shaktī, that is, she who represented all aspects and dimensions of the god's cosmic energy, and thereby was identified as *Durgā, *Kālī, *Pārvāti, and *Ūma. According to the *Varāka Purāna,* Mahadevi was a virgin renowned for her celestial beauty and who was distinguished by the three colors—white, red, and blue—from which she created the shaktīs of the Trimurti: white signifying *Saravastī as the shaktī of Brahman, red for *Lakshmī the shaktī of Vishnu, and blue for Pārvāti the shaktī of Shiva.

Mahamaya. Mother of Siddartha Gautama (c. 566–486 B.C.E.), the future historic Buddha. According to Buddhist tradition, Mahamaya miraculously conceived her special son as signified by her dream of a white *elephant entering her *womb. Birthed from his mother's side, the newborn Siddartha immediately revealed his extraordinary nature. Mahamaya died soon after her son's birth, and he was raised by his sister, *Prajapati, who later became his consort. In Buddhist art, Mahamaya was signified by the presence of a white elephant.

Maia. From the Greek for "little mother." Greek goddess of the land. According to Greek mythology, Maia was seduced by Zeus and bore his son, Hermes. In Roman mythology, she was the goddess of growth. Her cult was associated with Vulcanus and the fifth month, May, was dedicated to her.

Maidservant. A sign of wealth or of co-conspiracy. A symbolic protector of morality or of her mistress's chastity, the maidservant was normally depicted as a simply dressed woman older than her mistress as in depictions of *Susanna in *medieval and *renaissance Christian art; whereas if represented as a woman equal in age or younger than her mistress, the maidservant like *Abra suggested a coconspirator as in depictions of the story of *Judith in renaissance and *baroque Christian art.

Makosh. Slavonic goddess of water, fertility, and plenty.

Malleus Maleficarum. Most significant and sinister work on demonology, especially with regard to its misogynist interpretations of *witches. First published in 1486, the *Malleus Maleficarum* was a handbook for witchhunters that witnessed over twenty-nine editions in Latin by 1669 and multiple editions in English, French, German, and Italian; it was the source for all subsequent political and theological treatises on witchcraft in the western world. Premised on a fundamentalist reading of Exodus 22:18, the authors of the *Malleus Maleficarum* coordinated a stringent code of behavior for witchhunters that fused all known folklore and legends of black magic; ecclesiastical dogmas on heresy; and the methods and tenets of the *Inquisition. Two Dominicans, Jakob Sprenger, then Dean of Cologne University, and Heinrich Kramer, then Prior of Cologne University, were the acknowledged authors of this text; and their authority rested upon the Papal Bull of 1484 granted Kramer by Innocent VIII with the express directive to silence all opposition to witch-hunts. The *Malleus Maleficarum* was divided into three parts: (1) recognition of witchcraft, its relationship to the church, and explication of ecclesiastical rulings; (2) definition of the types of witches and methods of counteraction; and (3) formal legislation for secular courts, including the rules for conviction and punishment. Although premised as much on misogyny as upon religious conviction, the *Malleus Maleficarum* garnered tremendous public influence even into the nineteenth century. It was accepted by *Lutheranism, *Anglicanism, and the *Protestant traditions as both authority and the proper code against witches. The *Malleus Maleficarum* had widespread appeal and influence upon the arts including the immediate impact in terms of the "morality prints" popular in northern Europe from the fifteenth to the seventeenth centuries, as evidenced in the art of *Lucas Cranach and Hans Baldung Grien among other artists, and even including the art of Francisco Goya. *See also* Witches' Sabbat.

Mallophora. Epithet of *Demeter at her Temple in Megara. According to tradition, Demeter Mallophora taught city dwellers how to use wool. In classical Greek art, she was characterized either as holding a spindle in her hand, seated before a loom, or flanked by sheep.

Mama. Common child's name for mother. Mama was a Mesopotamian mother goddess whose role in the creation story was to form the first human beings from clay and *blood. Mama was the Akkadian epithet for a midwife; thereby, either identifying this function for a goddess, legendary or historical woman.

Māmitu. Akkadian goddess of oaths. According to legend, Māmitu was the female judge of the underworld, and the wife of Nergal. In classical Near Eastern art, she was identified as a female figure with the head of a goat.

Mama Ocllo. Legendary first queen of the Incas. Mama Ocllo was the sister and wife of Manco Capac, the first ruler of the Incas and the founder of the Cuzco.

Mammisi. From the Coptic for "place of birth." Egyptian temple annex in which the annual ritual of the birth of the child god or goddess was enacted. The mammisi was misidentified by the French archeologist and scholar, Jean-François Champollion (1790–1832), as the "birthing house" or sacred site to which pregnant women came to endure their labor and give birth.

Manash. Hindu snake goddess. Especially venerated in Bengal, Manash was invoked against snakebites and as a fertility goddess. She was identified with the Buddhist goddess, Jāngulī.

Manat. One of the triad of goddesses—*al-Lāt, *al-'Uzza, and Manat—venerated by the Arabs at the Ka'ba in Mecca in pre-Islamic times. One of the names of *Ishtar, Manat was the goddess of good fortune. She was particularly esteemed by the Aws and the Khazraj, the two main Arab tribes in Medina, and was worshiped in the form of a rock set up at the sacred site at Qudayd near Yathrib.

Mandala. From the Sanskrit for "essence." A sacred diagram and/or meditation symbol in *Hinduism and *Buddhism. The mandala took the form of the circle within the square and contained a variety of images and symbols appropriate to the individual's meditation tradition. A contemplative aide for the attainment of the mystical light, the production and ritual function of the mandala has often been compared to that of the *icon in *Eastern Orthodoxy.

Mandorla. From the Italian for "almond." An almond or oval-shaped *aureole (*glory), which surrounded the whole body of a holy or sacred person. In Buddhist and Hindu art, this enclosure of light signified the total sacrality of a holy person or goddess as for example in representations of *Avalokiteshvara or a *bodhisattva. This encasement of radiance was most common in Christian art in representations of *Mary as the *Immaculate Conception or at her *Assumption.

Mandrake. Narcotic plant traditionally employed in fertility potions, aphrodisiacs, virility potions, love charms, and aids to conception (Gn 30). According to popular folklore and legend, the mandrake root was formed from the union of a man and a woman, and reportedly made blood-curdling sounds when uprooted and inflicted either death or insanity on whoever was present.

Manicheanism. An extreme form of Persian dualism taught by Mani (215–275), which influenced the theological development of Early Christianity. According to Manicheanism, there were two eternal principles identified as Light and Dark or God and Matter. Light led the salvific spiritual quests of Primeval Man as the substance was trapped in Matter. The creation of Adam and later of *Eve was interpreted as a counterplot to retain the Light imprisoned in Matter through the process of sexual intercourse and reproduction. Jesus Christ was only one aspect of the savior known as Jesus of the Brilliant Light who redeemed through a vision of Light. Followers were known as "the elect," and abstained from meat and sex as central elements of the ascetic means towards gradual liberation. *Augustine was among "the elect" for ten years prior to his conversion to Christianity.

Mannerism. A transitional stylistic movement in Italian art between 1520 and 1600. As a reaction against the High *Renaissance, especially the art of *Raphael, and as a foreshadowing of the *Baroque, Mannerism emphasized the primacy of the figure, which it distorted and elongated, and a forced composition whose focal point was located in the background of the canvas. Mannerist colors were distinctive, acid (chartreuse, tangerine, cerise), and emotionally affective.

Mantegna, Andrea (c. 1431–1506). Painter of the Italian *Renaissance and iconographic innovator. Influenced by Donatello and classical antiquity, Mantegna included tinted stone or bronze into a position of prominence in his paintings. This visual motif provided both a sense of the sculptural (even in his renderings of the human figure) and a heightened awareness of perspective. He was an early exponent of placing the *Sacra Conversazione as a group of figures in a unified, comprehensible space as opposed to the format of the medieval triptych. Both a compositional and iconographic innovator, Mantegna was best known for paintings such as the *Madonna and Child* and his *Judith*.

Marama. Goddess of the *moon of the Maori of New Zealand. According to tradition, her body wastes away but was renewed whenever she bathed in the sacred water of life—thereby paralleling the lunar cycle of waning and waxing.

Margaret of Antioch, Saint (c. late third century). A legendary virgin *martyr who died during the Diocletian persecutions. Although of a delicate physical constitution and the daughter of a prince, she was raised in the country by a secret Christian. A beautiful young woman, Margaret was courted by Governor Olybrius, but refused him having dedicated herself to Christ. Denounced as a Christian, she was confronted by a *dragon in prison. Depending on the version of her legend, Margaret either forced the dragon to disappear by making the sign of the cross, or by cleaving the dragon in two with her pendant cross, which grew enormous when the monster swallowed the martyr whole. Witnesses to the trials of Margaret stood in awe of her constancy and faith, and were converted to Christianity. Ultimately she was beheaded. Hers was one of the voices heard by *Joan of Arc. One of the *Fourteen Holy Helpers, Margaret of Antioch was the patron of women in childbirth, nurses, and peasants. In western Christian art, she was represented as a beautiful young woman, often in peasant dress, wearing a caplet or crown of pearls, holding a *palm branch and a *cross, and accompanied by a dragon.

Margaret of Cortona, Saint (1247–97). Maltreated by her stepmother, Margaret sought refuge in the home of her lover. She lived with this nobleman for nine years and bore him a son. Her conversion to Christianity occurred when she discovered her lover's murdered body. A member of the Order of Franciscans Tertiaries, Margaret of Cortona led an exemplary life of prayer and devotion. She was honored when the Crucified Christ tilted his head towards her as a sign of forgiveness during an ecstatic vision. Credited with many miraculous healings, "La Povorella" lived a model life of Franciscan prayer, poverty, and humility. In western Christian art, Saint Margaret of Cortona was represented by a beautiful young woman wearing a *veil and the knotted *girdle of the Franciscan Order, and was accompanied by her faithful spaniel. The most popular narrative representation was the *Ecstasy of Saint Margaret of Cortona*, in which she was depicted in ecstatic prayer as the Crucified Christ nodded to her.

Margawse. Second member of the female triad of Arthurian legend. Based upon the Celtic tradition, this triad was composed of a virgin (Elaine), a mother (Margawse), and a *crone (Morgan). As a mother goddess, Margawse bore the four Aeons and a son, Modred, by her brother Arthur.

Marguerite. From the Latin for "pearl." A floral symbol for the suffering and death of Christian *martyrs, this member of the daisy family was associated with pearls and drops of blood in western Christian art.

Mari. Name of both a popular village goddess in Hindu mythology and the supreme female deity of Basque mythology. (1) Legendary mother goddess for the Dravidians of southern India. As

such, Mari had both a frightful and a beneficent nature: as the bringer of smallpox and of rain. (2) From the Basque for "queen." According to Basque tradition, Mari lived inside the earth. She was characterized as a beautiful woman who was attired in rich garments and bejeweled. She was reputed to fly through the air, to exhale fire, to ride on a ram, and to drive a chariot with four *horses. She was also described as traveling on white clouds or on a *rainbow. Mari was identified by her *attribute, the sickle, which she carried as an amulet against thunder.

Marīcī. From the Sanskrit for "beam of light" or "she who writes in the register of life" of "the shining one." Indian Buddhist goddess invoked at sunrise and characterized as a solar deity. Marīcī was portrayed as a beautiful woman surrounded by garlands of dazzling light rays, and as traveling in a vehicle drawn by seven boars. As the *Shaktī of Samvara, she was depicted a naked female figure with a crown of skulls who was postured dancing upon his lifeless body as she held a bowl, chopper, and a staff covered with skulls. In her manifestation as Ashokakantra, she was golden yellow in color, had two arms, rode a *pig, and held a branch of the Ashoka tree in her left hand. As Samksipta, Marīcī had three faces, one being that of a pig, and eight arms. In Tibetan and Nepalese Buddhism, she was identified with Vajrāvārāhi, that is "the diamond sow," and was represented as a female form with the head of a sow. In Tibet, Marīcī was also a companion of the Green *Tārā, and thereby was characterized as a seated female figure enthroned on a *lotus held by four boars or astride a boar. She has several forms including a multiheaded and armed yellow one, a three-headed and ten-armed red one, and a ten-armed and four-legged white one. In all of these forms, Marīcī held the branch of an ashoka tree and a variety of Tantric *attributes. In her Japanese form as *Marishi-ten*, she was invoked by warriors, especially archers, before they entered into battle as she could make them invisible. Favored with the devotion of the disciples of Zen Buddhism and Nīcheren Sho-shu, Marishi-ten had seven possible forms in Japanese art. Her most popular form was as a three-headed, including that of a sow, lady dressed in the Tang style, seated on a lotus carried by seven boars, with her feet resting upon a crescent *moon or another lotus. She was encased in an eight-beamed aureole. She had either six or eight arms in which she held a needle and thread, a *vajra, a hook, rope, and a *bow and *arrows. Marishi-ten also had a four-faced, including one of a sow, and two-armed form in which she tilted her head to the right and wore a glittering tiara. Her right hand gestured a *mudrā while she held a swastika-decorated fan in her left hand. In another posture, Marishi-ten took on a normal female form and sat on a lotus. She gestured a mudrā with her right hand and held a fan in her left hand. Whereas in her golden-yellow form, she wore a blue garment and had a small stūpā in her headdress. This eight-armed Marishi-ten held an arrow, needle, vajra, and lance in her right hands, and a bow, rope, lace, and an ashoka branch in her left hand. She had three heads each with a separate expression: infuriated with exposed fangs on her left head, serenity on her central head, and the head of a sow on her right head. A three-headed goddess stood on a running boar. Each of her three heads had three eyes. She was characterized as shooting an arrow, brandishing a sword, and holding a fan, staff, and spear in her six arms. This form of Marishi-ten was completely encircled in flames. In her simplest form, the goddess was represented as seated with a stūpā on her head. Marishi-ten was also portrayed as galloping on an *antelope in a three-headed, six-armed, and six-legged form. Again, each of her three heads had three eyes, oftentimes she wore a headdress decorated with three eyes and a skull. She was displayed in the act of shooting an arrow, and holding a staff, sword, spear, and *cakra in her many hands.

Marigold. A floral symbol for fidelity. This member of aster and sunflower families was a common and thereby humble flower that signified the Virgin *Mary.

Mariolatry. Worship of *Mary. Although not a theological doctrine or teaching of any Christian tradition, Mariolatry was an expression of popular devotions and faith. *Roman Catholicism proscribed *latria* (worship) of Mary but affirmed *hyperdulia* (special veneration); whereas most *Protestantism advocated severe and strict criticism of any popular devotions and cultic practices to Mary.

Mariology. Systematic theological study of teachings about *Mary including her person, and her role in Redemption with special reference to the Incarnation.

Marriage at Cana (Jn 2:1–12). The first public miracle of Jesus described in John's *Gospel. Jesus' presence at this event signified the Christian validation of marriage. Having attended a wedding ceremony with his mother and other followers in Cana, Jesus partook of the wedding banquet. Before the banquet ended, the host ran out of wine. *Mary told this to Jesus, who reminded her that his time had not yet arrived. Unperturbed, Mary instructed the servants to do whatever he asked. Six jars of *water were brought to him and then were miraculously turned into the finest wine. Several medieval texts, including *The Golden Legend* (96), followed the Venerable Bede in identifying the bridegroom as John the Evangelist. *The Golden Legend* (96) identified the bride as *Mary Magdalene. The Marriage at Cana had several *Old Testament foretypes, and was itself interpreted as a foretype of the miraculous feedings, varied feasts, Last Supper, and Celestial Banquet of the *New Testament. In the history of Christian art and devotion, the Marriage at Cana became important for both its eucharistic symbolism and its account of Mary's role as intercessor. The initial visual interest in the Marriage at Cana arose thematically, as it was considered one of the three festivals of Epiphany (with the Adoration of the Magi and Baptism of Jesus Christ). Established early in the history of Christian art, the *iconography of the Marriage at Cana was composed of the standing figure of Jesus who was either holding a thaumaturge or healer's staff (in the earliest images) or extending his right hand (in later images), over several large water jars in the presence of one or more servants. By the sixth century, the figure of Mary began to be included in this motif. In medieval art, the composition was expanded to include the bridal couple and the wedding guests.

By the thirteenth century, with its interest in *Mariology, Mary had become more influential, especially in her role as intercessor. Artistic representations of this theme diminished between the midfourteenth and midsixteenth centuries. Revived in *baroque art, this motif was transformed into a presentation of a great wedding banquet in which it became difficult to locate either Jesus or Mary.

Marriage of the Virgin Mary. *See* Betrothal and Marriage of the Virgin Mary.

Martha of Bethany, Saint (first century). An admirable woman of faith and action, sister of Lazarus and *Mary of Bethany, and friend of Jesus. Following tradition, her sister Mary of Bethany was conflated with *Mary Magdalene, and thereby Martha was identified as the person who led her sister to conversion (a popular motif among southern *baroque artists). In the Eastern Orthodox Church, she was included among the Holy Women who brought ointments and spices to anoint the body of the crucified Jesus at the tomb. According to *The Golden Legend*, Martha of Bethany accompanied her brother and sister to Marseilles, helped to evangelize Provence, and rescued the people of Aix from a terrible *dragon that she drove away with holy *water sprinkled from an *aspergillum. As the paragon of domestic virtues and skills, Martha was the patron of housewives and cooks. She was depicted in western Christian art as a mature, plainly dressed woman who was identified by one of her *attributes—*kitchen utensils, most often a *ladle; household *keys, usually on her *belt; an aspergil-

63. Joos van Cleve, *The Holy Family*

lum; or a dragon or jar of holy water at her feet.

Martha and Mary of Bethany (Luke 10:38). Sisters of Lazarus who entertained Jesus in their home. Martha complained vigorously that she had completed all the necessary work while her sister had sat at Jesus' feet and received spiritual instruction. Jesus countered that Mary had chosen the better part. Martha was thought of as the female personification of the active life, and was characterized as domestic, efficient, industrious, and pragmatic; while Mary was the female personification of the contemplative life, and was characterized as spiritual, passive, and mystical. Several early Church Fathers, including Tertullian, conflated Mary of Bethany with *Mary Magdalene. Representations of this scriptural event in western Christian art depicted Mary seated at the feet of Jesus while an erect Martha gestured angrily before him. A secularized presentation of the two sisters—one working in the kitchen while the other watches—became a popular motif in seventeenth-century northern art and nineteenth-century American art.

Mary, life and symbolism of. The mother of Jesus Christ and the model for Christian women in Christian art and devotion. (1) The minimal biblical references to Mary were supplemented by the many legendary and devotional books such as *The Golden Legend, and the *apocryphal gospels, especially the Protoevangelium of James. This scarcity of biblical evidence permitted the formation of many symbolic types of representation based purely on devotionalism and spirituality. Since the Early Christian Church was concerned with the issues of daily survival and the theology of the Resurrection, images and devotion to Mary were minimal. The cult of Mary began to flourish in the fifth century following both the establishment of the Imperial Church (325) and the decree of the Council of Ephesus (431). The *iconography of the *Theotokos (Mary as "God-bearer"; that is, with her son) developed according to the conciliar decree. The major events in the life of Mary were described in either the apocryphal gospels or legendary texts, and increased in mid-twelfth-century western art. In Christian art, the major events in the life of Mary that became identified as the narrative cycle of Mary were: *Meeting at the Golden Gate, *Nativity of the Virgin Mary, *Presentation of the Virgin Mary in the Temple, *Betrothal and Marriage of the Virgin Mary, *Annunciation to the Virgin Mary, *Visitation, *Nativity of Jesus Christ, *Purification of the Virgin Mary, *Marriage at Cana, Crucifixion, *Mourning (including *Deposition, *Lamentation, and *Pietà), Pentecost, *Annunciation of the Death of the Virgin Mary, *Dormition of the Virgin Mary, *Assumption of the Virgin Mary, and *Coronation of the Virgin Mary. (2) A major focus of Christian art as influenced by popular devotions, and by apocryphal and legendary texts. As the second most important personage in Christianity, the symbols and images of Mary proliferated throughout the history of Christian art. She was represented as the Ideal Woman, the Mother of God, the Second Eve, and the Ideal Mother (Madonna and Child). Her most common *attributes were the *lily, *rose, *book, *crown, *apple, *mirror, and *moon.

Christian art was influenced by the culture in which it was created, and was also responsive to or reflective of the evolving theological concerns of each cultural epoch. In earliest Christian art, there were minimal references to Mary, since the central theological concern was the Resurrection, not the Incarnation. The Cult of Mary developed in the fifth century following the establishment of the Imperial Church and the decree of the Council of Ephesus (431) that Mary was *Theotokos (from the Greek for "God-bearer"). At that time in Christian history, the most popular images of Mary were as Theotokos, that is, hieratic images of the Virgin and Child, in which their gestures and postures signified differing theological or spiritual meanings. By the seventh century, these Byzantine iconographic models were transferred to western art and further influenced by the legends that Luke the Evangelist had painted a portrait (series of portraits) of Mary. (3) Spiritual and devotional interest in Mary abounded during the twelfth century as she became the focus of much theological and iconographic innovations. At that time in Christian history, the most popular (and newest) images of Mary were as *Sedes Sapientiae* or *Virgo Sapientissima* (Throne of Wisdom), *Mater Ecclesia* (Mother Church), Queen of Heaven, Virgin and the *Unicorn, *Pietà (*Vesperbild*), *Maria Lactans* (Nursing Mother), Virgin of Mercy, Intercessor, *Madonna and Child in the Rose Garden, the *Holy Family, Madonna and Child with *Saint Anne, and the idealized images of the Madonna and Child, in which the objects held by the Christ Child signified the theological or spiritual intent. Other topics of importance to the growing interest in

Mary were reflected in the *Seven Joys and *Seven Sorrows of the Virgin Mary. The Renaissance interest in humanism and the theology of the Incarnation resulted in an interest in the spirituality of the *mater amabilis*, or maternal love, of Mary for her child. During that period, the most popular images of Mary were the Madonna of Humility, the Pietà, and the Madonna and Child. The resurgence of devotion to Mary in the *Counter-Reformation Church led to the development of new iconographic motifs including the *Immaculate Conception, Assumption of the Virgin Mary, Madonna and Child with Joseph (of Nazareth), Woman of the Apocalypse, Pietà, and Virgin of Solitude. Northern *baroque artists embellished the *iconography of the *Holy Kindred as a visual motif that diminished Mary's status in Christian spirituality. For other symbols of Mary, *see* individual entries on specific animals, flowers, fruits, plants, heroines of the Old Testament and classical Greco-Roman mythology, initials and monograms, saints, and narrative entries.

Mary of Bethany, Saint (first century). Sister of Lazarus and *Martha who received spiritual instruction at the feet of Christ. Mary of Bethany was identified as the anointer at Bethany, and was also present at the Resurrection of her brother Lazarus. She was often confused with *Mary Magdalene, and by the fifth century, the two women were identified in the West as one woman. The Eastern Orthodox Church identified Mary of Bethany as a person distinctive from Mary Magdalene. *See also* Anointing at Bethany, Martha of Bethany, and Mary Magdalene.

Mary Cleophas, Saint (first century). One of the Holy Women who followed Christ, stood witness at the foot of the *cross, and with *Mary Magdalene and *Mary Salome brought unguents and spices to the tomb. Mary Cleophas was identified as the sister of *Mary, the wife of Cleophas, and the mother of James Minor and Joses (Mt 27:56; Mk 15:40; Lk 24:10; Jn 19:25). Following the northern medieval tradition of the *Holy Kindred, she was the daughter of Anne by her second husband, Cleophas, and thereby the Virgin Mary's half-sister. Another tradition identified her as a companion to Lazarus, Martha, and Mary Magdalene in the mission to evangelize Provence. In western Christian art, Mary Cleophas was included in the relevant biblical narratives and the Holy Kindred, and was included as "one of the Marys."

Mary of Egypt, Saint (fifth century). A legendary Alexandrian prostitute who converted to Christianity. Mary of Egypt was mystically obstructed from entering the Church of the Holy Sepulcher in Jerusalem. She had a vision of *Mary, to whom she pledged renunciation of her unseemly lifestyle, and thereby was granted permission to enter the church. Once inside, Mary of Egypt heard a voice telling her she would find "peace" on the other side of the Jordan. She left Jerusalem with only three loaves of *bread, crossed the River Jordan, and became a hermit in the Syrian desert. During her solitary life of penance, her clothes rotted away and her *hair grew long to cover her wasted body. Zosimus, a priest on a Lenten retreat, saw her over the River Jordan. After he offered her a blessing, he watched in awe as she was carried across the river by angels

in order to receive the Eucharist. The following year he found her dead body, which he buried with the assistance of a *lion. A popular figure in medieval legends and devotions, Mary of Egypt was confused (and later conflated) with Mary Magdalene. In Christian art, Mary of Egypt was depicted as a haggard elderly woman with long, disheveled, white (gray) hair that covered her wrinkled body. Her wasted face was highlighted by sunken cheekbones and the loss of her teeth. She was usually postured in prayer and had three loaves of bread or a lion by her side.

Mary Magdalene, Saint (first century). Model of the female penitential *saint, first witness to the Resurrection, and one of the most popular and complex of all Christian saints. Following the model of the early church fathers, Western Christianity combined three women—Mary of Magdala, *Mary of Bethany, and an unnamed female sinner—into Mary Magdalene. The Eastern Christian Church recognized them as three separate women. Mary of Magdala was the woman from whom Jesus cast seven devils (Mk 16:9; Lk 8:2–7); she stood at the foot of the cross (Mt 27:56, Mk 15:40; Jn 19:25), was one of the Holy Women who brought spices and unguents to the tomb (Mt 28:1–8, Mk 16:1, Lk 24:1–10), and was the first witness to the Resurrection (Mt 28:9, Mk 16:9, Jn 20:4–18). Mary of Bethany received spiritual guidance at the feet of Jesus in the home she shared with her sister *Martha (Lk 10:38–42), was present at the Resurrection of her brother Lazarus (Jn 11:1–44), and anointed Jesus at Bethany (Jn 12:1–8). The unnamed repentant sinner who anointed Christ's feet in the *House of

64. Elisabetta Sirani, *Mary Magdalene*

Simon (Lk 7:36–50) was alleged to be a *harlot and was conflated with the unnamed *woman taken in adultery (Jn 8:1–11). All these women, due either to similarity in name or character, were fused into one female personality whom Western Christians came to identify as Mary Magdalene. Patron of penitents and flagellants, the Magdalene was invoked by women in childbirth and in cases of infertility. In early Christian art, Mary Magdalene was identified by her role as the first witness to the Resurrection, and was included in the appropriate narrative events in the life of Christ. By the early medieval period, however, she became an independent personality as the first witness to the Resurrection in the *Noli Me Tangere, as the disciple to the disciples, and as the archetypal female penitential saint. Medieval legendary and devotional texts, including *The Golden Legend, identified the Magdalene as the evangelist of Provence with Lazarus and Martha. According to tradition, she retired to a cave in the woods near Sainte Baume where she lived in solitude for thirty years meditating upon her sins, eating only celestial foods, and being serenaded by angelic songs during her daily "elevations." She received her last communion from Maximin just before her death. Her relics were reported to have been buried in the Cathedral of the Magdalene in Vézélay, an important twelfth-century pilgrimage site. *Medieval artists depicted the Magdalene as a preacher; a penitent with a *skull, *crucifix, and open *bible in front of her cave; on her daily assumptions (mystical elevations); and at her last communion. The Cult of Mary Magdalene developed, and individual images of the Magdalene as penitent, as contempla-

tive reader, and as miracle worker formed the devotional *iconography. Her legend and iconography became confused (and later conflated) with that of *Mary of Egypt, so that physical representations of the Magdalene alternated between those of a beautiful young woman either elegantly dressed (before her conversion) or simply attired (after her conversion), and those of a haggard, elderly naked woman with a sunken face, disheveled *hair, and wasted body covered with her long flowing hair. The *iconography of the Magdalene flourished anew in southern *baroque art as she became a symbol for the defense of and devotion to the sacraments, especially the sacrament of penance (Penitent Magdalene in the Wilderness, Conversion of the Magdalene), against the Reformers. Throughout the history of Christian art, Mary Magdalene was distinguished by her perennial trademarks of long, flowing red hair and an unguent jar.

Mary Magdalene of Pazzi, Saint (1566–1607). Carmelite nun of Florence and a Christian mystic. Mary Magdalene of Pazzi was a woman of passionate temperament matched by her religious mystical nature. As a young girl she decided to dedicate herself to God. Following her studies at St. John's Convent in Florence, she disobeyed her parents' wishes and refused the marriage they had arranged for her. Instead, she entered the Carmelite order of Saint Mary of the Angels Convent in Pazzi. Throughout a series of illnesses she had spiritual visions including one of *Mary as the Blessed Mother handing her a white *veil, a symbol of purity. A popular topic in the western Christian art created for seventeenth-century Carmelite churches and convents, Mary Magdalene of Pazzi was represented in the habit of her order and postured in one of the visionary episodes of her life. She was portrayed as kneeling before a vision of Mary and the Child as she took a veil from a dish held by an *angel and placing it on Mary Magdalene's head. In another vision, she knelt before *Augustine who was garbed in his episcopal robes and who wrote on her breast, "And the Word became flesh" (Jn 1:14). Variants of her visions depicted her receiving the Christ Child from Mary, receiving the Instruments of the Passion from the Resurrected Christ, or in the midst of her mystical marriage to the Christ Child.

Mary Salome, Saint (first century). One of the Holy Women who followed Christ, stood at the foot of the *cross, and with *Mary Magdalene and *Mary Cleophas carried unguents and spices to the tomb. Ostensibly Mary Salome was the mother of James Minor and John and the wife of Zebedee (Mt 20:20; 27:56). Following the medieval tradition of the *Holy Kindred, she was the daughter of Anne by her first husband, Salomas,. and thereby half-sister of *Mary. According to legend, she either accompanied the Magdalene to evangelize Provence, or traveled alone to evangelize Spain. She was not to be confused with the other *"Salomes"—the midwife at the Nativity of Christ according to the *Protoevangelium of James*, and the unnamed daughter of *Herodias who was identified as Salome by Flavius Josephus. In Christian art, Mary Salome was included in the relevant biblical narratives and in the Holy Kindred, and was identified as "one of the Marys."

Marys, The Three (Mt 28:1–8; Mk 16:1–8; Lk 24:1–11; Jn 20:1–9). The Holy Women who went with spices and unguents to anoint the *body of the crucified Christ. These women were identified as *Mary Magdalene, *Mary Cleophas, and *Mary Salome.

Marys at the Tomb (Mt 28:1–8; Mk 16:1–8; Lk 24:1–11; Jn 20:1–9). The holy women identified as the *Three Marys (ostensibly *Mary Magdalene, *Mary Salome, and *Mary Cleophas) who brought anointing spices for the body of Jesus to his tomb. Arriving at the tomb, they found the sepulcher stone moved away and the tomb empty except for a radiant *angel who advised them that Christ had risen from the dead. In early Christian and *byzantine art, this motif symbolized the Resurrection. After the thirteenth century, this event was fused with the Resurrection and Guarded Tomb into one visual motif.

Mask. A covering for the face in ceremonial rites and theatrical programs as a mode of disguising the identity of the actor. A tragic mask was an *attribute of *Melpomene as the *muse of tragedy, and a comic mask of *Thalia as the muse of comedy in classical Greek and *renaissance art.

Mātaras. The Ambikās, or "little mothers," of Indian art and mythology. According to Hindu tradition, these were seven or nine goddesses who were the *shaktis of Shiva and Ganesha. The mātaras were portrayed in postures of union, as appropriate to shaktīs, with either Shiva or Ganesha.

Māte. From the Latvian for mother. Epithet for mother goddesses or goddesses who were mothers in Latvian mythology.

Mater Matuta. Ancient Italic goddess of the dawn or morning light. A mother goddess, Mater Matuta was the patron of seafarers and became identified with *Ino.

Mati-syra-zemlya. Russian mythic female personification of the earth as mother. Mati-syra-zemlya was characterized as having dominion over evil powers and over nature. She was characterized as a female figure of justice and prophecy.

Matralia. Annual festival celebrated in honor of *Mater Matuta on June 11th.

Matres. Trio of maternal goddesses in the art and mythology of Roman Gaul, Britain, and the Rhineland. The matres were portrayed seated together with *baskets of *fruits or *cornucopias in their laps.

Matriarch. In the Hebraic tradition, there were four founding mothers of the Jewish peoples: *Sarah, *Rebecca, *Rachel, and *Leah. These were the wives of the Patriarchs and were the most important women in the early period of Jewish history.

Matriarchy. Society regulated by women and in which women were dominant in all aspects of life, power, and authority.

Matrilineal descent. Pattern of legal authority and identity through the female line only.

Matrona. Great goddess figure of Celtic mythology.

Matronalia. Annual festival celebrated in honor of *Juno on March 1st.

Maya. From the Sanskrit for "miraculous power." Vedic tradition described the power of the gods as created by Vishnu in terms of a primeval feminine principle from which the world was generated. This was maya. According to the *Upanishads*, the world engendered by magic was an illusion, that is maya, which was erased when the sole universal reality of Brahman was understood. Thereby, maya degenerated from "miraculous feminine power" to "feminine deception." Maya was also the name of the mother of the Buddha. *See also* Mahamaya.

Mayahuel. Ancient Mexican goddess of pulque, or the intoxicating drink usually reserved for the deities, the priests, and those about to undergo ritual ceremonies. In a well-known variant to her legend, Mayahuel was abducted by Quetzalcoatyl from heaven and brought to earth. When her body was torn into pieces by jealous demons of darkness, Quetzalcoatyl caused the first agave plants to rise from bones. In indigenous Mexican art, and later in Aztec images, Mayahuel was portrayed as seated upon a *tortoise in front of a blossoming agave plant.

Maypole. Symbolic residence of the spirit of vegetation and thereby, of fertility of the earth and humanity. Ancient European traditions and folklore espoused May as the month of fertility and new life. Ceremonies and festivals celebrating this spirit of new life, vegetation, and fertility were offered on May Day. Newly flowering branches were brought into homes on May Day morning to signify new life. The Maypole became the center of the ceremony with elaborate dances, usually circle dances around the pole, which were led by the "Queen of the May" identified as the most beautiful female virgin in the village. With the establishment of Christianity, the Maypole and other elements of indigenous fertility rituals slowly disappeared from use.

Ma-Zu. From the Chinese for "Queen of Heaven." Merciful mother goddess of southeast China. Ma-Zu was invoked by fishermen against disasters at sea. She was merged with *Kuan Yin.

Mechthild of Magdeburg (1210–82). Christian visionary and mystic. The child of noble parents, Mechthild had her first vision of the Holy Spirit at the age of twelve. At the age of twenty, she entered the Beguine convent in Magdeburg where she lived a quiet life of devotional prayer under the spiritual direction of Dominican monks. Reports of her extraordinary, and oftentimes bizarre visions resulted in her expulsion from Magdeburg and her refuge in the Cistercian convent at *Helfta where she befriended and mentored *Gertrude the Great. Among Mechthild's writings was the famed *Das fliessende Licht des Gottheit* (*The Flowing Light of God*) in which she emphasized the spirituality of fluids such as the Virgin's blessed milk. These devotional texts evoked much interest among the laity and later even influenced *Dante who named Mechthild in *Purgatory*, Canto 27–33. Although she herself was a rare independent topic in western Christian art, the mystical writings of Mechthild of Magdeburg were greatly influential on the representations of women, especially *Mary, *Mary Magdalene, and the female saints, in western Christian art.

Medb. Queen of Connacht in the Celtic Irish tradition. Medb was portrayed as a strong female warmonger who led the historic raid against Ulster in order to win a mystical *bull.

Medea. Renowned sorcerer of Greek mythology. The daughter of Aeëtes of Colchis, Medea was identified for her acts of sorcery, both good and evil magic. Besotted with her love for Jason, Medea used her magical skills to aide the Argonauts in their quest for the legendary Golden Fleece. She married Jason and traveled with him to Thessaly where he learned of his father's untimely death at the hands of Pelias. The sorcerer intervened to bring justice to her father-in-law's murderer and brought about her husband's ascent to the throne of Thessaly. Following Jason's abdication in favor of Acastus, they lived in Corinth with King Creon. For ten years, Medea lived happily with Jason, and eventually, she bore him two sons. In time, Jason betrayed Medea and replaced her with Glauce (Creusa), the beautiful young daughter of King Creon. Summoning her magical powers for her revenge, Medea pretended to make peace with Jason and his bride by presenting her with a golden crown and a regal robe. However, once Glaube put on the crown and the robe they were transformed into burning forces and she was killed. The betrayed Medea then killed her two sons by Jason. The sorcerer fled in a chariot drawn by winged *dragons or *serpents. She continued to practice her magic, for both good and evil, first in Athens and finally in Colchis where she reinstated her father as rightful king. According to tradition, Medea was believed to be immortal and was revered as patron of Corinth, which she delivered from famine.

Mediatrix. Tradition and popular devotion that *Mary as the Mother of Jesus Christ was the mediatrix of all graces. Following her *Assumption into heaven and her *Coronation as *Queen of Heaven, Mary was seated at the right hand of her son and became the one through whom all graces won by him were dispensed. Mary's exaltation as Mother Church was interpreted as symbolic of the role of the ecclesiastical hierarchy as the mediator between God and humanity.

Medica. Epithet of *Minerva as the patron of doctors.

Medeine. From the Lithuanian for "trio." According to medieval chronicles, Medeine was the goddess, if not simply the spirit, of the woods in Lithuanian mythology.

Medieval art. The umbrella identification for the varied artistic styles that developed in western Europe between the fifth and sixteenth centuries, including Italo-Byzantine, Carolingian, Ottonian, *Romanesque, and *Gothic. Medieval art was characterized as being predominantly Christian in content, nonnaturalistic in form, and without a sense of natural perspective. Medieval art excelled in the development of manuscript *illuminations and *cathedral architecture.

Meditations on the Life of Christ. An influential devotional text written in the late thirteenth century. Originally attributed to Saint Bonaventure, this book was written by an anonymous Franciscan (Giovanni de Caulibus) normally identified as Pseudo-Bonaventure. The elaborate, humanized descriptions of the events in the life of Jesus and *Mary were prepared as pious reflections on the meaning of being a Christian. The fictional life events as narrated in this text were accepted as true by *medieval and *renaissance Christians. Like *The Golden Legend* and *Revelations of Saint Bridget of Sweden*, the *Meditations on the Life of Christ* was influential in western Christian art.

Meditrina. Ancient Roman goddess of medicine whose role and *attributes were usurped by Asklepios.

Meditinalia. Annual festival celebrated in honor of *Meditrina on October 11th. One of the favored features of the ceremonies of the Meditinalia was the juice drinks squeezed from the recently harvested grapes. All those who partook of these juices were blessed with good health for the year.

Medium of Endor. *See* Saul and Witch of Endor.

Medusa. A beautiful maiden in Greek mythology who was identified as the only mortal Gorgon. She was transformed into an ugly winged *monster as punishment for defiling *Athena's temple with *Poseidon. Athena turned Medusa's *hair into hissing snakes because of her hubris in claiming that her hair was more beautiful than the goddess's. Medusa's face became so horrific that whoever looked upon her was turned into stone. The mythical hero Perseus tricked her into looking into a mirror and when she saw her reflection he decapitated her. Whoever held the *head of Medusa was able to destroy his or her enemies immediately. Eventually, Perseus gave the head of Medusa to Athena, who emblazoned it on her shield. Known as the gorgoneion, the severed head of Medusa was an apotropaic image and became popular as a decorative motif on temples, stelae, and ampHorae. In classical Greco-Roman art and *renaissance art, the youthful Perseus was depicted holding the head of Medusa by her snaky locks. This was the classical Greco-Roman foretype of David with head of Goliath, *Judith with the head of Holofernes, and *Salome with the head of John the Baptist.

Meeting at the Golden Gate (*Protoevangelium of James* 4:14 and *The Golden Legend* 131). The event that signified the conception of *Mary according to devotional and legendary texts. Although he was a pious Jew, the aged and childless Joachim was denied the right to sacrifice in the Temple. He retreated into the wilderness (*desert) for forty days of prayers and fasting in order to offer his sacrifice to God. One night, an *angel appeared simultaneously to Joachim in the wilderness and to his wife *Anne in her bedroom to announce the coming birth of a special child. Following the angel's instructions, Joachim and Anne met at the Golden Gate of Jerusalem. According to pious legend, when Joachim kissed Anne on the cheek she conceived Mary. Narratives of the life cycle of Mary flourished after the thirteenth century, but the motif of the Meeting at the Golden Gate became a

favored theme for late *medieval and *renaissance artists. This iconographic motif was replaced in the baroque period by the *iconography of the *Immaculate Conception.

Mefitis. Ancient Roman goddess venerated, and thereby depicted, at sulphur springs.

Megaira. One of the *Erinyes. A classical Greek term for an evil woman or a *Fury.

Meh-Urit. From the Egyptian language for "the great flood." Egyptian celestial goddess who birthed the sky. Meh-Urit was associated with *Isis as a protector of the dead. She was identified with the Greek goddess *Methyer, and merged by Plutarch with Isis. In Egyptian art, Meh-Urit was portrayed as a *cow.

Mehit. Lion-headed goddess of Egyptian art and mythology.

Melancholia. Legendary daughter of Saturn (Cronos) renowned for her introspective nature. The female embodiment of gloomy contemplation, Melancholia became associated with intellectual pursuits and medical problems attributed to excess bile. She was represented as a winged female figure, often seated with her head resting on one hand and holding a compass in the other, and an unopened *book rested in her lap. Melancholia was identified by a disorderly array of scholarly paraphernalia such as geometric tools, a sphere, writing instruments, and tablets.

Melania the Younger (383–439). Renowned Christian female philanthropist. A daughter of a pagan Roman father and a Christian mother, Melania the Younger was married against her will at the age of fourteen. Following the deaths of her first two children, she persuaded her husband to respect both her request for a celibate marriage and her dedication of her life to God. She inherited great wealth at the death of her father, and retreated from Rome to the country villa with her mother and her husband to establish a religious center. She sold off so much of her property for philanthropic purposes that she needed to obtain protection from Emperor Honorius from her family who were outraged as she continued her charitable donations to churches, monasteries, and orphanages, and to the sick, the poor, and pilgrims. For example, Melania supervised the manumission of over eight thousand slaves in two years. In 406, she and her family were forced to flee the invading Goths, and began a circuitous and dangerous four-year journey to Tagaste in North Africa. There, Melania established a dual monastery, for men and for women, and lived a life of great austerity. She made a pilgrimage to the Holy Land in 417 and also visited the desert monks of Egypt. Melania settled in Jerusalem where she visited her cousin, *Paula, regularly and eventually came to know her cousin's spiritual director, Jerome. Befriended by this *Church Father, Melania established a convent near the Mount of Olives and was superior for life. Following her burial of her mother and her husband in Jerusalem, Melania had a cell for meditation made for herself near their graves. Venerated in Eastern Orthodox Christianity, Melania the Younger was characterized by her *at-

tribute of a model of her convent on the Mount of Olives.

Melissa. Sister of *Amalthea and a nursemaid to Zeus in Greek mythology. Melissa nurtured Zeus with goat's milk, and later when she learned how to gather honey the young god transformed her into a *bee. She was portrayed in classical either in the posture of feeding the young Zeus or by her emblem, the bee. Melissa was also a common name for the priestesses of varied classical Mediterranean cults and for legendary nymphs.

Melpomene. From the Greek for "to sing." Greek *muse of tragedy and laments. One of the daughters of Zeus and *Mnemosyne, Melpomene was portrayed as a beautiful maiden dressed in long flowing garments and holding her *attributes of a tragic mask, a garland or *wreath of vine leaves, a club, or cothurii, the heavily soled and cord-bound shoes worn by actors.

Memento Mori. From the Latin for "reminder of death." A physical object that signified the transitory and fleeting quality of human existence. The most popular memento mori in western Christian art were a *skull, a skull with wings, a skull crowned with a *laurel wreath, a *skeleton, an hourglass, and a death's-head moth.

Mena. Roman goddess of menstruation. Mena was identified with *Juno.

Menat. Multilayered necklace with back counterweight worn by *Hathor, and later her priestesses, as an emblem of healing. The menat was also swung or shook by these priestesses to create percussion sounds during ritual processions.

Menopause. The physical cessation of a woman's menstrual cycle and a traditional sign of old age. No longer able to conceive a child and also no longer tainted by the monthly taboo of menstrual blood, menopause signified a transition into the role of "old woman" or "wise woman" in many world religions, and thereby made permissible participation in certain ritual activities previously denied to a menstruating woman. *See also* Crone.

Menstruation. The advent of the monthly cycle of bleeding announced a girl's transition into a woman and her ability to conceive a child. Simultaneously, menstruation had significant taboos associated with the woman's loss of menstrual blood, which was credited with the ability to produce sour milk, death, failure, and physical weakness. In some cultures, it was forbidden for a menstruating woman to touch food, participate in religious rituals, or engage in sexual intercourse. She was separated from the rest of society until her time had passed and then purified so she could reenter her normal daily life. However, in other cultures, a menstruating woman was interpreted as a powerful and positive force of love and creative magic whose touch could induce fecundity to vegetation, animals, and other human beings. In many cultures, artistic representations of a young woman, either dressed or naked, who pressed a white cloth to her genital area signified menstruation. For an example of the cultural attitudes towards menstruation and a menstruating woman, a brief examination of the Jewish tradi-

tion is offered. During her menstrual period, a Jewish woman was understood to be culturally and spiritually taboo. She could not participate in any ritual or ceremonial activities, including those at the Temple or *Synagogue; further physical contact with her husband was forbidden (Lev 20:18). At the end of her period, a Jewish woman was purified through the ritual bath known as a *mikveh*. According to Jewish tradition, menstruation was the direct result of Eve's sin, that is, her shedding of Adam's blood, thereby causing his death. It was believed that during the forty-year exile in the wilderness that Jewish women did not menstruate. The scriptural admonitions and regulations concerning menstruation had to be adhered to, disobedience was punished with death in childbirth. For example, it was believed that should a Jewish woman and her husband engage in sexual activity during her menstrual period that a "tainted"—that is, deformed or sick—child would result from this illicit union.

Meret. From the Egyptian language for "queen of the treasury." Ancient Egyptian goddess of song and rejoicing. Meret was represented standing upon the hieroglyph for *gold. A double representation of Meret signified the union of Upper and Lower Egypt.

Meretseger. From the Greek for "lover of friend of him who makes silence." Greek name for *Mert-Sekert.

Mert-Sekert. From the Egyptian hieroglpyhs for "mistress of the west." Egyptian goddess of the desert and its protector against snakes. Mert-Sekert was invoked as the protector of tombs and as a companion of the dead. According to tradition, Mert-Sekert was a companion of Osiris as the god of the dead as she was the female personification of the western desert, the land of the sunset and of the dead. She was also identified as a judge and the punisher of wrongdoers, and as protector of the good. She was venerated at the necropolis of Thebes. In Egyptian art, Mert-Sekert was represented as a female figure with the head of a snake, or as a snake with a woman's head, or as a snake. She wore a headdress composed of a disk encircled by *horns.

Mermaid. A mythical creature composed of a female torso and the lower body of a scaly *fish with a double tail. The mermaid's songs were so ethereal and enchanting that sailors were bewitched by them and allowed their boats to shatter on the *rocks. Riding a wave's crest while combing her *hair and looking in a *mirror, the mermaid was the feminine symbol of the seductive temptations that had to be conquered in order to achieve salvation. In the Mesopotamian tradition, the *kulittu*, or "fish-woman" was identified in contrast to the merman who was a symbol of protective magic.

Mesenet. Female personification of the "birth brick" in Egyptian art. According to Egyptian practice, a woman in labor crouched over the mesenet in order to give birth. The mesenet was inscribed with the image of *Meshkenit's head encircled by a double *spiral signifying the uterus.

Meshkenit. From the Egyptian language for "the place where one delivers." Egyptian goddess of childbirth. Meshkenit was identified with the

"birth brick" that was the two bricks used as footrests for pregnant women during their time in labor. Following Egyptian custom, it was believed that the destiny of the child-about-to-be-born was determined by Meshkenit who also fulfilled the role of character witness for the dead before Osiris. In Egyptian art, Meshkenit was represented by those birth bricks that terminated in the inscription of a human head. The motif on the birth brick might also take the form of a woman with a brick on her head, or of a brick with a woman's head.

Mesoamerican religions. Multiplicity of indigenous ritual and ceremonial practices, and belief systems of the indigenous peoples of regions of Mexico, Guatemala, Belize, El Salvador, Honduras, and Costa Rica prior to the importation of Christianity. Although difficult to characterize or identify without careful consideration of cultural histories and regional studies, there are a series of common elements which can be identified as "features of Mesoamerican religions." These include affirmation of an afterlife, usually horrific in character, and the eternality of the human spirit; a cosmology with carefully detailed mythology of the underworld; a code of sacred warfare; the central role of the rituals of sacrifice; sacred centers which marked an axis mundi; a series of annual and life-cycle rituals associated with human and agricultural fertility; and a hierarchy of ritual leaders and spiritual healers. Predominant among these varied indigenous religious systems are those of the Aztecs, Mayans, Olmecs, and Toltecs.

Mesopotamian and Near Eastern religions. Belief and ritual systems of the traditional peoples of the city states and empires of western Asia—Babylonia, Chaldea, Sumeria, Assyria—before the establishment of monotheistic traditions of *Judaism, *Christianity, and *Islam. Although there were regional distinctions and variations in the local deities and ritual customs, these religions shared commonalities in familial hierarchies in the pantheons of deities; the concept of each city having a major deity; official religion as an ideology of the state; private worship in homes and public rituals and festivals at temples; divination; rituals of sacrifice; life-cycle rituals, especially as associated with human and agricultural fertility; affirmation of an afterlife; and a mythological narration of the creation and the flood as well as of astral, cosmic, and national deities.

Metis. A Titan and the Greek female personification of good sense. Metis was the daughter of Oceanus and Tethys. According to tradition, she was the first wife of Zeus about whom *Gaia prophesied the birth of a daughter who would be equal to her father and a son who would supplant him. When Metis became pregnant, a fearful Zeus swallowed her and eventually gave birth to their daughter, *Athena, when Hephaestus used an *axe to alleviate a violent headache.

Michal. (1 Sam 14:49, 18:20–28, 19:11–17, 25:44; 2 Sam 3:13–14, 6:16–23; I Chr 15:29). From the Hebrew for "who is like God." Daughter of Saul and wife of David in the *Old Testament. Enamored of David, Michal was the younger daughter of Saul and sought her father's approval for marriage. The king consented on the condition that David provide him with proof of the death of two-hundred Philistines. Following his completion of this deed, David married Michal but unfortunately it did not prove to be the happiest of unions. Fiercely loyal to David, Michal defied her father and helped her husband escape the king's wrath and death warrant. She remained faithful to David during his exile and her forced marriage to a general loyal to her father. Following Saul's death, the couple were reunited but Michal was to remain childless throughout her marriage to David. She signified the disgust of traditional Judaism when David danced naked in joy before the Ark of the Covenant. A rare topic in western Christian art, Michal was represented within the context of the narrative cycles of David, especially as a female figure turning away in disgust as he danced before the Ark of the Covenant.

Michelangelo Buonarroti (1475– 1564). The greatest artist of the Italian *Renaissance. An extraordinarily gifted individual, Michelangelo excelled in painting, sculpture, and architecture. His interest in depicting the glories of human anatomy with a complex *iconography and a concern for the renaissance commitment to balance and harmony resulted in his masterful presentations of biblical and saintly figures, including *Mary, *Eve, and the *Sibyls. His lifelong spiritual quest was apparent in the innovative *iconography he created for the theme of the *Pietà, and the creation narrative. His most well-known works of western Christian art include his three versions of the Pietà, and the frescoes for the Sistine Ceiling.

Mikveh. Pool of living waters for ritual purification of *ablution. Created from the runoff of rain or a running spring, the mikveh provided the ritual purification required of a woman following her menstrual period, after tending to the bodies of the dead, or any other encounter with ritual impurity. According to Hebraic belief, whatever a woman sees upon leaving the mikveh will influence the child she is about to conceive.

Milcah. From the Hebrew for "queen." The name of two Jewish women in the *Old Testament: (1) wife of Abraham's brother Nahor and thereby the grandmother of *Rebekah (Gen 11:29, 22:20, 24:15, 24, 47); and (2) one of the five daughters of Zelophehad who successfully claimed their father's patrimony from Moses (Num 26:33, 27:1, 36:11; Josh 17:3).

Milk. A symbol for both physical and spiritual nourishment. Following Egyptian custom, milk was food simultaneously for the gods and for mortals. Depictions of the infant pharaoh suckling at the breast of the goddess signified his entry into the divine world, thereby aligning himself with the iconography and symbolism of *Isis suckling Horus. Simultaneously, milk was an appropriate ritual offering on the altars dedicated to Osiris. In the *Old Testament, the promised land was described as the land of milk and *honey. In the early Christian tradition, milk signified the Logos and simple spirituality for the newly baptized. The Eucharist of milk and honey was prepared by *deaconesses for distribution among the *children, the aged, and the sick in the early church. The *iconography of the *Maria Lactans* (Nursing Mother) signified

Mary as the good mother who nurses her child, as opposed to the bad mother who nursed *serpents. *See also* Charity.

Milky Way. From the Greek for "galaxy" or "milky way." When the mortal infant, Herakles, was suckled by *Hera (*Juno) he was granted the divine gift of immortality. He was both eager and hungry, and thereby sucked with such vigor that some of the goddess's divine milk spirited across the heavens creating new celestial bodies, and lilies on earth.

Millstone. A large, circular stone threaded by a *rope was an *attribute of Florian, *Christina, and Vincent.

Mīnākṣī. Manifestation of the Hindu goddess Pārvāti. Mīnāskī arose from the fires offered by a childless king. She was originally identified as a girl with three *breasts. Mīnāskī was venerated by fishermen. In Hindu art, she was portrayed as riding on a *fish, and as a wife of Shiva.

Minerva. The Roman virgin goddess of wisdom, war, industry, and the domestic arts. She was the patron of schoolmasters, school *children, artisans, poets, teachers, and physicians. In classical Greco-Roman and *renaissance art, Minerva was depicted as a majestic matron who wore a *helmet and a flowing toga with a coat of mail inscribed with an *owl. She held a *shield, *lance, or an image of Nike. Associated with the Greek goddess *Athena, Minerva was the classical Roman foretype for all Christian female warrior saints.

Minerva. Gallic goddess of handicrafts and arts. Inscriptions to Minerva abound throughout Gaul and Ireland.

65. *Medusa*

66. *Minerva*
67. Michelangelo Buonarroti, *The Delphic Sibyl*

She was best known as "Minerva Belisama," from the Celtic for "bright, shining, resplendent." In Gallic and Celtic art, Minerva was depicted as an armed female warrior or as a *medica* signifying medicinal springs. Her counterpart was the Irish Saint *Brigit.

Minervalia. Semiannual festivals celebrated in honor of the Roman goddess *Minerva on March 19th and June 13th. At the March events, artisans and teachers were feted, while flute players were feted in June.

Minotaur. From the Greek for "bull of Minos." Mythic monster composed of an adult male body and a *bull's head. Alleged to be the son of *Pasiphae and King Minos of Crete, the minotaur was retained in a *labyrinth underneath the royal palace of Knossos and was slain by Theseus with the intercession of *Ariadne. The myth of Pasiphae was interpreted as a form of an ancient fertility ritual that culminated in a *hieros gamos* between the king and the queen.

Miriam. Hebrew form of "Mary." Elder sister of Aaron and Moses, and one of the saviors of the Children of Israel. She suggested that her mother become the wet nurse for the newly adopted son (Moses) of Pharaoh's daughter (Ex 2:1–10). One of only two women identified in the *Old Testament as a *prophetess (the other being *Deborah), Miriam led the ceremonial dancing and singing of the Hebrew women following the crossing of the Red (Reed) Sea (Ex 15:20–21). Afflicted with leprosy as punishment for her criticism of Moses' marriage to an Ethiopian woman, she was healed by his intercession after seven days of suffering and ostracization

(Nm 12:1–15). In Jewish art, there were occasional representations of Miriam dancing in jubilation and celebration of Moses' triumph over pharaoh. In western Christian art, Miriam was depicted within the context of the life of Moses. In the nineteenth-century American and British art, there was interest in the theme of Miriam dancing before the Lord.

Mirror. A complex and ambiguous symbol with both negative and positive connotations. In Buddhist *iconography, the mirror signified emptiness, material things, and an illusion of reality. Among Japanese Buddhists, the mirror denoted the disk of the *sun or the goddess *Amaterasu Omikami. It was believed that the mirror was the repository of her spirit, the *shintai*. According to Japanese mythology and tradition, the mirror was one of the three sacred relics and an element in Japan's imperial regalia. In Greek art and mythology, *Athena's mirror symbolized her purity, wisdom, and *chastity, but was also the death sign of *Medusa. As an *attribute of the virtue *Prudence, a mirror signified self-knowledge, and as an attribute of the virtue Truth, reality; while as an attribute of Narcissus or *Venus it implied self-love, vanity, and lust in classical Greco-Roman and *renaissance art. In western *Christian art, penitential saints were depicted with a mirror as a sign of their meditation upon and penance for their sins. The spotless mirror, that is the *speculum sine macula*, was an attribute of *Mary and an integral element in the *iconography of the *Immaculate Conception.

Mistletoe. Evergreen plant associated with descents into the underworld in

Greek and Scandinavian mythology. As an eternally green plant with white berries, mistletoe was interpreted as a primal botanical embodiment of the life spirit and thereby a symbol of longevity and a talisman for good health. With the advent of patriarchal religions, mistletoe came to signify male virility and sexuality energies.

Mnemosyne. A Titan and the Greek goddess of memory. The daughter of *Gaea and Uranus, Mnemosyne was the mother of the nine *Muses by Zeus.

Modron. Great mother goddess of Celtic British myth and tradition. Based on the mother goddess, *Matrona, Modron was personified by the River Marne.

Moirai. From the Greek for "portion" or "share." Female personifications of fate in classical Greece. According to tradition, the three Moirai were the sisters known as *Atropos, *Clotho, and *Laschesis. Each had her distinctive duty to perform: Atropos cut the thread, sometimes identified as "the cord," of one's life; Clotho spun the thread; and Lachesis measured it. The Moirai were portrayed in classical Greek and *renaissance art as a grouping of three women identified by their *attributes of a *spindle, a *scroll, and *scales.

Mokoš. Fertility goddess of the indigenous eastern Slavic mythology. As the protector of women during childbirth, especially at the moment of delivery, Mokoš was assimilated into the iconography of *Mary.

Mole. Reported to be blind and deaf, this animal lived underground. In west-

ern Christian art, the mole signified the Devil.

Monica, Saint (c. 330–387). A pious Christian, mother of *Augustine of Hippo, and a model of Christian motherhood. The wife of a pagan, Patricius, Monica devoted her life to the nurture of her children and their acceptance of the Christian faith. She struggled with the many trials and tribulations of Augustine's varied experiments in philosophies, esoterica, and mystery religions. Rejoicing in his baptism by Ambrose of Milan on Easter Sunday 387, Monica died several days later in Ostia as she journeyed back to Africa. The patron of married women and of Christian motherhood, Monica was depicted in western Christian art as an elderly woman dressed in the black *habit and white veil of the much later Augustinian Order. She held a *book.

Monkeys. *See* Apes.

Monster. Sign of evil and danger, and ostensibly the Devil. These legendary *animals combined the shapes or body parts of several animals with human beings to display superhuman strength, thereby highlighting the hero or heroine who destroyed them. Common to Egyptian, Greek, Hindu, and Roman mythology as well as to Jewish apocalyptic literature, monsters were assimilated into Christian theology, legend, devotionalism, and art. *See also* Basilisk, Chimera, Crocodile, Dragon, Fabulous Beasts, Harpy, Mythical Beasts, Scorpion, Siren, Sphinx, Unicorn, and Wild Beast.

Monstrance. From the Latin "to show." A liturgical receptacle developed in the fourteenth century to display the consecrated Host for adoration and meditation. The monstrance was an *attribute of *Clare in western Christian art.

Moon. A complex and ambiguous symbol in religious art for the passage of time and of life, often of the female cycle, and of the night. Among many cultures, the moon had an ancient relationship with goddesses of fertility and virginity from *Cybele and *Isis to *Artemis and *Diana of Ephesus to *Heng-O. According to Egyptian mythology, the moon was the *sun shining at night. Lunar phases paralleled the life cycle of birth, growth, maturation, and death. Following the Council of Ephesus (431), many of the *attributes of Diana of Ephesus were assimilated into Marian symbolism in Christian art including the crescent moon, which was a sign of virginity and chastity. Representations of *Mary standing on the crescent moon signified the triumph of Christianity over paganism; and in Spanish art (after 1492), Mary stood on an inverted crescent moon to represent the victory of Christianity over *Islam. In depictions of the Crucifixion and more rarely the *Nativity, the moon signified night.

Morgan le Fay. Famed enchantress and bestower of death or immortality in Celtic-British legend and mythology. Morgan le Fay was the "queen of Avalon," that is, the underworld where fallen heroes were healed and where King Arthur retreated after his last battle. She was a medieval descendent of *Morrigan, the Irish goddess of war and death.

Morrigan. From the Irish for "queen of the ghosts." Ancient Irish war goddess who was transformed from a "bird in battle" into a goddess of the underworld. Morrigan was described as a weird and terrible figure who appeared at or just before a battle, and occasionally participated in the battle either by supporting or intimidating heroes.

Mosaics. Traditional but durable form of mural decoration created by the inlaying of small chips of stone, marble, and/or colored glass into cement to produce a design or figural representation. This medium survived into the thirteenth century, when it was surpassed by the development of *fresco.

Mother/Great Mother/Mother Goddess. Female embodiment of the life principle, destiny and wisdom, and the source of human life. Among many cultures, mother figures and mother goddesses were identified within the categories of earth mothers, earth goddesses, and fertility goddesses. According to tradition, any goddess could become a mother simply through the act of sexual intercourse; however, this was opposed to the very specialized concept of the mother goddess who was involved in the creation of the world as well as human life. There were three levels or activities of creation engaged in by mother goddesses: the act of sexual intercourse, the production of clay figures, and the role of midwife. *See also* Magna Mater.

Mother of God. From the Greek *Theotokos* and the Latin *Mater Dei*. Title ascribed to *Mary by the Council of Ephesus. *See also* Theotokos.

Mothering Sunday. Tradition associated with the visiting of one's mother and of the *cathedral as the mother church of a diocese on the fourth Sunday of Lent.

Mountain. An *Old Testament symbol for God the Father or the home of God.

Mourning (especially by the Virgin Mary). Deposition (Descent from the Cross), Lamentation, and Pietà.

Mouse. An *animal known for its gnawing away in the safety of the dark and as a sign of female sexuality, the mouse signified the Devil in western Christian art. *See also* Rat.

Mudrā. Symbolic gestures in the Buddhist art of India, Tibet, China, Korea, and Japan. The mudrā denoted the nature and function of a sacred being, and also represented their symbolic forces or divine manifestations. There were over one-hundred identifiable mudrās including over thirty for the Great Buddha, over fifty for the Buddhas, and over forty for the great deities and other significant personages.

Murillo, Bartolomé Esteban (1617/8–82). One of the leading painters of Spanish *baroque art along with *Jusepe de Ribera and Diego Velásquez. As a devout *Roman Catholic, Murillo employed his art to defend the Tridentine Church and to support the development of new iconographies, especially for Marian devotions. Renowned for his depictions of the *Immaculate Conception, Murillo softened and sweetened the dramatic tension of the baroque style to create an accessible image for popular and pious devotion.

Muses. The Greek goddesses of the arts and sciences. These feminine deities were the daughters of Zeus and *Mnenosyne, or alternately of Uranus and *Gaea. Residing on Mount Parnassus, they were lead by Apollo as the god of the arts. In classical Greco-Roman and *renaissance art, they were depicted as beautiful young women in flowing classical garments with *laurel wreaths on their heads. The individual Muses were identified by their *attributes. *Calliope was the chief of the Muses and the individual muse of epic poetry; her attribute was the *tablet, and *stylus, or a trumpet. The Muse of history, *Clio, was represented by a *book, *tablet and stylus, a *scroll, *swan, or a trumpet, while the Muse of music and lyric poetry, *Euterpe, held a double flute or a trumpet. *Thalia, the Muse of comedy and pastoral poetry, carried a comic mask, a scroll, a shepherd's staff, or an *ivy wreath, while the Muse of tragedy, *Melpomene, held a tragic mask, a *crown and scepter, an ivy wreath, a club, or a *sword. The Muse of choral dance and song, *Terpsichore, held a *lyre or viol, while *Polyphymnia, the Muse of heroic hymns and sacred dance, carried a *veil, a *lute, or an organ. Urania, the Muse of astronomy, held a celestial *globe and compass, while *Erato, the Muse of lyric and love poetry, carried a lyre, a tambourine, or a *swan.

Musical instruments. Musical instruments could be purely decorative elements in western Christian art, but the inclusion of a specific musical instrument such as an organ or *lute as an integral element of a work of art related to the theological meaning of the image. Musical instruments in the hands of *angels or the celestial choir signified the eternal and harmonious praise of

God. Musical instruments were *attributes of individual saints such as *Cecilia, the patron of music. Musical instruments also symbolized the varieties of human love from eros to agape. Reed instruments or pipes were seen as phallic symbols, while stringed instruments, like the lute, were viewed as vaginal symbols.

Mussels. *Attribute of *Aphrodite who was borne of sea foam in classical Greek art and mythology.

Mustard seed. Widespread symbol for female fertility.

Mut. Traditionally understood to be from the Egyptian language for "mother" or "vulture," but etymology is unclear. Although identified with a series of goddesses including *Bast, *Hathor, *Sekhmet, and *Uto, Mut was reputed to possess the necessary male and female reproductive organs. Her major cult was at Thebes. In Egyptian art, Mut was portrayed as a woman wearing the crowns of Upper and Lower Egypt, and holding a papyrus *scepter in one hand and the *ankh in the other. She may also be characterized as standing erect with her winged arms outstretched. At Mut's feet was the feather of *Maat and on her head was a vulture headdress. Alternately, she may be represented with the body of a woman and the head of either a man or a *vulture.

Myrrh. Fragrant herb sacred to *Hathor as "mistress of fragrance." Myrrh was employed in the purification rituals associated with the anointing of the dead, especially in preparation for sacred meals.

Myrtle. Dedicated to *Aphrodite and to *Venus, this evergreen plant was a classical Greco-Roman symbol of love and peace. Myrtle was combined with orange blossoms to form the bridal headpiece as a sign of auspiciousness. According to another classical Greek myth, Dionysus gave *Persephone as queen of the underworld a myrtle tree as an inducement to release his mother, *Semele; thereby it signified death. Further associations with mourning included the legendary description that the myrtle tree dripped blood when stabbed by Aeneas, and when its leaves were pierced by *Phaedra as she pined for Hippolytus. During the *Renaissance, the myrtle represented conjugal love and fidelity. In western Christian art, myrtle symbolized *Mary and the Gentile converts to Christianity (Zech 1:8). Christian *saints and martyrs wore a sprig of myrtle as a sign of their individual witness to Christian faith.

Mysteries. From the Greek for "hidden" or "veiled." Identification of varied groups of secret, or hidden, worship in classical Greco-Roman culture. Appropriate to the two modes of honoring the deities were the public worship that was open to all, and the mysteries that were revealed to the initiated select. The worship of *Demeter and *Persephone at Eleusis, that is the Eleusian mysteries, were among the most important of the mysteries dedicated to female deities.

Mystery Religions. From the Greek for "secret cult." Originally the secret initiation through a ritual of death and rebirth into a select group; later transformed into a generalization for secret teachings or divine wisdom accessible only to the initiated. Mystery religions are currently identified as those secret cults of an esoteric nature in ancient Greece and the Orient that involved an initiation rite, an oath of secrecy, and a theology of salvation in which the cultic deities participate and guarantee eternal life to the initiates. *See also* Eleusian Mysteries.

Mystical Winepress. *Medieval motif of Christ kneeling under the *winepress with a basin or tub prepared to receive his holy *blood. Following the writings of *Augustine, a cluster of *grapes from the Promised Land became symbolic of Christ. The visual and verbal metaphor of Christ in the Mystical Winepress was popular in the late medieval and southern *baroque devotionalism that rendered a literal reading to the doctrine of "real presence" in the Eucharist. There were two *Old Testament foretypes for this motif: the spies sent into Canaan who returned with the large clusters of grapes (Nm 13:17–19) and the metaphor of the angry God who treads his enemies in the wine press (Is 63:1–6).

Mythical Beasts. Composite *animals unlike any found in the natural world. These combinations of characteristics, shapes, or actual animal parts permitted freedom from the restrictive conventions of the phenomenal world, thus making the fearsome monsters more evil and the beautiful creatures more magnificent. Mythical beasts were common elements in early Christian, *byzantine, and *medieval art. Depending upon the narrative theme or context, the mythical (fabulous) beast was either a part of the general composition or had symbolic value intrinsic to the theological or spiritual intent of the work of art. *See also* Basilisk, Benu, Bestiary, Chimera, Dragon, Griffin, Harpy, Hippocampus, Mandrake, Monster, Phoenix, Sphinx, and Unicorn.

N

Naiads. Water nymphs who resided in springs, pools, and rivers in Greek mythology. The naiads were characterized as beneficent, musical, and cheerful female spirits. They were portrayed as beautiful young maidens wearing long flowing garments and crowns of flowers in classical Greco-Roman and *renaissance art. *See also* Dryads, Nereids, Nymphs, and Oceanids.

Nails. An instrument of the Passion and a symbol of the Crucifixion of Jesus Christ. Pious legend related that the Holy Nails were found by *Helena, mother of the Emperor Constantine, and that one of the Holy Nails was melted into his imperial crown and another in his bridle.

Nakedness. Natural condition of the human body without clothes or jewelry. Nakedness had multiple meanings in religious art including purity, innocence, truth, meekness, poverty, protest, fertility, ecstasy, shame, immodesty, shamelessness, death, and mourning. Among many cultures, it was believed that magic resided in the goddess's being not in her garments, *jewelry, or *attributes; and that creation was the natural and mysterious power of the female body. While among cultures, female nakedness was a sign of the evil and lascivious nature of women.

Namita. Principal female deity of Papua, New Guinea. According to tradition, Namita impregnated herself using her big toes, and gave birth to twins. She initiated arts and crafts for humanity, and also imposed death since it was blood that engendered human beings.

Nammu. From the Mesopotamian for "has given birth to heaven and earth." Mesopotamian mother goddess. Nammu was the female personification of the subterranean ocean, and the mother of An (heaven), Ki (earth), and En Kis.

Nanya. Babylonian goddess of love and fertility. Nanya with her daughters, Kamsura and *Inanna formed a feminine triad. She was later identified by the epithet of Inanna or *Ishtar.

Nanše. Sumerian goddess of divization and dreams. Nanše was the protector of the socially disadvantaged, goddess of birds and fishes, and caretaker of weights and measures. Nanše was the daughter of Enki, the sister of Ninurta, and the wife of Nindara in Sumerian mythology.

Nantosuelta. Gallic goddess of the dead. Nantosuelta was identified by the small round house she held in her hand as a signifier of her role as a protective domestic deity, and by her *attribute of the *cornucopia in classical Gallic and Roman art.

Naomi. Mother-in-law of *Ruth. Following the death of her husband and her sons in Moab, Naomi learned that the famine had ended in Israel. Accompanied by her daughter-in-law, Ruth, she returned to her hometown of Bethlehem. Originally a Moabite, Ruth converted to Judaism under Naomi's guidance. Solomon characterized her as "the woman of valor" (Prov 31:20).

Narcissus. A floral symbol for vanity and self-love in western Christian art. This lovely yellow spring flower was named after the Greek mythological figure who spurned the love of the nymph Echo, after which she faded away from unreciprocated love. He was condemned by *Aphrodite to fall hopelessly in love with his own reflection in the *water until he himself pined away. In late medieval and early *renaissance depictions of the *Annunciation or of the *Madonna and Child in the Paradise Garden, the narcissus represented the triumph of divine love and eternal love over human self-love and death.

Nativity of Jesus Christ (Mt 1:18–2:12; Lk 2:1–20). The narrative account of the birth of Jesus. Related by two of the four Gospels, this event was divided into four scenes—Journey of Joseph and Mary to Bethlehem, Nativity proper, *Annunciation to the Shepherds, and *Adoration of the Shepherds. Briefly reported in the *New Testament texts, the birth event was described in detail in the later *apocryphal gospels, and devotional and legendary texts. Throughout the history of Christian art, the Nativity of Jesus was conflated with representations of the *Annunciation to Mary, Annunciation to the Shepherds, Adoration of the Shepherds, and/or *Adoration of the Magi. The major *Old Testament foretypes of the Nativity were identical to those for the Annunciation to Mary— *Burning Bush, Gideon's Fleece, Shut Gate, and Aaron's Staff. The earliest images of the Nativity were from the fourth century and sought to display the miracle of the *Incarnation rather than the historical event itself. Even in the fourth century, images of the Nativity were rare in comparison to those of the Adoration of the Magi and the Baptism of Jesus, which directly represented the Incarnation. The newborn child was represented tightly wrapped in swaddling clothes and laying in a *basket or trough. Even in these earliest images, the *ox and the ass were present although *Mary might have been absent. Mary was present in those early images when the Nativity was conflated with the Adoration of the Magi and the Adoration of the Shepherds. The presence of the *ox and the ass, along with the Magi and the shepherds, signified the recognition of the uniqueness of this child and that all—the highest and the lowest—came together to glorify him. Following the decree of the Council of

Ephesus that Mary was *Theotokos, she became both a fixed element in representations of the Nativity and the second focal point of the composition. In byzantine art, the Nativity was depicted as occurring in a cave, signifying that Jesus was the philosopher-teacher—the one who brought the light (wisdom) to the world as Plato's philosopher did for those in the cave. Mary as Theotokos was seated on a *kline* (couch) to rest after having given birth to this special child (thereby emphasizing that this man was born of woman). The newborn infant, wrapped tightly in cloth simulating a shroud, rested atop a manger (resembling an altar, which emphasized that he was born to die) as the ox and the ass watched over him. Directly above was the Star of Bethlehem surrounded by *angels, and to the left of the cave were the shepherds and to the right the Magi. Joseph was seated or stood leaning on his staff "off center" supervising the activities. In the foreground, the two midwives bathed the newborn child (as reported in the *Protoevangelium of James*) as an affirmation of the Virgin Birth. Representations of the Nativity in early *medieval art were rare in comparison to depictions of the Adoration of the Magi, Baptism of Christ, and Crucifixion. By the twelfth century, however, the sacramental aspects of this event were emphasized as it was placed in a space parallel to the Last Supper. Between the twelfth and fourteenth centuries, two major shifts occurred in the *iconography of the Nativity, which related as much to the changing attitudes towards humanism in medieval culture as to the growing devotionalism to Mary. In northern medieval art, the relationship between Mary and the newborn child became more naturalistic. Although Mary continued to recline on a couch, the child was no longer separated from her and was placed upon a tablelike manger. Rather, Mary was depicted nursing her son or having him rest beside her on the couch. Joseph was an actor in the drama when he received the child from a midwife or passed the child to his wife. In the late medieval period, the image of the *Adoration of the Child developed as both a form of visual devotion and as a theological teaching. In his *Meditations on the Life of Christ*, Pseudo-Bonaventure (Giovanni de Caulibus) described a vision of the Nativity in which he saw Mary leaning against a *column as she painlessly gave birth. She then proceeded to wrap her child in swaddling clothes and rest him in the manger, where he received warmth from the breath of the ox and the ass. Joseph joined his kneeling wife in a prayer of celebration and adoration. *Bridget of Sweden reported her own vision of the Nativity in her *Revelations*. She too witnessed a painless birth after which Mary immediately knelt to celebrate and adore her naked newborn son, who rested on the ground. By the sixteenth century, the Nativity became conflated with representations of either the Annunciation to Mary, Annunciation to the Shepherds, Adoration of the Shepherds, and/or Adoration of the Magi.

Nativity of the Virgin Mary (*Protoevangelium of James* 5:2, and *The Golden Legend* 131): Having no scriptural authority, this event was recounted in the apocryphal *Protoevangelium of James* with an expanded account in *The Golden Legend*. Rarely depicted in Christian art before the fourteenth century, when it became a popular motif, the Nativity of Mary was signified by the presence of *Anne resting in her bed and being attended to by midwives. In the foreground, the infant Virgin Mary was being bathed and/or nursed by midwives. As a parallel to the *Adoration of the Magi, neighbors bearing gifts were included in this scene. A popular topic in sixteenth-century northern art, the Nativity of Mary occurred within an ecclesiastical interior, in reference to the fact that she was dedicated at birth to the service of God and would be raised in the Temple. Despite the efforts of the *Council of Trent to urge the avoidance in Christian art of apocryphal and legendary images, representations of the Nativity of Mary continued into the seventeenth and eighteenth centuries. These later images were distinguished by the presence of the aged Joachim leaning on his *staff for support and gazing adoringly at his newborn daughter.

Necklace. Jewelry worn around the neck, often as an amulet or as an *attribute of sacred power. Among many cultures, a necklace was interpreted as a fertility symbol as it repeats the visual forms of the female genitals at the base of the neck, thereby signifying sympathetic magic for sexual encounter. Within western cultures, mythological and artistic references to a sacred necklace from that formed by Hephaestus as a wedding gift for *Harmonia to *Ishtar's necklace of the "jewels of heaven" to the *Brisingamen were in relation to female deities, especially those of love and fertility. *See also* Menat.

Nectar. Unique drink of the Olympian deities in classical Greco-Roman my-

thology. According to tradition, nectar imbued immortality, and protection from decay and corruption.

Nehalennia. Germanic goddess of fertility and of the dead. A tutelary goddess of seafarers, Nehalennia was identified by her *attributes of *fruit or *baskets of fruits, and a *dog.

Nehem-t-auait. From the Egyptian language for "she who takes the part of the robbed." Ancient Egyptian goddess of Hermopolis. A wife of Thoth and mother of Neferhor, Nehem-t-auait was a protector of justice. She merged with *Hathor.

Nehushta (2 Kgs 24:8). From the Hebrew for "brazen." Daughter of Elnathan of Jerusalem, wife of Jehoiakim, king of Judah, and mother of Jehoiachin. A rare topic in western Christian art, Nehushta may be included as a proper Jewish matron in the narrative cycles of the royalty of Israel.

Neith. From the Egyptian language for "the terrible one." Egyptian goddess whose dual nature signified ferocity and gentility. Neith was a mother goddess figure who was a nourisher and sustainer of life, and a protector of the dead. As a mortuary goddess and patron of weaving and the domestic arts, she associated with the production of the mummy wrappings and the protection they offered the dead. According to tradition, Neith wove the earth on her loom. She was identified as the "first birth giver" having birthed the sun before the existence of the earth and the other planets. As the descendent of an ancient warrior goddess, Neith led the charge of the pharaoh's army into battle as she held her *attributes of crossed *arrows and her shield. Hereby she was known as "she who opens up the way." She also placed the weapons of a dead soldier around his coffin as a sign of her protection. She was associated with the creation mythology of Egypt, and thereby with *Hathor. According to Herodotus, the devotees of Neith burned a multitude of lights throughout the night of the Feast of Lamps which was sacred to the goddess (*History*, Book 2). The Greeks identified Neith with *Athena. In Egyptian art, she was portrayed as a female figure wearing the crown of Lower Egypt and holding a scepter and the *ankh, or a bow with two arrows. When she took on an animal form, Neith was represented by either a cow with eighteen stars placed at her side and a collar with the ankh around her neck, or as a cow suckling two *crocodiles to denote her powers over the Nile. Her attributes included the bow, arrow, shield, weaver's shuttle, and loom.

Nekhbet. Female symbol of nature and patron of childbirth in Egyptian mythology. As the vulture goddess of Upper Egypt, Nekhbet as the legendary mother of the pharaoh who was suckled at her breast. She was partnered by *Wadjet as goddess of Lower Egypt, thereby the pair of goddesses signified the unification of Egypt. The Greeks identified her with *Eileithyia. In Egyptian art, Nekhbet was represented by a female figure wearing a vulture skin on her head or as a sacred vulture. Her vulture headdress was surmounted by the white crown of Upper Egypt to which two plumes were attached. Nekhbet held a scepter or its symbolic equivalent as a staff of authority, a long-stemmed flower such as a lily entwined with a *snake, and the *ankh.

Nemesis. From the Greek for "apportionment of what is proper or due." Greek goddess responsible for the meting out of punishment for misdeeds and for hubris. The daughter of Nyx and Erebus, Nemesis was the female personification of compensatory justice and luck, and also the avenger of wickedness. She was also identified as the Hellenic goddess of *agone*, or sports competition, the Roman goddess of race courses and amphitheaters, and the patron of victorious Roman generals. In classical Greco-Roman and *renaissance art, Nemesis was depicted as either a youthful maiden dressed in a peplum holding a *wheel in one hand and a nosegay of herbs in the other, or as a winged creature with clawed legs and a female torso. Her other *attributes included a measuring staff, a bridle, a yoke, a sword, a scourge, *wings, wheels, and a chariot drawn by *griffins.

Nemetona. From the Celtic for "she who revered in the shrine." Celtic mother goddess.

Nephthys. Greek name for the Egyptian goddess who personified darkness, decay, and death. The daughter of Geb and *Nut, Nephthys was the sister of Osiris and *Isis, the wife of Seth, and the mother of Anubis. Identified in the *Book of the Dead* as the "friend of the dead," she was the protector of coffins and canopic jars. Nephthys was a faithful friend to Isis in her search for Osiris. Both goddesses were characterized as "healing deities" with Nephthys being skilled in magic and incantations. Thereby, Isis and Nephthys appeared together on coffins. She was the female counterpart of the ithyphallic god as life springs from death, consequently she was associated with the desert regions of the Nile, which became green after the floods. In Egyptian art, Nephthys was delineated as a woman with the hieroglyph for her name upon her head, according to any of the following variants: "mistress of the gods," "great goddess, lady of life," "sister of the gods," or "lady of heaven, mistress of the two lands."

Nepit. Ancient Egyptian wheat goddess. In Egyptian art, Nepit was characterized as a female figure who carried sheaves of wheat on her head. She was also depicted in the form of a *snake.

Nereids. Seamaidens dedicated to the service of Poseidon and to the protection of sea travelers. The nereids were the fifty daughters of Nereus and Doris. As seamaidens, they delighted sailors with their songs and dancing, and rescued them from dangerous seas. The most famed nereids were *Amphitrite and *Thetis. They were represented as beautiful young women, often with fish tails, who wore flowing garments, posing like ocean waves, and riding fanciful sea creatures. *See also* Dryads, Naiads, Nymphs, and Oceanids.

Nestorianism. Early Christological heresy condemned at the Council of Ephesus. Nestorius (d. 451) taught that there were two distinct persons in the incarnate Christ: one that was fully human, the other fully divine. Further he denied that *Mary was *Theotokos* in favor of her being identified as the *Christokos*, or "Christ bearer."

Net. Artistic images of heterosexual lovers under a net signified the capture of *Venus and Mars by her husband, Vulcan, or any other unfaithful couple captured by the irate spouse, in classical Greco-Roman and *renaissance art.

New Testament. Official canon of the Christian tradition that when combined with the *Old Testament, constituted the *Bible. The New Testament, consisting of texts ascribed to the apostles and evangelists, related the story of the life and the teachings of Jesus and his *disciples. It was identified as the New Testament in complement to the Old Testament of the Hebraic tradition (a New Covenant fulfilling an Old Covenant). In Christian art, the New Testament was signified by a *book or a *scroll in the hands of the evangelists or on a writing desk before each of them, or in the hands of Christ, *Mary, the saints, or theologians.

New Testament Apocrypha. Those second- and third-century writings rejected from inclusion in the canon of the *New Testament by the criteria of apostolic authorship and acceptance by the Christian churches. These rejected texts included material relating to the infancy, childhood, and Passion of Christ, the life cycle of *Mary, and activities of the apostles. The New Testament Apocrypha was accepted as spiritually inspirational but not canonical text, and retained a fascination and interest for Christians. Many of the stories of the New Testament Apocrypha were included in *The Golden Legend*, which was an influential text for medieval devotionalism and art. The most important books of the New Testament Apocrypha for Christian art were the

Protoevangelium of James, which details the Nativity and childhood of Mary, and the Nativity of Jesus Christ; the Gospel of Thomas, which described the childhood of Christ; and the *Gospel of Nicodemus* (also known as the *Acts of Pilate*), which elaborated upon the Passion and the Descent into Limbo.

Niddah. From the Hebrew for "menstruating woman." *See* Menstruation, Mikveh.

Night. *See* Nyx.

Nightingale. Avian symbol distinguished by its lament. Following the Greek myth, *Phaelmina was transformed into a nightingale as she fled Athens to escape the wrath of her brother-in-law, Tereus, after she served him his son, Itys, for meal as revenge for his rape of her sister, Procne. Alternatively, Procne became a nightingale as did Aedon who mistakenly killed her son, Itylus, and in her avian form she lamented his death every summer night. In western Christian art, nightingales signified the Christian faithful and *martyrs as this *bird's sweet and plaintive song signified the soul's longing for heaven.

Nike. From the Greek for "victory." Goddess of victory in Greek mythology. Daughter of the Titan Pallas and Styx, Nike delivered victory in battle or competition. A regular companion of *Athena, Nike was associated with the Roman goddess, *Victoria. In classical Greek and *renaissance art, Nike was portrayed as a beautiful winged maiden, most often dressed in a flowing garment, who held her *attributes of the *palm branch, *laurel *wreath, or garland of laurel, and a *caduceus.

Nimbus. From the Latin for "cloud." A technical name for *halo, the nimbus was a circle of light radiating from the *head of a holy individual.

Nine. A significant number relating to both the nine choirs of *angels and the nine *fruits of the Holy Spirit (Gal 5:22–3). Nine was a number of fulfillment as it was the result of the mystical number three multiplied by itself.

Ningyo. Legendary mermaid of Japanese popular belief. Ningyo warded off misfortune and preserved the peace. She was characterized in Japanese art as a female torso with a fish's tail.

Ninhuršaga. From the Sumerian for "queen of the mountains." Sumerian mother goddess. Ninhuršaga bore the gods and goddesses of the Sumerian pantheon thereby earning her epithet as "mother of the gods." As the wife of Enki, she was mother to the eight divinities favorable to humanity.

Ninišina. From the Sumerian for "great doctor of the black-headed (humans)." Female healing deity of ancient Sumeria.

Ninlil. From the Sumerian for "queen breeze." Compassionate mother goddess of ancient Mesopotamia.

Ninsun. From the Sumerian for "queen of the wild cow." Female leader of the Mesopotamian cult of wild cattle. Ninsun was the mother of Gilgamesh, and the interpreter of his dreams in the *Epic of Gilgamesh*.

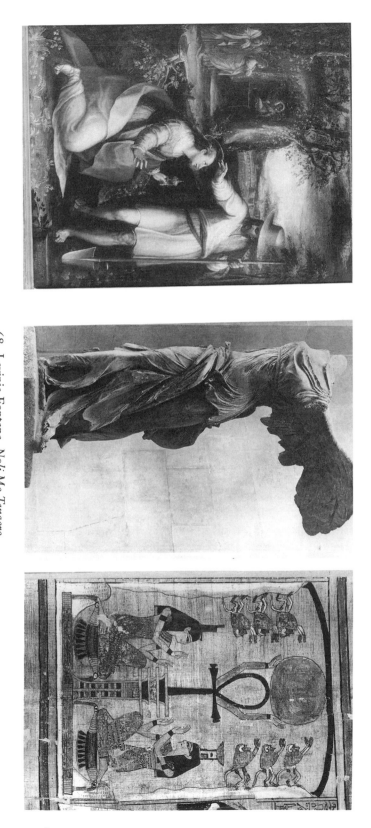

68. Lavinia Fontana, *Noli Me Tangere*
69. *Nike Samothrace*
70. *Isis and Nephthys, kneeling, assisting the sun to rise from the Djed column*

Ninšubur. Minor female deity associated with *Inanna.

Ninti. From the Sumerian for "Lady of Life" or "Lady of the Rib." Goddess of birth and protector of pregnant women in Sumerian mythology. According to tradition, Ninti taught pregnant women the sacred mystery that allowed them to create the bones of their unborn children from the mother's own rib. She was represented in Sumerian art with her *attribute a rib or being revered by pregnant women or women with newborn infants.

Niobe. Epitome of feminine tears and remorse in Greek mythology. Niobe bore her husband, Amphion of Thebes, twelve children—six sons and six daughters. Her act of hubris in insulting *Leto as "only the mother of two children" led to death of all her children. Leto's two children were Apollo and *Artemis who defended their mother's honor by killing Niobe's twelve children. Overwhelmed by grief, Niobe wept herself to death and was transformed into an eternal weeper, her face covered with tears, in the form of a marble statue.

Nirrti. From the Sanskrit for "annihilation." Nirrti was the goddess of destruction who threatened both the living and the dead in Hindu mythology. In Indian art, she was characterized as being black in color, and having as her *attribute and her messenger a *dove.

Nisaba. From the Sumerian for she who "opens men's ears," as in gives understanding. Sumerian grain goddess. Nisaba was transformed into the goddess of writing, accounting, and scribal knowledge. She was a popular figure in both Sumerian and Mesopotamian iconography. Nisaba was identified by her emblem, a *stylus.

Nixies. Female water sprites found in old German, Swedish, Slavic, Japanese, and Sanskrit legends. The nixies were characterized by a female torso and a fish tail.

Nokomis. From the Algonquin for "grandmother." Earth goddess of northeast American Indian tribes. Also known as "Grandmother Moon," Nokomis fed on all living things according to Alonguin and Ojibwan legends. She was represented as an old wise woman in tribal masks and totems.

Noli me tangere (John 20:17). From the Latin for "do not touch me." Episode in the Resurrection cycle in which *Mary Magdalene, mourning the loss of the body of the crucified Christ from the tomb, turned to respond to the query of the two *angels to find a man, ostensibly a gardener, standing before her. Thinking this man had been involved in the removal of the body, she asked where the body was. The man called her name and she recognized him as the Resurrected Christ. In awe, she reached out to touch him, but he warned her *"Noli me tangere,"* as he as not yet ascended to his Father. (Note that this was a different concept of Ascension than found in Luke.) This was the first reported scriptural appearance of the Resurrected Christ to anyone—disciple, follower, or family. He then called Mary Magdalene to be the "disciple to the disciples"—that is, to go and tell Peter and the other disciples that Jesus was risen from the dead. In Early Christian art, the *Noli me tangere* was a significant element in the Resurrection cycle but was conflated with the Guarded Tomb, *Three Marys at the Tomb, and the Resurrection. By the *medieval period, this theme became an independent topic due as much to the growing cult of the Magdalene as to the influence of the passion plays. The Magdalene was depicted fully clothed, and in a posture of kneeling before and reaching her hands forward with palms extended towards the Resurrected Christ. He stood before her displaying the wounds of the Crucifixion. With his left hand, he gestured her to stop, while his right hand pointed upwards towards *heaven. In *renaissance art, the theme of the *Noli me tangere* became a popular topic as it permitted the representation of the male nude (seminude). The naturalistic depiction of the resurrected body of Christ became the focal point of this image, whereas the medieval artists had concentrated on the gestures and the distance between Mary Magdalene and the Resurrected Christ. In southern *baroque art, presentations of this theme were numerous owing to both the rekindled interest in the cult of the Magdalene and the miraculous moment of the first sight of the Resurrected Christ. As with other themes in Christian art, the *Noli me tangere* was rarely depicted in western art after the midseventeenth century.

Nona. Several female figures shared this name. Most prevalent Nona was one of the *Parcae. Nona was also the name of the Roman goddess of birth.

Nordic religion. Belief and ritual systems of the indigenous peoples of northern Europe—Germanic, Icelandic, and Scandinavian—from approximately 3000 B.C.E. to the advent of Christianity. Although there were regional distinctions and variations in local deities and customs, Nordic religion shared commonalities in mythic sources, both oral and written traditions such as the *Elder Edda* and the *Younger Edda* (or *Prose Edda*); a pantheon of gods and goddesses, and local and regional divinities; public ceremonies and rituals in conjunction with the agrarian cycle, military endeavors, and civil crises; and private rites of passage and initiation. An elaborate mythology and series of funeral rituals supported a commitment to belief in the Afterlife as a critical aspect of this religious tradition, especially during times of wars and invasions. Between the tenth and the twelfth centuries, the majority of Nordic peoples were converted to Christianity, and the remnants of the traditional Nordic religion survived as folk belief and lore.

Norns. From the Old Norse for "she who whispers." Like the *Disir and the *Parcae, the Norns were a group of three maidens—Urd (the past), Verdandi (the present), and Skuld (the future)—who determined human fate. They were associated with the *Valkyries.

North. One of the four cardinal points. The region of the cold and the night, the north signified the barbarians and the pagans in early Christian praxis. The act of reading the gospel from a position north of the *altar represented the desire to bring the barbarian and the pagan to Christianity.

Nortia. Etruscan goddess of fate and fortune. According to tradition, the

New Year's rite celebrated at the Temple of Nortia included the ceremony of hammering a nail so as to nail down a bad year or good wishes for the new one. In classical Etruscan and Roman art, she was identified by her *attribute, a long nail.

Nott. From the Old Icelandic for "night." According to Nordic tradition, Nott was the daughter of a giant and the mother of Dag (Day). She was characterized in art and myth as driving her chariot across the sky as her lead stallion (the frost mane) bedewed the earth.

Nudity. Complex and ambiguous symbol for power, fecundity, delight, shame, truth, and poverty in religious art. Images of female nudity simultaneously signified abundance of nature, the source of life, and sensual delight; and were most often associated with goddesses of beauty and love. Representations of a nude woman whether as clay votive imagery or as an amulet was intended to promote fertility among Mesopotamian and Babylonian cultures. However a nude woman with a horned cap signified *Lilith, thereby a menacing figure, or *Ishtar. Nudity was an ambiguous and complicated symbol in Christian art. Classically, nudity signified the unconcealed truth. Given, however, the ambivalence of the Christian tradition's attitudes towards human sexuality, representations of nude figures in Christian art had multivalent and controversial meanings, such as abasement and glorification. A figure of a female nude, like *Eve, in a state of total undress was interpreted as lascivious and wanton, while one of a male nude, like David, was interpreted as the glorification of God's creation. Cultural and theological attitudes towards human sexuality governed the representation and the interpretation of nudity in Christian art, as did the character or metaphoric allusion of the person being represented; thus, the nudity of Eve signified the opposite of the nudity of *Mary of Egypt. In *medieval and *renaissance art, there were four clearly defined and understood types of nudity: *nuditas naturalis*, or the natural state of human birth (I Tm 6:7); *nuditas temporalis*, or the voluntary lack of worldly goods and possessions in a willing surrender to serve God; *nuditas virtualis*, or the quality of the virtuous life; and *nuditas criminalis*, or the lustful, vain absence of all virtue.

Nugua. Ancient Chinese creator deity who may be male or female in nature. Nugua formed the first human being from yellow clay and later invented the flute. In Chinese art, Nugua was characterized as having a human torso and a reptilian lower body.

Numbers, symbolism of. Numbers could be purely decorative elements in religious art, but the inclusion of a specific number, especially a mystical number, as an integral element of a work of art was related to the theological meaning of the image. In classical Mesopotamian art, the number three signified usefulness and perfection while the number seven was the most significant number although its meaning was ambiguous. According to the Egyptian system, the number one represented the beginning of time, the number two the duality of male and female, the number three the all-embracing nature (of the family), the number four spatial understanding, the number seven perfection, the number nine the whole of humanity, and the number one thousand the *lotus. The prevalent mystical numbers in Christian art were three, signifying the Trinity; four, the number of materials needed to create the earth; seven, the union of God and humanity (three plus four); eight, representing completion (*Easter, the eighth day of the week); and twelve signifying God's chosen people (the twelve Tribes of Israel or the twelve *apostles). These mystical numbers were included in Christian art in one of two ways—either by the inscription of their Arabic or roman numeral forms, or by the number of symbolic objects such as *fruits, *flowers, *animals, and so on.

Nungal. Female deity of the underworld in Mesopotamian mythology. Nungal was later identified with *Nintinuga (Gula).

Nuns. From the Greek and Latin for "(female) monk" and "single, solitary." Women who took "solemn vows" of dedication of their lives to the service of the *church as members of a religious order, who devoted themselves to lives of contemplation or personal perfection and to works of charity or education, and who lived within a communal religious life. In western Christian art, nuns were identified by the *habits of their individual orders. *See also* Beguines, Bridgettines, Poor Clares.

Nut. From the Egyptian language for "sow who eats up her piglets." Female personification of the sky or vault of heaven in Egyptian mythology. The daughter of Shu and sister of Geb, Nut was the mystical mother of Osiris, Horus, Set, *Isis, and *Nephthys. As the mistress of the heavenly bodies, Nut's children were believed to enter through her mouth and re-emerge through her womb. So for example she was reputed to swallow her son, Ra, the sun god, every evening and to give birth to him anew each morning. Nut was described as a "friend and protector of the dead" in the *Book of the Dead* for her acts of providing meat and drink in the tombs. She was delineated by a series of images in Egyptian art. She became associated with *Hathor. Nut was characterized as a monumental female figure who bent over the earth with her hands touching the eastern horizon and her feet the western horizon. She was also signified by the sow suckling her piglets, or as a woman with a *vulture's wings or a small round vase on her head. Her headdress was of a solar disk encased in *horns. Her *attributes were the papyrus and the *ankh. The *sycamore tree was sacred to Nut as its branches created a refuge from the summer sun for weary travelers. This was a classical foretype of the *tree that would shelter and feed *Mary and the child during the *Rest on the Flight into Egypt. A popular motif in sarcophagi and tomb chambers, Nut graced the ceilings otherwise decorated only with *stars. This motif of Nut symbolized the resurrection of the dead to new life.

Nuts. A classical Greco-Roman symbol for fertility. In western Christian art, specific types of nuts had individual meanings—the most important being the walnut, which was characterized by *Augustine as a symbol for the humanity and divinity of Jesus Christ. The shell of the walnut represented the humanity of Jesus while the fleshy meat of the walnut signified the divinity of Christ.

The walnut *tree was one of the many trees identified whose wood was used for the *cross.

Nymphs. From the Greek for "young woman." Feminine nature divinities in Greek mythology. The nymphs were the daughters of Zeus, and regularly inhabited forests, caves, springs, streams, and islands. They were benevolent spirits, popular with the common people, and often characterized as weaving, dancing, singing, reveling, or hunting. Traditionally, nymphs had the gifts of prophecy and poetic inspiration. These classical Greek figures were assimilated into Hindu and later Buddhist art and mythology as the *apsarases, water nymphs who became celestial musicians and attendants of Kama, Vedic god of love. In classical Greek and *renaissance art, nymphs were portrayed as youthful beauties most often attired in long flowing garments and wearing flowers in their hair. *See also* Dryads, Naiads, Nereids, and Oceanids.

Nyx. From the Greek and the Latin for "night." Female personification of Night and a primeval goddess in Greek and Roman mythologies. A daughter of Chaos and wife of Erebus, Nyx was the mother of *Nemesis, *Eris, Sleep, Death, and Dreams. She was venerated for her ocular gifts, and often prophesied from the darkness of a cave. In classical Greco-Roman and *renaissance art, she was portrayed as a beautiful maiden whose *veil was flung over her head and shoulders. Nyx wore a crown of poppies and a star-spangled cloak. Her owl and batdrawn chariot accompanied by *stars led her children, sleep and death, at the end of each day. Her *attributes included a mask, crescent *moon, owl, and a lit *torch that was turned upside down.

O

Oak. A classical Greco-Roman symbol of strength, *faith, and wisdom. The Celts and the *Druids worshiped the oak tree, that was associated with the Roman god Jupiter. In classical Greece and Rome, the *wreaths which crowned civil heroes were made of oak leaves. In western Christian art, the oak tree became a symbol for Jesus Christ or *Mary. The oak tree also signified the survival of Christianity against all adversity and challenge.

Obedience. One of the three virtues of Christian monastic life. The female personification of Obedience was identified in *Gothic art by her *attribute of an ass with a millstone and a camel motif on her shield. She was positioned opposite Rebellion on the jambs of the cathedral portals. By the Renaissance, the motif on Obedience's shield had been modified by the removal of the camel and inclusion of a yoke. She was especially popular within the context of western Christian art created for Franciscan churches, convents, and monasteries.

Obeisance. Female personification of the act of reverence or supplication in religious art. Obeisance was identified by her kneeling or prostrate posture.

Oceanic art. Ritual, ceremonial, decorative, and cultic objects created by the indigenous island peoples of the south and northwest Pacific from Melanesia, Micronesia, and Polynesia. The works of art, such as masks, totems, headdresses, figurines, and textiles, created by these artisans was designed and employed for ritual and ceremonial purposes, and never intended for either museum display or for posterity. Rather, the religious implications required periodic replacement of these ritual objects. These works of art can be characterized as distinctive and elegant in their design, complex in their iconographic patterns which included animal and human forms, bright in color tones, and with a spiritual significance to any distortion of the human or animal figure. As with African art, the elegance and spiritual aesthetic of Oceanic art influenced the development of many of the leading twentieth-century European artists, including Constantin Brancusi, Alberto Giacometti, Paul Gaugin, and Henry Moore.

Oceanic religion. Belief and ritual systems of the indigenous island peoples of the south and northwest Pacific from Melanesia, Micronesia, and Polynesia prior to the advent of Christian missionaries. Although difficult to characterize or identify without careful consideration of tribal and regional study, there are a series of common elements which can be identified as "features of Oceanic religion." These include affirmation of a cosmology with the three realms of human, physical, and suprahuman; the existence of magico-religious knowledge as a gift of the deities; ritual cycles that maintain the cosmic order; fertility (human and nature) rituals; acknowledged presence of ancestors, celestial spirits, and demons; and a hierarchy of ritual leaders and spiritual healers.

Oceanids. Mythic seamaidens capable of metamorphoses. The daughters of Oceanus and Tethys, there were five-thousand oceanids according to Greek mythology. These seamaidens lived in the oceans or on the earth, and had the gift of transformative powers. *See also* Dryads, Naiads, Nereids, and Nymphs.

Octopus. Eight-tentacled marine species. The octopus was a recurrent motif in classical Greco-Roman and *medieval art denoting thunder and rain.

Odilia, Saint (d. c. 720). Royal abbess and patron of Alsace and Strasbourg. Although born blind and identified as an unnecessary burden by her father, Odilia was brought to the Convent of Baûme-les-Dames, near Beşancon, by her beloved nurse. Acting on a divine vision to find and to support this blind child, Bishop Erhard of Bavaria baptized her, thereby restoring her sight.

Before his death, father and daughter reconciled, and she became heir to his fortunes. Odilia established two Benedictine convents, Höhenburg and Niedermünster. Her intercessory prayers were reputed to release her father from Purgatory. The patron of Alsace and of the blind, Odilia was portrayed in western Christian art dressed in a Benedictine habit that was trimmed in ermine to signify her earthly wealth. She was most often represented at her baptism or at her father's deathbed. Her *attributes included her eyes on a *book or a plate, and models of the convents she established.

Odudua. Yoruban earth goddess. Odudua was a bringer of fertility and a goddess of love among the Yoruba peoples. In Yoruban art, ceremonial rites, and dance, she was identified by her sacred color, black, as a signifier of fertility and sexuality.

Oholah (Ezek 23:4, 11). From the Hebrew for "tent." *Harlot used by Ezekiel to personify Samaria. The sister of *Oholibah, Oholah was a rare topic in western Christian art, and was represented dressed as an immoral yet seductive woman in narrative cycles of the prophets.

Oholibah (Ezek 23:4, 11). From the Hebrew for "my tent is in her." *Harlot used by Ezekiel to personify Samaria. A sister of *Oholah, Oholibah was a rare topic in western Christian art, and was represented dressed as an immoral yet seductive woman in narrative cycles of the prophets.

Oholibamah (Gen 36:2, 5, 14, 18). From the Hebrew for "my tent is in them." Wive of Esau in the *Old Testament. A rare topic in western Christian art, Oholibamah was included within the narrative cycles of Esau.

Oil. Signifier of God's grace and blessings. Oil was used as a sign of God's providence during the consecration of the believer during the Christian rituals of *baptism, confirmation, ordination, and unction.

Old Testament. The received canon of *Judaism that when combined with the Christian *New Testament was identified as the *Bible. The texts of the Old Testament recounted the history of the creation of the world, of humanity, and of the history of the Jewish people and their unique covenant with God. The writers of these texts were believed to have been inspired by God. Christian theologians and artists read the Old Testament both for its historical account of Jewish history and also for its prophecies relating to Jesus Christ. The heroes and heroines of the Old Testament were interpreted as foretypes of Christ and, later, of *Mary. Effort was made by Christian theologians and artists to parallel every prophecy or figure in the Old Testament with its fulfillment in Christ and Mary through the New Testament. In Christian art, the Old Testament was represented by a *scroll held in the hands of a *prophet, other Old Testament figures, a *saint, Mary, or Jesus Christ.

Old Testament Apocrypha. Those writings rejected from inclusion in the rabbinic canon of the *Old Testament by the criteria of appropriate historical authorship accepted by the Palestinian Jewish tradition. These rejected texts included a collection of approximately fifteen books or portions thereof written between 200 B.C.E. and 100 C.E. These included the texts relating the stories of *Judith and *Susanna. All fifteen books, except for 2 Esdras, were accepted into the Greek *Septuagint* of the Jewish community at Alexandria. While *Protestantism following the rabbinic canon inserted the Old Testament Apocrypha between the *Old Testament and the *New Testament of the *Bible, *Roman Catholicism following the *Septuagint* accepted all these excised texts as the Old Testament Apocrypha except for the Prayer of Manasseh and both books of Esdras, which formed a special appendix to the New Testament.

Olive. The olive, olive tree, and olive branch were general symbols for martyrdom, the *fruit of the *church, the faith of the just, and peace in Christian art. The olive tree was a tree whose thick trunk represented the wealth of its oil. This richness of oil signified God's providence for the blessed (Jgs 9:8–9). The olive branch was a classical Mediterranean symbol of peace, and was sacred to the goddesses *Athena and *Eirene. In the *Old Testament, this symbolic value was transformed into a sign of God's peace and a new covenant with the *earth when the *dove returned to Noah carrying an olive branch in its beak (Gn 8:11). The return of this dove represented the idea of the safe journey, and the image of the dove with an olive branch in its beak signified the peaceful departure of the soul at death. In paintings of the *Annunciation by Sienese artists, the Archangel Gabriel held an olive branch as opposed to the traditional *lily. The olive branch signified the city of Siena, while the lily symbolized Siena's bitterest enemy, the city of Florence.

Omikami Amaterasu. *See* Amaterasu Omikami.

Omphale. Lydian queen infatuated with Herakles. During his indentured one-year punishment performing menial tasks after killing Iphitos, Herakles served Queen Omphale. She fell in love with the Greek hero, and sought to keep him with her at the end of his time of servitude by the ruse of dressing him in women's clothing to suggest cowardice and other weaknesses.

Omphalos. Sacred stone identified as the "navel of the earth" and venerated in the Temple of Apollo at Delphi. According to legend, the two *eagles Zeus released in opposite directions met in Delphi, thereby determining it as the "center of the earth." The omphalos was believed to be the stone *Rhea gave Cronos to swallow in place of their infant son, Zeus. There was a direct connection between the inherent powers of the omphalos and of the prophecies of the oracle at Delphi.

One. A symbol for divinity, unity, and eternity. One hundred was a number of plenitude and one thousand a number of eternity.

Onion. Substitute for human heads in ritual sacrifice. According to Roman mythology, the legendary king Numa decreed that onions could be substituted for human heads during ritual sacrifices and offerings to the gods and goddesses. He announced this acceptable substitution following his celestial marriage to Egreria, a manifestation of the goddess *Diana.

Ops. Roman goddess of the harvest and the weather. Imperial Rome venerated Ops as a female personification of marriage and the family, and as the mother of Jupiter. She was identified with Consus, a wife of Saturn, and with *Rhea, and associated with *Cybele as a goddess of the harvest. Her annual festival was celebrated with the beginning of the harvests on August 25th.

Oracle. A means of communication with the divine, or the deities. Personified by female seers, the oracles instructed individual petitioners in ethics, mores, and the future. They signified the power of prophecy and foresight, and eventually were transformed into female mediums who communicated with the dead. Oracles were signified by a veiled female figure seated upon a tripod and flanked by a smoking vessel and a basket of scrolls.

Orange. The "golden apple" that wrought such havoc in Greek mythology by initiating the Trojan War. This symbolic connection was apparent when the *Tree of Knowledge was represented as an orange tree and *Eve held an orange, not an *apple. As a sign of purity, generosity, and chastity, the orange tree and its white, aromatic blossoms represented *Mary. During the late *medieval period, the Saracen custom of adorning a bride with a wreath of orange blossoms became accepted practice in western Europe.

Orans. The original position of prayer in Christianity. An individual stood straight with arms extended and *head held high in imitation of the position of Jesus on the *cross. This posture signified openness to God. In Christian art, persons represented in this posture were referred to as "orants." Female orants denoted both a specific person and a generic Christian soul.

Orb. A small globe surmounted by a *cross which denoted sovereignty and power. Christian monarchs, the Christ Child, and Christ as Pantocrator were identified by an orb that was held in their left hands.

Oreades. *Nymphs living in mountains and caves in Greek mythology.

Organ. The organ was an *attribute of Music as one of the *Seven Liberal Arts and of *Polyhumnia in classical Greco-Roman and *renaissance art, and of *Cecilia as both patron of music and reputed creator of this instrument in western Christian art. As a symbol of the praise continually offered to God, the organ was included within the heavenly concert and choirs of *angels.

Original Sin. According to the Talmud, original sin was the sin of Adam that resulted in death. Hebraic tradition affirmed that the *serpent had sexual intercourse with *Eve in the Garden of Eden. By this act, filth was injected into Eve and through her to the descendants of Adam. The western Christian doctrine as formulated by *Augustine that the effect of Adam and *Eve's fall from grace was transmitted to all successive generations of human beings through natural descent. As a result of Adam and Eve's surrender to the temptation of seeking to attain divine wisdom by eating of the *fruit of the *Tree of Knowledge, all men were condemned to labor, all women to pain in childbirth, and all human beings to eventual death. *Augustine, whose teaching on Original Sin became the basis for the church dogma, also taught that *baptism was both the sign of initiation into the Christian faith and the cleansing from Original Sin. The later Reformers taught that Original Sin produced the state of total depravity or corruption of human nature, rendering people completely unable to do good except by the intervention of God in Christ, who purged the evil from those who were destined for salvation through Grace. The Roman Catholic and Eastern Orthodox Churches held that the effect of Original Sin was a certain impairment of nature and an inclination to sin but not a total corruption. The varied interpretations of the meaning of this dogma paralleled the *iconography of the Temptation and the Fall in western Christian art.

Ostara. Germanic goddess associated with the spring. As the female personification of the rising sun, Ostara was associated both by etymology and attribution with the Greek goddess *Eos, the Roman *Aurora, and the Anglo-Saxon *Eostre. Her annual festival celebrating the advent of spring was assimilated into the Christian feast of Easter.

Ostrich. The concealment of the ostrich's head in the ground in moments of danger denoted the moral lesson that material concerns were unnecessary for the true believer—only *heaven was important (Jb 29:13–14). According to the *Physiologus, the ostrich did not brood its *eggs but watched over them until they hatched. In western Christian art, the ostrich egg signified both meditation and the virgin motherhood of *Mary. If hatched by the sun, these eggs represented the Resurrection.

Otter. An ambiguous symbol in western Christian art for both the righteousness of Christ and the evil of the Devil.

Oven. Widespread symbol for female lust, adulterous heat, unrighteous behavior, and motherhood. An oven was simultaneously a feminine metaphor and a symbol for sexual intercourse.

Owl. An avian symbol of ill omen and death, the owl was associated with *Lilith in Sumerian art and legend. Originally sacred to *Athena, this nocturnal animal had ambiguous meanings in Christian art. As an *animal that favored the night and feared the light, the owl denoted either the Devil or the *Jews, who in their blindness rejected Jesus as the Christ. Its presence in narrative events implied that the event depicted occurred at night. The owl's presence at the Crucifixion had a double meaning: as a positive sign, it indicated that the light of Christ was available to those who sat in the dark; as a negative sign, it signified that Christ was sacrificed as a decoy to the Devil in order to save humanity (as the owl was used as a decoy by hunters in quest of other *birds). Following the classical Greek association of the owl with Athena as the goddess (and female personification) of wisdom, the owl denoted the gift of wisdom in western Christian art, and in this context was depicted with scholarly *saints such as *Jerome. In *renaissance art, the owl denoted Night and Sleep.

Ox. An animal symbol of strength and fertility in religious art. In classical Chinese symbolism, the ox connoted agriculture and the spring; while in *Taoism, it was identified as the mount of Lao-Tzu. For its physical endurance, quietude, and humility, the ox became the emblem of *Zen Buddhism. The ox was a sacrificial *animal in the Hebraic culture, and a sign of docility, humility, patience, and strength. In the writings of several of the early church fathers, the ox was substituted for the *lamb as a symbol for Christ's sacrifice. As a powerful animal that voluntarily bore the yoke to plow the master's fields, the ox was a symbol for Christ as the Redeemer who worked and suffered for the good of humanity. The winged ox signifies Luke, whose *Gospel emphasized the sacrificial and redemptive aspects of the life and death of Christ. The ox was an *attribute of *Thomas Aquinas (mocked as a "dumb ox" by his academic opponents), *Lucia, Sylvester, and Luke. The ox characterized Sloth as one of the *Seven Deadly Sins in *renaissance art.

Ox and Ass. An essential and popular element in depictions of the *Nativity of Jesus Christ from the earliest representations in Christian art. Without canonical scriptural foundation as a part of the *Nativity, the ox and the ass were interpreted as both the recognition of this special child, and as symbols for the *Jews and Christians (Is 1:3). According to the apocryphal *Gospel of Pseudo-Matthew*, the ox and the ass were present at the Nativity, and knelt in recognition of the Christ Child. They were included in depictions of the *Flight into Egypt, *Rest on the Flight into Egypt, and *Return from Egypt.

Oya. From Yoruban for "good mother." Yoruban mother goddess. Oya was the goddess of storms and thereby capable of communicating with the spirits of the dead. As the goddess of dancing, she was represented on staffs carried by Yoruban women during ceremonial, folk, and ritual dances.

Oyster. Shellfish associated with *Venus (*Aphrodite); widespread symbol of female lust and fertility; and a popular aphrodisiac. According to classical Roman tradition, the oyster was the favored food of lustful, shameless women.

P

Ⓟ

Pachamama. From the Quechuan for "earth mother." Incan fertility and mother goddess revered in the Andean highlands of Peru and Bolivia.

Pachet. From the Egyptian language for "she who scratches." Egyptian goddess of the desert. Pachet was portrayed as a lion-headed woman in Egyptian art.

Padmapāni. From the Sanskrit for "the one who holds the lotus." Chief *bodhisattva of mercy in the Indian Buddhism. Originally characterized as a masculine figure, Padmapāni was fused into *Avalokiteshvara, and after the twelfth century, into the feminine figurations of the bodhisattva of mercy and compassion. In Indian Buddhist art, Padmapāni was identified by both the s-shape curve to his body posture and the small figure of Amitabha inscribed in his headdress or crown.

Paganism. From the Latin for the religion "of the country people." Identification of indigenous religious folk traditions prior to the advent of Christianity. Paganism was transformed into a generic term signifying all non-Christian religions.

Painting of the Virgin Mary or **Painting Materials (palette, brushes, easel, and canvas).** Representations of either a portrait of *Mary, an artist painting her portrait, or painting materials near Mary denoted Luke the Evangelist. According to pious legend, this apostle was both physician and artist, and had painted the only portrait "from life" of Mary. This legend and its ensuing images were used as a theological defense of Christian art.

Pales. Roman goddess protector of the flocks and herds. Pales was honored on her feast day of April 21st, which was also the birthday of Rome, and thereby was identified with the protection of the city.

Palladium. Cultic wooden statue of Pallas *Athena with the *aegis, her *shield, and raised *spear. According to tradition, Zeus threw the Palladium from Mount Olympus to the earth. Originally possessed by the city of Troy, the Palladium was revered as a talisman of protection of the city in the Temple of Athena. Following the fall of Troy, Odysscus and Diomedes removed the image as a sign of the victory of the Greeks, and it was placed in the Parthenon. According to an alternate version of the story of the Palladium, it was carried from the ruins of Troy by Anchises as he rode on his son's shoulders. Brought by Aeneas to Rome, the Palladium was venerated as the protective relic of the city. The Romans believed that their city would be rendered defenseless if the Palladium was lost or damaged. The Palladium became an *attribute of *Vestal and was cared for by the *Vestal Virgins.

Pallas. A daughter of Triton and childhood playmate of *Athena in Greek mythology; and an epithet used for the goddess. While they were wrestling, Athena accidently killed Pallas. As a sign of her grief, the goddess combined her own name with that of her deceased friend. According to tradition, the phrase "Pallas Athena" signified either the triumphant goddess following her victory over the giant named Pallas or the manner in which she swung her spear. A variation of the story suggested that Pallas was the son of Uranus and *Gaia. In the monumental battle between the deities of Olympus and the Titans, Athena defeated Pallas and stripped his skin to be used for her shield. In classical Greek and *renaissance art, Pallas Athena connoted an image of the goddess in full armor holding her shield in one hand and her spear in the other.

Palm. Prevalent symbol for fertility and sustenance, especially the fruit of the palm tree, in religious art. Egyptian art

and cultic practice identified the palm as the symbol of the New Year, a token of a long reign, of eternity, and of *Seshat. While Mesopotamian art and mythology identified the palm as an *attribute of the *mother goddess. In classical Greco-Roman and *renaissance art, the palm was an *attribute of *Fame, *Victoria, *Chastity, and *Artemis as an orgiastic nymph. It was a classical Greco-Roman symbol of military triumph adapted by Early Christianity as a sign of Christ's victory over death. The palm also signified immortality, divine blessings, triumph, *paradise, resurrection, *Flight into Egypt, Entry into Jerusalem, and *Immaculate Conception. An attribute of all Christian *martyrs, it also denoted Paul the Hermit, Onuphrius, Christopher, and Michael the Archangel.

Palm Tree. A symbol of immortality, nourishment, and the *paradise *garden. Associated with the Egyptian goddesses *Nut and *Hathor, the date palm was a source of food and drink for the dead who were sacred to Ra; and was also the sacred emblem of *Seshat. The palm tree connoted fertility and the *hieros gamos of Mesopotamian *mother goddesses. This evergreen tree signified the scriptural events of the *Rest on the Flight into Egypt and Entry into Jerusalem in western Christian art. The original *Tree of Life was often represented as a palm tree.

Panacea. From the Greek for "female healer." Greek goddess of health, and daughter of Asklepios and *Epione.

Panagia. From the Greek for "All Holy." Honorific title of *Mary in the Eastern Orthodox Church. The small icon of Mary worn by an Eastern Orthodox bishop was identified as a "Panagias."

Panathenaea. Festival dedicated to the goddess Athena thereby the most significant one held annually in July and August in the city of Athens. Cultic ritual activities and processions enveloped the city, especially every fourth year when this feast was celebrated as the "Great Panathenaea." A series of athletic and musical competitions complemented the religious ceremonies and the public parades, some of which were detailed on the friezes dedicated to Athena on the temples of the Acropolis. The great procession from the Agora to the Acropolis concluded with the adorning of the goddess's statue with a new woven and embroidered garment, and animal sacrifices.

Pañcaraksha. From the Sanskrit for "five-fold protection." Group of five Buddhist goddesses invoked for longevity and for the protection of villages. The Pañcaraksha were the female personifications of the five magical incantations, or *raksā*, uttered by the Buddha.

Pāndarā. From the Sanskrit for "the white one." Buddhist goddess and consort of Amitābha. Her identifying element was fire, especially as the passion of love.

Pandora. From the Greek for "all gifted" or "all endowed." In Greek mythology, this beautiful young woman was first female created by Hephaestus at Zeus's command. Distinguished by her beauty, she was given a series of gifts by the gods and goddesses. The messenger of the gods, Hermes,

brought Pandora to earth with a *box filled with evil and with hope in order to punish Prometheus. Her husband, Epimethius, who was Prometheus's brother, warned her not to open the box given her by Zeus. When she was alone, Pandora opened the box and all the evils, sorrows, and pain that would besiege the human race were released. She closed the box fast enough, however, to retain *hope. In both western Christian art and tradition, she was the classical Greco-Roman foretype for *Eve. For example, the early church fathers drew parallels between Pandora and Eve. In classical Greco-Roman and *renaissance art, Pandora was depicted as a beautiful nude young woman either seated or standing holding a box.

Pansy. From the French for "thought." Floral symbol for remembrance and meditation. This member of the *violet family was included in representations of penitential *saints and *Mary in *medieval art.

Panther. Animal symbol for Jesus Christ. According to the *Physiologus*, the panther slept for three days after eating a full meal, and upon arising exuded an aromatic belch that attracted friends but dispelled enemies.

Papyrus. From the Egyptian language for "green" or "to become green." In Egyptian art, papyrus symbolized the world risen from the primeval waters. It was also the emblem of Lower Egypt and its tutelary goddess, *Wadjet, whose scepter contained an amulet of the papyrus plant. The design on the columns of Egyptian temple architecture took on the pattern of the papyrus plant.

Paradise. From the Persian for "garden." Originally an enclosed park or pleasure *garden. This idealized garden of great physical beauty as the eternal dwelling place for the rightcous became a standard in Christian art for *heaven and the *Garden of Eden, especially in those representations of the *Expulsion from the Garden.

Parca. From the Latin for "to bear" or "to give birth." Roman goddess of birth, and one of the *Parcae.

Parcae. Roman goddesses of fate, or birth divinities, associated with the Greek *Moirai. The members of this triad were *Decima (Decuma), *Nona, and *Parca.

Parnashavarī. One of the thirty-three forms of *Avalokiteshvara. An ancient female deity of the indigenous tribes of India, Parnashavarī was transformed into a Buddhist female deity and depicted in either of two forms in Indian art: as a beautiful woman who held a lasso in one hand and a *pomegranate on a stick in the other, or as a four-armed woman who held a lasso, a pomegranate, and an axe, and gestured a *mudrā. In Tibetan Buddhism, she was identified as a follower of the *Tārās. Parnashavarī was portrayed as a female figure composed of a yellow body with three heads—white, yellow, and red in color—and six arms. Kneeling on her right knee, she held an axe, a *vajra, a *bow, *arrows, and a flowering branch in her many hands.

Parsley. Herbivorous symbol sacred to the *Great Goddess with the multiple meanings of fecundity, promiscuity, death, and springtime. According to ar-chaic legend, parsley beds were the natural source for babies. Parsley signified rest among the dead in Christian art. According to pious legends, parsley was identified as a magical plant capable of providing eternal peace to the restless souls of the dead. Given its association with the dead, it was incorporated into decorative motifs on funerary monuments. Medieval Christian legend affirmed that parsley can only be successfully planted on Good Friday.

Parthenon. Temple dedicated to *Athena on the Acropolis of Athens. Erected between 447 and 432 B.C.E., the Parthenon was designed by Icitinus and Callicrates. This sacred edifice housed the famous sculpture of the goddess by the Greek master, Phidias.

Parthenos. From the Greek for "without a man." Epithet identifying a virgin goddess.

Partridge. A favored avian sacrifice to the *Great Mother in festivals held at the spring equinox. In western Christian art, the partridge was an avian symbol for deceit, theft, and the Devil (Jer 17:11). In certain contexts, the partridge denoted the truth of Jesus Christ.

Pārvātī. From the Sanskrit for "daughter of the mountains." Hindu great goddess, and consort and *shaktī of Shiva and mother of Ganesha, the elephant-headed god of auspiousness and the remover of all obstacles. In Hindu art, Pārvātī signified the Indian ideal of female beauty with her sensuous nude body, contraposto pose, and the sacred cord between her breasts. By the second half of the tenth century, she was identified by the stylized pattern of her presentation with a straight head, her two feet surmounting a lotus, and the triple or s-shaped curvature to her posture. Her left hand was placed palm down upon her left thigh while her right hand held either a lotus flower or bud. Pārvatī became merged with *Durgā in both iconography and mythology.

Pasiphae. From the Greek for "she who shines on all." Greek moon goddess. A daughter of Helios, Pasiphae married Minos of Crete who was the father of her two daughters, *Ariadne and *Phaedra, and the surrogate father to her son, the Minotaur. According to Greek mythology, Minos requested a perfect white *bull to sacrifice in order of Poseidon. The god of sea accompanied the king's plea. When the extraordinary bull arrived on Crete, Minos was unable to sacrifice such an excellent animal and substituted a different one. An irate Poseidon originated a great passion in Pasiphae for the bull. The queen requested Daedalus to build her a secret place in which she and the bull could meet. As a result of this union, Pasiphae gave birth to her son, the Minotaur. Daedalus then created the *labyrinth in order to house and protect the queen's bull child. An incensed Minos imprisoned Daedalus in the labyrinth for his role in the queen's liaison with Poseidon's bull. The builder escaped with his son, Icarus, by flying on mechanical wings. In classical Greco-Roman and *renaissance art, Pasiphae was depicted as a beautiful woman wearing a regal crown and jewelry, and accompanied by either the white bull or the Minotaur.

Pasithea. Daughter of Zeus and Eurynome, and one of the *Graces.

Patience. Female personification of one of the minor virtues in the Christian cycles of the *Seven Virtues and *Seven Deadly Sins. In *Christian art, Patience was depicted as a woman holding her *attribute of a *lamb. An image of Job, oftentimes afflicted with boils, rested at her feet. In some medieval representations, Patience was signified by an ox and opposed by the vice of Wrath.

Patriarchy. Society regulated by men in which they had all dominance, power, and authority.

Patrilineal descent. Pattern of inheritance that was regulated by the male line only.

Patrons. *See* Donors.

Pattini. Singhalese goddess of marriage and protector from epidemic diseases. Pattini brought the cultivation of rice to Ceylon. According to tradition, she was born of a mango that had been struck by a divine arrow. Pattini was renowned for the cultic practice of fire walking.

Paul, Saint and Apostle (d. c. 67). Apostle to the Gentiles. Born into a Jewish Diaspora family in Tarsus, Paul was originally named Saul. As a Pharisee and a Roman citizen, he was trained in languages, philosophy, and law. He experienced an extraordinary call to become an apostle of Jesus Christ during his visionary conversion on the Road to Damascus. Following his recovery from the fall from his horse that was blinded by the bright light of the vision, Paul began a lifelong commitment to the development and promulgation of Christianity. Enormously influential throughout

71. *Pārvāti*
72. Rembrandt Peale, *The Roman Daughter* (Pero and Cimon)

73. *Demeter, Persephone, and Triptolomes*
74. *Phyllis and Aristotle*

Christian history, Paul became identified as the missionary to the Gentiles and was credited with the spread of Christian missions into the then known world. Identified as the "second founder" of Christianity, Paul has also been credited with initiating many of the misogynist tenets and later doctrines of Christianity including his influence upon *Augustine and *Martin Luther. Although modern scripture scholars have called into question the authorship of several of the texts attributed to Paul, he has been identified as the scriptural source for the following pronouncements which influenced the church's attitude toward women: that virgins should be single and celibate (1 Cor 7:25–38); that women should cover their hair (1 Cor 11:2–16); that a woman is the reflection of a man's glory (1 Cor 11:7); that women should be subordinate to men, especially in the home (Eph 5:22–23; Col 3:18; 1 Tim 5:24); that women's ministry be restricted (1 Cor 14:34–35; 1 Tim 2:11–14); and Eve's Deception (1 Tim 2:14). In Christian art, Paul was depicted as a physically small but stocky man with a balding head, short dark beard, and hooked nose. In *baroque art, he was represented like the other patriarchs—a tall man with long flowing white hair and beard. His *attributes included an inverted sword as a sign of his martyrdom and a *book (or scrolls) symbolic of his Epistles.

Paula, Saint (347–404). Roman matron converted to Christianity, and renowned for her charitable deeds and friendship with *Jerome. Widowed with five children, Paula dedicated herself to living the Christian life. In 385, she and her daughter, Eustochium, traveled to Jerusalem to live near Jerome. Literate and learned, these two Roman women directed Jerome's business affairs and managed the building of a monastery, convent, and guest house for *pilgrims. The patron of widows, Paula was interred in the Church of the Nativity in Bethlehem. A rare topic in western Christian art, she was represented as a nun and in the company of Jerome and her daughter.

Pax. Roman goddess of peace associated with the Greek *Eirene. As the divine female personification of peace, Pax was a favored motif on Roman coins, for example the "Pax Augustus." In classical Roman and *renaissance art, Pax was depicted as a winged female figure with a garland of *corn and crowned with a *laurel wreath, and holding a staff entwined with a *snake in one hand, and a *cornucopia and/or *olive branch in the other.

Peace. Female embodiment of stability and prosperity produced by periods of no warfare or military entanglements. A popular motif in western art from the Middle Ages into the present time, the feminine image of Peace illustrated the benefits of concord and celebrated the end of war. She was represented as a beautiful and strong woman dressed in a long flowing garment and surrounded by either children or the fruits of the earth. Her *attributes were a *cornucopia, sheaves of corn, garlands of *flowers, an *olive branch, and a *dove.

Peach. Fruit symbol for longevity, renewal, and the advent of spring in religious art. *Hsi Wang Mu guarded the peaches of immortality that grew in her garden of the Taoist *Paradise. The Chinese character, *t'ao*, connoted marriage and peach. In classical Greco-Roman and *renaissance art, the peach's double pit signified the virtue of silence and a steadfast heart. In western Christian art, the peach was a fruit *symbol for virtue, especially *charity. In the hands of the Christ Child, a peach signified salvation.

Peacock. A symbol of royalty, this solar bird greeted the dawn with a cry. The peacock was an avian *symbol for immortality from the legend that its flesh never decayed, while its tail's ability to renew itself perpetually represented resurrection. In classical Greco-Roman and *renaissance art, the peacock was the *attribute of *Hera (*Juno). In Taoist art, this bird symbolized *Hsi Wang-Mu, the Mother of the West. As a symbol of resurrection, the peacock was included in representations of the *Nativity of Christ. According to the *Physiologus, whoever ate an entire peacock by himself or herself would live forever (*Augustine reportedly tried three times to do so but failed). The many *eyes on the peacock's tail represented either God's (Christ's) ability to see all or vanity. Following tradition, the screeching of the peacock represented the pitiful cries of the Christian in need of God. The strutting and preening of the peacock was interpreted as a self-conscious display of a vain and narcissistic nature. Thereby, the peacock signified vanity and hubris, and in northern *medieval and *renaissance art was a symbol of the *Devil. The peacock was also an *attribute of *Barbara and of *Pride.

Pear. An *attribute of *Hera in classical Greco-Roman and *renaissance art. In western Christian art, the pear was a *fruit symbol for the Incarnation of Christ, or of his love for humanity.

Pearl. A classical Greco-Roman symbol for the goddess of love and beauty, *Venus, born of seafoam and carried to shore on an oyster *shell. The pearl also signified *Cleopatra. As the "tears of the oyster," the pearl was a symbol of sorrow but also a precious and rare jewel. According to the *New Testament, pearls signified the Word of God (Mt 7:6), and represented purity and spiritual wealth (Mt 13:45). As a symbol of purity, spiritual wealth, sorrow, and tears, the pearl became associated with *Mary in *medieval art. Pearls, especially a pearl tiara or diadem, were an *attribute of *Margaret of Antioch.

Peitho. Female personification of persuasion in the retinue of *Aphrodite in Greek mythology.

Pelagia, Saint. Common name for at least three early Christian virgin martyrs. Pelagia of Antioch (d. 311) dedicated herself to God and safeguarded her virginity from advancing soldiers by drowning herself in the sea. Another fourth-century woman identified as Pelagia of Antioch was an actress who was converted from her previous life, and devoted herself to a life of solitary prayer and penitence in a cave on the Mount of Olives. The third fourth-century woman identified as Pelagia was from Tarsus and was martyred when she refused to become an imperial concubine.

Pele. Hawaiian volcano and fire goddess. Identified as the "*Hina-ai-malama*," or "the Hina who eats the moon," this transplanted Polynesian goddess of the moon and the thunder-bolt had been expelled from Tahiti for an act of disobedience, or hubris. Pele was liable to unpredictable bursts of anger, which accounted for the erratic nature of thunderstorms and volcanic eruptions.

Pelican. An avian symbol for God the Father and the crucified Christ. According to tradition, baby pelicans violently flapped their *wings in their parents's faces, so that out of fear the father killed them. The mother pelican then pierced her *breast and revived her dead *children with her *blood. The pelican symbolized God the Father, who in anger punished his children and then repented and forgave them. The *Physiologus recounted the devotion of the mother pelican who pierced her breast to feed her young with her own blood. The pelican thereby symbolized both the sacrifice of Jesus Christ and the Eucharist. In *medieval and *renaissance art, the image of the mother pelican piercing her breast (with a nest of hungry young pelicans) would be placed atop or near the *cross in representations of the Crucifixion.

Pen. Instrument of authorship. The pen (quill) was an *attribute of any (all) of the four Evangelists, *Doctors of the Church, or Christian theologians and writers.

Penelope. Symbolic female personification of wifely devotion in Greek literature. The daughter of Icarius of Sparta, Penelope was the wife of Odysseus and the mother of Telemachus. She was a faithful and loyal wife to her husband even during his twenty-year absence due to the Trojan War and his circuitous journey home. She defended herself against the proposals of erstwhile young suitors by advising that she would choose a successor to her absent husband once she had finished weaving his funeral shroud. Each evening, once the suitors had departed, Penelope unwove the cloth she had woven together earlier that same day. She was reunited with her husband after he and Telemachus destroyed the youthful suitors and Odysseus publicly reclaimed both his throne and his queen. As the female personification of wifely devotion and fidelity, Penelope was portrayed in classical Greco-Roman and *renaissance art as a pious matron in the posture of weaving the alleged funeral shroud and surrounded by her youthful suitors.

Pentagram. A five-pointed, star-shaped form signifying either the followers of Pythagoras in classical Mediterranean culture or magicians in *medieval culture. The pentagram was used as an amulet to ward off sorcery. In western Christian art, the pentagram signified either protection from the Devil or the five wounds Christ received on the cross.

Penthesilea. Legendary beautiful *Amazon queen who fought for Troy following the death of Hector. Accompanied by twelve princesses, Penthesilea terrorized the Greek army. However when she engaged Achilles in battle, he killed her. Stripping her dead body of armor, the Greek warrior was amazed at Penthesilea's great beauty and was filled with a deep sorrow. Achilles delivered her body to Priam for an honorable burial in Troy. In classical Greco-Roman and *renaissance art, Penthesilea was represented as a beautiful and powerful woman warrior, or in scenes of Achilles mourning over her dead body.

Peony. Floral symbol identified as the "rose-without-thorns," and thereby an attribute of *Mary in *medieval Christian art.

Peppermint. An aromatic, herbal flower with medicinal properties symbolic of *Mary.

Perchta. Slavonic fertility goddess and bride of the sun. Perchta's feast celebration included the ritual wearing of masks, beautiful masks for those costumed as spring and summer, and grotesque masks for those costumed as autumn and winter.

Peri. Name associated with both the female demons of Ahriman, and good, kindly female sprites in Zoroastrian mythology.

Perit. Albanian folkloric female mountain spirit. This otherwise genteel fairy punished those who were wasteful with *bread by transforming them into crooked hunchbacks. Perit was depicted in Albanian and Slavic art as a mountain spirit clad in flowing white garments.

Periwinkle. Symbol for eternal life and fidelity. This evergreen plant with blue flowers signified protection from *witches and magicians.

Pero and Cimon. Legend of Roman Charity and idealization of filial piety. The beautiful Pero was the daughter of the aged Cimon, an unjustly accused and imprisoned Roman nobleman. In an attempt to avoid a trial, Cimon's powerful enemies arranged that no food or water be brought to the aged prisoner. However, Pero had recently given birth and she visited her father daily offering him her breast for nourishment. Cimon survived to be vindicated. A popular topic in *renaissance, *baroque, and *neoclassical art, Pero and Cimon were depicted with Pero offering her engorged breast to her father as a jailer looks on in amazement.

Perpetua and Felicity, Saints (d. 203). Carthaginian noblewoman and her servant woman, and renowned Christian martyrs. Perpetua was both the mother of a young child and a recent catechumen of Christianity. Arrested for refusing to sacrifice to the gods of Rome, the noblewoman and her maidservant were placed in prison. Following their arrest as Christians, Perpetua and Felicity were condemned to death with other Christians during the Imperial Games. Prior to their scheduled executions, Felicity underwent a lengthy and painful labor to give birth to a daughter. Her spiritual patience brought the jailer, Pudens, to Christianity. Perpetua received a series of spiritual visions during her imprisonment. Despite an attack by the animals in the arena, including the cow who mauled Perpetua, the two women survived and were beheaded at a later date. They were honored by *Augustine of Hippo in a series of sermons. In western Christian art, Perpetua and Felicity were identified respectively as a matron dressed as a noblewoman and a younger pregnant woman. Perpetua's *attribute was the *cow.

Persé. Greek female embodiment of the underworld aspect of the moon goddess. As the wife of Helios, Persé was the mother of Kirke and *Pasiphae. She was also known as *neaira*, from the Greek for "the new one," that is, the new moon.

Persephone. Greek goddess of the underworld and wife of Hades, famed as the daughter of *Demeter (*Ceres). The myth of Persephone explained the cycle of the seasons, and thereby of vegetation. The god of the underworld, Hades, was infatuated with this beloved and beautiful daughter of the earth mother. Unable to win Persephone's love, he abducted her from the earth and took her into his underworld kingdom. As her mother searched fruitlessly for her daughter, the earth lay fallow and the crops withered. After several months of desolation, Zeus ordered Hades to return Persephone to her mother so that the earth could be revived and the crops could grow. Hades agreed on the condition that the young daughter remain with him for the number of months equitable to the number of *pomegranate seeds she had eaten while in the Underworld. Persephone admitted to swallowing six seeds, thereby she was required to spend six months a year on the earth with her mother and the other six months with Hades in the Underworld. The youthful goddess was worshiped in association with her mother during the *Eleusian Mysteries, and was identified with the epithet of *kore. Persephone was the female personification of the birth and death of vegetation, and of new growth, as a goddess of fertility; whereas her mother was the female personification of ripened harvest. In classical Greco-Roman and *renaissance art, Persephone was portrayed as a beautiful young woman clad in a flowing white garment and her *at-tributes of *cornucopia, ears of *corn, sheaves of *wheat, *cock, *torch, and pomegranates.

Petronilla. Legendary Christian virgin martyr. Having dedicated herself to God, Petronilla refused to marry Flacco, a nobleman. She died as the result of constant prayer for release from this life, and was buried in front of Flacco. A rare topic in western Christian art, Petronilla was identified by her *at-tribute of a *palm branch.

Phaedra. Daughter of King Minos and Queen *Pasiphae of Crete, sister of *Ar-iadne, and wife of Theseus in Greek mythology. Phaedra's infatuation with her stepson, Hippolytus, had disastrous consequences when he rejected her ad-vances. Libeled by the queen, Hippoly-tus was banished from his father's kingdom. The young prince killed him-self by driving his chariot too fast. A remorseful Phaedra admitted her lies to Theseus, and then hanged herself. In classical Greco-Roman and *renais-sance art, Phaedra was represented either in the attempted seduction of Hippolytus or her own suicide.

Phaelmina. *See* Nightingale.

Pheasant. An avian symbol for fidelity and monogamy in marriage in western art, and of beauty and good fortune in eastern art. In western Christian art, two pheasants signified the sacrament of marriage in scenes of the *Nativity.

Pheme. Roman female personification of rumor and gossip. Ovid identified Pheme as the herald of truth and false-hood (*Metamorphosis*).

Philosophy. Queen of the Seven Liberal Arts. In classical Greco-Roman, *medieval, and *renaissance art, Philosophy was depicted as a tall slender but mature woman garbed in a flowing garment decorated with a tiered motif of flowers, fish, and stars, and with a *crown on her head and a *globe under one of her feet. An enthroned figure, she held *books in one hand and a scepter in the other.

Phoebe. An epithet of *Artemis as goddess of the moon.

Phoenix. Mythical bird of extraordinary beauty, composed of a *pheasant's *head and an *eagle's *body, which had a reputed life span of between three hundred fifty and five hundred years in the Arabian wilderness. Whenever it felt either old or its beauty waning, the phoenix burned itself upon a funeral pyre. In its *ashes was a small worm that in three days grew into a new youthful phoenix. The mythology and the iconography of the phoenix was known through the ancient world from Egypt to China. In Egyptian art and mythology, the phoenix was identified as the sacred bird of Heliopolis. It was associated with Ra and Osiris, and according to the *Book of the Dead (Chapter 13), the phoenix was a metaphor for the journey of the blessed dead. It was also known as a miraculous bird of long life, and was associated with the magical Egyptian *benu. In China, the phoenix was an *attribute of the Emperor, and in Imperial Rome, it signified the apotheosis of the Emperor. The classical Mediterranean legend and image of the phoenix was assimilated into Christian art, especially early Christian funerary art, as a symbol of the Resurrection.

Clement of Alexandria provided a Christian gloss of the legend of the phoenix in his First Epistle to the Corinthians. The phoenix remained a popular symbol in *byzantine and *medieval art.

Phryne. Classical Greek female embodiment of truth unveiled. Phryne was the beloved mistress of the classical Greek sculptor, Praxiteles. Unjustly accused of impiety, she was brought to trial. As the suit against her gained credence, her lawyer proceeded to uncover her in the middle of the courtroom—at which point the beautiful naked woman shielded her eyes in a gesture of modesty and earned an acquittal.

Phyllis. Legendary courtesan of Alexander the Great. According to popular tradition, Phyllis overheard the scholarly Aristotle as he lectured his young student that women were the downfall of men. He sought to persuade Alexander to abandon his favorite courtesan and to give his full attention to his studies. Phyllis, also identified as *Campaspe, decided to charm the erstwhile philosopher. After some time, Aristotle, besotted with the beautiful courtesan, agreed to prove the depth of his love for her by allowing her to ride him like a horse as she held the reins. Unknown to the philosopher, the entire court watched as he crawled on all fours with the triumphant Phyllis mounted on his back as Alexander exclaimed how woman could undo even the wisest of men! Representations of this episode were popular in medieval Christian art as an illustration that wisdom was only fruitful when combined with virtue. The story of Phyllis was a favored motif in classical Greco-Roman, *medieval, and *renaissance art.

Physiologus. From the Greek for "discourse of nature." A third-century Alexandrian anthology of curious and idiosyncratic stories about real and mythical animals. The anonymous "naturalist" who compiled this text drew upon the natural histories of Aristotle, Pliny, and other classical sources. Each story was constructed as a moral allegory and was assimilated into early Christian art and spirituality as symbols for Jesus as the Christ. In terms of Christian art, the symbolic importance of the *Physiologus* was revived in the middle ages as the foundation for the *medieval *bestiaries.

Pietà. From the Italian for "pity" or "compassion." This devotional variant of the Lamentation in western Christian art was the representation of *Mary mourning her dead son. Without any scriptural foundation, this motif developed in twelfth-century *byzantine art as a liturgical icon. As the *Vesperbild*, this motif of the mourning mother and her dead son developed in German art at the end of the thirteenth century and was related to the devotionalism of the Vespers for Good Friday. The *iconography of the Pietà traveled from German art into French art, and then into early fifteenth-century Italian art where it reached its artistic and spiritual fullness in the art of *Michelangelo.

Pig. A symbol of fertility and a favored sacrificial offering to the *mother goddess in classical Mediterranean world. In Egyptian art and mythology, the pig was a positive lunar symbol associated with *Isis and Osiris. The goddess *Nut was portrayed as a sow suckling her piglets as an amulet for maternal fertility and the season of spring. Pigs were sacrificed to *Isis, *Astarte, *Ishtar, and *Demeter (*Ceres). The pig was a symbol for lust and gluttony in western art. In classical Greco-Roman and *renaissance art, the pig was an *attribute of Gluttony, Lust, and Sloth of the *Seven Deadly Sins, and of *Melancholy. In western Christian art, the pig was an attribute of Anthony the Abbot who triumphed over lust and gluttony. In Tibetan Buddhist art, the popular *bodhisattva Mārīcī was portrayed seated on a throne drawn by seven pigs.

Pigeon. An avian *attribute of *Demeter (*Ceres).

Pilgrim. Personification of earthly life as a transition to spiritual life. This believer or devotee of a religious tradition undertook a journey (pilgrimage) to a sacred place or shrine out of a religious devotion or in search of spiritual renewal, a miraculous cure, a vision, or in fulfillment of a religious vow. In western Christian art, pilgrims were identified by their common *attributes of a *staff, a *wallet, a *scallop shell, a *gourd, and occasionally a broad-brimmed *hat.

Pilgrimage. Activity of earthly life symbolic of the transition to spiritual life. This often arduous journey was undertaken by a believer or devotee of a religious tradition to a sacred place or shrine to fulfill a religious vow or obligation, or spiritual devotion, to worship, or for a miraculous cure or spiritual vision. The Christian practice of pilgrimage reached its height during the Middle Ages. *Pilgrims and pilgrimage *saints were popular motifs in *medieval art.

Pillar. A symbol for multiple associations—steadfastness, spiritual fortitude, God, and flagellation—in western Christian art. Pillars of cloud and of fire led the Hebrews out of Egypt (Ex 13:21–2). The blinded but physically renewed Samson knocked down the pillars of the Philistine Temple (Jgs 16:23–31). The pillar was an Instrument of the Passion and signified the Flagellation of Jesus. According to the *Meditations on the Life of Christ*, *Mary rested against a pillar during the birth of Jesus. The pillar was an *attribute of Sebastian and Simon Stiletes.

Pillar, Our Lady of the. From the Spanish *"Nuestra señora del Pilar."* This iconographic motif identified both the *baroque cathedral in Zaragoza and the statue of the *Madonna and Child on a pillar (*La Virgen del Pilar*) enshrined within it. According to tradition, *Mary delivered the statue herself to the Apostle James who erected the sanctuary that protected it. Patron of the Spanish army, Our Lady of the Pillar was richly garbed and crowned with a diadem for special feastdays and liturgical celebrations. In her honor, newborn girls from Aragon were named Pilar. The basic iconography of Our Lady of the Pillar corresponded to that of the *Vièrge du Pilier*, a fifteenth-century *Black Madonna enshrined in Chartres Cathedral.

Pincers. An *attribute of *Agatha, *Apollonia, and Dunstan in western Christian art.

Pine. A symbol for strength of character, solitude, and vitality. As the goddess of wild forests, *Cybele had the *pine tree as an *attribute in classical Mediterranean art. This evergreen *tree was an allusion to the *Tree of Life in western Christian art.

Pinikir. Elamite mother goddess associated with *Ishtar.

Pink (as a flower). A variety of *carnation and a token of commitment, love, and betrothal. According to Flemish custom, the bride hid a pink somewhere on her body and permitted the bridegroom to search for it. When held in the hands of either newlyweds or a married couple, pinks denoted fidelity in marriage.

Pistis Sophia. Female redeemer figure of the third- or fourth-century Gnostic text, *Pistis Sophia*. The surviving version of the *Pistis Sophia* is a fourth-or fifth-century translation of the Greek original into Sahidic that reflects Egyptian Gnosticism. In this text, Pistis Sophia was the personification of Philosophy who was delivered from self-will or arrogance by Christ at his Ascension through the spheres and in conflict with the Aeons. She was led from Chaos by the Power of Light sent by Christ. A central role was also played by *Mary Magdalene who was identified as "Maria" or "Mariam" and who asked Christ the critical questions so that his disciples could properly interpret his teachings.

Pitcher. Handled vessel used for the storage or serving of liquids. In classical Greco-Roman and *renaissance art, the pitcher signified *Hebe, *Grammar, and *Temperance. The pitcher was a container for *water and a symbol for cleansing in western Christian art. A pitcher with a *basin and towel was included in representations of the *Annunciation (to Mary) as a sign of her perpetual virginity. A pitcher or small flask was employed by John the Baptist to baptize Jesus in northern *medieval and *renaissance art.

Plants, symbolism of. Botanical symbols for the cycle of life, death, and *resurrection as found in the natural order. As part of the produce of the earth, plants as *fruits, *flowers, and *vegetables, contained the seeds for each new and successive generation. As a generic symbol, plants indicated the productive energies of nature. In western Christian art, a grouping of plants was purely decorative while a specific plant was an integral element of the theological intent of the image; for example, *hyssop signified *baptism and repentance. *See also* Acanthus, Bramble, Bulrush, Burning Bush, Clover, Dandelion, Fern, Garlic, Hawthorn, Holly, Hyssop, Ilex, Ivy, Jasmine, Lady's Bedstraw, Lady's Mantle, Lady's Slipper, Lavender, Mandrake, Mistletoe, Myrtle, Peppermint, Reed, Rosemary, Sage, Tansy, Thistle, and Vine.

Pleiades. Seven daughters of Atlas and Pleione—Alycone, Asterope, Celaeno, Electra, Maia, Merope, and Taygete—in Greek mythology. The legendary hunter, Orion, became infatuated with them and when they spurned his advances, he began a five-year pursuit of these beautiful young women. To rescue them from Orion, Zeus transformed them into stars and placed them as the constellation, the Pleiades, in the heavens where they signified the spring and the harvest. In Greco-Roman and *renaissance art, the Pleiades were represented as seven beautiful women pursued by Orion, or as a series of seven stars in the shape of their constellation.

Plum. A botanical symbol for independence and fidelity.

Pluto. The ruler of the underworld in Greek mythology, famed for his roles in the abduction of *Persephone (the mythical explanation for the cycle of the seasons) and the story of Orpheus and *Eurydice. Pluto was the ruler of the area of Hades known as Tartarus where the wicked were tormented for eternity. In classical Greco-Roman and *renaissance art, he was depicted as a physically large and muscular man with a powerful, naked torso, and short dark *hair and *beard. He was the classical Greco-Roman foretype for images of the Devil, Satan, and Lucifer.

Poena. Roman goddess of punishment associated with the Greek *Nemesis.

Polyhymnia. From the Greek for "she who is rich in songs." Greek *muse of ceremonial song and dance. In classical Greco-Roman and *renaissance art, Polyhymnia was portrayed as a matron garbed in a heavy cloak and seated in the posture of learned meditation.

Pomegranate. A classical Mediterranean symbol for fertility, immortality, and resurrection. Due to its abundance of seeds and red juice, the pomegranate was used in Greek mythology to explain the cycle of the seasons. In classical Greco-Roman and *renaissance art, the pomegranate was an *attribute of *Persephone (Proserpina), *Demeter (*Ceres), and *Hera (*Juno). A common symbol in Christian art, this red fruit had several meanings. In the *hands of the Christ Child, the pomegranate signified either the Resurrection or the *church. Gregory the Great identified it as the sign of the unity of all Christians. In the hands of *Mary, the pomegranate represented the totality and unity of the Christian Church. An open pomegranate's seeds and red juice symbolized the general resurrection when all the tombs of the dead will be opened. The pomegranate was one of the fruits of the Promised Land (Dt 8:8).

Pomona. From the Latin for "fruit (of a tree)." Roman goddess of gardens and fruit trees. In classical Greco-Roman and *renaissance art, Pomona was represented as a nude woman holding a *basket of *fruit and a pruning knife. Pomona was also a wood nymph dedicated to the cultivation of fruit trees who fenced herself in the orchards to keep out the sartyrs. Vertumnus, a sartyr, fell in love with the beautiful nymph and disguised himself as an old woman in order to gain entry into the orchard. After praising the extraordinary trees the disguised sartyr described Vertumnus in glowing terms to the enchanted young nymph. He then revealed himself to her, and Pomona was filled with passion. The nymph Pomona was a popular topic in classical Roman art, and was depicted as a beautiful young nymph identified by a curved pruning knife.

Poor Clares. Sisters of Saint Clare, or the Second Order of Saint Francis, established in 1212 by *Clare of Assisi with the guidance of *Francis of Assisi. At their beginning, the Poor Clares were an enclosed contemplative order of women religious dedicated to poverty, mortification, prayer, and meditation. In 1804, permission to perform charitable work was added to their Conventual Rule. In western Christian art, the Poor Clares were identified by their dark brown habits and white waistcord tied with three knots of poverty, chas-

tity, and obedience; black *veils; and cloth sandals.

Pope Joan. *See* Joan, Pope.

Poppy. Floral symbol for sleep and death. The poppy was an *attribute of *Demeter (*Ceres), *Aphrodite (*Venus), and *Nyx in classical Greco-Roman and *renaissance art, and of the Passion of Jesus Christ in western Christian art.

Porcia (first century B.C.E.). Daughter of Cato and wife of Marcus Brutus, and a symbol of female fortitude and loyalty. Porcia was a devoted wife and a Roman matron dedicated to the virtues of loyalty and fidelity. In an effort to prove to her nervous husband that she was capable of bearing the pain of torture and thereby could share in the plan of the conspiracy against Julius Caesar, Porcia plunged a knife into her thigh and never made a sound (Plutarch, *Life of Brutus*). Following both the assassination of Caesar in which her husband participated, and his own suicide, Porcia as an honorable daughter of Rome took her own life by swallowing a mouthful of burning coals (Plutarch, *Lives* 46:53). She was a classical exemplar of conjugal love and fidelity. A popular topic in classical and *renaissance art, Porcia was portrayed as a mature and respectable Roman matron, thereby dressed simply and veiled, and postured in the act of either self-inflicting her thigh wound or her dramatic suicide.

Porta Clausa. Latin for "closed gate." Scriptural adage prefiguring *Mary's perpetual virginity (Ez 44:1–2). In western Christian art, the prophet Ezekiel was identified by a *scroll inscribed with the phrase, *"porta clausa erit."*

Potina. Roman goddess of medicine for *children.

Potiphar's Wife (Gn 39:1–22). Egyptian woman who unjustly accused the innocent Joseph of assault with intent to rape. The sincerity of her false witness and the evidence of Joseph's *cloak in her bedroom convinced her husband, Joseph's master and head of Pharaoh's bodyguards, of the *Hebrew's guilt. Joseph remained silent in his own defense, and was imprisoned for his "crime." In western Christian art, the theme of Joseph and Potiphar's Wife prefigured the chastity of Joseph in his marriage to *Mary.

Potter. Motif for the *Great Goddess as the creator of the human race out of clay. Originally associated with mythology and images of the Sumero-Babylonian goddess Aruru the Great, the motif of the potter was included in the iconographies of *Ishtar, *Inanna, *Kālī, *Mammītu, and *Ninhuršag.

Prajñā. From the Sanskrit for "wisdom" or "insight." Buddhist female principle of intuition that complements the male principle of meditation. In Buddhist art, Prajñā was represented as the integration of polarity achieved in *Yab-Yum.

Prajñāpāramitā. From the Sanskrit for "perfection of insight or wisdom." Female personification of text entitled *Prajñāpāramitā Sutras* in which the Buddha explains his teachings and which formed part of the scriptural canon of Mahāyāna Buddhism. According to tradition, this text was delivered by the Buddha to the guardianship of the Nāgas until the appropriate historical moment when the faithful were deemed to be ready for the fullness of its revelation. As the female reincarnation of the divine word, she was known by the epithet, "Mother of All Buddhas." In Indian Buddhist art, Prajñāpāramitā was represented as a female deity seated in a lotus posture on a lotus throne and holding an open book. Her Tantric form consisted of four to six arms, a third eye on her forehead, and attributes of a book, a *vajra, a *rosary, and a bowl. Most popular in Cambodian and Javanese Buddhist art, Prajñāpāramitā was a female counterpart of aspect of *Avalokiteshvara and had two distinct forms of presentation. She was portrayed as a female figure who wore a long sarong with an ornate belt around her waist and a naked torso. She had a crown and a high chignon signifying wisdom, and if she wore three crowns one bore the imprint of Amitābha Buddha. In her normal presentation she held the sacred text in one hand and a *lotus in the other, while in her Tantric form she had eleven heads and twenty-two arms. As her Tibetan Buddhist form of She-rab-pha-rol-tu phyin-na, she was characterized as white or yellow in color, dressed as a *bodhisattva, and with four arms in which she held a white lotus, a blue lotus, a sacred text, and a rosary. In her Japanese manifestation as Hannya Bosatsu (Haramitsu or Sai Hannya), she was the goddess of perfect wisdom who was seated on a lotus. Usually multiarmed, she held a sacred text, a blue lotus, a rosary, and a book, and gestured mudrās.

Prakriti. From the Sanskrit for "nature." *Kālī as the Triple Goddess that controlled the white, red, and black threads of creation, preservation, and destruction. More generally, the embodiment of all the cycles of nature and human existence.

Prende. Ancient Illyrian goddess of love. In Albanian folklore, Prende was identified as the "queen of beauty" for whom Fridays were sacred. With the advent of Christianity, Prende became a Roman Catholic saint.

Presentation of Jesus of Nazareth in the Temple (Lk 2:22–38). This scriptural event signified the dedication (not the circumcision) and "buying back" of the first-born male infant to God in the Temple following the Mosaic law (Ex 13:2). In accord with Jewish practice, five shekels were offered to God as the redemption price when the forty-day-old infant was presented to him (Nm 8:17; Lv 12:1–8). Both Christian art and scripture fused the presentation of the child with the purification of the mother, at which two *turtledoves were offered to God. The pious and blind Simeon was promised by God that he would live to see the *Messiah, and his blindness was cured when he "saw" the infant Jesus, whom he proceeded to carry into the Temple as a sign of his messiahship. The aged prophetess* Anna also witnessed that Jesus was the Messiah and praised God. Representations of this theme in eastern and western Christian art were rare before the eighth century; the earliest images represented the five major figures—the infant Jesus, Simeon, Anna, *Mary, and Joseph (holding two turtledoves)— within an ecclesiastical setting. Through the thirteenth century, the visual emphasis was on the manifestation of the

child's divinity through the acclamations of Simeon and Anna. Late medieval artists began to emphasize the theme of the *Purification of the Virgin Mary by depicting her as the physically dominant figure in the foreground, where she knelt with two turtledoves in a basket, and Simeon, Anna, and the infant Jesus in the background.

Presentation of the Virgin Mary in the Temple. (*Protoevangelium of James* and *The Golden Legend*). At the age of three, *Mary was dedicated formally to God's service by her parents. She was brought to the Temple to live and serve God until the age of twelve or fourteen, when she would be married. Although a part of the narrative cycle of the life of Mary, the theme of the Presentation of the Virgin Mary in the Temple developed as an independent topic in fourteenth-century western art. In the foreground of the composition, *Anne and Joachim watched as their small daughter walked the fifteen steps into the Temple where the High Priests waited to receive her into their care. Following *Josephus Flavius's report in his *History of the Jewish War*, there were fifteen steps from the Court of the Women to the High Temple of Jerusalem. According to *The Golden Legend*, little Mary danced joyously as she approached the Temple; some fourteenth- and fifteenth-century artists suggested this celebration by displaying her feet or allowing a billowing of her garments. In accord with the new devotionalism of the *Counter-Reformation Church, *baroque artists began to represent Mary kneeling before either the Temple steps or the High Priests.

Pride. One of the *Seven Deadly Sins. In *renaissance art, Pride was portrayed as a woman accompanied her *attributes of *lion, *eagle, *peacock, and *mirror. This female personification of Pride was assimilated into the motif of *Vanity.

Prie-Dieu. A kneeler or kneeling desk upon which *psalters, prayer books, or *books of hours were placed during private devotions. In *medieval art, the Virgin Annunciate was represented at a prie-dieu.

Priestess. From the Greek for "elder" and the Hebrew for "soothsayer." Female guardians of the temple and protectors of its laws. These women were trained and initiated into the sacred traditions of the temple and/or goddess they served. Priestesses oversaw divinatory, ritual, sacrificial, and healing ceremonies. They were administrative functionaries of the temple bureaucracy and also religious specialists who dealt with particular areas of the religious cult. Priestesses typically formed a female clergy devoted to the female deities except for the chaste high priestesses of certain cultures. Although they lived secluded lives in the temples, priestesses owned property, and engaged in business activities. They entered the priesthood through religious dedication and initiatory ceremonials. In some cults, the priestesses participated in temple prostitution. In religious art, priestesses were identified by their priestly vestments, especially the ritual hats or shaved heads, by ritual nudity, or by their gestures and ceremonial objects.

Primordial Goddess, religions. Current feminist research proposes a historical theory of a multiplicity of indigenous belief systems, and ritual and ceremonial practices of varied archaic peoples affirming a primordial goddess. Premised upon proposed matriarchal social structures and *matrilineal descent, such primordial goddess religions focused on the veneration of female deities, especially with regard to the female activities of conception, birth, and nurture of a child as the ultimate human metaphor for divinity. Given the distinctions between the diverse regional and tribal groups, the identifiable structure of any primordial goddess religions included a triad of female deities who individually represented the fundamental aspects of "the goddess": a goddess of generative life forces who signified fertility, birth, protection, and healing; a goddess of destruction who embodied the awesome powers of nature and death; and a goddess of regeneration who symbolized the life cycle of nature and rebirth. Within this framework, a lesser male deity represented the necessary stimulator for female fertility and thereby the regeneration of the dead; more rarely, he was the guardian of the forests and wild animals. Such religious traditions affirmed the centrality of an afterlife and accorded great importance to the rites of death, mourning, and burial (individual, familial, or communal). The sacred sites associated with primordial goddess religions denoted significant places for communication with the goddess or for extraordinary manifestations of her presence. According to this proposed historical theory, as human civilization progressed, the matriarchal society of the primordial goddess religions weakened and was replaced by the cultural system developed in later tribes with male-dominated social

75. Perino del Vaga, *Allegorical Figure of Prudence*
76. *Venus of Laussel* (Primordial Goddess)

77. Antonio Canova, *Cupid and Psyche*

structures including *patrilineal descent and a new pantheon of deities. Vestiges of these proposed primordial goddess religions may have survived in some of the folklore and legends associated with heroines, goddesses, and saints, and in the iconography of women in religious art.

Primordial Goddess, symbolism. Under the currently proposed theoretical framework of a primordial goddess, there were a variety of ritual, ceremonial, decorative, and cultic objects created by varied archaic indigenous peoples. These objects—including ceramic figurines, marble and stone reliefs and carvings, pottery decorations, wall paintings, and sculptures—were created for purposes of religious worship, rituals, and celebrations. A complex iconography delineated the varied manifestations of these primordial goddesses and visually characterized triadic powers of birth, life, and death. Fundamentally, primordial goddess symbolism favored abstractions and hieroglyphic forms with a special emphasis upon the triangle which was understood to be the essential female element. Although stylistic and media differences existed between the varied geographic and historical groups, there were identifiable symbols for the more generic category of primordial goddess including the iconography of the triad of goddesses. The iconography of the *Goddess of Generative Life Forces* was subdivided into three motifs as birth-giving, as pregnant, and as healing. Even the most elemental depiction of the goddess represented recognizable birthing postures and included a swollen vulva and breasts. Amulets with patterns of seeds and vulvas were given to barren women

and to those pregnant women who were about to give birth. As a pregnant figure, she was the symbolic female embodiment of fertility. In this mode, the goddess of generative life forces was signified by a nude woman whose hands were placed upon her pregnant belly. She was symbolized by her sacred animal, the pig, and by those amulets decorated with spirals, snakes, and rhomboids which were favored by barren women. Later civilizations viewed her as an agricultural deity who was also protector of grains and bread. In her proposed manifestation as the goddess of healing, she was characterized as a bird with an elongated neck, prominent beak, and an elaborate hairdo/headdress. If rendered as a waterfowl, she was characterized as nourishment, while the form of a spring bird represented the endless cycle of the seasons, especially of spring, and of the sacred energies of rebirth. As a protector of the family and the village, this aspect of the primordial goddess was identified by a variety of geometric motifs. Her sacred animal was the ram. As the goddess of healing, the goddess of generative life was represented by a *snake goddess who ensured family life, female fertility, and regeneration, especially with regard to human and nature life-cycles. *Goddess of Death:* Most often, this goddess of death was imaged as a bird-of-prey, such as a *vulture or an *owl. She was pictured as a nude woman without breasts posed in a stiff posture with tapered legs, her hands pulled tightly across her chest or extended at her sides. A series of inscribed triangles symbolized the pubic triangle as the bodily site of female fertility. *Goddess of Regeneration:* This female embodiment of rebirth was symbolized by the pubic triangle—triangles, hourglass forms, vulva (or seeds, herds, eggs, and the color red), the *uterus, and the fetus—in the varied motifs, *attributes, and themes of primordial mythology. Her animal attributes include the *bee, *butterfly, and *moth. *Primordial religious sites:* Within each of these regional and/or tribal variations of primordial goddess religions, there were ritual sites for worship. These sanctuaries served as both the locus for rituals and ceremonies, and for veneration of the goddess. Architecturally, these sites were premised upon floorplans characterized by female motifs such as the triangle, womb, labyrinth, and nests. Many of the postures, gestures, symbols, and motifs of these primordial goddesses were assimilated into the succeeding religions and social systems.

Primrose. A floral symbol for purity and youth. The primrose was an *attribute of Peter as the "keys of heaven in Christian art."

Prioress. Superior of a community of women religious, or the delegate of an *abbess, in Christianity.

Priscilla (before the third century). Legendary Christian martyr. Famed in early Christian art and archeology as the donor of the Catacombs of Priscilla in Rome, this legendary female convert and martyr may have been one and the same person as Tatiana and/or Martina. Less than minimal historical evidence supports her possible historical existence.

Prithivi. From the Sanskrit for "the wide (earth)." Indian earth goddess revered in the form of a cow. In the Vedic texts, Prithivi was the mother of the dawn, Usas, and of fire, Agni.

Procla (first century) (*Gospel of Nicodemus* and *Acts of Pilate*). Wife of Pontius Pilate and an early convert to Christianity. According to scriptural tradition, Procla had disturbing dreams and warned her husband not to sit in judgment of Jesus of Nazareth (Mt 27:19). Despite his wife's admonition, Pilate was involved with Jesus's execution. The *apocryphal gospels report that Procla accompanied her husband to the Imperial Court in Rome where she defended his action. Following his condemnation to death, the former Procurator of Judaea sought his wife's forgiveness. As a Roman citizen, Pilate was executed by decapitation and Procla was overjoyed when an *angel appeared to carry the severed head to heaven. The devoted wife fell down dead. A rare topic in western Christian art, Procla was portrayed as a proper Roman matron within the context of the narrative cycle of the Trials of and Crucifixion of Jesus of Nazareth.

Prophet(ess). From the Greek for "to speak for [a deity]." The inspired religious messengers of Israel in the *Old Testament who sought to purify and reform the people through their revelations, visions, and conversations with God. The four major prophets of Israel (Isaiah, Jeremiah, Daniel, and Ezekiel) prefigured the four Evangelists. The only female judge and prophetess of Israel was *Deborah. The oldest text in the Old Testament was "The Song of Deborah." In eastern and western Christian art, the prophets were idealized male figures of majesty and dignity with long flowing *hair and beards, dressed in long flowing garments, and carrying *scrolls (except for the prophet Jonah who was accompanied by the *whale or sea *monster). Deborah was represented as one of the female worthies (classical and biblical women of valor) or as an Old Testament foretype of *Mary. From the fifteenth century, the pairing of the Old Testament prophets with the classical *Sibyls became a common motif in eastern and western Christian art.

Proserpina. *See* Persephone.

Prostitution, Temple (Gen 38:21f; Jdg 5:22; 2 Sm 6:16ff; Ez 16:24, 20; Hos 4:14, 9:10). Generally prostitutes were understood to be women who engaged in sexual intercourse with men other than their husbands for some form of material gain or elevation of social or political status. Among many ancient cultures, priestesses, especially those dedicated to an aspect of the *Great Goddess, were identified as a form of temple prostitutes as they dispensed the goddess's grace through sexual activity. Traditionally, such a form of ritual prostitution was interpreted as a unique combination of beauty and kindness similar to the religious value of "compassion" or "charity" dispensed in the classical Greco-Roman world by the *Graces. As practitioners of the sensual magic of the sacred whore, temple prostitutes were understood to be healers of the sick. *Inanna was identified as the protective goddess of temple prostitutes as well as of midwives and wet nurses. During the Hellenistic period, the role of the temple prostitutes had been given over to the *Hetaerae who were respected for the learned skills, and given equal legal and political status to men,

while wives had the same rights and privileges as slaves. Generally, the Near Eastern and classical Mediterranean practice of sacred prostitution as a promotion of fertility through sympathetic magic was severely criticized by the Jewish and Christian traditions. In western Christian art and spirituality, *Mary Magdalene was *identified as a reformed prostitute and thereby her red *hair symbolized her former life as prostitutes either elegantly coiffed their hair or wore red wigs. *See also* Harlot; Hieros Gamos.

Protestantism. This theological and ecclesiastical movement separated from the Church of Rome in the sixteenth century primarily over the issues of the unique authority of the *Bible, justification by faith alone, and the rejection of papal authority. Protestantism emphasized the preaching and hearing of the Word, and lessened the role of the visual image except for religious pedagogy. The Protestant traditions have generally been regarded as iconoclastic for their denial of the devotional and sacramental aspects of western Christian art, the minimalization of liturgical art, and their emphasis on poetry and music in worship.

Prudence. One of the four Cardinal Virtues. In *medieval and *renaissance art, Prudence symbolized wise conduct and was depicted as a beautiful woman with the *attributes of a *snake, a *mirror, a *book, a compass, and a stag.

Psalter. A Christian liturgical book that was used for private devotions. A popular prayer book for the laity during the *medieval period, a Psalter contained an illuminated calendar as well as prayers. *See also* Book of Hours.

Psezpolnica. From the Serbian for "Lady Midday." Legendary black-haired woman, or a whirlwind, who appeared at the hottest part of the day during the harvest to dri°vi°ng the farmers insane from the heat of the sun or severing their heads with a sickle.

Psyche. From the Greek for "soul." Legendary Greek nymph whose beauty evoked jealousy in *Aphrodite. In anger, the goddess forced her son, Eros, to fill Psyche with love for the ugliest man on earth. However, the youthful messenger fell in love with Psyche; so he hid her in a beautiful palace and visited her every evening in the dark of night, so that she couldn't identify him. Goaded by her sister, Psyche betrayed her vow to Eros and woke him one night with a light. Recognizing him as the son of Aphrodite, Psyche was banished for her act of betrayal. Desperate, she went in search of Eros but when she reached the Temple of Aphrodite, Psyche was tormented with onerous tasks and treated harshly as she sought word and sight of her beloved. Zeus took pity on Psyche, immortalized her, and reunited her with Eros. In classical Greco-Roman and *renaissance art, Psyche was portrayed as a beautiful nymph, often nude, and within the context of an episode of her story, most usually the confrontation with Eros. As the female personification of the soul, Psyche was represented by a *butterfly or a young woman with butterfly wings.

Pudenziana, Saint (d. c. 160). Roman matron and Christian convert. Famed for her many acts of Christian *charity,

Pudenziana distributed her wealth among the poor and provided Christian burials for martyrs (2 Tm 4:21). A rare topic in early Christian art, she was the saint in whose honor the Church of Santa Pudenziana was named.

Pudicitia. From the Latin for "modesty." Female personification of chastity and demureness. With the fall of Rome, and the erosion of public and personal morality, the cult of Pudicitia vanished, but she was revived as an idealization of the feminine in medieval Christian art and spirituality. In classical Greco-Roman, *medieval, and *renaissance art, Pudicitia was represented as a heavily garbed, and often veiled, matronly figure.

Purification. Ritual and ceremonial ablution required for ritual effectivity. In all religious traditions, those individuals who performed services for the deities, took part in religious rites, or carried out religious rituals, entailed ritual and spiritual "purity." The rites of purification, which included the spraying or sprinkling of consecrated water, or the burning of incense, evoked purity and auspiciousness in the individual being cleansed.

Purification of the Virgin Mary (Lk 2:22–24). Following Mosaic law, the mother of a newborn male child was ritually unclean for a period of forty days (Lv 12:2–4). The new mother could be purified on the fortieth day by the sacrificial offering in the Temple of a yearling *lamb and a *pigeon or *dove; in situations of poverty, two *birds could be substituted for the originally proscribed sacrifice. In accordance with the law, *Mary accompanied by Joseph and the Christ Child came to the Temple with an offering of two turtledoves at the appropriate time for her purification. This event was celebrated on the Christian liturgical calendar as the Feast of the Purification of the Virgin Mary, or *Candlemas, on February 2nd. In Christian art, this event became conflated with the *Presentation of Jesus of Nazareth in the Temple.

Purim. Jewish Feast of Lots based upon the story of *Esther. Purim is the only festival originating in the heroic action of a woman and recognized by the Jewish tradition as a religious observance on the liturgical calendar.

Purple. A color that signified a variety of meanings: royalty, power, passion, suffering, and love of truth. Purple garments were worn by God the Father as a sign of his royal and powerful status, or by *Mary Magdalene as a sign of her penitence and her suffering during the Passion of Jesus Christ, and by *Mary as a symbol of her compassion during her son's Passion.

Purse. An ambiguous symbol for either avarice, *charity, or wealth. In classical Greco-Roman, *medieval, and *renaissance art, a purse signified *Vanity, *melancholy, and *Avarice. An *attribute of Judas Iscariot, the purse also signified those Christian saints known for their charitable acts, such as Nicholas of Tolentino and *Elizabeth of Hungary. Three purses identified Nicholas of Myra (or Bari).

Putti. These depictions of naked *children with *wings signified innocence in classical Greco-Roman art. Putti were incorporated into early Christian art as *angels. In *byzantine and *medieval art, angels were more often than not represented by adult figures. The image of the angelic putti returned with the *renaissance interest in classical Greco-Roman art, and flourished in *baroque and *rococo art.

Pyrrha (*Metamorphosis* 1:313–415). Legendary first mortal woman in Latin cosmology. Pyrrha was the wife of Deucalion. This primordial couple survived the great flood, and then became the parents of humanity by casting stones over their shoulders. The stones thrown by Pyrrha became female beings and those thrown by Deucalion male.

Pythia. *Prophetess and oracle of Apollo at Delphi. Pythia's oracular pronouncements were puzzling and difficult to interpret. In classical Greco-Roman and *renaissance art, Pythia was signified as a matronly woman dressed as a youthful nymph and seated by a steaming *omphalos that represented the oracle.

Pyx. A boxlike container used to store the Host or to distribute the Eucharist to the infirm and the elderly. The pyx was an *attribute of *Clare, Longinus, and Raphael the Archangel.

78. *Qodshu offers a Lotus to Min and Serpents to Resheph*

Q

⚜

Qadesh. Egyptian goddess of Syrian origin who was associated with *Hathor as a goddess of love. In Egyptian art, Qadesh was represented by a naked young woman holding *flowers and seated on the back of a *lion as she faced her devotees.

Qedeshet. Syrian goddess invoked for longevity and health. Worshiped in Egypt as a manifestation of *Hathor or *Astarte. In Egyptian art, Qedeshet was depicted as a naked woman standing on a striding *lion, holding a *mirror and a *lotus in her left hand, and two *serpents in her right.

Qodshu. Canaanite goddess of love and fertility. Qodshu was represented as a beautiful naked woman surrounded by sacred *animals.

Quail. An avian symbol of courage or love in eastern art. Two quails signified a loving couple. In classical Greco-Roman and *renaissance art, the quail symbolized *Artemis and her mother, *Leto. The quail was a symbol of lasciviousness, evil, and the Devil in western Christian art.

Queen. From the Old English for "owner." Female landowners especially during matriarchies. In Egyptian art and culture, the rank of queen was a singular position of rank and prestige for women. The pharaoh could have many wives, but only one queen. The term "queen" denoted "great wife" and it was her children who succeeded her husband on the throne. The queen's name was included in the hieroglyphic seal of the pharaoh's cartouche. As a widow, the queen became the Royal Mother, a position of both ceremonial function and political power.

Queen of Heaven, Mary as. The title of "Queen of Heaven" was used in relation to *Mary in the liturgies of the Eastern Orthodox and Roman Catholic Church. According to tradition, Mary was crowned Queen of Heaven following her *Assumption. The Roman Catholic Church recognized the Feast of Mary the Queen in 1954. In Christian art, the motif of Mary as Queen of Heavens was represented by a centrally positioned image of Mary crowned and enthroned as the surrounding groups of *angels, *apostles, *saints, *prophets, and other holy persons signal acclamation. This event was distinct from but coordinated with the *Coronation of Mary.

Queen of Sheba. A royal visitor from Ethiopia or southern Arabia (Saba) whose peaceful country was filled with *gold and *silver, and with vegetation watered by the river of *Paradise. Solomon, who learned of the queen and her country from a *bird, wished to meet her. In turn, the queen longed to meet the king renowned for his wisdom and who could answer her questions about magic and sorcery. According to tradition, *Lilith masqueraded as the Queen of Sheba until recognized by Solomon. Her descendants included the Falashas, the black Jews of Ethiopia, and Nebuchadnezzar, the legendary king of Babylon. An *Old Testament foretype of *Mary whose gifts to Solomon prefigured the *Adoration of the Magi and whose equality with Solomon signified the *Coronation of the Virgin Mary. The Queen of Sheba also denoted paganism recognizing Christianity as suggested by *Flavius Josephus's *Antiquities* (VI.5).

Quince. Yellow pear-shaped *fruit sacred to *Venus and a classical Greco-Roman symbol for marriage and fertility. A legendary aphrodisiac, the eating of quince before a sexual encounter was believed to guarantee the conception of sons of extraordinary ability and energy. In *medieval art, a quince held in the *hand of the Christ Child was a fruit of salvation.

Qur'ān. From the Arabic for "The Recitation"; Holy scriptures of *Islam. The Qur'ān contains the revelations that Allah granted to the prophet Muhammad through the archangel Gabriel. The first revelation occurred during Ramadan in 610 and the last revelation just prior to the Prophet Muhammad's death in 632. According to tradition, these revelations were collected in their final form within a generation of the prophet's death. The unifying theme of Allah's just governance over creation and the guidance to all humanity ensured salvation. The Five Pillars, the basic tenets of Islam, were outlined in the Qur'ān.

R

❦

Rabbit. A lunar animal symbol for fecundity, lust, and timidity, and an attribute of *Venus. In classical Greco-Roman and *renaissance art, the rabbit signified *Lust as one of the *Seven Deadly Sins. In the *hands of *Mary or the Christ Child, the *white *rabbit represented the triumph of chastity over lust in western Christian art.

Rachel (Gn 35:20). Beloved wife of Jacob, the mother of Joseph, one of the matriarchs of Israel, and a foretype of *Mary. She hid the "family gods" under her saddle at the departure for Canaan with Jacob and her sons, thereby prefiguring Mary on the *Flight into Egypt. After a period of barrenness, Rachel died giving birth to Benjamin. Her tomb and memorial pillar became a pilgrimage site for barren women. In western Christian art, Rachel was included in narrative paintings of the life of Jacob or Joseph, most especially in the departure for Canaan.

Radegonde of Poitiers, Saint (518–87). Christian visionary, and *abbess of the Convent of the Holy Cross at Poitiers. Daughter of the king of Thuringia, Ra-degonde was captured by Clothaire I of France, whom she married and eventually left after he killed her brother. A devout Christian, Radegonde earned the position of *deaconess, and established the convent of the Holy Cross at Poitiers, which was established to train women artists as copyists and illuminators. Famed for her charitable works and her visions, she became abbess at Poitiers. She was credited with ending the suffering of a group of prisoners who were released of *fetters by her prayers. Until her death, she retained a flagstone imprinted with the feet of Christ who visited her in response to her prayers that her secular crown be replaced with a crown of thorns. Radegonde was the patron of Jesus College, Cambridge. A rare topic in western Christian art, she was portrayed as she knelt in prayer before a crucifix and with the glorious vision of Christ's visit.

Radhā. Traditional beloved milkmaid and wife of Krishna in Hindu mythology. The love between Krishna and Radhā symbolized the relationship between the deity and the individual soul.

Rahab (Jb 9:13; 26:12). *Old Testament monster of chaos visualized as a sea serpent.

Rahab the Harlot (Jos 2:1–18). *Harlot of Jericho who saved the Israelite spies in the *Old Testament. Prior to the siege of Jericho, Joshua sent two spies to investigate the city. During the night, they hid in the house of Rahab the Harlot who hid them under stacks of flax from the army of the king of Jericho. Given the location of the house, it was possible for the spies to sneak out through a window and escape. Before they departed, they told Rahab to bind scarlet cloth around her windows so that her house and those within it would be spared when the Israelites conquered Jericho. In western Christian art and spirituality, she was recognized as a foretype of *Mary, and the scarlet ribbon as the redemption offered in the blood of Christ. A rare topic in western Christian art, Rahab was portrayed in *medieval art as a beautiful but pious woman prefiguring Mary's role in the salvation of humanity.

Rainbow. Mythological bridge between heaven and earth in religious art. In classical Mediterranean art, the rainbow was an *attribute of *Iris, the messenger of the deities. She was depicted with rainbow-colored wings in *renaissance art. In Chinese art and mythology, the rainbow connoted marriage as the union of *Yin and Yang. Following the Flood that destroyed the world, God told Noah that the rainbow was the sign of his new covenant with the *earth (Gn 9:8–17). According to Jewish tradition, the rainbow was a reflection of God's divine glory and should not be looked at for any length of time. Whenever a rainbow was seen, however, a Jew was to recite a prayer of benediction. The rainbow was a meteorological symbol for God's peace in western Christian art. The *wings of the Archangel Gabriel contained a rainbow motif in representations of the *Annunciation to Mary, and the *throne of God the Father, Jesus Christ, or *Mary in scenes of the Last Judgment and the *Coronation of the Virgin Mary.

Ram. Principle sacrificial animal and animal symbol for male deities of procreation and fertility in the classical Near East, Egypt, Greece, and Rome. The ram was also sacrificed to the *mother goddesses of classical Greece and Rome. The rite of the *crioboleum* which was dedicated to *Cybele included the sacrifice of a ram whose blood imparted vitality and immortality. As a goddess of fertility, *Aphrodite was accompanied by a ram.

Ran. Legendary Norse sea woman who fished up all drowning victims in her net. Ran acquired the status of a goddess of the dead who ruled over her own necropolis, in this case, the sea.

Rape. Forcible sexual intercourse against the will of the victim. Religious art and mythology was replete with episodes of this act of power and dominance, however, in the antique world, the term "rape" may have intended seduction. The cultural change in attitude and interpretation as to the meaning of the term and the act of "rape" was signaled by legal interpretation and punishment, especially in the cultural move from the classical Greco-Roman to the medieval Christian world that made a charge of rape punishable corporally. *See also* Rape of Europa; Rape of Helen of Troy; Rape of Lucretia; Rape of Persephone.

Rape of Europa. *See* Europa.

Rape of Helen of Troy. *See* Helen of Troy; Judgment of Paris.

Rape of Lucretia. *See* Lucretia.

Rape of Persephone. *See* Demeter; Persephone.

Raphael Sanzio (1483–1520). One of the three great masters of the High *Renaissance. A student of Perugino, Raphael creatively merged the innovations of *Leonardo and *Michelangelo into a distinctive and perhaps more immediately palatable style. His interest in superhuman naturalism and spiritual sentiment led to an artistic style that epitomized monumentality and devotionalism without sentimentality, as in his *Disputation Concerning the Blessed Sacrament*. Raphael was renowned for his representations of the *Madonna as an individualized ideal figure, as in his *Sistine Madonna*.

Rat. An animal symbol for destructiveness, decay, and evil in western art; and for prosperity in eastern art. In Indian art, the rat was a companion for the elephant god of auspiciousness, Ganesha; while in Japanese art, it was the messenger of Daikoku, one of the twelve gods of happiness. In western Christian art, the rat was an attribute of *Fina. *See also* Mouse.

Ratī. Feminization of the Egyptian sun god, Ra, and his wife. In Egyptian art, Ratī was portrayed as a female figure whose headdress included a solar disk encased in *horns and with a uraeus and, perhaps, two *feathers.

Rati. From the Balinese for "erotic delight." Goddess of love and fertility in Balinese art and mythology. Rati was imaged as a naked female figure characterized by her pendulant *breasts, pregnant belly, and mouth twisted in a form to represent a vulva.

Rātrī. Goddess of the night in Indian mythology. A sister of *Usas, Rātrī was a benevolent goddess and a protector against robbers and wolves.

Rat-taui. From the Egyptian language for "sun of the two lands." The wife of Monit and mother of Haipre, Rat-taui was associated with *Leto. In Egyptian art, she was represented as a female figure with a *vulture's crest and a headdress composed of a solar disk and cow's *horns.

Raudra. From Lapp for "mountain ash." A minor Lapp goddess and wife of the thunder god, Horagalles.

Raven. An ambiguous symbol for evil or spiritual blessings. Its black plumage and practice of scavenging identified the raven with evil and death, thereby making it a sign of the Devil or an omen of death. According to Greek mythology, the white plumage of the raven was turned black by *Apollo who punished the bird for being a tattletale in reporting on the infidelities of the god's beloved nymph, *Coronis, who was punished with death. The raven was an *attribute of the Celtic goddess of war and *Hera. According to Jewish legend, the raven turned black as punishment for its failure to return immediately to the Ark after Noah dispatched it as a test for the ebbing of the Flood. Like many Christian hermit saints, the Old Testament prophet Elijah was miraculously fed by a raven in the *desert. The raven was an *attribute of deacons, Onuphrius, Anthony the Abbot, Paul the Hermit, Benedict of Nursia, Vincent of Saragossa, Meinrad, and *Black Madonna of Einsiedeln in western Christian art.

Rebecca. Wife of Isaac and mother of Jacob and Esau, one of the matriarchs of Israel, and a foretype of *Mary. *Rebecca at the Well* (Gn 24): As the time approached for Jacob to be married, his father's servant Eliezer was sent to the family's ancestral home in search of a suitable bride. Arriving in Aram, Eliezer went to water the camels and came upon Rebecca filling her pitcher with water. As the bride of Isaac who was found by the *well, Rebecca prefigured the *Annunciation and the *Woman of Samaria. *Birthright of Jacob and Esau* (Gn 27:1–9): In her old age, Rebecca favored her younger son, Jacob, to receive Isaac's blessing, displacing Esau, the elder son from his rightful birthright and inheritance. She conspired with Jacob to confuse her aged and blind husband as to the identity of his sons, so that he gave the birthright blessing to Jacob. Thus, she prefigured Mary as *Wisdom.

Red. The color of passion, blood, and fire. An ambiguous symbol, red signified the emotional passion and lust of *Venus, the spiritual love of John the Evangelist, and the true love of *Mary. As a symbol for blood, red represented the life-sustaining energy of the Christian Eucharist, the life-giving possibility

of the menstrual cycle, and the faithfulness of martyrdom. As a sign of royalty and sovereign power, red was associated with the crown of Lower Egypt and the cardinals of the Roman Catholic Church; and in relation to the color of fire, red signified the Christian liturgical feast of Pentecost.

Reed. A common symbol and ritual offering to fertility goddesses in the Ancient Near East. Bundles of reeds signified *Inanna, *Ishtar, and *Anu. The reed was an Instrument of the Passion and a sign for the Mocking of Jesus (the *Ecce Homo*) in western Christian art. Flourishing on riverbanks, the reed symbolized the just who lived by the *waters of grace, as well as the multitudes seeking Christian *baptism. John the Baptist often carried a small *cross made of reeds.

Regina Caeli. Latin for "Queen of Heaven." *See* Mary; Queen of Heaven, Mary as.

Reliquary. A small, ornamented *box, casket, or shrine used as a depository for sacred relics in world religions. The design motifs on the reliquary related to the nature of the relic contained therein.

Rembrandt van Rijn (1606–69). The leading northern artist of the *baroque period. Influenced by *Michelangelo Merisi da Caravaggio and Adam Elsheimer, Rembrandt extended their interest in tenebrism and dramatic theatricality to new heights. An extraordinary portrait painter, Rembrandt was gifted in his psychological penetration of his sitters. He transferred this ability to depict psychological insight and deep emotional content into biblical and mythological subject matter as in his *Danaë*. Although he lived in a Reformation country, biblical themes dominated in Rembrandt's oeuvre, and he was identified as the great Protestant painter (as evidenced by his *Bathsheba at the Bath*). His engravings and drawings, such as his famed *Hundred Guilder Print*, became popular as bible illustrations. His careful readings and renderings of biblical narratives extended further the Protestant *iconography initiated by *Lucas Cranach I.

Renaissance art. From the Italian for "rebirth." The mid-fifteenth to mid-sixteenth-century style of painting and sculpture influenced by the retrieval of interest in classical humanism and the dignity of the human person. This cultural shift towards anthropocentrism (as opposed to medieval theocentricism), permitted both a retrieval of classical Greco-Roman art and philosophy as well as an acceptance of "modern" medicine and science. Renaissance art was characterized by its concern for a classical sense of balanced compositional harmony, a central vanishing point, natural perspective and light, a recognition of human anatomy, and fidelity to nature.

Renenti. An epithet of *Isis as goddess of heaven.

Renenut. From the Egyptian language for "food, nourishment" and for "snake." Egyptian goddess of agriculture, fertility, and the harvest. Following the harvesting of the crops and the pressing of grapes, special sacrifices were made Renenut as they were made to *Demeter in Greece. She was also identified as the special nourisher of

children. In Egyptian art, Renenut was represented as either a *snake or as a female figure with the head of a snake.

Rennit. World nurse and mother goddess in Egyptian art and mythology.

Renpet. Egyptian goddess of spring and of youth.

Repanse de Joie. French for "Dispenser of Joy." Legendary fairy queen entrusted with the *Holy Grail. Originally an epithet for the ancient priestess who practiced ritual sex, the Repanse de Joie became associated with the Lady Elaine as the "Lily Maid" of the Arthurian legends. Representations of *Elaine in *medieval, *renaissance, and nineteenth-century art emphasize her white garments and have her either holding or standing by a lily.

Reparata, Saint (third century). A virgin martyr from Caesarea who was paraded naked in the streets of Palestine, tortured, and beheaded. According to legend, a *dove (signifying her *soul) came out of her mouth (decapitated torso) and ascended into *heaven. Reparata was a patron of Florence. In early Christian art, she was depicted as a young girl with a dove coming out of her mouth. Her *attributes included a dove, a *palm, a *book, and a *banner of resurrection.

Reret. From the Egyptian language for "sow." Egyptian goddess of maternal fecundity which tirelessly created new life. In Egyptian art, Reret was represented by either a *hippopotamus or as a female form with the head of a hippopotamus.

79. Raphael Sanzio, *The Sistine Madonna*
80. Dante Gabriel Rossetti, *Beata Beatrix*

81. Rembrandt van Rijn, *Danaë*

Rest on the Flight into Egypt. *See also* Flight into Egypt, Rest on.

Restitua, Saint. Legendary Christian female virgin martyr. According to tradition, Restitua was martyred by being burned in a boat covered with pitch while she sought to bring Christianity to Africa. The burned boat with her charred body floated to Ischia where her remains were consecrated and revered by the Christian community. More than likely this legend was based upon the historical reality of a burned image of the *Great Goddess that was damaged during an invasion, and revered as "the restored one." As with other images, characteristics, sacred sites, and attributes of the Great Goddess, this one was assimilated into Christianity and became associated with either *Mary or a female saint.

Return from Egypt (Mt 2:19–23). In a third dream, the Archangel Gabriel advised *Joseph that Herod was dead. Thus, the *Holy Family returned safely to Nazareth. *See also* Flight into Egypt.

Revelations of Saint Bridget of Sweden. The record of this fourteenth-century visionary's prophecies and communications from *Mary who related her perspective of the *Nativity and Passion of Jesus. A popular text of pious devotions, the *Revelations of Saint Bridget of Sweden* influenced *medieval and *renaissance Christian art. For example, this *book was the source for the motif of the kneeling Virgin Mary in depictions of the Nativity that eventually gave rise to the *iconography of the *Adoration of the Child. *See also* Bridget of Sweden, Saint.

Rhea. Great *mother goddess of Greek mythology, daughter of Uranus and *Gaea, consort of Cronos, and parent of most of the gods and goddesses of Mount Olympus, especially *Hera, *Hestia, and *Demeter. Originally worshiped as an earth mother, Rhea was associated with the Roman Magna Mater (Great Mother) or *Ops, and the Phrygian mother goddess, *Cybele. In classical Greco-Roman art, Rhea was represented as a matron wearing a *crown of *towers, enthroned between two *lions, and holding a small drum in her hand. She was a classical Greek foretype for *Anne. *See also* Bona Dea.

Rhea Silvia. *Vestal virgin raped by Mars and thereby the mother of Romulus and Remus. When her dishonor was discovered, Rhea Silvia was cast into prison and her twin sons were thrown into the River Tiber from whence they were saved by a she wolf.

Rhine Maidens. River *nymphs in Teutonic mythology. The Rhine Maidens were associated with the *Valkyries who cared for the bodies of the dead, the Greek *Sirens whose enchanting songs drove sailors to their deaths, and the female deities who protected the karmic wheel in Hindu and Buddhist art and mythology.

Rhinoceros. Animal symbol of good fortune in Chinese Taoist art. The *horns of the rhinoceros were believed to have magical properties, including the use of the pulverized horns as an aphrodisiac.

Rhoda (Acts 12:15–17). From the Greek for "rose." Woman who recognized the voice of Peter following his escape from prison in the *New Testament. Rhoda was both servant and portress at the house of Mary, the mother of John Mark, in Jerusalem. This home served as the headquarters of the Christian community on Mount Zion and was its first synagogue. Following Peter's arrest, the leaders of the Christian community met to discuss their future actions and to pray. During this time, Rhoda heard a knock at the door and recognized the voice of the petitioner as that of Peter. However in her joy at his release she forgot to unlock the door and went instead to tell the others what she knew. Like *Mary Magdalene's initial report of the Resurrection of Jesus Christ, Rhoda was disbelieved and thought to be overcome with female emotions. However as Peter continued to knock until the door was opened to him, the others believed only when they had seen. A rare topic in western Christian art, Rhoda was included as a matron dressed in servant clothes in representations of the narrative cycles of Peter.

Ribera, Jusepe (1591–1652). One of the leading painters of Spanish *baroque art. Influenced by the northern Caravaggesti in Rome in 1615, Ribera blended Spanish realism with Italian idealism and *Caravaggio's chiaroscuro. His paintings, including tender renderings of the *Nativity, and strongly characterized depictions of scenes from the lives of the *saints, became visual defenses for the teachings and doctrines of the *Counter-Reformation *church. Ribera's art was categorized as a balanced blend of emotion and devotionalism, as in his *The Penitent Magdalene*.

Rice. Food symbol of fertility and happiness. According to Indonesian mythology, the Rice Mother was the guardian goddess of crops and its soul. It was believed that her incarnation was found in the last sheaf of the harvest that was tied and then dressed as a doll.

Rind. From the old German for "ivy." Indigenous northern Germanic earth goddess characterized by the powers of generation.

Ring. A completed circle symbolizing eternity and union. In Christian art, two rings represented the *earth and the sky, while three rings signified the Trinity. A symbol of permanent union, a wedding ring was an *attribute of *Catherine of Alexandria, *Catherine of Siena, and *Francis of Assisi. As a sign of their spiritual marriage to the church, ecclesiastical officials wore rings that identified their hierarchical position: plain metal bands were worn by *nuns, and simple gemmed bands by *abbesses.

Ritual Sex. Act of sexual intercourse either being a god and goddess, or mimetically between a king and temple priestess. A form of the *hieros gamos*, acts of ritual sex were engaged in to induce the fertility of the earth. In religious art, depictions of ritual sex can be distinguished from the *hieros gamos* as the former was represented as occurring on an altar and the latter on a bed. *See also* Prostitution, Temple.

River. Prevalent symbol for female fertility and nourishment in religious art. The majority of rivers were personified by feminine deities such as *Ishtar, *Inanna, *Ganga, *Jumna, and *Sarasvatī. Most often, rivers were signified in religious art as overflowing vases or containers either held by or placed next to the figure of the goddess. Further, the river signified the ritual purification simultaneously available through *ablutions and/or *bathing. The river was a symbol for both journey or *pilgrimage, and the ritual cleansing associated with *baptism in Christianity. According to tradition, the four sacred rivers—Pison, Gihon, Tigris, and Euphrates—were the four rivers of *paradise; they were depicted in western Christian art as flowing from a single *rock (*mountain) and signified the four gospels. *See also* Mikveh.

Rizpah (1 Sam 3:7; 21:8–12). From the Hebrew for "hot stone." Concubine of Saul and faithful mother of two of his sons. Following Saul's death, a great famine caused by a drought descended upon Israel. David had become king and believed that this devastation was divine retribution for Saul's slaughter of the Gibeonites. Therefore in an attempt to appease the Gibeonites and God's justice, David turned over to them the two sons of Saul and Rizpah, and five of Saul's grandsons. All these persons were hanged by the Gibeonites, and Rizpah sat on a sackcloth she had spread across a large rock to guard the bodies from desecration until the rains came. Once the drought, and thereby the famine, was ended, David ordered the hanged bodies removed and given proper burial. A rare topic in western Christian art, Rizpah was represented as a proper matron with her head veiled as she sat on the large rock and guarded the bodies of her dead sons.

Robe. A garment associated with the Passion of Jesus. A scarlet or purple robe was an Instrument of the Passion, and symbolized the Mocking of Jesus (the *Ecce Homo*) (Mt 27:27–30). A seamless robe signified the Crucifixion (Jn 19:23–24).

Robigo. Roman goddess of the grain, or conversely of the rust that could destroy the grain crop.

Rocks. Prevalent symbol for the sacred abode of the deities in religious art. Sacred rocks, signified by either their size or unusual formations, denoted the presence of *Cybele as the principal *mother goddess of the ancient Middle East. In Taoist art, rocks connoted the qualities of *Paradise: serenity, eternality, and stability. While in the classical Chinese art and mythology, they communicated friendship and longevity; and were invoked to produce rain and sons. Rocks were geological symbols of strength, solidity, power, Christian fortitude, and Jesus Christ as the *church in western Christian art. In the *Old Testament, rocks signified God, while the *New Testament emphasized the metaphor of Peter as the rock (Mt 16:18). Rocks with gushing *water denoted both *baptism and the church, while a large rock with four streams of water indicated Christ with the four gospels.

Rococo art. From the French for "rock work." Popular in the mid-eighteenth century, this delicate, light, airy, and curvaceous style of art emphasized pastel colors and pastoral storybook themes.

Roman art. Classical forms and styles of art originating with the seventh-century B.C.E. Etruscans and flourishing during the Roman Imperium. Although stylistic distinctions existed between the varied eras of classical Rome from the Etruscan, Roman Italy, Hellenistic, and Augustan periods to the Roman Imperial times, there were identifiable characteristics to the more generic category of classical Roman art including realism, psychological penetration, pictorial refinement, linear perspective, voluminous forms, bold decorative colors, and an alliance with the political ideal of service to the state. Influenced by classical Greek, Hellenistic, and Eastern art, the tenets and styles of classical Roman art were assimilated into western European art, especially in Christian iconography and *renaissance art.

Roman Catholicism. The Christian communion historically centered on the office of the Primacy of Peter, accounted as the first bishop of Rome, and which identified itself as the universal and apostolic *church. Roman Catholicism affirmed that the successive bishops of Rome were the supreme teachers, pastors, and governors of the Church as Vicars of Christ on *earth; the authority of church councils and bishops, and the authentic teaching of doctrine derived from their union with the popes as Petrine Bishops of Rome. As the Christian tradition in western Europe from the fourth century through the Reformation, Roman Catholicism was a powerful political, social, and economic force in the development of cultural attitudes and western Christian art.

Roman Charity. *See* Pero and Cimon.

Roman religion. Indigenous belief system of the ancient Romans, later identi-

fied as the Roman Empire. This organization of local and national ceremonies, rituals, festivals, and myths revolved around the maintenance of peace, or good relations, between the deities and humanity. As with other religious traditions, classical Roman religion integrated the sacred with the secular, in its support of the state, eventually developing into a formal state religion. Traditionally, Roman religion never required adherence to a code of ethics or a profession of faith. Among the common identifiable characteristics of classical Roman religion were its syncretism as evidenced by the pantheon of gods and goddesses who either were accompanied by or conflated with the divine figures of classical Greece, the Eastern Mediterranean, and Egypt. During the first century, the establishment of the Imperial Cult with its ritual and ceremonial trappings led to the tenet of the divine mandate of rule by the emperors. A priestly hierarchy, divination ceremonials, ritual precision, ritual sacrifice, and the simultaneous practice of a public and private cult characterized classical Roman religion. The legacy of classical Roman religion shaped the cultural and philosophic attitudes of "the west," that is, Europe and North America.

Romance of the Rose. Elaborate medieval allegory of lovers's pursuits and a brutal attack on women. The *Romance of the Rose* was the foremost and influential medieval poem of the late thirteenth and early fourteenth century. The first half of the text was written by Guillaume de Lorris by 1240 and reflected the medieval attitudes towards woman as the idealization of love. However the second part of the poem was written by Jean Chapenil de Meun by 1280 and presented a brilliant but devasting attack on the evils of the female sex. His reading of women provoked both transformations in the iconography of women in *medieval art, and *Christine de Pizan's rebuttal in her *City of the Ladies*.

Romanesque art. A form of *medieval art that dated from the late tenth century into the thirteenth century. Its stylistic characteristics—thick-walled and low-ceiling churches, sharp architectural lines, and stylized, heavy figures in carved and illuminated works of art—sought to retrieve the imperial tradition of the Roman Empire. Deeply influenced by *byzantine art and *iconography, romanesque art represented sovereignty and power.

Rosalia. Imperial Roman festival celebrated in May or June. Characteristic of the Rosalia was the procession of women who adorned the graves and tombs of the death with *roses.

Rosalia, Saint. *See* Rosalie, Saint.

Rosalie, Saint (twelfth century). Christian virgin *saint carried by *angels to an inaccessible *mountain where she lived for many years a life of Christian prayer and devotion. Rosalie was the patron saint of Palermo. In western Christian art, she was depicted as a young woman kneeling in prayer inside a cave with a crucifix (*cross) and *skull. She was also represented receiving a gift of *roses or a *rosary from *Mary.

Rosary. A string of beads, usually numbering between one-hundred-and-eight and one-hundred-and-twelve, used for meditation and contemplation on the merciful compassion of Buddha. In Buddhist art, the rosary was an *attribute of *Avalokiteshvara, *Kuan-yin, and *Kwannon. In western Christian art and spirituality, the rosary was a string of one-hundred-and-fifty small beads (on which were said "Aves") and fifteen larger ones (on which were said "Pater Nosters") that served as an aide to prayer and devotions to *Mary. The rosary was an *attribute of *Dominic, *Catherine of Siena, and Mary.

Rose. A floral symbol sacred to *Venus and signifying love, the quality and nature of which was characterized by the color of the rose. A symbol of purity, a *white rose represented innocence (nonsexual) love, while a pink rose represented first love, and a red rose true love. When held by a *martyr, the red rose signified "red martyrdom" or the loss of life, and the white rose "white martyrdom" or celibacy. According to Ambrose, the thorns of the rose were a reminder of human finitude and guilt as the roses in the *Paradise Garden had no thorns. A thornless rose was an attribute of *Mary as the Second *Eve. A garland of roses denoted the rosary. Roses were an *attribute of *Elizabeth of Hungary, *Dorothea of Cappadocia, and Benedict of Nursia.

Rose of Lima, Saint (1568–1617). First native-born individual in the Americas to be canonized a *saint (1671). A dedicated, poor young woman, Rose provided support for her aged parents. After joining the Dominican Order, she was renowned for the torturous penances she inflicted upon herself as well as her mystical visions. Rose committed her life to the care of sick Indians and

82. Properzia de' Rossi,
*Joseph and
Potiphar's Wife*

83. Workshop of
Peter Paul Rubens,
*Saint Teresa of Avila
Interceding for
Souls in Purgatory*

slaves, and was identified as the founder of social services in Peru. In western Christian art, Rose of Lima was depicted as a beautiful young woman who knelt in prayer and wore the *crown of thorns or had a scourge nearby.

Rosemary. From the Latin for "rose of the sea." Botanical memory charm. Associated with *Venus, the goddess who rose from the sea, rosemary was also sacred to the *fairies. In this capacity, it was believed to be an appropriate love token that never allowed the lover to forget his beloved. Rosemary became transformed into a memory charm for the dead, and became a favored decorative motif on funerary art.

Rosmerta. Gaelic goddess of fertility and prosperity. Rosmerta was identified by her *attributes of the *cornucopia and the *caduceus.

Rossetti, Dante Gabriel (1828–82). A founder of the *Pre-Raphaelite Brotherhood. The son of an expatriate Italian Dante scholar, Dante Gabriel Rossetti dedicated his artistic vision to the retrieval of the medieval synthesis, especially with regard to art and religion. He joined with *William Holman Hunt and John Everett Millais to establish the Pre-Raphaelite Brotherhood. Although influenced by *Dante and medieval art, Rossetti's paintings were of a poetic and neurotic intensity matched only by his poetry. His major contribution to the iconography of women in western art, and in western religious art, was his development of the iconic type identified as "a stunner," that is, a beautiful woman with loose flowing hair, melancholy eyes, and pursing lips as exemplified in his painting entitled *Beata*

Beatrix. His interest in western Christian art survived his role in the Pre-Raphaelite Brotherhood, as evidenced by his painting of *The Annunciation*.

Rossi, Properzia de' (c. 1490–1530). Only significant woman sculptor of the Italian Renaissance. An accomplished musician and scientist, Properzia de' Rossi was a prodigy who produced her first sculpture, a carving of the Crucifixion of Jesus Christ, on a peach pit. She was commissioned to sculpt several works for the facade of the Church of San Petronio, including several *angels and *Sibyls that were finished successfully. Unfortunately, her excellent relief on the theme of Joseph and Potiphar's Wife was rejected not for her artistic skill but because of the allegations of a jealous male sculptor, Amico Aspertini. He claimed that Rossi's inspiration came from her own involvement with a young nobleman, Anton Galleazo Malvasia. This scandalous behavior on the part of a woman caused the superintendents of the Church of San Petronio to reject Rossi's carved relief. According to tradition, she died shortly thereafter from the grief and mortification she suffered from both Aspertini's allegations and the superintendents's discriminating actions. She did die soon after her work was rejected, but more likely from a terminal illness such as cancer or tuberculosis for which she was treated at a hospice.

Rubens, Peter Paul (1577–1640). Leading Roman Catholic painter of Flemish *baroque art. Influenced by *Caravaggio, Rubens developed his own personal and passionately dramatic style, which was highlighted by his use of high florid colors, as evidenced by his *Lamentation*

valiter Ruth manipulos suos excutit qoteu sie redacta. socrus sue ostendens narrat ei omnem Booz erga se humanitate

est si eam inueneriv ... Ruth min. sua monet eā ut ... cuous sichat. er ecce nadat ad Boozi area atq illo dormiente se sub palio ei absconoat. q ea ... apigrans sin more hebreorū accipiat muxorem.

84. *Story of Ruth*

over the Dead Christ and *Adoration of the Kings*. Affiliated with the Jesuits in Antwerp, Rubens was an iconographic innovator of the highest level as witnessed by his interpretations of *Mary and *Mary Magdalene, and his innovative presentations of Marie de Medici.

Rudder. Emblem signifying *Isis in Egyptian art and *Fortune in classical Greco-Roman and *renaissance art.

Rumina. From the Latin for "mother's breast." Indigenous Italic goddess of nursing or suckling; patron of nursing mothers. Sacrificial offerings of milk were placed upon altars dedicated to Rumina, especially by new mothers or those with meager flows of milk. Rumina was characterized as a physically powerful female figure whose naked full breasts were engorged with milk, and most often, was represented with one child nursing at her breast while others surrounded her awaiting their turns.

Her iconography was assimilated into that of *Charity.

Ruth. Moabite heroine of the *Old Testament Book of Ruth and renowned as the faithful daughter-in-law of *Naomi. The impoverished and widowed Ruth cared for her mother-in-law in Bethlehem by gleaning after the reapers cut the harvest of grains on the fields owned by Naomi's kinsman, Boaz. Recognized for her filial devotion and her beauty, Ruth became Boaz's wife. Despite the fact that Boaz was twice her age and she was past the normal age of childbearing, Ruth conceived a son, Obed, on their wedding night, thereby becoming an ancestor of David. She was an Old Testament foretype of *Anne. A rare topic in western Christian art, Ruth was included in Old Testament narrative cycles in *medieval and *renaissance art. Otherwise, she was identified either as the companion of her aged mother-in-law, or by the gleaned wheat she held in her hands.

S

⚜

S. A letter symbol for the Holy Spirit.

Sa. From the Egyptian language for "wise blood." Sacred blood of *Isis. According to Egyptian tradition, those who partook of sa became wise and immortal. Composed of the goddess's menstrual blood, sa was the fundamental component necessary in the creation of a pharaoh or a great hero.

Sabina, Saint (d. 126). Roman martyr to Christianity. Brought to the Christian faith by her maidservant Serapia, the wealthy widow Sabina became a devoted and fervent practitioner of her new religion. Initially saved from persecution because of her social position, Sabina was arrested and condemned to death for her faith. She was martyred in Rome, and her relics were translated in the Basilica of Santa Sabina in the fourth century. In early Christian art, especially the carved doors of her basilica, Sabina was portrayed as a Roman matron wearing the *laurel crown of martyrdom and holding a *palm branch.

Sabine Women (Plutarch, *Lives*, *Romulus*). Legendary victims of *rape and abduction by the Romans. Following the famous quarrel between the legendary founders of Rome, Romulus and Remus, and the death of Remus, the city of Rome prospered. However, there were no women for the followers of Romulus; so the Sabine men from the neighboring village were invited for an athletic festival. During the competition, the Romans invited the village and abducted all available women. The war that ensued resulted in the Sabines being equals in the establishment and the development of Rome.

Saci. From the Sanskrit for "power." Epithet of the Goddess as wife or consort of Indra.

Sacra Conversazione. From the Italian for "holy conversation." Motif for the *Madonna and Child credited to *Fra Angelico. This representation of the Enthroned Madonna and Child with *saints and/or *donors who, while cognizant of each other's presence and united in a common action, were also aware of the spectator. All hierarchical barriers, social and historical, were removed as all the figures within the canvas functioned within a single unified space.

Sacred Heart of Jesus. A popular devotion to Jesus Christ as compassionate love incarnate represented in images of either a standing Resurrected Christ with his bleeding or flaming *heart exposed or the heart of Jesus Christ pierced by *arrows. This iconographic motif was widely popularized by the mystical visions of *Margaret Mary Alacoque, a seventeenth-century contemplative *nun of the Visitation Order.

Sacred Marriage. *See* Hieros Gamos.

Sage. An aromatic mint signifying healing and symbolic of *Mary in medieval Christian art.

Sail. *Attribute of *Aphrodite (*Venus) and *Fortuna in classical Greco-Roman art.

Saint. From the Latin for "holy." Heroes and heroines of Christianity served as intermediaries and advocates between humanity and God the Father. Although originally applied to all Christians as it had been to all the faithful of the *Old Testament, the term "saint" became an honorific title reserved for outstanding holiness. The process of being canonically recognized as a saint (canonization) was a lengthy process during which the character and orthodoxy of the individual and the miracles attributed to him or her were investigated by the *church. The study of the lives of the saints was known as hagiography. Saints who had special relationships with individual cities, towns, countries, occupations, or guilds were defined as patrons. In Christian art,

saints were identified by the distinguishable *attribute or symbol that related to the method of their martyrdom and/or their most important miracle or teaching.

Sala. Cherry tree as sign of both *virginity and the botanical sign under which *Maya gave birth to the Buddha. The fruit of this tree was a worldwide symbol for the feminine in religious art.

Salacin. Roman epithet for *Venus (*Aphrodite) as the female embodiment of the sea, especially of the fecundity of the sea as womb.

Salamander. Believed to be nonflammable and able to extinguish flames with its breath, the salamander symbolized Fire in classical *Mediterranean art and mythology. According to Jewish tradition, it connoted protection against fire; and alternately was a symbol for Torah, and of the scholar protected by God. This small amphibious animal similar to a lizard signified faith over passion in western Christian art. Medieval *bestiaries described the salamander as impervious to *fire and capable of extinguishing *flames with its cold breath. In northern *medieval art, the salamander was depicted in either the *Annunciation to Mary as a sign of faith or the Temptation and the Fall as a variant of the *serpent.

Salome (Mt 14:1–12; Mk 6:14–29; Lk 9:7–9). According to the *New Testament, the unnamed daughter of *Herodias danced at the birthday celebration for her stepfather, Herod Antipas. Her dance so pleased him that she was promised anything she wished unto half of his kingdom. Consulting her mother, the obedient daughter requested the head of the imprisoned John the Baptist, who had denounced Herodias for adultery. Despite Herod's pleas, his stepdaughter would not accept any other prize. As a result, the Baptist was beheaded, and the severed head was placed upon a silver platter for her. The Jewish historian Josephus Flavius identified this unnamed dancing daughter of Herodias as Salome in his *Antiquities of the Jews* (18.137), but made no mention of her dance or of her guilt in the death of John the Baptist. Rarely depicted in early Christian and *byzantine art, Salome and her dance became an artistic topic as the role of the Baptist (and the ritual of Baptism) gained importance in Christian theology. In the earliest medieval images, Salome was represented as prepubescent girl engaged not in an erotic dance but in acrobatic or gymnastic feats. Herod, his guests, Herodias, John the Baptist, and the executioner(s) were included in these narrative representations, which conflated the *Banquet of Herod*, the *Dance of Salome*, and the *Execution of John the Baptist* into one scene. In *renaissance and *baroque art, artists focused not on the banquet or the dance, but rather on the depiction of the beautiful young Salome, often regally dressed, as she accepted the severed head of the Baptist on a silver platter. From the scriptural context these images of Salome emphasized the contrast between her youthful loveliness and the grotesque head of the Baptist. The iconographic distinction of Salome with the head of the Baptist from *Judith with the head of Holofernes was that the former held a platter while the latter held the severed head by its hair. In nineteenth- and twentieth-century west-ern art, the theme of Salome was rediscovered within the context of the *femme fatale* and the eroticism of orientalism, including oriental dances.

Salome (Mary Salome). *See* Mary Salome, Saint.

Salome the Midwife. First witness to the newborn Jesus as the Messiah. According to the apocryphal *Protoevangelium of James*, Joseph, after settling *Mary into the stable, went in search of a midwife to assist in the imminent birth. He found two midwives who debated the possibility of a virgin conceiving and bearing a child. One of them, Salome, was punished for her doubt with a searing pain in her *hands, which shriveled after she physically examined the new mother's virginity. Urged to place her painful hands upon the newborn infant, Salome recognized the singularity of his birth and her hands were healed in this apocryphal first miracle of Christ. In *byzantine and Italo-Byzantine art, the two midwives were represented *bathing the newborn child in the foreground of *Nativity scenes. This iconographic motif became rare after the fourteenth century and was one of many nonscriptural topoi banned by the *Council of Trent.

Salt. Symbol for protection against decay and evil. Salt was placed in the mouths of infants at their *baptisms (bread and salt in the mouths of adults) as an emblem of the scriptural injunction to be "salt of the earth." In the Hebraic, Arabic, and many other cultures, bread and salt were offered as a sign of hospitality.

Salus. From the Latin for "salvation rescue." Roman goddess personifying the salus publica, or welfare of the state. Salus was identified with the Greek *Hygeia as a protector of health. In classical Greco-Roman and *renaissance art, she was characterized by her *attributes of a *snake and a *bowl.

Samaritan Woman. *See* Woman of Samaria.

Sandals. A symbol for hermit and *pilgrim *saints. Discarded sandals signified humility and a recognition of holy ground.

Sapientia. From the Latin for "Lady Wisdom." Roman counterpart to the classical Greek *Sophia. Sapientia was the form of the Goddess worshiped by the *Gnostics as well as other spiritualists and philosophers throughout western history. Signifying the hidden mysteries and sacred wisdom otherwise only known in the mind of God, Sapientia was understood to be the female embodiment of the primordial mind. During the High Middle Ages, it became an epithet of *Mary.

Sapphira (Acts 5:7–11). From the Aramaic for "beautiful." Wife of Ananias the Hypocrite in the *New Testament. After her husband sold some property but only gave a small tithe to the Christian community, he was severely rebuked by Peter. Ananias' remorse and guilt caused his sudden death. Several hours later, Sapphira was questioned about this same monetary issue, and she too died instantly from regret over her "sin against the Holy Spirit." A rare topic in western Christian art, Sapphira was represented with her husband or with Peter in the narrative cycles of Peter.

Sappho (sixth century B.C.E.). Greatest classical poetess. A resident of the island of *Lesbos, Sappho lived a disciplined and chaste life. Although married to a man from the island of Andros, she provoked scandal by gathering together a group of young women for companionship and artistic conversations. Famed for her poetry, beauty, and violence of passions, Sappho drowned herself following the rejection of her love by Phaon. Unfortunately, only a fragment of her poetry survived the Christian persecutions of women and of alleged lesbians.

Šapš. From the Ugaritic for "light of the gods." Ugaritic goddess of the sun.

Sara-Kali. Form of the Goddess venerated as giver of life and queen of heaven by the gypsies. Among those European gypsies who were practicing *Druids, Sara-Kali took the form of a black woman in the posture of childbirth.

Sarah. From the Hebrew for "princess." Wife of *Abraham, mother of *Isaac, the first matriarch of Israel, and a foretype of *Mary. Having failed to conceive a child, Sarah followed the custom of her people by offering her servant, Hagar, to her husband in hopes of an heir. Hagar bore a son, Ishmael, and grew haughty in her attitude towards her mistress. Past the age of childbearing, Sarah laughed when the three angels who visited Abraham announced that she would have a special son who would be heir to the covenant and father of a great nation. Some time later, Sarah gave birth to Isaac (Gn 17:15–16). No longer having to accept the mocking of Hagar and Ishmael, Sarah persuaded Abraham to drive them into the desert. In western

Christian art, Sarah was represented within the context of the narrative episodes in the life of Abraham, especially the Philoxeny (Hospitality) of Abraham. Sarah prefigured both *Anne and Mary.

Sarama. Indigenous Indian goddess of the hunt and of death.

Saranyu. Indigenous Indian goddess and protector of horses. Saranyu was characterized as a mare in Indian religious art.

Sarasvatī. Originally three indigenous Indian river goddesses who were transformed into the Hindu goddess of arts, language, letters, and music. Sarasvatī was both the creation and wife of Brahmā, and oftentimes the consort of Mañjushri. As the goddess of music and poetry, she ruled over the two basic elements to all Indian rituals. In Hindu art, she was depicted as riding on a *swan or *peacock, and as having two or four arms in which she held a *book, a *rosary, a *lotus bud, a plow, and/or a vina, the Indian form of a *lute, and also gestured a *mudrā. In the guise of Vajrasarasvatī, she was represented as a three-faced and six-armed female form seated on a *lotus. In her Tibetan form as Dbyangs-chan-ma, she took on the Tantric form of a red body with three faces and six arms in which she held a variety of Tantric *attributes. As Benzai-ten, she was venerated by artists, musicians, poets, and geishas in Japan, and in more modern times by Japanese businessmen, gamblers, and jealous women. Her iconography was transformed between the fifteenth and sixteenth centuries as a result of an error in translation so that she became a goddess of the virtue of

good luck and thereby one of the seven goddesses of happiness in Japanese Buddhism. Benzai-ten had three forms of presentation: as a pretty young woman who played the *biwa*, a Japanese lute, or held a sword; as a large white serpent or a feminine male figure; and as an eight-armed female figure who brandished a trident, *vajra, *bow, and a rope in her right hands, and a *cakra, chopper, sword, and *arrows in her left. Her sacred companions were the *peacock, white serpent, or *Mārīcī. Usually characterized as being white or pale green in color, Benzai-ten's attributes included a sword, key, hook, rope, arrow, bow, lance, cakra, jewel, and trident.

Sarcophagus. From the Latin for "flesh eater." An aboveground stone or terracotta casket for the burial of the dead. The exterior of the sarcophagus was decorated, more or less elaborately depending upon the financial resources of the deceased, with symbols or iconographic motifs that identified the religious belief of the deceased. In Egyptian burial practice, a sarcophagus was a manifestation of the Lord of Life who granted eternal power to the deceased by means of symbols and images. *Isis, *Nut, and *Nephthys were among the most popular motifs on Egyptian sarcophagi.

Sarpenitu. Akkadian for "she who shines silver." A goddess of pregnancy and wife of the Babylonian Marduk.

Sati. Hindu goddess who sought death because of the ongoing dispute between Daksha, her father, and Shiva, her husband. Her corpse was dismembered by Vishnu and Sati was reborn as *Pārvāti.

Satis. From the Egyptian language for "she who runs like an arrow." Egyptian female personification of the giver of waters for the purification of the dead, and as the life-giving waters of the Nile. Satis was the queen of Elephantine, donor of the waters of the cataracts, and the wife of Khnum, the creator god. Originally identified as a goddess of the hunt, Satis became associated with *Hathor as a goddess of women and of love. In Egyptian art, she was portrayed as a female figure who wore the white crown of Upper Egypt and carried the *ankh in her right hand. Satis was flanked by two *antelopes, her animal *attribute.

Saule. From the Latvian for "sun-virgin" or "mother sun." Latvian goddess of the sun. Saule was courted by both the sky god, Dievs, and the moon god, Mēness. She lived on an agrarian estate on the top of the mountain of heaven, and was invoked to foster the growth and harvest of the fruits of the earth.

Saŭska. From the Hurrian for "she who is armed." Hurrian goddess of love and healing. Saŭska became associated with *Ishtar as both a warlike goddess and as a giver of health and fertility. In Near Eastern art, she was characterized as wearing a long slit skirt that permitted freedom of movement, a war cap similar to those of the gods of battle, and *wings. Saŭska was accompanied by her sacred animal, the *lion.

Saw. A carpenter's tool that became an *attribute of *Joseph (of Nazareth), Simon Zelotes, *Euphemia, and Isaiah.

Scales. A symbol for judgment, along with a *sword of equality and justice.

Scales were an *attribute of Michael the Archangel and the Last Judgment in Christian art, and of *Themis in classical Greco-Roman art.

Scallop Shell. A symbol of *pilgrimage and thereby an *attribute of James Major and Edward the Confessor. In southern European art, John the Baptist was depicted using a scallop shell at the Baptism of Jesus Christ.

Scarlet Woman. Accustomed reference for the *Whore of Babylon whom John described as dressed in scarlet (Rev 17:3–6).

Scepter. A symbol of royal power and authority. The scepter was an *attribute of *Gabriel the Archangel, monarch *saints, Christ as King of Heaven, and God the Father in western Christian art, and of the goddesses *Hera and *Hestia in classical Greek art.

Scholastica, Saint (c. 480–c. 543). Twin sister of *Benedict of Nursia and founder of an order of Benedictine *nuns. Dedicated to God at an early age, Scholastica was a devout and pious woman who met with her brother once a year at Monte Cassino. According to tradition, she and her brother spoke of the joys of *heaven into the morning of their last meeting. When she died three days later, Benedict reportedly had a vision of a *dove ascending into heaven. Scholastica was the leading female *saint of the *Benedictine Order. In western Christian art, she was depicted as a mature woman dressed in a Benedictine *habit with a dove either issuing from her mouth or hovering over her *head and/or *book. Her *attributes included the *crucifix and the *lily.

Scivias. From the Latin for "Know the Ways of the Lord." One of the most remarkable religious compilations created by a woman, and second only to *Herrade of Landsburg's *Hortus Deliciarum*. *Scivias* was written by *Hildegard of Bingen between 1142 and 1152. She was also credited minimally with the design directions, if not the actual creation, of the illustrative materials for this text. Based on her thirty-five visions, this book formed a history of salvation. In an almost classical manner, Hildegard identified herself as a weak and passive vehicle for the Word of God. She claimed divine inspiration for this work and for her visions that undermined the medieval church in its claims of authority over women. For Hildegard, men and women were complementary and female otherness was an appropriate form of the human condition. The *Scivias* was the first medieval manuscript beyond the *Beatus Apocalypse* illuminated by *Ende in which line and color were employed to indicate supernatural contemplation. Among Hildegard's illustrations for the *Scivias* were representations of the church in a female form, the *Virtues and the *Vices, the struggles of the soul, and the fallen angels.

Scorpion. As a harmful creature with a painful sting, the scorpion became a protective image against evil in Mesopotamian and Babylonian art, and was accorded veneration. The Egyptian goddess *Selket was depicted wearing a crown of scorpions as the protector of the Pharaoh's throne, and as the guardian of the canopic jars, and of the underworld. She was worshiped in the form of a scorpion or as a female figure with a scorpion head. Selket was associated with *Isis as a protector of the young Horus, and thereby, of all children. According to popular belief, she killed only men because of her reverence for Isis. The scorpion was a symbol of treachery, evil, the Devil, and Judas Iscariot (Rev 9:5), in western Christian art. During the medieval period, it was an animal symbol for the *Jews or the *Synagogue. Tibetan Buddhist practice advocated the eating of scorpions as a protection against injurious demons. In Tibetan Buddhist art, the scorpion was an *attribute of Padmasambhava, the founder of Lamaism and a destroyer of demons.

Scotia. From the Greek for "darkness." Form of the Goddess venerated in ancient Scotland.

Scroll. A symbol of authorship. The scroll was an *attribute of the *Muses, *Calliope and *Clio, in classical Greco-Roman and *renaissance art. It denoted either classical philosophy or the *Old Testament in Christian art. An inscribed scroll identified individual *saints, fathers of the church, or the Evangelists as authors. A scroll of music was an attribute of *Cecilia, *Ambrose, and Gregory the Great. A scroll inscribed with scriptural text was commonplace in northern *medieval and renaissance art.

Scultore, Diana Ghisi (1530–90). Italian woman artist. Diana Ghisi Scultore was trained in the studio of her father and brothers in Mantua. She was recognized for her paintings and engravings of religious subjects, which were rendered in a simple mannerist style. She married the architect and sculptor, Francesco Ricciarelli, in 1579.

Scylla. A terrifying female sea monster who resided in a cave directly opposite to the whirlpool, Charybdis, in Greek mythology. The sea god, Glaucus, became enamored of the beautiful sea nymph named Scylla. When he sought a love potion from *Circe, the sorcerer fell in love with him. In an attempt to garner Glaucus's love, Circe created a potion of magical herbs for Scylla to bathe in. However contrary to the god's desire, when the beautiful nymph bathed those parts of her lower body touched by the herbal potion were transformed into grotesque horrors including a girdle of the heads of hideous *dogs, and a *dolphin's tail that replaced her legs. Scylla retreated to a cave from which the dogs's heads would capture and devour seaman whose ships went past too close; their alternative was to venture too close to Charybdis. A variant of this story related that the beautiful Scylla was the daughter of Nisus of Megara, and enamored of Minos of Crete. In order to win Minos's love, she defied her father by cutting off his long red hair as he slept and thereby denied him immortality. When Minos conquered Megara, he killed Nisus but scorned Scylla for her act of filial betrayal. He had her tied to the stern of his ship and dragged her through the sea until she sought refuge in the cave opposite Charybdis. In this latter version, Scylla and Nisus were a classical Greek foretype of *Delilah and Samson.

Sea Nymphs. Female figures in Greek and Roman mythology identified by the collective terms: *Oceanids, *Nereids, or *Nymphs.

Seal. A symbol of the mark or signature of God (Rv 7:2, 3) in western Christian art.

Sechat-Hor. From the Egyptian language for "she who remembers Horus." Egyptian cow goddess and *queen of the herds. Sechat-Hor was a foster mother to Horus while *Isis went in search of Osiris.

Securitas. Roman female personification of security, Securitas was the goddess empowered with the continuation, or permanence, of the Roman Empire.

Sedna. From the Aleutian for "mother of the sea." Sea goddess and *queen of sea creatures in Eskimo art and mythology.

Sekhmet. From the Egyptian language for "the mighty one." Egyptian goddess of war who with her consort, Ptah, and their son, Neferteni, formed the "Triad of Memphis." In the guise of the divine protector armed with *arrows, Sekhmet accompanied the Pharaoh into battle and thereby guaranteed military victory. As a destructive form of *Hathor, Sekhmet's fiery breath signified the dangerous hot winds of the desert; while as the friendly form of *Bast, this goddess was a mistress of magic as a healing art. In later Egyptian art and mythology, she fused with the goddess *Mut into the deity identified as Mut-Sekhmet. She was portrayed as a lioness or a female figure with a lion's head in Egyptian art. Sekhmet's attributes included arrows and desert winds.

Seléne. From the Greek for "light, brightness, and radiance." Greek goddess of the moon. According to legend, Seléne became enamored of the handsome youth Endymion as he slept on Mount Latmus. Her nocturnal visits resulted in their fifty daughters. One ver-

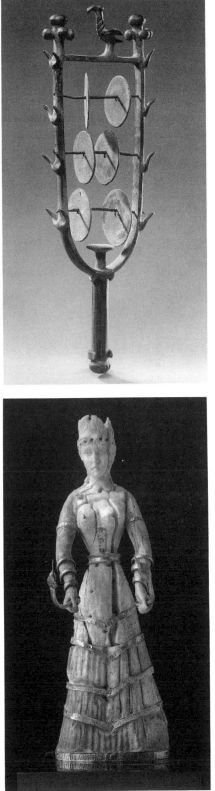

86. *Sistrum*

85. *Sekhmet*

87. *Snake Goddess*

sion of her legend claimed that Seléne brought eternal sleep to her husband so that his physical beauty would never fade away with age. She was a tutelary goddess of magic and sorcery. She was identified with *Artemis and *Hecate; and later with the Roman *Diana and *Luna. In classical Greco-Roman and *renaissance art, Seléne was depicted as a beautiful winged maiden dressed in a long flowing white garment and wearing a golden diadem. She rode in a chariot drawn by two white *horses or cows whose *horns signify the crescent moon, or on a mule.

Selket. From the Egyptian language for "she who lets throats breathe." Egyptian tutelary goddess of the dead. An ally of Ra, the sun god, Selket used her powerful magic to defeat his enemies. She was the guardian of the Pharaoh's throne, the canopic jars, and the underworld. Selket was associated with *Isis as a protector of Horus, and thereby of all children, while his mother went in search of Osiris. In Egyptian art, she was characterized as either a female figure with a scorpion head or crown, or as a *scorpion.

Semele. Beloved of Zeus and mother of Dionysus in Greek mythology. The daughter of Kadmos (Cadmus) and *Harmonia, Semele was persuaded by a disgruntled *Hera disguised as a nursemaid, to appeal for an unimpinged vision of her lover who otherwise camouflaged himself. Unable to refuse his beloved's request, Zeus revealed himself in his full divinity and glory, and Semele was burned by his radiance. A frantic Zeus sought to rescue their unborn child by removing it from Semele's womb and placed the fetus in his thigh

until the appointed time for the birth. After he attained maturity, Dionysus led his mother from the underworld to eternal life on Mount Olympus as the minor deity named *Thyone.

Semeriamis, Queen. Famed Babylonian queen. Following her birth, the daughter of the Syrian fish goddess, *Astargartis, and the Babylonian god of wisdom, Oannes, was reportedly nursed by the sacred *doves of *Ishtar until the infant was placed in the loving care of the loyal shepherd known as Simmos. Semeriamis married Menones, a general in the army of Ninus, king of Assyria. Following his death, the still beautiful widow attracted the attention of King Ninus, and they married. After Ninus's death, she became regent for their son and conquered what was the then-known eastern world. A rare topic in classical Near Eastern art, Semeriamis was portrayed as a beautiful woman either dressed as a queen or armed for battle.

Semnai Theai. From the Greek for "exalted goddesses." Collective title for the earth goddesses identified as embodiments of fertility. The Semnai Theai were later known as the *Erinyes.

Sengen. Indigenous Japanese goddess of Mount Fugiyama.

Šentait. Minor Egyptian cow goddess. Šentait was a protector of the dead and an embodiment of maternal fertility. In Egyptian art and mythology, she became merged with *Isis.

Sequana. Goddess of the River Seine and of the tribe known as the Sequanae in the art and mythology of Gaul.

Sequana was identified with her *attribute, a *duck.

Serah (Gen 46:17; Num 26:46; 1 Chr 7:30). From the Hebrew for "lady." Only woman in the *Old Testament named in the genealogy of the tribes of Israel during the time in the wilderness. Serah was the daughter of Asher and the granddaughter of Jacob and *Zilpah. She traveled to Egypt with Jacob. A rare topic in western Christian art, Serah was depicted as a proper Jewish matron in the narrative cycles of the history of the Tribes of Israel.

Seraphim. The six-winged, fiery-red celestial beings that guard the throne of God the Father. Described as burning with love for God, the seraphim were led by Uriel the Archangel (Is 6:2).

Šerida. Mesopotamian goddess of light and consort of Utu/Šamaš.

Serpent. A worldwide symbol of duality evoking adoration and abhorrence simultaneously. The serpent was a common sign for speed, beauty, mystery, and danger. Among the Egyptians, the serpent was recognized as being equally demonic and beneficent, and was associated with several goddesses including *Buto, *Isis, *Meretseger, *Nephthys, and *Wadjet. According to the *Book of the Dead (Chapter 87), it was the symbol of survival after death. The image of the *ouroboros*, that is, of the serpent creating a *circle by swallowing her own tail, denoted eternity and the soundless sea in Egyptian art. A classical Mediterranean chthonic symbol for the fertility and curative powers of mother goddesses like *Demeter, and the *wisdom associated with virgin goddesses

such as *Athena. The serpent also signified the seasonal death and rebirth of *Persephone. For the Hebraic tradition, the serpent was the king of the beasts who walked upright but whose jealously of Adam, especially of his relationship with *Eve, caused him to bring about the fall of humanity. According to the *Old Testament, the serpent tempted (tricked) *Eve into eating the forbidden *fruit, and thereby was cursed by God to crawl on the ground (Gn 3). The Talmud recorded that the serpent had sexual knowledge of *Eve, and thereby the descendants of Adam and Eve were born in filth. The staff of Moses was transformed into a serpent that swallowed the snakes of Pharaoh's priests (Ex 4:2–4). The Brazen Serpent fashioned by Moses was a foretype of the Crucifixion (Nm 21:8). In western Christian art, the serpent signified the evil tempter of the Garden of Eden who was depicted as a reptile until the mid-twelfth century, when it became a composite figure of a serpentine body and tail with a female head, and in later *medieval and *renaissance art, a female head and torso. The serpent was an *attribute of George of Cappadocia, *Margaret, Benedict of Nursia, John the Evangelist, and Patrick. A serpent entwined around a *cross denoted the Crucified Christ, while a serpent with an *apple in its mouth encircling the *globe represented human sinfulness overcome by the *Immaculate Conception.

Sešat. From the Egyptian language for "she who presides over the house of records." Egyptian goddess of literature and of writing. Sešat's chief responsibility was to write the history of Thoth as the god of wisdom. As queen of builders and patron of the library, Sešat was accountable for the care and preservation of books and thereby, of history and wisdom. She recorded the story of each pharaoh noting the years and events of his reign, and supervised his jubilees. In Egyptian art, Sešat was portrayed as a woman wearing a dress made of panther skins and a headdress composed of a seven-pointed star that was surmounted by a *bow or a crescent *moon crowned with two *falcon *feathers. She held a *palm leaf in one hand, and a scribe's palette and writing reed in the other.

Seven. A mystical number of completion and perfection, and a symbol for the *Holy Spirit, grace, and *charity.

Seven Deadly Sins. A popular didactic topic in *medieval and *renaissance art that identified the greatest offenses against God, and paralleled the *Seven Virtues. The Seven Deadly Sins were pride (*superbia*), envy (*invidia*), anger (*ira*), lust (*luxuria*), sloth (*accidia*), avarice (*avaritia*), and gluttony (*gula*). Although there was not a common and regular set of anthropomorphic symbols or personifications for the Seven Deadly Sins, they were most often identified symbolically as female figures engaged in dramatic actions.

Seven Joys and **Sorrows of the Virgin Mary.** These medieval didactic and spiritual topics were represented either as a narrative cycle on medieval *churches or as a unified composition in *renaissance and southern *baroque art. The Seven Joys of the Virgin Mary were the *Annunciation, *Visitation, *Nativity, Epiphany (Baptism), Christ among the Doctors, Resurrection, and *Assumption. The Seven Sorrows of Mary were

Simeon's Prophecy, *Flight into Egypt, Jesus lost in Jerusalem, Meeting Jesus on the Road to Calvary, Crucifixion, *Descent from the Cross, and Entombment.

Seven Liberal Arts. This popular medieval and renaissance didactic topic paralleled the *Seven Virtues and the *Seven Deadly Sins in *medieval art, and the classical Mediterranean gods and goddesses in *renaissance art. Normally personified as women, the Seven Liberal Arts were grammar, dialectic, rhetoric, arithmetic, music, geometry, and astronomy. Grammar was distinguished by her toga and her *attributes of inkpots, *pens, *candlesticks, and scalpel. Rhetoric was depicted as a beautiful female warrior who wore a *helmet and carried a *shield. Dialectic was a delicate woman with an elaborate hairstyle who held a *serpent, a wax *tablet, and a fishhook. Geometry wore a *robe inscribed with *stars and the signs of the *Zodiac, and held a *globe and a pair of compasses. Arithmetic had elegant, long fingers for her computations. Astronomy had great golden *wings and held a book and astronomical instruments. Music led the procession of musicians, poets, goddesses, and graces.

Seven Virtues. This popular medieval and renaissance didactic topic paralleled the *Seven Deadly Sins. The Seven Virtues were prudence (*prudenza*), *justice (*justicia*), *faith (*fides*), *charity (*caritas*), *hope (*spes*), fortitude (*fortitudo*), and temperance (*temperanza*). Normally personified as female figures, the Seven Virtues had a prescribed *iconography. The Theological Virtues were Faith, who held a chalice or a *cross with Peter seated at her *feet; *Hope, who elevated her *hands to *heaven with James Major at her feet; and *Charity, who held *flames and a *heart, and was surrounded by *children, with John the Evangelist at her feet. The Cardinal Virtues were Prudence, often depicted as two-headed, who held a *snake or *mirror with Solon seated at her feet; Fortitude, who held either a *shield, *globe, *column, *sword, or lion's skin, with Samson seated at her feet; Justice, who held *scales, sword, and cross with Trajan seated at her feet; and Temperance, who held two *vases or a sword with Scipio Africanus seated at her feet.

Shai and Renent. Female personifications of *Fate and *Fortune who were deified as goddesses in Egyptian art and mythology. Shai was characterized as "determined fate" and *Renent as "good fortune." Following the *Book of the Dead, Shai was portrayed in Egyptian art as a female figure who stood erect near the pillar of balance where the dead were judged.

Shaktī. From the Sanskrit for "power." Female creative energies personified as the consort to the male creative principle. Shaktī was embodied in the great goddesses of Hinduism: *Durgā, *Lakshmī, and *Pārvati. According to popular religious practices, *Kāmāksī was revered as the supreme Shaktī. In Hindu art, Shaktī was represented by the depictions of Durgā, Lakshmī, Pārvāti, or Kāmāksi, or by any of their symbolic images or *attributes. In Tantric Buddhist art and spirituality, Shaktī was denoted by the symbolic union of the *yoni with the Shiva lingam, or the sexual posture of the *Yab-yum.

Shamrock Leaf. A symbol of the Trinity and an *attribute of Patrick in western Christian art.

Shayba. From the Arabic for "old woman." Spirit of the *Great Goddess resident in the sacred stone in Mecca according to ancient Arabic tradition.

Shears. *Attribute of *Atropos in classical Greco-Roman and *renaissance art, and of *Agatha in western Christian art.

Sheba, Queen of. See Queen of Sheba.

Sheep. A single sheep signified a Christian *soul, while twelve sheep represented the twelve apostles in Christian art.

Sheila-na-gig. Female demon from early Celtic art and mythology. Like the classical figure of *Baubo, the Sheila-na-gig was portrayed as a naked female figure in a display of her pudenda as an apotropaic gesture. Representations of the Sheila-na-gig were standard talismen against evil on the walls of medieval British cathedrals.

Shekhinah. From the Hebrew for "indwelling." Divine presence or immanence of God, often characterized as feminine in nature, in Judaism. According to the *Kabbalah, the Shekhinah was the most overtly female of all the sefirah, or last of the ten sefirot; and was referred to as "the daughter of God." Throughout the Kabbalah's descriptive texts and images of the Shekhinah, sexual imagery was employed and she was interpreted as the archetypal woman mourning at the Wailing Wall. The Shekhinah maintained a harmonious relationship with the preceding six sefirot, so that the world was sustained by their divine energy.

Shell. In Hinduism and Buddhism, the conch shell's spiral design signified the female principle and the womb, and was an *attribute of *Lakshmi, *Saravastī, and *Avalokiteshvara. In Chinese art and mythology, the conch shell denoted royalty. While the *scallop shell identified *Aphrodite (*Venus) in classical *Greco-Roman, *renaissance, and *baroque art; it was the sign of the *pilgrim in western Christian art.

Shelomith. From the Hebrew for "peace." Name of two women in the *Old Testament. A daughter of Dibri, Shelomith and her Egyptian husband were the parents of a son punished for his impiety by stoning (Lev 24:11). Shelomith was also the name of a daughter of Zerubbabel of the tribe of Judah and leader of the return from the Babylonian exile (1 Chr 3:19). Both women were rare topics in western Christian art, but were included as proper Jewish matrons in the narrative cycles of the Old Testament in *medieval art.

Shibboleth. From the Hebrew for "ear of corn." Originally the sacred image revealed during the ceremonial rites associated with *Astarte and *Demeter as goddesses of fertility. Identified as a sign of Baal, the shibboleth represented the *hieros gamos that resulted in a plentiful harvest. As an unpronounceable word, shibboleth became a secret code among the tribes of Israel in the *Old Testament (Jdgs 12:6).

Shield. *Attribute of *Artemis (*Diana), *Athena (*Minerva), and *Chastity in classical Greco-Roman and *renaissance art, and of *Joan of Arc in western Christian art.

Shin-Mu. From the Chinese for "Mother of Perfect Intelligence." Ancient Chinese mother goddess famed for the miraculous conception of her first-born son. Following this extraordinary pregnancy, Shin-Mu was transformed into a Great Mother birthing over thirty thousand creatures. The characterization of her without a vagina and as a perpetual virgin mother eventually permitted identification with *Mary.

Shintoism. From the Japanese for the "way of the *kami* (divine presences)." Ancient and cohesive religious traditions based upon the interpretation of ancient mythology and reevaluation of folk ways in Japan. As both cultic ritual practices in shrines and an attitude towards the sacrality of nature, Shintoism was an indigenous religious heritage of the Japanese people and became centered on the creation myth of the islands of Japan and the descent of the emperor from *Amaterasu Omikami. With the eventual introduction of Buddhism and Chinese religions into Japan, Shintoism established a priestly hierarchy, formalized its rituals, and codified cultic practices.

Ship. Worldwide symbol for journey. In Egyptian art and mythology, a ship was a classical symbol for the transition from one stage of life to another. It was the imaginative, visual, and poetic metaphor for rites of passage. The ship was a symbol for the *church in Christian art. The biblical foundation of the association between a ship and the church was Noah's Ark (Gn 6:11–8:19), and the Stilling of the Water (Mt 14:22–33; Mk

6:45–52; Lk 6:15–21). Among other early church fathers, Tertullian and Ambrose employed the metaphor of the ship to describe or characterize the church. A ship was an attribute of *Mary, *Mary Magdalene, and *Ursula.

Shrew. According to Herodotus, *History* (Book II), the shrew was sacred to the Egyptian goddess, *Buto, and symbolized protection and rebirth.

Sibylline Books. Collection of prophecies about the future of the human race as found in the nine (ten) *books ascribed to the *Sibyl of Cumaea and preserved in the Temple of Jupiter Capitolinus in Rome. These books were consulted by the High Priests of Rome during those states of emergency as defined by the Senate. According to tradition, the original books were destroyed in a fire in 83 B.C.E. but were later replaced and transferred for safekeeping to the Temple of Apollo on the Palatine Hill on the order of the Emperor Augustus. The Sibylline Books were believed to have been finally destroyed by decree of the Christian general, Stilicho, in 405.

Sibyls. Oracular priestesses of antiquity each of whom made a pronouncement about Jesus Christ or *Mary. Famed for their powers to see the future in states of ecstasy or trance, the Sibyls were paralleled to the male *prophets of the *Old Testament in *medieval and *renaissance art. Each Sibyl was reported to have made at least one recorded prophecy that related to Jesus Christ; thus, the Sibyls represented the fact that the classical, or, pagan, world had a vision of the Messiah. In classical Greco-Roman, early Christian, *medieval, and

*renaissance art, the Sibyls were portrayed as extremely old female mortals identified by their *attributes. The Delphic Sibyl was denoted by her attribute of the *crown of thorns as she forecast the Mocking of Christ. The European Sibyl held a *sword signifying her prophecy of the Massacre of the Innocents, the *Flight into Egypt, and Christian missions to the Gentiles. The Agrippine Sibyl's *whip foretold the Flagellation, while the Hellespontic Sibyl's *nails and a *cross anticipated the Crucifixion. The Phrygian Sibyl's *banner and cross prophesied the Resurrection, and the Samian Sibyl's cradle and *rose predicted that the Messiah would be born among the lowly. The Cumean Sibyl held a bowl and a *sponge for her omens of the Crucifixion while the Libyan Sibyl's lighted taper suggested that the Messiah would be the light of the world. The Persian Sibyl's *lantern foretold the birth of Jesus while the Erythrean Sibyl's *lily predicted the *Annunciation to Mary. The Cumean Sibyl was distinguished by her *cornucopia, which predicted that a human mother would nurse her divine son, and the Tiburtine Sibyl's severed *hand signified the Betrayal of Christ. Perhaps the two most famous Sibyls were the Erythraean Sibyl whose prophecies prefigured the Annunciation, and the Tiburtine Sibyl who foretold at the moment of the Nativity the virgin birth of a king who would be greater than Augustus.

Siduri Sabitu. Legendary proprietress of the alehouse at the edge of the world (*Epic of Gilgamesh*). Siduri Sabitu attempted to dissuade the heroic Gilgamesh from his quest for immortality in order to enjoy his earthly life.

Sieve. A symbol of virginity and truth. The sieve was the *attribute of mortal and legendary women famed for their integrity and/or their virginity, such as *Chastity, *Tuccia, and Elizabeth I.

Sif. Germanic goddess of vegetation. This legendary wife of Thor was identified by her golden hair, which signified the silks of the golden grain.

Sigyn. Legendary wife of Loki in German mythology. As a symbol of marital devotion, Sigyn protected her husband by collecting in a *bowl the poisonous venom dripping from the *snakes seated above Loki's head, which was the punishment for his involvement in Balder's death.

Sikhism. From the Sanskrit for "a learner." Religious tradition of northern India established by the sixteenth-century Guru Nanak who proclaimed monotheism and the need for loving devotion to the formless and nonanthropomorphic deity. Religious exercises and devoted meditation on the divine name resulted in direct experience of God. The Sikh holy scriptures, known as the *Adi Granth*, presented the teaching of the Gurus including opposition to idolatry, the caste system, a hierarchy of priests, and elaborate rituals; while the *Rahit Maryada* was the definitive code for spirituality and ethics. By the late seventeenth century, the tenth and final guru, Govind Singh, established the characteristic Sikh identity which included the initiatory rituals, the taking of the name Singh, the wearing of white turbans, preservation of long hair and beards, and the ever present dagger of the military fraternity known as the Khalsa.

Siliwe Nazarata. Indonesian goddess of life and dweller on the moon. Siliwe Nazarata was the wife of the creator god, Lawalangi.

Silver (as a color). Symbolic of glory, innocence, purity, joy, and virginity.

Silver (as an element). Tested by fire, this precious metal signified chastity and purity.

Sipe Gyalmo. From the Tibetan for "queen of the world." Tibetan Bon goddess. In Tibetan art, Sipe Gyalmo was identified as a three-eyed and six-armed woman holding her *attributes of a *sword, *banner of victory, royal sunshade, swastika, skull-bowl, and trident. She was normally represented riding on a red mule.

Sirani, Elisabetta (1638–65). Bolognese painter famed for her depictions of heroic women. Daughter of the minor painter, Giovanni Andrea Sirani, Elisabetta studied music, the Bible, classical Greco-Roman mythology, and the lives of the saints as well as art. Stylistically, her paintings and engravings show the influence of the Italian *baroque painter, Guido Reni. A prodigy, she completed over one hundred ninety paintings before her premature death at the age of twenty-seven, reputedly from poison. The financial support of her family, Elisabetta established her own atelier specifically for women students. Renowned for her religious, allegorical, and mythological themes, she completed several major public commissions including a *Baptism of Christ, Saint Anthony of Padua*, and a version of the *Repentant Magdalene*. Elisabetta is best remembered for her feminist presentations of three classical heroines: *Porcia Wounding Her Thigh, Timoclea,* and *Judith Triumphant.*

Siren. A mythical female creature who was either half *bird or half *fish and half female, and gifted with the power of bewitching song. The siren was capable of charming a man to sleep with her music in order to destroy him. Most often, she was reputed to have enchanted passing sailors with her song and then, like a demon of death, sucking their blood. The only sailors known to survive the charms of the sirens were the Argonauts who were protected by Orpheus, and Odysseus and his companions who were cautioned by *Circe to put wax into their ears so they could not hear. According to medieval legends, *Eve was charmed by a siren in the *Garden of Eden to eat of the forbidden *fruit. In classical Mediterranean art, the sirens were common figures on funerary monuments and symbolized mourners; as such they were assimilated into early Christian art as signs of the Resurrection. In classical Greek art, the sirens were characterized as beautiful maidens like the *Muses; while on classical Roman *sarcophagi, they were depicted as vampirelike tomb spirits who as servants of Hades and *Persephone led the souls of the dead to the underworld. In early Christian art, Odysseus was the classical foretype of the virtuous man who was not tempted by sensuous pleasures into mortal pleasures, or as the wise man not deceived by false doctrines or heresies. In Asian art, the sirens assimilated the characteristics of the *Harpies and *Ceres as embodiments of the sensuality and allurement of this world.

Sister. Women religious who take "simple vows" and thereby are not committed to the office of prayer as the focus of their daily lives. Sisters were deeply involved in the everyday work of the church in the world, such as health care, social welfare, education, and missionary work. However, they are not necessarily affiliated with a religious house. *See* Nun.

Sistrum. Egyptian musical instrument common to both ancient rituals and iconography. This rattlelike instrument had a handle formed from the head of *Hathor with *cow's ears and a horseshoe-shaped metal frame that had loose crossbars. The sound of the sistrum frightened away the demons and other evil spirits. It was an *attribute of *Bastet, *Hathor, *Isis, and *Nephthys.

Sītā. From the Sanskrit for "furrow." Incarnation of the Hindu goddess, Lakshmi. A wife of Rāmā, Sītā was abducted by the King of Raksos (Rāvana) and following her release became mother earth.

Sītalā. From the Sanskrit for "the cool one." Bengali goddess of smallpox. In Indian art, Sītalā was depicted as an ugly woman who rode a *donkey and carried a switch.

Sitātapatrā. Powerful protector of *Avalokiteshvara's white parasol. An esoteric female deity, Sitātapatrā was portrayed in *mandalas, and had two forms: a normal female body or one with three or four heads and six to eight arms. In both manifestations, she held a series of Tantric symbols and a white parasol.

Six. A mystical number of creation (the six days) and perfection. Six signified mercy, justice, love, divine power, majesty, and *wisdom. It was the sum of three and three, the number of the Trinity in western Christian art.

Skadi. From the Old English for "shade." Ancient Celtic and Teutonic goddess of death and the underworld. The destructive manifestation of the Goddess, Skadi was characterized as bathing in the blood of her victims and imaged as a dark female figure often decorated with a necklace of skulls or penises.

Skeleton. A symbol for death. A skeleton with a *scythe or *hourglass denoted the transitory nature of human life. In western Christian art, the skeleton was found in depictions of the Last Judgment, *Dance of Death, *Danse macabre, and the penitential *saints (David, *Mary Magdalene, Peter, and *Jerome).

Skull. A symbol of the transitory nature of human life and material wealth. A skull was an *attribute of hermit and penitential *saints including Paul, *Jerome, *Mary Magdalene, Peter, and *Francis of Assisi. As a sign of vanity and death, a skull was an integral element to pictorial compositions of the memento mori and *vanitas, and was an attribute of Melancholia. Placed below (or beneath) a *cross, a skull and crossbones denoted the medieval legend that the *cross of Jesus was placed on the grave of Adam.

Sky. A symbol for the heavenly realm, the home of God the Father and the heavenly hosts of *angels and *saints in western Christian art.

Sloth. Female embodiment of one of the *Seven Deadly Sins. Characterized by physical or mental illness or *melancholia, Sloth was represented as a woman either dozing or daydreaming, and accompanied by an *ass or a *pig.

Smashana-Kali. Manifestation of *Kālī as protector of places of burial and/or cremation. As Smashana-Kali, she was served by the *dakinis who nursed the dying and supervised the rites of death and burial. Her emblem was the eight-petaled *lotus inscribed with multiple inverted triangles simultaneously signifying a vagina and rebirth.

Smoke. An ambiguous symbol for all things transitory and ephemeral, vanity, the anger and wrath of God, and prayers and petitions to God the Father in Christian art.

Snail. According to Buddhist tradition, the visual or verbal image of the snail crawling over broken matter signified the transcience of earthly power. An ambiguous symbol in Christian art, used either to represent laziness and sinfulness or the Resurrection. The snail signified an *attribute of Touch, as one of the Five Senses, and of Sloth, as one of the *Seven Deadly Sins, in *renaissance art and literature.

Snake. A contradictory but worldwide symbol in religious art. As an animal symbol related to solar worship, the shedding of the snake's skin signified death and rebirth. According to its nature, it was an earthbound creature and thereby identified as a chthonic deity and as an enemy of the sun deities. As the snake's bite resulted in injury or death, the snake was ritually placated with offerings and prayers, and in this mode was denoted as the protector of the deities, or of royal persons. With reference to its phallic form, the snake was a regular offering in ancient fertility rites and as an *attribute of fertility deities. Further, the regular shedding of its skin signified healing, hence its attribution with the healing deities. In Egyptian art and mythology, the snake played a central role in the creation story, and as an attribute of the goddesses *Wadjet, *Meretseger, and *Renenutet. In Mesopotamian art, a pair of entwined snakes in a form of stylized copulation symbolized the divine source of the earth's fertility. Snake-headed female figurines were located in excavations of Ur dating 4000 B.C.E. The image of the snake swallowing its own tail (ouroboros, from the Greek for "tail devouring") signified eternity in classical Mediterranean and *renaissance art. In classical Greece, snakes were interpreted as the reincarnations of the spirits of the dead, most especially in instances of heroic ancestors, and also of rebirth and immortality. The Oracle of Delphi employed snakes in the rituals associated with her prophecies and predictions. According to popular legend, the first king of Attica, Cecrops, had a human body that ended in a snake's tail. *Athena entrusted his daughters with the nurture and upbringing of Erichthonius, a son of *Gaea. The adult Erichthonius took on the form of a snake and drove Cecrops's daughters to madness and to suicide. In classical Greek art, the snake was an attribute of Athena, *Demeter, and *Hecate; and in its negative form, of *Medusa. The snake was associated with the fertility goddesses, such as *Ishtar, of Near Eastern art and mythology. Since the snake characteristically shed its own skin each year, it signified renewal or resurrection in Christian art. Conversely as the *serpent, it played a central role in the Temptation and Fall of Adam and Eve. One of the plagues set upon Egypt was of snakes (Ex 7:8–13). The snake signified Deceit, Earth, Logic, Prudence, Africa, Envy, and Lust in renaissance art. According to popular legend and ritual practices, the snake was a votive image for female infertility in India. In China and Japan, its association with water, especially as the form taken on by river deities, was crucial as was its attribution to the goddess *Benten.

Snow, Our Lady of the. Honorific title for *Mary derived from the fourth-century legendary origin of the Basilica of Santa Maria Maggiore. Invoking the Virgin for counsel on the best employment of his wealth, Giovanni Patricio had a vision of her appearance to him, his wife, and Pope Liberius in which *Mary told him to build a church in her honor where he found snow the next morning. Therefore on August 6, 352, Giovanni, his wife, and the Pope located snow on the Esquiline Hill, and the latter took his crosier to outline a design for the basilica in the snow.

Snowdrop. A floral symbol of purity and hope in western Christian art. One of the earliest of spring flowers, the little *white snowdrop was a medieval *attribute of *Mary.

Sopdet. Egyptian goddess who incorporates Sirius, the dogstar, and thereby was crucial to the flooding of the Nile. As a female personification of life-giving waters and of fertility, Sopdet was assimilated into *Isis.

Sophia. From the Greek for "wisdom." A symbol for the wisdom of the virgin goddesses such as *Athena in classical Mediterranean art, and for the allegorization of wisdom in the *Holy Spirit and *Mary in Christian art. Mistakenly identified as a female *saint. *See also* Sophia, Saint.

Sophia, Saint (second century). The legendary mother of three daughters—*Faith, *Hope, and *Charity—who were female personifications of the three theological *virtues. All four women were reportedly martyred in Rome in the second century. The Greek theological title, *Hagia Sophia*, should correctly be translated as the "Holy Wisdom of God," not as "Saint Sophia."

Sophonisba (Livy, *The History of Rome* 30:15). Female embodiment of virtue. During the Second Punic War, the beautiful daughter of the Carthiginian General Hasdrubal, Sophonisba, fell captive to Rome. Her husband's entreaties convinced her that death was better than any dishonor Sophonisba might encounter during her captivity. Thereby, she willingly drank poison. A popular topic in classical Roman and *renaissance art, she was represented as a beautiful and proper matron who with great dignity received and/or drank a cup of poison.

Soteira. From the Greek for "female savior." An epithet of *Persephone as the bride of Hades.

Soul. This immaterial principle proper to each human separated from the physical body at death. In Christian art, the soul was signified by either a small winged figure (usually female) or a *dove.

South. One of the four cardinal points and a symbol both for light and warmth, as well as the *New Testament, in particular the Epistles.

Sparrow. A bird symbolic of *Aphrodite and *Venus. An avian symbol for the lowly (that is, the multitudes), who were nurtured and protected by God the Father (Mt 10:29; Lk 12:6) in western Christian art. The sparrow was an *attribute of *Dominic and *Francis of Assisi.

Spear. Weapon signifying battle, the hunt, or spiritual ardor in religious art. The *spear was an *attribute of the *Shakti, *Izanami-ni-mikoto, and *Teresa of Avila.

Speculum Humanae Salvationis. Latin for *The Mirror of Human Salvation.* Illustrated textbook developed from the iconographic method of *Old Testament foretypes prefiguring events in the lives of Jesus Christ and *Mary. Initially developed by the Dominican friar, Ludolph of Saxony, in a Latin version of 1324, translations appeared soon thereafter. Fifteenth-century *block-book editions were influenced on the Christian symbolism employed in stained glass, sculpture, painting, and tapestry.

Spes. From the Latin for "hope." Roman female personification of Hope and the goddess of gardens. Spes was represented as a young girl carrying flowers of grain in classical Roman art.

Sphinx. From the Greek for "the strangler." Fabulous creature composed of a

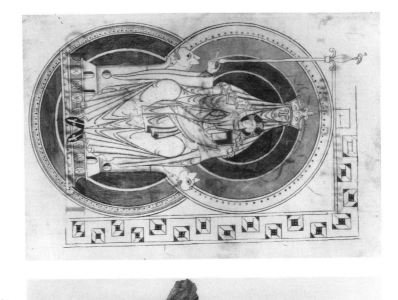

88. *Mary as Sophia on the Lion Throne*
89. *Sphinx*
90. Upper Rhenish Master, *Mary Spinning*

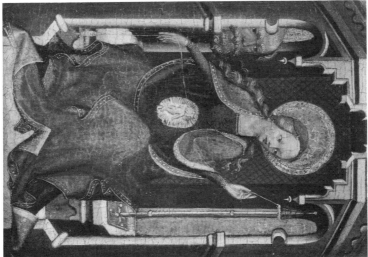

lion's body and a human head, or occasionally the head of a hawk or of a ram. According to legend, this daughter of Typhon and Echidna was a demon of death who sat at a crossroad and only permitted passage to those who could answer her riddles, while those who could not were swallowed. The sphinx was an emblem of sovereign power in Egypt, thereby a symbol of the Pharaoh. Bearded, male-headed sphinxes guarded the front of Egyptian temples. The female-headed sphinxes of Syrian art traveled to Crete and entered classical Greek art. Popular as a funerary or votive offering, the sphinx was characterized by its canine body with a *snake's tail, birdlike wings, lion's paws, and woman's head. According to Greek mythology, the sphinx was ordered by *Hera to stand guard at the gates of Thebes and the marketplace to quiz every person passing by until Oedipus answered her question and the grief-stricken sphinx plunged to her death.

Spider. Symbol of those deities who spin and weave human destinies like a spider's web. In Egyptian art, the spider was an *attribute of Neith who wove the universe and for whom mummy wrappings were sacred. In classical Greek art and mythology, *Athena, *Arachne, and the *Moirai were connoted by the spider. A spider on a thread signified good fortune coming from heaven in Chinese art, while the spider produced the "five potions" of Chinese folk medicine. Tsuchi-Gumo was the famed malevolent earth spider of Japanese mythology. The spider was a symbol of the *Devil and evil in western Christian art.

Spindle, spinning, spinning wheel. A symbol of the gestation of an idea or new life. The spindle or distaff was an *attribute of *Athena as the virgin goddess of wisdom, war, and weaving; *Clotho one of the three Fates of classical Greco-Roman mythology who spun the thread of life; and *Mary. In byzantine *iconography, the Virgin Annunciate was depicted with a spindle in her *hands to signify both her task of weaving a sacred cloth for the Temple and the gestation of new life inside her womb. *See also* Distaff.

Spiral. Widespread sign of fertility and birth. The spiral was a customary sign for the womb, and thereby of gestation and birth. As a design motif on funerary art, the spiral connoted rebirth. In Egyptian art, the double spiral identified *Meshkenet, simultaneously the birth brick and the goddess of childbirth. In its visual allusion to a coiled snake, the spiral was a line of life.

Sponge. An Instrument of the Passion in western Christian art.

Square. A symbol of the *earth and earthly things in western Christian art.

Square halo. An *earth-connected symbol that signified in western Christian art that the person being depicted was alive at the time the painting or sculpture was made.

Squirrel. A symbol of avarice and greed. The red squirrel was a sign of the Devil in western Christian art.

Śridevi. Terrifying goddess of Tibetan Buddhism, and tutelary goddess of the Dalai Lama. According to tradition, Śri-

91. Sabina von Steinbach, *Ecclesia*

92. Sabina von Steinbach, *Synagoga*

devi oversaw the judgment of the dead and kept records of human sins. In Tibetan Buddhist art, she was portrayed as a beautiful woman with an eye in her forehead, mounted on a mule, and holding a skull bowl in her left hand.

Staff. A symbol for power, magic, authority, identity, hermits, and *pilgrims in religious art. Among the Buddhist traditions, there were two symbolic staffs: the staff of wisdom signified the infinite treasure of the wisdom of the Buddha, and the beggar's staff had several metal rings across the top that chimed to announce the arrival of the holy beggar. The staff was an *attribute of James Major, *Ursula, Raphael the Archangel, Philip, John the Baptist, Roch, Christopher, and *Jerome in Christian art. A flowering staff signified either Aaron or Joseph (of Nazareth). A bishop's staff or *crosier signified his role as the shepherd of his flock. A staff in the *hand of Jesus Christ represented his role as the Good Shepherd.

Staff, Budding or **Flowering.** A symbol of prayer and God's favor, and an *attribute of Aaron and Joseph (of Nazareth) in Christian art.

Stag. Sacred animal of Indo-European traditions. The stag was an *attribute of *Artemis and *Diana in classical Greco-Roman and *renaissance art.

Star. Stellar symbols signified deities in religious art. *Ishtar was identified with the eight-pointed star known as the planet *Venus. The Egyptian goddesses—*Sothis, *Seshat, and *Nut—had stellar *attributes. The star was an astronomical symbol for divine guidance or an epiphany in Christian

art. The starry sky signified Abraham's progeny (Gn 22:17). In western Christian art, there was the Star of David, Star of Bethlehem, Star of the Sea, and a series of twelve stars that represented the twelve tribes of Israel, the twelve apostles, the *crown of the Queen of Heaven, and the *Immaculate Conception. The star was an *attribute of *Dominic, *Thomas Aquinas, and Nicholas of Tolentino.

Starfish. An aquatic symbol for the Holy Spirit and *charity. An *attribute of *Mary, who as the *star of the *sea (Stella Maris) guided Christians through the rough waves and storms of faith.

Steinbach, Sabina von (fl. 1225–40). Medieval woman sculptor. The daughter of the sculptor, Erwin von Steinbach, Sabina was trained in his studio. Following her father's death, she completed his work on Strasbourg Cathedral. She was credited with the design and execution of a series of angels and Sibyls, and most particularly for her images of *Synagoga and *Ecclesia. Despite contemporary thirteenth-century attempts to suggest that she was the patron not the artist of these works, recent research has confirmed her historical authenticity.

Stella Maris. From the Latin for "star of the sea." A prevalent epithet of mother goddesses including *Aphrodite, *Astarte, *Ishtar, *Isis, and *Venus, thereby foretypes of *Mary in Christian art.

Stigmata. Plural of stigma meaning "mark." These marks signified the five wounds of the Crucified Christ. The stigmata appeared miraculously upon the bodies of certain extraordinary persons associated with devotion to the Passion of Jesus Christ, such as *Francis of Assisi, *Catherine of Siena, and *Catherine of Genoa.

Still Life. This replacement motif for traditional western Christian art developed in the seventeenth-century Dutch and Flemish art. Ostensibly, the still life concentrated upon the representation of a grouping of natural objects such as *flowers, *fruits, *vegetables, or foods. Early still lives were either symbolic or allegorical in theme. Those that were symbolic emphasized the transient quality of material objects and the inevitability of death. The most common symbolic still lives were the *vanitas and the *memento mori. Allegorical still lives developed from what had previously been details of flowers, fruits, vegetables, or other natural objects in fifteenth- and sixteenth-century western Christian art, such as the *vase of flowers in *Annunciation or *Nativity scenes.

Stones. Geological symbols for resolution and strength. According to Egyptian art and legend, the hardness and immutability of the stone was a manifestation of absolute being in contrast to human frailty and finitude. They were symbols of eternity and immortality. Stone(s) held by penitential *saints, such as *Jerome, *Mary Magdalene, and Barnabas, denoted mortification of the flesh in western Christian art. As a sign of his martyrdom, stones are an *attribute of Stephen.

Stork. A migratory bird symbolic of piety, prudence, chastity, and vigilance in western religious art, and of longevity in Chinese art. As a harbinger of spring, the stork was associated with *Hera and *Juno as goddesses of marriage and childbirth in classical Greco-Roman and *renaissance art; and with the *Annunciation (and hence with the universal delivery of babies) in western Christian art. According to classical legend and the medieval *bestiaries, the stork protected and cared for its aged parents, and became a symbol of filial piety and devotion. According to the *Physiologus, the stork as a slayer of *serpents signified Jesus Christ.

Strawberry. A botanical symbol for *Mary in her sweetness, purity, and righteousness. The blood-red fruit signified Jesus Christ and the Christian *martyrs. The trefoil leaves of the strawberry plant represented the Trinity, while the five-petaled blossom the wounds of Christ. A combination of strawberries and *violets denoted the true humility of the spiritual and righteous believers.

Strigae. From the Latin for "she who screeches." Roman birdlike demons, or old women, who stole babies. Also identified as the offspring of the *Harpies, the Strigae were characterized as vampirelike birds who shrieked over infants in their cradles and then fell upon the infant to suck his or her blood. Apotropaic measures, such as threshold amulets or blessings, were deemed necessary in classical Rome to circumvent the entry of the strigae in an infant's nursery.

Stylus. Writing instrument *attribute of the Greek *Muses *Calliope and *Clio, in classical Greco-Roman and *renaissance art.

Succubus. From the Latin for "to lie under." Female demon who besets a man sexually while he sleeps to conceive a demon child and to pollute his future semen, which can be cleansed by special morning prayers. Those women on trial as witches were identified as "the devil's succubus."

Sul. Celtic goddess worshiped in Bath, and whose eternal fire burned in her temple. Sul was assimilated into *Athena.

Sun. The source of light, heat, and energy, the sun represented spiritual illumination and glorification in religious art. Typically, solar deities were male as lunar deities were female. The major exception to this rule was *Amaterasu Omikami, the Shinto sun goddess. The sun was a symbol for Jesus Christ (Mal 4:2) and for *Mary as the *Woman Clothed with the Sun (Rv 12:1) in Christian art. The sun and the moon signified the passage from night into day at the *Nativity and from day into night at the Crucifixion. The sun was an *attribute of *Thomas Aquinas.

Sunflower. A floral symbol for the Christian *soul in search of Jesus Christ (as the *sun) in western Christian art.

Sun Goddess. Oriental or Asian modality of the *Great Goddess. In western art and mythology, sun deities were male and moon deities were female, with the singular exception of Scandinavia where the sun was female and the moon male. However in the eastern traditions, the sun was female and the moon male. Sun goddesses included *Aditi, *Amaterasu Omikami, and *Mārīcī.

Susanna. From the Hebrew for "lily." According to the Roman canon of the *Old Testament, Susanna was the beautiful wife of Joachim, a prominent member of the Diaspora Jewish community in Babylon. One afternoon as she walked through her husband's garden, Susanna decided to bathe and sent her handmaidens for her bathing oils. After they returned, Susanna entered the *water as the servants departed to leave her in solitude. She was then accosted by two elders who were infatuated with her beauty. They threatened to bring false witness against her and accuse her of adultery with an unnamed youth. Despite the imminent danger of death by stoning (the penalty for adultery), Susanna refused the elders' demands that she have sexual relations with them, and called out for her servants. The elders then unjustly accused her of adultery and brought false witness against her in the courts. Found guilty of adultery, Susanna was sentenced to death by stoning. As Susanna approached the place of judgment, the young boy *Daniel cried out in her defense. All present returned to court where Daniel interrogated each elder separately and proved they had lied against Susanna. Her innocence was glorified and the elders were punished. Prefiguring *Mary, the chaste Susanna became a paradigm of wifely virtues and an example of God's divine intervention on behalf of the innocent and the just. In earliest Christian art, Susanna signified the triumph of innocence and was symbolized by a *lamb between two *wolves (the elders). Narrative figural compositions emphasized the trial in which the young prophet Daniel defended Susanna from unjust accusation. Since she had placed her trust in God, *Augustine characterized

Susanna as the epitome of wifely virtue and Christian womanhood as opposed to *Lucretia, who committed suicide to protect her honor and the honor of her family. In *medieval art, the trial sequence was emphasized, as Susanna was interpreted both as a foretype of Mary and an example of legal justice. In *renaissance and *baroque art, the emphasis in depictions of the Susanna story shifted to representations of the *bathing scene. During the seventeenth century, Susanna was described as more virtuous than Lucretia, and as the appropriate model for Christian women as honorable wives and mothers in the moralizing prints and engravings popular in Protestant countries.

Swallow. A regular avian signifier of spring and thereby of new life or rebirth in religious art. The swallow was a popular harbinger of the spring in Chinese art; while in Japanese art, it was a bird symbolic of infidelity because of its practice of changing its mate on a regular basis. A common motif in Egyptian funerary art, the swallow represented the deceased's desire to be transformed into a bird in order to permit easy entry through the gates of the underworld into new life. It was also an *attribute of *Isis in her search for Osiris. In classical Greco-Roman and *renaissance art, the swallow connoted *Aphrodite and *Venus. It was an avian symbol for the Incarnation and the Resurrection in western Christian art.

Swan. Avian symbol of magical power, prophecy, enchantment, and transformation in religious art. According to the Hindu tradition, the *asparases were modulated into swans; while in Norse mythology, the *Valkyries became swans in order to accompany Odin into battle. In classical Greco-Roman and *renaissance art, the swan was an *attribute of *Aphrodite, *Clio, *Erato, and *Venus, and also signified the disguise of Zeus when he ravished *Leda. It was also an emblem for Music and Touch in renaissance art. The swan was an ambivalent symbol for deceit, death, Jesus Christ, and *Mary in western Christian art. The trumpeter swan only sang immediately before its death (the famed "swan song"), and thereby signified both the crucified Jesus and his last words on the *cross. A white swan was an *attribute of Mary.

Swastika. Ancient and widespread symbol for the sun's journey through the heavens. The swastika signified light, fertility, and good fortune. Its anticlockwise pattern denoted feminine energy, the *Yin, and the *moon. In classical Greek art, the swastika was an *attribute of *Artemis, *Demeter, and *Hera.

Swine. Swine were an animal symbol for gluttony, sensuality, and Satan, and an *attribute of Anthony the Abbot in western Christian art.

Sword. A symbol of military and spiritual warfare and Christian martyrdom. As an *attribute of Ares, *Athena, and the *virtues of fortitude and justice, the sword was assimilated into Christian art as an attribute of James Major, Michael the Archangel, George of Cappadocia, Louis of France, *Cecilia, Paul, *Euphemia, *Agnes, Alban, Cyprian, Peter Martyr, *Lucia, *Catherine of Alexandria, Julian the Hospitaler, Thomas à Becket, Pancras, Martin, Boniface, and *Justina of Padua.

Sword and scales. A symbol of virtue and Justice, and an *attribute of Michael the Archangel.

Sword Lily. *See* Iris (as a flower).

Sybil. From the Latin for "cavern dweller." Roman form of *Cybele as both a Great Mother and an oracular spirit. Variant spelling of *Sibyl. *See also* Sibylline Books.

Sycamore. Celestial tree of Egyptian art and mythology. The sycamore was sacred to the Egyptian goddesses *Hathor, *Isis, and *Nut. In eastern and western Christian art, it was a referent to the *Rest on the Flight into Egypt.

Synagoga. This blindfolded or veiled allegorical female figure represented the unbelief of *Judaism in *medieval art. She was contrasted to *Ecclesia, who was wide-eyed.

Synagogue. The place of assembly for the Jewish community, a House of Prayer, for religious, educational, and social functions. Following the destruction of the Temple of Jerusalem (70), the synagogue became the primary meeting place for Jewish community throughout the Diaspora.

Syntyche (Phil 4:2). From the Hebrew for "fortunate." One of the two women in the Christian community of Philippi entreated by Paul to stop quarreling. A rare topic in western Christian art, Syntyche was represented as a proper matron engaged in a verbal debate with *Euodia in the narrative cycles of Paul.

Syrinx. Virginal mountain nymph and hunter in Greek mythology. During her legendary pursuit by the god Pan, Syrinx invoked the deities to be transformed into a reed. Later the grieving suitor heard the musical sound of the reed, and proceeded to cut the reeds into uneven lengths with which to create his syrinx or panpipes.

T

Tabitha (Acts 9:40–42). From the Aramaic for "gazelle." Early Christian whose resurrection encouraged conversions in Joppa. A devout and pious woman famed for her *charity, Tabitha died. Following the traditions of burial, her body was cleansed and anointed; and then laid out for a final viewing by her sorrowing friends. Two men sought out Peter and brought him to the upper room where Tabitha's body was being mourned by a group of wailing women. Peter prayed, and then told Tabitha "rise." The previously believed-to-be-deceased woman sat up and opened her eyes. A rare topic in Christian art, the story of Tabitha was included in the narrative cycles of apostolic miracles in *byzantine and *medieval art.

Tabiti. Scythian goddess of fire and queen of the animals. Portrayed as a "great goddess," Tabiti was characterized as being winged and surrounded by *animals. She was assimilated to the Roman goddess *Vesta.

Tailtice. Irish female deity as the embodiment of tellurian and natural forces. According to tradition, Tailtice participated in the festival known as *Lugnasad*, or the espousal of the god Lug, which was an Irish form of the *hieros gamos*.

Tait. Egyptian goddess of linen weaving. Tait was associated with *Isis, especially in her creation of swaddling cloth for the burial of Osiris.

Tamar (Gen 38). In the *Old Testament, two women were called Tamar, the daughter-in-law of Judah and the sister of Absalom. The lesser known figure was the childless widow of the two elder sons of Judah. According to Jewish law, she should have become the wife of Judah's surviving son. When her father-in-law refused her her right, Tamar disguised herself as a *prostitute, and deceived him into having sexual relations with her (Gn 38:6–11, 13–30). The daughter of King David, the beautiful Tamar was lusted after by her half-brother Amnon. He lured her into his bedchamber under false pretenses of illness, raped her, and then with loathing, sent her away. Tamar's brother Absalom avenged her rape and mistreatment (2 Sam 13). When Tamar was concealed by Satan, Gabriel came to her rescue. She was rewarded for her trials and tribulations by becoming an ancestor of the Messiah.

Tanit. Manifestation of the Great Goddess in the art and mythology of Carthage. Associated with *Aphrodite, *Astarte, *Ashtoreth, *Athena, *Juno, and *Venus, Tanit was virginal, maternal, and lunar. The priestesses who served her at the Shrine of the Heavenly Virgin where famed astrologers whose prophecies were reputed to rival those of the *Sibyls. In Carthagian iconography, Tanit was represented as a female figure garbed in a full triangular shaped skirt and postured with her arms extended vertically. She wore an image of the full *moon on her head. Tanit was a classical foretype of *Mary.

Tansy. An aster whose spicy fragrant oil had medicinal and magical powers, and thereby became an *attribute of *Mary in *medieval art. According to pious legend, the tansy was consecrated at the *Assumption of the Virgin Mary, and henceforth was used as a protection against magicians, *witches, and the Devil.

Tantra. From the Sanskrit for "to extend." Shamanistic cultic and ritual practices premised on the powerful creative energies of the goddess, and thereby, of woman. Also the name of the sacred scriptures of *Tantrism.

Tantrism. Esoteric tradition of *Buddhism, especially as practiced in Nepal, Tibet, and Bhutan; and premised upon female energy. The basic principle of Tantrism was the fundamentality of female energy as a metaphor for spiritual energy. Male believers could realize this spiritual energy through emotional and sexual union with a woman. However, this form of ritual sexual intercourse was clearly defined by the Sanskrit term *maithuna*, or "controlled sex," during which the man must retain not expel his bodily fluids but learn rather to extend the act of sexual union and to redirect his seminal flow internally so as to increase his level of wisdom. Tantric Buddhist art identified this form of sexual union as the *Yab-Yum, that is, the divine embrace of the mother-father in a state of eternal and blissful union.

Taoism. From the Chinese for "the way." Cohesive Chinese tradition of moral, social, philosophical, and religious values premised upon the sixth-century B.C.E. writings of Lao-tzu known as the *Tao-te Ching.*

Taphath (1 Kgs 4:11). From the Hebrew for "drop." A daughter of Solomon and wife of Benabinadab, a leader of Israel. A rare topic in western Christian art, Taphath was included in the narrative cycles of Solomon and of the royal house of Israel.

Tārā. From the Sanskrit for "she who delivers" and for "star." Most significant Buddhist goddess. According to tradition, Tārā was born from a tear of *Avalokiteshvara. She incorporated the concept and all the characteristics of female divinity. The name, Tārā, connoted the generic term for "goddess." There are twenty-one forms of Tārā represented in Tibetan Buddhist art; they are distinguished by their colored forms. *White Tārā* (Sgrol-dkar, Sitātārā) signified transcendent knowledge and perfect purity. She was portrayed as a seated female figure with flowing hair and dressed as a *bodhisattva. With her right hand she gestured a *mudrā, and in her left she held either a *lotus, a *lute, or a white *serpent. Invoked against snake bites, the White Tārā was a manifestation of *Sarasvatī. *Green Tārā* (Sgrol-ljan, Shyāmatārā) was the original Tārā who conceived and gave birth to all the other Tārās. Associated with Avalokiteshvara, the Green Tārā was represented as a female figure seated on a throne carried by *lions. Dressed as a bodhisattva, she held a blue lotus and was invoked for good fortune. *Yellow Tārā* (Bhrikutī, Bikuchi, Kilingtü eke, Kro-gnyer Ch-ma) was the Tantric form of Avalokiteshvara as the "goddess that frowns." As such, she was a wrathful emanation of Amitābha and a fearsome form of the Green Tārā. The Yellow Tārā had four styles of presentation: a female figure with a third eye and four arms in which she held a lotus and rosary in the right ones, and a trident and a vase in the left; a female figure with three heads and six arms in which she held Tantric symbols; a female figure with four heads and eight arms in which she held a *vajra, a conch shell, a blue lotus, a bow, an elephant skin, and a rope; and finally a seated female figure who held a blue lotus. The *Blue Tārā* (Ekajatā Ugrā Tārā, Ral-gchig-ma) was known as "she who has but one chignon." A ferocious Tārā, she was a fearsome aspect of the Green Tārā who was characterized as a short, stout female figure on the order of a deformed dwarf. Her open laughing mouth revealed a forked tongue and large teeth. She wore a necklace of skulls and a tiger's skin. The Blue Tārā had anywhere from four to twenty-four arms in which she held a variety of *attributes including a chop-

per, a skull cup, a sword, a knife, a blue lotus, and a vajra. She was postured so that her right foot crushed several corpses. The *Red Tārā* (Ku-ru-ku-li, Kurukullā) symbolized the power of love present in the original Tārā. A beautiful female figure, she had eight arms in which she held a bow and arrow, a lasso, and a variety of Tantric attributes. Her crown was composed of skulls with a wheel in the center. The Red Tārā was either seated or in the midst of a dance as her left foot held down Rāhu, the demon-devourer of the sun.

Tašmetu. From the Mesopotamian for "she who hears prayers." Mesopotamian female deity as the female personification of divine accessibility.

Taweret. Egyptian hippopotamus goddess of childbirth and maternity. Taweret was associated with *Hathor, and was identified in the *Book of the Dead* as a protector of the dead. In Egyptian art, she was depicted as a female hippopotamus with large udders. Taweret stood erect with her left paw on the Sa, symbolic of protection. Taweret was represented as papyrus and as the symbol of life preserved as worn by travelers, especially religious pilgrims.

Tcheft. Epithet of *Isis as a goddess of the foods selected for offering to the deities.

Tecla, Saint. *See* Thecla, Saint.

Teeth. An *attribute of *Apollonia in western Christian art.

Tefnut. Egyptian goddess personifying humility and world order. Daughter of the primeval sun god Atum who self-created the primordial couple of Tefnut and Shu, Tefnut represented the power of sunlight. As the wife of Shu, she was mother to *Nut and Geb. In Egyptian art, Tefnut and Shu were portrayed as a pair of *lions; while Tefnut herself was signified by the solar or lunar eye, or as a female figure with the head of a lioness surmounted by a disk or *uraeus, or both the disk and uraeus.

Tellus. From the Latin for "earth." Festival honoring *Tellus Mater, which was celebrated annually on April 15th.

Tellus Mater. From the Latin for "earth" and "mother." Roman goddess invoked against earthquakes, for fertility and marriage, and during the rites for the dead. Tellus Mater was the Roman equivalent of *Gaea. As the goddess of the earth and of the cornfields, Tellus Mater was associated with *Ceres. In classical Greco-Roman art, she was portrayed as a respectable but dominant matron who might be suckling *snakes, a symbolic act signifying healing and the fertility of the earth. *See also* Lust.

Temperance. Female personification of one of the four cardinal virtues. Temperance, like her sister virtues *Justice, *Prudence, and *Fortitude, was a popular topic in *medieval and *renaissance art. She was represented as an erect young woman who poured liquid from one container into another as an act of abstinence from drink. Her *attributes included a pitcher, a torch, a *cloak, a sheathed *sword, and a bridle.

Ten. A mystical number of fulfillment and perfection as in the Ten Commandments and *Ten Bridesmaids in western Christian art. The number ten was a combination of three (signifying the *Trinity or God the Father) and seven (representing Humanity).

Ten Bridesmaids (Mt 25:1–13). One of the better known parables of Jesus Christ. The ten bridesmaids who retired for the night with their lamps awaiting the bridegroom were like the Kingdom of Heaven. When the bridegroom arrived at midnight, the five bridesmaids who had wisely filled their lamps with oil rose and lit them, while the other five bridesmaids who were foolishly unprepared begged for oil to light their lamps. As the wise bridesmaids had no oil to spare, the foolish bridesmaids went in search of oil at midnight. The bridegroom came in and went with the wise bridesmaids, and shut the bedroom *door. The foolish bridesmaids arrived some time later and knocked, but the bridegroom responded that he didn't know them.

Tenenit. Egyptian goddess of beer according to the *Book of the Dead*.

Teresa of Avila, Saint (1515–82). One of only two women named a *Doctor of the Church. This young Spanish woman entered a Carmelite convent against the wishes of her aristocratic but pious parents. An extraordinary devout woman, Teresa began having spiritual visions and conversations during her practice of spiritual exercises. In 1555, she reportedly experienced a "second conversion," which led to her fame as a mystic. As an ascetic reformer she initiated the austere order of the Discalced (barefooted) Carmelites, and was responsible for a resurgence of lay piety and spirituality in Counter-Reformation Spain. She worked with her confessor, *John of the

Cross, to effect a reformed order of Carmelite Monks. An intense and brilliant woman, Teresa recorded her mystical and spiritual experiences with great clarity. Her books, including the *Interior Castle*, became a foundation for postmedieval mysticism. In western Christian art, Teresa was depicted as a tall, physically large woman dressed in the white and brown *habit of the Discalced Carmelites. A popular topic in seventeenth-century southern *baroque art, Teresa was depicted within the context of three major spiritual episodes in her life: her ecstasy, the receipt of the Holy Nail from the Resurrected Christ, and the receipt of the *white *cloak from *Mary and Joseph (of Nazareth).

Teresa of Lisieux, Saint (1873–97). Carmelite nun and spiritual writer. At a young age, Marie François experienced both suffering with the death of her mother and religious devotion. Following her two elder sisters, she entered the Carmelite Convent in Lisieux where she was professed in 1890 and later served as mistress of novices. Suffering from tuberculosis, Teresa dedicated her life to prayer and at the direction of her prioresses, wrote the story of her childhood and then the story of her life in the convent. These two texts were eventually combined into the inspirational autobiography, *Histoire d'une âme (The Story of a Soul)*. Teresa's emphasis on what she called her "little way" of the childlike simplicity of faith as a trust and absolute self-surrender to God accounted for the book's enormous popularity and influence. A rare topic in western Christian art, Teresa of Lisieux was depicted as a fragile young woman dressed in the Carmelite habit and kneeling in a posture of prayer.

Terpsichore. From the Greek for "she who delights in dancing." Greek *muse of solemn and ceremonial dance, and later of lyric poetry. In classical Greco-Roman and *renaissance art, Terpsichore was portrayed as a beautiful young woman in a flowing garment who held a *lyre in her left hand and plucked its strings with a plectrum in her right hand.

Terra Mater. From the Latin for "earth mother." *See* Tellus Mater.

Teteo innan. From the Aztec for "mother of the gods." Aztec goddess of childbirth and child care. Teto innan was identified as the divine warrior in the guise of Quauhcihuatl, or "eagle woman," and as the goddess of love in the guise of *Cihuacoatl or *Tlazalteoth.

Thais. Famed Athenian courtesan and lover of Alexander the Great. According to tradition, Thais pressured Alexander into the incineration of the palace at Persepolis. Following the young emperor's premature death, she became mistress to Ptolemy, the Egyptian pharaoh, to whom she bore two sons.

Thaïs, Saint (d. c. 348). Archetypal reformed prostitute and Christian penitent. The beautiful and illustrious prostitute of Alexandria, Thaïs was brought to Christianity by the holy Bishop Paphnutius. As a public display of her rejection of her previous lifestyle, she dispersed her jewels to the poor, burned her material possessions, and rejected any economic rewards earned from prostitution. She spent the remainder of her life in poverty and penitent prayer living in a cell whose door had a small hole through which Thaïs received a daily ration of *bread and *water. Following the bishop's dream that the reformed prostitute's sins had been absolved, Thaïs died. A rare topic in western Christian art, she was portrayed as a beautiful woman in the act of dispersing her objects of wealth or as a shrunken and haggard figure in a posture of prayer.

Thalassa. From the Greek for "sea." An ancient form of *Aphrodite as a protector of marriage and of sexuality, especially as expressed in marital union.

Thalia. From the Greek for "she who blossoms." Greek *muse of comedy and the light-hearted art of letters. In classical Greco-Roman and *renaissance art, Thalia was portrayed as a beautiful young woman in a flowing garment who held her *attributes of a comic mask, a *wreath of *ivy, and a crooked staff.

Thalna. Etruscan goddess of birth. In Etruscan and later art, Thalna was represented as a beautiful young woman who was clad in voluptuous garments, and often held a newborn infant in her arms.

Thecla, Saint (first century). This first female *martyr converted to Christianity by hearing the *gospel at the *feet of Paul. The story of her conversion and her martyrdom were reported in the apocryphal *Acts of Paul and Thecla*. Having rejected her fiancee, Thecla gained permission to accompany Paul on a dangerous mission after she cut her *hair short and dressed in men's clothing. Although she suffered many tortures, including *flames and wild

*beasts, Thecla survived to become a famed healer. Local physicians believed her curative powers were generated by her *chastity. They sought to defile Thecla in their jealousy but were defeated when a *rock opened up to receive her as she fled from them. According to tradition, she died from old age inside the rock. In western Christian art, Thecla was depicted as either a beautiful young woman, usually in a state of partial undress, who was tied to a *stake with *serpents or *lions at her *feet signifying an attempted execution, or as an old woman dressed in a flowing *mantle holding either a *palm or a *pillar.

Theia. From the Greek for "the divine one." A Titan, wife of Hyperion, and a goddess of light. Theia was the mother of Helios, *Selene, and *Eos in Greek mythology.

Thekla the Nun (ninth century). Byzantine *abbess and poet. A defender of *icons, Thekla the Nun was famed for her poetry in praise of *Mary as *Theotokos*. A rare topic in eastern Christian art, Thekla the Nun was represented as an abbess with her books of poetry.

Themis. Greek goddess of justice, order, and morality. The daughter of Uranus and *Gaea, Themis was a goddess of oracles, most especially of Delphi, and of hospitality. As a wife to Zeus, she was mother to the *Horae and the *Moirai. She was portrayed as a dominant female figure identifiable by her *attributes of the *scales and the *cornucopia.

Thenenet. Epithet for *Isis as the goddess of the underworld.

Theotokos. From the Greek for "God" and "to give birth to." This title was ascribed to *Mary by the Council of Ephesus (431) to distinguish her, her role, and her veneration. As a result of this decree identifying her as the Mother of God or the God-bearer, Mary began to be depicted only with the Child (either as an infant or an adult) in Christian art. The byzantine iconographic types of the Virgin and Child were identified as the Theotokos, and distinguished as to their spiritual or devotional intent by the gestures and postures of Mary and the Child.

Thesan. Etruscan goddess of the dawning of both the day and of new life, that is, of childbirth.

Thesmophoria. Festival sacred to *Demeter. As an annual celebration of the mysterious gifts of agriculture and of life, the Thesmophoria included sacrifices of *pigs, a day of fasting followed by a banquet, ritual ingestion of *pomegranates, and public gatherings of women.

Thet. *Girdle or knot of *Isis in Egyptian art. The thet was a conventional symbol of the uterus with its ligature and the vagina represented by a red stone signifying the blood of life. During the Egyptian burial ceremony, the thet was to be dipped in water and placed around the neck of the deceased.

Thetis. Greek sea goddess and mother of Achilles. In the midst of pursuit by her husband, Peleus, Thetis transformed herself into fire, water, a *lion, a *serpent, and a *fish, but Peleus won the day, so they married. She bore him several children, all of whom she im-mersed in the flames to destroy their mortality and then dispatched them to Olympus to live with the gods and goddesses. About to complete this fiery ritual with her infant son, Achilles, Thetis slipped, dropped her son, and fled off into the sea. Alternatively, she dipped her infant sons into the river Styx, thereby making them invulnerable except for the heel by which the mother held her newborn.

Thirteen. Numerical symbol for faithlessness and betrayal. Thirteen was interpreted as an unlucky or evil omen.

Thisbe (*Metamorphosis* 4:55–166). Beloved of Pyramus in Greek mythology. As childhood sweethearts, Thisbe and Pyramus were forbidden marriage by their parents. They planned a night elopement and agreed to meet by a mulberry tree near a tomb. Thisbe arrived first and as she waited for her beloved, a bloodied lion scared her off and she fled, losing her veil that was chewed by the animal. Pyramus came in time to see the lion departing and found his beloved's bloodied veil. Believing Thisbe to be dead, the erstwhile young lover plunged his sword into his side and died. Thisbe returned to find Pyramus dead, and then killed herself. According to tradition, their blood stained the roots and thereby the fruit of the mulberry tree for all eternity.

Thistle. A botanical symbol for sin or sorrow as in God's curse on Adam (Gn 3:17–18) in western Christian art. A thorny plant, the thistle was also a sign of the Passion and the sufferings of the Christian *martyrs. In the *hands of the Christ Child, the *goldfinch denoted the Passion as the *bird fed on thistles and *thorns.

Thoeris. From the Egyptian language for "she who is great." Hippopotamus goddess of childbirth. A protective deity, Thoeris was represented on beds, headrests, and in the *Book of the Dead. In Egyptian art, she was depicted as a female hippopotamus with her arms and breasts upright. Her *attribute was the sa-loop, an emblem of protection, this torch warded off demons and other evil spirits.

Thomas Aquinas, Saint (c. 1225–74). The "Angelic Doctor" of the *Church and the master systematizer of scholastic theology. A Dominican, Aquinas studied with the leading Dominican scholar Albertus Magnus (Albert the Great) at the University of Paris. Aquinas was identified as the "Prince of the Scholastics" because of his masterful efforts to combine Aristotelian philosophy with Christian theology. The author of many significant theological books, Aquinas's most noted writing was the *Summa Theologica*. He was the patron of universities, centers of learning, and Roman Catholic schools. In western Christian art, Thomas Aquinas was depicted as a short, portly man dressed in a Dominican habit with the *sun embroidered on his chest. His *attributes included a *book, a *lily, a *dove, a *chalice, and an *ox.

Thorn. Symbol for sin, tribulation, and grief. According to early Christian tradition, the thorn was interpreted as a result of the Fall, so that *Mary was described as a "rose without thorns," thus denoting her place in the *paradise garden. An Instrument of the Passion,

the crown of thorns was a parody upon the Roman Emperor's *crown of *roses. The tonsure of a priest or monastic was an allusion to the crown of thorns. *Saints were depicted wearing or holding a crown of thorns as a sign of their martyrdoms, while *Catherine of Siena and *Francis of Assisi wore or held the crown of thorns as a sign of their receipt of the *stigmata.

Three. A mystical number of completion (a beginning, a middle, and an end), and supreme power. An indivisible number, three signified the Trinity (God the Father, God the Son, and God the Holy Spirit), the three days that Jonah lay in the belly of the *whale (*sea monster), and the three days Jesus lay in the *tomb.

Three Marys at the Tomb. *See* Marys, Three, and Marys at the Tomb.

Thyrsus. Long staff that ended in a pine cone entwined with vine leaves. The thyrsus was a sign of the Greek god Dionysus and also of his followers, the *Bacchantes and the *Maenads.

Tiāmat. From the Akkadian for "the sea." Mesopotamian great mother and the female personification of salt water. As the primeval dragonlike monster of the original chaos, Tiāmat was defeated by Marduk, and from her remains he formed the heavens and the earth. According to the Babylonian epic, *The Tale of Gilgamesh*, Tiāmat birthed eleven monsters including the *snake, the bison, and the *lion, which she loosed on the earth in revenge for the killing of Apsu. These monsters were all destroyed by Marduk. In classical Near Eastern art, Tiāmat was characterized

93. *Posthumous effigy of the wife of Jayavarman VII as the divinity Tārā or Prajñāpāramitā, personification of Divine Wisdom.*
94. *The Goddess Thoueris (Thoeris), on a pedestal, holding before her the Symbol of Isis*

95. *Saint Thecla with Wild Beasts and Angels*

96. Eutychides, *Tyché of Antioch*

by depictions of magical incantations and images of protective magic.

Tiara .From the Greek for "headdress." An elegant turban or peaked cap denoting nobility among the Persians; later the ritual headdress of a Jewish high priest. A gem-studden or ornamental headband worn in a woman's *hair above her forehead, the tiara signified nobility, and identified female deities in religious art. The elaborate headpiece composed of three successive crowns surmounted by a cross, the tiara became a symbol of the pope or God the Father in western Christian art.

Tinnit. Supreme goddess of Carthage, virgin and mother, and queen of heaven. Tinnit conferred fertility upon her devotees, and as Dea Caelesis, she had a direct relationship with the moon. She was a classical foretype of *Mary. In classical Mediterranean art, Tinnit was identified by her *attributes of the *pomegranate, *figs, sheaves of wheat, and the *dove. Her emblem was a triangle with horizontal beams of light.

Tirzah (Num 26:33, 27:1, 36:11; Josh 17:3). From the Hebrew for "pleasing." One of the five daughters of Zelophehad who successfully claimed her patrimony before Moses. A rare topic in western Christian art, Tirzah was included as a proper Jewish woman in the narrative cycles of Moses.

Tlaltecuhtli. From the Nahuatl for "earth monster." Female personification of the mystic yet destructive source of the earth including all its geological and botanical growth in Nahuatl and later Aztec art and mythology. Tlaltecuhtli devoured the sun every evening at sunset, retained it overnight in her belly, and then regurgitated it at dawn. She was portrayed as an enormous toadlike creature oftentimes in a squatting posture as she devoured either the sun or a human heart.

Tlazolteotl. From the Nahuatl for "goddess of filth." Nahuatl love goddess, especially in terms of illicit sexual relationships. Tlazolteotl was the mother of the maize god, Cinteoth. Ritual adultery was confined to her priests and priestesses. A patron of midwives, healers, and weavers, she favored black magic and was reputed to absorb the sins of her devotees as a form of ritual purification. In Nahuatl iconography, Tlazolteotl was identified by her cotton earrings and bound forehead, oftentimes with a *spindle whirling in her headdress.

Toad. Amphibian symbol for death, vices of lust, and greed. Related to the *frog, the toad was also a creature of dark and moist places. The toad was an attribute of the Devil.

Toilet. Generic term for a woman's daily preparation with cosmetics, hairdressing, *jewelry, and perfumes. In the classical world, the ritual character of this daily routine of accentuating a woman's beauty and sexuality was interpreted as a recognition of the spirit of the goddess that resided in each woman.

Toilet Scenes. A ritual motif symbolic of the preparation of the goddess for the *hieros gamos. A prevalent theme in classical western art, the toilet scene derived from the Egyptian model of the "Toilet of Hathor" who as the goddess of love and joy was simultaneously the protector of women and the deity who presided over the bridal toilet. Typical components of a "toilet scene" were a beautiful young woman often in a state of partial or total undress with long flowing *hair (which may be being combed or dressed either by the woman herself or by her maidservant), a *mirror, hair-dressing implements, ointment jars and perfume bottles, *jewelry, cosmetic jars and brushes, flowers and/or fruits, a little *dog or *cat, and a maidservant. All these elements have direct relationship to traditional cultural interpretations of being female and of the initiation of a virginal young girl into womanhood. These visualizations signified female generative powers and the cycle of human procreation. Featured in toilet scenes, the varied goddesses of love including *Aphrodite, *Hathor, and *Venus were assimilated into western Christian art as foretypes of *Bathsheba and *Susanna in the *Old Testament. These women sat either facing her own reflection in a *mirror, combing her hair, or arranging her jewels, flowers, or makeup. Oftentimes, these scenes incorporated either a *bath(ing) or a bed. The iconographic motif of *Aphrodite washing her hair can be read as a classical Greek variant of the story. The ritual toilet of both young *virgins and holy women was a religious act signifying the sacred power of sexual intercourse as a terrestrial equivalent of the hieros gamos. In western *medieval art, the toilet scenes was transformed into a secular depiction of the bridal toilet while *renaissance art revealed a "return to mythological roots" given the ascent in popularity to the mythological "Toilet of Venus." By the sixteenth century in western Europe, however, the toilet scene became

a common topos for the artist's portrait of his beloved or for his admiration of female beauty and sexuality. From the eighteenth-century until the present day, the transformation of the sacred toilet of a goddess in advance of her sexual union with a god (or mortal) into the secular topic of the "boudoir painters," as for example in the art of Jean-Honoré Fragonard. This motif served as the foundation for Pablo Picasso's visual meditations upon female beauty and fecundity as found in his painting, *Girl Before a Mirror*. Throughout its artistic transformations and evolution from a sacred and ritual motif into secularized boudoir paintings, the toilet scene remained fundamentally a homage to female beauty, and has served as a visual metaphor for the ambiguity of sacrality and secularity, sexuality and sensuality, reality and illusion, and vanity and contemplation.

Tomb. A symbol for death and/or burial of the dead. In Christian art, the tomb (*sarcophagus) was integral to the *iconography of the Resurrection of Lazarus, the Entombment, and the Resurrection of Jesus Christ.

Tomyris (Herodotus 1:214). Headhuntress and *queen of ancient Asia. Historical queen of the nomadic peoples of central Asia, Tomyris was famed for her role in the death of Cyrus the Great. In the midst of a war, Tomyris's son and the leader of her army invited his opponent, Cyrus the Great, and his army to a feast. The senior general saw his opportunity and grabbed it by slaughtering the queen's army. Disgraced and ashamed, Tomyris's son committed suicide. The anguished queen declared blood vengeance for both the slaughter of her army and the death of her son. She successfully witnessed the death of Cyrus the Great in battle and then demanded that his corpse be brought directly to her. She proceeded to abuse the dead body even to the act of ritual decapitation and then rolled Cyrus's severed head in blood as a sign of her complete revenge. Interpreted as a symbolic act of justice in classic Greco-Roman art and culture, Tomyris's revenge was transformed into a classical foretype of *Mary's triumph over the devil as was Judith's triumph over Holofernes. A popular motif in classical Greco-Roman, *renaissance, and *baroque art, Tomyris was portrayed as a regal queen who was dressed in oriental garments and wore a turban decorated with a crown on her head. She held the severed head of her enemy in her hands as a servant knelt nearby with a blood-filled urn. This image of Tomyris as a female embodiment of *Justice was a popular topic for the art commissioned for the law courts.

Tonacacihuatl. From the Toltec for "queen of our flesh." Aztec goddess of pregnancy and childbirth. Tonacacihuatl and her spouse, Tonacatecutli, transferred souls from heaven into the womb of a pregnant woman.

Tortoise. A common and worldwide symbol in eastern religious art for longevity, endurance, and strength. In Indian art and mythology, river goddesses were characterized as mounted on tortoises. The tortoise was a symbol for chastity and reticence, especially in the *hands of either *Mary or the Christ Child in western Christian art; while in *renaissance art, it signified Touch.

Towel. A symbol for rituals of cleansing, and spiritual purity. A spotless white towel was a symbol of the Virgin Annunciate. A towel and a *basin signified either *Mary or Pontius Pilate.

Tower. Architectural symbol of virginity, vigilance, and inaccessibility. Gateways to Egyptian temples were formed by two identical towers that signified *Isis and *Nephthys as guardians of the sanctuary. A tower denoted *Danaë in classical Greco-Roman and *renaissance art. In western Christian art, the tower was an *attribute of *Barbara, the Virgin Annunciate, and the *Immaculate Conception.

Tree of Jesse. A decorative motif created to display the genealogy of Jesus Christ according to Matthew and Isaiah in western Christian art. In these depictions, Jesse, the father of David, sat or reclined on the ground as a tree grew from his genitals. The *flowers or *fruits of this tree represented the Christ's ancestors, and at the top of the tree was a depiction of *Mary and the Christ Child. This *iconography was introduced into western Christian art in a stained-glass window designed by the Abbot Suger for the Cathedral of Saint Denis, Paris. According to medieval tradition, the Tree of Jesse was a dead *Tree of Life that was resurrected by Christ's blood. In northern *medieval and *renaissance art, the Tree of Jesse had a representation of *Anne, the Virgin, and Child at the top. In southern renaissance art, the tree took on the physical characteristics of a *vine, suggesting eucharistic symbolism.

Tree of Knowledge. Legendary arboreal symbol for the identification of good from evil in the *Old Testament. The *fruit of this tree was believed to provide the consumer with instanteous attainment of this gift of moral distinctions. Planted by God in the *Garden of Eden, the Tree of Knowledge played a central role in the story of the Temptation, Fall, and Expulsion of Adam and *Eve. According to pious legend, the wood from this tree was miraculously preserved and used for the cross upon which Jesus of Nazareth was crucified.

Tree of Life. A decorative motif from Middle Eastern art that signified immortality. In Egyptian art, the Tree of Life was connoted by either a *sycamore or a date *palm tree; and was sacred to the goddesses *Hathor, *Isis, and *Nut. The Tree of Life was depicted as filled with green leaves and flowers; in contrast the Tree of Good and Evil (Tree of Knowledge) was represented as being on the edge of death like humanity after the Fall. According to popular tradition, the Tree of Life was believed to be used for the *cross of Jesus Christ. In western Christian art, the Tree of Life symbolized *paradise and eternal life.

Trees, symbolism of. Symbols for the cycle of life, death, and resurrection in the fullness of the four seasons. As the one of the "fruits of the earth," trees—like *flowers and *plants—contained the seeds for each new and successive generation. As a generic symbol, a tree indicated growth, creative power, and immortality as its vertical thrust signified a link between *heaven and *earth. As a mother goddess, *Ishtar was signified by a sacred tree in Mesopotamian art. In Egyptian art and mythology, trees denoted the sites of origin and of sacred rites, and the abodes of the deities.

*Sycamores and date *palms were sacred to the Egyptian goddesses, *Hathor, *Isis, and *Nut. In Christian art, trees were purely decorative while a specific tree was an integral element of the theological intent of the image; for example, the *oak tree signified God the Father while the evergreen tree symbolized the Resurrected Christ. Trees played a central role in many biblical, apocryphal, and legendary stories including the Temptation and Fall, the trial of *Susanna, the *Annunciation to Mary, and the Entry into Jerusalem. Created on the third day, trees denoted meaning by their physical conditions, so that flourishing and flowering trees represented the positive values of life, hope, holiness, and health while a withering or dead tree suggested the negative values of diminishing powers and death. *See also* Acacia, Almond Tree, Aspen, Cedar, Cherry, Chestnut, Cypress, Elm, Fig Tree, Fir Tree, Hemlock, Holly, Ilex, Laurel Tree, Oak, Olive, Palm Tree, Sycamore, and Willow.

Trefoil. A symbol for the Trinity and an *attribute of Patrick in western Christian art.

Trial of Bitter Waters (Nm 5:11–31). A test devised to gauge the guilt or innocence of a woman accused of adultery according to the Hebraic tradition. According to the apocryphal *Protoevangelium of James* (15:1–4, 16:1–3), the High Priests demanded that *Mary and Joseph (of Nazareth) take the Trial of Bitter Waters to prove their innocence as she was pregnant and had been a temple maid (and thereby in the care of the High Priests). Although rare, depictions of the Trial of Bitter Waters existed in early Christian and *byzantine art.

Mary was represented drinking the bitter herbs; to the amazement of the High Priests, she survived her ordeal without sickness or death. This event became conflated with Joseph's first dream in *medieval art but was rarely depicted after the early medieval period.

Triangle. Worldwide symbol for three-fold Nature in religious art. The equilateral triangle signified gender in Hindu iconography. If the apex was at the base of the triangle, it connoted the *yoni*, or Shiva's *shakti; while the apex at the top of the triangle denoted the Shiva lingam. In classical Greek and Hellenistic art, the representation of the delta, or a triangle positioned with the apex up, was identified as an image of woman, that is, the *eidolon gynaikeion*. According to Tantric Buddhism, the triangle represented the *shri yantra*, or merger of the lingam and yoni; as such it was a contemplative object that released psychic energy and heightened the devotee's consciousness. Triangular-shaped musical instruments were an *attribute of *Erato, the Greek *muse of poetry, in classical Greco-Roman and *renaissance art. The triangle was a geometric symbol for God the Father or the Trinity in Christian art. A triangular *halo was reserved for God the Father.

Tripod. Ancient Greek altar composed of a triangular slab of wood or marble resting upon three legs. The priestess of Apollo at Delphi, better known as the *oracle, sat on a tripod when she received and uttered her sacred communications.

Trivia. Epithet of *Diana and of *Hecate as goddesses of the crossroads.

Truth. Female personification of virtue and honesty. A legendary daughter of Time, Truth was represented in varied forms including a naked woman who held the book in which truth was written or who stood on a globe to signify her superiority to material concerns.

Tryphaena (Rom 16:12). From the Greek for "dainty." One of the two Christian women greeted by Paul in his letter to the Church of Rome. Tryphaena and her sister, Tryphosa, were identified as "workers in the Lord." A rare topic in western Christian art, Tryphaena and Tryphosa were depicted as proper Christian matrons in the narrative cycles of Paul.

Tuccia (Pliny, *Natural History*, 28:12). Legendary *vestal virgin and female embodiment of abstinence. Unjustly accused of adultery, Tuccia defended her innocence by filling a sieve with water and demonstrating that this sieve did not leak. A classical foretype of the Christian virtue of *Chastity and of *Mary, Tuccia was a popular motif for female portraiture indicating the moral virtue of the sitter in classical Greco-Roman and *renaissance art.

Turan. Etruscan goddess of love. In Etruscan and Roman art, Turan was portrayed as a winged great mother figure whose *attributes included the *swan, the *dog, a twig, and a blossom.

Turtledove. An avian symbol for purity. Two turtledoves in a basket were offered by Joseph (of Nazareth) at the *Purification of the Virgin Mary in eastern and western Christian art.

Twelve. A mystical number of maturation or natural fulfillment, as in the twelve months of the year, the twelve disciples, the twelve signs of the *Zodiac, the twelve tribes of Israel, the twelve *prophets, the twelve *Sibyls, and the twelve *stars in the *crown of the *Woman Clothed with the Sun.

Two. A numerical symbol for the humanity and the divinity of Jesus Christ, and the male and the female species of human and animal life.

Tyché. From the Greek for "that which happens." Greek goddess of fate and fortune. In classical Greco-Roman and *renaissance art, Tyché was identified by her *attributes of the helmsman's rudder (as director of fate), the *cornucopia (as bringer of good fortune), and the wheel and the globe (inconstancy and transitoriness, and as Fortuna). In classical Greco-Roman and *renaissance art, she was portrayed as beautiful young woman dressed in long flowing garments, wearing a mural crown, and holding a cornucopia in one hand and the wheel of fortune in the other.

Tyet. Amulet identified with *Isis in Egyptian art and ritual practice. Characterized as the "knot-amulet of red jasper" in the *Book of the Dead, the tyet was installed in the tomb as a sign of the goddess's protection.

U

Ukemochī. Shinto fertility goddess. According to tradition Ukemochī was slain by the moon god, Tsuikiyomi. In Japanese art, she was identified by her *attributes of rice, oats, beans, a *cow, a *horse, and silkworms.

Ūma. Hindu female personification of light, beauty, and the life of heavenly wisdom. In Hindu art and mythology, Ūma was assimilated into Devī, Durgā, and Pārvāti.

Umbilical Cord. Symbol of motherhood, female creative energy, and nurture. The physical cord or connection between fetus and the mother's placenta that thereby provides nourishment and removes waste. This cord is cut at birth and the newborn's fragment forms the navel.

Umilità de Faenza (1226–1310). *See* Humility, Saint (Humilitas).

Ummati. From the Assyrian for "mothers of creation." Honorific bestowed upon Assyrian priestesses who had met the criteria of the spirit of fertility and the "wisdom of motherhood."

Uni. Tutelary goddess of Perugia in Etruscan mythology. Uni was assimilated into *Juno.

Unicorn. A *mythical beast composed of *head and body of a *horse, the *beard of a *goat, the legs of a buck, and the tail of a *lion, with a single *horn in the middle of its forehead. In eastern religious art, the unicorn was a sign of benevolence and its appearance was a portend of an auspicious event, such as the birth of Confucius. It was also associated with longevity, happiness, and the gift of a large family of children. Described in a variety of literature including the *Old Testament, the *Physiologus, and *The Golden Legend, the unicorn was believed to have had magical, medicinal, and curative powers that were accentuated by the fact that a unicorn would only appear to (and allow itself to be captured by) a young virgin. In western Christian art, the unicorn signified purity and chastity, and was a symbol of Jesus Christ, the Virgin Annunciate, the Perpetual Virginity of Mary, and all virgin *saints. It was an *attribute of *Justina of Padua and *Justina of Antioch.

97. *Umā-Maheśvara*

Unut. Egyptian goddess of protection against demons and other evil spirits. Unut was portrayed in the form of a hare or a *lion, and as armed with knives in Egyptian art.

Uraeus. From the Egyptian for "cobra" and from the Greek for "of the tail." Reptilian symbol of sovereignty, and of power over life and death. Divine *snake of Egyptian art and mythology, the uraeus was most often interpreted as a cobra, and was identified with the goddess, *Buto. This terrifying sacred snake appeared on the heads or head-dresses of deities and pharaohs in the act of spitting flames and thereby de-stroying the wearer's enemies. The white crown of Lower Egypt was known as a uraeus as it took on the shape of a rearing cobra with an inflated hood. It was an *attribute of *Hathor, *Tefnut, and *Wadjet.

Urania. Greek *muse of astronomy. Urania was represented by a beautiful young woman in long flowing garments who held a celestial globe and a pointer in classical Greco-Roman and *renais-sance art.

Urd. Variant name for the Earth Mother and for the oldest *Norn in Norse mythology.

Urit-hekau. From the Egyptian lan-guage for "she who is rich in magic." Urit-hekau was the female personifica-tion of mysterious and supernatural powers in Egyptian art and mythology. She was portrayed as a lioned-headed female figure wearing a sovereign's crown. Urit-hekau was also an epithet for a goddess, such as *Isis.

Urme. Female gypsies of Polish, Rus-sian, and Serbian legends. Usually grouped as three, the urme were female spirits who determined human fate, in the manner of the *Fates or *Moirai.

Urn. A container for oils, ointments, perfumes or *water, and a feminine symbol for cleanliness, fertility, and death. Funeral urns were *attributes of *Artemisia and *Agrippina, classical symbols of conjugal fidelity, in classical Greco-Roman and *renaissance art. An elegantly decorated urn signified *Mary Magdalene and *Susanna in eastern and western Christian art.

Ursula, Saint (fifth century). A medieval princess whose legendary life and mar-tyrdom were reported in the chronicles of Geoffrey of Monmouth and *The Golden Legend. A beautiful young prin-cess, Ursula consented to marry Prince Conon on three conditions: that he and his court converted to Christianity, that she be granted ten noble virgin compan-ions, each of whom had one thousand virgin handmaidens, and that she and her companions be allowed a three-year *pilgrimage to the shrines of all the Christian *saints of Europe. Following her final pilgrimage to Rome, Ursula and her eleven thousand virgin compan-ions were slain by the Huns in Cologne. According to tradition, Ursula was spared by the leader of the Huns, but after she rejected him, he killed her with three *arrows. She was the patron of chastity, marriage, drapers, and teach-ers, and was invoked against the plague. In western Christian art, Ursula was de-picted as a beautiful young woman dressed in regal *robes with a jeweled *crown. She held an arrow or pilgrim-age *staff with a *white *banner inscribed with a red cross. She was accompanied by her eleven thousand virgin companions, who were represented either kneeling at Ursula's *feet, enclosed in the protection of her royal robes, or lying dead around her.

Ushas. Hindu goddess of the early dawn. Ushas was the daughter of Dyaus and the beloved of Surya. She was portrayed in a style appropriate to the description in the Vedas: as a delicate bride dressed in rose-red garments with a golden *veil. Her car was pulled by reddish cows signifying morning clouds.

Usert. An epithet of *Isis as an earth goddess.

Ushnīśavijayā. From the Sanskrit for "the victorious goddess of the usnīsas" and "she who has the intelligence of the most splendid Perfect One." A popular Buddhist goddess possessing the virtues of all the Buddhas. Popular in Tibetan and Mongolian art, Ushnīśavijayā was portrayed as white in color with three faces—yellow, white, and black—and with eight hands in which she held a *vajra, ambrosia vase, and small image of the Buddha, and gestured *mudrās, while seated within a white mandala.

Usnīsa. Skull protuberance, oftentimes identified or characterized as a chignon, on the head of the Buddha to signify his perfect wisdom and his enlightenment. Similarly, the smaller chignons on the heads of *bodhisattvas or divinities in recognition of their attainment of enlightenment and/or wisdom.

Uto. From the Egyptian language for "she who is papyrus-colored," that is, the green one. Egyptian goddess of regeneration and of the forces of vegetation. Uto was identified with the snake goddess *Buto, and was a tutelary goddess of Lower Egypt as the counterpart to *Nechbet of Upper Egypt. In Egyptian art, Uto was identified by the *uraeus as a manifestation of the solar eye.

Uttu. Sumerian goddess of weaving. In classical Near Eastern art, Uttu was denoted by a spider in the act of spinning her web.

Uzume. Japanese goddess of jollity. Uzume was renowned for her obscene dancing, which enticed the goddess *Amaterasu Omikami from her cave, thereby ensuring the return of spring sunshine for new life and virility.

V

*

Vāch. From the Sanskrit for "speech." Hindu female personification of speech, especially as invested with magical powers; the mother of the Vedas. The wife of Prajāpati, Vāch signified the feminine world principle on which all actions of the deities were grounded. She became assimilated into *Saravastī.

Vagina Dentata. From the Latin for "toothed vagina." Worldwide, classic symbol of the "devouring mother goddess." The vagina dentata signified the paradigmatic male fear that the vagina is lined with teeth that will sever the penis during sexual intercourse. Representations of this bodily metaphor were found among varied cultures, and indicated the universality of this fear as well as the widespread association between the mouth and the vagina, and also a gate or doorway; for example the classic Christian ascetic image of the vagina as "the mouth of Hell."

Vajra. Thunderbolt scepters characteristic of deities in Tantric Buddhist, Chinese, and Japanese religious art. The vajra was also used in the preparatory rituals for Vedic rites to ward off evil, to invoke the spiritual forces, and to instill a firmness of spirits within the participants.

Vajrāvārāhi. From the Sanskrit for "Diamond Sow." Buddhist supernatural female being. In Buddhist art, Vajrāvārāhī was portrayed as a naked woman whose body was colored *pomegranate red and who held a *vajra in her right hand and a *skull and a *club in her left. By her right ear, there was a growth in the form of a pig's head.

Vājrāyoginī. Buddhist goddess of initiation and one of the *Dākinīs. In Buddhist art, Vājrāyoginī had two forms: yellow in which she was represented as headless carrying her severed head in her hands and with blood streaming from her buttocks; and red in which her *attributes were the *thunderbolt, *skull, and *club.

Vala. Northern European name for a *sibyl or seeress.

Valkyries. From the Norse for "she who selects the dead." Legendary female military beings who conducted the heroic war dead to Valhalla, "hall of the dead." The Valkyries were originally the priestesses of *Freya as the *Mother Goddess, and were associated with the *Amazons as a northern European tribe of women warriors. In later mythology, they were transformed into the servants of Odin. In northern European art, the Valkyries were represented as golden-haired warrior maidens with dazzling white arms who carried spears or naked swords, and rode swift horses over land and sea. Their *attributes included *ravens and *wolves.

Vanir. Group of northern Germanic fertility deities—Freyr, *Freya, and *Njörd—whose battle with Aesir ended in peace-making ceremony when Kvasir, the wisest being, was created out of the spittle that Aesir and Vanir spat in a jar. The Vanir were master magicians.

Vanitas. From the Latin for "empti-ness." A *still-life painting that had religious overtones and that flourished in northern European art after the Reformation. A collection of objects were chosen and arranged to remind the viewer of the transitory and uncertain nature of human existence. From Ecclesiastes 1:2 ("*vanitas vanitatum . . .*" or "vanity of vanities"), a vanitas was identified by its hourglass with sand running out, *skulls, *mirrors, *butterflies, *flowers, and guttering *candles. The vanitas was derived from the northern European fascination with the *memento mori depictions of Jerome, which led to the variant known as *Melancholia*.

Vanth. Etruscan goddess of the underworld and a messenger of death. In classical Etruscan and Roman art, Vanth was portrayed as a winged female figure

who held her *attributes of a *snake, *torch, and *key.

Vase. A generic feminine symbol of containment having multiple meanings in religious art such as female fertility, female sexuality, and the source of life. Mesopotamian images of the goddess included a vase that signified the womb. However, the vase also denoted the treasured gifts and sacrificial offerings made to the deity. In Egyptian art a vase had myriad meanings including the womb, the new day, and the water of life. Sacrificial offerings of milk, water, and wine were presented in vases. Egyptian funeral practices included the use of the canopic jars and the funerary urn. In classical Greco-Roman and *renaissance art, the vase was an *attribute of *Charity, *Nemesis, *Pandora, and *Psyche. In Christian art, an empty vase signified the body separated from the *soul. A vase rimmed with *birds quenching their thirst symbolized eternal bliss. A vase with a *lily (lilies) was an emblem of the *Annunciation to Mary. A clear glass vase, in Annunciation or *Nativity scenes, implied the perfect purity and perpetual virginity of Mary. A vase of ointment or perfumes was an *attribute of *Mary Magdalene, the *Myrrophores* (*Three Maries), *Irene, and *Susanna. In Hindu and Buddhist art, deities were portrayed with a vase signifying either immortality or life. In particular, the variously shaped *amrita vase contained the divine drink of immortality, and thereby, was an attribute of several *bodhisattvas and saints, including *Avalokiteshvara, *Kuan-Yin, and *Kwannon.

Vashti. From the Persian for "beautiful." Queen of Persia and consort of

King Ahasuerus in the *Old Testament. When Vashti refused to appear without her veil before the King and his court, he divorced her and married *Esther (Es 1:9–21). Rarely a separate topic in western Christian art, Vashti was occasionally included in narratives of the Esther story.

Vasudhārā. From the Sanskrit for "she who holds treasures." Buddhist goddess of wealth and consort of Vaiśravana. In Buddhist art, Vasudhārā was portrayed as a seated youthful female figure with two to six arms, white or yellow in color, and heavily bedecked with rich jewelry. In her left hand(s), she held ears of *corn, three *peacock *feathers, a *vase, a text of *Prajñāpāramitā sutras*, and a *box filled with jewels or a *cintāmani; while she gestured with her right hand(s) the *mudrā of the gift of largesse. Vasudhārā was depicted standing on the *moon and above a double *lion. In Nepalese and Tibetan Buddhist art, Vasudhārā also signified abundance.

Veela. Northern European Sibyls who were transformed into wood sprites. Veela had second sight and were gifted in the healing arts of flowers and herbs. These wood sprites were partial to dancing and music. Most often, Veela were positively inclined towards human beings, unless their dancing was disturbed.

Vegetables, symbolism of. Botanical symbols for the cycle of life, death, and *resurrection in the fullness of the four seasons. As the produce of the earth, vegetables like *fruits and *flowers contained the seeds for each new and successive generation. As a generic symbol, vegetables indicated the abundance of harvest, fertility, and earthly desires (as associated with fecundity and creation of new life). In western Christian art, vegetables could be purely decorative, but a specific vegetable had an integral meaning with regard to the theological intent of the image; for example, the combination of *cucumbers, *peaches, and *pears signified good works. *See also* Beans, Garlic, Gourds, Mustard Seed, Olive, Parsley, and Thistle.

Veil. From the Latin for "covering." A piece of cloth, often translucent, which concealed the wearer's hair or face, denoting modesty, chastity, submission, and renunciation of the world. In classical Greco-Roman and *renaissance art, the enthroned *Hera (*Juno) was veiled, while the female personification of Truth was "un-veiled." As a religious garment, the veil was the outer covering of a *nun's headdress in Christian culture. As a sign of modesty, *Rebecca upon meeting Isaac and *Mary enthroned were veiled. A veil with the *head of Jesus Christ, technically a *vernicle, was an *attribute of *Veronica. It was also an attribute of *Agatha, whose veil on a spear stemmed the flow of lava from Mount Etna, thereby saving Catania.

Veil of Veronica. Representation of the *head of Jesus Christ depicted on a veil and one of the best-known *acheiropaeic images in Christian art. The veil was an *attribute of *Veronica, who was reputed to have dried Christ's face with her handkerchief as he carried his *cross to *Calvary. The imprint of his face remained miraculously on this sweat cloth (*sudarium*) or *vernicle, creating an *acheiropoitos. The narrative source for the Veil of Veronica was the apocryphal *Gospel of Nicodemus*.

Veja māte. From the Latvian for "wind mother." Latvian goddess of winds and ruler of the weather. Veja māte nurtured the forests and the *birds.

Velu māte. From the Latvian for "mother of the dead." Latvian goddess of the dead. In northern European art, Velu māte was portrayed as a matron clad in a white woolen wrap who received the bodies of the dead at the entrance to their earthly burial places.

Venevalid. Roman feast of *Venus celebrated on April 1st.

Venus. From the Latin for "love, especially as sensual desire." The Roman goddess of love, grace, fertility, and beauty. Several classical Greco-Roman myths were the basis of Venus as the foretype of both *Eve and *Mary. She won the golden *apple thrown into the wedding feast of Thetis by offering Paris the most beautiful woman in the world, thereby initiating the Trojan War. From the blood of her beloved Adonis sprang the *anemone. His death was interpreted in Ovid's *Metamorphoses* as a prime example of a metamorphosis—the death and rebirth of flowering nature. As the mythical mother of Aeneas, Venus became the "Mother of All Romans." *Sacred and Profane Love*: Formulated by Plato in his *Symposium*, and reformulated by the Renaissance Humanists, this theme of the twin Venuses representing the dual natural of love has a long history in western art. The two artistic styles of representing the nude Venus as either the "crystalline" Venus or the "vegetable" Venus denoted the classical concepts of Sacred and Profane Love. The gestures, postures, and attributes of the "crystalline" Venus were assimilated into images of Mary, while those of the "vegetable" Venus became associated with Eve. In *renaissance art, these two forms of Venus were distinguished by their styles of dress: the "crystalline" Venus was represented in the classical nude, as a sign of purity and innocence, and held a *vase usually containing the flame of sacred love; while the "vegetable" Venus was elegantly garbed and bejeweled, symbolizing the materialism of earthly vanities. *Triumph of Venus*: Enthroned Venus rides her chariot drawn by *doves and *swans; and often accompanied by her son, Cupid. A popular theme in *baroque art and representative of civic processions. *Toilet of Venus*: Depictions of Venus in the act of preparing herself either for the day or for a sexual encounter with one of her many lovers. The goddess displays her beauty in her mirror as she perfumes her body, applies her makeup, and dresses her hair. Most often, she was accompanied by a maidservant and Cupid. *Jewels, perfume bottles, and instruments of feminine beauty such as the *mirror and the comb were displayed on the table or bed before her. In late fifteenth-century Venetian painting, this theme became identified as a representation of the recumbent Venus who looks into the mirror being held by Cupid. *Venus and Adonis*: Enflamed with love for the beautiful Adonis, Venus was horrified when she realized that he had been slain by a wild boar during a hunt. The goddess arrived in her chariot to hear her beloved's final death throes and everywhere his blood had dropped *anemones burst forth. In classical Greco-Roman and *renaissance art, the two most popular presentations of this topos were the departure of Adonis for the

Hunt and the Death of Adonis. *Birth of Venus*: According to tradition, Venus was borne of the foam of the sea. She was represented as an erect figure floating on a *scallop shell and wringing the seawater from her long *hair. *Venus and Mars*: There were two episodes in the relationship between the goddess of love and the god of war that were favored by classical Greco-Roman and *renaissance artists—the scene of Venus and Mars captured in the act of infidelity in a net made by her husband, Vulcan; and the scene of the Conquest of War by Love in which the amorous couple lay together usually in a pastoral setting. A popular image in art, Venus was depicted as a beautiful young nude woman. Her special *attributes were the red *rose, the pearl, *doves, *swans, scallop shell, *dolphins, *girdle, *torch, flaming heart, and *myrtle.

Venus Genetrix. Cult of *Venus as the "life giver," which was inaugurated by Julius Caesar who understood himself to be a direct descendent of the Trojan hero, Aeneas, and a son of the goddess.

Venus Observa. Posture of sexual intercourse Adam attempted unsuccessfully to impose upon *Lilith. According to several patriarchal religious traditions, including Roman Catholicism, this placement of the man upon the woman was the only appropriate sexual relation for both marital intercourse and the conception of a child. Reversal of the Venus Observa, that is with the woman in the superior position, was included in the iconography and ceremonial rites of many mother and/or fertility goddesses as it afforded both sexual pleasure and control to the female partner. Eventually, the Venus Observa became

associated with goddesses of darkness such as *Hecate, and was transformed into the sexual posture favored by *witches who thereby were capable of turning the world upside down as evidenced in *medieval, *renaissance, and *baroque art.

Vernicle. Medieval title for the *Veil of Veronica, which was a representation of the *head of Jesus Christ depicted on a veil and one of the best-known *acheiropaeic images in Christian art. The veil was an *attribute of *Veronica, who was reputed to have dried Christ's face with her handkerchief as he carried his *cross to Calvary. The imprint of his face remained miraculously on this sweat cloth (*sudarium*) or vernicle, creating an *acheiropoitos. The narrative source for the Veil of Veronica was the apocryphal *Gospel of Nicodemus*.

Veronica, Saint. A legendary woman whose story of her encounter with Jesus on the *Road to Calvary had no canonical scriptural authority, but could be found in the apocryphal *Gospel of Nicodemus*. An unnamed pious woman offered her linen handkerchief to Jesus on his way to *Calvary to wipe the sweat from his brow. When the cloth was returned to her, she found the imprint of his visage. Her name thereby became Veronica, from the Latin *vera icon* for "true likeness." By the *medieval period, she was conflated with the unnamed *Woman with the Issue of Blood (*hemorrissha*). Also identified as the vernicle or *sudarium* ("sweat cloth"), the *Veil of Veronica has been preserved at Saint Peter's Basilica Church since the eighth century. This miraculous portrait was an *acheiropaeic image, that is, "one not made by hands." The patron

98. Sandro Botticelli, *Birth of Venus*

of linen drapers and washerwomen, Veronica's *attribute was the cloth bearing Christ's portrait.

Vesica Piscis. From the Latin for "fish bladder." Oval- or almond-shaped encasement of sacred persons or objects, similar to the *mandorla.

Vesta. Ancient Italic goddess of the domestic hearth and its fire. In her Roman form, Vesta was identified with the Greek goddess *Hestia and thereby came to signify both domestic hearth and the stability of the state. In classical Greco-Roman and *renaissance art, Vesta was depicted as a matron garbed in a flowing white toga and veil, and crowned with garlands of *flowers and pieces of *bread. The *ass (*donkey) was her sacred *animal. Her *attributes included the *torch, cup, scepter, and *Palladium, the sacred statue brought from Troy by Aeneas.

Vestal Virgins. Virginal priestesses dedicated to Vesta and caretakers of the sacred eternal fire of Rome. To be a Vestal Virgin was one of the most honorable roles for a Roman woman, especially as there were not less than two and no more than six Vestals at any given time. Between the ages of six and ten years of age, young girls from the noblest Roman families were chosen to become Vestal Virgins. Pledged to absolute chastity and faithful duty of the eternal fire, these young girls entered the Temple of Vesta for a ten-year training period which was followed by a ten-year term of service to the goddess and to the state. At the end of this twenty-year interval, the Vestal Virgin was offered the option of returning to secular life and to a possible marriage, or of

remaining as a Vestal Virgin unto her death. The superior priestess who oversaw the selection and training of new Vestals, and who directed the daily activities of the initiated priestesses was known as the *Vestalis Maxima*. Although denigrated as "pagans" by Augustine, the Vestal Virgins were interpreted as a foretype of *Mary by medieval Christians. In classical Greco-Roman and *renaissance art, Vestal Virgins were identified as beautiful but pious women garbed in long flowing white garments and veils, and with coronet-shaped headpieces. The *laurel and the sacred fire of Rome, sometimes represented by a torch or a flame, were their *attribute. *See also* Claudia, Rhea Silvia, and Tuccia.

Vestalia. Roman feast of *Vesta celebrated on June 9. This festival was famed of the procession of barefoot *Vestal Virgins and other devoted Roman matrons to the goddess's sanctuary at the foot of the Palatine Hill.

Vices. Abstract personifications of evil were depicted in *medieval and *renaissance art, especially in cathedral carvings, and prints and engravings. The Seven Vices were Pride, Covetousness, Lust, Anger, Gluttony, Envy, and Sloth. Unlike the Seven *Virtues, the *attributes of the Seven Vices were neither clearly defined nor regularized. *See also* Seven Deadly Sins.

Victoria. Roman goddess of victory identified with the Greek *Nike. Victoria was the maiden protector of Rome and her Empire, and patron of the Roman legions and the emperor. A divine messenger, she came to earth to crown the victor of wars, battles, sports competitions, and arts contexts. A popular winged figure in classical Greco-Roman and *renaissance art, Victoria was garbed in a long flowing toga and had a *laurel wreath or crown on her head. She may be shown either holding a *palm branch, or in the act of untying her sandal or awarding the victor a laurel wreath or palm branch. On Roman coins, Victoria was depicted as a youthful woman with an exposed left *breast, and who held a palm branch in her right hand and a laurel wreath in her left hand. Her *attributes included the laurel wreath, palm branch, weapons, shield, or a defeated enemy at her feet. Victoria was the classical model for the *angel in western Christian art.

Vidyujjvālākarāli. From the Sanskrit for "she who is as terrible as the fire of lightning." Buddhist goddess of lightning and death. Vidyujjvālākarāli was represented as a fearsome black figure with twelve heads, twenty-four arms, brown hair bursting into flames, and a mouthful of fangs. She was armed with a *sword, *thunderbolt (*varjā*), *arrow, *spear, *hammer, *club, *knife, noose, and/or *skull.

Vigilance. Virtue of royal and public officials. Vigilance was characterized as a proper maiden, that is, one modestly dressed and whose head and face were covered with a *veil. Her *attributes included a *crane and a lamp. During the Renaissance, Vigilance was represented holding the *apples of the *Hersperides and with a *dragon by her side.

Vijaya. From the Sanskrit for "she who is victorious." Manifestation of *Pārvāti as the Hindu goddess of war.

Víly. Slavonic folklore spirits of the winds and storms. The Víly were identified as the souls of dead girls who led young men to their deaths. In northern European art, these beautiful female figures who had supernatural powers were depicted as *swans or *horses. Their *attribute was the *arrow that might be used to disturb human reason.

Vina. Indian form of the *lute. The vina was an *attribute of varied female deities and personifications found in Buddhist and Hindu *iconography.

Vindhya-vasini. From the Sanskrit for the "dweller in the Vindhyas." Manifestation of *Pārvāti as a terrifying goddess. According to tradition, the blood never stops flowing before her image in her temple at Mirzapur.

Vine and Vine Leaves. Ancient symbols of peace and plenty. In classical Greco-Roman and *renaissance art, *Melpomene wore vine leaves. The vine and vine leaves were widely used in the *Old and *New Testaments to denote the relationship between God and his people. The vineyard was the sheltered site where the Keeper of the Vineyard (God) tended his vines (the children of God) (Is 5:7). As an emblem of Christ, it was the "true vine" (Jn 15:1, 5, 8). Vine and vine leaves referred to the Christian *church—God was the keeper of the vineyard—and were also a symbol of the Eucharist.

Violet (as a color). The color alternately of love and truth, or of passion, penitence, sorrow, and suffering. It was worn by penitential saints such as *Mary Magdalene, and by *Mary following the Crucifixion.

Violet (as a flower). Small and common flower denoting humility, modesty, and hidden virtue. Violets grew low to the ground with its blossoms dropping in shyness. It was a floral *attribute of *Mary, who was described by Bernard of Clairvaux as the "violet of humility." This flower implied the humility associated with Christ's humanity. White violets were the attribute of *Fina.

Virago. From the Latin for "manlike or heroic woman," "female warrior;" and the French for "man." Originally a vigorous and heroic female warrior such as an *Amazon. Conversely, virago came to mean a bold, impudent, and/or wicked woman.

Virāj. From the Sanskrit for "she who extends herself in might." According to Hindu mythology, Virāj was the female creative principle arising from Purusha. She was later identified as the primeval female being in the form of a cow generated by Brahman. In Hindu art, Virāj was represented as the sacred *cow.

Virgin. From the Latin for "without a man." A state of inviolate chastity applicable to either man or woman. However, in widespread religious usage, the term virgin signified an unmarried and sexually chaste woman who was distinguished for her purity or steadfastness in religion, and regarded as having a special place among members of the religious community on accounts of her personal merits.

Virgin Birth. The miraculous conception of Jesus Christ. Following Roman Catholic and Eastern Orthodox Church teaching, *Mary was believed to have conceived by the Holy Spirit, and there-fore her virginity was not damaged. A series of miraculous conceptions and virgin births in classical Mediterranean mythology prefigured this event. The scriptural foundation for the miraculous conception derived from Isaiah 7:14, Matthew 1:18, and Luke 1:34–5, 3:23. The story of the testimony of *Salome the midwife was found in the apocryphal *Protoevangelium of James*.

Virginia (Livy, *The History of Rome* 3:44–48). Legendary heroine of ancient Rome and feminine symbol of justice. One of the leading legislators of Rome, Appius Claudius, lusted after Virginia, the young daughter of an honorable Roman centurion. Against every precept of Roman justice and honor, Appius ordered one of his servants to claim Virginia as a rightful slave. Following the expected familial protests, the servant was to bring the case before Appius for judgment. However, her father stabbed her to death rather than see her condemned to dishonor with Appius. The story of Virginia was a popular theme in *renaissance and *baroque art.

Virginity. From the Latin for "without a man." Worldwide and multivalent condition of either a transitional or temporary period of sexual renunciation for spiritual cleansing in order to attain a condition of ritual purity, that stage of life prior to marriage, or a permanent state of being "without" due either to personal choice or religious vow. Although this condition of being was applicable to either a man or a woman, virginity became a honorific description or category by which women were singled out in many world cultures and religions. For example, in the antique Mediterranean world, virginity was a condition of primordial innocence that signified inviolable purity and a closer connection with nature; thereby, a virgin was a mediator between humanity and the heavens. Virgin goddesses had awesome creative powers of renewal and regeneration, and were not subordinate to a god or a man. Their virgin priestesses had parallel energies. Those virgin goddesses who were also mother goddesses, such as *Hera and *Cybele, had their virginity renewed annually in ritual *bath(ing)s. Virginity was signified in classical western cultures by long, loose flowing hair; flowing white garment; androgynous-formed body; and the following *attributes: crescent *moon, white *flowers, clear glass jar/bottle, and a little *dog. During the Early Christian period, the concept and iconography of virginity was transformed into a lifestyle that reduced a woman's special penalties from the *Fall. The earliest virgin martyrs sought to be "like man" in action and in body. The unique and perpetual virginity of *Mary became a focal point of Christian devotions, art, and theology in the fourth century and the concept of "being a virgin" came to signify a life of self-denial and ascetic renunciation of the flesh to overcome a woman's decadent and depraved nature as outlined in Ambrose of Milan's "Instructions to a Virgin" and *Jerome's "Letter to Eustochium." Visual depictions of Christian virgins followed the pattern of the idealized model of Mary's "disembodied" bodiliness. As the iconography and devotions to Mary increased through the next centuries of Christian history, so did the parallel development of the iconography of "secular" virginity even unto the Renaissance transformation of classical Greco-Roman and early Chris-

tian characteristics of virginity into the symbolism of a bride, and the more modern self-appropriation of one's own body.

Virtues. Abstract personifications of good were popular in *medieval and *renaissance art, especially in *cathedral carvings, and in prints and engravings. Personified as female, the *Seven Virtues were *Faith, *Hope, *Charity, *Temperance, *Prudence, *Fortitude, and *Justice. Faith, Hope, and Charity were identified as the Theological (Christian) Virtues, which were attained through faith, while the other four were known as the Cardinal Virtues, which were attained through training and discipline. During the Renaissance, the allegorical virtues—strength, true religion, wisdom, liberality, and history—were added to the original classical Seven Virtues. These allegorical virtues were depicted in art as majestic female figures with identifiable attributes.

Virtus. From the Latin for "courage, manliness." Roman goddess who personified virile manhood. In classical Roman art, Virtus was characterized as a maiden wearing a short tunic and helmet, and holding a *sword or a *lance in her right hand.

Visitation (Luke 1:39–56). Scriptural event denoting the visit of *Mary, immediately following the *Annunciation, to her elder cousin *Elizabeth, then pregnant with her son, John the Baptist. Elizabeth and her unborn child acknowledged through word and deed the special child in Mary's womb; the unborn John reportedly leapt with joy, while his mother proclaimed the greeting that has been incorporated into the

Ave Maria. Mary responded with the poetic hymn that became identified as the *Magnificat. In early Christian and *byzantine art, the depiction of the Visitation was part of the narrative cycle of the *Nativity. The two women were depicted either in an embrace or in conversation. In the fourteenth century, due to the influence of Bonaventure, the Visitation became an independent and important Marian feast. The *iconography of the Visitation was distinguished from the Nativity cycle, and became an independent topic. In the High Middle Ages, a new motif developed in which the two infants were displayed in their respective mother's womb (later proscribed by the *Council of Trent). In fifteenth-century Flemish manuscript illuminations, Elizabeth was depicted kneeling before Mary, who reached out to embrace her cousin.

Vixen. From the Old English for "(female) fox." Originally an identification of the female members of the fox species, a vixen was transformed into an ill-tempered, querulous woman who might otherwise be called a shrew or a termagant.

Volumna. Roman goddess of the nursery. Volumna cared for the health and welfare of infants and young children.

Volva. From the Old German for "seeress." Women who practiced the magic, *seior*, associated with *Freya. The volva attained a condition of ritual ecstasy and was thereby capable of foretelling the future and of casting spells. Throughout German folklore and popular legends, the gods consulted the volva who revealed the knowledge of the world.

Vör. From the old German for "she who is cautious." Indigenous Germanic goddess of contracts, oaths, and pledges. Vör was the protector of marriage, especially of the marriage vows, and of married women.

Vulgate. *Jerome's fourth-century translation of the *Bible into Latin, or the vulgar (common or vernacular) language. His occasional faulty translations, such as Moses' *horns instead of rays of light, were important in the development of Christian *iconography. A revised version of the Vulgate was approved by the *Council of Trent.

Vulture. Avian symbol of sexual lust and prowess, and greed. In Egyptian art and mythology, the vulture was the emblematic *animal of Upper Egypt, and was the symbol for the female principle as the beetle or scarab was of the male principle. According to tradition, vultures were female birds that were impregnated while in flight if they turned their backs into a south or southeast wind. The gestation period for a vulture was three years. The vulture was an associated with the Egyptian goddesses, *Mut, *Neith, and *Nekhebet. In Greek and Roman mythology, the vulture was the symbol of rapacious lust as exhibited by the attempted rapist of *Leto, Tityus who was condemned to the eternal torture of having his liver (the seat of sexual passion) ripped out daily by two vultures; and also the symbol of hubris as it performs a similar function of eating the liver of Prometheus who was chained to a rock as punishment for bringing the divine fire to earth.

W

⚜

Wadjet. From the Egyptian language for "papyrus-colored one." National goddess of Lower Egypt and a solar goddess. Wadjet was the female embodiment of the forces of growth, and was identified as *Buto, and assimilated into *Isis. In Egyptian art, she was represented as a woman with a lioness head surmounted by a disk with the uraeus. Her sacred animal was the cobra.

Walburga, Saint (c. 710–79). Niece and companion to Boniface during his missions to Germany. Schooled in the healing arts, Walburga established convents in Germany and headed a monastic house of monks and nuns in Heidenheim. After her death, her remains were interred in Eichstätt, which became a pilgrimage center for the sick as Walburga's famed healing oil was reputed to flow from the rock under her reliquary. In western Christian art, Walburga was portrayed as an abbess garbed in a Benedictine habit and holding a *crosier. Her *attributes included a *crown and *scepter at her feet, and a container of her famed curative oils.

Walpurgisnacht. Celebration of *witches orgies in Blocksberg on May 1st. This misnomer of a diabolical festival occurred from a variant spelling of the name *Walburga and further confusion with the pagan fertility goddess Waldborg. This confusion led to celebration coinciding with the feast day of *Walburga.

Wand. A slender staff that possessed magical powers such as those used in classical Mediterranean art and mythology by the healers, like Asklepios, and magicians, like *Circe. In the *Old Testament, Aaron's staff was transformed into a *serpent that swallowed the serpents of Pharaoh's sorcerers, and Moses used his staff to strike the *rock and bring forth *water. The many suitors for *Mary left their staffs overnight in the Temple, but only Joseph's flowered as a sign that God had chosen him to be Mary's husband.

Washbasin. A symbol for cleanliness. This was a frequent *attribute of the Virgin Annunciate in northern, especially Flemish, *medieval art.

Water. Symbol for cleansing and purification, especially in relation to the ritual cleansing of *baptism. In Egyptian art and cultic practice, water signified simultaneously life and purification. The particular Christian rite of baptism involved the washing away of sin and the birth into a new life as a preparation for the Last Judgment. The act of washing, or the accessories of *water and washing, implied innocence, for example, when Pontius Pilate washed his hands (Mt 27:24–26) or the Christian catechumen was immersed into the baptismal waters. In the *Old Testament, water suggested struggle, trial, and tribulation like the Flood (Ps 69:1,2; Gn 21:7). The *ewer and basin, *pitcher, transparent *vase, *fountain, and *well were symbols related to water that also signified the virginity and purity of Mary. When mixed with wine during the Zéon rite of the sacrament of Eucharist in the Eastern Orthodox Church, water denoted the humanity of Jesus Christ as the wine was his divinity. This rite was represented in depictions of the Last Supper and Communion of the Apostles by the liturgical vessels of a wine ewer and a water pitcher, and in representations of the Crucifixion by the red and white streams from the wounded side of Christ.

Waters, Clara Erskine Clement

(1834–1916). American art historian and writer on Christian art, and the role of women as artists and artistic motifs. A representative of late nineteenth-century New England literary culture, Clara Erskine Clement Waters had an active mind and a relentless pen that she utilized in her vision of the high values implicit in great art and in Christianity. A bright, wealthy, and genteel lady, Mrs. Waters wrote a series of popular and engaging studies on the religious symbolism and significance of art including *Handbook of Legendary and Mythological Art* (1871); *A Handbook of Christian Symbols and the Stories of the Saints as Illustrated in Art* (1886); *Angels in Art* (1898); and *Saints in Art* (1899). Among her other significant books were her politely feminist versions of the lives of women artists and of Biblical heroines: *Heroines of the Bible* (1900) and *Women in the Fine Arts* (1904).

Weasel. In the *Old Testament, this was an unclean *animal that was reputed to conceive through its *ear and to give birth through its mouth (Lv 11:29). According to *medieval *bestiaries, the weasel was familiar with herbs and could cure its young of illnesses with rue. In western Christian art, it signified Christ's victory over Satan as the weasel's traditional enemy, the *basilisk, was a symbol of evil.

Weaving. Act prevalent among female embodiments and deities that was symbolic of either the gestation of an idea (plan) or of new life. For example, *Athena was simultaneously goddess of wisdom, weaving, and war; *Penelope, *Circe, *Parcae, *Isis, and Athena all wove a garment of protection for a king/hero; the *Valkyries "weave the web of the spear" as a metaphor for the decision as to who dies in battle; and in *byzantine iconography, *Mary was depicted in the act of weaving at the moment of the *Annunciation. *See also* Distaff, Spindle.

Weird Sisters. From the Anglo-Saxon for the *Crone or death goddess. The triad of three sisters variously described as *witches, death goddesses, or crones in both religious art and mythology. Shakespeare has them identify themselves as the Weird Sisters in Act I, Scene III, of *Macbeth*. The Weird Sisters correspond to the *Fates, *Moirai, *Norns, and *Parcae.

Well. In Christian art, the well was a symbol of *baptism, salvation, and of life and rebirth (Rv 22:1). The *waters of eternal life were depicted as a flowing well, whereas a sealed well alluded to the perpetual virginity of *Mary. Three wells, or fountains, grouped together were an *attribute of Paul, for according to pious legend his severed *head hit the ground in three places after his martyrdom. In those three places, three wells, or fountains, sprang up.

Werburg, Saint (seventh century). British nun who reformed and established convents. According to pious legends, this daughter of King Wolfhere and niece of King Aethelred reputedly saved a village whose crops were being decimated by a flock of hungry geese. Once the marauders proved their remorse, Werburg released them from their imprisonment. In an variant of this story, she revived a dead goose. She established a series of convents throughout her uncle's kingdom, and was herself abbess at Repton. During a Danish invasion, Werburg's relics were translated to Chester in the late ninth century for protection and it became a pilgrimage center. In western Christian art, she was represented garbed as an *abbess but crowned as a princess. As the builder of a series of convents, Werburg held a model of an abbey, and was accompanied by her *attribute, the *goose.

West. One of the four cardinal points that specified darkness and the home of *demons. The west *rose *window of the *gothic *cathedral made the light of the *gospel accessible to those seated in darkness.

Weyden, Rogier van der (1399/ 1400–64). The leading Flemish painter in the middle of the fifteenth century. With minimal extant biographical evidence, Rogier was identified as a student of Robert Campin or the Master of Flemalle. His work was filled with a depth of religious feeling and expressed in linear and sculptural terms. His work was influential in Flanders and Germany into the late fifteenth century. Concerned with human emotion, Rogier had a personalized sense of color tending towards gold and pale, bright colors that combined with his stylizations of gestures and facial expressions. His masterpiece, *The Deposition*, was filled with iconographic innovations, including the depiction of tears and the swooning *Madonna whose bodily contortions signified her compassion for her son's passion. Rogier initiated a series of iconographic motifs or types central to the forms of contemporary fifteenth-century Christian piety and devotionalism especially in relationship to women; these included the crying face, or the iconography of tears, *Mary embracing the cross, Mary's *com-passio*, the reading *Magdalene, and the visualization of devotion. Technically proficient, Rogier was an iconographic innovator of the highest caliber.

Whale. This aquatic mammal signified containment and concealment in western Christian art. As a symbol of the Devil, whose cunning enticed unbelievers into the depths of Hell, the whale's huge body was interpreted as an island

and the *ships that anchored there were destroyed when the whale dove into the *waters. His open mouth represented the gates of Hell. In the *Old Testament, Jonah was swallowed by the whale and rested there for three days as a foretype of the Entombment and Resurrection. The whale denoted the tomb of Jesus and symbolized the passion, death, and resurrection experience (Jon 1:17, 2:1–2, 10). In early Christian art, the whale was a popular symbol of the faithful who trusted in God and were saved.

Wheat. Symbol of the bounty of the *earth. In classical Greco-Roman and *renaissance art, wheat signified *Demeter (*Ceres) and *Persephone (*Proserpina). As the source of the *bread of life, sheaves of wheat signified both the Eucharist and *Mary, metaphorically the container of the grains from which came the flour for the Eucharist, in Christian art.

Wheel. A never-ending, rotating circular force that symbolized supreme power. As a customary solar symbol in the art of world religions, the wheel further signified the calendar year and the cycle of human existence. In *Buddhism and in Buddhist art, the wheel of the Law (of phenomenal existence) represented the endless cycle of birth, death, and rebirth. Simultaneously, it signified the absolute weapon necessary for the conquest of the passions and the annihilation of all human desires. In classical Greco-Roman and *renaissance art, the wheel identified those goddesses, like *Nemesis and *Fortuna, who rotated the year and administered chance. In *medieval and *renaissance art, it was used to expel *Adam and *Eve from the *Garden of Eden. The burning or flaming wheel with eyes and wings supported the Throne of God according to the vision of *Ezekiel (Ez 1:1–28). An *attribute of *Catherine of Alexandria, the Catherine Wheel was a sign of her martyrdom. The Wheel of Fortune was a medieval allegory for the transitoriness of human existence, wealth, and the futility of worldly goods.

Whip. Signifier of punishment, penance, and/or authority. In classical Greco-Roman and *renaissance art, the whip was an *attribute of *Hecate, Eros (Cupid), *Grammar, and *Envy. In western Christian art, the whip was an Instrument of the Passion, and used as a symbol for punishment by whipping or flagellation. An attribute of Ambrose of Milan, it signified the expulsion of the heretics from Italy. The whip was also an attribute of Vincent, who was martyred by being beaten with a whip. As a penitential saint, *Mary Magdalene was represented either holding the whip or with it lying near her.

White. In Egyptian art and cultic practice, white was the color of the crown of Upper Egypt and signified joy. In Christian art, white was a color that symbolized innocence, light, joy, purity, virginity, faith, glory, holiness of life, and the soul (Ps 51:7; Mt 17:2; Mt 28:3). Christ wore white after the Resurrection, while *Mary wore white in the *Immaculate Conception, *Assumption, her *Presentation in the Temple, and scenes prior to the *Annunciation. The white garments of Roman *vestal virgins signified their innocence and purity and led to the customs of white garments for brides, those receiving first communion, and for baptism. If worn by a judge, a white robe denoted integrity; by a wealthy man, humility; and by a woman, chastity. Early Christian clergy wore white, a practice that was continued as the liturgical color for Christmas, Easter, Ascension, and other joyous feast days (including the feasts of the Blessed Sacrament and the feasts of Mary and *angels, confessors, virgins, and women not martyred). This was also the liturgical color from Holy Saturday through Pentecost. White vestments were worn for the burial of *children and the clergy, and since Vatican II for all funerals as liturgies of resurrection, and for marriage ceremonies. The color of light, white was also represented by silver.

Whore of Babylon (Rev 17:1–8). *New Testament female personification of evil and decadence in the apocalyptic vision of John the Evangelist. In western Christian art, the Whore of Babylon was represented as a beautiful woman dressed in the purple and scarlet cloths dyed from the blood of the martyrs. Following the scriptural image, she was seated on a scarlet beast that had ten *horns and seven heads symbolic of the seven hills of Rome. Her golden cup overflowed with filth of fornication and abominations. A symbol of the decadence and evil of Imperial Rome to the early Christians, the Whore of Babylon became a verbal and visual metaphor for the papacy in the polemic of the Reformers. *See also* Scarlet Woman.

Wild Beast. A zoological symbol for the conversion of savage pagans or barbarians to Christianity.

Wilgefortis, Saint. From the Latin for "steadfast virgin." Legendary Christian virgin martyr. Daughter of the King of Portugal, Wilgefortis pledged herself to God and vowed perpetual virginity. Her father commanded her to marry the King of Sicily, but she refused and prayed for divine intervention in the form of physical ugliness and a beard. When his beautiful daughter was physically transformed into a bearded and ugly creature, the irate king ordered her crucifixion. While on the cross, Wilgefortis prayed that any Christian who invoked her name would be freed from troubles. According to pious tradition, she became the liberator of wives with difficult husbands. Both her physical existence and her story were mythical, and her name was a series of word plays upon freedom—i.e., she was Liberata in Latin, and Uncumber in English. The cult of Wilgerfortis was instituted in fourteenth-century Flanders following the development of crucifixes with the likeness of a bearded and clothed female figure. In western Christian art, Wilgerfortis was portrayed as a bearded and clothed woman crucified on a Latin cross.

Willow. Arboreal symbol for mourning, meekness, or submission. In Chinese and Japanese art, the weeping willow signified the spring, feminine beauty, and grace. If depicted in the context of a wind, the weeping willow represented a wife's submission to her husband. As an *attribute of *Kuan-Yin, the willow signified meekness. The willow was a symbol for the gospel of Christ in western Christian art. Although widely distributed among the peoples of the world, the gospel remained intact like the willow tree, which survived no matter how many of its branches were cut off. In depictions of the Crucifixion or

Lamentation, the willow signified the tears shed in grief and over the dead; and became a popular motif on funerary art.

Wimple. A linen covering wrapped around the head, neck, and cheeks of a medieval woman for warmth. Popular in fourteenth- and fifteenth-century Flanders, the wimple is found in late medieval northern art. As a sign of modesty, it was adapted as part of a *nun's *habit.

Window. In the Near East, representations of a woman's face looking out a window was a popular motif for *Astarte (*Ishtar) or her priestess as signaling to those outside the temple, or to signify that ritual prostitution that was part of the goddess's cult. In western Christian art, the window was an opening in a wall implying penetration without destruction or violation of the integrity of the wall. The clear glass used in windows symbolized the perpetual virginity of *Mary, and was popular in northern medieval art, especially in depictions of the *Annunciation.

Wings. Symbolic of divine motion and movement between the heavens and the earth. In Egyptian art, wings signified the ability or power to provide protection. In classical Greco-Roman art, varied categories of deities had wings to facilitate their activities and their purposes. For example, *Iris had wings as the messenger of the gods while *Nike (*Victoria) as the goddess of victory, *Eos (*Aurora) as the goddess of the dawn, and *Nemesis (*Fortuna) as the goddess of fate and chance. In Christian art, wings were symbolic of divine mission; hence the *angels, archangels,

seraphim, and cherubim have wings. The emblems of the four Evangelists all have wings: the winged *lion of Mark, the winged *ox of Luke, the winged young man of Matthew, and the winged *eagle of John.

Winifred, Saint (seventh century). Welsh virgin martyr and saint. Winifred vowed her perpetual virginity and dedication to God. When confronted by a disappointed suitor identified as Caradoc of Hawarden, she opted for death rather than seduction or marriage. He decapitated Winifred at the entrance to a church, supposedly at Holywell, where a fountain with curative powers spurted up from the site where her severed head touched the earth. Miraculously, Bruno replaced the young nun's head and restored her to life; although she bore a white (red) mark around her neck as an emblem of her trial. She dedicated the remainder of her life to God's work on earth, and became Abbess at Gwytherin. In western Christian art, Winifred was portrayed garbed as an abbess and with her attributes, the *sword signifying her martyrdom and the *fountain (well) her cure.

Wisdom. Intellectual capacity as personified by the allegorical figure, Sapientia, who was characterized as a lady of nobility, or the Greek goddess *Athena (*Minerva). One of the *Seven Gifts of the Holy Spirit, Wisdom was personified in Christian art and theology as *Sophia (Greek for "wisdom") who was the mother of three female virgin *saints: *Faith (Fides), *Hope (Spes), and *Charity (Caritas).

Witch. From the Old English for "to cast a spell." Original concept related

99. Rogier van der Weyden, *The Deposition*

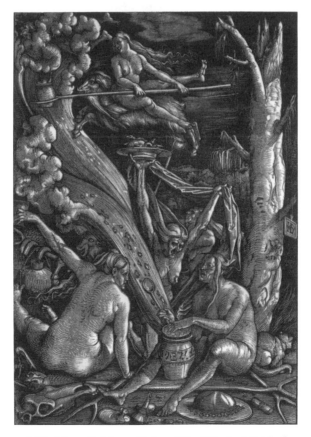

100. Hans Baldung Grien, *The Witches' Sabbath*

to the descendants of the priestesses dedicated to the *Great Goddess, that is those who dealt with fertility and death, and who operated at night. These women had knowledge of the medicinal and magical powers of vegetation and herbs, adored the horn god, were storm spirits, had the power of transformation and prophecy, and had as their powerful weapon, menstrual blood. With the advent of Christianity, the definition and the role of the witch was transformed from an almost sacerdotal function first to that of a sorcerer and then to that of a heretic aligned with the *Devil. Prior to 1350, the sorcerer acquired the necessary magical skills to control nature including barrenness of both the land and humans, illness, and death. After 1350, the concept of the witch was transformed into that of a person, male or female, who made a pact with the Devil by signing over body and soul in return for power or wealth. The Devil granted them magical powers, including the gift of flight, the ability to transform themselves into animals or beautiful young women, invisibility, sympathetic magic that harmed, and companions that were usually *toads or *cats. Female witches were lascivious, uncontrollably lustful creatures who sought out unhappy husbands and unmarried young men, and were represented in the superior position in sexual copulation as a sign of their ability to "turn the world upside down." Witches were depicted as naked elderly women with sagging breasts and bellies and straggly *hair. They were popular in late *medieval northern and *baroque art, especially after the publication of the *Malleus Maleficarum, and the Reformed traditions' teachings on women's fundamentally evil nature.

Witch of Endor (1 Sm 28:3–25). This necromancer was visited by Saul on the eve of a crucial battle against the Philistines. At his pleading, she conjured up the spirit of the dead *prophet Samuel who advised that neither the king nor any of his three sons would survive the battle. Learning that his sons had been killed, a seriously wounded Saul fell on his own *sword.

Witches' Sabbat. Ostensibly derived from a misunderstanding of the Hebrew and the Moorish for "an occasion of power" and intended to connote more than an assembly of witches who honored the *Devil but also a celebration of diabolical rites and licentious orgies. Sabbat signified a clandestine and anti-Christian ritual conducted within the confines of a Christian church. The term, "Witches' Sabbat," was an intentional association and denigration of Jews, Muslims, and *witches. According to investigations and rulings of the *Inquisition, the Church of Rome decreed that *witches occasioned four major Sabbats annually on *Candlemas, *Walpurgisnacht, *Lammas, and Halloween with Midsummer and the Winter Solstice being variant dates. Following the pagan ceremonies and rites, especially those related to fertility, which it was believed witches followed, the Sabbat was characterized as an extraordinary presentation of female power highlighted by *dance, incantations, invocations, ritual offerings, celebration, and orgiastic encounters. The Witches' Sabbat was composed of a variety of elements including an assembly that met after the normal bedtime of respectable Christians on Friday evening; ceremonial "Homage to the Devil," which included the "kiss of shame" (*osculum in fame* or *osculum obscoenum*) and the reading of the names of the Devil; a banquet which was characterized as an orgy of gluttony and lust including the eating of magic cakes, drinking of potions; festivities that involved music making and dancing; and finally indiscriminate intercourse throughout the entire evening. Appropriately, witches also joined together in their covens for a weekly witches' sabbat every Friday night, the day associated with a variety of goddesses from *Venus to *Freya to *Eve. Popular in late *medieval art, representations of witches and of witches' sabbat became both prevalent and more instilled with an evil eroticism following the publication of the *Malleus Maleficarum*.

Wolf. The male wolf signified avarice, greed, and sexual lust, while the she wolf denoted a prostitute or a depraved wife. In Chinese art, the wolf represented rapaciousness and cruelty. Among the Romans, this animal was honored as the she wolf who suckled Romulus and Remus, the mythological founders of Rome. In western Christian art, the wolf was a symbol for heretics and pagan barbarians (Mt 7:15). According to the *Fioretti*, *Francis of Assisi converted the wolf of Gubbio from a killer into a friend; the wolf thereby implied the ability to convert savage pagans. In Scandinavian mythology, one wolf would devour the sun and another the moon at the end of the world while the Fenriswolf killed Odin in the final battle.

Woman Clothed with the Sun (Rv 12:1–6). A revelatory vision of *Mary, particularly in relation to the teachings and *iconography of the *Immaculate Conception and *Assumption, as recorded by John the Evangelist on Patmos. When he consulted the Tiburtine *Sibyl, the emperor Augustus had a similar vision of a "woman clothed with the sun," which was interpreted as the classical Greco-Roman foretype of Mary. Many of her *attributes—including the *crown of *stars, crescent *moon, and the *dragon and *serpent under her feet—were described by the author of the Book of Revelation.

Woman with the Issue of Blood (Mt 9:20–22; Mk 5:25–34; Lk 8:43–48). For twelve years, a certain woman had been plagued by a continuous flow of blood. Any medical treatment she received only worsened her condition. Hearing of Christ, she sought him out in hope of a cure. As he passed her in the crowd, she reached out and touched the hem of his garment. Immediately, the flow of blood stopped. Sensing the cure, Jesus turned to ask who had touched his garment. Frightened, the woman prostrated herself and confessed. Affirmed by her faith, Jesus told her to go in peace. This event was rarely depicted in Christian art except in the narrative cycles of early Christian and *byzantine art. This miraculous cure can be distinguished from other encounters Jesus had with women as this woman (the *hemorrhissa*) was depicted kneeling behind him and touching the hem of his garment.

Woman of Samaria (Jn 4:1–30). As a sign that his mission spread beyond the *Jews and of his transformation of the cultural subjugation of women, Jesus spoke to a Samaritan woman and asked her to give him a drink of *water from a *well. In response to her query—how a Jew could permit a Samaritan to give him water—Jesus replied that he would give her living water and she would never thirst again if she only asked. Recognizing that he was the *Messiah, the Samaritan woman brought together as many citizens as she could find. During his two day stay, he converted many of the Samaritans. This event was rarely depicted as a separate topic in Christian art; rather, it was included in the context of the narrative cycle of the life of Christ. The traditional presentation depicted Jesus and the woman standing or sitting by the well. She held a jug or a bucket, and offered him a drink.

Woman Taken in Adultery (Jn 8:1–11). In an effort to trick Jesus into blasphemy and thereby end his *ministry, the Pharisees brought a "woman taken in adultery" to him for judgment according to the Mosaic Law (Lv 20:10; Dt 22:22–24). Recognizing the implicit danger of their query, Jesus said that the one among them without sin must cast the first stone. Jesus bent down and made marks in the ground (an indication of frivolousness on the part of the rabbi who was being asked to pass capital judgment) with his writing. When Jesus looked up, only the woman remained. Having no accusers, Jesus told her he would not condemn her and sent her home. According to tradition and Christian devotion, this anonymous woman became conflated with *Mary Magdalene. The theme of the Woman Taken in Adultery had a sporadic history in Christian art. The earliest images dated from the fifth century, and emphasized the final scene between Jesus and the accused woman. Rarely depicted in *byzantine and *medieval art, this theme was retrieved by Michael

Packer in 1481 when the scene shifted to the accusation of the woman before the crowd. This was the only scriptural story in which Jesus wrote, but few artists depicted this action. The theme of the Woman Taken in Adultery became popular in *renaissance and *baroque art.

Womb. From the Teutonic for "belly." Also identified as the uterus, this hollow muscular female organ of the pelvic region was the site for the maturation of a fertilized ovum. The womb was a female bodily metaphor for sexual intercourse, pregnancy, or the cycle of birth, death, and rebirth. Worldwide symbol for the *Great Goddess and the creative energies and power of the feminine. The oldest Greek oracle was at Delphi (*delphos* being Greek for "womb").

Woodpecker. Sacred bird of Ares (Mars), the god of war. This ambiguous aviary symbol represented the Devil, heresy, and Christ in western Christian art. The woodpecker's consistent search for worms was a symbol for incessant prayer. As a destroyer of worms, the woodpecker denotes Christ as the enemy of the Devil.

Worms. A symbol for the *serpent and the Devil.

Wormwood. Herbal intoxicant sacred to the *Great Mother. Wormwood, or *artemisia absinthium*, came from a tree sacred to *Artemis, and which was elsewhere associated with manifestations of the Goddess such as the *vilas. The intoxicating and addictive drink identified as *absinthe* was derived from the wormwood tree.

Woyset. From the Egyptian language for "she who is strong." Egyptian goddess-protector of the youthful Horus, and patron of Thebes.

Wrath. One of the *Seven Deadly Sins, and also listed among the Vices. Wrath was represented by an irate female figure in the act of attacking an innocent person in classical Greco-Roman, *medieval, and *renaissance art. Her *attributes included a dagger or a *sword.

Wreath. A sign of spiritual glorification. In Egyptian art and cultic practice, the "wreaths of justification" were originally places on the mummy cases of the Pharaohs, and eventually became a common iconographic motif on mummy cases. This action evolved from the mythic tradition of Atum giving Osiris a wreath as a sign of triumph over the enemy that was eventually interpreted as death. These "wreaths of justification" were usually composed of *olive leaves. In Christian art, this circle of leaves or *flowers held in the hands of *angels glorifies a saint or a holy person. The exact meaning of a wreath was related to the identification of the leaves or flowers. A *laurel wreath signified either victory over death, or distinction in writing Christian poetry or literature. An *oak wreath meant physical and spiritual strength, a *yew wreath immortality, and a *cypress wreath mourning.

X

⚜

Xi-Wang-Mu. From the Chinese for "Queen Mother of the West." Chinese (Taoist) goddess of immortality and female embodiment of *Yin. As queen mother of the western paradise, Xi-Wang-Mu was an amiable being who guarded immortality and rewarded her favorites with the *peaches of eternal life. In the indigenous Chinese mythology, she was a menacing figure with a tiger's fangs and a leopard's tail who sent infectious diseases, calamities, and/or the five disasters into the world of human beings. In her Taoist form, Xi-Wang-Mu was identified by her *attribute, the *phoenix.

Xilonen. Aztec goddess as young maize mother.

Xochiquetzal. From the Aztec for "Flower Feather." Aztec goddess of love, patron of female handicrafts, and queen of *flowers. Originally an indigenous Mexican lunar goddess and wife of the sun god, Xochiquetzal became the mother of the great god, Quetzalcoatyl, in Aztec mythology. Characterized as the first woman in the Aztec cosmology, Xochiquetzal was later identified as the patron of *prostitutes.

Y

❧

Yab-Yum. From the Tibetan for "father-mother." Cultic practice and images of this ritual position of sexual intercourse, which was practiced by Hindu and Buddhist Tantric deities in their "fierce" appearance. This union of the god as a symbol of eternality and of the goddess as temporality, the Yab-Yum signified the divine merger of the dual aspects of the universe. As a ritualistic and artistic form of *hieros gamos, the Yab-Yum had counterparts in the classical Mediterranean and Near Eastern religions.

Yakshas. Collective identification for the mysterious female spirits that frequented the fields, forests, and jungles of India, and fostered fertility. According to Hindu folklore, the Yakshas must be propitiated with gifts and sacrifices as they could be either beneficent or malevolent beings. They were eventually assimilated into the Jain and Buddhist traditions. In Indian art, the Yakshas were represented as beautiful young women often standing near a favored tree.

Yang and Yin. Negative and positive principles pervading all things in the dualistic universe of Chinese cosmology. The Yang signified the male principle, and thereby represented heaven, light, sun, and activity; whereas the *Yin denoted the female principle, and thereby represented earth, darkness, moon, and passivity.

Yashodā. From the Sanskrit for "beauty, worth." Foster mother of Krishna. A *gopī, Yashodā was the wife of the cowherd Nanda who lived on the banks of the Yamunā River. To safeguard the infant Krishna from assassination by Kamsha, the tyrant ruler of Mathurā, the divine infant was placed in the care of Yashodā; thereby following the ancient indigenous custom of protecting infants from evil and childhood diseases. According to the *Bhāgavata Purāna*, Yashodā shook a cow's tail over Krishna to protect him from the night fiend, Putana; then she anointed the twelve symbolic parts of his body with cow urine. In Hindu art and mythology, Yashodā was characterized as the ideal foster mother with her placid nature, sensuous body, and full breasts. The most common depictions of Yashodā represent her seated as she suckled the infant god.

Year. The annual cycle of the sun and the seasons was a symbol of fulfillment corresponding the twelve months with the twelve signs of the *zodiac, the twelve tribes of Israel, the twelve disciples, the twelve apostles, and so on. The Church (Liturgical) Year included the annual religious observances and holy days, beginning with Advent, which narrated the Christian story through the liturgical services in conjunction with the life cycle of Jesus Christ.

Yellow. Color with two opposite symbolic meanings dependent upon the context. In its primary meaning, yellow was an emblem of the *sun and suggested divinity. Yellow signified illuminated truth; that is, the truth removed from the shadows. The golden yellow background of *byzantine and *renaissance paintings symbolized the sacredness of the space. Joseph (of Nazareth) and Peter both wore yellow as a symbol of revealed truth. However, yellow could also denote infernal light, degradation, jealousy, treason, cowardice, instability, and deceit, such as when Judas wore yellow. Medieval heretics and nonbelievers wore yellow garments, while yellow *crosses denoted the contagious areas during the plagues. In the medieval ghetto, the Jews were required to wear yellow badges.

Yemaja. Goddess of the lakes and rivers among the Yoruba peoples.

Yin. Female principle in Chinese Dualism; fundamental partner of the Yang.

Yo. Japanese mythic equivalent of the Chinese *Yin.

Yoke. Symbol of control over the brute strength of the animals, e.g., oxen. In classical Greco-Roman art, the yoke was an *attribute of *Nemesis as goddess of law and order.

Yoni. From the Sanskrit for "vulva." Hindu symbol for the womb of the goddess as the source of all creation. As a worldwide sign of both the female and the goddess, some form of the yoni was found in all world religions as either a devotional or votive image, symbol of the mother goddess, or ritual object. In western Europe, depictions of the goddess postured or in the act of displaying her vulva were common before the advent of *Christianity; while the sign of the vulva, i.e., the yoni, signified woman in Egyptian hieroglyphs.

Z

⚜

Zana. An indigenous Balkan goddess revered for her beauty and courage. According to tradition, Zana was protected by three goats each one having a pair of golden *horns. She was assimilated into the Roman *Diana.

Zebidah (2 Kgs 23:36). From the Hebrew for "given." Daughter of Pedaiah of Rumah and mother of Jehocakim, king of Judah, in the *Old Testament. A rare topic in western Christian art, Zebidah was included as a proper Jewish matron in the narrative cycles of the monarchs of Israel and/or in the ancestors of Jesus Christ.

Zemes māte. From the Latvian for "earth mother." Indigenous earth and mother goddess of the Baltic peoples. Fundamentally concerned with human welfare, Zemes māte nurtured the fertility of the fields and human life, and was ruler of the dead. She merged with *Velu māte, and with the advent of Christianity was assimilated into the imagery and spirituality associated with *Mary.

Zemyna. Lithuanian earth goddess and mother of all plant life. Zemyna nur-tured human and animal life, but demanded appropriate animal sacrifices at both the seeding and harvesting times.

Zenenet. From the Egyptian language for "the exalted one." An Egyptian solar goddess, Zenenet was assimilated with *Ra-Tanit.

Zero. This numerical symbol for nonbeing was also a symbol of potential force, like an *egg.

Zeruah (1 Kgs 11:26). From the Hebrew for "leperous." Mother of Jeroboam, king of Northern Israel, and widow of Nebat the Ephraimite in the *Old Testament. A rare topic in western Christian art, Zeruah was portrayed as a proper Jewish matron in the narrative cycles of the monarchs of Israel and/or of the ancestors of Jesus Christ.

Zilpah (Gen 29:24, 30:9–12, 35:26, 37:2, 46:18). *Leah's servant woman in the *Old Testament. A wedding gift from Laban to his daughter, Zilpah served Leah throughout her years of marriage to Jacob. Once her mistress was past the age of childbearing, Zilpah was sent on her behalf to Jacob, and thereby became the mother of his two sons, Asher and Gad. A rare independent topic in western Christian art, Zilpah was included as a female figure dressed in the garments of a servant in the narrative cycles of Jacob, and/or the ancestors of Jesus Christ.

Zipporah (Ex 2:21, 4:25, 18:2). Wife of Moses in the *Old Testament. One of the seven daughters of Jethro, a Midramite priest with whom Moses took refuge following his exile for the murder of an Egyptian. He first encountered Zipporah and her sisters by a well as they strove to fight off an erstwhile group of young shepherds. Moses ensured the safety of these women and their supplies of water. In a gesture of both gratitude and hospitality, Zipporah invited Moses to her father's tent for the evening meal. They married and Zipporah bore Moses several children including a son named Eliezer who had not been circumcised given the haste with which the family decided to return to Egypt. Once Moses fell ill on this journey, Zipporah, believing the Lord's anger was upon her, quickly circumcised her youngest son with a sharp flint. Moses recovered and decided to send Zipporah and their children back to Jethro until he had successfully led the Israelites out of Egypt. Husband and wife were later reunited on the journey to the Land of Milk and Honey, and Zipporah was with Moses at his death. A rare independent topic in western Christian art, Zipporah was depicted as a proper Jewish matron within the context of either the narrative cycles of Moses or the cycles of the Exodus.

Zita, Saint (1218–72). Pious Christian maidservant and saint. Zita was a devoted Christian woman who worked as a maidservant for the Fatinelli Family of Lucca for over forty years. She dedicated her life to the Christian "good works." She was renowned for a miraculous ability to aid the poor; for example, once without her master's permission she took some bread to feed a starving family, when confronted by her master the bread Zita was carrying was transformed into roses. The water she gave a thirsty pilgrim turned into wine, her unbaked loaves of bread were miraculously placed into the oven, and her master's coat loaned to a trembling old man was returned by an angel. Following her death, her attic window was lit by a heavenly brilliance signifying her entrance into heaven. She was the patron of the city of Lucca and of domestic servants; and was invoked for lost keys. In western Christian art, Zita was dressed as a maidservant and identified by one or more of her *attributes: *keys, *pitcher, *book of devotions, *rosary, and loaves of bread.

Zodiac. From the Greek for "life" and for "wheel." The symbolic wheel of life, an *attribute in Christian representations of *Father Time. It was a circular diagram showing the Zodiac signs used in astrology. The Zodiac was an imaginary band of *stars in the *heavens, including the paths of the *sun and the *moon; it was divided into twelve parts, each named for a constellation. It described the annual cycle of the sun and the seasons. The signs of the Zodiac corresponded to the Labors of the Months and signified the omnipotence of God through time and space. The motif of the Zodiac was popular in *me-

101. Francisco de Zurbarán, *The Young Virgin*

dieval art, especially in the *illumina-tions for *Books of Hours, decorative carvings in churches, and in Flemish paintings, especially on the themes of the *Annunciation to Mary and the *Nativity.

Zoë. Daughter or aspect of *Sophia as the Gnostic Goddess. According to leg-end, Zoë was identified by the epithet, "Mother of All Living," as a result of her breathing life into Adam.

Zohar. From the Hebrew for "splen-dor." Together with the *Sefer Yetzirah*, the central text of *Kabbalah written as Aramaic midrash on the *Old Testa-ment and ascribed to the followers of Simeon bar Yochai (second century). Reputed to be the mystical teachings of the prophet Elijah, the *Zohar* was published in the thirteenth century by Moses de Leon who claimed that this ancient manuscript was sent to Spain by Nachmanides. The text described the esoteric reality of everyday life. It ad-vised that the fundamental human task was to unify the male aspect of the di-vine with the female aspect, identified as the *Shekhinah, which was continually under attack by the forces of evil.

Zoolatry. Worship of animals as deities in and of themselves in classical Greece and Rome. A variation of zoolatry in which the animals embodied the dei-ties and the deities were characterized by their animal aspects was central to Egyptian religious tradition and practice.

Zoroastrianism. Persian religion of ethical and ritual purity based on the teachings of its founder, Zoroaster (Zar-athustra) (nineteenth century B.C.E.). An ethical dualism, Zoroastrianism fo-cused on the struggle between the good represented by Spenta Mainyu and evil by Angra Mainyu (Ahriman), which was paralleled by the ethical struggle of everyday human experience as overseen by the creator god, Ahura Mazda. The eschatology of Zoroastrianism, espe-cially its teaching of the Final Judgment, including the resurrection of the dead and the condemnation of evil to eternal torment, influenced Judaism and Chris-tianity. The sacred texts of Zoroastri-anism were identified as the *Avesta*, and its priests as Magi.

Zurbarán, Francisco de (1598–1664). A master of devotional images, and one of the great painters of the Spanish *ba-roque. He lived in Seville and in reli-gious houses of Spanish colonies of the New World. Zurbarán's early style fa-vored bleak, austere piety. As a painter of elemental doctrinal works that were expressed in clear, sober colors and massive, solemn figures. Zurbarán was influenced by the southern Spanish tra-dition of unidealized representation. His *Adoration of the Shepherds* typified his painterly quest to implement the union of realism with mysticism (follow-ing Tridentine teaching). The success of *Murillo in the 1640s caused Zurbarán to create a series of works that were softer and more saccharine in expres-sion. To obtain these painterly goals, Zurbarán developed a smoother tech-nique and an *iconography of romantic devotions, especially to *Mary.

Selected Bibliography

❧

Achtemeier, Paul J. *Harper's Bible Dictionary.* Harper and Row, 1985.

Apostolos-Cappadona, Diane. *Dictionary of
Christian Art.* Continuum, 1994.

Attwater, Donald. *The Penguin Dictionary
of Saint.* Revised by Catherine Rachel
John. Penguin Books, 1983.

Bachman, Donna G. and Sherry Peland.
*Women Artists: An Historical, Contem-
porary, and Feminist Bibliography.* The
Scarecrow Press, 1978.

Badawy, Alexander. *Coptic Art and Archae-
ology: The Art of the Christian Egyptians from the Late Antique to the
Middle Ages.* MIT Press, 1978.

Baring, Anne and Jules Cashford. *The Myth
of the Goddess: Evolution of an Image.*
Viking, 1991.

Bell, Robert E. *Dictionary of Classical Mythology: Symbols, Attributes and Associations.* ABC-CLIO, 1982.

————. *Women of Classical Mythology: A
Biographical Dictionary.* Oxford University Press, 1991.

Bernen, Satia and Bernen, Robert. *A Guide
to Myth and Religion in European Painting, 1270–1700.* George Braziller, 1973.

Biedermann, Hans. *Dictionary of Symbolism: Cultural Icons and the Meanings
behind Them.* Translated by James
Hulbert. Meridian Books, 1994.

Blundell, Sue. *Women in Ancient Greece.*
British Museum Press, 1995.

Bowden, John. *Who's Who in Theology.*
Crossroad Publishing, 1992.

Brownrigg, Ronald. *Who's Who in the New
Testament.* J. M. Dent, 1993 (1971).

Butler's Lives of the Saints. Edited by Michael Walsh. HarperCollins, 1991.

Carr-Gomm, Sarah. *The Hutchinson Dictionary of Symbolism in Art.* Helicon,
1996 (1995).

Chadwick, Whitney. *Women, Art, and Society.* Thames and Hudson, 1990.

Chetwynd, Tom. *A Dictionary of Symbols.*
Paladin/Grafton, 1982.

Chevalier, Jean and Alain Gheerbrant, eds.
A Dictionary of Symbols. Revised and
translated by John Buchanan-Brown.
Blackwell Reference, 1994 (1982).

Chilvers, Ian. *The Concise Oxford Dictionary
of Art and Artists.* Oxford University
Press, 1990.

————, Harold Osborne and Dennis Farr.
The Oxford Dictionary of Art. Oxford
University Press, 1994 (1988).

Cirlot, J. E. *A Dictionary of Symbols.* Philosophical Library, 1962.

Comay, Joan. *Who's Who in the Old Testament, Together with the Apocrypha.* J.
M. Dent, 1993 (1971).

Cooper, J. C. *An Illustrated Encyclopedia of Traditional Symbols.* Thames and Hudson, 1978.

Coptic Encyclopedia. 8 vols. Macmillan Publishing Company, 1991.

Cotterell, Arthur. *A Dictionary of World Mythology.* Putnam, 1980.

———. *The Macmillan Illustrated Encyclopedia of Myths and Legends.* Macmillan, 1989.

Coulson, John, ed. *The Saints: A Concise Biographical Dictionary.* Hawthorn, 1958.

Craven, Roy C. *Indian Art: A Concise History.* Thames and Hudson, 1995 (1976).

Daniel, Howard. *Encyclopedia of Themes and Subjects in Painting.* Thames and Hudson, 1971.

Davidson, Gustav. *A Dictionary of Angels, Including the Fallen Angels.* Free Press, 1967.

Day, Peter D. *The Liturgical Dictionary of Eastern Christianity.* The Liturgical Press, 1993.

De Bles, Arthur. *How to Distinguish the Saints in Art by Their Costumes, Symbols, and Attributes.* Gale Research, 1975.

Delaney, John J. *Dictionary of Saints.* Image Books, 1983.

Dictionary of Art. 34 vols. Macmillan of London, 1996.

Didron, Adolphe Napoléon. *Christian Iconography: The History of Christian Art in the Middle Ages.* 2 vols. Frederick Ungar Publishing, 1965.

Drake, Maurice and Wilfred. *Saints and Their Emblems.* Burt Franklin, 1971.

Duchet-Suchaux, Gaston and Michel Pastoureau. *The Bible and the Saints: A Flammarion Iconographic Guide.* Flammarion, 1994.

Earls, Irene. *Renaissance Art: A Topical Dictionary.* Greenwood Press, 1967.

Ehrenberg, Margaret. *Women in Prehistory.* British Museum Publications, 1989.

Ellis, Peter B. *Dictionary of Celtic Mythology.* Constable and Company, Ltd., 1992.

Elm, Susanna. *"Virgins of God": The Making of Asceticism in Late Antiquity.* Clarendon Press, 1994.

Encyclopedia of Archetypal Symbolism. 2 vols. Shambhala, 1991–1996.

Encyclopedia of the Early Church. 2 vols. James Clarke and Company, 1992.

Encyclopedia Judaica. 16 vols. Keter Publishing, 1971.

Encyclopedia of Religion. 16 vols. Macmillan, 1987.

Encyclopedia of World Art. 15 vols. McGraw Hill, 1959–1963.

Esposito, John L. *The Oxford Encyclopedia of the Modern Islamic World.* 4 vols. Oxford University Press, 1995.

Ettinghausen, Richard and Oleg Grabar. *The Art and Architecture of Islam 650–1250.* Penguin Books, 1987.

Evans, Joan. *Monastic Iconography in France from the Renaissance to the Revolution.* Cambridge University Press, 1970.

Every, George. *Christian Legends.* Paul Hamlyn, 1987.

Farmer, David Hugh. *The Oxford Dictionary of Saints.* Clarendon Press, 1978.

Feest, Christian F. *Native Arts of North America.* Thames and Hudson, 1993 (1980).

Ferguson, George. *Signs and Symbols in Christian Art.* Oxford University Press, 1966.

Fine, Elsa Honig. *Women and Art: A History of Women Painters and Sculptors from the Renaissance to the 20th Century.* Allanheld and Schram, 1978.

Frédéric, Louis. *Buddhism: A Flammarion Iconographic Guide.* Flammarion, 1995.

Funk and Wagnall's Standard Dictionary of Folklore, Mythology and Legend. Funk & Wagnall's, 1949–1950.

Glassé, Cyril. *The Concise Encyclopedia of Islam.* Harper and Row, 1989.

Goldenson, Robert and Kenneth Anderson. *The Wordsworth Dictionary of Sex.* Wordsworth Reference, 1994 (1986).

Goldsmith, Elizabeth Edwards. *Ancient Pagan Symbols.* AMS Press, 1973.

Grabar, André. *Christian Iconography: A*

Study of Its Origins. Princeton University Press, 1968.

Grant, Michael and John Hazel. *Who's Who in Classical Mythology.* J. M. Dent, 1993 (1973).

Graves, Robert. *Greek Myths.* Penguin Book, 1955.

———. *The White Goddess.* Farrar, Straus, and Giroux, 1982 (1948).

Green, Miranda. *Celtic Goddesses: Warriors, Virgins, and Mothers.* British Museum Press, 1995.

Grimal, Pierre. *The Dictionary of Classical Mythology.* Penguin Books, 1991.

Hale, J. R., ed. *A Concise Encyclopedia of the Italian Renaissance.* Oxford University Press, 1981.

Hall, James. *Dictionary of Subjects and Symbols in Art.* Harper and Row, 1979.

———. *A History of Ideas and Images in Italian Art.* Harper and Row, 1983.

———. *An Illustrated Dictionary of Symbols in Eastern and Western Art.* HarperCollins, 1994.

Hamilton, Edith. *Mythology.* Little, Brown and Company, 1963.

Harris, Ann Sutherland and Linda Nochlin. *Women Artists: 1550–1950.* Knopf, 1976.

Hart, George. *A Dictionary of Egyptian Gods and Goddesses.* Routledge and Kegan Paul, 1986.

Hawthorne, Gerald F., and Ralph P. Martin, eds. *Dictionary of Paul and His Letters.* Intervarsity Press, 1993.

Herder Dictionary of Symbols. Translated by Boris Matthews. Chiron Publishing, 1993.

Hinks, Roger. *Myth and Allegory in Ancient Art.* Kraus, 1976.

Hulme, F. Edward. *The History, Principles, and Practice of Symbolism in Christian Art.* Gale Research, 1969.

Jacobus de Voragine. *The Golden Legend: Readings on the Saints.* 2 vols. Translated by William Granger Ryan. Princeton University Press, 1993.

Jameson, Anna Brownell (Murphy). *The History of Our Lord as Exemplified in*

Works of Art. 2 vols. Longmans, Green, and Company, 1872.

———. *Legends of the Madonna as Represented in the Fine Arts.* Riverside Press, 1887.

———. *Legends of the Monastic Orders.* Longmans, Green, and Company, 1890.

———. *Sacred and Legendary Art.* 2 vols. Longmans, Green, and Company, 1890.

Jobes, Gertrude. *Dictionary of Mythology, Folklore, and Symbols.* 3 vols. Scarecrow Press, 1961.

Jones, Alison. *Larousse Dictionary of World Folklore.* Larousse, 1995.

Kadel, Andrew. *Matrology: A Bibliography of Writings by Christian Women from the First to the Fifteenth Centuries.* Continuum, 1995.

Kaftal, George. *Iconography of the Saints in Italian Painting from Its Beginnings to the Early XIVth Century.* 5 vols. Sansoni, 1952–1985.

Kaster, Joseph. *Putnam's Concise Mythological Dictionary.* Perogee Books, 1990.

Katzenellenbogen, A.E.M. *Allegories of the Virtues and Vices in Medieval Art from the Early Christian Times to the Thirteenth Century.* 2 vols. University of Toronto Press, 1989.

Kelly, Joseph F. *The Concise Dictionary of Early Christianity.* The Liturgical Press, 1992.

Knipping, John Baptiste. *Iconography of the Counter-Reformation in the Netherlands.* 2 vols. B. de Graar, 1974.

Kravitz, David. *Who's Who in Greek and Roman Mythology.* C. N. Potter, 1976.

Lurker, Manfred. *Dictionary of Gods and Goddesses, Devils and Demons.* Routledge and Kegan Paul, 1987 (1984).

———. *The Gods and Symbols of Ancient Egypt.* Thames and Hudson, 1980 (1974).

Martha Ann and Dorothy Myers Imel. *Goddesses in World Mythology: A Bio-*

graphical Dictionary. Oxford University Press, 1995 (1993).

Mathews, Thomas F. *The Clash of Gods: A Reinterpretation of Early Christian Art.* Princeton University Press, 1993.

Meracante, Anthony S. *The Facts on File Encyclopedia of World Mythology and Folklore.* Facts on File, 1988.

———. *Who's Who in Egyptian Mythology.* Clarkson N. Potter, 1978.

Metford, J. C. J. *Dictionary of Christian Lore and Legend.* Thames and Hudson, 1983.

Miller, Mary Ellen. *The Art of Mesoamerica from Olmec to Aztec.* Thames and Hudson, 1996 (1986).

Murray, Peter and Linda Murray. *The Penguin Dictionary of Art and Artists.* Penguin Books, 1988.

Neumann, Erich. *The Great Mother.* Princeton University Press, Bollingen Series #47, 1974 (1955).

New Catholic Encyclopedia. 15 vols. McGraw Hill, 1967.

New Dictionary of Christian Theology. SCM Press Ltd., 1983.

New International Dictionary of the Christian Church. Zondervan Publishing House, 1978 (1974).

New Larousse Encyclopedia of Mythology. Putnam, 1968.

Notable American Women 1607–1950: A Biographical Dictionary. 3 vols. Belknap Press, 1971.

Petersen, Karen and J. J. Wilson. *Women Artists: Recognition and Reappraisal from the Early Middle Ages to the Twentieth Century.* Harper and Row, 1976.

Pettys, Chris. *Dictionary of Women Artists.* G. K. Hall, 1985.

Physiologus. Translated by Michael J. Curley. University of Texas Press, 1979.

Power, Kim. *Veiled Desire: Augustine's Writings on Women.* Darton, Longman and Todd, 1995.

Prebish, Charles S. *Historical Dictionary of Buddhism.* Scarecrow Press, 1993.

Pye, Michael, ed. *The Continuum Dictionary of Religion.* Continuum Publishing, 1993.

Rawson, Philip. *The Art of Southeast Asia.* Thames and Hudson, 1995 (1967).

Réau, Louis. *Iconographie de l'art chrétien.* 6 vols. Presses Universitaire de France, 1955–1959.

Reid, Jane Davison, ed. *The Oxford Guide to Classical Mythology in the Arts, 1300–1990s.* 2 vols. Oxford University Press, 1993.

Rice, David Talbot. *Islamic Art.* Thames and Hudson, 1996 (1965).

Robbins, Rossell H. *The Encyclopedia of Witchcraft and Demonology.* Crown Publishers, 1972 (1959).

Robins, Gay. *Women in Ancient Egypt.* British Museum Press, 1993.

Rochelle, Mercedes. *Mythological and Classical World Art Index.* McFarland, 1991.

Schiller, Gertrud. *Iconography of Christian Art, Volume I.* Translated by Janet Seligman. New York Graphic Society, 1971.

———. *Iconography of Christian Art, Volume II.* Translated by Janet Seligman. Lund Humphries, 1972.

Schreckenberg, Heinz. *The Jews in Christian Art: An Illustrated History.* SCM and Continuum, 1996.

Seyffert, Oskar. *The Dictionary of Classical Mythology, Religion, Literature, and Art.* Gramercy, 1995 (1882).

Sill, Gertrude Grace. *A Handbook of Symbols in Christian Art.* Macmillan Publishing Company, 1975.

Smith, Jonathan Z., ed. *The HarperCollins Dictionary of Religion.* HarperCollins, 1995.

Smith, Susan L. *The Power of Women: A Topos* in Medieval Art and Literature. University of Pennsylvania Press, 1995.

Speake, Jennifer. *The Dent Dictionary of Symbolism in Christian Art.* J. M. Dent, 1994.

Stanley-Baker, Joan. *Japanese Art.* Thames and Hudson, 1995 (1984).

Steinberg, Leo. *The Sexuality of Christ in*

Renaissance Art and in Modern Oblivion. Pantheon Books, 1983.

Stone-Miller, Rebecca. *Art of the Andes.* Thames and Hudson, 1995.

Stutley, Margaret and James. *A Dictionary of Hinduism: Its Mythology, Folklore, and Development, 1500 B.C.—A.D. 1500.* Routledge and Kegan Paul, 1977.

Stutley, Margaret and James. *Harper's Dictionary of Hinduism.* Harper and Row, 1977.

Sykes, Egerton. *Who's Who in Non-Classical Mythology.* Revised by Alan Kendall. Oxford University Press, 1993 (1952).

Thomas, Anabel. *Illustrated Dictionary of Narrative Painting.* John Murray in association with The National Gallery, London, 1994.

Unterman, Alan. *Dictionary of Jewish Lore and Legend.* Thames and Hudson, 1991.

Vries, Ad de. *Dictionary of Symbols and Imagery.* North-Holland Publishing Co., 1974.

Waal, Henri van de. *Iconclass: An Iconographic Classification System.* North-Holland, 1973–84.

Walker, Barbara G. *The Woman's Dictionary of Symbols and Sacred Objects.* Harper and Row, 1988.

———. *The Woman's Encyclopedia of Myths and Secrets.* Harper and Row, 1983.

West, Edward N. *Outward Signs: The Language of Christian Symbolism.* Walker and Company, 1989.

Whittlesey, E.N. *Symbols and Legends in Western Art.* Scribners, 1972.

Whone, Herbert. *Church, Monastery, Cathedral: A Guide to the Symbolism of the Christian Tradition.* Enslow Publishers, 1977.

Willett, Frank. *African Art.* Thames and Hudson, 1995 (1971).

Winternitz, Emanuel. *Musical Instruments and Their Symbolism in Western Art.* Yale University Press, 1979.

Young, Serenity, ed. *An Anthology of Sacred Texts by and about Women.* Crossroad, 1993.

List of Illustrations
and Credits

❦

1. *The Goddess Isis with the Child Horus on her Lap* (Ptolemaic Period, 305–330 B.C.E.: The Metropolitan Museum of Art, New York). Egyptian sculpture. Blue faience statuette; 6¾ inches high. The Metropolitan Museum of Art, Purchase, Joseph Pulitzer Bequest, 1955. (55.121.5). ©1996 The Metropolitan Museum of Art, New York.

2. *Yashodā with Krishna* (Vijayanagar Period, c. 14th century: The Metropolitan Museum of Art, New York). Indian Sculpture. Copper; 13⅛ inches high (33.3 cm). The Metropolitan Museum of Art, Purchase, Lita Annenberg Hazen Charitable Trust Gift, in honor of Cynthia Hazen and Leon Bernard Polsky, 1982. (1982.220.8). ©1996 The Metropolitan Museum of Art, New York.

3. *Virgin and Child* (School of Normandy, early 14th century: The Metropolitan Museum of Art, New York). French sculpture. Limestone, painted, 61½ inches high. The Metropolitan Museum of Art, Bequest of George Blumenthal, 1941. (41.190.279). ©1996 The Metropolitan Museum of Art, New York.

4. Gerard David, *The Saint Anne Altarpiece* (c. 1500–20: National Gallery of Art, Washington, D.C.). Oil on cradled oak, painted surface: left panel 2.340 (including addition at top) x .749; center panel, 2.325 (including addition at top) x .960; right panel, 2.340 (including addition at top) x .738. Widener Collection. ©1996 Board of Trustees, National Gallery of Art, Washington, D.C. 1942.9.17 (613)/PA.

5. *The Birth of Aphrodite* from the Ludovisi Throne (c. 470–460 B. C. E.: Museo Nazionale Romano delle Terme, Rome). Courtesy, Alinari/Art Resource, N.Y.

6. Antonio Vivarini, *Saint Apollonia Destroying a Pagan Idol* (c. 1450: National Gallery of Art, Washington, D.C.). Tempera on panel, .597 x .343 (23½ x 13½ inches). Samuel H. Kress Collection. ©1996 Board of Trustees, National Gallery of Art, Washington, D.C. 1939.1.7 (118)/PA.

7. *Asherah, or Goddess of Fertillity, from a cover of a box which contained unguents and medicine* (14th century B. C. E.: Musée du Louvre, Paris). Myceneaen. Courtesy, Scala/Art Resource, N.Y.

24. Nerocci de' Landi and Master of the Griselda Legend, *Claudia Quinta* (c. 1494: National Gallery of Art, Washington, D.C.). Tempera on panel, 1.048 x .460 (41¼ x 18⅛ inches). Andrew W. Mellon Collection. ©1996 Board of Trustess, National Gallery of Art, Washington, D.C. 1937.1.12.(12)/PA.

25. Master of the Saint Lucy Legend, *Mary, Queen of Heaven* (c. 1485–1500: National Gallery of Art, Washington, D.C.). Oil on oak(?), painted surface: 1.992 x 1.618 (78 ⁷⁄16 x 63¾ inches); panel: 2.015 x 1.638 (79⅜ x 64½ inches). Samuel H. Kress Collection. ©1996 Board of Trustees, National Gallery of Art, Washington, D.C. 1952.2.13.(1096)/PA.

26. Antoine Dufour, *Cleopatra,* detail from *Vie des Femmes Celebres,* Ms. 17 (c. 1505: Musée Dobree, Nantes). Courtesy, Giraudon/Art Resource, N.Y.

27. Lucas Cranach the Elder, *The Nymph of the Spring* (after 1537: National Gallery of Art, Washington, D.C.). Oil on panel, .484 x .728 (19¹⁄16 x 28⅝ inches); framed: .628 x .876 (24¾ x 34½ inches). Gift of Clarence Y. Palitz. ©1996 Board of Trustees, National Gallery of Art, Washington, D.C. 1957.12.1.(1497)/PA.

28. *Cybele Enthroned on a Cart Drawn by Two Lions* (c. 2nd century: The Metropolitan Museum of Art, New York). Roman sculpture. Bronze, 22⅛ inches high x 3 feet 5 inches long (56.2 x 10.4 cm). The Metropolitan Museum of Art, Gift of Henry G. Marquand, 1897. (97.22.24). ©1996 The Metropolitan Museum of Art, New York.

29. *Veiled Dancer* (early 2nd century B. C. E.: The Metropolitan Museum of Art, New York). Greek sculpture. Bronze, 8⅛ inches high. The Metropolitan Museum of Art, Bequest of Walter C. Baker, 1971. (1972.118.95). ©1996 The Metropolitan Museum of Art, New York.

30. *Dancing Celestial Figure (Apsarās)* (late 11th century: Museum of Fine Arts, Boston). Cambodia. Bronze, 39.3 cm high. Denman Waldo Ross Collection. (22.686). Courtesy, Museum of Fine Arts, Boston.

31. Fra Angelico, *Dance of the Angels,* detail from *The Last Judgment: Paradise* (14th century: Museo di San Marco, Florence). Courtesy, Alinari/Art Resource, N.Y.

32. *Demeter of Cnidus* (late 4th century B. C. E.: The British Museum, London). Copyright by The Trustees of The British Museum, London. (LXIXC44).

33. *Diana the Huntress* (Roman: Vatican Museums, Vatican City State). Courtesy, Alinari/Art Resource, N.Y.

34. *Diana of Ephesus* (Roman: Vatican Museums, Vatican City State). Courtesy, Alinari/Art Resource, N.Y.

35. *Durgā as the Slayer of the Buffalo Demon (Durga Mahishasuramardini)* (c. 8th century: Museum of Fine Arts, Boston). Southern India, Tamilnadu, Pallava Dynasty. Granulite, 150 cm high. Denman Waldo Ross Collection. (27.171). Courtesy, Museum of Fine Arts, Boston.

36. Jean Cousin the Elder, *Eva Prima Pandora* (16th century: Musée du Louvre, Paris). Courtesy, Giraudon/Art Resource, N.Y.

37. Rembrandt van Rijn, *Flora* (17th century: The Metropolitan Museum of Art, New York). Oil on canvas, 39⅜ x 36⅛ inches (100 x 91.8 cm). The Metropolitan Museum of Art, Gift of Archer M. Huntington in memory of his father, Collis Potter Huntington, 1926. (26.101.10). ©1996 The Metropolitan Museum of Art, New York.

38. Fede Galizia, *Judith with the Head of Holofernes* (1596: The John and Mable Ringling Museum of Art, Sarasota, Florida). Oil on canvas, 47½ x 37 inches. (State Number 684). Courtesy, The John and Mable Ringling Museum of Art, Sarasota, Florida.

39. Artemisia Gentileschi, *Susanna and the Elders* (1610: Schloss Weissentstein, Pommersfelden). Courtesy, Foto Marburg/Art Resource, N.Y.

40. Giotto di Bondone, *The Meeting of Joachim and Anne at the Golden Gate* (c. 1305: Scrovegni Chapel, Padua). Courtesy, Alinari/Art Resource, N.Y.

41. *Cycladic Idol* (c. 2600–2500 B. C. E.: Museum of Fine Arts, Boston). Early Cycladic II. Marble, 0.159 m. high. William Amory Gardener Fund. (35.60). Courtesy, Museum of Fine Arts, Boston.

42. *Etruscan Mother Goddess (Mater Matuta)* (5th century B. C. E.: Museo Archeologico, Florence). Courtesy, Alinari/Art Resource, N.Y.

43. *Three Goddesses from East Pediment of the Parthenon: Hestia, Dione, and Aphrodite* or *Hestia, Thalassa, and Gaea* (Greek: The British Museum, London). Marble, East Pediment K, L, and M. Copyright by The Trustees of The British Museum, London. (B3281).

44. *The Goddess Hathor and Pharaoh Seti I* (Egyptian: Museo Archeologico, Florence). Courtesy, Alinari/Art Resource, N.Y.

45. *Hatshepsut Enthroned* from the Valley Temple of Hatshepsut at Deir-el-Bahri, Thebes (Dynasty 18, 1490–1480 B. C. E.: The Metropolitan Musuem of Art, New York). Egyptian sculpture. Marble. The Metropolitan Museum of Art, Rogers Fund and Edward S. Harkness Gift, 1929. (29.3.2). ©1996 The Metropolitan Museum of Art, New York.

46. *Hieros Gamos* (6th century B. C. E.: Museo-di Villa Guilia, Rome). Etruscan sarcophagus. Courtesy, Alinari/Art Resource, N.Y.

47. Hildegard of Bingen, Manuscript Illumination from *The Seasons,* Cod. lat. 1942, fol. 38r (n.d.: Biblioteca Statale, Lucca). Courtesy, Scala/Art Resource, N.Y.

48. *Hygeia* (Roman: Liverpool Museum, Liverpool). Courtesy, Giraudon/Art Resource, N.Y.

49. Lucas Cranach the Elder, *The Holy Kindred* (16th century: Stadtkirche, Wittenberg). Courtesy, Foto Marburg/Art Resource, N.Y.

50. *Inanna-Ishtar, crowned with a star and holding a bow, with the Image of Sirius and the Tree of Life* (c. 700 B. C. E.: The British Museum, London). Neo-Assyrian cylinder seal. Copyright by The Trustees of The British Museum (89769).

51. *Pectoral in the form of Winged Isis* (late 6th century B. C. E.: Museum of Fine Arts, Boston). Nubian, Sudan, Nuri, Kushite, Tomb of King Amarinataki-lebte, Third Ethiopian Dynasty. Gold, 6½ inches. Harvard University-MFA Expedition. (20.276). Courtesy, Museum of Fine Arts, Boston.

52. *The Priestess or Female Pope ("Pope Joan"),* M.630, f.2, detail (15th century: The Pierpont Morgan Library, New York). Italian tarot cards made for the Visconti-Sforza family. Courtesy, The Pierpont Morgan Library/Art Resource, N.Y.

53. Artemisia Gentileschi, *Judith* (c. 1612–13: Museo di Capodimonte, Naples). Courtesy, Alinari/Art Resource, N.Y.

54. *Juno* (Roman: Museo Nazionale di Capodimonte, Naples). Courtesy, Alinari/Art Resource, N.Y.

55. *Kālī Slaying the Demon Generals Chand and Munda. In the background she presents their severed heads to the goddess Chandi.* Illustration from the *Markandeya Purana, Canto 87.* (c. 1800–20: Victoria and Albert Museum, London). Guler style. Gouache. Courtesy, Victoria and Albert Museum, London/Art Resource, N.Y.

56. *Vishnu and Lakshmi Riding on Garuda* (n.d.: Victoria and Albert Museum, London). Courtesy, Victoria and Albert Museum, London/Art Resource, N.Y.

57. School of Leonardo da Vinci, *Leda and the Swan* (15th century: Private Collection, Rome). Courtesy, Alinari/Art Resource.

58. Edmonia Lewis, *Hagar* (1875: National Museum of American Art, Washington, D.C.). Carved marble, 52⅝ x 15¼ x 17 inches. Courtesy, National Museum of American Art, Washington, D.C./Art Resource, N.Y.

59. Barbara Longhi, *Madonna Adoring the Child* (17th century: The Walters Art Gallery, Baltimore, Maryland). Courtesy, The Walters Art Gallery, Baltimore (37.1068).

60. Guido Reni, *Lucretia* (17th century: Galleria Corsini, Florence). Courtesy, Alinari/Art Resource, N.Y.

61. *Maat* (Egyptian: Museo Archeologico, Florence). Bas-relief. Courtesy, Scala/Art Resource, N.Y.

62. *Maenad Leaning on her Thyrsos* (5th century B. C. E., last quarter: The Metropolitan Museum of Art, New York). Roman copy of a Greek original, perhaps by Kallimachos. Pentellic marble. The Metropolitan Museum of Art, Fletcher Fund, 1935. (35.11.3). ©1996 The Metropolitan Museum of Art, New York.

63. Joos van Cleve, *The Holy Family* (16th century: The Metropolitan Museum of Art, New York). Oil on wood, 16¾ inches high x 12½ inches wide (42.5 x 31.8 cm). The Metropolitan Museum of Art, The Friesdam Collection, Bequest of Michael Friesdam, 1931. (32.100.57). ©1996 The Metropolitan Museum of Art, New York.

64. Elisabetta Sirani, *Mary Magdalene* (1660: Pinacoteca Nazionale, Bologna). Courtesy, Alinari/Art Resource, N.Y.

65. *Medusa* (6th B. C. E.: Acropolis Museum, Athens). Mask. Courtesy, Alinari/Art Resource, New York.

66. *Minerva* (Roman: Musée du Louvre, Paris). Courtesy, Alinari/Art Resource, N.Y.

67. Michelangelo Buonarroti, *The Delphic Sibyl,* detail (1510–15: Sistine Chapel, Vatican Palace, Vatican City State). Courtesy, Alinari/Art Resource, N.Y.

68. Lavinia Fontana, *Noli Me Tangere* (1571: Galleria degli Uffizi, Florence). Courtesy, Alinari/Art Resource, N.Y.

69. *Nike Samothrace* (Greek: Musée du Louvre, Paris). Courtesy, Foto Marburg/Art Resource, N.Y.

70. *Isis and Nephthys, kneeling, assisting the sun to rise from the Djed column,* from *Papyrus of Ani* (Dynasty 18, c. 1250 B. C. E.: The British Museum, London). Copyright by The Trustees of The British Museum, London. (10470/2).

71. *Pārvāti* (Chola Dynasty, c. 900: The Metropolitan Museum of Art, New York). South Indian sculpture. Bronze, 27⅜ inches high. The Metropolitan Museum of Art, Cora Timken Burnett Collection of Persian Miniatures and other Persian Art Objects, Bequest of Cora Timken Burnett, 1956. (57.51.3). ©1996 The Metropolitan Museum of Art, New York.

72. Rembrandt Peale, *The Roman Daughter* (1811: National Museum of American Art, Washington, D.C.). Oil on canvas, 84¾ x 62⅞ inches. Courtesy, National Museum of American Art, Washington, D.C./Art Resource, N.Y.

73. *Demeter, Persephone, and Triptolomes* (440 B. C. E.: National Archeological Museum, Athens). Relief from the Temple of Demeter at Eleusis. Courtesy, Alinari/Art Resource, N.Y.

Museum of Art, Rogers Fund, 1953. (53.120.2). ©1996 The Metropolitan Museum of Art, New York.

90. Upper Rhenish Master, *Mary Spinning* (c. 1400: Gemaldegalerie, Staatliche Museen, Berlin). Courtesy, Foto Marburg/Art Resource, N.Y.

91. Sabina von Steinbach, *Ecclesia* (c. 1230: Cathderal of Our Lady, Strasbourg). Courtesy, Foro Marburg/Art Resource, N.Y.

92. Sabina von Steinbach, *Synagoga* (c. 1230: Cathderal of Our Lady, Strasbourg). Courtesy, Foro Marburg/Art Resource, N.Y.

93. *Posthumous effigy of the wife of Jayavarman VII as the divinity Tārā or Prajñāpāramitā, personification of Divine Wisdom* (12th–13th century: Musée Guimet, Paris). Cambodia. Courtesy, Giraudon/Art Resource, N.Y.

94. *The Goddess Thoueris, on a pedestal, holding before her the Symbol of Isis* (Ptolemaic Period, c. 332–330 B. C. E.: The Metropolitan Museum of Art, New York). Egyptian figure. Glass, 11 cm high. The Metropolitan Museum of Art, Purchase, Edward S. Harkness Gift, 1926. (26.7.1193). ©1996 The Metropolitan Museum of Art, New York.

95. *Saint Thecla with Wild Beasts and Angels* (5th century: The Nelson-Atkins Museum of Art, Kansas City). Egyptian (Coptic) sculpture. Limestone rondelle, 3¾ x 26 inches (d x diam) (10.0 x 66.0 cm). The Nelson-Atkins Museum of Art, Kansas City, Missouri (Purchase: Nelson Trust). (48.10).

96. Eutychides, *Tyché of Antioch* (Roman copy: Vatican Museums, Vatican City State). Courtesy, Alinari/Art Resource, New York.

97. *Umā-Maheśvara* (c. 13th century: Museum of Fine Arts, Boston). Nepal. Gilt copper, 24.5 cm high x 21.2 cm wide x 10 cm deep. Marshall H. Gould and Frederick L. Jacks Funds. (68.3). Courtesy, Museum of Fine Arts, Boston.

98. Sandro Botticelli, *Birth of Venus* (15th century: Galleria degli Uffizi, Florence). Courtesy, Alinari/Art Resource, N.Y.

99. Rogier van der Weyden, *The Deposition* (15th century: Museo del Prado, Madrid). Courtesy, Alinari/Art Resource, N.Y.

100. Hans Baldung (called Grien), *The Witches' Sabbath* (1510: Museum of Fine Arts, Boston). Charoscuro woodcut; block: 14⅞ x 10 inches. Bequest of W.G. Russell Allen. (69.1064). Courtesy, Museum of Fine Arts, Boston.

101. Francisco de Zurbarán, *The Young Virgin* (17th century: The Metropolitan Museum of Art, New York). Oil on canvas, 46 x 37 inches (116.8 x 94 cm). The Metropolitan Museum of Art, Fletcher Fund, 1927. (27.137). ©1996 The Metropolitan Museum of Art, New York.

Appendices

⚜

Appendix 1.a:
Guide to Variant Names of Goddesses

A

Acca Larentia: Acca Laurentia, Larentia,
  Laurentia
Aditi: Addittu, Adit, Aditya
Adraste: Andate, Andrasta, Andraste
Aibell: Aiobell, Aiobhell
Alcestis: Alceste, Alkeste, Alkestis
al-Lāt: al-Lat, Allat, El-Lat
Almathea: Almatheia
Alpan: Alpanu, Alpnu
al-'Uzza: El-'Uzza
Amaterasu Omikami: Ama-terasu-ō-mi-
  kami, Ama-terasu-oho-hiru-me-no-
  mikoto, Omikanu Amaterasu
Amentit: Amenit, Ament, Amenti
Ammit: Amemait, Am-met, Ammut
Anat: Anahita, Annuthat, Anthat,
  Anthrati, Antit
Anukis: Ank, Anouke, Anoukis, Anqet,
  Anqt, Anquet, Anuket, Anukit, Anuqet
Anunītu: Annunītum
Aranhod: Arianhod, Arianrhod
Ariadne: Aridela
Armaiti: Armait, Armati
Āryajangulī: Jañgulī, Jōguri-dōnyō
Asera: Aserat
Asertu: Aserdus, Atirat

Asherah: Asherath, Ashirah, Ashirath,
  Ashtaroth, Ashtoreth, Ashtoroth
Ashokakāntā: Aśokakāntā
Ashthābhujā-Kurakulla: Astabhujā-
  Kurakulla
Astarte: Astar, Astart, Astert, Astlik,
  Ataecina, Athtar, Attart
Atalanta: Atalante
Athena: Athenaia, Athene, Athena Nike,
  Athena Parthenos
Avalokiteshvara: Avalokita, Avalokiteśvara,
  Lakeśvara, Lakeshvara

B

Baalath: Baalat, Belet
Baba: Bau, Bawu
Baba-yaga: Baba Yaga, Jezi Baba, Yaga
  Vasilisa
Bacchantes: Bacchae
Banshee: Banshie, Bansith
Bast: Bastet, Bastis, Bubastis
Bean Sídhe: Bean Nighe, Bean Sôdhe
Befana: Saint Befana, La Strega, La
  Vecchia
Bēletsēri: Belet Seri, Beleterseteri, Beli
  Sheri, Belisheri, Belit Seri
Benten: Benzaiten, Benzai-tennyo
Bercht: Berchta, Berchte, Berkta, Bertha,

Bertie, Berty, Brechta, Eisenberta, Frau
Berchta, Frau Berta, Percht, Perchata,
Perchta, Precht, Vrou Elde, Yrou-Elde
Blodeuwedd: Blodenwedd, Blodeuedd,
Blodewedd
Boadicea: Boudicea
Bodhisattva: Bo-satsu, Pu-sa
Brigantia: Brigentis, Brighid, Brigidu,
Briginda, Brigindo
Brigid: Bride, Bridgit, Brig, Brighid
Britomartia: Aphaea, Car, Car-Dia, Carme,
Carmenta, Carna, Dutyima, Laphira
Brynhild: Brunhild, Brunhilda, Brunhilde,
Brunnehilde
Buana: Ana, Buanann, Buan-ann
Buto: Bouto, Edjo, Inadjet, Uajyt,
Uatchura, Uazet, Uazit, Udjat, Uzoit,
Wadjet

C

Calliope: Kalliope
Callisto: Kallisto
Calypso: Kalypso
Caménae: Casménae, Kaménae, Kasménae
Cerridwen: Ceridwen, Keridwen
Chalchihuitlicue: Aticpac Calquicihuatl,
Huixtocihuatl
Chensit: Khensit
Chicomecoatl: Chalchiuhclihuatl
Chimalman: Chimalma
Chinna-mastā: Chinnamasta,
Chinnamastakā
Circe: Kirke
Clio: Cleio, Kleio, Klio
Clytemnestra: Klymentestra
Clytie: Klytie
Coronis: Koronis
Cundī: Candrā, Cundā, Cunti, Juntei
Kannon Bosatsu
Cybele: Kubele, Kybele
Cynthia: Kynthia

D

Dākinīs: Daginis, Daini, Khecara, Mkna'-
'gro-ma
Damgalnuna: Damgalnunna, Damkina
Dana: Ana, Anu, Dana-Ana, Dana-Anu,
Danu, Danube, Deenitsa, Don,

Donann, Donau, Donmnu, Dunay,
Tuatha Dé Danaan
Danann: Danu
Decuma: Decima
Deianira: Dejanira
Demeter: Damatres, Demetra, Dimitra
Despoina: Despina, Despoena
Devana: Diiwica, Dziewona
Diana of Ephesus: Artemis Ephesus,
Diana of the Ephesians, Ephesian
Artemis
Dimu: Diya
Durgā: Doorga, Durgha, Durja

E

Egeria: Etheria, Silvia of Aquitaine
Eirene: Irene
Ekajatā: Ral-g Cig-na, Ugra-Tārā,
Vidyujjvālākarāli
Electra: Elektra
Ereshkigal: Ereskigal, Ereskigala
Erinyes: Eumenides
Eris: Discordia
Estanathlehi: Estana Hehi

F

Fates: Fata, Parcae
Flidhais: Flidais
Fortuna: Fortune
Freya: Freyja, Freyjia
Furies: Furiae
Fylgir: Fylgjur

G

Gabija: Gabeta, Gabieta
Gabjauja: Gabjaiya
Gaea: Gaia, Ge, Gea
Gatumdu: Gatumdug
Geštinana: Geshtinanna, Gestinanna,
Mother Geštinana
Graces: Gratiae
Graeae: Graiae, Graii
Great Mother: Magna Mater
Gula: Meme, Ninisina, Ninkarrak,
Nintinuga
Gul-šeš: Gul-ašeš, Gulšeš

H

Hāriti: He-li Di, Karitei-mo
Hathor: Athir, Athor, Athyr, Hether
Hebat: Hapatu, Hepat
Hecate: Hekate
Heket: Hekt, Heqet, Heqt, Heqtit,
  Hequet, Hiqit, Hiquet
Hemsut: Hemuset
Heng-O: Chang-E, Chang-Ngo, Chang-O,
  Heng-E
Hine-ahuone: Hine-ahu-one
Hine-titama: Hine-tītama, Hine-titamauri
Hippolyta: Hippolyte
Hlodyn: Fjorgyn, Hlödin, Hlothyn
Holle: Frau Holle, Hoide, Holda
Hsi Wang Mu: Seiobo
Hygeia: Hygea, Hygia, Hygieia

I

Ilazki: Illargi, Illargui, Iratagi, Iretagi,
  Iretargui
Inanna: Inana
Išhara: Ešara, Išara
Ishtar: Alpha, Ashtart, Estar, Istar, Istara,
  Istaru
Isis: As, Aset, Ast, Au Set, Ese, Eset, Esi,
  Hesi
Iusas and Nehbet Hotep: Iussaet and
  Nebt-Hotep
Iustitia: Justitia
Ix Chel: Ixchel, Ix Ch'up, Ix Hun Zipit
  Caan
Ix Chiup: Ix Ch'up
Izanami-No-Mikoto: Isanami-No-Kami,
  Isanami-No-Mikoto, Izanami-No-Kami

J

Ju-i: Nyo-i
Juno Lucina: Juno Opigena
Juturna: Iuturna
Juventas: Iuventas

K

Kālī: Kali-Ma, Kamakshi, Kumari
Kaménae: Caménae
Kuan-yin: Guan-yin, Guanyin, Kuanyin,
  Kwan-yin, Kwanyin
Kubaba: Gupapa, Kupapa
Kwannon: Kannon

L

Lakshmi: Lakśmi, Laxmi
Latona: Leto
Lauka-māte: Laukamat, Laukamāte,
  Lauka-mäte
Leto: Lato, Latona

M

Maat: Maa, Maât, Maati, Maet, Maht,
  Mait, Maut, Mayet
Mahamaya: Maya
Mama: Mami
Māmitu: Mammetu, Mammit, Mammitu
Manat: Manāt
Mārīcī: Hod-zu Chen-Ma, Malizhi,
  Marishi-ten, Tiannu, Vajravārāhi
Matrona: Modron
Mayahuel: Mayauel
Meh-Urit: Mehet-Uret, Mehturt,
  Mehueret, Meh-Urt, Mihi-urit
Mehit: Mechit
Meret: Mert
Meretseger: Meresegir, Merseger,
  Mertseger
Meshkenit: Maskhonit, Mersekhnet,
  Meshkent, Meshkhent, Meshkoni
Mīnākṣī: Minau
Minerva: Meneruva, Menerva, Menrfa,
  Menvra
Moirai: Moera, Moerae, Moirae, Moires,
  Morae
Morrigan: Morrigu
Mother/Great Mother/Mother Goddess:
  Magna Mater
Mut: Mauit, Maut, Mooth, Mout, Muit,
  Muth

N

Naiads: Naiades
Namita: Namite
Nechmetawaj: Nehmet-Awai
Neith: Neg, Neit, Neither, Net, Nit
Nekhbet: Nechbet, Nekhabit, Nekhebet,
  Nekhebit

Nephthys: Nebhat, Nebthet, Nebt-hat,
Nephys, Nepte, Nephthys
Nisaba: Nidaba, Nissaba
Nugua: Nü-gua
Nungal: Munungal
Nut: Net, Nit, Noot, Nuit

P

Parnashavarī: Hiyoi-ten, Lo-na-gym-ma,
Parnaśvarī
Persé: Perseis
Persephone: Persephassa, Persephoneia,
Phersephassa, Proserpina
Pinikir: Pinenkir
Prajñāpāramitā: Billig-un Chinadu
Kichaghar-a Kürük-sen, Dai Hannya,
Hannya Bosatsu, Haramitsu, Shes-teb-
pha-rol-tu-phyin-na
Proserpina: Persephone, Proserpine
Pszpolnica: Poldunica, Polednica,
Poludnitsa, Poludnitza, Prez-poludnica

Q

Qedeshet: Qedeshat

R

Rat-taui: Rat-tawi, Rattus
Renenut: Ranin, Raninit, Ranut, Ranno,
Rannuit, Renenet, Renenit, Renen-uret,
Renunet, Renute
Renpet: Renph, Renpit
Rhea: Rheia
Rind: Rhind, Rinda, Rinde, Rindr

S

Sarasvatī: Benzai-ten, Dabiacaitin Nü,
Dhyangr-chan-ma, Kele-yinükin Tegu,
Ngag-gi Tha-mo, Sarasvati
Sauska: Sausga, Sawuska
Sekhmet: Sachmet, Sakhmet, Sakhmis,
Salchmet, Sechmet, Sehmet, Sekhait,
Sekhauit, Sekhautet, Sekhmen, Sekmet,
Sokhit
Seléne: Méne, Selena

Selket: Selkhet, Selkis, Selkit, Selqet,
Selquet, Serket, Serket-heter, Serkhit,
Serq, Serqet
Sengen: Ko-No-Hana, Siku-a-Hime
Šerida: Aya
Sešat: Sefkhet-Aabut, Seshat, Sesheta
Shakti: Śakti
Sitātapatrā: Byakusangai, Chagham
Sigürtei, Gdags-dkar Chan-Ma

T

Tārā: Dara eke, sGrol-mas, Tārini, Tārini
Bosātsu, Tuoluo
Taweret: Tauerat, Taueret, Taur, Taurt,
Tawerat
Tefnut: Tefenet, Tefnoot, Tefnuit
Tellus Mater: Terra Mater
Thalia: Thalaeia, Thaleia
Thoeris: Ta-uret, Theoris, Thoueris
Tinnit: Tanit, Thinit, Tinit

U

Umā: Uma, Umā-Maheśvara
Urme: Ursitory
Ushnīśavijayā: Butchō, Foding, gTtsug-tor
Rnam-par rGyal-ma, Rasinan Usnir-tu
Uto: Wadjet
Uzume: Ame-no-uzume, Ame-no-uzume-
no-mikoto, Udzume

V

Vāch: Vac, Vak
Vala: Veela, Vila, Völva
Vasudhārā: Vasundhārā
Veela: Vala, Völva
Venus: Venus Genetrix, Venus Observa
Vör: Vara

Y

Yashodā: Jesodha, Josodha, Yaśodā,
Yaśodha, Yashodara, Ysodha

Z

Zemyna: Zem Ynele, Zemynele, Zied Kele

Appendix 1.b:
Guide to Variant Names of Metaphorical Female Figures

Eirene: Irene, Peace

Eris: Discordia

Fates as a group: Fata; Fatit; Moera, Moerae, Moirae, Moirai, Morae; Parcae

Fates as individuals: Clotho, Klotho; Decuma, Decima

Fortuna: Fortune

Furies: Erinyes, Eumenides

Graces: Charites, Gratiae

Graeae: Graiae, Graii

Great Mother: Magna Mater

Isutitia: Justitia

Muses as individuals: Calliope, Kalliope; Clio, Cleio, Klio, Kleio; Polyhymnia, Polymnia

Naiads: Naiades

Nereids: Nereides

Nixies: Der Nixen, Nix, Nixe, Nixy

Oceanids: Oceanides

Vices: Seven Deadly Sins, Seven Vices

Appendix 1.c:
Guide to Variant Names of Celestial Female Beings

Apsarās, Apsarāses: Feitian, Hiten, Lha'i Bu-mo, Nang-fa, Tennin, Tepanom, Tevoda, Tiannü

Bercht: Frau Berchta, Frau Berta, Berchta, Berchte, Berkta, Bertha, Bertie, Berty, Brecata, Eisenberta, Percht, Perchta, Precht, Vrou Elde, Yrou-Elde

Bodhisattva: Bo-satsu, Pu-sa

Dākinīs: Daginis, Dainis, Khecara, Mkna'-'gro-ma; Buddha Dākinī; Vajradākinī; Ratnadākinī; Padmadākinī; Vishvadākinī; Karmadākinī; Simhavaktrā; Dākinī-ten; Lāsyā: Sgeg-pa-ma; Mālā: Phreng-ba; Gītā: Ghe-ma; Puspā: Me-tog-ma; Dhūpā: Bdug-spas-ma; Dīpā: Snang-gsal-ma; Gandhā: Dri-chab-ma.

Hāriti: He-li Di, Karitei-mo

Houri: Hur

Naiads: Naiades

Nereids: Nereides

Nixies: Die Nixen, Nix, Nixe, Nixy

Oceanids: Oceanides

Pleiades: Plaiades

Tārā: Dara eke, Sgrol-ma, Tārini, Tārini Bosātsu, Tuoluo; White Tārā: Sgrol-dkar; Green Tārā: Sgrol-ljan, Shyāmatārā: Yellow Tārā: Bhrikuti, Bikuchi, Kilingtü eke, Kro-guyer Ch-ma; Blue Tārā: Ekajatā Mgrā Tārā, Ral-gehig-ma; Red Tārā: Ku-ru-ku-li, Kurukullā

Yakshas: Yakśas, Yakśī, Yakshī, Yakshinī, Yakśinī

Appendix 1.d:
Guide to Variant Names of Demonic Female Beings

Baalath: Baalat, Belet

Baba: Bau, Bawu

Baba-yaga: Baba Yaga, Jezi Baba, Yaga-Vasilisa

Banshee: Banshie, Bansith

Furies: Erinyes, Eumenides, Furiae

Lama: Lamassu

Lilith: Lilit, Lilitu

Sheila-na-gig: Sheela-na-gig, Sheelanagyg, Shela-no-gig

Witch of Endor: Medium of Endor

Appendix 1.e:
Guide to Variant Names for Old Testament Women

Abishag the Shulamite: Abisag the
 Shulamite
Eve: Eva
Hannah: Hanna
Jehosheba: Jehoshabeath

Rebecca: Rebekah
Sarah: Sara
Sheba: Queen of Sheba
Susanna: Susannah
Witch of Endor: Medium of Endor

Appendix 1.f:
Guide to Variant Names of New Testament Women

Anne: Ann, Anna
Herodias: Herodiade
Mary: Blessed Virgin Mary, Maria, La
 Vierge, La Vierge Marie, Marie, Mary
 the Mother, The Virgin Mary
Mary Cleophas: Mary Clophas
Mary Magdalene: Maddalena, Marie
 Madeleine, La Maddalena, La

Madeleine, Mary Magdalen, Mary of
 Magdala
Salome: Saloma, Salomé
Salome (the Midwife): Mary Salome
Samaritan Woman: Woman of Samaria
Veronica: Beranike, Bernice, Veronike
Woman with the Issue of Blood:
 Hemorrissha

Appendix 1.g:
Guide to Variant Names for Historical and Legendary Women

Agnes: Ines, Inez
Anastasia: Anastacia
Bacchantes: Bacchae, Maenads, Maenades
Befana: Befana, La Strega, La Vecchia
Bercht: Frau Berchta, Frau Berta,
 Berchta, Berchte, Berkta, Bertha,
 Bertie, Berty, Brechta, Eisenberta,
 Perchata, Percht, Perchta, Precht, Vrou
 Elde, Yrou-Elde
Berenice II: Berenice Eugertes, Berenike,
 Bernike, Bernice
Bernadette of Lourdes: Marie Bernarde
 Soubiros
Bridget of Sweden: Birgitta of Sweden
Brigid: Bride, Bridgit, Brig, Brighid
Catherine of Bologna: Caterina dei Vigri
Christine de Pizan: Christine de Pisan,
 Christine of Pisa
Cleopatra VI: Cleopatra VII, Cleopatra
 Ptolemy
Dorothea of Cappadocia: Dorothy of
 Cappadocia
Egeria: Etheria, Silvia of Aquitaine

Elaine: Lady of Shalott, Maid of Astolat
Elizabeth of Hungary: Elizabeth of
 Thuringia
Eudocia of Constantinople: Athenaïs,
 Eudociae
Fata Morgana: Morgana, Morgain La Fee,
 Morgaine La Fay, Morgaine La Faye,
 Morgan La Fay, Morgan the Fate
Fatima: Al-Zahrā, Fatimah
Fina: Serafina
Francesca Romana: Frances of Rome
Geneviève: Genovefa
Gertrude the Great: Gertrud von Helfta,
 Gertrude von Helfta
Guinevere: Guanhumara, Guenever,
 Guenhuvara, Guinevire, Gvenour,
 Gwenhwyfar, Gwenhwyvar
Hatshepsut: Hashepsowe, Hatasu,
 Hatshopsiti
Helena: Helen
Herrade of Landsburg: Herrad of
 Landsburg, Herrad von Landsburg,
 Herrade von Hohenburg, Herrade von
 Landsburg

Holle: Frau Holle, Hoide, Holda
Hourbout, Susannah: Horenbout,
 Hornebolt
Humility: Humilitas, Umilità de Faenza
Joan, Popess: Papess Joan, Pope Juan
Leocritia: Lucretia
Lucia: Lucy
Lucrece: Lucretia
Lucretia: Leocritia, Lucrece
Lucy: Lucia
Maenads: Bacchae, Bacchantes, Maenades,
 Thyiades
Mahamaya: Maya
Mary Magdalene of Pazzi: Maria
 Maddalena del Pazzi
Mechthild of Magdeburg: Mechtilde of
 Magdeburg
Morgan Le Fay: Fata Morgana, Morgan
 the Fate, Morgana, Morgain La Fee,
 Morgaine La Fay, Morgaine La Faye,
 Morgan La Fay
Odilia: Ottila

Phyllis: Campaspe
Pope Joan: Papess Joan, Popess Joan
Porcia: Portia
Priscilla: Priscia
Procla: Procula
Pudenziana: Pudens
Radegonde of Poitiers: Radegundis of
 Poitiers
Rosalia: Rosalie
Semeriamis: Sammuramat
Thecla: Tecla
Teresa of Lisieux: Thérèse of Lisieux,
 Marie François Martin
Umilità de Faenza: Humility
Vestal Virgins: Vestales
Walburga: Gauburge, Vaubourg,
 Waldburg, Walpurgis
Werburg: Werburga
Winifred: Gwenfrewi, Wenefred,
 Winifrede
Yashodā: Jesodha, Yashodha, Yaśodā,
 Yaśodha, Yasodha, Ysodha

Appendix 2.a:
Topical Guide to Goddesses

Abundance: Copia, Demeter
Agriculture: Abuk, Asnan, Ceres, Ceres
 Africanus, Chicomecoatl, Demeter,
 Gabjauja, Lauka-māte, Nepit, Nisaba,
 Ops, Pomona, Renenut, Robigo
Animals: Artemis, Artio, Britomartia,
 Diana, Epona, Ninsun, Pales, Saranyu,
 Sechat-Hor, Tabiti
Art: Beset, Minerva, Sarasvatī
Beauty: Aphrodite, Hathor, Umā, Venus,
 Zana
Beer: Tenenit
Birth, including Pregnancy, Childbirth,
 and Lactation: Anunītu, Artemis,
 Atchet, Auge, Bast, Beset, Ceres,
 Cihuacoatl, Diana, Eileithyia,
 Hannahanna, Heket, Hera, Ix Chel,
 Juno, Kalteš, Lucina, Meshkenit,
 Nekhbet, Ninti, Parca, Rumina, Sara-
 Kali, Taweret, Teteo innan, Thalna,
 Thesan, Thoeris, Tonacacihuatl
Ceremonies: Kebechet

Children: Chalchihuitlicue, Hemsut, Isis,
 Kwannon, Potina, Volva, Woyset
Compassion and Mercy: Kuan-yin,
 Kwannon, Ma-Zu, Ninlil, Tārā
Cosmic Energy: Lalita Tripurasundarī,
 Mahadevi, Maya, Shaktī, Urit-hekau
Creation: Bulaing, Estanathlehi,
 Jugumishanta, Luonnotar, Nugua, Nut
Dance: Bast, Hathor, Laka, Oya
Dawn: Aurora, Aya, Chasca, Eos, Eostre,
 Mater Matuta, Thesan, Ushas
Death, including Protection of the Dead:
 Agrona, Ala, Armaiti, Badb, Ceres,
 Dakini, Freya, Gilitine, Hathor, Hel,
 Hine-nui-te-po, Isis, Ixtab, Kālī,
 Libitina, Meh-Urit, Mert-Sekert,
 Namita, Nantosuelta, Nehalennia,
 Nephthys, Oya, Sarama, Selket, Šentait,
 Skadi, Smashana-Kali, Tellus Mater,
 Vidyujjvālākarāli
Desert: Mert-Sekert, Pachet, Velu māte
Destruction: Caillech, Cāmundā, Kālī,
 Nirrti, Tlaltecuhtli

Disaster: Até, Ekajatā
Discord: Discordia, Eris
Disease: Cihuateotl, Lamatšu, Sītalā
Divinization and Dreams: Nanše
Drought: Ba
Earth: Ana, Armaiti, Britomartia, Coatlicue, Demeter, Gaea, Hecate, Jian Lao, Ki, Larunda, Lur, Mati-syra-zemlya, Nokomis, Odudua, Prithivi, Rhea, Tailtice, Zemes māte, Zemnya
Eloquence: Benten, Vāch
Evil: Lamaštu, Sekhmet
Fate: Ananke, Atropos, Clotho, Decima, Fates, Fatit, Gul-šeš, Lachesis, Hemsut, Išduštaya and Papaya, Laima, Moirai, Nona, Norns, Nortia, Parca, Parcae, Shai and Renent, Tyché
Fertility: Aditi, Aine, Ala, al-Lāt, Anahit, Anukis, Aphrodite, Armaiti, Artemis, Asera, Asherah, Astarte, Brigit, Ceres, Coatlicue, Cybele, Demeter, Despoina, Diana of Ephesus, Epona, Feronia, Fjörgyn, Flora, Freya, Gefjon, Har, Heket, Hera, Hlodyn, Ilamatecuhtli, Laima, Larunda, Lauka-māte, Libera, Luperca, Makosh, Manash, Mokoš, Nanya, Nehalennia, Pachamana, Perchta, Qodshu, Rati, Renenut, Rosmerta, Semnai Theai, Šentait, Sopdet, Tellus Mater, Tinnit, Ukemochī, Uto, Vanir, Venus
Fire: Brigit, Chantico, Coatlicue, Feronia, Gabija, Itzpaployl, Pāndarā, Pele, Tabiti, Vesta
Fish: Hat-mehit
Food: Anna-Purna, Atchet, Chicomecoatl
Freedom of the Roman People: Libertas
Good Luck and Fortune: Fortuna, Gefjon, Laima, Lakshmī, Manat, Nortia, Shai and Renent, Tyché
Great Goddess: Asherah, Astarte, Balaath, Caillech, Fatima (legendary), Hathor, Ishtar, Isis, Mahadevi, Tanit
Health and Healing, including protection against disease: Aditi, Aryajangulī, Baba, Bast, Brigit, Ganga, Gula, Hygeia, Isis, Juturna, Kamrušpo,

Meditrina, Ninišina, Panacea, Pattini, Potina, Qedeshet, Rennit, Salus, Sauska, Tlazolteotl
Hearth and Home: Brigit, Chantico, Hestia, Vesta
Heaven, including the Afterlife: Hebat, Nut
Human Destiny: Kalteš
Hunt: Artemis, Artio, Devana, Diana, Sarama
Immortality: Xi-Wang-Mu
Jollity: Uzume
Justice: Adrasteia, Astraea, Iustitia, Nehem-t-auait, Nemesis, Poena, Themis
Law: Maat
Light: Šerida, Theia, Umā
Lightning and Thunder: Fugora, Hine-titama, Lei-zi, Vidyujjvālākarāli
Literature: Sešat
Love: Aine, Alpan, Aphrodite, Asera, Astarte, Astlik, Belili, Flora, Freya, Hathor, Inanna, Išhara, Kadeš, Kubaba, Kurukullā, Nanya, Prende, Qadesh, Qodshu, Rati, Sauska, Tlazolteotl, Turan, Venus, Xochiquetzal
Marriage and the Family: Ceres, Chalchihuitlicue, Freya, Hera, Isis, Juno, Kilya, Pattini, Tellus Mater, Vör
Memory: Mnesmosyne
Menstruation: Mena
Misfortune: Cihuateotl
Monarchy, including Sovereignty and the Throne: Hanwašit
Moon: Artemis, Belili, Chia, Cynthia, Diana, Fatima (legendary), Heng-O, Hina, Holle, Ilazki, Isis, Ix Chel, Ix Chiup, Kilya, Luna, Marama, Pasiphae, Persé, Seléne, Tanit, Tinnit
Mother: Achamoth, Aditi, Akka, Alom, Amentit, Ammavaru, Anna, Aranrhod, Ataecina, Atargaris, Bachue, Buana, Chandashi, Cybele, Dana, Danaan, Demeter, Durgā, Gaea, Gatumdu, Gaurī, Hannahanna, Hathor, Hera, Hina, Hsi Wang Mu, Ishtar, Isis, Izanami-No-Mikoto, Jörd, Juno, Kubaba, Lahar, Magna Mater, Mama,

Mari, Matrona, Meh-Urit, Modron, Nammu, Neith, Nemetona, Ninhuršaga, Ninlil, Pachamama, Pārvāti, Rennot, Rhea, Shin-Mu, Tanit, Tiāmat, Zemes māte

Mountain: Adrasteia, Fjörgyn

Music, including Song: Bast, Benten, Beset, Hathor, Laka, Meret, Sarasvatī

Nature: Abuk, Astlik, Britomartia, Fauna, Fjörgyn, Flidhais, Hine-titama, Isis

Night, including Sunset and the Dark: Hecate, Nott, Nyx, Rātrī

Oaths and Loyalty: Fides, Išhara, Māmitu, Vör

Order: Maat, Tefnut

Peace: Eirene, Pax

Poetry: Brigit, Sarasvatī

Rainbow: Iris

Religious Purification: Lua

Salt: Huitocihuatl

Security and Protection: Securitas, Unut

Sexuality, including Female Sexual Energy and Power: Anukis, Aparājīta, Aphrodite, Hera, Isis, Juno, Kadeš

Silence: Angerona

Spring: Blodeuwedd, Flora, Hebe, Ostara, Renpet

Storms, including Protection from: Oya

Sun: Aditi, Amaterasu Omikami, Atirat, Mārīcī, Ratī, Šapš, Saule, Wadjet, Zenenet

Thieves and Vagabonds: Laverna

Time: Kālī

Truth: Maat

Twilight: Chasca

Underworld, including the Afterlife: Ala, Alpan, Ataecina, Bēletsēri, Belili,

Epona, Ereshkigal, Gestinanna. Hecate, Hel, Izanagi-No-Mikoto, Laverna, Nungal, Persephone, Skadi, Vanth

Vegetation: Chalchihuitlicue, Duillae, Hine-rau-wharangi, Isis, Sif, Uto, Zemnya

Victory: Anahit, Brigantia, Nike, Victory

Vine: Libera

Virgin Mother: Chimalman, Shin-Mu, Tanit

Virginity, including Protection of: Artemis, Athena, Blancheflor, Diana, Tinnit

Virile Manhood: Virtus

War: Adraste, Agrona, Anat, Anath, Athena, Bachue, Bellona, Chimalman, Enyo, Freya, Inanna, Išhara, Minerva, Morrigan, Sekhment

Water: Anahit, Astarte, Boiuna, Caménae, Cyhiraeth, I, Juturna, Kaménae, Makosh, Satis, Sedna, Sopdet, Thalassa, Yemaja

Wealth: Vasudhārā

Weather: Ops, Veja māte

Weaving and Domestic Arts: Athena, Ixazalvah, Ix Chel, Minerva, Namita, Neith, Tait, Tlazolteotl, Uttu

Welfare of the State: Salus

Wisdom: Athena, Isis, Minerva, Prajñā, Prajñāpāramitā, Sapientia, Sešat, Shin-Mu, Sophia, Tārā, Ūma

Witches: Holle

Women, including Nurture and Protection of: Demeter, Eileithyia, Hera, Isis, Juno, Kwannon, Vör

Woods: Artemis, Diana, Flidhais, Medeine

Writing, including History, Literature, and Poetry: Sešat

Youth: Flora, Hebe, Juventas, Renpet

Appendix 2.b:
Topical Guide to Metaphorical Female Figures

Individual figures: Baubo, Blancheflor, Blodeuwedd, Bona Dea, Chloris, Concord, Constancy, Deceit, Ecclesia, Fama, Fides, Flora, History, Humility, Innocence, Inspiration, Iustitia, Melancholia, Metis, Obediance,

Obeisance, Peitho, Philosopy, Pheme, Phryne, Pudicitia, Spes, Synagoga, Truth

Group figures:

Deadly Sins: Anger, Avarice, Envy, Gluttony, Lust, Pride, Sloth

Fates: Atropos, Clotho, Fatit, Lachesis, Moriai, Nona, Norns, Nortia, Parca, Parcae, Skuld, Urd, Urme, Verdandi

Graces: Aglaia, Charites, Euprosyne, Thalia

Horae: Auxo, Dike, Eirene, Eunomia, Karpo, Thallo

Liberal Arts: Arithmetic, Astronomy, Dialectic, Geometry, Grammar, Music, Rhetoric

Muses: Calliope, Clio, Erato, Euterpe, Melpomene, Polyhymnia, Terpsichore, Thalia, Urania

Vices: Anger, Covetousness, Envy, Gluttony, Lust, Pride, Sloth

Virtues: Charity, Faith, Fortitude, Hope, Justice, Prudence, Temperance

Appendix 2.c:
Topical Guide to Celestial Female Beings

Bodhisattvas: Avalokiteshvara, Batō Kwannon, Cundī, Junei Kannon Bosatsu, Kuan-yin, Kwannon

Dancers and Musicians: Apsarās, Apsarāses, Dākinīs, Gopīs

Fairies: Aibell, Bean Sídhe, Befana, Bercht, Elves, Eumenides, Fairy, Mab, Perit, Repanse de Joie

Forest Spirits: Caipora, Dryad, Hamadryad, Nymph, Veela, Yakshas

Guardian Spirits: Aibell, Da-shi-zhi, Empusa, Fylgir, Fravasi, Hāriti, Lama, Laumé, Pañcaraksha

Maidservants: Houri, Lasas

Water Spirits: Naids, Nereids, Ningyo, Nixies, Nymph, Oceanids, Rhine Maidens, Sea Nymphs

Appendix 2.d:
Topical Guide to Demonic Female Beings

Avengers: Erinyes, Eumenides, Furies, Harpy

Dancers and Musicians: Bacchantes, Korybantes, Maenads

Demons: Agrat Bat Mahalat, Ammit, Culsu, Lamaštu, Lilith, Lilītu, Ljubi, Megaira, Peri, Psezpolnica, Sheila-na-gig, Strigae, Succubus

Enchanctresses: Circe, Medea, Mermaids

Guardian Spirits: Graeae

Headhuntresses: Salome, Herodiade

Monsters: Gorgons, Medusa, Scylla

Seductresses: Calypso, Circe

Sorcerers: Circe, Medea

Underworld: Galla

Witch: Baba-yaga, Cerridwen, Weird Sisters

Appendix 2.e:
Topical Guide to Old Testament Women

Daughters: Athaliah, Dinah, Jehosheba, Jemimah, Jephthah's Daughter, Keziah, Lo-ruhamah, Lot's Daughters, Milcah, Serah, Shelomith, Tamar, Taphath, Tirzah

Daughters-in-law: Ruth

Harlots: Oholah, Oholibah, Rahab the Harlot

Headhuntresses: Jael, Judith

Heroines: Deborah, Esther, Jael, Judith

Idolators: Athaliah, Jezebel, Queen of Sheba

Judge: Deborah
Maidservants: Abra, Hagar, Zilpah
Mistresses: Abishag the Shulamite,
    Bathsheba, Delilah, Rizpah
Mothers: Bathsheba, Eve, Hagar, Hannah,
    Leah, Rachel, Rebecca, Sarah, Zeruah
Mothers-in-law: Naomi
Prophetess: Deborah, Huldah
Queens: Athaliah, Bathsheba, Esther
Seductresses: Bathsheba, Delilah, Eve,
    Jezebel, Queen of Sheba

Sisters: Miriam
Unfaithful Wives: Gomer
Wise Women: Witch of Endor
Wives: Abigail, Adah and Zillah,
    Bathsheba, Elisheba, Esther, Eve,
    Hannah, Jecoliah, Leah, Lot's Wife,
    Michal, Milcah, Nehushta, Oholibamah,
    Potiphar's Wife, Rachel, Rebecca,
    Sarah, Susanna, Tamar, Taphath,
    Zipporah

Appendix 2.f:
Topical Guide to New Testament Women

Daughters: Mary, Jairus's Daughter
Faithful Followers: Joanna, Julia, Lydia,
    Mary Magdalene, Rhoda, Tabitha,
    Three Maries, Tryphaena, Woman with
    the Issue of Blood, Woman of Samaria,
    Woman Taken in Adultery
Headhuntresses: Herodias, Salome
Matrons: Euodia, Syntyche
Mothers: Anne, Elizabeth, Eunice, Lois,
    Mary, Mary Cleophas, Mary Salome

Prophetesses: Anna
Queens: Candace
Seductresses: Herodias, Salome, Scarlet
    Woman, Whore of Babylon
Sisters: Bernice, Martha of Bethany, Mary
    of Bethanyt
Wives: Elizabeth, Mary, Mary Cleophas,
    Mary Salome, Procla, Sapphira

Appendix 2.g:
Topical Guide to Historical and Legendary Women

Artists: Catherine of Bologna, Ende,
    Margaretha van Eyck, Lavinia Fontana,
    Fede Galizia, Artemisia Gentileschi,
    Guda, Caterina van Hemessen, Herrade
    of Landsberg, Hildegard of Bingen,
    Susannah Hourbout, [Mary] Edmonia
    Lewis, Judith Leyster, Barbara Longhi,
    Properza de' Rossi, Diana Ghisi
    Scultore, Sabina von Steinbach
Beauties: Cleopatra VI, Galatea, Helen of
    Troy, Pandora, Phryne, Psyche, Radhā
Courtesans: Hetaera, Phyllis, Thais
Daughters: Alcestis, Antigone, Danaë,
    Electra, Hesperides, Ino, Pero, Pleaides
Deaconesses: Apollonia, Radegonde of
    Poitiers
Doctors of the Church: Catherine of
    Siena, Teresa of Avila

Enchantesses: Morgan Le Fay
Femmes Fatales: Circe, Cleopatra VI,
    Siren, Thais
Foster Mothers: Acca Larentia, Almathea,
    Lupa, Melissa, Yashodā
Headhuntresses: Tomyris
Heroines: Angelica, Claudia, Cloelia,
    Deidre, Lucretia, Sophonisba, Tuccia,
    Virginia
Hunters: Atalanta, Daphne
Ideal Feminine: Beatrice (Portinari)
Maidens in distress: Andromeda, Clytie,
    Coronis, Daphne, Echo, Elaine,
    Erminia, Europa, Eurydice, Hero,
    Lamia, Sabine Women, Syrinx
Midwives: Acca Larentia, Salome the
    Midwife
Mothers: Aedon, Agrippina, Alcmene,

Althaea, Amphitrite, Andromache, Ariadne, Asteria, Callisto, Cassiopoeia, Cornelia, Danaë, Dimu, Embla, Eurynome, Jecuba, Latona, Leda, Leto, Lucretia, Mahamaya, Monica, Niobe, Rhea Silvia, Semele

Musicians: Cecilia, Hildegard of Bingem, Kassiane, Thekla the Nun

Nuns and/or Abbesses: Agnes of Assisi, Margaret Mary Alacoque, Beatrice of Nazareth, Bernadette of Lourdes, Bridget of Sweden, Brigid, Catherine of Bologna, Clare of Assisi, Elizabeth of Hungary, Gertrude, Gertrude the Great, Herrade of Landsberg, Hildegard of Bingen, Mechtild of Madgeburg, Melania the Younger, Radegonde of Poitiers, Rose of Lima, Scholastica, Teresa of Avila, Teresa of Lisieux, Walburga, Werburg

Patrons of the Arts: Galla Placidia

Priestesses: Alma Mater, Amata, Dakini, Io, Umati, Vestal Virgins

Princesses: Cassandra, Coronis, Erminia, Europa, Iphigenia, Ursula

Prophetesses: Cassandra, Pythia, Sibyls

Queens or Empresses: Boadicea, Berenice II, Cassiopoeia, Cleopatra VI, Clytemnestra, Cunegunda, Dido, Eudocia of Constantinople, Galla Placidia, Guinevire, Hecuba, Helen of Troy, Hippolyta, Medb, Omphale, Penthesilea, Phaedra, Semiriamis, Tomyris, Vashti

Religious leaders: Catherine of Siena, Clare of Assisi, Fatima (historical), Francesca Romana, Hildegard of Bingen, Popess Joan

Sacrifices: Ipighenia

Saints: Agape, Agatha, Agnes, Agnes of Assisi, Margaret Mary Alacoque, Anastacia, Apollonia, Artemidos, Bernadette of Lourdes, Bridget of Sweden, Brigid, Catherine of Alexandria, Catherine of Bologna, Catherine of Genoa, Catherine of Siena, Cecilia, Charity, Chionia, Christina, Clare of Assisi, Colomba of Córdoba, Cunegunda, Dorothea of Cappadocia, Elizabeth of Hungary, Eugenia, Euphemia, Faith, Felicity, Fina, Flora, Francesca Romana, Geneviéve, Gertrude, Gertrude the Great, Irene (third century), Irene (fourth century), Joan of Arc, Justina of Antioch, Justina of Padua, Kassiane, Lucretia, Lucy, Macrina, Margaret of Antioch, Margaret of Cortona, Mary of Egypt, Mary Magdalene of Pazzi, Monica, Paula and Eustochium, Pelagia, Perpetua and Felicity, Petonilla, Priscilla, Radegonde of Poitiers, Restituta, Rosalie, Rose of Lima, Sabina, Scholastica, Sophia, Teresa of Avila, Teresa of Lisieux, Thaïs, Thecla, Thekla the Nun, Ursula, Veronica, Walburga, Werburg, Wilgefortis, Winifred, Zita

Seductresses: Calypso, Circe, Cleopatra VI

Sorcerers: Calypso, Medea

Warriors: Amazons, Antiope, Boadicea, Brynhild, Clorinda, Hippolyta, Joan of Arc, Penthisilea, Valkyries

Weavers: Arachne, Athena

Witches: Aradia, Circe

Wives: Aedon, Agrippina, Alcestis, Althaea, Amphritrite, Andromache, Artemisia, Baucis, Berenice II, Chloe, Cornelia, Deianira, Eurydice, Griselda, Harmonia, Hecuba, Helen of Troy, Lucretia, Penelope, Porcia, Psyche, Pyrrha, Radhā, Sigyn

Writers: Beatrice of Nazareth, Bridget of Sweden, Catherine of Bologna, Catherine of Genoa, Christine de Pizan, Egeria (late fourth century), Eudocia of Constantinople, Gertrude the Great, Hadewijch, Herrade of Landsberg, Hildegard of Bingen, Anna Brownell Murphy Jameson, Julian of Norwich, Mechtild of Magdeburg, Sappho, Teresa of Avila, Teresa of Lisieux, Thekla the Nun, Clara Erskine Clement Waters

Index of Subjects

ᘐᐧᘑ

NOTE: This is basically a *subject index* comprised of iconographic themes, images, artists, religions, and historical and legendary figures. It is designed to assist the reader to find her way to specific topical entries, and to support comparative study between topics treated as separate entries (for instance: Animals, Flowers, Metaphorical female figures, Women artists, Women writers). Employed comparatively, this index may stimulate further thought and research on the part of readers.

A

Abisag the Shulamite, *see* Abishag the Shulamite.
Abundance, goddesses of, *see* Appendix 2.a: Topical Guide to Goddesses.
Acca Laurentia, *see* Acca Larentia.
Addittu, *see* Aditi.
Adit, *see* Aditi.
Aditya, *see* Aditi.
African goddesses, *see* Abuk, Ala, Ceres, Africanus, Chandaski, Odudua, Oya, Yemaja.
Agriculture, goddesses of, *see* Appendix 2.a: Topical Guide to Goddesses.
Aiobell, *see* Aibell.
Aiobhell, *see* Aibell.
Air, *see* Four Elements.
Akantha, *see* Acanthus.
Alceste, *see* Alcestis.
Alkeste, *see* Alcestis.
Alkestis, *see* Alcestis.
al-Lat, *see* al-Lāt.
Allat, *see* al-Lāt.
Almatheia, *see* Almathea.
Alpanu, *see* Alpan.
Alpha, *see* Ishtar.
Alphabetical symbolism, *see* A(ve) M(aria), M with a Crown, MA.

Alpnu, *see* Alpan.
Al-Zahrā, *see* Fatima (historical).
Ama-terasu-ō-mi-kami, *see* Amaterasu Omikami.
Ama-terasu-oho-hiru-me-no-mikoto, *see* Amaterasu Omikami.
Ame-no-uzume, *see* Uzume.
Ame-no-uzume-no-mikoto, *see* Uzume.
Amemait, *see* Ammit.
Amenit, *see* Amentit.
Ament, *see* Amentit.
Amenti, *see* Amentit.
Am-met, *see* Ammit.
Ammut, *see* Ammit.
Ana, *see* Buana.
Ana, *see* Dana.
Anahita, *see* Anat.
Anastacia, Saint, *see* Anastasia.
Andate, *see* Adraste.
Andrasta, *see* Adraste.
Andraste, *see* Adraste.
Animal, symbolism of, *see* Ant, Antelope, Apes, Asp, Ass, Basilisk, Bat, Bears, Beaver, Bee, Bestiary, Boar, Buffalo, Bull, Camel, Cat, Chamelon, Chimera, Cow, Crab, Crocodile, Deer, Dog, Donkey, Dragon, Elephant, Ermine, Fabulous Beasts, Fish, Fly, Fox, Frog, Gazelle,

Giraffe, Goat, Grasshopper, Griffin,
Gryphon, Hare, Hart, Hedgehog, Hind,
Hippocampus, Hippopotamus, *Historia
Animalium,* Hog, Horse, Hyena, Ladybug,
Lamb, Leopard, Lion, Lizard, Lynx,
Minotaur, Mole, Monkeys, Mythical
Beasts, Ox, Ox and Ass, Panther,
Physiologus, Pig, Rabbit, Ram, Rat,
Rhinoceros, Salamander, Scorpion,
Serpent, Sheep, Shrew, Snail, Snake,
Sphinx, Spider, Squirrel, Stag, Starfish,
Swine, Toad, Tortoise, Unicorn, Vulture,
Weasel, Whale, Wild Beast, Wolf, Worms.

Animals, goddesses of, *see* Appendix 2.a:
Topical Guide to Goddesses.

Ank, *see* Anukis.

Ann, Saint, *see* Anne, Saint.

Anna, Saint, *see* Anne, Saint.

Annunītum, *see* Anunītu.

Annuthat, *see* Anat.

Anouke, *see* Anukis.

Anoukis, *see* Anukis.

Anqet, *see* Anukis.

Anqt, *see* Anukis.

Anquet, *see* Anukis.

Anthat, *see* Anat.

Anthrati, *see* Anat.

Antit, *see* Anat.

Anu, *see* Dana.

Anuket, *see* Anukis.

Anukit, *see* Anukis.

Anuqet, *see* Anukis.

Aphaea, *see* Britomartia.

Appearance to Mary Magdalene (Noli Me
Tangere)

Arabian (pre-Islamic) goddesses, *see* al-Lāt,
al-'Uzza, Fatima (legendary), Manat,
Shayba.

Arbor Vitae, *see* Tree of Life.

Arianhod, *see* Aranhod.

Arianrhod, *see* Aranrhod.

Aridela, *see* Ariadne.

Armait, *see* Armaiti.

Armati, *see* Artmaiti.

Armenian goddesses, *see* Anahit, Astlik.

Art, goddesses of, *see* Appendix 2.a: Topical
Guide to Goddesses.

Art historical terms, *see* Achieropaeic image,
Achieropoitos, African art, Aniconism,
Australian Aboriginal art, Baroque art,
Buddhist art, Byzantine art, Christian art,
Christian iconography, Deesis, Egyptian
art, Fresco, Genre, Gothic art, Greek art,
Hindu art, Icon, Iconoclasm, Iconography,

Iconostasis, Illumination, Illustration,
International Gothic, Islamic art, Jain art,
Jewish art, Kore, Landscape, Mandala,
Mandorla, Mannerism, Medieval art,
Memento Mori, Mosaics, Oceanic art,
Pietá, Reliquary, Renaissance art, Rococo
art, Roman art, Romanesque art, Still Life,
Vanitas.

Artemis of Ephesus, *see* Diana of Ephesus.

Artists, *see* Fra Angelico, Jacopo Bellini,
Gentile Bellini, Giovanni Bellini, Gian
Lorenzo Bernini, Sandro Botticelli,
Michelangelo Merisi da Caravaggio,
Catherine of Bologna, Lucas Cranach,
Donatello, Duccio di Buoninsegna,
Albrecht Dürer, Ende, Hubert van Eyck,
Jan van Eyck, Margaretha van Eyck,
Lavinia Fontana, Fede Galizia, Artemisia
Gentileschi, Giotto di Bondone, El Greco,
Mathias Grünewald, Guda, Caterina van
Hemessen, Herrade of Landsberg,
Hildegard of Bingen, Hans Holbein the
Elder, Susannah Hourbout, Leonardo da
Vinci, [Mary] Edmonia Lewis, Judith
Leyster, Barbara Longhi, Andrea
Mantegna, Michelangelo Buonarotti,
Bartolomé Esteban Murillo, Raphael
Sanzio, Rembrandt van Rijn, Jusepe
Ribera, Dante Gabriel Rossetti, Properzia
de' Rossi, Peter Paul Rubens, Diana Ghisi
Scultore, Sabina von Steinbach, Rogier
van der Weyden, Francisco de Zurbarán.
See also Appendix 2.g: Topical Guide to
Historical and Legendary Women.

As, *see* Isis.

Aserat, *see* Asera.

Aserdus, *see* Asertu.

Aset, *see* Isis.

Asherath, *see* Asherah.

Ashirah, *see* Asherah.

Ashirath, *see* Asherah.

Ashtart, *see* Ishtar.

Aśokakāntā, *see* Ashokakāntā.

Ashtaroth, *see* Asherah, Astarte.

Ashtoreth, *see* Asherah, Astarte.

Ashtoroth, *see* Asherah, Astarte.

Ast, *see* Isis.

Astabhujā-Kurakulla, *see* Ashthābhujā-
Kurakulla.

Astar, *see* Astarte.

Astart, *see* Astarte.

Astert, *see* Astarte.

Astlik, *see* Astarte.

Ataecina, *see* Astarte.

Atalante, *see* Atalanta.
Athenaia, *see* Athena.
Athenaïs, *see* Eudocia of Constantinople.
Athene, *see* Athena.
Athir, *see* Hathor.
Athor, *see* Hathor.
Athtar, *see* Astarte.
Athyr, *see* Hathor.
Aticpac Calquicihuatl, *see* Chalchihuitlicue.
Atirat, *see* Asertu.
Attart, *see* Astarte.
Au Set, *see* Isis.
Australian goddesses, *see* Bulaing.
Avalokita, *see* Avalokiteshvara.
Avalokiteśvara, *see* Avalokiteshvara.
Avengers, *see* Appendix 2.d: Topical Guide
   to Demonic Female Beings.
Aya, *see* Serida.
Aztec goddesses, *see* Chalchihuitlicue,
   Chantico, Chicomecoatl, Cihuateotl,
   Coatlicue, Huixtocihuatl, Ilamatecuhtli,
   Itzpapaloyl, Mayahuel, Teteo innan,
   Tlaltecuhtli, Tlazolteotl, Tonacacihuatl,
   Xilonen, Xochiquetzol.

B

Baalat, *see* Baalath.
Baba Yaga, *see* Baba-yaga.
Bacchae, *see* Maenads.
Bacchantes, *see also* Maenads.
Banshie, *see* Banshee.
Bansith, *see* Banshee.
Bar-Do-Thos-Grol, *see* (Tibetan) Book of the
   Dead.
Basque goddesses, *see* Lar.
Bastet, *see* Bast.
Bastis, *see* Bast.
Bau, *see* Baba.
Bawu, *see* Baba.
Bdug-spas-ma, *see* Dākinīs.
Bean Nighe, *see* Bean Sídhe.
Bean Sôdhe, *see* Bean Sídhe.
Beauties, *see* Appendix 2.g: Topical Guide to
   Historical and Legendary Women.
Beauty, goddesses of, *see* Appendix 2.a:
   Topical Guide to Goddesses.
Beer, goddesses of, *see* Appendix 2.a: Topical
   Guide to Goddesses.
Befana, Saint, *see* Befana.
Belet, *see* Baalath.
Belet Seri, *see* Bēletsēri.
Beleterseteri, *see* Bēletsēri.
Beli Sheri, *see* Bēletsēri.

Belisheri, *see* Bēletsēri.
Belit Seri, *see* Bēletsēri.
Benzaiten, *see* Benten.
Benzai-ten, *see* Sarasvatī.
Benzai-tennyo, *see* Benten.
Beranike, *see* Veronica.
Berchta, *see* Bercht.
Berchte, *see* Bercht.
Berenice Eugertes, *see* Bernice II.
Berenike, *see* Bernice II.
Berkta, *see* Bercht.
Bernice, *see* Berenice II, Veronica.
Bernike, *see* Berenice II.
Bertha, *see* Bercht.
Bertie, *see* Bercht.
Berty, *see* Bercht.
Bhrikuti, *see* Tārā.
Bikuchi, *see* Tārā.
Billig-un Chinadu Kichaghar-a Kürük-sen,
   see Prajñāpāramitā.
Birgitta of Sweden, Saint, *see* Bridget of
   Sweden.
Birth goddesses, including pregnancy,
   childbirth, and lactation, *see* Appendix
   2.a: Topical Guide to Goddesses.
Blessed Virgin Mary, *see* Mary.
Blessed Mother, *see* Mary.
Blue Tārā, *see* Tārā.
Blodenwedd, *see* Blodeuwedd.
Blodeuedd, *see* Blodeuwedd.
Blodewedd, *see* Blodeuwedd.
Boat, *see* Ship.
Bodhisattvas, *see* Appendix 2.c: Topical
   Guide to Celestial Female Beings.
Books, *see* Apocrypha, Apocryphal Gospels,
   Bible, Biblia Pauperum, Book of Hours,
   Book of the Dead, (Tibetan) Book of the
   Dead, Divine Comedy, Golden Legend,
   Gospel of Mart, Historia Animalium,
   Hortus Delicarium, Malleus Maleficarium,
   Physiologus, Pistis Sophia, Psalter,
   Revelations of Saint Bridget of Sweden,
   Romance de la Rose, Scivias, Sibylline
   Books, Speculum Humanae Salvationis.
Book of Psalms, *see* Psalter.
Bo-satsu, *see* Bodhisattva.
Boudicea, *see* Boadicea.
Bouto, *see* Buto.
Brecata, *see* Brecht.
Bride, *see* Brigid, Saint.
Bridgit, *see* Brigid, Saint.
Brig, *see* Brigid, Saint.
Brigentis, *see* Brigantia.
Brighid, *see* Brigantia, Brigid, Saint.

Brigidu, *see* Brigantia.
Briginda, *see* Brigantia.
Brigindo, *see* Brigantia.
Brigittines, *see* Bridgettines.
British goddesses, *see* Agrona, Modron.
Brunhild, *see* Brynhild.
Brunhilda, *see* Brynhild.
Brunhilde, *see* Brynhild.
Brunnehilde, *see* Brunhild.
Buanann, *see* Buana.
Buan-ann, *see* Buana.
Bubastis, *see* Bast.
Buddha Dākinī, *see* Dākinīs.
Buddhist goddesses, *see* Aparājīta,
   Āryajangulī, Ashokakāntā, Ashthābhujā-
   Kurakulla, Avalokiteshvara, Batō
   Kwannon, Benten, Bhrkuti, Bodhisattva,
   Chinna-mastā, Cundī, Dakini, Ekajatā,
   Jian Lao, Juntei Kannon Bosatsu, Kuan-
   yin, Kurukullā, Kwannon, Lalita
   Tripurasundarī, Locana, Mahamaya,
   Mārīcī, Marishi-Ten, Pāndarā,
   Parnashavarī, Prajñā, Prajñāpāramitā,
   Śridevi, Tārā, Vajrāvārāhi, Vajrāyoginī,
   Vasudhārā, Vidyujjvālākarāli.
Bull of Minos, *see* Minotaur.
Butchō, *see* Ushnīsavijayā.
Byakusangai, *see* Sitātapatrā.

C

Campaspe, *see* Phyllis.
Candrā, *see* Cundī.
Car, *see* Britomartia.
Car-Dia, *see* Britomartia.
Carme, *see* Britomartia.
Carmenta, *see* Britomartia.
Carna, *see* Britomartia.
Carthaginian goddesses, *see* Tinnit.
Carthaginian women, historical and
   legendary, *see* Dido.
Caritas, *see* Charity.
Casménae, *see* Caménae.
Castitas, *see* Chastity.
Caterina dei Vigri, *see* Catherine of Bologna,
   Saint.
Celestial female beings, *see* Aglaia, Aibell,
   Angels, Apsarās, Apsarāses, Bean Sídhe,
   Beata, Befana, Bercht, Beset, Bdug-spos-
   ma, Blancheflor, Buddha Dākinī, Caipora,
   Dākānās, Dākinī-ten, Da-shi-zhi, Decuma,
   Dhupā, Dīpā, Disir, Cri-chab-ma, Dryads,
   Fairy, Fatit, Fylgir, Gabija, Gandhā, Gītā,
   Glu-ma, Gopīs, Hamadryad, Houri,

Karmadākīnī, Lama, Lasas, Lāsyā, Lhamo,
   Mab, Māla, Me-tog-ma, Naiads, Nereids,
   Ningyo, Nixies, Nymphs, Oceanids,
   Oreades, Padmadākīnī, Peri, Perit,
   Phreng-ba, Pleiades, Prende, Puspā,
   Ratnadākīnī, Rhine Maidens, Sea Nymphs,
   Sgeg-pa-ma, Shaktī, Snang-gsal-ma,
   Valkyries, Vajradākīnī, Veela, Víly,
   Vishvadākīnī, Yakshas.
Celestial female dancers and musicians, *see*
   Appendix 2.c: Topical Guide to Celestial
   Female Beings.
Celestial maidservants, *see* Appendix 2.c:
   Topical Guide to Celestial Female Beings.
Celtic goddesses, *see* Adraste, Aranrhod,
   Brigantia, Cyhiraeth, Danann, Epona,
   Flidhais, Margawsae, Matrona, Modron,
   Nemetona, Skadi, Sul.
Celtic women, legendary and historical, *see*
   Boadicea, Deidre, Medb, Morgan Le Fay.
Cerealia, *see* Cerialia.
Ceremonies, goddesses of, *see* Appendix 2.a:
   Topical Guide to Goddesses.
Ceridwen, *see* Cerridwen.
Chagham Sigürtei, *see* Sitātapatrā.
Chalchiuhclihuatl, *see* Chicomecoatl.
Ch'an Buddhism, *see* Buddhism.
Chang-E, *see* Heng-O.
Chang-Ngo, *see* Heng-O.
Ch'ang-O, *see* Heng-O.
Chang-O, *see* Heng-O.
Charites, *see* Graces.
Children, goddesses of, including nurture
   and protection, *see* Appendix 2.a: Topical
   Guide to Goddesses.
Chimalma, *see* Chimalman.
Chinese female deities, *see* Feng-Po,
   Heng-O, Hsi Wang Mu, Lei-zi, Ma-Zu,
   Nugua, Shin-Mu, Xi-Wang-Mu.
Chinnamasta, *see* Chinna-mastā.
Chinnamastaka, *see* Chinna-mastā.
Christ Appearing Before His Mother, *see*
   Appearance to His Mother.
Christian Scriptures, *see* New Testament.
Christian women, historical and legendary,
   see Agape, Angelica, Beatrice (Portinari),
   Clorinda, Elaine, Erminia, Eudocia of
   Constantinople, Eustochium, Galla
   Placidia, Griselda, Guinevere, Helena,
   Héloïse, Joan of Arc, Macrina, Melania
   the Younger, Monica, Paula, Popess Joan,
   Radegonde of Poitiers, Scholastica, Teresa
   of Avila, Thekla the Nun.
Christine de Pisan, *see* Christine de Pizan.

Disaster, goddesses of, *see* Appendix 2.a: Topical Guide to Goddesses.

Discord, goddesses of, *see* Appendix 2.a: Topical Guide to Goddesses.

Discordia, *see* Eris.

Disease, goddesses as bringers of, *see* Appendix 2.a: Topical Guide to Goddesses.

Divina Commedia, *see* Divine Comedy.

Divinization and dreams, goddesses of, *see* Appendix 2.a: Topical Guide to Goddesses.

Diya, *see* Dimu.

Doctors of the Church, *see* Appendix 2.g: Topical Guide to Historical and Legendary Women.

Dominations, *see* Angels.

Dominions, *see* Angels.

Don, *see* Dana.

Donann, *see* Dana.

Donau, *see* Dana.

Donmnu, *see* Dana.

Donkey, *see* Ass.

Doorga, *see* Durgā.

Dormition, *see* Falling Asleep of the Virgin Mary.

Dorothy of Cappadocia, *see* Dorothea of Cappadocia.

Dress, *see* Clothing.

Dri-chab-ma, *see* Dākinīs.

Drought, goddesses of, *see* Appendix 2.a: Topical Guide to Goddesses.

Dunay, *see* Dana.

Durgha, *see* Durgā.

Durja, *see* Durgā.

Dutyima, *see* Britomartia.

Dziewona, *see* Devana.

E

Earth, *see* Four Elements.

Earth, goddesses of, *see* Appendix 2.a: Topical Guide to Goddesses.

Edjo, *see* Buto.

Egyptian goddesses, *see* Amentit, Ammit, Anat, Anukis, Bast, Buto, Chensit, Hathor, Hat-mehit, Hedetet, Heket, Hemsut, Isis, Iusas and Nehbet Hotep, Junit, Kebechet, Maat, Mafdet, Meh-Urit, Meret, Meretseger, Mert-Sekert, Meshkenit, Mut, Nehem-t-auait, Neith, Nekhbet, Nephthys, Nepit, Nut, Pachet, Qadesh, Renenut, Rennit, Renpet, Reret, Satis, Sechat-Hor, Sekhmet, Selket, Šentait, Sešat, Shai and

Renent, Sopdet, Tait, Taweret, Tefnut, Thoeris, Uut, Urit-hekau, Uto, Wadjet, Woyset, Zenenet.

Egyptian women, historical and legendary, *see* Berenice II, Cleopatra VI, Hatshepsut, Ratī, Rat-Taui.

Eisenberta, *see* Bercht.

Ekajatā Mgrā Tārā, *see* Tārā.

Elektra, *see* Electra.

Elements, Four, *see* Four Elements.

Elizabeth of of Thuringia, Saint, *see* Elizabeth of Hungary, Saint.

El-Lat, *see* al-Lāt.

Eloquence, goddesses of, *see* Appendix 2.a: Topical Guide to Goddesses.

El-'Uzza, *see* al-'Uzza.

Enchantresses, *see* Appendix 2.d: Topical Guide to Demonic Female Beings, Appendix 2.g: Topical Guide to Historical and Legendary Women.

Ephesian Artemis, *see* Diana of Ephesus.

Ereskigal, *see* Ereshkigal.

Ereskigala, *see* Ereshkigal.

Erinyes, *see also* Furies.

Ešara, *see* Išhara.

Ese, *see* Isis.

Eset, *see* Isis.

Esi, *see* Isis.

Eskimo female deities, *see* Sedna.

Estana Hehi, *see* Estanathlehi.

Estar, *see* Ishtar.

Etheria, *see* Egeria.

Etruscan goddesses, *see* Alpan, Feronia, Nortia, Thalna, Thesan, Turan, Uni, Vanth.

Eudociae, *see* Eudocia of Constantinople.

Eumenides, *see also* Erinyes, Furies.

Eustochium, *see* Paula.

Eva, *see* Eve.

Evil, goddesses of, *see* Appendix 2.a: Topical Guide to Goddesses.

F

Fabulous Beasts, *see* Mythical Beasts.

Fairies, *see* Appendix 2.c: Topical Guide to Celestial Female Beings.

Faithful Followers, *see* Appendix 2.f: Topical Guide to New Testament Women.

Fama, *see* Pheme.

Fata, *see* Fates.

Fata Morgana, *see* Morgan Le Fay.

Fate, goddesses of, *see* Appendix 2.a: Topical Guide to Goddesses.

Fates, see also Atropos, Clotho, Lachesis, Norns, Urme.

Fatimah, see Fatima (historical).

Feitian, see Apsarās, Apsarāses.

Felicity, see Perpetua and Felicity.

Femmes Fatales, see Appendix 2.g: Topical Guide to Historical and Legendary Women.

Fertility, goddesses of, see Appendix 2.a: Topical Guide to Goddesses.

Festivals, see Cerialia, Eleusian Mysteries, Matralia, Matronalia, Meditinalia, Minervalia, Panathenaea, Purim, Rosalia, Thesmorphoria, Venevalid, Vestalia, Walpurgisnacht, Witches' Sabbat.

Fire, see Four Elements.

Fire, goddesses of, see Appendix 2.a: Topical Guide to Goddesses.

Fish, goddesses of, see Appendix 2.a: Topical Guide to Goddesses.

Fjorgyn, see Hlodyn.

Flidais, see Flidhais.

Flowers, symbolism of, see Almond, Anemone, Blancheflor, Blodeuwedd, Bluebell, Carnation, Cherry, Columbine, Convolvulus, Cyclamen, Daffodil, Daisy, Dandelion, Flora, Forget-me-not, Hyacinth, Iris, Jasmine, Lady's Bed Straw, Lady's Mantle, Lady's Slipper, Lavender, Lily, Lily-of-the-Valley, Lotus, Marigold, Myrtle, Narcissus, Pansy, Peony, Periwinkle, Poppy, Primrose, Rose, Snowdrop, Sunflower, Sword Lily, Violet.

Foding, see Ushnīśavijayā.

Food, including nourishment and nurture, goddesses of, see Appendix 2.a: Topical Guide to Goddesses.

Forest spirits, see Appendix 2.c: Topical Guide to Celestial Female Beings.

Fortune, see Fortuna.

Foster Mothers, see Appendix 2.g: Topical Guide to Historical and Legendary Women.

Fountain, see Well.

Frances of Rome, see Francesca Romana.

Frau Berchta, see Bercht.

Frau Berta, see Bercht.

Frau Holle, see Holle.

Freyja, see Freya.

Freyjia, see Freya.

Fruits, symbolism of, see Apple, Apples of the Hesperides, Cherry, Date, Fig, Grapes, Lemon, Orange, Peach, Pear, Plum, Pomegranate, Quince, Strawberry.

Furiae, see Furies.

Fylgjur, see Fylgir.

G

Gabeta, see Gabija.

Gabieta, see Gabija.

Gabjaiya, see Gabjauja.

Gaelic goddesses, see Rosmerta.

Gaia, see Gaea.

Galaxy, see Milky Way.

Gallic goddesses, see Minerva, Nantosuelta, Sequana.

Gandhā, see Dākinīs.

Garden, Enclosed, see Enclosed Garden.

Garden of Delights, see Hortus Delicarium.

Gatumdug, see Gatumdu.

Gauburge, see Walburga.

Gdags-dkar Chan-Ma, see Sitātapatrā.

Ge, see Gaea.

Gea, see Gaea.

Genovefa, see Geneviève.

Germanic goddesses, see Eostre, Fjörgyn, Freya, Gefjon, Holle, Idun, Nehalennia, Ostara, Sif, Sigyn, Skadi, Vanir, Volva, Vör.

Gertrud von Helfta, see Gertrude the Great.

Gertrude von Helfta, see Gertrude the Great.

Geshtinanna, see Geštinana.

Geštinanna, see Geštinana.

Ghe-ma, see Dākinīs.

Giovanni da Fiesola, Fra, see Angelico, Fra.

Gītā, see Dākinīs.

Gnostic goddesses, see Achamoth, Pistis Sophia, Zoë.

Golden Calf, see Calf, Golden.

Good Luck and Fortune, goddesses of, see Appendix 2.a: Topical Guide to Goddesses.

Gorgonaion, see Gorgoneion.

Gothardt, Mathis Neithardt, see Grünewald, Mathias.

Graces, see also Aglaia, Euphrosyne, Thalia.

Graiae, see Graeae.

Graii, see Graeae.

Gratiae, see Graces.

Great Goddesses, see Appendix 2.a: Topical Guide to Goddesses.

Greek goddesses, see Adrasteia, Anake, Aphrodite, Artemis, Astraea, Até, Athena, Auge, Auxo, Britomartia, Chloris, Cynthia, Demeter, Despoina, Discordia, Eilaithyia, Eirene, Enyo, Eris, Gaea, Hebe, Hecate,

Hera, Hestia, Hygeia, Karpo, Maia, Mnemosyne, Moirai, Nemesis, Nike, Nyx, Panacea, Pasiphae, Persé, Persephone, Seléne, Semnai Theai, Thalassa, Theia, Themis, Thetis.

Greek women, historical and legendary, *see* Aedon, Alcestis, Alcmene, Almathea, Althaea, Amazons, Amphitrite, Andromache, Andromeda, Antigone, Antiope, Arachne, Arethusa, Ariadne, Asteria, Atalanta, Atropos, Bacchantes, Baucis, Calliope, Callisto, Calypso, Cassandra, Cassiopeia, Chloe, Circe, Clio, Clotho, Clytemnestra, Clytie, Coronis, Danaë, Daphne, Deianira, Echo, Electra, Europa, Eurydice, Eurynome, Galatea, Harmonia, Helen of Troy, Helle, Hero, Hetaera, Hippolyta, Ino, Io, Iphigenia, Lamia, Leda, Leto, Maenads, Medea, Melissa, Metis, Niobe, Omphale, Pallas, Pandora, Pasithea, Penelope, Phaedra, Phryne, Phyllis, Psyche, Pythia, Rhea, Sappho, Semele, Syrinx, Thais, Thisbe.

Green Tārā, *see* Tārā.

Grey, *see* Gray.

Gryphon, *see* Griffin.

gTsug-tor Rnam-par rGyal-ma, *see* Ushnīsavijayā.

Guanahumara, *see* Guinivere.

Guan-yin, *see* Kuan-yin.

Guanyin, *see* Kuan-yin.

Guardian Spirits, *see* Appendix 2.c: Topical Guide to Celestial Female Beings; Appendix 2.d: Topical Guide to Demonic Female Beings.

Guenever, *see* Guinevere.

Guenhuvara, *see* Guinevere.

Guinevire, *see* Guinevere.

Gul-ašeš, *see* Gul-šeš.

Gulšeš, *se* Gul-šeš.

Gupapa, *see* Kubaba.

Gvenour, *see* Guinevere.

Gwenfrewi, *see* Winifred.

Gwenhwyfar, *see* Guinevere.

Gwenhwyvar, *see* Guinevere.

H

Hammer of Witches, *see* Malleus Malleficarum.

Hanna, *see* Hannah.

Hannya Bosatsu, *see* Prajñāpāramitā.

Hapatu, *see* Hebat.

Haramitsu, *see* Prajñāpāramitā.

Harlots, *see* Appendix 2.e: Topical Guide to Old Testament Women.

Hashepsowe, *see* Hatshepsut.

Hatasu, *see* Hatshepsut.

Hatshopsiti, *see* Hatshepsut.

Headhuntresses, *see* Appendix 2.d: Topical Guide to Demonic Female Beings; Appendix 2.e: Topical Guide to Old Testament Women; Appendix 2.f: Topical Guide to New Testament Women; Appendix 2.g: Topical Guide to Historical and Legendary Women.

Health and Healing, including protection against disease, goddesses of, *see* Appendix 2.a: Topical Guide to Goddesses.

Hearth and Home, goddesses of, *see* Appendix 2.a: Topical Guide to Goddesses.

Heaven, including the Afterlife, goddesses of, *see* Appendix 2.a: Topical Guide to Goddesses.

Hebrew Scripture, *see* Old Testament.

Hekate, *see* Hecate.

Hekt, *see* Heket.

Hekuba, *see* Hecuba.

Helen, Saint, *see* Helena, Saint.

He-li Di, *see* Hariti.

Hemorrissha, *see* Woman with the Issue of Blood.

Hemuset, *see* Hemsut.

Heng-E, *see* Heng-O.

Hepat, *see* Hebat.

Heqet, *see* Heket.

Heqt, *see* Heket.

Heqtit, *see* Heket.

Hequet, *see* Heket.

Hermaphroditus, *see* Hermaphrodite.

Herodiade, *see* Herodias.

Heroines, *see* Appendix 2.e: Topical Guide to Old Testament Women, Appendix 2.g: Topical Guide to Historical and Legendary Women.

Herrad of Landsburg, *see* Herrade of Landsburg.

Herrad von Landsburg, *see* Herrade of Landsburg.

Herrade von Hohenburg, *see* Herrade of Landsburg.

Herrade von Landsburg, *see* Herrade of Landsburg.

Hesi, *see* Isis.

Hether, *see* Hathor.

Hinayna Buddhism, *see* Buddhism.

Hindu goddesses, *see* Aditi, Ammavaru,
Armaiti, Cāmundā, Danu, Devi, Durgā,
Ganga, Gaurī, Kāmāksī, Kālī, Korrawi,
Lakshmī, Mahadevi, Manash, Mari,
Mātaras, Maya, Nirrti, Padmapāni,
Pārvāti, Prithivi, Rātrī, Sarama, Saranyu,
Saravastī, Sati, Sītā, Sītalā, Sitātapatrā,
Ūma, Ushas, Ushnīsaviyayā, Virāj.
Hindu women, historical and legendary, *see*
Gopīs, Radhā, Yashodā.
Hine-ahu-one, *see* Hine-ahuone.
Hine-tītama, *see* Hinw-titama.
Hine-titamauri, *see* Hine-titama.
Hippolyte, *see* Hippolyta.
Hiqit, *see* Hcket.
Hiquet, *see* Heket.
Hispanic goddesses, *see* Ataecina, Duillae.
Hiten, *see* Apsarās, Apsarāses.
Hiyoi-ten, *see* Parnashavarī.
Hlödin, *see* Hlodyn.
Hlothyn, *see* Hlodyn.
Hod-zu Chen-Ma, *see* Mārīcī.
Hoide, *see* Holle.
Holda, *see* Holle.
Holy Women, *see* Maries, The Three.
Horenbout, Susannah, *see* Hourbout,
Susannah.
Horn of Plenty, *see* Cornucopia.
Hornebolt, Susannah, *see* Hourbout,
Susannah.
Hortus Conclusus, *see* Garden Enclosed.
Hōshu, *see* Cintāmani.
Human Body, *see* Breast, Eye, Foot, Hand,
Head, Heart, Skeleton, Skull, Teeth.
Human Destiny, goddesses of, *see* Appendix
2.a: Topical Guide to Goddesses.
Humilitas, *see* Humility.
Hunt, goddesses of, *see* Appendix 2.a:
Topical Guide to Goddesses.
Hunters, *see* Appendix 2.g: Topical Guide to
Historical and Legendary Women.
Hur, *see* Houri.
Hygea, *see* Hygeia.
Hygia, *see* Hygeia.
Hygieia, *see* Hygeia.

I

Icelandic goddesses, *see* Hlodyn, Jörd.
Ideal Feminine, *see* Appendix 2.g: Topical
Guide to Historical and Legendary
Women.
Idolaters, *see* Appendix 2.e: Topical Guide
to Old Testament Women.

Ilex, *see* Holly.
Illargi, *see* Ilazki.
Illargui, *see* Ilazki.
Immortality, goddesses of, *see* Appendix 2.a:
Topical Guide to Goddesses.
Inadjet, *see* Buto.
Inana, *see* Inanna.
Incan goddesses, *see* Chasca, Kilya, Mama
Occlo, Pachamama.
Ines, Saint, *see* Agnes.
Inez, Saint, *see* Agnes.
Invidia, *see* Envy.
In-zō, *see* Mudrā.
Iratagi, *see* Ilazki.
Irene, *see* Eirene.
Iretagi, *see* Ilazki.
Iretargui, *see* Ilazki.
Irish goddesses, *see* Aine, Ana, Badb, Banta,
Brigit, Buana, Caillech, Dana, Danaan,
Morrigan, Tailtice.
Isanami-No-Kami, *see* Izanami-No-Mikoto.
Isanami-No-Mikoto, *see* Izanami-No-Mikoto.
Išara, *see* Ishara.
Islamic women, historical and legendary, *see*
Fatima (historical), Fatima al-Ma'sumah.
Istar, *see* Ishtar.
Istara, *see* Ishtar.
Istaru, *see* Ishtar.
Italic goddesses, *see* Camÿnae, Kamÿnae,
Mater Matuta, Rumina, Vesta.
Iussaet and Nebt-Hotep, *see* Iusas and
Nehbet Hotep.
Iuturna, *see* Juturna.
Iuventas, *see* Juventas.
Ixchel, *see* Ix Chel.
Ix Ch'up, *see* Ix Chiup.
Izanami-No-Kami, *see* Izanami-No-Mikoto.

J

Jañgulī, *see* Āryajangulī.
Jehoshabeath, *see* Jehosheba.
Jesodha, *see* Yashodā.
Jewelry, *see* Brisingamen, Cintāmani,
Comma, Coral, Cowrie Shells, Crown,
Gold, Hand-of-Fatima, Hand-of-Ishtar,
Menat, Necklace, Pearl, Silver, Tiara.
Jezi Baba, *see* Baba-yaga.
Jōguri-dōnyō, *see* Āryajangulī.
Jollity, goddesses of, *see* Appendix 2.a:
Topical Guide to Goddesses.
Josodha, *see* Yashodā.
Judges, *see* Appendix 2.e: Topical Guide to
Old Testament Women.

Magna Mater, *see* Mother/Great Mother/ Mother Goddess.

Mahayna Buddhism, *see* Buddhism.

Maht, *see* Maat.

Maid of Astolat, *see* Elaine.

Maidens in Distress, *see* Appendix 2.g: Topical Guide to Historical and Legendary Women.

Maidservants, *see* Appendix 2.e: Topical Guide to Old Testament Women.

Mait, *see* Maat.

Mālā, *see* Dākinīs.

Malizhi, *see* Marīcī.

Mami, *see* Mama.

Mammetu, *see* Māmitu.

Mammit, *see* Māmitu.

Mammitu, *see* Mamitu.

Manāt, *see* Manat.

Mani, *see* Cintāmani.

Mantovana, *see* Diana Ghisi Scultore.

Maria, *see* Mary.

Maria Maddalena, *see* Mary Magdalene.

Maria Maddalena dei Pazzi, *see* Mary Magdalene of Pazzi.

Marie, *see* Mary.

Marie Madeleine, *see* Mary Magdalene.

Marishi-ten, *see* Marīcī.

Marriage and the Family, goddesses of, *see* Appendix 2.a: Topical Guide to Goddesses.

Martin, Marie François, *see* Teresa of Lisieux.

Mary, life and symbolism of, *see* Meeting at the Golden Gate, Nativity of the Virgin Mary, Presentation of the Virgin Mary in the Temple, Betrothal and Marriage of the Virgin Mary, Annunciation to the Virgin Mary, Visitation, Nativity of Jesus Christ, Purification of the Virgin Mary, Marriage at Cana, Mourning (including Deposition, Lamentation, and Pietá), Pentecost, Annunciation of the Death of the Virgin Mary, Dormition of the Virgin Mary, Assumption of the Virgin Mary, Coronation of the Virgin Mary.

Mary Clophas, Saint, *see* Mary Cleophas.

Mary Magdalen, *see* Mary Magdalene.

Mary of Magdala, *see* Mary Magdalene.

Mary the Mother, *see* Mary.

Maskhonit, *see* Meshkenit.

Matrons, *see* Appendix 2.f: Topical Guide to New Testament Women.

Mauit, *see* Mut.

Maut, *see* Maat, Mut.

Maya, *see* Mahamaya.

Mayan goddesses, *see* Alom, Caquixaha, I, Ixazalvah, Ix Chel, Ix Chiup, Ixtab.

Mayauel, *see* Mayahuel.

Mayet, *see* Maat.

Mechit, *see* Mehit.

Mechtilde of Magdeburg, *see* Mechthild of Magdeburg.

Medium of Endor, *see* Witch of Endor.

Mehet-Uret, *see* Meh-Urit.

Mehturt, *see* Meh-Urit.

Mehueret, *see* Meh-Urit.

Meh-Urt, *see* Meh-Urit.

Meme, *see* Gula.

Memory, goddesses of, *see* Appendix 2.a: Topical Guide to Goddesses.

Méne, *see* Seléne.

Meneruva, *see* Minerva.

Menevra, *see* Minerva.

Menrfa, *see* Minerva.

Menstruation, goddesses of, *see* Appendix 2.a: Topical Guide to Goddesses.

Menvra, *see* Minerva.

Meresegir, *see* Meretseger.

Merseger, *see* Meretseger.

Mersekhnet, *see* Meshkent.

Mert, *see* Meret.

Mertseger, *see* Meshkent, Meretseger.

Meshkent, *see* Meshkenit.

Meshkhent, *see* Meshkenit.

Meskhoni, *see* Meshkenit.

Mesoamerican goddesses, *see* Alom, Caquixaha, Chalchihuitlicue, Chantico, Chicomecoatl, Cihuateotl, Coatlicue, Huixtocihuatl, I, Ilamatecuhtli, Itzpapaloyl, Ixazalvah, Ix Chel, Ix Chiup, Ixtab Mayahuel, Teteo innan, Tlaltecuhtli, Tlazolteotl, Tonacacihuatl, Xilonen, Xochiquetzol.

Mesopotamian and Near Eastern goddesses, *see* Akka, Anath, Anunītu, Asera, Asherah, Asnan, Astarte, Atargatis, Atirat, Aya, Bēletsēri, Belili, Damgalnuna, Diana of Ephesus, Dumuziabzu, Ereshkigal, Gatumdu, Geštinana, Gestinanna, Gula, Gulšeš, Hannhanna, Hanwašit, Har, Hebat, Inanna, Išduštaya and Papaya, Išhara, Ishtar, Kamrušpa, Kadeš, Kadi, Kubata, Lahar, Mama Nammu, Māmitu, Nanše, Nanya, Ninhuršaga, Ninišina, Ninlil, Ninšubur, Ninsun, Ninti, Nungal, Qedeshet, Qodshu, Šapš, Sarpenitu, Sauska, Šerida, Tabiti, Tašmetu, Tiāmat, Uttu.

Nepthys, *see* Nephthys.
Nereides, *see* Nereids.
Nesbit, *see* Mut.
Net, *see* Neith, Nut.
New Testament women, *see* Anna, Anne, Bernice, Canaanite Woman's Daughter, Candace, Elizabeth, Eunice, Euodia, Hemorrhissa, Herodias, Jairus' Daughter, Joanna, Lois, Lydia, Peter's Mother-in-Law, Procla, Rhoda, Salome, Sapphira, Scarlet Woman, Syntyche, Tabitha, Tryphaena, Whore of Babylon, Woman Clothed with the Sun, Woman with the Issue of Blood, Woman of Samaria, Woman Taken in Adultery.
Ngag-gi Tha mo, *see* Sarasvatī.
Nidaba, *see* Nisaba.
Night, *see* Nyx.
Night, including Sunset and the Dark, goddesses of, *see* Appendix 2.a: Topical Guide to Goddesses.
Ninisina, *see* Gula.
Ninkarrak, *see* Gula.
Nintinuga, *see* Gula.
Nissaba, *see* Nisaba.
Nit, *see* Neith, Nut.
Nix, *see* Nixies.
Nixe, *see* Nixies.
Nixy, *see* Nixies.
No-Ko-Hana, *see* Sengen.
Noot, *see* Nut.
Nordic goddesses, *see* Dana, Freya, Hel, Luonnotar, Nott, Raudra, Urd.
Nordic women, historical and legendary, *see* Gullveig.
Nü-gua, *see* Nugua.
Nuit, *see* Nut.
Numbers, symbolism of, *see* Eight, Fifteen, Five, Forty, Four, Fourteen, Nine, One, Seven, Six, Ten, Thirteen, Three, Twelve, Two, Zero.
Nuns and Abbesses, *see* Appendix 2.g: Topical Guide to Historical and Legendary Women.
Nyo-i, *see* Ju-i.
Nyo-i-shu, *see* Cintāmani.

O

Oaths and Loyalty, goddesses, *see* Appendix 2.a: Topical Guide to Goddesses.
Oceanic and Polynesian female deities, *see* Hainuwele, Haumea, Hina, Hine-ahuone, Hine-nui-te-po, Hine-ram-wharangi, Hine-titama, Hintubuhet, Jugumishanta, Laka, Marama, Namita, Pele, Rati, Siliwe Nazarata.
Oceanides, *see* Oceanids.
Old Testament women, *see* Abigail, Abishag the Shulamite, Abra, Adah and Zillah, Athaliah, Bathsheba, Deborah, Delilah, Dinah, Elisheba, Esther, Eve, Gomer, Hagar, Hannah, Hoglah, Hokmah, Huldah, Jael, Jecoliah, Jehosheba, Jemimah, Jephthah's Daughter, Jezebel, Judith, Keziah, Leah, Lo-ruhamah, Lot's Daughters, Lot's Wife, Michal, Milcah, Miriam, Naomi, Nehusta, Oholah, Oholibah, Oholibamah, Potiphar's Wife, Queen of Sheba, Rachel, Rahab, Rahab the Harlot, Rebecca, Rizpah, Ruth, Sarah, Serah, Shelomith, Shibboleth, Susannah, Tamar, Taphath, Tirzah, Vashti, Witch of Endor, Zebidah, Zeruah, Zilpha, Zipporah.
Omikami Amaterasu, *see* Amaterasu Omikami.
Order, goddesses of, *see* Appendix 2.a: Topical Guide to Goddesses.
Ottila, *see* Odilia.

P

Padmadākinīs, *see* Dākinīs.
Panakeia, *see* Panacea.
Panathenaia, *see* Panathenaia.
Papess Joan, *see* Joan.
Parcae, *see* Fates.
Parnaśavarī, *see* Parnashavari.
Parsee goddesses, *see* Anahit.
Patrons, *see* Donors.
Patrons of the Arts, *see* Appendix 2.g: Topical Guide to Historical and Legendary Women.
Peace, including Prosperity, goddesses of, *see* Appendix 2.a: Topical Guide to Goddesses.
Penthesilea, *see* Penthesileia.
Percht, *see* Bercht.
Perchta, *see* Bercht.
Perseis, *see* Persé.
Persephassa, *see* Persephone.
Persephoneia, *see* Persephone.
Persian (pre-Islamic) goddesses, *see* Daēnā.
Phaelmina, *see* Nightingale.
Phersephassa, *see* Persephone.
Phreng-ba, *see* Dākinīs.
Pinenkir, *see* Pinikir.

Uatchura, *see* Buto.
Uazet, *see* Buto.
Uazit, *see* Buto.
Udjat, *see* Buto.
Udzume, *see* Uzume.
Ugra-Tārā, *see* Ekajatā.
Uma, *see* Umā.
Umā-Maheśvara, *see* Umā.
Umilità de Faenza, *see* Humility, Saint.
Underworld, including the Afterlife, goddesses of, *see* Appendix 2.a: Topical Guide to Goddesses.
Underworld spirits, *see* Appendix 2.d: Topical Guide to Demonic Female Beings.
Unfaithful wives, *see* Appendix 2.e: Topical Guide to Old Testament Women.
Ursitory, *see* Urme.
Uzoit, *see* Buto.

V

Vac, *see* Vach.
Vajradākinī, *see* Dākinīs.
Vajryna Buddhism, *see* Buddhism.
Vajravārāhi, *see* Mārīcī.
Vak, *see* Vāch.
Vara, *see* Vör.
Vasundhārā, *see* Vasudhārā.
Vaubourg, *see* Walburga.
Veela, *see* Vala.
Vegetables, symbolism of, *see* Beans, Garlic, Gourds, Mustard Seed, Olive, Parsley, Thistle.
Vegetation, goddesses of, *see* Appendix 2.a: Topical Guide to Goddesses.
Venus Genetrix, *see* Venus.
Venus Observa, *see* Venus.
Veronike, *see* Veronica.
Vesperbild, *see* Pietá.
Vestales, *see* Vestal Virgin.
Victory, goddesses of, *see* Appendix 2.a: Topical Guide to Goddesses.
Vidyujjvālākarāli, *see* Ekajatā.
Vila, *see* Vala.
Vine, goddesses of, *see* Appendix 2.a: Topical Guide to Goddesses.
Virgin Mary, *see* Mary.
Virgin Mother Goddesses, *see* Appendix 2.a: Topical Guide to Goddesses.
Virginity, including Protection of, goddesses of, *see* Appendix 2.a: Topical Guide to Goddesses.
Virile Manhood, goddesses of: *see* Appendix 2.a: Topical Guide to Godesses.

Vishvadākinī, *see* Dākinīs.
Völva, *see* Vala.
Vrou Elde, *see* Bercht.

W

Wadjet, *see* Uto.
Waldburg, *see* Walburga.
Walküren, *see* Valkyries.
Walpurgis, *see* Walburga.
War, goddesses of, *see* Appendix 2.a: Topical Guide to Goddesses.
Warriors, *see* Appendix 2.g: Topical Guide to Historical and Legendary Women.
Water, *see* Four Elements.
Water, goddesses of, *see* Appendix 2.a: Topical Guide to Goddesses.
Water Spirits, *see* Appendix 2.c: Topical Guide to Celestial Female Beings.
Weather, goddesses of, *see* Appendix 2.a: Topical Guide to Goddesses.
Weavers, *see* Appendix 2.g: Topical Guide to Historical and Legendary Women.
Weaving and Domestic Arts, goddesses of, *see* Appendix 2.a: Topical Guide to Goddesses.
Wenefred, *see* Winifred.
Werburga, *see* Werburg.
White Tārā, *see* Tārā.
Winifrede, *see* Winifred.
Wisdom, goddesses of, *see* Appendix 2.a: Topical Guide to Goddesses.
Wise Women, *see* Appendix 2.e: Topical Guide to Old Testament Women.
Witches, *see* Appendix 2.d: Topical Guide to Demonic Female Beings, Appendix 2.g: Topical Guide to Historical and Legendary Women.
Witches, goddesses of, *see* Appendix 2.a: Topical Guide to Goddesses.
Wives, *see* Appendix 2.e: Topical Guide to Old Testament Women, Appendix 2.f: Topical Guide to New Testament Women, Appendix 2.g: Topical Guide to Historical and Legendary Women.
Women, including Nurture and Protection of, goddesses of, *see* Appendix 2.a: Topical Guide to Goddesses.
Women artists, *see* Catherine of Bologna, Ende, Margaretha van Eyck, Lavinia Fontana, Fede Galizia, Artemisia Gentileschi, Guda, Caterina van Hemessen, Herrade of Landsburg, Hildegard of Bingen, Susannah Hourbout,

[Mary] Edmonia Lewis, Judith Leyster, Barbara Longhi, Properzia de' Rossi, Diana Ghisi Scultore, Sabina von Steinbach. *See also* Appendix 2.g: Topical Guide to Historical and Legendary Women.

Women religious, *see* Abbess, Anchoress, Bridgettines, Canoness, Dakini, Desert Mothers, Nuns, Priestess, Prioress, Prophet(ess), Poor Clares, Sisters, Vestal Virgin.

Women religious leaders, *see* Agnes of Assisi, Margaret Mary Alacoque, Beatrice of Nazareth, Bridget of Sweden, Brigid, Catherine of Siena, Clare of Assisi, Elizabeth of Hungary, Francesca Romana, Gertrude the Great, Hildegard of Bingen, Humility, Marina, Melania the Younger, Radegonde of Poitiers, Scholastica, Teresa of Avila, Walburga. *See also* Appendix 2.g: Topical Guide to Historical and Legendary Women.

Women writers, *see* Beatrice of Nazareth, Bridget of Sweden, Catherine of Bologna, Catherine of Genoa, Christine de Pizan, Egeria (late fourth century), Eudocia of Constantinople, Gertrude the Great, Hadewijch, Herrade of Landsberg, Hildegard of Bingen, Anna Brownell Murphy Jameson, Julian of Norwich, Mechthild of Magdeburg, Sappho, Teresa of Avila, Teresa of Lisieux, Thekla the Nun, Clara Erskine Clement Waters. *See also* Appendix 2.g: Topical Guide to Historical and Legendary Women.

Woods, goddesses of the, *see* Appendix 2.a: Topical Guide to Goddesses.

Writers, *see* Augustine, Beatrice of Nazareth, Bridget of Sweden, John Calvin, Catherine of Bologna, Catherine of Genoa, Christine de Pizan, Dante Aligheri, Egeria (late fourth century), Eudocia of Constantanople, Gertude the Great, Hadewijch, Herrade of Landsberg, Hildegard of Bingen, Jacobus da Voragine, Anna Brownell Murphy Jameson, Jerome, Flavius Josephus, Julian of Norwich, Martin Luther, Mechthild of Magdeburg, Paul, Sappho, Teresa of Avila, Teresa of Lisieux, Thekla the Nun, Thomas Aquinas, Clara Erskine Clement Waters.

Writing, including History, Literature, and Poetry, goddesses of, *see* Appendix 2.a: Topical Guide to Goddesses.

Y

Yaga-Vasilisa, *see* Baba-yaga.
Yakśas, *see* Yakshas.
Yakshī, *see* Yakshas.
Yakshinī, *see* Yakshas.
Yakśī, *see* Yakshas.
Yakśinī, *see* Yakshas.
Yashodhara, *see* Yashodā.
Yaśodā, *see* Yashodā.
Yaśodha, *see* Yashodā.
Yellow Tārā, *see* Tārā.
Yin, *see* Mudrā.
Youth, goddesses of, *see* Appendix 2.a: Topical Guide to Goddesses.
Yrou-Elde, *see* Bercht.
Ysodha, *see* Yashodā.

Z

Zem Ynele, *see* Zemyna.
Zemynele, *see* Zemyna.
Zen Buddhism, *see* Buddhism.
Zied Kele, *see* Zemyna.

Also published by Continuum

Diane Apostolos-Cappadona
DICTIONARY OF CHRISTIAN ART

"A tour de force. Containing over 1000 alphabetized entries and exhaustive cross-references, the volume promises to be an indispensable reference to Christian motifs, subject matter, iconography and theology in visual art. In addition, over 160 reproductions of classic art illustrate the entries."

—*Publishers Weekly*

"A must for every college, university, and school library. It would also make a nice addition to one's private library."

—*American Reference Book Annual*

"It's combination of appeal to a wide variety of readers, engaging subject, and lack of up-to-date competitors makes [it] an essential purchase for academic, public, and seminary libraries."

—*Booklist*

Diane Apostolos-Cappadona and Lucinda Ebersole, Editors
WOMEN, CREATIVITY, AND THE ARTS

"The editors of this energetically intelligent anthology have selected essays about and by women in the arts. The first section contains nine essays by psychologists, art historians and critics, literary critics and sociologists. . . . In the second half of the book, the editors have collected eloquent and stirring autobiographical writings by such twentieth-century arts pioneers as Georgia O'Keefe, Martha Graham, Louise Nevelson, Ursula K. Le Guin, and Audre Lorde."

—*Booklist*

Also published by Continuum

Heinz Schreckenberg
THE JEWS IN CHRISTIAN ART
An Illustrated History

This unique encyclopedic collection of more than one thousand pictures, some in color, is of the utmost importance for understanding Christian attitudes to Jews over the past two thousand years. *The Jews in Christian Art* is one of the first books to consider art as a serious source of historical knowledge about the Jews and the ideological constructs developed around them by Christian thinkers and artists.

Gurtram Koch
EARLY CHRISTIAN ART AND ARCHITECTURE
An Introduction

"What makes Koch's book so valuable? First, it is rigorously and consistently an introduction, which means that it presents information as systematically as possible. . . . I can easily imagine this book in one's pocket while touring museums and historical sites. . . . Secondly, throughout the text there are regular line drawings, giving vivid illustration to the points and themes being discussed in the text. . . . Thirdly, the book is generously provisioned with 32 black and white plates, again covering a variety of different artistic and architectural features. . . . Koch's work is almost above criticism, so successfully has he achieved his aim."
—*Reviews in Religion and Theology*